THE WORD LEAPS THE GAP

Richard B. Hays

The Word Leaps the Gap

*Essays on Scripture and Theology
in Honor of Richard B. Hays*

Edited by

J. Ross Wagner
C. Kavin Rowe
&
A. Katherine Grieb

WILLIAM B. EERDMANS PUBLISHING COMPANY
GRAND RAPIDS, MICHIGAN / CAMBRIDGE, U.K.

Published 2008 by

Wm. B. Eerdmans Publishing Co.

2140 Oak Industrial Drive N.E., Grand Rapids, Michigan 49505 /

P.O. Box 163, Cambridge CB3 9PU U.K.

Printed in the United States of America

13 12 11 10 09 08   7 6 5 4 3 2 1

Library of Congress Cataloging-in-Publication Data

The Word leaps the gap: essays on Scripture and theology in honor of Richard B. Hays /
   edited by J. Ross Wagner, C. Kavin Rowe & A. Katherine Grieb.
      p.   cm.
   Includes bibliographical references and index.
   ISBN 978-0-8028-6356-0 (cloth: alk. paper)
   1. Bible — Criticism, interpretation, etc.   I. Hays, Richard B.
   II. Wagner, J. Ross.   III. Rowe, Christopher Kavin, 1974-
   IV. Grieb, A. Katherine.

   BS511.3.W665   2008
   220.6 — dc22

                                                        2008039496

www.eerdmans.com

Contents

v

For Richard Hays

At the heart of all your words is silence.
In the night of the world you hear bells
Chiming. It is silence you hear. You sense
Peace underneath earth's noise, wells
Of stillness far down under the daily slog
Through wetlands of knowledge, your life,
The tramp through swamps of books in heaps, log-
Piles, bogs of words, teeming, sweaty . . . And rife
Too with truth for those hearing beneath the buzz
Of ceaselessly concatenating syllables
The Origin, the Source who IS, who does
Unheard his work, generating multiples
Of being, infinitely, in silence.
His Word you hear. You hear inside night
Melodies mute to most ears, intense
Notes populating scores of starry light.

These you share with us in love, wise guide
To many, to me old friend most dear, seen
Too seldom in the long years, alas, this side
Or that of the ocean, yet in heart near, keen
Brother, in Christ mated long ago,
The night you sang to welcome Christopher to earth,

With joyful, wild chords greeting him: "Hello!" —
Young father exulting at your new son's birth.

Then Sarah, much-loved daughter — girl! — breaking
On life's stage — her heart, like yours, like Judy's,
Set to range God's wide creation seeking
That place — *hers* — to plant her tent, send melodies
Skyward, dance, deploy her lively art.

And Chris himself is father now. The years swing
Swiftly. Walk now with Judy to the end,
Listening to the silence. Sing to God, to us. Sing.
And you shall hear Him one day speak: "Welcome, friend."

GEORGE HOBSON
July 2006

Contributors

Dale C. Allison Jr.
Errett M. Grable Professor of New Testament Exegesis and Early Christianity
Pittsburgh Theological Seminary

Gary A. Anderson
Professor of Old Testament
University of Notre Dame

John M. G. Barclay
Lightfoot Professor of Divinity
Durham University

Markus Bockmuehl
Professor of Biblical and Early Christian Studies
University of Oxford

Douglas A. Campbell
Assistant Professor of New Testament
Duke Divinity School

Stephen B. Chapman
Associate Professor of Old Testament
Duke Divinity School

Sarah Hays Coomer
Daughter

Brian E. Daley, SJ
Catherine F. Huisking Professor of Theology
University of Notre Dame

Ellen F. Davis
Professor of Bible and Practical Theology
Duke Divinity School

James D. G. Dunn
Lightfoot Professor of Divinity Emeritus
Durham University

Susan G. Eastman
Assistant Professor of the Practice of Bible and Christian Formation
Duke Divinity School

Bruce N. Fisk
Professor of New Testament
Westmont College

Beverly Roberts Gaventa
Helen H. P. Manson Professor of New Testament Literature and Exegesis
Princeton Theological Seminary

Joel B. Green
Professor of New Testament Interpretation
Fuller Theological Seminary

A. Katherine Grieb
Associate Professor of New Testament
Virginia Theological Seminary

Stanley Hauerwas
Gilbert T. Rowe Professor of Theological Ethics
Duke Divinity School

Christopher B. Hays
D. Wilson Moore Assistant Professor of Ancient Near Eastern Studies
Fuller Theological Seminary

Judith C. Hays
Associate Professor
Duke University School of Nursing

George Hobson
Poet, friend

Luke Timothy Johnson
Robert W. Woodruff Professor of New Testament and Christian Origins
Candler School of Theology, Emory University

Leander E. Keck
Winkley Professor of Biblical Theology Emeritus
Yale University

Joel Marcus
Professor of New Testament and Christian Origins
Duke Divinity School

Walter Moberly
Professor of Theology and Biblical Interpretation
Durham University

David P. Moessner
Professor of Biblical Theology
University of Dubuque Theological Seminary

Associate Faculty
Faculty of Theology, Department of New Testament Studies
University of Pretoria

C. Kavin Rowe
Assistant Professor of New Testament
Duke Divinity School

E. P. Sanders
Arts and Sciences Professor Emeritus of Religion
Duke University

D. Moody Smith
George Washington Ivey Professor of New Testament Emeritus
Duke Divinity School

David C. Steinmetz
Amos Ragan Kearns Professor of the History of Christianity
Duke Divinity School

Marianne Meye Thompson
George Eldon Ladd Professor of New Testament Interpretation
Fuller Theological Seminary

Allen Verhey
Professor of Christian Ethics
Duke Divinity School

J. Ross Wagner
Associate Professor of New Testament
Princeton Theological Seminary

Francis Watson
Professor of Biblical Interpretation
Durham University

N. T. Wright
Bishop of Durham, England

Abbreviations

A1CS	The Book of Acts in Its First Century Setting
AARSR	American Academy of Religion Studies in Religion
AB	Anchor Bible
ABD	*Anchor Bible Dictionary* (ed. D. N. Freedman)
ABRL	Anchor Bible Reference Library
AGJU	Arbeiten zur Geschichte des antiken Judentums und des Urchristentums
AnBib	Analecta biblica
ANET	*Ancient Near Eastern Texts Relating to the Old Testament,* 3rd ed. (ed. J. B. Pritchard)
ANETS	Ancient Near Eastern Texts and Studies
ANF	*Ante-Nicene Fathers*
AnGr	Analecta Gregoriana
ANRW	*Aufstieg und Niedergang der römischen Welt: Geschichte und Kultur Roms im Spiegel der neueren Forschung* (ed. H. Temporini and W. Haase)
ANTC	Abingdon New Testament Commentaries
APOT	*The Apocrypha and Pseudepigrapha of the Old Testament* (ed. R. H. Charles)
ARG	*Archiv für Reformationsgeschichte*
ASTS	ArtScroll Tanach Series
AThR	*Anglican Theological Review*
Aug	*Augustinianum*
AV	Authorized Version
BA	*Biblical Archaeologist*
BASOR	*Bulletin of the American Schools of Oriental Research*
BCL	Bohn's Classical Library

BCNH.E	Bibliothèque copte de Nag Hammadi, section "Études"
BDAG	Bauer, Danker, Arndt, and Gingrich, *Greek-English Lexicon of the New Testament and Other Early Christian Literature*, 3rd ed.
BDF	Blass, Debrunner, and Funk, *A Greek Grammar of the New Testament and Other Early Christian Literature*
BECNT	Baker Exegetical Commentary on the New Testament
BETL	Bibliotheca ephemeridum theologicarum lovaniensium
BHT	Beiträge zur historischen Theologie
Bib	*Biblica*
BibSem	The Biblical Seminar
Bijdr	*Bijdragen: Tijdschrift voor filosofie en theologie*
BLS	Bible and Literature Series
BNTC	Black's New Testament Commentaries
BS	Bollingen Series
BTB	*Biblical Theology Bulletin*
BTCB	Brazos Theological Commentary on the Bible
BU	Biblische Untersuchungen
BWANT	Beiträge zur Wissenschaft vom Alten und Neuen Testament
BZ	*Biblische Zeitschrift*
BZAW	Beihefte zur Zeitschrift für die alttestamentliche Wissenschaft
BZNW	Beihefte zur Zeitschrift für die neutestamentliche Wissenschaft
CBET	Contributions to Biblical Exegesis and Theology
CBQ	*Catholic Biblical Quarterly*
CBQMS	Catholic Biblical Quarterly Monograph Series
CBR	*Currents in Biblical Research*
CCSL	Corpus Christianorum: Series latina
CEJL	Commentaries on Early Jewish Literature
CHANE	Culture and History of the Ancient Near East
CNTC	Calvin's New Testament Commentaries
COS	*The Context of Scripture* (ed. W. W. Hallo)
CQ	*Classical Quarterly*
CRINT	Compendia rerum iudaicarum ad Novum Testamentum
CS	Cistercian Studies Series
CSCO	Corpus scriptorum christianorum orientalium
CSEL	Corpus scriptorum ecclesiasticorum latinorum
CTL	Cambridge Textbooks in Linguistics
DNP	*Der neue Pauly: Enzyklopädie der Antike* (ed. H. Cancik and H. Schneider)
DOP	*Dumbarton Oaks Papers*
DRev	*Downside Review*
ECF	Early Church Fathers
ECLS	Early Christian Literature Series
EDNT	*Exegetical Dictionary of the New Testament* (ed. H. Balz and G. Schneider)

EJL	Early Judaism and Its Literature
EKKNT	Evangelisch-katholischer Kommentar zum Neuen Testament
EncJud	*Encyclopaedia Judaica*
ESV	English Standard Version
ET	English translation
ETL	*Ephemerides theologicae lovanienses*
EvQ	*Evangelical Quarterly*
ExpTim	*Expository Times*
FAT	Forschungen zum Alten Testament
FC	Fathers of the Church
FOTL	Forms of the Old Testament Literature
FRLANT	Forschungen zur Religion und Literatur des Alten und Neuen Testaments
GCS	Die griechische christliche Schriftsteller der ersten [drei] Jahrhunderte
H&T	*History and Theory*
HBM	Hebrew Bible Monographs
HBT	*Horizons in Biblical Theology*
HDR	Harvard Dissertations in Religion
HICLR	*Hastings International and Comparative Law Review*
HNT	Handbuch zum Neuen Testament
HNTC	Harper's New Testament Commentaries
HTKNT	Herders theologischer Kommentar zum Neuen Testament
HTR	*Harvard Theological Review*
HUCA	*Hebrew Union College Annual*
IBC	Interpretation: A Bible Commentary for Teaching and Preaching
IBS	*Irish Biblical Studies*
ICC	International Critical Commentary
IJST	*International Journal of Systematic Theology*
IMSS	Institute of Mennonite Studies Series
Int	*Interpretation*
IR	*Iliff Review*
ISBL	Indiana Studies in Biblical Literature
JAL	Jewish Apocryphal Literature Series
JANESCU	*Journal of the Ancient Near Eastern Society of Columbia University*
JAOS	*Journal of the American Oriental Society*
JB	Jerusalem Bible
JBL	*Journal of Biblical Literature*
JCM	Jews, Christians, and Muslims from the Ancient to the Modern World
JECS	*Journal of Early Christian Studies*
JETS	*Journal of the Evangelical Theological Society*
JPT	*Journal of Pentecostal Theology*
JPTSup	Journal of Pentecostal Theology Supplement Series

JQR	*Jewish Quarterly Review*
JR	*Journal of Religion*
JRE	*Journal of Religious Ethics*
JRS	*Journal of Roman Studies*
JSCE	*Journal of the Society of Christian Ethics*
JSNT	*Journal for the Study of the New Testament*
JSNTSup	Journal for the Study of the New Testament: Supplement Series
JSOT	*Journal for the Study of the Old Testament*
JSOTSup	Journal for the Study of the Old Testament: Supplement Series
JSP	*Journal for the Study of the Pseudepigrapha*
JTI	*Journal of Theological Interpretation*
JTS	*Journal of Theological Studies*
JTSA	*Journal of Theology for Southern Africa*
KEK	Kritisch-exegetischer Kommentar über das Neue Testament (Meyer-Kommentar)
KJV	King James Version
LCL	Loeb Classical Library
LD	Lectio divina
LEC	Library of Early Christianity
LSJ	Liddell, Scott, and Jones, *A Greek-English Lexicon,* 9th ed. with revised supplement
LXX	Septuagint
MNTC	Moffatt New Testament Commentary
MNTS	McMaster New Testament Studies
ModTh	*Modern Theology*
MT	Masoretic Text
NAL	New American Library
NASB	New American Standard Bible
NBf	*New Blackfriars*
NEB	New English Bible
NIB	*The New Interpreter's Bible*
NICNT	New International Commentary on the New Testament
NICOT	New International Commentary on the Old Testament
NIGTC	New International Greek Testament Commentary
NIV	New International Version
NJPS	*Tanakh: The Holy Scriptures: The New JPS Translation according to the Traditional Hebrew Text*
NovT	*Novum Testamentum*
NovTSup	Supplements to Novum Testamentum
NPNF[1]	*Nicene and Post-Nicene Fathers,* Series 1
NPNF[2]	*Nicene and Post-Nicene Fathers,* Series 2
NRSV	New Revised Standard Version
NSBT	New Studies in Biblical Theology
NTAbh	Neutestamentliche Abhandlungen

NTD	Das Neue Testament Deutsch
NTG	New Testament Guides
NTS	*New Testament Studies*
OBO	Orbis biblicus et orientalis
OBT	Overtures to Biblical Theology
OCD	*Oxford Classical Dictionary*, 3rd ed. (ed. S. Hornblower and A. Spawforth)
OECT	Oxford Early Christian Texts
OG	Old Greek
OTL	Old Testament Library
OTM	Oxford Theological Monographs
OTP	*Old Testament Pseudepigrapha* (ed. J. H. Charlesworth)
PaThSt	Paderborner Theologische Studien
PBSR	*Papers of the British School at Rome*
PEQ	*Palestine Exploration Quarterly*
PG	Patrologia graeca [= Patrologiae cursus completus: Series graeca]
PGM	*Papyri graecae magicae: Die griechischen Zauberpapyri*
PH	Papyrusinstitut Heidelberg
PhLit	*Philosophy and Literature*
PL	Patrologia latina [= Patrologiae cursus completus: Series latina]
ProEccl	*Pro Ecclesia*
PTL	*Poetics and Theory of Literature*
QJS	*Quarterly Journal of Speech*
RAC	*Reallexikon für Antike und Christentum* (ed. T. Kluser et al.)
RAI	Rencontre Assyriologique Internationale
RB	*Revue biblique*
REB	Revised English Bible
RelArts	*Religion and the Arts*
RevQ	*Revue de Qumran*
RNT	Regensburger Neues Testament
RST	Regensburger Studien zur Theologie
RSV	Revised Standard Version
RTR	*Reformed Theological Review*
SAAB	*State Archives of Assyria Bulletin*
SANE	Sources from the Ancient Near East
SB	Sources bibliques
SBET	*Scottish Bulletin of Evangelical Theology*
SBLAB	Society of Biblical Literature Academia Biblica
SBLDS	Society of Biblical Literature Dissertation Series
SBL Forum	*Society of Biblical Literature Forum*
SBLSCS	Society of Biblical Literature Septuagint and Cognate Studies
SC	Sources chrétiennes
SCJ	Studies in Christianity and Judaism
SCT	Studies in Continental Thought

SEÅ	*Svensk exegetisk årsbok*
SHR	Studies in the History of Religions (supplement to *Numen*)
SJLA	Studies in Judaism in Late Antiquity
SJT	*Scottish Journal of Theology*
SNTSMS	Society for New Testament Studies Monograph Series
SNTW	Studies of the New Testament and Its World
SP	Sacra Pagina
SR	*Studies in Religion*
SSEJC	Studies in Scripture in Early Judaism and Christianity
StCH	Studies in Comparative History
STI	Studies in Theological Interpretation
Str-B	*Kommentar zum Neuen Testament aus Talmud und Midrasch* (ed. H. Strack and P. Billerbeck)
TBS	Tools for Biblical Study
TD	*Theology Digest*
TDNT	*Theological Dictionary of the New Testament* (ed. G. Kittel and G. Friedrich)
TEG	Traditio Exegetica Graeca
Tem	*Temenos*
THKNT	Theologischer Handkommentar zum Neuen Testament
TM	The Making of Europe
TNIV	Today's New International Version
TNTC	Tyndale New Testament Commentaries
TOTC	Tyndale Old Testament Commentaries
TRu	*Theologische Rundschau*
TS	*Theological Studies*
TSAJ	Texte und Studien zum antiken Judentum
TT	Texts and Translations
TynBul	*Tyndale Bulletin*
UF	*Ugarit-Forschungen*
VT	*Vetus Testamentum*
VTSup	Vetus Testamentum Supplements
WA	*D. Martin Luthers Werke: Kritische Gesamtausgabe* (Weimar, 1883ff.)
WATR	*D. Martin Luthers Werke: Kritische Gesamtausgabe: Tischreden* (Weimar, 1912-21)
WBC	Word Biblical Commentary
WUNT	Wissenschaftliche Untersuchungen zum Neuen Testament
YCS	*Yale Classical Studies*
ZNW	*Zeitschrift für die neutestamentliche Wissenschaft und die Kunde der älteren Kirche*

Editors' Preface

Perhaps no modern biblical scholar has argued more eloquently or more compellingly than Richard Hays that those who would read Holy Scripture rightly must be prepared to engage in a thrilling, unpredictable, and even perilous endeavor. The Word of God, he cautions us, is alive and powerful: it crackles and glows with an energy that will not be suppressed or contained; repeatedly it "leaps the gap" between the worlds of its first hearers and the lives of those who patiently and expectantly attend to it still.[1] Through field-defining monographs and thought-provoking essays, Richard has apprenticed a generation of exegetes in the art of reading Scripture, sensitizing their ears to intertextual echoes, focusing their vision through the interpretive lenses of community, cross, and new creation, and directing their attention to the narrative of God's righteousness displayed through the faith of Jesus Christ that runs like a golden thread through the Christian Bible.

This *Festschrift* is offered to Richard Hays, in celebration of his sixtieth birthday, as a token of gratitude from colleagues and friends whose scholarly imaginations have been sparked in numerous ways by his generative insights. Many of the essays dialogue with Richard's work explicitly — indeed, several pose rather vigorous challenges to his views. Others take up topics that fall within the wide scope of Richard's interests in biblical studies, theology, and the history of interpretation. But all of them are offered in the hope

---

1. Cf. *The Moral Vision of the New Testament* (New York: HarperSanFrancisco, 1996), pp. 298-304; *Echoes of Scripture in the Letters of Paul* (New Haven: Yale University Press, 1989), p. 33.

of advancing the important conversations about the Bible, Christian theology, and the shape of the Christian life that Richard cares about so passionately. The quality of the discussion within the pages of this volume stands as a clear token of the affection and esteem with which Richard is regarded by his many conversation partners in the academy and the church.

Those who conspire to assemble a collection of essays such as this accrue a heavy debt of gratitude. Our coterie of contributors enthusiastically responded to the invitation to join us in honoring Richard and over many months kept the compact of silence unbroken. Greg Jones, Dean of the Divinity School at Duke University, cheerfully colluded in the project from the outset, offering wise counsel in the conception of the volume and providing generous editorial support. Ryan Bonfiglio and David Beary, both seniors in the Master of Divinity program at Princeton Theological Seminary, assisted us in getting the manuscript into its final form. Ryan painstakingly checked citations from ancient sources, while David rendered yeoman's service in compiling the indexes under a tight deadline. Two of our doctoral candidates, Amy Peeler (Princeton) and T. J. Lang (Duke), kindly helped us through the final crunch of the proof stage. In addition to producing a beautiful book, Sam Eerdmans, Linda Bieze, Jim Chiampas, and their colleagues at Wm. B. Eerdmans publishing house have made the process of moving from proposal to publication as smooth and painless as possible. Our heartfelt thanks to them all. A special word of gratitude goes to Carol Shoun, Faculty Editorial Associate at Duke Divinity School and a true master of the craft. Her careful attention to detail and her finely tuned ear for the English language have left their mark on nearly every page.

We join our colleagues, Richard, in wishing you many more years of joyful and fruitful labor for the advancement of scholarship, for the upbuilding of the church, and most of all, for the glory and praise of the God whose you are, and whom you serve.

THE EDITORS

Why "The Way the Words Run" Matters:
Reflections on Becoming a "Major Biblical Scholar"

Stanley Hauerwas

If we understand deeply enough the way in which the promise of the Holy Spirit is linked to the church's gathering to bind and loose (Matt. 18:19-20), this may provide us as well with a more wholesome understanding of the use and authority of Scripture. One of the most enduring subjects of unfruitful controversy over the centuries has been whether the words of Scripture, when looked at purely as words, isolated from the context in which certain people read them at a certain time and place, have both the clear meaning and the absolute authority of revelation.

To speak of the Bible apart from people reading it and apart from the specific questions that those people reading need to answer is to do violence to the very purpose for which we have been given the Holy Scriptures. There is no such thing as an isolated word of the Bible carrying meaning in itself. It has meaning only when it is read by someone and then only when that reader and the society in which he or she lives can understand the issue to which it speaks.[1]

---

1. John Howard Yoder, "Binding and Loosing," in *The Royal Priesthood: Essays Ecclesiological and Ecumenical,* ed. Michael G. Cartwright (Grand Rapids: Eerdmans, 1994), p. 353. I am indebted to Chris Huebner for calling attention to this quotation from Yoder in his essay "Mennonites and Narrative Theology: The Case of John Howard Yoder," which appears in Huebner's book *A Precarious Peace: Yoderian Explorations on Theology, Knowledge, and Identity* (Scottdale, Pa.: Herald, 2006), p. 61.

I. Hays's Challenge

In *The Moral Vision of the New Testament,* Richard Hays was kind enough to attend to my account of the role of the Bible in theological and ethical reflection.[2] Hays notes the diverse sources that shape how I read Scripture — Barth, Aristotle, Aquinas, Yoder, Fish — but then observes that it is not at all easy to see how I can hold "these different elements together in a coherent hermeneutical position; indeed, given his [Hauerwas's] rather freewheeling approach to biblical interpretation, it is not at all clear that he has done so."[3]

I have never responded to Hays's criticism, but now that I am a "major biblical scholar," that is, I have written a commentary on the Gospel of Matthew, I am in a position to attempt — or at least I owe Richard — a response to his challenge to my "freewheeling approach" to the Bible.[4] I fear that I will not be able to satisfy Richard's suggestion that I need to articulate a "coherent hermeneutical position," but I hope to make clear why I do not believe a "coherent hermeneutical position" is much help for reading the Bible.[5]

---

2. Richard Hays, *The Moral Vision of the New Testament* (New York: HarperSanFrancisco, 1996), pp. 253-66. The very grammar of our speech often betrays us. For example, I use the word "role" to avoid the word "use." I also do not like to have to use the locution "theology and ethics," because I do not think they are two "things." But given the conventions, I feel it necessary to refer to both.

3. Hays, *Moral Vision,* p. 254.

4. Stanley Hauerwas, *Matthew,* BTCB (Grand Rapids: Brazos, 2006). This book is dedicated to David Aers, Ellen Davis, and Richard Hays — close friends and close readers who have taught me much about how to read and, in particular, how to read Scripture. I continue to doubt, however, whether the *art* of reading, particularly the art of reading the Bible, can be taught. Richard Hays is obviously a talented reader of Scripture, but I have always thought he is so not because of his training as a historian. Rather, his reading skills, I suspect, reflect his love of poetry. Of course, it helps to know Scripture as well as Richard knows Scripture. I only wish I had his familiarity with the text, because such familiarity is crucial for making the connections that good readings exemplify.

5. My worries about hermeneutical theories derive from philosophical concerns about the "self" such theories too often presuppose. Paul DeHart rightly suggests that Hans Frei resisted the kind of hermeneutical theory represented by Gadamer and Ricoeur because he was convinced they continued to reproduce romantic conceptions of the self; see DeHart, *The Trial of the Witnesses: The Rise and Decline of Postliberal Theology* (Oxford: Blackwell, 2006), p. 200. In *Theology and Narrative,* ed. George Hunsinger and William Placher (New York: Oxford University Press, 1993), Frei observes:

> In regard to understanding, . . . I find myself influenced increasingly by Wittgenstein and J. L. Austin rather than by the Idealistic tradition that has dominated the field for so long, whether in its pure form (e.g., in Dilthey), in existen-

However, I first need to say more about Hays's "bill of particulars" concerning my approach to the Bible. Hays calls attention to my argument in *Unleashing the Scripture,* which is built on the claim that fundamentalism and historical criticism are but two sides of the same coin: they are both developments of the Protestant stress on *sola scriptura,* transformed by the printing press into *"sola* text." These developments were given ideological formation by democratic social orders that created something called the individual citizen, which presumed the ability to read the Bible without spiritual formation and moral guidance. As a result, the Bible was separated from the community necessary for it to be read as the word of God, that is, the church.[6]

Hays quite rightly characterizes my position as entailing the view that the community already formed by the story of the kingdom of God is both prior and necessary if the Bible is to be rightly read. Such a community is constituted by the "enacted story" of the liturgy and the exemplary lives of the saints. I therefore argue that it is a methodological mistake to ask how Scripture should be "used" in Christian ethics. Such a question assumes that the ethicist has some epistemological privilege external to the Bible, a privilege often based on the "latest" historical reconstruction of the text, allowing the ethicist to determine the "meaning" of the text and then to ask how the text might be "used."

Hays worries that my emphasis on the church as the politics necessary for the reading of Scripture fails to do justice to "the classic Protestant idea

---

tialist form, in a more historical form like that of Pannenberg, or in a more ontological form like that of Heidegger, Gadamer, and among theologians Fuchs and Ebeling. There is, it seems to me, a variety of descriptions for any given linguistic phenomenon, and hence, above all, no ontological superdescription or explanation for it. Furthermore, the "grammar" (use according to rules of such a construct) is more readily exhibited or set forth than stated in the abstract. (p. 33)

In an odd way — odd because hermeneutical theories often claim to be political — hermeneutical theories of "meaning" involve an attempt to avoid making explicit the politics of reading.

6. Stanley Hauerwas, *Unleashing the Scripture: Freeing the Bible from Captivity to America* (Nashville: Abingdon, 1993). I am quite sympathetic with Kevin Vanhoozer's recent attempt to rehabilitate the notion of *sola scriptura,* viewing the Bible as an authoritative script not merely for intellectual assent but for live performance: "To practice *sola scriptura* means to participate in the canonical practices that form, inform, and transform our speaking, thinking, and living — practices that the Spirit uses to conform us to the image of God in Christ." See Vanhoozer, *The Drama of Doctrine: A Canonical-Linguistic Approach to Christian Theology* (Louisville: Westminster John Knox, 2005), p. 237.

that Scripture can challenge and judge tradition."[7] Indeed, he even suggests that the logic of my position should require me to become a Roman Catholic, although that would mean belonging to a church with positions on major ethical issues such as war and the role of women that are at odds with my commitment to Christian nonviolence and my support of the ordination of women.[8] Hays concludes that, finally, in my hands "the New Testament falls mute, muzzled by the unfaithful church, and Hauerwas finds himself with no theoretical grounds for an appeal to Scripture against the church's practices."[9]

Hays acknowledges that I do provide "sermonic exhibits," which I claim to be evidence that I am not "muzzling" the text. However, he is not impressed by my sermons, observing that I am less inclined to exposit the text than to propose conditions that must be met if the text is to be rightly read. For example, in my sermon on the Sermon on the Mount, Hays notes that

> nowhere does Hauerwas engage in exegetical discussion of the structure and logic of the six antitheses in Matthew 5:21-48; nowhere does he explore the first-century historical background of such practices as turning the other cheek and going the second mile (Matt. 5:39-41); nowhere does he ask what source in Scripture or elsewhere might be said to instruct Jesus' hearers to hate their enemies (Matt. 5:43); nowhere does he investigate the meaning of the word *teleios* ("perfect"; Matt. 5:48). In short, he does not undertake any of the exegetical practices necessary to demon-

---

7. Hays, *Moral Vision,* p. 263. Of course, it was my contention that the development of historical criticism was also in service to a politics, namely, the developing nation-states of modernity. For example, Jon Levenson argues that "historical criticism is . . . the realization of the Enlightenment project in the realm of biblical scholarship. Like citizens in the classical liberal state, scholars practicing historical criticism of the Bible are expected to eliminate or minimize their communal loyalties, to see them as legitimately operative only within associations that are private, nonscholarly, and altogether voluntary"; see Levenson, *The Hebrew Bible, the Old Testament, and Historical Criticism* (Louisville: Westminster John Knox, 1993), p. 118. For substantiation of Levenson's argument that biblical criticism not only mirrored the liberal state but served as an ideology for its legitimation, see Thomas Howard, *Protestant Theology and the Making of the Modern German University* (New York: Oxford University Press, 2006), pp. 207-11.

8. Hays, *Moral Vision,* p. 265.

9. Hays, *Moral Vision,* pp. 265-66. Hays at one time thought it crucial to maintain the distinction between "what it meant" and "what it means" in order to ensure that the Scripture can judge the church. I do not know whether he still thinks that necessary, but from my perspective such a distinction ensures only that members of the Society of Biblical Literature can judge the church.

strate how the specific language of the text might or might not warrant an ethic of nonviolence.[10]

Finally, Hays argues that I fail to deal with texts that stand in tension with my synthetic construal of the New Testament message. According to Hays, I feel no necessity to show how the Pastoral Epistles or Revelation fits within my story of the kingdom. Nor do I ever try to resolve the tensions within the canon. I use the category of story as an elixir to gloss over discrepancies in the Gospels by stressing journey and cross as focal points around which everything in the Gospels can be organized.[11] From Hays's perspective, I — unlike John Howard Yoder — ride roughshod over the Bible, making it mean what I have predetermined it to mean. In short, I do not do what anyone who intends to be faithful to the Bible must do; that is, I do not do exegesis.

II. In My Own Defense

I cannot help but feel just a wee bit defensive in the face of Hays's criticisms of my "use" of the Scripture. I should like to think my sermons are not as devoid of exegetical display as he suggests, but I do not think trying to show how I was reading the texts I used in the sermons will be much help for responding to Hays.[12] Moreover, given the developments in Hays's position

10. Hays, *Moral Vision*, p. 259. Hays further notes that I have an overt hostility toward historical criticism even though my account of Jesus in "Jesus: The Story of the Kingdom" (in *A Community of Character* [Notre Dame: University of Notre Dame Press, 1981]) draws on the work of such biblical scholars as Tinsley, Harvey, Riches, and Dahl.

11. Hays speaks of "focal images," drawing on the work of David Kelsey, to provide shape to the diversity of the scriptural texts (*Moral Vision*, pp. 193-205). It is not a language I use, just to the extent that the "image" threatens to become isolated from the way the words run. Hays's discussion of the images of community, cross, and new creation is subtle, but on the whole I worry that "cross" abstracted from Jesus' crucifixion (an abstraction Hays resists) too easily becomes a "symbol" to illumine the human condition.

12. I should like to think the sermons Hays has included in *The Art of Reading Scripture* (Grand Rapids: Eerdmans, 2003), the book he edited with Ellen Davis, might suggest he would now find my sermons not quite as exegetically deficient as when he wrote *The Moral Vision of the New Testament*. For example, in a wonderful sermon on Daniel he calls attention to the fourth figure that appears in the furnace, suggesting that this figure prefigures Christ. Hays acknowledges that prior to his participation in the Scripture Project (which produced *The Art of Reading Scripture*) he would not have been able to preach Daniel this way, but he now finds it impossible not to see Daniel as a prophecy of Christ. He is careful to avoid any

exemplified in the book he edited with Ellen Davis, *The Art of Reading Scripture,* I think it may be the case that we increasingly share a fundamental outlook about how the Bible is to be read.[13] Yet the criticisms Hays made of my work in *The Moral Vision of the New Testament* are important, and I need to respond to them for no other reason than to get straight for myself what I re-

---

suggestion that the author of Daniel intended to write a christological prophecy, arguing rather that the author wrote figuratively, making such a reading possible (pp. 306-10). I do not disagree with his christological reading, but I would not have worried at all about what the author of Daniel might have "intended." I assume that even if the author were available to us now, he or she would have as much trouble saying what he or she intended as I have trying to say what I intend in writing this paragraph. Moreover, Daniel is now Scripture, which means that issues of "authorship" are more complex than questions about "intention."

I would contend, however — a contention well developed by John Wright in his book *Telling God's Story: Narrative Preaching for Christian Formation* (Downers Grove, Ill.: InterVarsity, 2007) — that preaching is the appropriate practice for biblical reading. Wright argues that contemporary preaching too often takes as its task to find "applications" for the text, when its task should be to lead a congregation away from one narrative world and into another. Wright's book is both a brilliant analysis of how we got where we are and a practical guide for a constructive way forward.

13. See especially Hays's essay "Reading Scripture in Light of the Resurrection" (*Art of Reading Scripture,* pp. 216-38). The "Nine Theses on the Interpretation of Scripture" set out at the beginning of the book say better some of the points I was trying to make in *Unleashing the Scripture.* In particular, theses 2 ("Scripture is rightly understood in light of the church's rule of faith as a coherent dramatic narrative") and 6 ("Faithful interpretation of Scripture invites and presupposes participation in the community brought into being by God's redemptive action — the church") are expressions of the argument of *Unleashing the Scripture.* Hays, however, continues to try to have it both ways; that is, he wants a theological reading of Scripture without calling into question the work of historical criticism. For example, he argues that "the New Testament's resurrection accounts teach us to read the Old Testament as Christian Scripture," but this does not mean "to deny its original historical sense, nor does it preclude responsible historical criticism. Christians have a stake in seeking the most historically careful readings of the Old Testament that we can attain. At the same time, however, in light of the New Testament witness, we cannot confine the meaning of the Old Testament to the literal sense understood by its original authors and readers, for these ancient texts have been taken up into a new story that amplifies and illumines their meaning in unexpected ways" ("Reading Scripture," p. 233). I have quoted Hays at length because his wording continues to betray assumptions that, given his agreement with the "Nine Theses," he should leave behind. It is not the "accounts" of the resurrection that teach us to read the Old Testament as Christian Scripture. It is the resurrection testified to by the Holy Spirit. "Accounts" may indicate what we learn from walking with Jesus to Emmaus, but we are able to make that walk because of his resurrection. There is, moreover, no "original historical sense," and it is not at all clear why the "literal sense" should be identified as that which the "original" authors and readers understood. The very presumption of "original" needs to be left behind. Furthermore, I have no idea what might count as "responsible historical criticism."

ally think about how the reading of the Scripture matters for the upbuilding of the holiness of the church.[14]

I am very sympathetic with Hays's criticism that I am not sufficiently exegetical. I do not, however, think that has to do with the argument I made in *Unleashing the Scripture* for why the church is the necessary politics for reading the Scripture. After all, the church insists that the words matter.[15] But when I wrote *Unleashing the Scripture,* I did not know how to show how the words matter, because, as Rusty Reno observes, most theologians in modernity (including me) have lost competency in exegesis. As a result, accord-

14. The reader will note that I avoid using the language of "interpretation," because I think such language suggests that the text has "a meaning," which then must be interpreted. Such a view reproduces the habits of liberal Protestant theologians who assume that the language of Scripture needs to be demythologized to meet the epistemic standards of modernity. This view is nicely exemplified in a "Comment" by William Schweiker in the *Journal of Religious Ethics* (*JRE* 34 [2006]: 711-19), written in response to an article by Michael O'Neil. O'Neil had criticized Schweiker for basing his critique of misuses of power on universal epistemic principles rather than the practices and authority of the church. Schweiker notes in his defense that he employs a hermeneutical "method" because he assumes that "claims to truth about *meaning*," including "the *moral meaning* of Christian faith," are different from the kinds of knowing found in sensible experience or logical truths (p. 712, emphasis original). He observes, moreover, that "the non-reducibility of understanding to empirical and/ or logical knowledge claims is crucial to sustain. I may 'know,' for instance, that the sun is shining through my window, but that does not in itself determine its meaning for me or anyone else, or that I understand its possible range of meanings" (p. 713). You know you are in the grip of a theory, a bad one at that, when you think "the sun is shining through my window" has a "meaning" or "meanings." As I will suggest below, such a view of language continues to assume a dualism between language and world that is profoundly mistaken.

15. George Lindbeck puts it as well as it can be put, noting that we do not and should not choose between the priority of church and Scripture. Rather, we best think of their "co-inherence, . . . their mutually constitutive reciprocity." Lindbeck observes that the canon is closed for those who believe in the eschatological decisiveness of Jesus Christ, so that the balance between church and Scripture has shifted. Originally, the church formed Scripture, but now the church is formed by Scripture. "Yet the Bible's community-forming role . . . is not independent of community. It helps constitute the *ecclesia* only when interpreted communally in accordance with a community-constituting hermeneutics." See Lindbeck, *The Church in a Postliberal Age* (Grand Rapids: Eerdmans, 2003), p. 205. "A community-constituting hermeneutics" may sound like a "general hermeneutical theory," but it is crucial not to overlook the indefinite article, "a." The "a" means that different communities will produce different readings, some of which may be in conflict. Attempts to develop a hermeneutical theory that can resolve such differences in advance are doomed to failure. The church did not develop a theory to resolve conflicting readings; rather, the church was given an office to ensure that one church's readings would be tested by other churches. The name of that office is "bishop."

ing to Reno, "each decade finds new theories of preaching to cover the nakedness of seminary training that provides theology without exegesis and exegesis without theology."[16] Indeed, that exegesis and theology are now thought to be two separate enterprises indicates a sea change in theology just to the extent that prior to recent times — to be sure, in quite different ways — theology was exegesis.[17]

Put simply, I did not know how to go on to show what the arguments I had made about the ecclesial practices that should shape exegetical practice might look like in actual exegesis.[18] The best I could do was to try to display how the words mattered through the sermonic exhibits. But Hays is quite right that given the character of sermons, or at least the form sermons usually take in our day, the sermons I used as exhibits did not exemplify the kind of close reading of texts he thinks crucial for responsible biblical interpretation.

I have now, however, at least tried to do the kind of work Hays thinks I needed to do by writing a theological commentary of the Gospel of Mat-

---

16. R. R. Reno, series preface (to the Brazos Theological Commentary on the Bible), in my *Matthew*, p. 13. Commenting on the work of Karl Rahner, Lindbeck observes that while Rahner may have developed an authentically Christian idealist-existentialist-evolutionary *Weltanschauung*, "one can learn to think well in his categories while remaining biblically illiterate"; see *Church in a Postliberal Age*, p. 212. Lindbeck's characterization of Rahner applies to most modern theologians. Our problem is that even if we want to make exegetical work constitutive of our theology, we do not know how.

17. How and why theologians began to do theology as a systematic discipline that required no extensive reading of biblical texts is doubtless a story that needs telling. I have no special insight to account for this development, but surely it has something to do with theology finding its primary home in the universities of modernity; see (e.g.) my *State of the University: Academic Knowledges and the Knowledge of God* (Oxford: Blackwell, 2007). As theologians began to seek academic "respectability," theology began to look more and more like philosophy. Furthermore, I suspect theologians' loss of exegetical skill has to do with the diminishment of biblical authority and literacy among Christians in the mainline churches. How do you make an argument that turns on the exegesis of a particular passage when those to whom you are making the argument have little knowledge of the Scripture? As a result, the Bible cannot help but be a resource of "ideas" that become the primary focus of theology.

18. Of course, I did have an example of what such exegesis might look like in the work of John Howard Yoder and, in particular, in his book *The Politics of Jesus: Vicit Agnus Noster,* 2nd ed. (Grand Rapids: Eerdmans, 1994). For those interested, I need to report that I tried to convince John not to "update" the scholarship in the second edition, in the new "epilogues" to each chapter. I thought such "updating" gave the impression that his readings of the texts depended on developments in historical scholarship. Yet he always thought, or at least said, that *The Politics of Jesus* was nothing more than a report of where the scholarship had taken us. I have no doubt John thought that, but I do not think what he did in *The Politics of Jesus* can be shown to be only a "report."

thew.[19] By discussing some of the decisions I made in writing that commentary, I hope to provide at least a partial response to Hays's criticism of my work. However, before I do so, I want to challenge a presumption Hays seems to have held when he wrote *The Moral Vision of the New Testament,* which apparently shaped some of his criticism of me. For as the quotation above concerning my sermon on the Sermon on the Mount suggests, Hays seems to have thought knowing more about the "historical background" was crucial for sustaining the "close readings" he found lacking in my work. Historians will do what historians will do, and often we may learn something from them that may be of use, but I remain unconvinced that the so-called historical knowledge is a trump or even is necessary for how the Scripture is to be read by the church.

For example, I simply do not believe that I will learn from word studies the "meaning" of the word *teleios*. I do not believe that I will learn the meaning of the word *teleios* because I believe it is a philosophical mistake to think that *the* word has *a* meaning.[20] Such views about the meaning of words re-

---

19. I do not think I would have been able even to begin work on Matthew if I had not been asked to preach on the seven last words of Christ at Saint Thomas Church Fifth Avenue in New York City. I do not know what Hays might think about those meditations, but I know they forced me to attend to the words as witnesses to the Word in a manner I am not sure I had done in my previous work. See my *Cross-Shattered Christ: Meditations on the Seven Last Words* (Grand Rapids: Brazos, 2004).

20. Happily, the fourth thesis in Davis and Hays's *Art of Reading Scripture* reads: "Texts of Scripture do not have a single meaning limited to the intent of the original author. In accord with Jewish and Christian traditions, we affirm that Scripture has multiple complex senses given by God, the author of the whole drama" (p. 2). The very fact that Christians presume our Scriptures can be translated challenges the assumption that a word can be isolated for its "meaning." I believe the necessary act of translating to be a faithful way of enacting Matt. 28:19. Every translation is a new reading, requiring that each translation be tested by other translations. The words matter, but that the words are a translation means that no "meaning" can be determined by a word isolated from the way the words run. Attempts to show what a word had to "mean" by comparison with what the word may or may not have meant in other texts are not entirely without use, but such "word studies" cannot in themselves determine what the word "meant." For example, if I wrote that Hays was an "asshole," most would think I was making a very negative judgment about him. But where I come from, Texas, "asshole" is a term of endearment males use after they have scored a touchdown. Languages in use cannot be definitively translated, but rather we can, in Alasdair MacIntyre's way of stating it, learn a "second first language." The church has quite rightly asked some to learn Hebrew and Greek to test translation, but we must remember that the Hebrew and Greek being learned is not the "original language." Ellen Davis and Richard Hays have an extraordinary "feel" for the respective languages of the texts over which they work, but the languages they know so well come to life only through the life they bring to

produce presumptions that words depend on ostensive references that I simply do not think can be sustained after Wittgenstein. To try to isolate the "meaning" of a word from its use is to assume that language is one thing and what the language depicts is something quite other. It is to understand language and the world as externally related to one another, such that language users are positioned as spectators rather than performers.[21] The presumption that a dualism exists between language and the world hides from us that "the world" is constituted by language and that there is no way to transcend language to speak about language.[22]

These are deep philosophical issues that require fuller development than I can provide for the purpose I want to achieve in this paper. The reason is not simply a matter of space. Rather, the defense of claims concerning the practical force of language and correlative theological reading of Scripture is best done indirectly and through example. I will try to provide some examples below, but first I want to call attention to the argument Markus Bockmuehl makes in his recent book *Seeing the Word: Refocusing New Testa-*

---

them. "Life," of course, names the work of the Holy Spirit. For an example of how the study of words should be done, see C. Kavin Rowe, *Early Narrative Christology: The Lord in the Gospel of Luke* (Berlin: de Gruyter, 2006). George Lindbeck also calls attention to the significance of the Christian presumption that our Scripture can be translated in his *Church in a Postliberal Age,* pp. 231-36.

21. My general rule is to avoid the grammar entailed in questions about "meaning." To ask the "meaning" of a word or sentence or paragraph is to tempt us to think the meaning is separable from what the words do; that is, it is to tempt us to think the "meaning" can be abstracted from description and/or depiction. Hans Frei's work stands as a challenge to the presumption that "meaning" can be isolated from how the story runs. For the best account of Frei's argument, see David Dawson, *Christian Figural Reading and the Fashioning of Identity* (Berkeley: University of California Press, 2002), pp. 141-85.

22. It is tempting to footnote some remark by Wittgenstein to confirm this conclusion, but such a footnote would betray the character of the training Wittgenstein provides that is necessary to acknowledge the contingent character of ourselves as language users. For example, many allegedly influenced by Wittgenstein seem to think that he puts forward some theory about meaning as use or that he provides a philosophy of ordinary language. Wittgenstein certainly does say, in the *Philosophical Investigations:* "For a *large* class of cases — though not for all — in which we employ the word 'meaning' it can be defined thus: the meaning of a word is its use in the language" (§43, trans. G. E. M. Anscombe [New York: Macmillan, 1953], emphasis original). Please note, however, that he is not putting forward a theory of meaning but rather some characteristics of the employment of the word "meaning." For those tempted to find a position in Wittgenstein, they should at least attend to his remark that "to understand a sentence means to understand a language. To understand a language means to be master of a technique" (§199). For Wittgenstein, training is the heart of the matter.

ment Study, because he helps us see — and the very title of his book reminds us that we must learn to see — why theological readings are not an afterthought once we have done our historical homework.

Bockmuehl argues that Scripture requires "the wisdom of the implied exegete."[23] According to Bockmuehl, both Testaments of Scripture clearly presuppose such an interpreter, but the interpreter that is a reader of the Old and New Testaments, "the Christian Scripture," is a disciple, that is, a witness to the Christ. Bockmuehl, therefore, argues that

> the object of biblical interpretation . . . is the interpreter as much as it is the text, and it is *performative* as much as it is hermeneutical. Taking a cue from John Webster, one might even say that this presumption of discipleship involves the interpreter in the kind of theological anthropology that the New Testament itself envisages: it presumes to engage an exegete whose very interpretation serves, is judged by, and is *converted* to the evangelical truth that inheres in Scripture's witness.[24]

Which means that the right reading of the gospel requires an ecclesial location. Thus, Bockmuehl argues, "in spite of its foundational significance for Christianity, the New Testament does not *create* the church but rather *presupposes* and confirms it at every turn."[25] The very survival of what we know as the New Testament indicates that speculation about the origin of the texts of the New Testament will be inadequate to determine the meaning of the same texts. For the New Testament is not a ragtag collection of ill-conceived political agendas and diverse ecclesiologies, but "the New Testament as a whole and in its parts *presupposes* an implied readership and a *Sitz im Leben* in which it functions as the abiding deposit of the apostolic witness to the gospel."[26] Accordingly, theological themes are not "added on" after exegetical work is done, but rather theological and ethical loci such as Trin-

---

23. Markus Bockmuehl, *Seeing the Word: Refocusing New Testament Study,* STI (Grand Rapids: Baker Academic, 2006), pp. 75-99.

24. Bockmuehl, *Seeing the Word,* p. 92, emphasis original.

25. Bockmuehl, *Seeing the Word,* p. 113, emphasis original. I began this paper with the quotation from Yoder because in *The Moral Vision of the New Testament,* Hays quite rightly gives a very sympathetic account of Yoder's work that seems to suggest that Yoder's focus on the text is an alternative to my focus on the church. Yet Yoder is no less insistent that the kind of church matters for the right reading of the text. I think it would be quite instructive to compare Bockmuehl's understanding of the implied reader with Yoder's understanding of discipleship.

26. Bockmuehl, *Seeing the Word,* p. 114, emphasis original.

ity, sanctification, judgment, the inspiration of Scripture, or the doctrine of heaven are the direct result of the New Testament text's continuing in the church.[27]

Such a view does not mean that the many-splendored thing called the historical-critical method must be abandoned, but no longer can such a method — and it is by no means clear what it means for it to be a "method" — claim that the work done in its name must precede a theological reading. Like Bockmuehl, I think the historical work that has helped us see the Jewish character of Jesus' life and ministry has been a singular contribution of recent historical scholarship.[28] But I remain unconvinced that the kind of theological reading Bockmuehl argues the New Testament demands is compatible with many of the readings that shape work done in the name of the historical reconstruction of the texts of the New Testament.

For example, from the perspective of what is claimed to be "history," we are taught to ask as well as answer:

> Why was Matthew written? He wanted to restate Mark to justify the existence of Jewish Christianity. Why did Luke write? To convince Rome that Christianity was not dangerous and so assure its existence. Or to establish his theology over and against Mark's. Why did the resurrection narratives arise? Because they needed a way to justify the continued existence of the Jesus community after his death. Why does Acts include the ascension? To justify the fact that Jesus was no longer with them. Why does Paul claim such a low status in 2 Corinthians? Because he's actually trying to regain control of the community. Why were early Christian communities attractive? Because they offered increased status. Why did Paul write anything? To get his congregations to do what he wanted. Why is Revelation written? To assure Christians that God will have his revenge on the beast. Why do the New Testament authors interpret the

27. Bockmuehl, *Seeing the Word*, p. 118.

28. Bockmuehl, *Seeing the Word*, pp. 200-201. Indeed, it is my view that historical criticism was a gift from God to counter the tendency in Protestantism to lose the life of Jesus because of the overemphasis on justification by grace. So the liberal Protestant attempt to recover the lives of Jesus at least had the virtue of reminding us that Jesus had a life. I do not think there is a necessary correlation between the emphasis on "doctrine" and the failure to account for the significance of Jesus' life, but they have often gone hand in hand. That historical critics will not let the church avoid the bits of Scripture that do not confirm our contemporary sensibilities is also a contribution we dare not ignore. Of course, I do not believe that historical criticism was necessary for the recovery of the significance of Jesus' life or for forcing us to attend to the unpleasant parts of Scripture. It just worked out that way.

Old Testament out of context? To justify their own positions by whatever means possible.[29]

From my perspective, these questions and answers are simply not helpful for shaping the kind of reading Bockmuehl argues Scripture demands of the "implied exegete," if what we read is to be read for the upbuilding of the church. That does not mean the words do not matter, but how the words matter is to be determined, as Davis and Hays suggest, "in light of the church's rule of faith as a coherent dramatic narrative."[30] Our problem, quite simply, is that few of us know what such a reading of the Scripture disciplined by the rule of faith might look like. I tried at least to begin to work in that direction in my commentary on the Gospel of Matthew, but I have no illusions that I accomplished what I set out to do. However, I want to call attention to some of the ways I tried to work in the hope that others may learn from my mistakes.[31]

III. Reading Matthew

In his series preface to the volumes coming out in the Brazos Theological Commentary on the Bible, Rusty Reno declares that this commentary series is based on the assumption that the Nicene tradition, in all its diversity and controversy, provides the proper basis for the interpretation of the Bible as Christian Scripture. God the Father Almighty, who sends his only begotten

---

29. I am indebted to Mr. Colin Miller for this paragraph, which is to be found in his paper "Reading Scripture with Milbank and Saint Paul," written for my seminar in philosophical theology (Fall 2006).

30. Davis and Hays, *Art of Reading Scripture*, p. 1.

31. As he comes to the end of his chapter entitled "Scripture, Consensus, and Community," in his book *The Church in a Postliberal Age*, George Lindbeck notes his acute awareness that his essay is "a counter-instance of what it recommends"; that is, in making his argument he does not refer the reader to the biblical text (p. 284). Desiring to avoid that result, a result I have often exemplified, I will try to explain some of the decisions I made in writing the commentary on Matthew. I am hesitant to do so, however, because (1) I do not want to blow my own horn, even though it is a very little horn; and (2) I do not think I can do justice to the details. One of the things I learned in writing *Matthew* is the inexhaustibility of the text, and I fear that whatever I say here might look like a "point" I was trying to make when I wrote the commentary. I wish I could think of an alternative, but I cannot. I thank the readers for their patience with my attempt to "spell out" the way I approached the task of writing a commentary.

Son to die for us and for our salvation and who raises the crucified Son in the power of the Holy Spirit so that the baptized may be joined in one body — faith in *this* God with *this* vocation of love for the world is the lens through which to view the heterogeneity and particularity of the biblical texts. Doctrine, then, is not a moldering scrim of antique prejudice obscuring the meaning of the Bible. It is a crucial aspect of the divine pedagogy, a clarifying agent for our minds fogged by self-deceptions, a challenge to our languid intellectual apathy that will too often rest in false truisms and the easy spiritual nostrums of the present age rather than search more deeply and widely for the dispersed keys to the many doors of Scripture.[32]

Reno contends that such an approach to Scripture does not mean that doctrine becomes a substitute for exegesis but rather that Scripture is to be read as the living language of faith: "To put the matter in a formula, the more readily exegesis enters into the life and practice of the church, the more fully theological is the interpretation."[33] These were the conditions I assumed I was obligated to try to fulfill in the commentary I was to write on the Gospel of Matthew.

In order to force myself to write, and thus to think, differently, I gave myself certain rules: (1) I would make no reference to the so-called Synoptic Problem; (2) I would try to avoid all "consciousness" words in reference to Jesus or Matthew; (3) I would try to write, not "about" Matthew, but "with" Matthew; and (4) I would try to respect the reticence of Matthew by avoiding any attempt to provide "explanations." Each of these rules in a different way was an attempt to avoid the temptation to "get behind" the text.[34]

---

32. R. R. Reno, series preface, in Hauerwas, *Matthew*, p. 12. Reno quite rightly and helpfully also insists that doctrine is a habit of mind rather than a list of propositions.

33. R. R. Reno, "Apostolic Legitimacy and Apostolic Vitality," *Center for Catholic and Evangelical Theology Report*, Fall 2006, p. 6.

34. Bockmuehl reads the temptation of Jesus, like the temptation of Eve, as an attempt to make Jesus assume the position of an autonomous reasoning subject, isolated from the ecclesial context. Bockmuehl suggests that the tempter's strategy is not unlike some of the rhetorical strategies surrounding Scripture, just to the extent that we are asked to assume a "more objective" stance than the "plain sense of the divine word." Thus the conditional:

> "*If* you really are the Son of God . . ." (Matt. 4:3). A divine Son surely is and does all that pleases him! Never mind that the baptismal heavenly voice in fact affirmed Jesus to be the Son who is and does all that pleases *the Father* (3:17). But unlike his foremother in the garden, this Son does *not* rise to the bait and does *not* produce the invited distortion of what God has "really" said. Instead, the Word

To the extent that I had or have a hermeneutic, I simply tried to display, in the words of Gene Rogers and Lewis Ayres, "the way the words run."[35] According to Ayres, "the way the words run" names the way a community has learned to read texts through training in the grammatical and figural reading habits necessary for the discovery of the plain sense of what is being read.[36] The "plain sense" is not a restrictive reading, but rather it names the inexhaustible richness of the way the words run given that the words are inspired by God. To read the way the words run, therefore, is to let the words

---

himself turns to find in Scripture the true representation, the textual icon, of God's life-giving and all-nourishing presence: "Man . . . shall live by every word that proceeds from the mouth of God" (4:4). (*Seeing the Word,* p. 95, emphasis original)

Unfortunately, I did not have Bockmuehl's book prior to writing the commentary on Matthew, but I did read the temptation of Jesus as a "hermeneutical" lesson that teaches us to resist questions that would have us "go behind the text" in an effort to discover what God must have "really meant" (see *Matthew,* pp. 52-54).

35. Ayres's account of "the way the words run" is to be found in his *Nicaea and Its Legacy: An Approach to Fourth-Century Trinitarian Theology* (New York: Oxford, 2004), p. 32. Ayres borrowed the phrase from Gene Rogers's essay "How the Virtues of an Interpreter Presuppose and Perfect Hermeneutics: The Case of Thomas Aquinas," *JR* 76 (1996): 64-81.

36. Ayres argues that this understanding of reading was not unique to Christians but rather reflected the Roman understanding of the relation between moral formation and reading. Ayres observes that

Roman educators wanted students to learn the right lessons from the right texts. Education in reading technique, therefore, became a contested cultural area and Christians eventually if slowly sought to adapt these teaching techniques by focusing them on Scripture. This feature of Roman education also helps to explain why Christians so naturally read scriptural texts as shaping a form of life, and it reminds modern readers to be clear about the distinction between figural practices — especially allegory — and moral readings. (*Nicaea and Its Legacy,* p. 36)

The significance of training is crucial to understanding Wittgenstein. Thus Wittgenstein's suggestion:

It disperses the fog to study the phenomena of language in primitive kinds of application in which one can command a clear view of the aim and functioning of the words. A child uses such primitive forms of language when it learns to talk. Here the teaching of language is not explanation, but training. (*Philosophical Investigations* §5)

For a good exposition of the *Investigations* that emphasizes the significance of training, see Andrew Lugg, *Wittgenstein's Investigations, 1-133: A Guide and Interpretation* (London: Routledge, 2000).

shape our imaginations such that we are forced to read the world scripturally rather than vice versa.[37]

Accordingly, I begin my commentary on Matthew by observing that Matthew's beginning, "The book of the genesis of Jesus Christ," is to indicate that the story he will tell, like Genesis, is a creation account. Is this an imposition on the text? If Matthew is beginning with creation, why does he not, as Luke does, trace the genealogy back to Adam? Moreover, why does he identify Jesus the Messiah first as the son of David and then as the son of Abraham?

Rather than trying to "explain" the first verse of Matthew, I read the beginning in light of Jesus' apocalyptic announcement that a new age is being inaugurated through his ministry, death, and resurrection. The beginning of Matthew's Gospel is therefore read in light of Jesus' whole life, which is nothing less than the new creation. This is a king, the son of David, sitting in judgment on all the nations of the world (Matt. 25:31-32). But unlike other kings, this king will be sacrificed, because he is also the son of Abraham. I do not, therefore, think it accidental that Jesus the Messiah is first identified as the son of David before he is also designated as the son of Abraham. The way the words run matters, making clear from the very beginning that we will learn what it means for Jesus to be the Messiah only by the hard and painful lesson of the cross.

Some may object that I am making far too much out of what may have been nothing more than Matthew's attempt to assure a community in tension with a synagogue that they were inheritors through David of Israel's promises.[38] Yet given the way the words run, given the way the story is told by the way the words run, it is theologically significant that Jesus is first identified as the son of David before he is identified as the son of Abraham. This son of David, who is also the son of Abraham, will soon be identified as the very Son of God (Matt. 3:17), transfiguring every presumption about what the rule of this king entails. For this is a king who will be sacrificial.

37. I hope this claim exemplifies the argument Hays makes in *The Conversion of the Imagination: Paul as Interpreter of Israel's Scripture* (Grand Rapids: Eerdmans, 2005). "Imagination" names for Hays the poetic character of Paul's reading of the Bible, which he associates with Paul's use of "images." But such "images" are constructed by words, which means that our imaginations depend on how the words run.

38. See Warren Carter, *Matthew and the Margins: A Socio-Political and Religious Reading* (New York: Orbis, 2000), p. 57. I footnote Carter because I deeply admire his readings of Matthew. He is, of course, an extremely skillful historian, but in the manner of many skillful historians, his reading of Matthew depends less on his historical reconstructions than his theological insights. He is quite simply a very fine Christian preacher.

That is why Matthew helps us see that the "what" that is Jesus cannot be separated from how we come to know the what. And so it is telling that Jesus' baptism and temptation is followed by his calling of the disciples. Matthew is a manual for discipleship, requiring that those who would follow Jesus as king learn that this is a king who will rule from a cross. Therefore, it is not accidental that after Jesus went up the mountain and sat down, "his disciples came to him" to be taught (Matt. 5:1). The Sermon on the Mount is the constitution for the creation of a new people. These are not ideals impossible to live but rather descriptions of a community Jesus has made possible.

But the descriptions and the life are inseparable. I therefore read the beatitudes christologically, which means I think it a mistake to speculate about what it means or who might exemplify what it means to be poor in spirit, or what it means to mourn, to be meek, to hunger and thirst for righteousness, to be merciful, pure in heart, a peacemaker, or persecuted. We know what each of those descriptions entails only by attending to the life of Jesus. No word studies can do what only a christological reading makes possible. For example, I suggest that Philippians 2:5-8 is the text we best read to understand what it means to be poor in spirit. Of course, "poor in spirit," even read through the incarnation, remains vague, but vagueness is required just to the extent that the absence of specificity means we will need many readings of this beatitude.[39]

In a similar fashion, we learn what it means to be perfect only through participation in Christ's love of enemies. The assumption that we might know what "perfect" entails abstracted from the one who has loved us — and we must not forget that we are the enemy — results in turning the Sermon on the Mount into an "ethic" or a "law" about which we get to make up our minds. In contrast, I read the sermon as the conditions for a community being called into existence through the life and work of Jesus. Hays may well have found the argument I made in my sermon on the Sermon on the Mount in *Unleashing the Scripture* insufficiently exegetical, but the readings of the Sermon on the Mount in my commentary on Matthew reflect, I hope, the sermon in *Unleashing the Scripture*. Of course, I do not assume simply because my reading of Matthew 5 in the commentary is more detailed that I have satisfied the suggestion that I need to be more exegetical — the good news is that the reading can never come to an end.

---

39. For an account of the significance of the unavoidable character of vagueness, see Peter Ochs, "Morning Prayer as Redemptive Thinking," in *Liturgy, Time, and the Politics of Redemption,* ed. Randi Rashkover and C. C. Pecknold (Grand Rapids: Eerdmans, 2006), pp. 71-74.

Lest it be thought that my theological exegesis means no reading is excluded, I do not think that attempts to negotiate Jesus' underwriting of the law, as well as the righteousness of the scribes and Pharisees, by drawing a distinction between the "ceremonial," the "juridical," and the "moral" do justice to the way the words run. I simply do not find in Scripture a basis for such a distinction. More important, however, than whether the distinction exists in Scripture is how it creates a gulf between Jews and Christians that results in a misreading of Paul.[40]

Markus Bockmuehl entitles the last chapter of his book "Seeing the Son of David," insisting that "no theologically conscionable construal of Jesus's identity . . . can finally bypass this vital and personified commitment to the salvation of Israel, centered on the city over which Jesus lamented."[41] What this means, at the very least, is that Christians cannot protect themselves from questions about why they think they can pick and choose which parts of the law apply to their lives as Christians. How Christians answer such challenges, challenges as basic as the day set aside to worship God, will necessarily be christological. But that does not mean the current practice of Christians can be assumed to settle what we should say to Jews or ourselves when challenged about how we read the law.

I conclude by calling attention to what is perhaps the most daring reading I offer in my commentary on Matthew, namely, that the desolating sacrilege Jesus tells the disciples they will see (Matt. 24:15) is not the destruction of the temple but rather his crucifixion. I believe that is the way the words run once you begin, as Matthew begins, by announcing that "this is the gen-

---

40. Hays's refusal to "leave the Jews behind" in his exegetical practice I believe to be one of his great achievements. In particular, see his chapter "Christ Prays the Psalms: Israel's Psalter as Matrix of Early Christology," in *Conversion of the Imagination*.

Among other well-known exegetical tactics I challenge in the commentary are those that try to deal with Matt. 5:38-41 by invoking the distinction between private and public forms of retaliation. The distinction between the private and the public simply cannot be sustained by the way the words run. That such a distinction has seemed to many a "natural" reading of the sermon reflects a politics quite different from the church I think must exist if we are to avoid importing foreign categories to shape the reading of the gospel.

41. Bockmuehl, *Seeing the Word*, p. 222. Elsewhere, Bockmuehl has shown that Jesus' and Paul's thinking on the law reflected modes of argumentation well within the presumptions of the practice of halakah. See his *Jewish Law in Gentile Churches: Halakhah and the Beginning of Christian Public Ethics* (Edinburgh: T. & T. Clark, 2000). It may be objected that to use this earlier work of Bockmuehl is to undercut my criticism of historical analysis. But such a view presumes I have a stake in denying in principle that historical studies can be of use, which is certainly not the case.

esis of Jesus Christ." Jesus has already told his disciples that the temple will be torn down (Matt. 24:1-2), so calling the destruction of the temple the "desolating sacrilege" adds nothing to what he has already said. There can be no sacrilege more desolating than the death of the Messiah, the Son of God. To be sure, such a reading is theological all the way down, but that does not mean it is any less "exegetical."[42]

I am aware that my reading of Matthew is at best only a beginning for what it might mean for some of us to learn to read Scripture theologically. We are dying — and I mean quite literally we are dying — for examples of what reading Scripture theologically might look like. Scripture, vivified by the Holy Spirit, is the heart of the church. Without a heart we cannot live. I suspect we are in a time of transition when some trained in historical criticism are attempting to work theologically and some trained in theology are attempting to reason "scripturally" through exegetical practice.[43] Richard Hays has had the talent and courage to work both sides of that street and as a result has provided some of the examples, the heart, we so desperately need.[44]

42. I have not addressed Hays's criticism that I impose an order on the discordant texts that constitute the Christian Scriptures. I can do no better than to quote thesis 2 from *The Art of Reading Scripture*'s "Nine Theses": "Though the Bible contains the voices of many different witnesses, the canon of Scripture finds its unity in the overarching story of the work of the triune God. While the Bible contains many tensions, digressions, and subplots, the biblical texts cohere because the one God acts in them and speaks through them: God is the author of Scripture's unity for the sake of the church's faithful proclamation and action" (p. 1). I note that each of the theses is followed by a paragraph in which questions are posed for ongoing discussion, indicating that the theses are not so much a conclusion as an agenda.

43. "Scriptural reasoning" is the name Peter Ochs has given to the work of a group of Jewish, Christian, and Islamic theologians' commitment to read Scripture together. For an introduction to their work, see the July 2006 issue of *Modern Theology*, "The Promise of Scriptural Reasoning," edited by C. C. Pecknold and David F. Ford. The word "reasoning" is crucial, because I am sure one of the difficulties for theologians' arguing exegetically is that such "arguments" do not look like "reason." Peter Ochs, in an essay for the issue entitled "Philosophic Warrants for Scriptural Reasoning" (*ModTh* 22 [2006]: 465-82), provides a wonderful account of what such reasoning entails.

44. I am indebted to Ellen Davis and Kavin Rowe for critical comments on this paper.

Echoes of the Ancient Near East?
Intertextuality and the Comparative Study
of the Old Testament

Christopher B. Hays

One of Richard Hays's contributions to biblical studies has been his advancement of the study of intertextuality. His sensitive readings of specific New Testament texts have served as models, and he has even offered criteria for recognizing "echoes" of the Old Testament in the New, initially in his *Echoes of Scripture in the Letters of Paul*.[1] He restated these criteria with some clarification in a later article, "'Who Has Believed Our Message?' Paul's Reading of Isaiah."[2] This contribution came to mind recently in a conversation with a colleague about Isaiah's appropriation of the ancient Near Eastern historical and religious environment. She asked: "How do you recognize a reference to ANE backgrounds?"

To frame the issue as one of comparative methodology, my colleague's question might be restated as follows: "When, and on what grounds, is comparison valid?" A number of different answers have been proposed (more or less explicitly) to that question, but the overall direction of the field of comparative studies has been a progressive narrowing of scope, to the point that

---

1. Richard B. Hays, *Echoes of Scripture in the Letters of Paul* (New Haven: Yale University Press, 1989).

2. Richard B. Hays, "'Who Has Believed Our Message?' Paul's Reading of Isaiah," in *SBL Seminar Papers 1998* (Atlanta: Scholars Press, 1998), pp. 205-25; reprinted in *The Conversion of the Imagination: Paul as Interpreter of Israel's Scripture* (Grand Rapids: Eerdmans, 2005), pp. 25-49.

I would like to thank Carol Newsom for prompting this study, and David Petersen and Brent Strawn for reading and commenting on it.

our research is conducted primarily within form-critical (i.e., generic) boundaries.[3] As a scholar of biblical prophecy, I am particularly troubled by this trend, because the literary creativity of the prophets is such that one expects old motifs to be employed in new ways, that is, in new *Gattungen* with different *Sitze im Leben*.[4] The prophets frequently subverted and transformed genres (as in the mock lament for the "king of Babylon" in Isaiah 14); moreover, as subtle and artful interpreters of their times and cultures, they wove into their words countless allusions to the literary texts and the sociohistorical "texts" of their worlds. T. N. D. Mettinger has referred to some of these phenomena as the "metamorphic use of conventional motifs and genres."[5] Insofar as intertextuality offers a more robust critical model for addressing these matters, I would like to argue that the comparative study of the Old Testament would be enriched by a fuller engagement with the concept — and perhaps vice versa.

After briefly reviewing comparative studies' limited interaction with intertextual methods, this essay surveys some recent conflicts about the proper understanding of intertextuality and then returns *ad fontes* — to Julia Kristeva's foundational statements about intertextuality — to note that in

---

3. To substantiate this point fully would be another project; however, it can be seen in the tables of contents of standard reference works such as Pritchard's *Ancient Near Eastern Texts* and Hallo and Younger's *Context of Scripture*. A primary classification strategy in all such texts is genre: e.g., "hymns," "legal texts," "historiography." In *ANET*, genre is *the* primary means of classification. In *COS*, it is the third principle, after "Hallo's threefold taxonomy" and language; see Younger's discussion in "The Production of Ancient Near Eastern Text Anthologies from the Earliest to the Latest," in *Orientalism, Assyriology, and the Bible*, ed. Steven W. Holloway, HBM 10 (Sheffield: Sheffield Phoenix, 2006), p. 214. However, the threefold taxonomy (canonical, monumental, archival) is in effect another layer of generic differentiation. Extended comparative studies also seem to be conducted primarily within genres: law codes are compared with other law codes, creation stories are compared with other creation stories, laments are compared with other laments, etc. This is in keeping with Hallo's own observation that "the most fruitful literary comparisons and contrasts can be drawn on the level of genre, that is, of a compositional type conforming to a given pattern and serving a specific function"; see Hallo, "Compare and Contrast: The Contextual Approach to Biblical Literature," in *The Bible in the Light of Cuneiform Literature: Scripture in Context III*, ed. Hallo et al., ANETS 8 (Lewiston, N.Y.: Edwin Mellen, 1990), p. 8. Nor is there any question of Hallo's being exceptional in this opinion; he speaks for the mainstream of the field.

4. So also James Muilenburg, "Form Criticism and Beyond," *JBL* 88 (1969): 5.

5. Tryggve N. D. Mettinger, "Intertextuality: Allusion and Vertical Context Systems in Some Job Passages," in *Of Prophets' Visions and the Wisdom of Sages: Essays in Honour of R. Norman Whybray on His Seventieth Birthday*, ed. H. McKay and D. Clines, JSOTSup 162 (Sheffield: JSOT, 1993), pp. 257-80, quotation p. 275.

some of its less celebrated details, Kristeva's theory is more hospitable to historical approaches than most presentations of it might suggest. I will argue that Hays's guidelines, which are in line with Kristeva's vision in important ways, might mark a promising starting point for an intertextual-comparative method. A final reflection will observe how a particular dimension of Kristeva's view of intertextuality pushes beyond Hays's model in ways that may be useful in the comparative study of the Old Testament.

Intertextuality and Biblical Studies

James Muilenburg's exhortation in his SBL presidential address to move "beyond form criticism" is now a familiar watershed, championing sensitive readings of individual texts and warning against the overgeneralization to which form criticism is prone. Less often noted about the speech is Muilenburg's perception that he was also reopening the question of the comparative task, although he could not answer it in the same context:

> There is another question into which we have not gone. How are we to explain the numerous and extraordinary literary affinities of the *Gattungen* or genres and other stylistic formulations of Israel's literature with the literatures of the other peoples of the Near East? Were the prophets and poets familiar with these records? If not, how are we to explain them? If so, in what ways?[6]

These were hardly new questions, but Muilenburg seems to have been asking for a more carefully reasoned understanding of the intertextual affinities between biblical texts and those of their ancient environs.

A survey of theory and practice in comparative studies since 1969 would show that Muilenburg's suggestion has not been pursued with much alacrity. Indeed, comparative studies, with its steep philological price of entry, is a strong contender for the prize of most refractory subdiscipline in biblical studies when it comes to adopting new methods. As Steven Holloway has bluntly remarked, "The narrow training of specialists as hard-core philologists and archaeologists tend[s] to leave them unprepared to grapple with broader intellectual issues. . . . Assyriology has been particularly hostile to abstract theories originating in other disciplines."[7]

6. Muilenburg, "Form Criticism and Beyond," p. 18.
7. Holloway, introduction to *Orientalism, Assyriology, and the Bible*, p. 33.

One might object that intertextuality has in fact breached the field of Old Testament comparative studies already. It is true that the term is used, but rarely with any theoretical reflection; H. F. Plett bemoans scholars who "use the term 'intertextuality' without having critically examined the concept."[8] As an example, one might take the volume *Intertextuality in Ugarit and Israel,* introduced by its editor, J. C. de Moor, with the observation that "'intertextuality' crops up more and more often in biblical scholarship."[9] Indeed it does, but unfortunately neither de Moor nor any of the nine contributors wrestles in those pages with the question of what intertextuality *is,* or precisely how it ought to influence Old Testament or comparative scholarship.[10] Kristeva and the other pioneers of the idea are not cited once. The volume and the meeting on which it was based seem to have been primarily an opportunity for each scholar to iterate his or her familiar project under a new buzzword. Intertextuality becomes, in Ellen van Wolde's phrase, "a modern literary theoretical coat of veneer over the old comparative approach."[11]

In the present day, however, we may be witnessing a new wave of interest in "theory" among comparative scholars.[12] One would hope that intertextuality would be a facet of this new interest, since it has proved fruitful in New Testament studies — and indeed in literary studies of many sorts

8. Heinrich F. Plett, "Intertextualities," in *Intertextuality,* ed. Plett (Berlin: de Gruyter, 1991), p. 4.

9. Johannes C. de Moor, ed., *Intertextuality in Ugarit and Israel* (Leiden: Brill, 1998), p. ix.

10. I do not mean to single out one book for criticism; one could easily multiply examples. Only one of thirty-three contributors to *The Quest for Context and Meaning: Studies in Biblical Intertextuality in Honor of James A. Sanders,* ed. C. Evans and S. Talmon (Leiden: Brill, 1997) engages with the theoretical underpinnings of the method.

11. Ellen van Wolde, "Trendy Intertextuality?" in *Intertextuality in Biblical Writings: Essays in Honour of Bas van Iersel,* ed. S. Draisma (Kampen: Kok, 1989), p. 43. It should be noted that van Wolde means something rather different by "comparative approach" than what is discussed here.

12. I think of Holloway's above-cited work engaging with Orientalism; Zainab Bahrani with aesthetics in *The Graven Image: Representation in Babylonia and Assyria* (Philadelphia: University of Pennsylvania Press, 2003); Tremper Longman with genre theory in *Fictional Akkadian Autobiography: A Generic and Comparative Study* (Winona Lake, Ind.: Eisenbrauns, 1991); Neal Walls with myth theory in *Desire, Discord, and Death: Approaches to Ancient Near Eastern Myth* (Boston: American Schools of Oriental Research, 2001); or Elnathan Weissert with intertextuality in "Creating a Political Climate: Allusions to Enuma Eliš in Sennacherib's Account of the Battle of Halule," in *Assyrien im Wandel der Zeiten,* RAI 39 (Heidelberg: Heidelberger Orientverlag, 1997), pp. 191-202. One should also mention, even in this very incomplete list, the various contributions of F. W. Dobbs-Allsopp.

— as a category in which to discuss the relationship of texts and ideas to other texts and ideas. A "minimal" definition of intertextuality would be that "in one artistic text there coexist, more or less visibly, several other texts."[13] In its "thicker" manifestations, intertextuality allows an admirable breadth of possibilities for what counts as "other texts" — offering, perhaps, a way for the comparative method to frame and name the broadening of its horizons.

The field is indebted to W. W. Hallo for taking up the methodological question of intertextuality in an essay from 1990[14] — at which time he could locate only a handful of studies in which a scholar of the ancient Near East had employed the term "intertextuality." (Not much has changed since that time. Steven Holloway wrote in 2002 that the "study of 'intertextuality' in Assyrian royal inscriptions is in its infancy,"[15] and the same could still be said of other genres as well.) Unfortunately, the definition from which Hallo was working seems impoverished by the standards of more recent studies:

> Intertextuality has been defined broadly as "a text's dependence on and infiltration by prior codes, concepts, conventions, unconscious practices, and texts," in short, as an alternative to — indeed a weapon against — contextuality. As such it replaces or complements synchronic by diachronic considerations.[16]

13. Hans-Peter Mai, "Bypassing Intertextuality: Hermeneutics, Textual Practice, Hypertext," in *Intertextuality,* ed. Plett, p. 47. Jacob Neusner's view that intertextuality's imperative is to "read everything in light of everything, everywhere, all at once" would indeed be an "invitation to chaos," as he observes in *Canon and Connection: Intertextuality in Judaism* (Lanham, Md.: University Press of America, 1987), p. xiii. Thankfully, it is at best a reflection of one extreme on the spectrum of intertextual theory, and at worst a caricature of the same.

14. W. W. Hallo, "Proverbs Quoted in Epic," in *Lingering over Words: Studies in Ancient Near Eastern Literature in Honor of William L. Moran,* ed. T. Abusch et al. (Atlanta: Scholars Press, 1990), pp. 203-17. An earlier reference to intertextuality is found in William L. Moran's "Some Considerations of Form and Interpretation in Atra-ḫasīs," in *Language, Literature, and History: Philological and Historical Studies Presented to Erica Reiner* (New Haven: American Oriental Society, 1987), p. 253. Although Moran's use of the term suggests that he understands its meaning in a manner closer to Kristeva's, it is no more than a passing note.

15. Steven W. Holloway, *Aššur Is King! Aššur Is King! Religion in the Exercise of Power in the Neo-Assyrian Empire,* CHANE 10 (Leiden: Brill, 2002), p. 93. (It is worth mentioning again, however, Weissert's "Creating a Political Climate" — an excellent example of intertextual research within Assyriology.) The situation for biblical comparativists is arguably still even more impoverished. Peter D. Miscall feints toward biblical/ANE intertextuality but ultimately ends up only discussing biblical texts in detail in "Isaiah: New Heavens, New Earth, New Book," in *Reading Between Texts: Intertextuality and the Hebrew Bible,* ed. D. N. Fewell (Louisville: Westminster John Knox, 1992), pp. 41-56.

16. Hallo, "Proverbs Quoted in Epic," p. 203.

The fact that Hallo viewed intertextuality as "a weapon against contextuality" demonstrates his acquaintance with certain examples of poststructuralist employment of the concept, but he does not develop such aspects at all. Seen from a certain perspective, it is a gracious and accommodating move for a champion of "contextuality" to try to assimilate the contributions of a method that could be understood to subvert his own. Nevertheless, his remarks seem to limit intertextuality to "literary influence," which is properly only a subcategory of intertextuality: "The question of literary influence has, of course, always occupied a considerable place in the study of Western literature. But it is only recently that it has begun to be considered seriously by students of ancient Near Eastern literature."[17] Thus, when Hallo speaks of intertextuality in cuneiform literature, he means what most refer to as "allusion": "the apparently deliberate harking back from one genre to another or from one context to a thoroughly different one, with at least the implication that the source of the allusion is familiar to the 'author,' perhaps even to the audience."[18] This is confirmed by his remarks in his introduction to *The Context of Scripture,* in which he describes intertextuality as a "vertical," diachronic dimension distinct from the "horizontal," contextual dimension.[19] This is rather too narrow a definition of intertextuality, since a text's appropriation of its ("horizontal") context may also quite rightly be described as intertextual.

Hallo's reference to "allusion" may lead to confusion for other reasons as well. Allusion, as Robert Alter has observed, is distinguished by intentionality.[20] By restricting himself to the canonical stream of cuneiform literature, within which he can assume scribes' familiarity, Hallo is able to avoid having to argue for intention, and to gloss over the dissonance between the different theories of intertextuality. In the case of the Hebrew Bible and its ancient Near Eastern "backgrounds," it is profoundly difficult to achieve consensus on mechanisms of historical influence or intention. Not only are texts difficult to date with certainty, but even the basic events of ancient Is-

---

17. Hallo, "Proverbs Quoted in Epic," p. 203.

18. Hallo, "Proverbs Quoted in Epic," p. 207.

19. W. W. Hallo, introduction to *The Context of Scripture,* vol. 1 (Leiden: Brill, 1997), pp. xxv-xxvi.

20. Robert Alter, *The Pleasures of Reading in an Ideological Age* (New York: Simon & Schuster, 1989), pp. 112, 115. On the topic of allusion, see also Ziva Ben-Porat, "The Poetics of Literary Allusion," *PTL* 1 (1976): 105-28; Earl Miner, "Allusion," in *The Princeton Handbook of Poetic Terms,* ed. A. Preminger (Princeton, N.J.: Princeton University Press, 1986), pp. 10-11.

rael's history are contested. This is partly why most who employ the concept of intertextuality with regard to the Old Testament focus on intrabiblical connections where the direction of influence is clearer (e.g., Deutero-Isaiah's use of earlier Isaianic traditions[21]). Yet as long as it is strictly founded on arguments about diachronic development, even intrabiblical research is not safe. Michael Fishbane's influential study of "innerbiblical exegesis" has come under criticism for its assumptions about the historical priority of texts.[22] Similarly, it has proved quite possible to argue a reverse relationship between Deutero-Isaiah and some sections of First Isaiah. If we are willing to accept a limitation of intertextuality to cases where there is an undisputed "pre-text," then the fund of applicable cases will be vanishingly small; and we should also ask what has been gained by the mere employment of the label "intertextuality."

History, Authority, and Intertextuality

Given the lack of clarity about intertextuality in comparative studies, it may be helpful to reframe the matter before proceeding. Plett has remarked that intertextuality "is a fashionable term, but almost everybody who uses it understands it somewhat differently."[23] Intertextuality is most helpful as a category, in my view, when it is defined broadly, as comprising both allusion and other possible relationships among texts. One helpful typology of intertextuality is offered by Stefan Alkier, to whose work Hays has sought to draw attention.[24]

21. E.g., Benjamin D. Sommer, *A Prophet Reads Scripture: Allusion in Isaiah 40-66* (Stanford: Stanford University Press, 1998); H. G. M. Williamson, *The Book Called Isaiah: Deutero-Isaiah's Role in Composition and Redaction* (Oxford: Oxford University Press, 1994). Similarly, Marvin A. Sweeney perceives "debates" with Isaiah on the part of Micah and Zechariah in *Form and Intertextuality in Prophetic and Apocalyptic Literature*, FAT 45 (Tübingen: Mohr Siebeck, 2005), pp. 210-35.

22. Lyle Eslinger, "Inner-Biblical Exegesis and Inner-Biblical Allusion: The Question of Category," *VT* 42 (1992): 47-58.

23. Plett, "Intertextualities," p. 3. In addition to Plett's *Intertextuality*, good introductions to the concept include Ulrich Broich and Manfred Pfister, eds., *Intertextualität: Formen, Funktionen, anglistische Fallstudien* (Tübingen: Niemeyer, 1985); and Michael Worton and Judith Still, eds., *Intertextuality: Theories and Practice* (Manchester, N.Y.: Manchester University Press, 1990).

24. I am particularly indebted to Hays's lecture "Intertextuality: A Catchall Category or a Specific Methodology?" delivered at the SBL Annual Meeting, San Antonio, Texas, November 21, 2004. His work with Alkier has resulted in *Die Bibel im Dialog der Schriften: Konzepte intertextueller Bibellektüre*, ed. Alkier and Hays (Tübingen: Franke, 2005).

Alkier suggests that one should distinguish between three types of intertextual interpretation: the *production-oriented* perspective, the *reception-oriented* perspective, and the *experimental* perspective.[25] The first two types are bounded by what we can know or credibly hypothesize about the actual knowledge, intentions, and interpretations of the author, or of actual communities of readers, respectively. The third, which could also be described as a purely text-oriented perspective, opens the field to intertextual readings of two or more texts that may have no direct historical linkage and may never before have been connected by any community of readers. In each case, the text is read within a particular *discursive universe (Diskursuniversum)* that shapes the interpretive understandings of a particular reading community. Danna Nolan Fewell has suggested that the web of intertexts is "bounded only by human culture and language itself."[26] Alkier might be understood to pose the next logical questions: *Whose culture? And whose language?*

One could take Isaiah 22:13b as an example of Alkier's typology. From a production-oriented perspective, the comment "Let us eat and drink, for tomorrow we die" may well have been a reflection of actual funerary-cult feast language, perhaps Mesopotamian or Egyptian in origin, something that would have been known at least to Judean scribes and perhaps to other hearers.[27] From a reception-oriented perspective, the phrase was referenced by Paul (1 Cor. 15:32) to emphasize the importance of faith in the resurrection of the dead, so that Christian gospel became an intertext for the ancient saying. Finally, from an experimental perspective, a scholar in the present day might take up the saying as a way of illustrating more modern Materialist philosophical positions. In this third case the scholar need not show that the philosophies in question have any knowledge of the biblical text at all; instead, the intertextual event takes place in the mind of the scholar. The text would function in rather different ways in each of these discursive universes.

Although Alkier and others view all three of the aforementioned perspectives as legitimate and necessary, others have made the very study of intertextuality into a battleground. If we recall the parable of the blind men

---

25. Stefan Alkier, "Die Bibel im Dialog der Schriften und das Problem der Verstockung in Mk 4: Intertextualität im Rahmen einer kategorialen Semiotik biblischer Texte," in *Die Bibel im Dialog der Schriften,* pp. 1-22, esp. 6-11.

26. Fewell, "Introduction: Writing, Reading, and Relating," in *Reading Between Texts,* p. 17.

27. For a full list of similar sayings, see Hans Wildberger, *Isaiah 13–27,* trans. T. H. Trapp (Minneapolis: Fortress, 1997), pp. 373-74.

and the elephant, intertextuality is the elephant, and some of the blind men, disagreeing on its nature, have begun to beat each other with their canes. The battle lines are drawn primarily between the historical and ahistorical ("experimental") approaches.[28] Historical scholars tend to manifest this controversy through a simple disdain for ahistorical readings.[29] Since in biblical studies historicism is still the dominant perspective, the assaults from the ahistorical perspective have been more overt. For example, the editors of a *Semeia* volume on intertextuality sought "to challenge the tendency especially among certain biblical scholars to employ intertextuality . . . as a restrictive tool for nailing down authorial intent and literary influence (for example, see . . . Hays)."[30]

One might ask: Do projects like Hays's, with their historical interest in the *Diskursuniversum* and intentions of the author, have any claim to being intertextual?[31] One could parse minutely the myriad ways in which intertextuality has been understood, but I would instead like to return *ad fontes,* to look at Julia Kristeva's original formulation of the concept. I do not wish to gloss over the differences between Kristeva's ideology and that of Hays and other biblical scholars who employ the notion of intertextuality,[32]

---

28. Plett, "Intertextualities," pp. 3-4, refers to these two groups as "traditionalists" and "progressives," terms whose political baggage is probably better avoided.

29. The situation is different in comparative literature and English departments, where the great popularity of intertextual approaches has spawned somewhat vitriolic rejections such as William Irwin, "Against Intertextuality," *PhLit* 28 (2004): 227-42. Excerpt: "The term *intertextuality* is at best a rhetorical flourish intended to impress, at worst it is the signifier of an illogical position" (p. 240).

30. George Aichele and Gary A. Phillips, "Introduction: Exegesis, Eisegesis, Intergesis," *Semeia* 69/70 (1995): 7. The authors are inspired by similar attacks in other parts of the humanities, citing, e.g., Manfred Pfister, "How Postmodern Is Intertextuality?" in *Intertextuality,* ed. Plett, who argues that "a reduction of intertextuality to distinct and pointed references from one particular text to another runs counter to the vitally expansive nature of this principle. It is no more than a futile academic attempt to tame the indomitable, a bourgeois attempt to defuse its explosive and revolutionary potential that aims to expose all notions of autonomy and unity of the subject and the text as ideological fictions" (p. 211).

31. Interestingly, *Echoes of Scripture* was criticized when it first appeared for being equivocal about the role of history in hermeneutics (see Karl Donfried's review in *TS* 52 [1991]: 732-34). The problem seems to have been the sometimes-implicit distinction that Hays made between the *Diskursuniversum* of Paul's letters (which interested him) and their specific historical date and setting (which interested him less in the context of that project).

32. These differences should not be drawn too starkly. Kristeva may be perceived as something of a Marxist revolutionary, but Hays's readings of the biblical text have revolutionary implications as well. The constant self-critique that Kristeva envisions for semiotics

but I believe one finds support in Kristeva's writings for the historical study of texts and authors, and thus for a critique of the antihistorical comments I have just cited. As Kristeva says quite clearly, to study a text intertextually is to consider it "within (the text of) society and history."[33]

Kristeva's theory, in its original formulation, is *not* particularly at home in a literary world where the author is dead, or where the reader is the measure and meaning of all things. Her concept of intertextuality was inspired in large part by her reading of Bakhtin and his theories of "dialogism" and "polyphony."[34] In Bakhtin's writings, these terms work in two ways: First, they name conditions of all reality — the world is characterized by a multiplicity of individual voices and perspectives (polyphony), and reality can be truly grasped only when it is expressed as a dialogue among these multiple voices (dialogism). But second, in literary terms, dialogism and polyphony are the product of authorial genius. In Bakhtin's view, only a *virtuoso* writer could capture these voices on the page and thereby portray reality faithfully. For example, polyphony was characteristic of Dostoevsky's novels, but not of most novels, let alone of all writing. The author and the world of the text's production mattered to Bakhtin, and apparently to Kristeva as well.

Kristeva's intertextuality had roots in her social and (one might say) ethical interests, since a text interacts with the "social text" of its environment:

> The structure of the French novel in the 15th century might be considered as the result of a transformation of many other codes. . . . The transformational method thus leads us to situate the literary structure within the social ensemble considered as a textual ensemble. We shall give the name INTERTEXTUALITY to this textual interaction that is produced within a single text. For the knowing subject, intertextuality is the indication of the way in which a text reads history and inserts itself into it. The concrete manner of intertextuality's realization in a text will

---

is not so different from what Hays understands in the NT term μετανοέω. For both, reading intextextually should be a "politically transformative practice" (cf. Mai, "Bypassing Intertextuality," p. 41).

33. Julia Kristeva, "The Bounded Text" (1966-67), in *Desire in Language: A Semiotic Approach to Literature and Art*, ed. L. S. Roudiez, trans. T. Gora, A. Jardine, and L. S. Roudiez (New York: Columbia University Press, 1980), p. 37.

34. On the connection of Bakhtin and Kristeva, see Graham Pechey, "Bakhtin, Marxism, and Post-Structuralism," in *The Politics of Theory: Proceedings of the Essex Conference on the Sociology of Literature, July 1982* (Colchester: University of Essex Press, 1982), pp. 234-47; also Pfister, "How Postmodern Is Intertextuality?"

determine the primary characteristic ("social," "esthetic") of a textual structure.[35]

The term "transformational method" might be adopted to describe the way in which Kristeva, like Bakhtin, believed that texts do not merely reflect history but affect it ("insert themselves into it"). Because texts do this, one can, or rather must, consider the ways in which their implied authors *intended* to use the texts, both literary and social, that made up their environment.

It is true that Kristeva was not terribly interested in persuading her reader of specific allusions, influences, or sources. Intertextuality, she wrote, is not to be misunderstood in "the banal sense of 'study of sources.'"[36] She might even have sympathized with Harold Bloom's impatience with "the wearisome industry of source-hunting."[37] But a great disservice is done to her theory if this aversion is amplified beyond recognition by later writers, so that one gets the impression that it is just as well not to know anything about the world in which literary works took shape. Intertextuality as she conceived it does *not* seem to have been "a weapon against context" — she was indeed interested in context, but primarily in the way in which texts are transposed in a given context. At the end of one of her first essays on intertextuality, Kristeva called for the construction of a typology of cultures based on historical study, in order that "in studying the signifying practices in relationship to the sign, we may situate them in history."[38] This interest is

35. ". . . la structure du roman français au 15e siècle peut-elle être considérée comme le résultat d'une transformation de plusieurs autres codes. . . . La méthode transformationnelle nous mène donc à situer la structure littéraire dans l'ensemble social considéré comme un ensemble textuel. Nous appellerons INTERTEXTUALITÉ cette inter-action textuelle qui se produit à l'intérieur d'un seul texte. Pour le sujet connaissant, l'intertextualité est une notion qui sera l'indice de la façon dont un texte lit l'histoire et s'insère en elle. Le mode concret de réalisation de l'intertextualité dans un texte précis donnera la caractéristique majeure ('sociale,' 'esthétique') d'une structure textuelle." Julia Kristeva, "Narration et transformation," *Semiotica* 1 (1969): 443. Translations from the French are my own.

36. "le sens banal de 'critique des sources.'" Kristeva, *La révolution du langage poétique* (Paris: Éditions du Seuil, 1974), p. 60.

37. Harold Bloom, *The Anxiety of Influence: A Theory of Poetry* (New York: Oxford University Press, 1973), p. 31.

38. ". . . en étudiante les pratiques signifiantes dans leur rapport avec le signe, nous les situerons dans l'histoire." Kristeva, "Narration et transformation," p. 448. On the connection of this passage to Bakhtinian ideas, see J. Féral, "Kristevan Semiotics: Towards a Semanalysis," in *The Sign: Semiotics Around the World,* ed. R. W. Bailey et al. (Ann Arbor: Michigan Slavic, 1980), p. 275.

quite comprehensible in light of the Marxist influence on her work of this period; Marxism is among other things a theory of history, after all.

Situating "transformational practice" in history is not, of course, an exotic concept in biblical studies. It is akin to the hermeneutical procedure Samuel Sandmel called for some years ago. Granted, he said, there may be hundreds of places where Paul used similar language to that of the rabbis; however, this hypothetical situation does not imply that Paul and the rabbis were in thorough agreement. He suggests that scholars press on to "the next question, namely, what is the significance in the context of Paul's epistles of these parallels?"[39] That is, how does Paul transform rabbinic language to serve his own ends? The answer to that question is naturally debated today. Yet while the significance of ANE parallels in specific Old Testament texts is certainly a subject of study, this is not typically done in a systematic fashion. One suspects that the "transformational practice" of the prophetic texts would prove to be very different from that of wisdom texts.

Another possible objection to my portrait of Kristeva is the undeniable fact that her "dialogue with Bakhtin . . . was mediated by the texts of Derrida and Lacan."[40] For that reason, she sometimes made intertextuality sound like a poststructuralist concept, as when she called the text a *tissu* ("fabric") of woven citations of other texts: "The 'literary word' is not a point (a fixed sense), but an intersection of textual surfaces, a dialogue of many writings: that of the writer, that of the addressee (or the individual), or that of the present or earlier cultural context."[41] But this literary act of weaving appears to have been for Kristeva a deliberate one on the part of the author; in an admiring study of Bakhtin's dialogism, she wrote: "Bakhtin situates the text within history and society, which are then seen as texts read by the writer, and into which he inserts himself by rewriting them."[42] Even Kristeva's rejec-

---

39. Samuel Sandmel, "Parallelomania," *JBL* 81 (1962): 5.

40. Jay Clayton and Eric Rothstein, "Figures in the Corpus: Theories of Influence and Intertextuality," in *Influence and Intertextuality in Literary History*, ed. J. Clayton and E. Rothstein (Madison: University of Wisconsin Press, 1991), p. 18. A fuller discussion of Kristeva's interaction with these thinkers may be found in Mai, "Bypassing Intertextuality." In "How Postmodern Is Intertextuality?" Pfister critiques efforts to conflate "intertextuality" with other postmodern projects.

41. "[L]e 'mot littéraire' n'est pas un *point* (un sens fixe), mais un *croisement de surfaces* textuelles, un dialogue de plusiers écritures: de l'écrivain, du destinataire (ou du personnage), du contexte culturel actuel ou antérieur." Kristeva, "Le mot, le dialogue, et le roman" (1966), in *Semeiotiké: Recherches pour une sémanalyse* (Paris: Éditions du Seuil, 1969), p. 144; cf. also "La productivité dite texte" (1967), in *Semeiotiké*, p. 225.

42. Kristeva, "Word, Dialogue, and Novel" (1966), in *Desire in Language*, p. 65.

tion of the term "intertextuality" in favor of "transposition" emphasizes her belief in some version of *author*-ity; it "indicates her continued interest in the positionalities of writing rather than the responses of reading."[43] After all, "transpose" can be an active, transitive verb — you can transpose a text, whereas (to quote Robert Alter) "you can't 'intertextual' it."[44] As Kristeva wrote, "We prefer the term *transposition* because it specifies that the passage from one signifying system to another demands a new articulation of the thetic — of enunciative and denotative positionality."[45] Whichever metaphor is used, weaving or transposing, Kristeva's terminology emphasizes the agency of an author — not an author whose intention can restrict the significance of his or her text, but *apart from whom there can be no transposition of sign systems.* Minimally, one might compare the Kristevan author to a scientist who scoops up a bucket of chemicals and dumps it into another vat of chemicals: he may not be able to predict or control the reactions that ensue, yet he is still the *sine qua non* of the experiment, and his actions and motivations are subject to investigation. Indeed, even this image perhaps slights authorship too much, since, like Bakhtin, Kristeva was an appreciative reader. In short, it seems that readings of Kristeva that identify her too closely with poststructuralist theorists — even (as is commonly done) with her friend and mentor Roland Barthes — obscure these historical aspects of her thought.

The effects of such conflation can be seen in an account of intertextuality such as Timothy K. Beal's. Beal has repeatedly called into question the value and legitimacy of historical readings of the biblical text, and instead identifies the interpreter as the primary locus of meaning:

> The tracing out of intertextual relations is endless and, quite literally, pointless. Therefore, any interpretive conclusion is a matter of giving up, shutting down, or maybe petering out. The interpreter makes a de-cision, a cut, which cuts off other possible relations, positions roadblocks against other intersections. And where I make my cuts and set up my roadblocks is likely determined not only by accident and oversight but also by the hermeneutical and ideological norms — spoken and unspoken — estab-

---

43. Clayton and Rothstein, "Figures in the Corpus," p. 21.

44. Alter, *Pleasures of Reading*, p. 112: "You can allude to a text, but you can't 'intertextual' it."

45. "Nous . . . préférerons [le terme] transposition, qui a l'avantage de préciser que le passage d'un système signifiant à un autre exige un nouvelle articulation de thétique — de la positionalité énonciative et dénotative." Kristeva, *La révolution du langage poétique,* p. 60.

lished within my academic discipline and within my other networks of affiliation and accountability.[46]

In this model, the interpreter's decisions are based on "accident," "oversight," and the norms of a community. For Beal, the interpreter is the one who "make[s] sense" of the text.[47] The text is a "production of meaning," which produces a surplus of meaning for the interpreter to use. But interpreters, according to Beal's Marxist frame of reference, use their control over the productivity of texts to cement their own power. Thus, the task of the intertextual interpreter is to "dynamite the established strategies of containment."[48]

Is this a good account of intertextuality? The implications of Beal's description should be drawn out. In the first place, it devalues the norms of academic disciplines and other networks by equating them with the arbitrary decisions of the individual interpreter; that is, it assumes that there is no greater wisdom in such communities and traditions.[49] It devalues the text itself by claiming that any conclusion one draws about its meaning is at best a failure of energy and at worst a purposeful hindrance to the ongoing interpretive process. (Paradoxically, it may also *overvalue* the text if it makes it the only check on the interpreter's fancy.) Such a view is likely to be attractive to interpreters who feel oppressed and constrained by the traditions and communities that precede and surround them, but this picture of the futility of drawing interpretive conclusions is not convincing. Such conclusions are futile only to the extent that any and all human knowledge is futile. In fact, much of the scholarship on historical relationships among texts is rather convincing and impressive. Furthermore, for a scholar who perceives that a text *means something* (i.e., that it allows for certain interpretations and not others), who believes that meaning is outside him- or herself, and who seeks to grasp that meaning, there is no other way to proceed than to ask historical questions. One might agree with Beal that texts have a surplus of meaning

---

46. Timothy K. Beal, "Intertextuality," in *Handbook of Postmodern Biblical Interpretation*, ed. A. K. M. Adam (St. Louis: Chalice, 2000), p. 129.

47. Timothy K. Beal, "Ideology and Intertextuality: Surplus of Meaning and Controlling the Means of Production," in *Reading Between Texts*, p. 31.

48. Beal, "Ideology and Intertextuality," p. 36.

49. Note the objection to reader-oriented literary theories in Simon B. Parker, *Stories in Scripture and Inscriptions: Comparative Studies on Narratives in Northwest Semitic Inscriptions and the Hebrew Bible* (New York: Oxford University Press, 1997), p. 4: "Rather than seeking to let the literature of ancient Israel address us on its own terms, . . . it too easily makes of biblical literature a reflection of our own concerns at the end of the twentieth century, whether secular or theological."

but still notice that their surplus is not limitless and thus that they do exercise controls on the reader.

Historically inclined scholars do not, of course, believe their historical arguments to be mathematical in their certainty; as with all *Wissenschaft,* their results are subject to revision in light of better information. Benjamin Sommer, in a defense of Fishbane, granted that historical judgments about texts "may place the critic in a precarious situation" in requiring difficult decisions about dating and the "sufficient conditions for terming a parallel a borrowing." But he steadfastly insisted that the proper response to this situation is not a flight from historical concerns but rather the "careful construction of an argument."[50] And even with our best efforts, the same caveats that Hays conceded must be maintained: The identification of echoes is a "daunting challenge" that makes great claims on the historical imagination in order to reconstruct the *mundus significans* of the text; furthermore, it is "not a strictly scientific matter lending itself to conclusive proof" but an art requiring aesthetic judgment.[51]

Even aesthetic judgments require persuasive argumentation, however, at least in academia. How should a historical argument about one text's use of another be constructed? H. G. M. Williamson has recently offered some useful methods by which the approximate historical date of texts may be established to the satisfaction of reasonable minds. One of his principles is a text's appearance in "quotations and allusions by later writers."[52] But here he focuses on intrabiblical examples such as Deutero-Isaiah's references to earlier Isaianic texts, where the sheer volume of allusions is overwhelming. What of subtler cases such as we often find in the Bible's allusions to the ancient Near East? Sommer offers guidelines:

> I think scholars can develop criteria to distinguish between cases in which texts share vocabulary by coincidence or by their independent use of a literary tradition, on the one hand, and cases in which one author borrows vocabulary from an older text, on the other. . . . If two texts share vocabulary items that are commonplace in Biblical Hebrew, the parallel between them is most likely coincidental. If they share terms that often appear together in biblical or ancient Near Eastern texts, then there is a strong like-

---

50. Benjamin D. Sommer, "Exegesis, Allusion, and Intertextuality in the Hebrew Bible: A Response to Lyle Eslinger," *VT* 46 (1996): 489.

51. Hays, "Who Has Believed?" pp. 29-30.

52. H. G. M. Williamson, "In Search of the Pre-Exilic Isaiah," in *In Search of Pre-Exilic Israel,* ed. J. Day, JSOTSup 406 (London/New York: T. & T. Clark, 2004), p. 191.

lihood that they independently draw on traditional vocabulary clusters. If the vocabulary is neither common nor part of a known vocabulary cluster, then the possibility of genuine borrowing is strong. If a text repeatedly alters the wording or ideas of earlier texts in certain ways, or if it displays a particular preference for certain texts, then examples of shared vocabulary which display those tendencies are likely to represent genuine cases of borrowing.[53]

These are useful criteria, to be sure, but they are too narrow, grounded solely in vocabulary. As one moves to comparative work, one must take account of borrowing *across linguistic barriers,* which in many cases necessitates appeal to other criteria.[54] In fact, I do not think Sommer would wish to proceed so narrowly as this passage suggests, even with inner-biblical research: elsewhere in the article, when he speaks of the "cumulative" nature of arguments for allusions, or the "likelihood that the author would allude to the alleged source," he shows his inclination to employ a broader model.[55]

A Broader Application of the Seven Principles of *Echoes*?

I would like to investigate whether Hays's model might provide a starting point for an intertextual-comparative method in Old Testament scholarship. It would not be surprising if this model were useful in pressing beyond the form-critical impasse, since it is non-generic by nature; that is, Paul's letters are not of the same genre as the scriptural texts that they echo. Let us recall Hays's seven criteria for recognizing echoes of Scripture in Paul's writings

---

53. Sommer, "Exegesis, Allusion, and Intertextuality," pp. 483-85.

54. It can entail significant labor to deal with this problem and establish "corresponding expressions," as Peter Machinist did regarding Assyrian rhetoric in "Assyria and Its Image in First Isaiah," *JAOS* 103 (1983): 719-37; or as I did regarding terms for "yoke" in "Kirtu and the 'Yoke of the Poor': A New Interpretation of an Old Crux (KTU 1.16 VI:48)," *UF* 37 (2005): 361-70. It appears to me that a broader method would be desirable in various ANE fields; consider Leonard Lesko's comment about two Egyptian texts: "Although there are no overlapping phrases in the two texts, and the surviving manuscripts are separated by hundreds of years, it is not impossible that there would be some connection between these two prophecies." Lesko, "The End Is Near," in *Through a Glass Darkly: Magic, Dreams, and Prophecy in Ancient Egypt,* ed. Kasia Szpakowska (Swansea: Classical Press of Wales, 2006), p. 67.

55. Sommer, "Exegesis, Allusion, and Intertextuality," p. 485. Sommer cites *Echoes of Scripture* at length on p. 484 but does not otherwise allude to the "echoes" model.

and reflect on how they would need to be adapted. In each case, I have modified pieces of his explanation to speak to a wider audience.

1. *Availability: Was the proposed source of the echo available to the author and/or his original readers?*[56] This is of course the great differentiating factor between Hays's project and the one I am proposing. Whereas New Testament scholars can quite safely assume that the authors of their texts had access to most or all of the Old Testament, Old Testament scholars must always proceed cautiously in assuming what cultural knowledge was possessed by Israelite and Judean authors. It is the rare instance when — as in the case of Proverbs 22:17–24:22 and the Egyptian text Wisdom of Amenemope — a direct literary relationship can easily be argued (and even in this case it cannot be proven). Nevertheless, scribes at the royal courts of Samaria and Jerusalem were no doubt quite familiar with the cultures of the surrounding nations.[57] Then as now, commerce and diplomacy were powerful drivers of international contact, and there is no doubt that the Judean court in the monarchic era had contact with Egypt, Mesopotamia, and the Syro-Palestinian seacoast — in other words, with all of the great cultural powers to whose texts biblical texts are often compared. In contrast to the situations in Egypt and Mesopotamia, the majority of the literary production of Judah and Israel (i.e., apart from the curated records found in the Bible) has been essentially obliterated and so is inaccessible to direct study, but it behooves the comparativist to keep a very open mind about the availability of influences.

2. *Volume: How "loud" is the echo; that is, how explicit and overt is it?*[58] Occasionally, the Old Testament scholar encounters a text that explicitly announces its incorporation of other voices from the ancient Near East, such as the speech of the Assyrian *rab šaqeh* at the wall of Jerusalem in 2 Kings 18–19//Isaiah 36–37; Peter Machinist has verified that significant portions of the biblical account do reflect genuine Assyrian rhetoric.[59] There are other "loud" echoes of the surrounding ANE cultures, of course.

---

56. Cf. Hays, "Who Has Believed?" p. 34.

57. Kaufmann's old claim that the ancient Israelites did not even understand the religions of their neighbors can safely be dismissed; see Yehezkel Kaufmann, *The Religion of Israel: From Its Beginnings to the Babylonian Exile,* trans. and abr. Moshe Greenberg (Chicago: University of Chicago Press, 1960), pp. 7-20. The biblical critique of paganism, whatever its vintage, is rhetorical — that is, intended to convince, not instruct — and thus not necessarily reflective of what its authors actually knew.

58. Cf. Hays, "Who Has Believed?" p. 34.

59. Machinist, "Assyria and Its Image in First Isaiah."

For example, Psalm 29 has such affinities with Syro-Palestinian theology that some have proposed that it could be a "Baal hymn brought over into Yahwism."[60]

Hays's distinction between allusion and echo may be instructive here (*"allusion* is used of obvious intertextual references, *echo* of subtler ones").[61] Echoes of the ancient Near East are certainly more numerous than allusions in the Old Testament — indeed, they are pervasive. As an example of an echo, it can be shown that the bird imagery of Daniel 4:30 (4:33 Eng.) — which is merely mysterious on a first reading — owes much to a long tradition of such imagery in Mesopotamian laments.[62] It is predominantly the quieter echoes of the ancient Near East that remain to be noticed, and other criteria may outweigh sheer volume. The task requires wide knowledge, both of texts and of languages. Where the New Testament scholar may identify louder echoes by means of "verbatim repetition of words and syntactical patterns"[63] from the Greek versions of the Jewish Scriptures, the Old Testament comparativist typically faces the problem of linguistic gaps between cultures.[64] Still, one should not despair or set the bar unduly high for "commensurate terms"; in her influential article on literary allusion, Ziva Ben-Porat demonstrates an allusion by T. S. Eliot to John Donne that is marked by only two words, "hair" and "bracelet."[65]

3. Recurrence or Clustering: How often does the author cite or allude to the same text?[66] In sections of the Old Testament where the Bible's relationship to ancient Near Eastern patterns is extensive, it will be easier to establish a literary reference in a specific location. For example, knowing that the Psalms have much in common with the prayers of neighboring cultures may prompt the scholar to expect echoes. And knowing that Deuteronomy has a shape akin to that of Assyrian (or perhaps Hittite) treaties invites closer comparison of its legal materials.[67] But this should not be limited to in-

60. Patrick D. Miller, *They Cried to the Lord: The Form and Theology of Biblical Prayer* (Minneapolis: Fortress, 1994), p. 373 n. 123.

61. Hays, *Echoes*, p. 29.

62. Christopher B. Hays, "Chirps from the Dust: The Affliction of Nebuchadnezzar in Daniel 4:30 in Its Ancient Near Eastern Context," *JBL* 126 (2007): 305-25.

63. Hays, "Who Has Believed?" p. 35.

64. See Plett's discussion of linguistic "transcoding" ("Intertextualities," p. 11). The NT scholar must sometimes refer to the Hebrew or Aramaic Scriptures in order to assess an echo, but the problem is much more pervasive in ancient Near Eastern comparative studies.

65. Ben-Porat, "Poetics of Literary Allusion," pp. 118-21.

66. Cf. Hays, "Who Has Believed?" p. 37.

67. See, e.g., Eckart Otto, *Das Deuteronomium: Politische Theologie und Rechtsreform in*

stances of generic similarity; for example, prophetic books that make extensive reference to the political "texts" of their time (i.e., events and their representations) require scrutiny to identify, insofar as it is possible, how they transpose those texts and thus insert themselves into the historical text. As an example of the transposition of a historical text, one might take the biblical treatments of Cyrus. Rather than asking whether Daniel, Isaiah, Ezra, or Chronicles portrays him most accurately, or seeking to harmonize those accounts into one "historical" portrait, the intertextual scholar might ask, "How does each of the biblical authors transpose Cyrus in his writings?" In this way Cyrus's historical interactions with the Jews become intertexts. It goes without saying that this will not be as tidy (or as literary) an enterprise for the Old Testament scholar as the identification of scriptural echoes is for the New Testament scholar.

4. *Thematic Coherence: How well does the alleged echo fit into the line of argument of the passage in question? Does the proposed precursor text fit together with the point the author is making?*[68] Old Testament comparativists must employ this criterion carefully. There *are* instances in which biblical echoes of the ancient Near East appear with largely the same thematic content, such as the aforementioned example from Proverbs. But a case like Deuteronomy, which seems to employ the trope of an Assyrian treaty in order to emphasize allegiance to Yahweh rather than the Assyrian emperor, demonstrates that the biblical authors often adopted foreign forms and themes precisely in order to *subvert* them; in such a case there is an *inverse* thematic coherence. Another example is Isaiah 14:4-27, which references ANE lament forms and burial practices in order to mock and curse the one who is being "lamented." Or again, if it is true that Genesis 1 makes reference to the Babylonian creation myth, then it is an example of a subtler subversion of prior texts, since it obviously makes very different claims about the origin of the world. Of course, Hays is aware that "the rebounds of intertextual echo generally . . . distort the original voice in order to interpret it,"[69] but it seems to me that biblical authors typically reevaluate extrabiblical material more radically than earlier biblical material.[70] (This is true of the

---

Juda und Assyrien (Berlin: de Gruyter, 1999); George E. Mendenhall, "Ancient Oriental and Biblical Law" and "Covenant Forms in Israelite Tradition," *BA* 17 (1954): 25-46, 49-76.

68. Cf. Hays, "Who Has Believed?" p. 38.

69. Hays, *Echoes,* p. 19, quoting John Hollander, *The Figure of Echo: A Mode of Allusion in Milton and After* (Berkeley: University of California Press, 1981), p. 111.

70. This would be a topic for further reflection; but even a text like Jer. 31:29-30, in which one biblical author flatly contradicts another, at least acknowledges the intention and

New Testament as well — one thinks of Paul's sermon on the "unknown god" in Acts 17.)

5. Historical Plausibility: Could an author in fact have intended the alleged meaning effect of any proposed allusion, and could contemporaneous readers have understood it?[71] This question raises tricky issues akin to those surrounding availability. Hays explains that this criterion should force the scholar to take seriously the biblical authors' "historical situatedness";[72] one should ideally be able to confirm that the interpretation given is consonant with those of other writers of the same time period. Can a given reading have made sense in a given sociocultural world? Here again scholars of later periods, with more extensive catalogues of texts, are at a great advantage. Who *were* the first readers of a given Old Testament text? Questions about how these texts were written and read in their ancient contexts are often glossed over by scholars,[73] but the answers will have a radical impact on one's conclusions about plausible "reader-competence."[74] The literary corpora of other ANE cultures may suggest how scribes from other cultures "read" texts and historical events, but the textual remains from Syria-Palestine are comparatively limited. Our best evidence for ancient reading practices in Israel may be the way that biblical texts read other biblical texts, which has been the topic of numerous recent studies.[75]

Advancing beyond this present state of the art to incorporate extrabiblical ancient Near Eastern evidence will test the creativity of the comparativist. For example, ritual objects and cylinder seals from Israel and Judah shed light on cultural and religious developments that we usually reconstruct only from texts. If iconographic and literary influence are correlated, then the valuable studies of ANE iconography by the Fribourg School

---

authority of the earlier saying. The reclamation of the original meaning of extrabiblical intertexts is often much trickier.

71. Cf. Hays, "Who Has Believed?" p. 41.

72. Hays, "Who Has Believed?" p. 41.

73. This is by no means a universal oversight. One might mention James W. Watts's *Reading Law: The Rhetorical Shaping of the Pentateuch*, BibSem 59 (Sheffield: Sheffield Academic, 1999); David M. Carr's *Writing on the Tablet of the Heart: Origins of Scripture and Literature* (Oxford: Oxford University Press, 2005); or William Schniedewind's *How the Bible Became a Book: The Textualization of Ancient Israel* (Cambridge: Cambridge University Press, 2004).

74. Hays, "Who Has Believed?" p. 42.

75. E.g., the works of Sommer, Williamson, Watts, Carr, Schniedewind, etc., that are cited above.

(i.e., Keel, Uehlinger, et al.)[76] may help guide textual scholars to expect influence from specific foreign cultures in specific periods. Keel and Uehlinger report that Judahite crafts during the Iron IIB era (ca. 925-725) give "evidence of an intense fascination with Egyptian power symbols,"[77] accelerating in Judah by the second half of the eighth century. This increase, they note, "relates indirectly to the encroachment of the Assyrians and to the related fact that Judah established considerably closer ties with Egypt under Hezekiah . . . when it faced the threat from [Mesopotamia]."[78] In other words, Judean adoption of Egyptian religious motifs accelerated as the political relationship between the two nations grew warmer. Since this finding correlates with other archaeological data as well,[79] it establishes a locus of possible cultural intercourse for textual scholars to investigate.

6. History of Interpretation: Have other readers in the tradition heard the same echoes that we now think we hear?[80] Here the comparativist is somewhat handicapped by the relative youth of the field. By contrast, the study of intertestamental echoes is ancient; the New Testament itself insists upon its relationship to the Old, and Christian interpreters have been making these connections for so long that some of their interpretations are taken for granted or forgotten and must be uncovered again by modern scholars. Hays writes: "Traditional readings will need to be supplemented by new readings that benefit from a scholarly recovery of the 'cave of resonant signification' within which Paul's voice originally sounded"[81] — how much more is this true of Old Testament comparative studies! Although the Old

76. Among other works, one might mention Othmar Keel and Christoph Uehlinger, *Gods, Goddesses, and Images of God in Ancient Israel*, trans. T. H. Trapp (Minneapolis: Fortress, 1998); or Keel's *Symbolism of the Biblical World: Ancient Near Eastern Iconography and the Book of Psalms*, trans. T. J. Hallett (New York: Seabury, 1978).

77. Keel and Uehlinger, *Gods, Goddesses, and Images*, p. 266.

78. Keel and Uehlinger, *Gods, Goddesses, and Images*, p. 272. One might add John Strange's argument that the lotus pattern on the walls and doors of Solomon's temple (1 Kings 6:18-35) suggests that monarchic Jerusalem knew of Egyptian beliefs about the afterlife, since the lotus was an Egyptian symbol of resurrection; see Strange, "The Idea of the Afterlife in Ancient Israel: Some Remarks on the Iconography in Solomon's Temple," *PEQ* 117 (1985): 35-40. Of course, the status of this theory is tenuous since the temple has never been unearthed and the date of the texts in 1 Kings cannot be ascertained.

79. Ephraim Stern, *Archaeology of the Land of the Bible*, vol. 2, *The Assyrian, Babylonian, and Persian Periods* (New York: Doubleday, 2001), pp. 228-35.

80. Cf. Hays, "Who Has Believed?" p. 43.

81. Hays, "Who Has Believed?" p. 43, using a phrase from Hollander, *Figure of Echo*, p. 65.

Testament also clearly broadcasts its immersion in its cultural backgrounds, most of the primary records of its surrounding cultures were already lost even in antiquity, and so it is mostly in the past 150 years or so that one can speak of a "tradition of interpretation." Our understanding of the ancient Near Eastern context has certainly been transformed more radically in recent years than our understanding of the New Testament's Greco-Roman context.

At the same time, the classical histories do contain comparative observations about the ancient Near East that should be weighed by modern interpreters. For example, Lucian's study of Syrian religion in *De Dea Syria*,[82] or the references to the religious practices of the Babylonians in Ctesias, Herodotus,[83] Berossus[84] or Manetho[85] — texts such as these represent early studies in comparative religion, and they may, when supported by primary data, open up new understandings of biblical texts.

7. Satisfaction: Does the proposed intertextual reading illuminate the surrounding discourse and make some larger sense of the author's argument as a whole? Do we find ourselves saying, "Oh, so that's what the author meant"?[86] This is, of course, a personal and subjective measure; it is best understood to reflect the satisfaction of informed readers, those well versed in the periods and cultures under investigation. It is an understatement to say that comparative study of the Old Testament can offer satisfaction. It is prone to produce epiphanic moments, as the Bible comes to life in new ways.

If the reaction of Old Testament scholars to the enumeration of these principles is that they are not new, well and good. It is certainly true that the best comparative work in the field already asks most of these same questions implicitly. But just as Talmon's earlier essay consolidated and enunciated the best methodology of the years that preceded it, so might we hope to do the same, thirty years later. Hays's criteria seem to help, although they remain to be tested in a way that space will not allow here.

---

82. If this text is indeed by Lucian. See discussion in *On the Syrian Goddess*, ed. J. L. Lightfoot (Oxford: Oxford University Press, 2003).

83. On Ctesias and Herodotus, see references at John McGinnis, "A Neo-Assyrian Text Describing a Royal Funeral," *SAAB* 1 (1987): 9.

84. Stanley Mayer Burstein, *The Babyloniaca of Berossus*, SANE 1.5 (Malibu: Undena, 1978).

85. Gerald P. Verbrugghe and John M. Wickersham, *Berossos and Manetho, Introduced and Translated: Native Traditions in Ancient Mesopotamia and Egypt* (Ann Arbor: University of Michigan Press, 1996).

86. Cf. Hays, "Who Has Believed?" p. 44.

While strictly linguistic and generic criteria may feel more secure to scholars with extensive linguistic training, comparative studies that overlook literary and sociohistorical questions (such as those laid out by Hays) do not thereby avoid them but merely *presume certain conclusions without argument*. Rare indeed is the Old Testament text for which this is a safe way to proceed. Comparative scholars should be prepared to offer answers, however provisional, to these questions. They should also be as explicit as possible about their methods and criteria for identifying echoes, so that they are not left in the position of the late Supreme Court justice Potter Stewart, who famously said of obscenity: "I know it when I see it."

Beyond *Echoes*

There are a number of ways, then, in which Hays's method would have to be re-imagined in order to be used in Old Testament comparative study. However, the dimension in which Kristeva's concept of intertextuality most radically exceeds the reach of Hays's project in *Echoes of Scripture* is in its definition of "text." It is clear that when Kristeva speaks of a text, she is not referring merely to literary texts but to historical and social *contexts*. In this way intertextuality would be understood not only as a literary theory but as a historical and contextual one. As Simon Parker has remarked, the common "separation of the two disciplines is unfortunate."[87]

Here, finally, the poverty of Old Testament comparative studies becomes its advantage: the very shortage of comparative literary texts forces us to employ artistic, historical, and social data to fill out our comparative picture, the *Diskursuniversum* of the "biblical world" (or better, *worlds*). Furthermore, our necessary uncertainty about the biographies of our authors should allow us to welcome Kristeva's reduction (though not abolition) of the author. That is, it is probably appropriate that we accord less weight to perceived "authorial intentions" than might, say, scholars of T. S. Eliot's poetry, who in advancing a particular interpretation must reckon with the author's well-known biography and assorted writings. Without this baggage, our interpretation of our ancient biblical authors must creatively employ the scraps that we have, from art to our reconstructions of religion

---

87. Parker, *Stories in Scripture*, p. 4. Cf. also pp. 5-6: "While the focus is of necessity on the written texts, I seek to bring into peripheral view their social background: the speakers and hearers of these stories which were recorded in writing."

and history; we must reconstitute the soil in which our texts grew as if we were paleobotanists.[88]

To say that we should take up the unwritten voices of a text's world and look at how they are transposed in the text is not a radical suggestion; but it does leave us with few methodological guides. Scholars of later periods have often been allowed, by the bounty of literary material from their periods, to construct a world without reference to nonliterary data. On the other end of the spectrum, social historians have too often dismissed texts as elite products that distort material reality. The beauty of Kristeva's vision of intertextuality is that it is both literary and historical; it can account for the ways in which Old Testament texts transpose the social and historical texts of their environs. Although it is beyond the scope of this project to argue, it might be that one could specify the typical intertextual functioning of wisdom versus that of prophecy — or, more likely, of one text or author versus another. There will be no single, static answer, but rather in every one of the many instances in which the Old Testament takes up its cultural surroundings, there may be a different purpose, a different way in which the biblical authors transpose the culture around them in the service of their stories about God's work.

*   *   *

I note with satisfaction that in a recently published article, Jeremy Hutton takes up the suggestion of explicitly employing Hays's methodology in the comparative study of biblical and ancient Near Eastern texts. See Hutton, "Isaiah 51:9-11 and the Rhetorical Appropriation and Subversion of Hostile Theologies," *JBL* 126 (2007): 271-303.

---

88. This phrase is not entirely metaphorical. Paleobotany has recently been used to help reconstruct the economy of the Neo-Assyrian period by Avraham Faust and Ehud Weiss in "Judah, Philistia, and the Mediterranean World: Reconstructing the Economic System of the Seventh Century B.C.E.," *BASOR* 338 (2005): 71-92.

On Interpreting the Mind of God: The Theological Significance of the Flood Narrative (Genesis 6–9)

Walter Moberly

I would like in this essay briefly to consider the meaning of one of the best known of all biblical stories, that of Noah and the flood (Genesis 6–9).[1] The fame of the story has many roots. On the one hand, it is the first extended narrative sequence within Scripture, situated near the outset, and its treatment of the fate of the world as a whole gives it obvious resonance. On the other hand, it has regularly over the centuries been depicted in the literature, art, and music of the Western world, and it has impacted upon the development of the science of geology.[2] The general history of the reception of the story is astonishingly rich.[3] Even if contemporary cultural movements mean that these factors are no longer as influential as they used to be, pictures of Noah, his ark (in the form of a nice houseboat), and pairs of animals still feature in countless children's books and pictures — though more, one suspects, for the animals than for the theology.

I hope to do three things in this paper. First, to say something about the nature and purpose of the flood story as a whole. Second, and most extensively, to examine a particular exegetical and theological crux. Third, to touch on some of the characteristic difficulties that an increasing number of

---

1. Or, more precisely, Gen. 6:5–9:19. The issues posed by 6:1-4 and 9:20-29 (and also 5:28-29) cannot be dealt with here.

2. It still features prominently in "creation science."

3. An entrée to this history is provided by Norman Cohn, *Noah's Flood: The Genesis Story in Western Thought* (New Haven/London: Yale University Press, 1996); J. David Pleins, *When the Great Abyss Opened: Classic and Contemporary Readings of Noah's Flood* (Oxford: Oxford University Press, 2003).

people today seem to have with the story. All of this is with a view toward enabling a fresh reappropriation of the story in contemporary Christian thought.

It is a particular pleasure to write this in honor of Richard Hays, whose own work has so notably contributed to a more robust engagement with the Bible as Christian Scripture. I offer this essay as a small token of my great indebtedness and gratitude to a valued friend.

I. On Reading the Flood Narrative

Because my basic concern has to do with the understanding and appropriation of the flood narrative as a whole,[4] a few preliminary words about what is involved in reading the narrative may perhaps be useful.

First, are we reading one story or two? The flood narrative has become a parade example in modern scholarship of a composite narrative, whose internal difficulties are best resolved when it is recognized that the story comprises two originally separate accounts, one Yahwistic (J) and the other Priestly (P).[5] Although this view has sometimes been queried, recently on the grounds that the story as it stands displays an elaborate chiastic structure that could hardly be the result of the poor editing usually hypothesized,[6] such an alternative has not generally commended itself.[7] For the present I

---

4. Sadly, there is insufficient space to discuss the use made of the story within the NT, even though that would be particularly appropriate in relation to Richard Hays's work.

5. For example, Ernest Nicholson observes: "In spite of many attempts to challenge it, the evidence in favour of the two-source theory of the composition of this narrative remains compelling"; see Nicholson, *The Pentateuch in the Twentieth Century: The Legacy of Julius Wellhausen* (Oxford: Clarendon, 1998), p. 205. Works that popularize scholarship on this story tend to present the J and P strands as a given; so André Parrot, *The Flood and Noah's Ark,* trans. Edwin Hudson (London: SCM, 1955), pp. 15-22; Lloyd R. Bailey, *Noah: The Person and the Story in History and Tradition* (Columbia: University of South Carolina Press, 1989), pp. 146-58 (with nuance); Pleins, *Great Abyss,* pp. 23-30, 115-28.

6. So Bernhard W. Anderson, "From Analysis to Synthesis: The Interpretation of Genesis 1–11," *JBL* 97 (1978): 23-39; and, more ambitiously, G. J. Wenham, "The Coherence of the Flood Narrative," *VT* 28 (1978): 336-48.

7. So especially J. A. Emerton, "An Examination of Some Attempts to Defend the Unity of the Flood Narrative in Genesis," *VT* 37 (1987): 401-20; *VT* 38 (1988): 1-21. Wenham responds to Emerton with "Method in Pentateuchal Source Criticism," *VT* 41 (1991): 84-109. My main difficulty with Wenham's proposed chiasm is that it does not sufficiently illuminate one's reading by directing one's attention to what matters most in the story. It is at its most persuasive in terms of those aspects of the story that are clearest on any reckoning: a pattern

would simply say that, whatever the nature of the compositional process, Genesis presents the story as one story, and so we should attempt as far as we can, that is, without resorting to special pleading, to make sense of it as such.

Thus, the apparently pleonastic repetitions, with differences of vocabulary, at the beginning and end of the story become a kind of narrative equivalent to Hebrew poetic parallelism. A preliminary formulation is followed by a repetition and extension; the determinative divine decisions, which YHWH first resolves in His[8] own mind (6:5-8; 8:21-22), are subsequently communicated in a fuller and slightly different way to a human recipient, Noah (6:11-13; 9:8-17).

Alternatively, the apparently conflicting chronologies do not really conflict, for the only exceptions to the detailed overall chronological framework are the references to "forty days and forty nights" (7:12) or "forty days" (7:17; 8:6);[9] since "forty days/years" is the Hebrew idiom for an indefinite long period of time,[10] this is not the same kind of chronology as the specific count of months and days such that one should infer two competing time scales. Rather, the "forty" is a different kind of notation, a generalizing statement — "a long time" — within the one chronology.[11] So, despite some undoubted internal unevenness, it remains possible and appropriate to read the text as one story.

Second, what kind of material is this narrative? Some reflection as to the kind of question that the narrative does and does not fruitfully sustain is illu-

---

of opening divine pronouncements, humans and animals entering the ark, and steadily increasing flood waters, which are then balanced by steadily decreasing flood waters, humans and animals leaving the ark, and closing divine pronouncements, a pattern whose specific turning point comes at 8:1. Yet the chiasm entirely fails to bring out, for example, the fundamental significance of Noah's sacrifice and the divine pronouncement in 8:20-22.

8. I am not unaware of difficulties in the use of gendered language for God. I use the masculine pronoun largely because it is the Bible's own usage; but I capitalize it, partly in implicit recognition that God is beyond gender in human categories, and partly in continuity with traditional reverential usage.

9. I do not include the "seven days" of 7:4, 10 and 8:10, 12, as these do not in any way appear to compete with the overall chronology. The locations of 7:10 and 8:12 within the overall schema are pinpointed by the dates that immediately follow.

10. Three days/years is the corresponding expression for an indefinite short period of time.

11. Curiously, this possibility is usually not even raised in standard discussions, e.g., Niels Lemche, "The Chronology in the Story of the Flood," *JSOT* 18 (1980): 52-62; Lloyd M. Barré, "The Riddle of the Flood Chronology," *JSOT* 41 (1988): 3-20; Reinhard G. Kratz, *The Composition of the Narrative Books of the Old Testament,* trans. John Bowden (London/New York: T. & T. Clark, 2005), pp. 235-36.

minating for recognizing its genre. On internal grounds, it is clearly uninterested in those issues that have fascinated many interpreters who have sought to construe it as "historical," even if one or two of its details may appear to be so.[12] The narrator reports the inner thoughts and words of YHWH but says nothing about Noah's thoughts or words; indeed, Noah says nothing throughout. Practicalities such as, which animals? what of the living conditions? what sort of food, how much, and how preserve it as edible? — while often appealing to interpreters across the centuries and still amenable to ingenious resolution[13] — are entirely ignored in favor of a narrative interest in entry to and exit from the ark and in the steady increase and decrease of the flood waters. Humans and animals appear to live in darkness within the ark, which (as far as we are told) has only one openable hatch in addition to the door.[14] Or there is the freshly plucked olive leaf, which shows that the waters have subsided. Within the general storyline this makes perfect sense, and is memorable and moving. But the narrator appears to assume that when the waters go down, growing things reappear in the same condition they were in before the waters came; the "realistic" question as to the likely state of an olive tree and its foliage after a year under the sea cannot be sustained.[15]

12. For example, if one takes the all-too-brief instructions in 6:14-16 to indicate that a transverse section of the ark would be virtually triangular — so that the ark should be envisaged "like a giant Toblerone bar," as one of my students, Lizzie Hartley, nicely put it — then such a vessel would apparently be stable in floating, which is all that it would be required to do (so E. D. Morgan, "Noah's Ark Was a Masterpiece: A Mystery of Correct Engineering Design before the Flood," *Meccano Magazine,* December 1926, p. 767). The contention that the design of the ark would give it stability is an ancient one; see M. Zlotowitz and N. Scherman, *Bereishis/Genesis,* 2 vols., ASTS (New York: Mesorah, 1986), 1:231. However, the instructions in 6:14-16 are open to widely differing construals of the shape and seaworthiness of the ark.

13. See, e.g., John Woodmorappe, *Noah's Ark: A Feasibility Study* (Santee, Calif.: Institute for Creation Research, 1996).

14. The meaning of צהר (6:16a) is unclear. Given its position in the instructions, which are still dealing with the overall structure of the ark, and given that it is "for" (ל) the ark and not "in its side" (בצדה) as is that opening that is the door, the sense of "window" would be inappropriate; "roof" is more likely. The "window" (חלון) out of which Noah sends the birds (8:6) is not a window in the sense that one might readily imagine, because it does not allow Noah to see out — for if he could see, then it is not obvious why he would need to dispatch the dove. Most likely, it is an openable hatch in the roof, made of wood to keep the rain out, not with glass or air to let the light in. Noah reaches up through this hatch to dispatch and receive the birds.

15. The realistic condition of any part of a tree after a year under the sea, even when newly emerged from the waters, would presumably be indistinguishable from flotsam or seaweed — it would not show fresh life and so would fail to make the point that the story

Third, what is the interpretative significance of flood narratives from other cultures, narratives that no doubt originate to some extent from lingering ancient memories of calamitous flooding conditions in various regions of the world? The best-known of these from the wider world of ancient Israel is Tablet XI of the Epic of Gilgamesh, which tells of Utnapishtim and a flood.[16] This account has sufficient commonality with the Genesis account to make comparison illuminating. To be sure, since we do not know the actual relationship between the two, their possible relationship can be, and has been, argued any which way. In general terms, however, it is not, I think, greatly controversial to suggest that the Genesis account be read as a Hebrew retelling of a common story, whose details are shaped by the concern to set the well-known story in a particular light: think about it *this* way, and one will understand more truly the situation of the world under God. As one of the prime twentieth-century Christian theological interpreters of the Old Testament, Gerhard von Rad, put it, concluding a brief comparison of the Genesis story with that in the Epic of Gilgamesh, "the biblical story of the Flood has been made a witness to the judgment and grace of [the] living God."[17]

II. Toward Interpreting the Narrative via an Exegetical and Theological Crux

Introducing the Issue

Although the interpretation of the flood narrative at first sight appears relatively straightforward, my impression is that the longer one studies it, the more complex an understanding of it becomes. This can be seen by focusing upon a famous crux within the story.

Most commentators have recognized that an important key to understanding the story's meaning is provided by the repetition of certain weighty words within the thoughts of YHWH. At the outset (Gen. 6:5) we learn the reason why YHWH decides to send a flood:

---

needs. To try to deal with the difficulty by appealing in any way to the irregular or miraculous would undermine the point of the text, that the leaf shows the return of regular conditions upon earth.

16. See, e.g., *ANET,* pp. 93-97.

17. Gerhard von Rad, *Genesis,* trans. John Marks, 3rd ed. (London: SCM, 1972 [ET from 9th German ed.]), p. 124. The German reads "des lebendigen Gottes," so the absence of "the" before "living God" is a typographical error.

The LORD saw that the wickedness of humankind was great in the earth, and that every inclination of the thoughts of their hearts was only evil continually.[18]

Yet this evil within human inclinations not only remains unchanged by the flood; it is also explicitly appealed to in the context of YHWH's subsequent decision never again to send a flood (8:21):

And when the LORD smelled the pleasing odor, the LORD said in his heart, "I will never again curse the ground because of humankind, for *(ki)* the inclination of the human heart is evil from youth; nor will I ever again destroy every living creature as I have done."

The puzzle is why one and the same thing should, apparently, be the reason for (in conventional theological shorthand) both judgment and grace.[19] Is this a deliberate theological paradox? Or what? Chrysostom, for example, comments on 8:21 that this is "a strange form of loving kindness." Luther observes: "It seems that God can be accused of inconsistency here." Calvin notes that "this reasoning seems incongruous. . . . God seems to contradict himself."[20] More recently, von Rad sees something highly significant at stake:

This saying of Yahweh [8:21] without doubt designates a profound turning point in the Yahwistic primeval history, in so far as it expresses with surprising directness a will for salvation directed towards the whole of Noachite humanity, "although" (the Hebrew particle כִּי can be translated in this way) "the imagination of man's heart is evil from his youth." So far as that is concerned — Calvin says in his exposition of the passage — God would have to punish man with daily floods. In its hard paradox this v. 21

18. Unless otherwise specified, the English rendering is NRSV.

19. John Goldingay criticizes conventional use of "judgment" on the grounds that it is not an OT idiom; rather, God is the subject of the verb "judge" (שׁפט) in contexts of adjudicating or delivering, not punishing. See Goldingay, *Old Testament Theology*, vol. 1, *Israel's Gospel* (Downers Grove, Ill.: InterVarsity, 2003), pp. 169-70. This is a helpful reminder of potential drawbacks in familiar theological shorthand, though I do not think it need rule out its use.

20. John Chrysostom, *Hom. Gen.* 27.10, trans. Robert C. Hill, *Homilies on Genesis 18-45*, FC 82 (Washington, D.C.: Catholic University of America Press, 1990), p. 170; Martin Luther, *Luther's Works*, vol. 2, *Lectures on Genesis, Chapters 6-14*, ed. Jaroslav Pelikan (Saint Louis: Concordia, 1960), p. 120; John Calvin, *A Commentary on Genesis*, 2 vols. (London: Banner of Truth, 1965 [ET Calvin Translation Society, 1847, from Latin of 1554]), 1:283-84.

is one of the most remarkable theological statements in the Old Testament: it shows the pointed and concentrated way in which the Yahwist can express himself at decisive points. The same condition which in the prologue is the basis for God's judgment in the epilogue reveals God's grace and providence. The contrast between God's punishing anger and his supporting grace, which pervades the whole Bible, is here presented almost inappropriately, almost as indulgence, an adjustment by God towards man's sinfulness.[21]

Recognition that the collocation of 6:5 and 8:21 is in some way theologically significant is thus well established in interpretations of the flood narrative.

The Distinctive Nature of the Evil-Thought Clause in Genesis 8:21

Within YHWH's climactic words in 8:21, I wish to look more closely at the subordinate clause — "for the inclination of the human heart is evil from youth" — a clause that I will refer to as the "evil-thought clause."

It is important to note that the specific verbal resonances between YHWH's resolution for the future and His initial reasons for sending the flood come *only* in the evil-thought clause, which restates less emphatically, but definitely nonetheless, the opening characterization of humanity:

6:5 וכל־יצר מחשבת לבו רק רע כל־היום
and that every inclination of the thoughts of their hearts was only evil continually

8:21 כי יצר לב האדם רע מנעריו
for the inclination of the human heart is evil from youth

The puzzle or paradox of the text is particularly focused upon these few words and their construal.

It is also significant that the divine words in 8:21 would read entirely smoothly without the evil-thought clause. While such smoothness in omission by itself shows little, two further factors may encourage a heuristic reading of the divine words without this clause.

We note, first, that without the clause the divine words of 8:21 can be seen as poetic, with both parallelism and a clear 3:3 pattern:

---

21. Von Rad, *Genesis*, pp. 122-23.

לא־אסף לקלל עוד
I will never again curse

את־האדמה בעבור האדם
the ground because of humankind

ולא־אסף עוד להכות
nor will I ever again destroy

את־כל־חי כאשר עשיתי
every living creature as I have done

One of the striking characteristics of the early chapters of Genesis is that most of the significant pronouncements are made in poetry, a heightened mode of speech appropriate to memorable moments (as in much Hebrew prophecy) — so the first human words (2:23), the divine curses (3:14-19), Lamech's boast (4:23-24), the pronouncement about bloodshed (9:6), and Noah's curse and blessing (9:25-27). So also, in the immediate context of 8:21, are the divine words about the seasons that directly follow (8:22). Without the evil-thought clause, one can straightforwardly see the whole divine pronouncement in 8:21-22 as poetic. Interestingly, however, the presence of the evil-thought clause in 8:21 has, I would suggest, so effectively obscured this poetic form that no modern translation of which I am aware sets 8:21 as poetry, though the continuation in 8:22 is almost invariably set thus.[22]

We can note, second, that the affirmation of the regularity of the seasons and the harvests with which YHWH's words continue in 8:22 picks up the divine forbearance as articulated in 8:21, expressing its consequences for the temporal structuring of life — but showing no further interest in the theological paradox represented by the evil-thought clause. Similarly, in Genesis 9, the divine communication to Noah about the significance of the rainbow makes no reference to continuing human sin.

It seems to me, therefore, that there is a case for seeing the evil-thought clause as a distinct addition to an otherwise already complete and rounded divine pronouncement.[23] Although my concern is not redaction criticism as such, there are times when to think in terms of tradition and redaction can

22. So, e.g., NEB, REB, JB, NIV, NJPS. The ESV sets 8:21-22 as prose throughout.

23. Thus, I disagree with Claus Westermann, who infers from a somewhat complex discussion of von Rad, Rendtorff, and Steck that all the divine words in 8:21a are a Yahwistic addition to antecedent tradition. I think Westermann misses the distinctive role of the evil-thought clause, though the tenor of his discussion remains illuminating; see Westermann, *Genesis 1–11: A Commentary*, trans. J. Scullion (Minneapolis: Augsburg, 1984), pp. 454-56. A recent discussion that recognizes the likely redactional role of the evil-thought clause and its interruption of an otherwise poetic divine speech is Markus Witte, *Die biblische Urgeschichte: Redaktions- und theologiegeschichtliche Beobachtungen zu Genesis 1,1-11,26*, BZAW 265 (Berlin/New York: de Gruyter, 1998), p. 181 (who lists other scholars with a similar proposal in n. 133).

be heuristically useful in helping one to think freshly about the possible force of the text in its received form. Insofar as a redaction-critical hypothesis serves this purpose, it will be justified.

How then would the text read without the evil-thought clause? Noah is, in effect, the sole representative of the human race, since his wife, sons, and sons' wives are narratively formulaic; they are extensions of Noah as paterfamilias, whose role — other than being there "for the ride" — is to enable Noah to be the fruitful father of post-flood humanity. Throughout the flood Noah has been a model of obedience to YHWH's instructions.[24] Now he offers a sacrifice whose pleasingness to YHWH is emphasized (vv. 20-21a). In response, therefore, to this sacrifice, YHWH makes two inner resolutions.[25] First (v. 21a), YHWH resolves never again to curse the earth (recalling His pronouncement in Eden, Gen. 3:17).[26] Second (v. 21b), He resolves never again to destroy all life, as had happened in the flood. There is a difference in the positioning of עוֹד ("again") in the two divine resolutions, which is probably significant. In 8:21a it qualifies לְקַלֵּל ("curse") in a way that probably means that the existing curse remains but will not be increased ("I will not curse the ground any further . . ."), while in 8:21b it qualifies וְלֹא־אֹסִף ("destroy") in such a way as to rule out any repetition of the verbal action that follows ("I will not again destroy").[27] On this basis, the regular conditions of life upon earth, its seasons and its harvests, will continue (v. 22).[28] Part of the logic implicit in moving from the resolutions not to disable life upon earth to the promise to maintain the regular pattern of seasons and harvests would appear to be the maintenance of conditions for sacrifice, so that humanity can continue to make right offerings to YHWH. YHWH's pleasure in Noah's sacrifice becomes a fundamental determinant for the continuance of human life upon earth, so that others may do as Noah has done.

When one reads the text thus, one of the difficulties in the received text

24. If my construal of Noah's sending of the raven is correct, then it furthers the portrayal of Noah as in harmony, symbolically expressed, with the will and action of God; see Moberly, "Why Did Noah Send Out a Raven?" *VT* 50 (2000): 345-56.

25. YHWH's responsiveness to sacrifice here is analogous to His responsiveness elsewhere to prayer and repentance, all of which are understood to *matter* to YHWH.

26. There has been much discussion of the precise force of קלל and its relation to ארר in 3:17; 5:29, but for my purposes little, I think, hangs on it.

27. Cf. Moberly, *At the Mountain of God*, JSOTSup 22 (Sheffield: JSOT Press, 1983), p. 113; Gordon Wenham, *Genesis 1–15*, WBC 1 (Waco: Word, 1987), p. 190.

28. For an illuminating account of 8:22 as a calendar of the agricultural year, see Theodore Hiebert, *The Yahwist's Landscape: Nature and Religion in Early Israel* (Oxford: Oxford University Press, 1996), pp. 45-47.

disappears — namely, that YHWH's resolutions in response to Noah's sacrifice seem somehow disproportionate when juxtaposed with the continuing evil in the human disposition. As von Rad put it, "his supporting grace . . . is here presented almost inappropriately, almost as indulgence, an adjustment by God towards man's sinfulness."[29] For if there is no mention of human sinfulness in the evil-thought clause, and righteous Noah, making an appropriate sacrifice, is the only significant human on earth (a kind of second Adam), YHWH's pleasure in him and corresponding resolutions about life hereafter do not jar within the narrative's own frame of reference.

The Significance of the Evil-Thought Clause within Genesis 8:21

What then is the difference made by the presence of the evil-thought clause? It changes the tenor of the whole divine speech by bringing to the fore two weighty issues that otherwise are at most only implicit in the story at this point. In convenient theological shorthand, these can be characterized as divine mutability and human depravity.

The issue of divine mutability is not explicit but rather a natural inference. If, according to the evil-thought clause, humanity has not changed and is the same post-flood as pre-flood, then what is the reason for the fact that the condition of humanity that brought on the flood does so no longer? As Campbell and O'Brien put it, "because nothing has changed in human nature, the change must be placed in God"; or as Brueggemann puts it, "humankind is hopeless. . . . Hope will depend on a move from God."[30] If humanity will not change in thinking and living in such a way as to corrupt God's good creation, then God will change in not enacting the judgment that that corruption might be expected to bring upon itself.[31] The nature and implications of such divine change, in terms of what may and may not appropriately be predicated of God, is of course an enduring issue within biblical theology more generally.[32]

---

29. Von Rad, *Genesis,* p. 123. Compare Derek Kidner's "If God seems too lightly propitiated . . ."; Kidner, *Genesis,* TOTC (London: Tyndale, 1967), p. 93.

30. Antony F. Campbell and Mark A. O'Brien, *Sources of the Pentateuch* (Minneapolis: Fortress, 1993), p. 97 n. 17; Walter Brueggemann, *Genesis,* IBC (Atlanta: John Knox, 1982), pp. 80-81.

31. This formulation echoes the play on שחת in 6:11, 12, 13.

32. The poles of the discussion are far apart. On the one hand, Philo is deeply uneasy with the notion of divine mutability and focuses upon an exposition of Gen. 6:4-12 in his trea-

To be sure, the issue of divine mutability is explicit at the outset of the story (6:6-7) and is implicit in YHWH's response to Noah's sacrifice. Yet were it not for the evil-thought clause in 8:21, I do not think that interpreters would raise the issue at this point in the story; for divine responsiveness in relation to sacrifice is so common that it would not merit more attention here than in the context of any other acceptable sacrifice.

The second issue arises in the clause's explicit strong statement about enduring evil in human thought, engagement with which readily leads into larger theological debates: for Christians, about "original sin," and for Jews, about the "evil tendency."[33] Calvin, for example, in his commentary at this point has an extended discussion of human depravity:

> Since God here declares what would be the character of men even to the end of the world, it is evident that the whole human race is under sentence of condemnation, on account of its depravity and wickedness. Nor does the sentence refer only to corrupt morals; but their iniquity is said to be an innate iniquity, from which nothing but evils can spring forth. . . . God does not merely say that men sometimes think evil; but the language is unlimited, comprising the tree with its fruits. . . . And the clause which is added, "from youth," more fully declares that men are born evil; in order to show that, as soon as they are of an age to begin to form thoughts, they have radical corruption of mind. . . .[34]

By way of contrast, Nahum Sarna comments from a Jewish perspective:

> As compared with 6:5, the language is considerably modified and is no longer all-inclusive. The statement is not a judgment but an observation that a proclivity for evil is woven into the fabric of human nature. The key phrase is "from his youth," not from birth or conception, implying that the tendency to evil may be curbed and redirected through the discipline of laws. Hence, the next section deals with the imposition of laws upon postdiluvian humanity.[35]

---

tise *On the Unchangeableness of God,* which greatly influenced the Christian Fathers. On the other hand, Brueggemann (perhaps influenced by Moltmann's *The Crucified God*?) straight-forwardly celebrates the capacity for change in Israel's God (*Genesis,* pp. 78-79, 81, 84-86).

33. The long history of Jewish theology and spirituality concerning the "evil tendency" (היצר הרע) in humanity finds its prime biblical derivation in Gen. 6:5 and 8:21.

34. Calvin, *Genesis,* 1:284-85.

35. Nahum Sarna, *The JPS Torah Commentary: Genesis/Bereishith* (Philadelphia/New York/Jerusalem: Jewish Publication Society, 5749/1989), p. 59.

I do not, however, wish to get involved in the well-worn Jewish-Christian debate about original sin, as in, for example, Robert Gordis's formulation, "For Christianity, man sins because he is a sinner; for Judaism, man becomes a sinner when he sins"[36] — not least because I find myself wanting to affirm both parts of Gordis's antithesis. Generally speaking, in most such debate there is a danger of ahistorical generalizations that fail to do justice to the diversity of positions and emphases within both Judaism and Christianity.[37] In the context of my heuristic thesis about the significance of the evil-thought clause, I wish rather to ask whether or not it develops an issue already present within the story.

For the logic of the evil-thought clause is hardly straightforward in the context of 8:21. In Genesis 6:5 it is straightforward, in the context of the corruption that had afflicted the world as a whole. But in 8:21 the corrupt humanity has been wiped out. There are only eight representatives of humanity left, and of these only one is significant: Noah, who is righteous (צדיק), who is a person of integrity and walks with God (6:9), who has been obedient to YHWH throughout. That is, Noah is surely the very person of whom it *cannot* be said that "the inclination of his heart/mind is evil from his youth." Yet it is the humanity represented by Noah that is thus characterized. How is this to be understood?

If one seeks to remain within the narrative's own frame of reference, a possible narrative hook could be Noah's family, with probably his sons as the prime suspects.[38] Although they are passive and formulaic within the flood story proper, they subsequently take an active role, and Ham's voyeurism (or whatever it was) with regard to his father brings a curse (9:18-27). Noah's drunkenness in this later story could also be seen to place Noah in a more

36. Robert Gordis, *Judaic Ethics for a Lawless World* (New York: Jewish Theological Seminary of America, 1986), p. 69. Gordis's discussion of sin focuses on Genesis 3 without reference to Genesis 6–9.

37. One might note, for example, that early Christian Antiochene exegetes appealed to "from youth" in 8:21 so as "to restrict the wickedness of mankind to a clearly defined period in a person's life: 'from youth,' not 'from birth'"; see Hagit Amirav, *Rhetoric and Tradition: John Chrysostom on Noah and the Flood,* TEG 12 (Leuven: Peeters, 2003), p. 125. Conversely, Rashi shows no reluctance to root the evil tendency more deeply within human nature: ". . . from the moment the embryo bestirs itself to have an independent existence the evil inclination is given to it"; see A. M. Silbermann, ed., *Pentateuch with Rashi's Commentary: Genesis* (Jerusalem: Silbermann, 5733/1972), p. 36.

38. Or possibly their wives. Rabbinic tradition argued for the continuity of the descendants of Cain in terms of one or more of the women among them having married into Noah's family; see Zlotowitz and Scherman, *Bereishis/Genesis,* 1:187.

ambiguous light than would be evident from the flood story proper. These subsequent developments could perhaps be considered implicit within the preceding narrative — though such a move seems to me distinctly forced.

Alternatively, one might just argue in dogmatic terms. If human thought is generically corrupt, then so must be Noah's thought, too; Noah cannot be an exception but must be included within sinful humanity. This would mean that the positive qualities he displays are the result of his responsiveness to God; and so these qualities do not deny human depravity but rather show how, by God's grace, such depravity may be overcome.[39] Yet such a move seems to me to introduce the kind of theological discrimination of a later period that does not really resonate with the story's own portrayal of Noah as a צדיק.

I am therefore inclined to suggest that the real reason for the evil-thought clause is not the logic of the story in its own terms but rather *the context and world of the scribe responsible for the clause*. A Hebrew scribe is surely engaging with the question of why the world of his own day, which might well have appeared no less corrupt and heedless of God than the generation of the flood — the kind of scenario articulated in, say, Jeremiah 5:1-5 or Psalm 14, or expressed in various ways by many Jews and Christians down the ages — is the recipient of divine forbearance rather than judgment. This scribe recognizes that the main point of the existing flood narrative is to offer an account of divine maintenance of regular human life. Yet he wishes to deepen an understanding of what is at stake in such maintenance. Thus, by adding the evil-thought clause to YHWH's resolution about His future dealings with humanity, he makes explicit that the post-flood world familiar to him is no improvement on the notorious pre-flood world; the humanity that now receives the divine forbearance has not changed from the humanity that was swept away.

To be sure, the introduction of evil-thinking humanity into a context where only Noah, the צדיק, is significant does indeed stretch the logic of the story. Yet it does so in the kind of way that is indicative of the use of traditional narrative for articulating a contemporary existential reality. The potent legends are precisely those in which an ancient story can become a mirror for better understanding a problematic present.

---

39. So, with interesting nuances, David Clines, "The Theology of the Flood Narrative," in *On the Way to the Postmodern: Old Testament Essays, 1967-1998*, vol. 2, JSOTSup 293 (Sheffield: Sheffield Academic, 1998), pp. 520-21; Goldingay, *Old Testament Theology*, pp. 172-73, 177. The implications of the story's specifying that Noah "found favor" with YHWH (6:8) before it mentions that he was righteous (6:9) can be developed in a variety of ways, not solely in certain familiar categories of Protestant theology.

The Origin and Location of the Evil-Thought Clause

If this account of the nature and purpose of the evil-thought clause commends itself as at all on the right lines, there remain three further interpretative issues to address.

First, there is the standard exegetical question of whether the clause qualifies "because of humankind" or "I will never again curse." If the former, then the sense would be that humanity's evil thoughts constitute a reason why YHWH *might* be moved to curse the ground, even though in fact He will not do so; in this case the opening particle כִּי is probably best rendered concessively as "although" (as by von Rad). If the latter, then the sense would be that humanity's evil thoughts are the specific reason for YHWH's pronouncement of mercy; in which case כִּי has a causative sense, "for/because." Theological first principles might naturally incline the Christian interpreter to the former option; as Derek Kidner puts it, "Theologically it must be the former: . . . man's incorrigibility . . . never counts in the sinner's favour."[40] It seems to me, however, that the exegetical issue eludes clear resolution. Either way the unambiguous point remains that YHWH's maintenance of regular human life is combined with full recognition of the deeply corrupt tendencies of that human life.

Second, is it possible and helpful to try to locate the scribe? If this is taken as a question about date and social/religious context, then I suspect that little useful can be said, other than that the complete lack of any text-critical uncertainty over the evil-thought clause would most likely preclude a date significantly subsequent to Israel's reception of Genesis as a whole. More helpful, I think, is to locate the scribe textually and conceptually through noting the comparable phenomenon of a paradoxical כִּי clause in relation to God's merciful purposes for stiff-necked Israel in Exodus 34:9. There are in fact numerous verbal and conceptual parallels between Genesis 6-9 and Exodus 32-34, and it is likely that there is a deliberate strategy to construe the situation of Noah and the world in general by analogy with the construal of the situation of Moses and Israel in particular — a narrative parallelism that is now well recognized.[41] The way God deals with a sinful world is not different from the way in which He deals

---

40. Kidner, *Genesis*, p. 93.

41. See Moberly, *At the Mountain of God*, pp. 91-93; Terence Fretheim, *Exodus*, IBC (Louisville: John Knox, 1991), pp. 303-5; Rolf Rendtorff, *The Canonical Hebrew Bible: A Theology of the Old Testament*, trans. David E. Orton, TBS 7 (Leiden: Deo, 2005), pp. 61-63.

with a sinful chosen people; and the meaning of election is significantly illuminated thereby.

Third, there is an oddity about the clause that I have deliberately passed over until now. This is that — to put it crudely — the evil-thought clause may appear to have been inserted into the wrong part of the divine speech. For the first affirmation within the divine words in 8:21 relates not to the flood but to the curse upon the ground in Eden (3:17). As already noted, the point of the pronouncement appears to be that the curse upon the ground will remain in place but will not be added to. It is only the second affirmation that refers specifically to the flood, in which YHWH promises never again to do what on this occasion He has done; YHWH's resolution of Genesis 6:7 has been enacted but will never be enacted again. If there is a paradox that the reason for the divine wrath in sending the flood reappears in the context of divine mercy for the future, then the clause that gives rise to the paradox ought, one might think, to have been added to the pronouncement about the flood, and not to the pronouncement about the curse in Eden. For the precise paradoxical point to be made clearly, the text should surely read:

> I will never again curse the ground because of humankind,
> nor will I ever again destroy every living creature as I have done,
> for the inclination of the human heart is evil from youth.

So why does the text not say what it "should" say? One can, of course, always appeal to possible textual dislocation. Maybe in this case the interpretative clause was added originally, as in typical textual annotation, between the lines or in the margin. A subsequent scribe then worked the clause into the text but perhaps did not quite see its point, and so introduced it into the wrong part of the sentence.

A possible analogy of wording that is most likely a marginal gloss introduced into the text in a "wrong" or at least less-than-ideal location, thus obscuring the nature of the gloss, can be found in Isaiah 40:20. Here it is likely that the rare, and puzzling, word מסכן has been well-meaningly glossed with עץ לא־ירקב ("wood that will not rot"), to make clear its nature as material used in idol manufacture. But the gloss is not directly adjacent to מסכן but to the word that follows it, תרומה ("offering"/"gift"). This placement, *ex hypothesi*, is the work of a scribe who introduced the marginal/interlinear gloss into the text but not into its best location, which has led to numerous interpreters not seeing the nature of the gloss. Thanks to Hugh Williamson,[42] the likelihood of עֵץ לֹא־יִרְקַב as a gloss on מְסֻכָּן has been established as persuasively as is ever possible in such cases, and recent translations have adopted his proposal.[43]

If one accepted that the evil-thought clause was a misplaced addition to the text, what would follow? Quite possibly nothing. That is, whether or not one suggests that "curse the ground" must now be read as a reference not to Eden but to sending a flood,[44] many interpreters appear consciously or unconsciously to have done what one regularly does with oral speech — instantly to correct the words when the speaker stumbles or puts them together infelicitously, by giving them the sense that seems to be intended in context.

Nonetheless, the basic principle that we must attend to what a text actually does say, rather than what we expect it to say or would like it to say or have thought it to say, means that we still need to ask whether there is significance in the precise placement of the clause.

Reading the Narrative with the Evil-Thought Clause as Integral

Why say that YHWH will not extend the curse on the ground pronounced in Eden even though human thoughts are evil from early life? At face value, it would seem that the real anxiety addressed by the clause is not another flood but an intensification of the already hard conditions of daily agricultural life. Human corruption might make the worsening of regular daily conditions seem a more likely divine response than the entire sweeping away of life; and so this is the issue related to the divine forbearance. Contextually,

42. Hugh Williamson, "Isaiah 40:20 — A Case of Not Seeing the Wood for the Trees," *Bib* 67 (1986): 1-20.

43. NRSV and REB respectively modify RSV and NEB at this point. This does not of itself resolve whether the glossator was right to interpret מְסֻכָּן as a kind of wood, and various other construals of the word are possible. See K. van Leeuwen, "An Old Crux: הַמְסֻכָּן תְּרוּמָה in Isaiah 40,20," in *Studies in the Book of Isaiah: Festschrift Willem A. M. Beuken*, ed. J. van Ruiten and M. Vervenne, BETL 132 (Leuven: Leuven University Press, 1997), pp. 273-87. Nonetheless, the glossator's construal is as likely as any and is clearly ancient, and it has become part of the received text.

44. Terence Fretheim mentions as an option (which he rejects) that "'never again curse the ground' . . . could refer to no more floods"; see Fretheim, *Genesis, NIB* 1 (Nashville: Abingdon, 1994), p. 393. The option is long established. Already in the seventeenth century, Cornelius a Lapide glossed YHWH's resolution not to curse the earth with *Non amplius terram perdam diluvio, ut feci;* see Lapide, *Commentaria in Pentateuchum Mosis* (Antwerp, 1623), p. 126.

this construal of the first divine resolution could be linked with the assurance of regular agricultural life in 8:22. Thus, the evil-thought clause can shift a reading of the overall emphasis of the divine speech away from "no more flood" to "no worsening of regular agricultural life" despite continuing human sin.

In immediate narrative context, the subsequent divine communication to Noah (9:8-17) emphasizes "no more flood." God, after giving certain instructions, communicates to Noah His commitment never again to use a flood to destroy life; the commitment, designated as a covenant, is symbolized by the mysterious and beautiful rainbow, which appears in the sky (usually) when the sun shines in the presence of threatening rain clouds. God will be mindful of the binding covenantal significance of the rainbow in the way that Israel is to be mindful of its obligations (9:8-17; cf. Num. 15:37-41). All of this can clearly incline interpreters to find the same emphasis in 8:21. Nonetheless, one can read the text more incrementally. An initial emphasis upon the conditions of agricultural life, which also mentions "no more flood," is followed by a narrative expansion of the latter element. Although the prime thrust of the story as a whole is that there will never again be a life-obliterating flood, there is also a subordinate emphasis upon YHWH's not adopting the lesser but perfectly possible expedient of making regular life more difficult.

On any reckoning, the divine speech with the evil-thought clause is a more complex utterance than without it. The clause poses tensions for one's reading that are open to more than one way of construal. Nonetheless, we are perhaps enabled to see something of how a paradigmatic narrative was adapted and appropriated already within the time frame of the Old Testament period.

To conclude this phase of the essay, how might one read the flood narrative as a whole if the preceding discussion about the introduction of the evil-thought clause is used heuristically? In addition to the important narrative analogy between Noah:world and Moses:Israel that the evil-thought clause highlights, several other emphases become apparent. First, the exemplary role of Noah remains clear. He has been faithful throughout, and YHWH's words about the future of life on earth come in the context of response to Noah's acceptable sacrifice. The specific implication that YHWH wishes to maintain life upon earth so that acceptable sacrifice may continue to be offered also remains. This means that human responsiveness to God in appropriate form is central to the continuing purpose of life upon earth. When Noah's own appropriate form, sacrifice, is seen to be supplemented and paralleled by prayer,[45] and indeed eventually displaced altogether by prayer,[46] then the imaginative and figural potential of Noah as the faithful human whose faithfulness opens up possibilities of life for others lies readily open to be developed.

The clear recognition of human corruption post-flood is most naturally read as referring not to Noah but to others. The world in which the narrative is read and appropriated is a world in which there is a strong human tendency not to respond rightly to God. The righteousness of Noah is not representative of humanity generally. Right human responsiveness, and corresponding divine blessing, can never be taken for granted. So, as we read elsewhere, life upon God's earth is a constant struggle between life and death, blessing and curse, even for the people of YHWH (Deut. 30:15-20).

The text's overall emphasis remains YHWH's resolution to sustain life upon earth in the future. This resolution, however, is a paradoxical expression of merciful divine forbearance in the face of recognition of human life post-flood as no improvement upon life pre-flood. Humanity remains undeserving of the gift of manageable life in a regular world order; but the gift is given nonetheless. Part of the logic of saying this, however, is surely akin to that of prophetic utterances that seek to engender an appropriate response. That is, YHWH's forbearance, rightly understood, should lead not to complacency or the heedless exercise of evil thinking but rather to the living of life in a way that recognizes its quality as gift.

III. On Using the Flood Story in a Contemporary Context

I would like finally to move beyond the exegetically based discussion to two other questions.[47]

---

45. For example, there is the figural parallel between Noah's sacrifice and Moses' prayer at Sinai; see Moberly, *At the Mountain of God,* p. 92.

46. Passages such as Ps. 51:19 (17 Eng.) and 141:2 became important in distinct ways within both rabbinic Judaism and patristic Christianity for moves to construe prayer as the true form of sacrifice.

47. There are, of course, many other questions that could be asked. Richard Bauckham, for example, fruitfully asks how we can use the Bible to address the genuinely novel features of the modern world, especially the fact that, for the first time in history, "*we* can now do what the Flood did." See Bauckham, "The Genesis Flood and the Nuclear Holocaust," in *The Bible in Politics: How to Read the Bible Politically* (London: SPCK, 1989), pp. 131-41, quotation p. 137, emphasis original.

Is the Flood Narrative a Good Story to Use?

First, why use *this* story? Undoubtedly, a number of people today have anxieties about the religious use of a story that envisages God's wiping out the whole of life upon earth (except eight people, and animals in pairs). Does not such a story risk cheapening life, and does such a deity deserve worship? Not untypical is Richard Dawkins:

> The legend of the animals going into the ark two by two is charming, but the moral of the story of Noah is appalling. God took a dim view of humans, so he (with the exception of one family) drowned the lot of them including children and also, for good measure, the rest of the (presumably blameless) animals as well.[48]

To observe that earlier generations tended not to have this kind of problem, and do not seem to have used the story as an argument for cheapening life, can be valuable in reminding us that our contemporary perspectives are not the only significant ones. Moreover, it is entirely false to suppose that contemporary readers are the first to find difficulty with the biblical text.[49] Yet these recognitions do not necessarily help us make progress with the difficulties in the form that we today encounter them.

There is an obvious sense in which this kind of question may sometimes express little more than a superficial reading of the text (not attending to or understanding the story's own concerns) and a somewhat sentimental attitude (finding it hard to comprehend death and disaster within the purposes of God; though this, of course, is always demanding, as recurrent disasters and tragedies — most recently, in the public mind, the tsunami in the Indian Ocean on December 26, 2004 — remind us). The instinct of the Parisians in 1945 to mark the liberation of Paris from German occupation with a performance of André Obey's comedy play *Noah* suggests to me a deeper intuition than that of those who feel the story to be unsuitable for general use.[50] Yet

48. Richard Dawkins, *The God Delusion* (London: Bantam, 2006), pp. 237-38.

49. Let the contemporary reader study Origen and Luther! Even Calvin, who was not given to downplaying the moral difficulties within Scripture, notes in his comments on Gen. 6:7 that the inclusion of animals within the divine judgment "seems to exceed the bounds of moderation" (*Genesis,* 1:250), though he proceeds to offer a justification of sorts.

50. Writing in the late 1940s about his play of 1929, Obey refers to numerous correspondents who marvelled that he "should have been able to predict the catastrophe of 1939, to foretell the ruins from which were born the spirit of hope, the desire to begin all over again, of which my ancient patriarch is the very incarnation" (though Obey disclaims any such pre-

the underlying issue has to do with *assumptions* — those things that the biblical writers and premodern readers were happy to assume, but that have in one way or another become problematic in a contemporary context (one thinks of extensive recent debate in relation to ancient and contemporary assumptions about gender).

Rather than try to engage at that general level, it may be helpful to reflect in two preliminary ways upon certain aspects of Hebrew narrative, whose internal conventions indicate a spare mode of narrating. On the one hand, this affords many opportunities for the interpretative imagination to expatiate about that on which the text is silent — opportunities of which classic midrash made the most. There is, for example, a recurrent minority tradition among Jewish interpreters to find fault with Noah. Either they fix on the phrase "righteous . . . in his generation" (6:9), and suggest that since that generation was so corrupt, righteousness in that context was, crudely, no big deal.[51] Or they construe Noah's lack of speech throughout the story suspiciously: his failure to warn others, to express compassion for them, or to ask God to spare them shows that his sympathies are too narrow and self-centered.[52] (It is somewhat analogous to those who find fault with Abraham in Genesis 22 for not being the Abraham of Genesis 18: why obey God in an extreme situation when one might remonstrate with Him instead?) For whatever reasons such moves may be made, they suggest a dissatisfaction with the story's assumption that it is appropriate for Noah to display his integrity and obedience with never a word. It is an interesting precedent for the feeling that a differently told story would be a better or more usable story.

On the other hand, if a story of a flood is in some way a given in the world of ancient Israel (as the survival of other flood stories indicates), then there is the intrinsic constraint that the storyline necessarily entails the extensive obliteration of life upon earth. Here some of the characteristic moves within the Old Testament come into sharper focus when compared with, say,

---

dictive meaning in his writing); quoted by Michel Saint-Denis, introduction to Obey's *Noah: A Play in Five Scenes*, trans. Arthur Wilmurt (Melbourne/London/Toronto: Heinemann, 1949), p. vii.

51. See J. P. Lewis, *A Study of the Interpretation of Noah and the Flood in Jewish and Christian Literature* (Leiden: Brill, 1968), p. 133.

52. Noah's being at fault for not warning his contemporaries is a tradition in the *Zohar;* see *The Chumash: The Stone Edition* (Brooklyn: Mesorah, 1993), p. 31. For a modern example, see Morris Adler as cited in W. Gunther Plaut, ed., *The Torah: A Modern Commentary* (New York: Union of American Hebrew Congregations, 1981), p. 65.

the Utnapishtim story in the Epic of Gilgamesh. The Old Testament will not allow that there is any power other than YHWH who could bring and remove such a flood, which involves unmaking and remaking creation. Yet the reasons for YHWH's actions are charged with moral concern for the integrity of creation (Gen. 6:5, 11-13), and the text strikingly depicts YHWH at the outset as acting more in sorrow than in anger (Gen. 6:6-7);[53] and thereafter, despite the extensive divine instructions to Noah, the text says nothing about the divine thoughts or attitude, until the turn of the tide (Gen. 8:1). Thus, the Old Testament concern seems to be how to envisage the ultimate disaster that the flood represents — which is a given — within the morally demanding and life-bestowing purposes of YHWH.

If one observes that the story's opening portrayal of human sin leading to unlimited calamity is not the only thing to say about human life upon earth, then something similar is central to the point of the story itself, in that its purpose is to underline God's graciousness and patience with creation. To be sure, the story's concept of a small faithful remnant that survives overwhelming judgment and disaster and is the basis for hope for the future is hardly congenial[54] — yet it may nonetheless be salutary.[55]

Divine Revelation and Human Construction

Second, there are old questions that are being newly asked about the nature and status of the biblical text. In brief, what is the relationship between (a) recognizing the words of Genesis 8:21 as human words ascribed to God, and subsequently expanded by an anonymous scribe, in the context of an

53. The portrayal of YHWH in Gen. 6:6-7 is perhaps the more striking when it is compared with the briefer allusion to the story in Isa. 54:8-9, which does implicitly depict YHWH's action in the flood as marked by "anger" (קצף). The ethos of the Genesis narrative is far removed from, say, Jonathan Edwards's notorious depiction of "sinners in the hands of an angry God."

54. But is it so different from a popular scenario of contemporary science fiction? This scenario envisages some general catastrophe overtaking civilization on earth as we know it, and focuses on the struggle of a few to reestablish worthwhile life in the face of immense obstacles. These are stories of courage and hope against the odds, and the viewer or reader is implicitly meant to identify with those who demonstrate these positive qualities rather than thinking about the catastrophe as such.

55. Although "remnant theology" is often primarily associated with prophecy, the flood is its prime narrative depiction, both in general concept and in terminology (the use of שאר in 7:23).

ancient Hebrew retelling of a familiar story; and *(b)* taking the words as in some way genuinely representing the mind of God? On what grounds should one really trust the omniscient narrator, rather than just grant imaginative credence for the duration of one's reading? What is the relationship between literary artifact and reality? Although I sometimes get the feeling that some postmodern colleagues think that one should simply "tell the story," I confess to being unable to escape the salutary discomfort posed by modernity's characteristic critique: Is not all this talk of God merely the projection of human values and aspirations onto the big screen? Is not biblical language ultimately no more than human ideology?

Although sometimes people speak as if the discovery of the complexities of human processes involved in the formation of the Bible somehow disqualifies the Bible from being regarded any longer as the word of God, those who are more theologically literate will rightly insist that one should conceive the human and the divine as complementary rather than competitive. It is vital to avoid easy polarities between divine revelation and human imagination, or between that which is divinely given and that which is humanly constructed, or between divine sovereignty and human freedom, when the real challenge is to grasp how these may belong together. Or, in other terms, it is clear that the flood story — like the Bible as a whole — is a work of human construction. The question becomes whether this human construction is itself a response to antecedent divine initiative and so mediates a reality beyond itself, and if so, how fidelity in mediation should be understood and evaluated; or whether it is human construction "all the way down," with no reality beyond itself — a question not readily answered via the familiar agendas of biblical scholarship!

One potentially useful way of trying to avoid competitive understandings of the divine and the human is the proposal, periodically advanced, that Scripture (word of God) should be seen as somehow both human and divine, by analogy with the humanity and divinity of Jesus (Word of God). Nonetheless, the question of what is "acceptably" human needs more attention than it sometimes receives. That is, there is sometimes a tendency to suppose that writers singly composing narratives of historical factuality are acceptable in a way that editors and scribes reworking legends preserved by a community are not. Yet surely *any* significant mode of human communication should in principle be acceptable as a vehicle for the divine word, unless and until it can be clearly shown that it is problematic in the kind of way that might disqualify it.

I conclude by briefly and baldly indicating how I think a fuller engagement with this issue might be developed. In short, what is at stake in a Christian engagement with the flood story need be neither a display of naïve literalism nor a wistful nostalgia for bygone certainties nor a stubborn clinging to the morally objectionable. For such engagement, rightly understood, should represent a trusting commitment to work in a self-opening way with the wider moral and theological tradition — both biblical and postbiblical — of which this flood story forms a part. Such a commitment would be intrinsically indebted to the past and present fruitfulness of that tradition in its various Christian (and/or Jewish) forms. Within this context, searching and critical questions are put to text and tradition as a corollary of allowing text and tradition, received as mediators of a divine reality, to put searching and critical questions to us. When, and only when, the Genesis flood story is thus contextualized can it be appropriate to read it as in some way genuinely conveying the mind of the living God.

The Book of Tobit and the Canonical Ordering of the Book of the Twelve

Gary A. Anderson

The plot of the book of Tobit can be neatly summarized in the travels of its main characters. Tobit himself hails from the tribe of Naphtali (1:4), at the northern end of the northern kingdom of Israel. At the very beginning of the book we learn of his exemplary behavior in making the long, arduous trip to Jerusalem for the pilgrimage festivals (1:5-8). By doing so he was refusing to participate in the local bull cult that Jeroboam had put in place to obviate travel to the chosen city (1:5, cf. 1 Kings 12:25-33). When the kingdom of Israel fell in 721 BCE, Tobit was taken, along with his neighbors, to the Assyrian capital of Nineveh. Initially, he enjoyed considerable favor and rose to a position of considerable prominence within the royal household (1:10-13). During that time, Tobit made frequent business trips to Media. On one trip he left ten talents of silver in trust with a fellow Israelite by the name of Gabael (1:14).

During the reign of King Sennacherib (ca. 701 BCE), things turned sour. Tobit was forced to abandon his home and possessions and flee for his life (1:18-20). While he was in exile, Sennacherib was murdered and his son Esarhaddon came to the throne. Tobit's nephew Ahiqar, himself a prominent official in the royal court, interceded, and Tobit was allowed to return home (1:21-22). Back at home, however, his fortunes took another turn for the worse; Tobit became blind and eventually prayed that his life would come to an end (2:7–3:6). He bid his son Tobias to travel to Media and secure the funds he had left in deposit with Gabael, so that after his death Tobias would have the means to support his mother and to continue to give alms (4:1–5:3). This trip constitutes the very heart of the book.

When he reached Media, Tobias — guided by an angel — met and married his wife, Sarah. They obtained the funds and returned to Nineveh, where, with the angel's assistance, Tobit's eyes were healed. In thanksgiving over the restoration of all that he had, Tobit foresaw the journey of journeys that would take place after his death: the return of captive Israel to a restored Jerusalem (13:1-17).

Now, with the protagonists' problems solved, the story should be ready to draw to a close. But there is one further wrinkle in the geographical detail. Tobit knew that Nineveh was doomed to fall in the near future, and he feared for his son and family (14:3-4). His advice was to the point: "So, my boy, you must leave Nineveh; do not stay here. On the day that you bury your mother alongside of me, on that very day spend not a night within its borders. For I note that there is much wickedness in it, and much dishonesty is perpetrated here, and no one is ashamed of it" (14:9-10).[1] And so it happened that when Tobit and his wife died, Tobias and Sarah returned to Media and cared for Sarah's parents in their old age. After their death, Tobias tended to their burial and inherited their estate. The book then closes with these words: "Before he died, he saw and heard about the destruction of Nineveh. He saw its captives being led into Media, those whom the king of Media, Achiacharos (Cyaxares), carried off. Tobias praised God in all that He did for the people of Nineveh and Assyria. Before he died, he rejoiced over Nineveh and praised the Lord God for ever and ever" (14:15).

The crucial piece of information that I would like to explore is Tobit's knowledge that the city of Nineveh would fall. Though it occurs in the epilogue of the story, after the tension in the plot has reached its resolution, one should not miss the important role it plays. For had Tobias remained in Nineveh, all of the blessing and beatitude that had been visited upon this family as a result of Tobit's religious virtuosity would have been lost.

But how was Tobit so confident that Nineveh would fall? Here is the rub. The different textual versions of our tale provide us with three different ways of solving the problem. And in each of them the reason is embedded in Tobit's address to his son in 14:3-4.[2]

---

1. Translations of Tobit are from Joseph A. Fitzmyer, *Tobit*, CEJL (Berlin: de Gruyter, 2003).

2. Greek[I] (G[I]) is the shorter recension of the book that is found in Vaticanus and Alexandrinus. Greek[II] (G[II]) is the longer recension and is found in Sinaiticus. It is generally considered to be the more original form of the book. On this problem, see D. C. Simpson, "The Chief Recensions of the Book of Tobit," *JTS* 14 (1912-13): 516-30; Fitzmyer, *Tobit*, pp. 4-5. The Old Latin (VL) is thought to follow Greek[II].

- Greek[I]: Take your children, my child; I have now grown old and am about to depart from this life. Go to Media, my child, because I believe what the prophet Jonah said about Nineveh, that it will be overthrown.
- Greek[II]: Take your children, my boy, and hasten off to Media, because I believe the word of God about Nineveh, which He spoke to Nahum.
- Old Latin: My son, love your children, and hasten off into the region of the Medes, because I believe God's word, which he uttered about Nineveh.[3]

Of these three texts, Greek[II] and the Old Latin are fairly straightforward and easy to understand. Greek[II] cites the prophet Nahum, a figure who spoke directly to the city's impending fall of 612 BCE. Indeed, this is highlighted in the superscription of the book of Nahum: "A pronouncement on Nineveh: The Book of the Prophecy of Nahum the Elkoshite" (Nah. 1:1).[4] Given that Tobit was sent into exile as a relatively young man in 721 BCE and that his son lived well beyond the century mark, it is not at all unexpected that Tobias would have witnessed this cataclysmic event. The Old Latin is a bit more unusual, because it provides no specific source for the knowledge. It is true that the book can speak in this sort of general fashion when addressing the rebuilding of Jerusalem: "God's house will be rebuilt in [Jerusalem], just as the prophets of Israel have said of it" (Tob. 14:5). But this seems less jarring to the ear, because the tradition of Jerusalem's restoration was not limited to a single prophet but was part of a much larger eschatological tradition. The reader would recognize it as a common trope. But the same cannot be said for the expectation that Nineveh would fall. The singularity of this prediction makes the attribution of it to a specific prophet much more natural.[5]

What then do we make of the Greek[I] version, which claims that Tobit's knowledge came from what the prophet Jonah had said when he visited Nineveh?[6] Every commentator whom I have checked is certain that this tex-

---

3. The variant in the Vulgate is very similar to the Old Latin: ". . . the destruction of Nineveh will be at hand, for God's word does not fail."

4. OT translations are from the NJPS.

5. Dr. Ronnie Goldstein of the Hebrew University in Jerusalem graciously read this manuscript and suggested to me that the text tradition represented by the Latin came first, which names no prophet. The two Greek versions were bothered by this "gap" in the story and each filled it in a different way. This explanation has the advantage of being the simplest, which is often the hallmark of the best text-critical decision. Yet a nonspecific reference to the future fall of Nineveh still strikes me as odd.

6. For the canonical reader, Jonah is generally identified with the prophet of the same

tual tradition is secondary. Frank Zimmermann writes that this is "a clear case of substitution by one who was more familiar with Jonah as a story than the fulfillment of the prophecy. Actually, of course, the latter's prophecy was not realized because the people of Nineveh repented and the city was not destroyed. Therefore there is no point in Tobit's saying that Nineveh will be destroyed as predicted by Jonah."[7] Carey Moore, in his recent commentary on the book, supports this judgment as well.[8] Fitzmyer agrees with Zimmermann but provides a further explanation of why the prophet Jonah cannot be the correct reference:

> In the OT the prophet Nahum of Elkosh is the author of a triumphal ode composed against the Assyrians and their capital, Nineveh. It is certainly the more fitting allusion for Tobit to cite, as he does in G^{II}, than the oracle of Jonah, which is found in G^{I} instead. Nahum foretold indeed the coming destruction of Nineveh (Nah 1:1; 2:8-10, 13; 3:18-19), whereas at the preaching of Jonah (3:4: "Yet forty days, and Nineveh shall be overthrown!") the king, nobles, and people of Nineveh repented; and so they escaped judgment (Jonah 3:10). Tobit recalls Nahum's words against Nineveh and so recommends that [Tobias] leave it as soon as he can to go to Media.[9]

The solution to the problem would seem to be assured. The reference to Jonah must be secondary. But if so, what would account for its inclusion?

Zimmermann's argument that Jonah was cited instead of Nahum because the scribe wanted to include a more familiar name sounds convincing at first. Copyists do substitute common names for those less well known, and for most modern readers the figure of Jonah is better known than that of Nahum. But who is to say that the same was true in the era of Tobit? I can think of no evidence that would suggest such. One might note that from Qumran we have a pesher on Nahum but none on Jonah. The explanation of Zimmermann is clearly ad hoc and should not be considered satisfactory. We should also note that there are problems with the reference to Nahum.

---

name who is mentioned in 2 Kings 14:23-27 and lived during the reign of Jeroboam II (786-746 BCE). This would place Jonah in Nineveh about a generation prior to the arrival of the Israelite exiles (see 2 Kings 17:5-23).

7. Frank Zimmermann, *The Book of Tobit: An English Translation with Introduction and Commentary*, JAL (New York: Harper, 1958), pp. 118-19.

8. Carey A. Moore, *Tobit*, AB 40A (New York: Doubleday, 1996), p. 290.

9. Fitzmyer, *Tobit*, pp. 325-26.

How could Tobit have heard this prophet, given that he was of Judean origin? Nahum's oracles are clearly directed to the citizens of Jerusalem.[10] To be sure, Tobit may have learned of his words from a Judean who had been deported to Assyria. But are not the odds better that he would have heard about Jonah, who had just a couple of decades earlier preached in his own town?

One might counter that Fitzmyer's objection that Jonah's prediction about the fall of Nineveh clearly failed is a far more difficult problem. In his own day, Jonah was decisively shown to be wrong. But would not an ancient scribe be just as aware as the modern scholar that the city of Nineveh had escaped the harsh penalty Jonah had prophesied? Why would he insert such a blatantly inferior reading into his text?

Two considerations may solve this problem. First of all, it is not clear that Jonah was wrong in *every* respect. The book closes not with the restoration of Nineveh but with Jonah's anger over this display of divine mercy. In a fit of pique, Jonah heads out of the city in an easterly direction (Jonah 4:5). As Uriel Simon has shown, this is a wonderful piece of literary irony in that it matches Jonah's disposition at the beginning of the book.[11] There God orders him to go to Assyria in the east, and in rebellion Jonah heads west (1:3). Now that his duty is finished, one would expect him to return home to Israel in the west, but in his rage he heads east. There he builds a booth in order to see whether the Ninevites will return to their pernicious behavior and prove him right. Certainly, Jonah imagines, God has gotten the matter wrong. His disposition to be merciful (4:2) has allowed him to be persuaded by the Ninevites' temporary turn from evil. Given sufficient time, Jonah reasons, Nineveh will revert to its sinful ways and God will have to reconsider and destroy the city (4:5). Justice will win out in the end.

But God, for his part, never directly addresses Jonah's worries about the relationship of justice to mercy. And Simon observes: "The Lord's last speech does not refer to the moral argument [of Jonah], and the question of the Ninevites' future conduct does not come up at all."[12] When God does speak to Jonah at the end of the book, he ignores the fact of Nineveh's repentance and tells Jonah that he has granted this city a reprieve because of the number of innocents who reside therein (4:11). At the end, the book of Jonah

10. See Nah. 2:1 (1:15 Eng.): "Celebrate your festivals, O Judah, / Fulfill your vows. / Never again shall scoundrels invade you, / They have totally vanished."

11. Uriel Simon, *The JPS Bible Commentary: Jonah* (Philadelphia: Jewish Publication Society, 1999), p. 39.

12. Simon, *Jonah*, p. 41.

leaves the reader hanging. The plot does not come to closure: we remain ignorant as to how Jonah will respond to God and ignorant as to whether the divine mercy toward Nineveh will continue.[13]

A second consideration is even more important for our purposes. The book of Jonah in the Masoretic collection is the fifth book among the Minor Prophets. It is preceded by Obadiah and followed by Micah and Nahum. The antiquity of this order is confirmed by the Minor Prophets scroll found in Wadi Murabbaʿat, which dates to the second century CE. The order no doubt reflects the imagined historical sequence of the prophets. Jonah was identified with a figure of the same name who was active during the reign of Jeroboam II (2 Kings 14:23-25), in other words, during the middle of the eighth century. Obadiah preceded Jonah because that book was attributed to Obadiah the servant of Ahab (1 Kings 18:3). Micah prophesied during the reigns of Jotham, Ahaz, and Hezekiah, that is, at the end of the eighth century, while Nahum was active during the seventh century. The implications of placing Micah and Nahum after Jonah should not be missed. As Simon observes: "Micah prophesied the fall of Assyria (5:4-5) and Nahum the destruction of Nineveh (2:4–3:19). *Thus the placement of these two books after Jonah expresses the view that Assyria returned to its evil ways after its short-lived repentance in the time of Jonah.*"[14] For any ancient reader, it would be impossible to ignore the canonical shaping of the Minor

---

13. See Alan Cooper's article "In Praise of Divine Caprice: The Significance of the Book of Jonah," in *Among the Prophets*, ed. P. R. Davies and D. J. A. Clines, JSOTSup 144 (Sheffield: JSOT Press, 1993), pp. 144-63. Cooper shrewdly observes that the closing verse of the book (4:11), which is normally translated as a question, "Should I not care about Nineveh?" could just as easily be rendered as a declarative sentence, "As for me, I do not care about Nineveh . . ." (p. 158). His conclusion, which may be a bit extreme, is nevertheless instructive: "The implication would be that God cares no more about that huge city full of ignoramuses and beasts than he had about the קיקיון [plant]. Their repentance means nothing to him, and he has kept his real reason for sparing them (if, indeed, he had one) to himself" (p. 158). My own opinion is that God is not so much indifferent to the citizens of Nineveh as he is reluctant to reveal to Jonah the precise reasons for why he has forgiven them. It is not appropriate for human beings to know when and why God will forgive. Indeed, both the sailors and the king of Nineveh are quite circumspect in this regard and concede to God the freedom to ignore their pleas. Note the words of the king: "*Who knows* but that God may turn and relent?" (3:9). And compare this with the captain of the boat in chapter 1: "Up, call upon your god! *Perhaps* the god will be kind to us and we will not perish" (1:6). It should be emphasized that Cooper's translation of 4:11 and its theological implications are not due to his reading of the book on its own terms but derive from reading Jonah in light of Nahum.

14. Simon, *Jonah*, p. xiv, emphasis mine.

Prophets scroll.[15] One could not hear the warnings of Jonah without weighing them against the testimony of Micah and Nahum. In the end, the canonical reader must concede that Jonah was not completely wrong; Nineveh returned to its sinful ways and did fall by prophetic decree.

It might be added that this point is made even more emphatically in the Septuagintal text of the Minor Prophets, for there the prophet Nahum comes immediately after Jonah. Consider the literary effect of juxtaposing the end of Jonah with the beginning of Nahum:

> "And should not I care about Nineveh, that great city, in which there are more than a hundred and twenty thousand persons who do not yet know their right hand from their left, and many beasts as well!" A pronouncement on Nineveh: The Book of the Prophecy of Nahum the Elkoshite. "The LORD is a passionate, avenging God. / . . . The LORD is slow to anger and of great forbearance, / But the LORD does not remit all punishment." (Jonah 4:11; Nah. 1:1-3)

What is striking here is that Jonah had believed that God's merciful nature — "I know that You are a compassionate and gracious God, slow to anger . . ." (Jonah 4:2) — meant that he would not deal appropriately with Nineveh. But the very opening verses of Nahum show us a different side of God. Yes, God is "slow to anger" but he also "does not remit all punishment." This canonical placement cannot be accidental. Whoever placed Nahum right after Jonah was providing a window into how early Judaism heard the two books. Jonah's own prediction that the city of Nineveh would fall in forty days may have proved wrong in terms of its overly optimistic time frame, but his words did eventually come to pass. The canonical placement of the prophet Nahum is witness to this fact.

It should not occasion surprise that interpreters up to now have not given this particular reading in the book of Tobit its due. The hallmark of the modern reader of the Bible is the desire to hear each book on its own terms. Only in the last decade or so have scholars begun in earnest to hear the biblical books in relationship to one another. Consider what Rolf Rendtorff has to say about the canonical ordering of Jonah and Nahum:

> God sent Jonah with a message that was *true*. Nineveh will be destroyed because of its wickedness. But the announcement of the divine judgment

---

15. And indeed, this is how some moderns are now interpreting the book; see the proposal of Cooper in n. 13 above.

always also contains the possibility of the repentance of sinners and the resultant repentance of God. This makes the prophetic message (apparently) *untrue*. It is this ambiguity that Jonah cannot stand. It was because he had this possibility in mind that he fled. . . .

The reader of this text, living after the end of the Assyrian empire, must, however, wonder how this hopeful expectation of the future fate of the capital, Nineveh, given narrative shape in Jonah, relates to Nineveh's actual fate. Will Nineveh really repent and be saved? This question is picked up again later in Nahum.[16]

I could cite any number of other recent commentators on Jonah to a similar end. The point is that modern readers of the prophets are only now rediscovering what ancient readers had long known. The canonical ordering of the biblical books does make a difference for the interpreter. The problem of Nineveh was not read solely from the perspective of Jonah's idiosyncratic mission. Rather, God's final message about that city transcended whatever Jonah himself might have personally thought. In the view of Tobit, Jonah had the message right — Nineveh will fall — but the time frame wrong — not in forty days but after a number of decades.

If we understand the reference to Jonah as original, then I think the text-critical questions fall neatly into place. The earliest reading for the verse in question is that represented by Greek[I], the shorter recension.[17] According to this version, Tobit heard about Jonah's prophecy while residing in Nineveh and inferred its correct, divine intent. It was these words that he recalled for the benefit of his son. Later copyists saw that the reference to Jonah was not without its problems and did one of two things. In the case of the longer Greek recension, Greek[II], the scribe altered the name to Nahum ("Take your children, my boy, and hasten off to Media, because I believe the word of God about Nineveh, which He spoke to Nahum") to provide the reader with a prophet who clearly got it right without any ambiguity. In the Old Latin version, we see a different solution. The source of Tobit's knowledge is left without specific attribution (". . . hasten off into the region of the Medes, *because I believe God's word*, which he uttered about Nineveh"). But even those who would quibble with this reconstruction of the textual history must still pro-

16. Rolf Rendtorff, *The Canonical Hebrew Bible: A Theology of the Old Testament* (Leiden: Deo, 2005), p. 292.

17. I should note that I am in agreement with most scholars that for the overall shape of the book the longer recension is the earliest, but that does not mean that for any given verse this recension should always be given priority.

vide a reason why one of the Greek versions believed that Tobit had learned of Nineveh's eventual demise from the prophet Jonah.[18]

I have argued that there are two reasons why this reading works. First, Jonah prophesied in the city of Nineveh just a decade or two before Tobit's arrival. Clearly, the ancient scribe must have imagined, Tobit would have been familiar with this famous figure. Second, the book of Jonah ends on an ambiguous note; as the reader finishes the book, Jonah is waiting to see what the ultimate fate of Nineveh will be. That fate is revealed in the next two books, Micah and Nahum: Nineveh is doomed. Some critics of the canonical method have argued that ancient readers of the Bible took no interest in such matters and that canonical criticism is thoroughly anachronistic.[19] There is some truth to this piece of criticism. But the shorter recension of the book of Tobit shows us that ancient scribes could be very good canonical readers. And the ability of those ancient writers to read canonically was missed by a whole generation of commentators on the book of Tobit.[20]

18. See my n. 5, above. Whether the original reading named no prophet (Old Latin) or Nahum (Greek[II]), one would still need to explain why that original reading was altered in favor of Jonah in Greek[I].

19. See John Barton, *Reading the Old Testament: Method in Biblical Study* (Louisville: Westminster John Knox, 1996), pp. 97-98.

20. It is my honor to dedicate this article to my dear friend and colleague Richard B. Hays, who has spent so much of his scholarly career laboring over the implications of a canonical reading of Scripture.

Faithfulness and Fear, Stumbling and Salvation: Receptions of LXX Isaiah 8:11-18 in the New Testament

J. Ross Wagner

The past century has witnessed a steadily growing scholarly interest in the collection of Greek texts and translations of Israel's Scriptures commonly known as the Septuagint (LXX). This still-evolving discipline, like its subject matter, is complex and multifaceted.[1] Among the variety of approaches to the study of the Septuagint, one that holds great promise for New Testament studies regards these translations not merely as vehicles for recovering an earlier Hebrew *Vorlage* but as sacred texts in their own right — texts that have significant histories of effects in both Jewish and Christian communities of faith.

As careful investigation of scriptural citations in the New Testament has revealed, early Christian authors were well acquainted with the Septuagint.[2] What has not yet been fully explored is the extent to which reading the Scriptures *in Greek* shaped early Christian ways of understanding and articulating what God has done for Israel and for the world in and through Christ. In the present essay, I seek to make a modest contribution to the investigation of this

---

1. Karen H. Jobes and Moisés Silva provide a learned and accessible overview of the discipline in their *Invitation to the Septuagint* (Grand Rapids: Baker, 2000), pp. 258-72. More narrowly focused is the valuable introduction by R. Timothy McLay, *The Use of the Septuagint in New Testament Research* (Grand Rapids: Eerdmans, 2003).

2. For a convenient display of the data, see the multivolume work of Hans Hübner, *Vetus Testamentum in Novo* (Göttingen: Vandenhoeck & Ruprecht, 1997-). Hübner goes so far as to speak of the *"Prädominanz der Septuaginta im Neuen Testament"*; see Hübner, *Biblische Theologie des Neuen Testaments I: Prolegomena* (Göttingen: Vandenhoeck & Ruprecht, 1990), p. 64, emphasis original.

question by exploring one aspect of the *Wirkungsgeschichte* of LXX Isaiah in the New Testament. It is a singular privilege to be able to do so in the context of a *Festschrift* honoring my *Doktorvater*, mentor, and friend Richard Hays, whose groundbreaking studies have revitalized and reoriented contemporary investigation of the reception of Israel's Scriptures in early Christianity.

This study focuses on a single text, LXX Isaiah 8:11-18, and its interpretation in three New Testament letters: Romans, 1 Peter, and Hebrews.[3] The Septuagint version of Isaiah 8 presents an interesting case study because of the striking differences between this Greek translation and the Hebrew text attested, in somewhat different forms, in 1QIsaᵃ and in the MT.[4] However, my interest here lies not in the question of the translator's *Vorlage* or style of translation[5] but in the "meaning potential" of the Greek text itself.[6] Attention to how these three quite different New Testament interpreters understood, appropriated, and transformed the words of Greek Isaiah offers intriguing insights into the range of possible meanings of this text for ancient readers. At the same time, it affords a striking glimpse of the dynamic process of interpretation set into motion within early Christian communities by the resurrection of Jesus Christ from the dead.[7]

---

3. In this essay, "Septuagint Isaiah" refers to the critically reconstructed text of the Göttingen Septuagint (Joseph Ziegler, *Isaias,* 3rd ed., Septuaginta 14 [Göttingen: Vandenhoeck & Ruprecht, 1983]) as the best available approximation of the original translator's opus.

4. There is good reason to believe that the *Vorlage* of LXX Isaiah was fairly close to the Hebrew text represented by the MT; so Arie van der Kooij, "Isaiah in the Septuagint," in *Writing and Reading the Scroll of Isaiah: Studies of an Interpretive Tradition,* ed. Craig C. Broyles and Craig A. Evans, 2 vols. (Leiden: Brill, 1997), 2:517, 529 n. 48. On 1QIsaᵃ, see van der Kooij, "1QIsaᵃ Col. VIII, 4-11 (Isa 8,11-18): A Contextual Approach of Its Variants," *RevQ* 13 (1988): 569-81.

5. For discussion of LXX Isa. 8:11-18 that devotes closer attention to the Isaiah translator's method of translation, in dialogue with previous scholarship, see J. Ross Wagner, "Identifying 'Updated' Prophecies in Old Greek (OG) Isaiah: Isaiah 8:11-16 as a Test Case," *JBL* 126 (2007): 251-69. Whether or not the question of the translator's understanding of his *Vorlage* can ever be adequately addressed apart from critical attention to the reception of the translation remains an important — and debated — issue. See the illuminating study by Philippe Lefebvre, "Les mots de la Septante ont-ils trois dimensions?" in *KATA TOYΣ O': Selon les Septante,* ed. Gilles Dorival and Olivier Munnich (Paris: Cerf, 1995), pp. 299-320.

6. Cf. the approaches of William Loader, *The Septuagint, Sexuality, and the New Testament* (Grand Rapids: Eerdmans, 2004), pp. 1-4; and Stanley E. Porter and Brook W. R. Pearson, "Isaiah through Greek Eyes: The Septuagint of Isaiah," in *Writing and Reading the Scroll of Isaiah,* ed. Broyles and Evans, 2:531-46.

7. On the resurrection as decisive for early Christian hermeneutics, see Richard B.

LXX Isaiah 8:11-18

We begin with a brief exploration of the text of LXX Isaiah 8:11-18. This discussion will serve as a reference point for our subsequent examination of the variety of ways in which the meaning potential of this passage has been actualized in the particular arguments of Romans, 1 Peter, and Hebrews.

11 Οὕτως λέγει κύριος· τῇ ἰσχυρᾷ χειρὶ ἀπειθοῦσι τῇ πορείᾳ τῆς ὁδοῦ τοῦ λαοῦ τούτου λέγοντες· 12 μήποτε εἴπητε σκληρόν· πᾶν γάρ, ὃ ἐὰν εἴπῃ ὁ λαὸς οὗτος, σκληρόν ἐστι· τὸν δὲ φόβον αὐτοῦ οὐ μὴ φοβηθῆτε οὐδὲ μὴ ταραχθῆτε· 13 κύριον αὐτὸν ἁγιάσατε, καὶ αὐτὸς ἔσται σου φόβος. 14 καὶ ἐὰν ἐπ' αὐτῷ πεποιθὼς ᾖς, ἔσται σοι εἰς ἁγίασμα, καὶ οὐχ ὡς λίθου προσκόμματι συναντήσεσθε αὐτῷ οὐδὲ ὡς πέτρας πτώματι. ὁ δὲ οἶκος Ιακωβ ἐν παγίδι, καὶ ἐν κοιλάσματι ἐγκαθήμενοι ἐν Ιερουσαλημ. 15 διὰ τοῦτο ἀδυνατήσουσιν ἐν αὐτοῖς πολλοὶ καὶ πεσοῦνται καὶ συντριβήσονται, καὶ ἐγγιοῦσι καὶ ἁλώσονται ἄνθρωποι ἐν ἀσφαλείᾳ ὄντες. 16 τότε φανεροὶ ἔσονται οἱ σφραγιζόμενοι τὸν νόμον τοῦ μὴ μαθεῖν. 17 καὶ ἐρεῖ· μενῶ τὸν θεὸν τὸν ἀποστρέψαντα τὸ πρόσωπον αὐτοῦ ἀπὸ τοῦ οἴκου Ιακωβ καὶ πεποιθὼς ἔσομαι ἐπ' αὐτῷ. 18 ἰδοὺ ἐγὼ καὶ τὰ παιδία ἅ μοι ἔδωκεν ὁ θεός. καὶ ἔσται εἰς σημεῖα καὶ τέρατα ἐν τῷ Ισραηλ παρὰ κυρίου σαβαωθ, ὃς κατοικεῖ ἐν τῷ ὄρει Σιων.[8]

11 Thus says the Lord, "With a strong hand they reject walking in the way of this people, saying,

> 12 No longer say, '[It's] hard'; for everything this people says is: '[It's] hard.' Do not fear what they fear and do not be troubled. 13 The Lord — sanctify him, and he will be your fear. 14 And if you trust in him, he will be for you a sanctuary, and you will not encounter him as the obstruction of a stone or as the obstacle of a rock.

But the house of Jacob is in a snare, and they are lying in a trap in Jerusalem. 15 For this reason many among them will become weak, and they will fall and be broken, and people dwelling in safety will draw near and be captured. 16 Then those who seal up the law in order not to learn [it] will be exposed."

Hays, "Reading Scripture in Light of the Resurrection," in *The Art of Reading Scripture,* ed. Ellen F. Davis and Richard B. Hays (Grand Rapids: Eerdmans, 2003), pp. 216-38.

8. The text is from Ziegler's edition (see n. 3 above), although I have not followed his punctuation in every respect.

17 And he will say, "I will wait for God, who has turned his face away from the house of Jacob, and I will trust in him. 18 Here am I and the children that God has given me; and they will be for signs and wonders in Israel from the Lord Sabaoth, who dwells in mount Zion."

The oracle of the Lord in LXX Isaiah 8:11-18 speaks of a sharp division in Israel between two parties: one termed "this people" (8:11, 12), the other unnamed but marked by their refusal to follow "the way of this people" (8:11). The appellation "this people" — a jarring repudiation of the covenant formula "my people" found in many of Isaiah's oracles of consolation — has already appeared three times in Isaiah 6 as the Lord's designation for those to whom the prophet is to bring his message of judgment. "This people" is characterized by spiritual insensibility: their hearts have grown calloused, their ears dull of hearing, and they have closed their eyes (6:8, 9, 10). Elsewhere in LXX Isaiah, "this people" is similarly depicted as recalcitrant and rebellious (8:6; 9:16; 28:11, 14; 29:13, 14). Rather than walking "in the true way," they determinedly "follow . . . after their sins" and continually provoke God with their idolatrous practices (65:2-3).

Not surprisingly, then, in Isaiah 8:11-18 too "this people" (further identified as "the house of Jacob" and those "in Jerusalem," 8:14; cf. 8:17) names those who oppose Israel's God. They are marked by rebellious speech and by abject fear in the face of Judah's enemies (8:12). Instead of fearing God and trusting him to deliver them, they place their hope in foreign powers as a shield against Assyrian aggression (8:6; cf. 7:1-2, 5-6). They offer their devotion not to Israel's God but to foreign deities who can be consulted via mediums and soothsayers (8:19).

In LXX Isaiah 8 "this people's" refusal to trust in the Lord is further manifested in their repudiation of the law. The Greek version of the oracle charges that they "seal up the law in order not to learn [it]" (8:16). Although God has given the law to his people as a "help" (βοήθεια, 8:20), "this people" chooses instead to rely on the vain hope offered by divination (8:19). The faithlessness of "this people" toward God's law resonates with the accusations of lawless behavior and outright rejection of the law leveled in the opening lines of the book and repeated throughout LXX Isaiah.[9]

The second, unnamed group rebels against "walking in the way of this

---

9. "Woe to a sinful nation, a people full of sins, evil seed, lawless children (υἱοὶ ἄνομοι)" (Isa. 1:4). For opposition to the law, see Isa. 5:24; 8:16; 24:5, 16; 30:9; 42:24. On the translator's particular interest in the law, see further Isaac Leo Seeligmann, *The Septuagint Version of Isaiah: A Discussion of Its Problems* (Leiden: Brill, 1948), pp. 104-8.

people" (8:11). They exhort one another not to "fear what [this people] fear" (8:12)[10] but rather to honor the Lord as holy, to fear the Lord alone (8:13), and to trust confidently in their God (8:14). By implication, they, unlike "this people," devote themselves to learning and obeying God's law (8:16; cf. 51:7), regarding the law as a divine "help" on which to rely (8:20).

Their summons to confident trust, "If you trust in him" (ἐὰν ἐπ' αὐτῷ πεποιθὼς ᾖς, 8:14), finds a strong echo in the response of the speaker in 8:17-18, who resolves, "I will wait for God, . . . and I will trust in him" (πεποιθὼς ἔσομαι ἐπ' αὐτῷ, 8:17).[11] Just who is speaking these lines is unclear.[12] The voice could be identified as Isaiah's, for the reference to children as "signs and wonders" from the Lord recalls earlier episodes in which the prophet's sons figure prominently (7:3; 8:1-4). At the same time, the third-person καὶ ἐρεῖ is somewhat puzzling in view of Isaiah's first-person self-references earlier in the chapter (8:1, 3, 5; cf. ch. 6 passim). In any case, it is clear that the speaker distances himself from the disobedient "house of Jacob" and supports the resolve of the faithful to put their hope in the Lord. As subsequent oracles continue to emphasize, this attitude of confident trust in God marks those whom the Lord will redeem.[13]

Isaiah 8:11-18 promises deliverance for those who trust in the Lord, but certain judgment for those who reject his law. The Lord will be a "sanctuary" for those who trust in him, and they will *not* encounter their God "as the obstruction of a stone or as the obstacle of a rock" (8:14). In contrast, "this people," the rebellious "house of Jacob" from whom God has turned his face

---

10. The Greek construction τὸν φόβον αὐτοῦ could also be understood as an objective genitive, "do not fear *it* (i.e., this people)."

11. In Isa. 8:14 the translator solved what was apparently for him a problem both theologically (God as stone of offense) and syntactically (the need for a clear break between למקדש and ולאבן) by borrowing the phrase πεποιθὼς ἔσομαι ἐπ' αὐτῷ from v. 17 and transforming 8:14 into a conditional sentence (cf. *Tg. Isa.* 8:14). The effect is to give prominence in LXX Isaiah 8 to the theme of trust as the faithful response to God. On the translator's concern to moderate Isaiah's portrayal of God as Israel's adversary in 6:9-10; 8:11-16, and elsewhere, see Johan Lust, "The Demonic Character of Jahweh and the Septuagint of Isaiah," *Bijdr* 40 (1979): 2-14; cf. Douglas A. Oss, "The Interpretation of the 'Stone' Passages by Peter and Paul: A Comparative Study," *JETS* 32 (1989): 181-200, esp. pp. 185-86.

12. See below for the possibility that the author of Hebrews has exploited this ambiguity in identifying the speaker as Christ.

13. In Isa. 10:20, restored Israel is characterized as those who "trust in God (ἔσονται πεποιθότες ἐπὶ τὸν θεόν), the Holy One of Israel, in truth." The opening section of the book (Isaiah 1–12) closes with the affirmation of the redeemed, "See, my God, my Savior, is the Lord; I will trust in him (πεποιθὼς ἔσομαι ἐπ' αὐτῷ) and not be afraid" (12:2); the translator's addition of ἐπ' αὐτῷ in 12:2 creates a tighter link with 8:14, 17, and 10:20.

(8:17; cf. 1:15), is "in a snare," and those who live in Jerusalem lie "in a trap" (8:14). The passage clearly implies that because they do not trust in the Lord, they *will* encounter the God of Israel as a stumbling block (8:14), with the result that "they will fall and be broken, they will draw near and be captured" (8:15).[14] As the final verse of the section emphasizes, this fate will expose the fact that they have not submitted to God's law but have refused to hear and to learn it (8:16).[15] In this way, LXX Isaiah closely associates trust in God with understanding and obeying God's law.[16]

This brief survey of LXX Isaiah 8:11-18 has sought to display something of the "meaning potential" of the passage for a reader viewing Isaiah "through Greek eyes." We turn next to examine what a number of early Christian interpreters actually did with this Greek text.

LXX Isaiah 8:11-18 in Early Christianity

Sources and Traditions

The interpretation of Scripture by New Testament writers belongs to a complex and dynamic process of appropriating and transforming Israel's traditions in a quest to understand and proclaim the significance of God's redemptive work in Christ. Early Christian authors encountered Israel's Scriptures in a variety of forms, both oral and written, including Jewish and Christian oral traditions, biblical manuscripts, collections of scriptural testimonies, personal notebooks of *excerpta,* and scriptural texts committed to memory.[17] Conse-

---

14. That the LXX translator, despite his rendering of 8:14a (see n. 11 above), nevertheless preserves the Hebrew text's clear prediction of stumbling and destruction for "this people" (8:14b-15) is often overlooked by those who seek to draw a sharp contrast between the sense of the LXX and that of the MT; see, e.g., C. H. Dodd, *According to the Scriptures* (London: Nisbet, 1952), p. 42 n. 1; Steve Moyise, "Isaiah in 1 Peter," in *Isaiah in the New Testament,* ed. Steve Moyise and Maarten J. J. Menken (London: T. & T. Clark, 2005), p. 179.

15. A similar doom is pronounced in LXX Isa. 24:16-17, a rather freely rendered passage (with echoes of Isa. 8:13-14) into which the translator has introduced "the law": "Woe to those who reject, to those who reject the law. Fear and a pit and a snare upon you who dwell on the land."

16. Note also the link between trust and understanding established by the translator in Isa. 7:9: "If you do not believe, you will surely not understand" (καὶ ἐὰν μὴ πιστεύσητε οὐδὲ μὴ συνῆτε).

17. See further J. Ross Wagner, *Heralds of the Good News: Paul and Isaiah in Concert in the Letter to the Romans,* NovTSup 101 (Leiden: Brill, 2002), pp. 20-27.

quently, before examining the use of Isaiah 8 in Romans, 1 Peter, and Hebrews, it is necessary to address, if only in cursory fashion, two preliminary questions: (1) What source or sources lie behind the citations of Isaiah 8 in our three New Testament texts? and (2) Are there early Jewish or Christian traditions of interpretation that illuminate the authors' readings of these texts?

Although it is relatively unproblematic to infer the dependence of Hebrews 2:13 on a Greek text of Isaiah 8 much like that of the LXX,[18] the situation is quite a bit more complex in the case of Romans 9:33 and 1 Peter 2:8, both of which cite Isaiah 8:14 in close connection with Isaiah 28:16. The striking correspondences in wording between Paul's conflated citation of Isaiah 28:16/8:14 in Romans 9:33 and the serial (unconflated) quotation of these same texts in 1 Peter 2:6, 8 have long been noted, as have the divergences of both citations from the LXX (see p. 83). The fact that direct literary dependence of one of these New Testament authors on the other is highly unlikely has sparked the search for a common (probably written) tradition or source.[19] The form of the citations suggests that they originally derive from a manuscript of LXX Isaiah that was revised — though only unsystematically — toward a Hebrew exemplar similar to the MT.[20] Paul may well have drawn his citations directly from such a manuscript, although his use of a traditional collection of scriptural excerpts cannot be ruled out.[21] In either

18. See Martin Karrer, "The Epistle to the Hebrews and the Septuagint," in *Septuagint Research: Issues and Challenges in the Study of the Greek Jewish Scriptures,* ed. W. Kraus and R. G. Wooden, SBLSCS 53 (Atlanta: SBL, 2006), pp. 335-53.

19. For detailed discussions of the problem, see Dietrich-Alex Koch, *Die Schrift als Zeuge des Evangeliums,* BHT 69 (Tübingen: Mohr Siebeck, 1986), pp. 57-60, 69-71, 161-62, 249-50; Christopher D. Stanley, *Paul and the Language of Scripture,* SNTSMS 74 (Cambridge: Cambridge University Press, 1992), pp. 119-25; Florian Wilk, *Die Bedeutung des Jesajabuches für Paulus,* FRLANT 179 (Göttingen: Vandenhoeck & Ruprecht, 1998), pp. 22-24, 31-34; Wagner, *Heralds,* pp. 126-36.

20. Note the close correspondences between the citation of Isa. 8:14 in Rom. 9:33 and 1 Pet. 2:8 and the later translations of Aquila, Symmachus, and Theodotion. On the sporadic alteration of LXX texts toward Hebrew exemplars in the centuries before Aquila's more thorough revision, see Stanley, *Paul and the Language of Scripture,* pp. 37-51. Wilk, *Bedeutung,* p. 34 n. 27, convincingly refutes Koch's hypothesis that the citation of Isa. 28:16 reflects a Christian reworking of LXX Isa. 28:16 as a christological proof text; see Koch, *Schrift,* pp. 69-71; idem, "Beobachtungen zum christologischen Schriftgebrauch in den vorpaulinischen Gemeinden," *ZNW* 71 (1980): 178-84.

21. Although the evidence does not support the earlier theory of J. Rendel Harris, *Testimonies,* 2 vols. (Cambridge: Cambridge University Press, 1916-20) that a single "testimony book" stands behind these citations, a strong case has now been articulated by Martin Albl, *"And Scripture Cannot Be Broken": The Form and Function of the Early Christian* Testimonia

LXX Isaiah 28:16	Romans 9:33	1 Peter 2:6
διὰ τοῦτο οὕτως λέγει κύριος·	καθὼς γέγραπται·	διότι περιέχει ἐν γραφῇ·
ἰδοὺ ἐγὼ ἐμβαλῶ	ἰδοὺ τίθημι	ἰδοὺ τίθημι
εἰς τὰ θεμέλια Σιων	ἐν Σιὼν	ἐν Σιὼν
λίθον	λίθον	λίθον
	προσκόμματος	
	καὶ πέτραν σκανδάλου,	
πολυτελῆ		
ἐκλεκτὸν ἀκρογωνιαῖον		ἀκρογωνιαῖον ἐκλεκτὸν
ἔντιμον		ἔντιμον
εἰς τὰ θεμέλια αὐτῆς,		
καὶ ὁ πιστεύων ἐπ’ αὐτῷ	καὶ ὁ πιστεύων ἐπ’ αὐτῷ	καὶ ὁ πιστεύων ἐπ’ αὐτῷ
οὐ μὴ καταισχυνθῇ	οὐ καταισχυνθήσεται	οὐ μὴ καταισχυνθῇ

LXX Isaiah 8:14	Romans 9:33	1 Peter 2:8
καὶ οὐχ		καὶ
ὡς λίθου προσκόμματι	λίθον προσκόμματος	λίθος προσκόμματος
συναντήσεσθε αὐτῷ		
οὐδὲ	καὶ	καὶ
ὡς πέτρας πτώματι	πέτραν σκανδάλου	πέτρα σκανδάλου

Isaiah 8:14 σ’ (Eus. frg.)	εἰς δὲ λίθον προσκόμματος καὶ εἰς πέτραν σκανδάλου
Isaiah 8:14 α’ (Q)	καὶ εἰς λίθον προσκόμματος καὶ εἰς στερεὸν σκανδάλου
Isaiah 8:14 θ’ (Q)	καὶ εἰς λίθον προσκόμματος καὶ εἰς πέτραν πτώματος

Collections, NovTSup 96 (Leiden: Brill, 1999) that various scriptural anthologies circulated widely among early Christian teachers and preachers.

83

case, Paul is almost certainly responsible for the conflation of the two texts.[22] The appearance of Isaiah 8:14 and 28:16 in 1 Peter may, in turn, reflect the influence of Pauline tradition.[23] The author's use of a revised manuscript of LXX Isaiah similar in character to that employed by Paul or his dependence on a traditional anthology of quotations would account for the close verbal correspondences between the citations in 1 Peter 2:6, 8 and those in Romans 9:33.[24]

Intertwined with the problem of the source of our authors' citations of Isaiah 8:14 and 28:16 is the question of the influence of earlier interpretive traditions on their readings of these texts. A number of scholars have suggested that Paul and the author of 1 Peter build on an existing christological interpretation of the "stone" image.[25] Although evidence for a pre-Pauline messianic interpretation of Isaiah 8:14 and 28:16 is neither abundant nor weighty,[26] there are traces of an eschatological/messianic interpretation of the rejected and vindicated stone of Psalm 118:22 in some strands of early Judaism and early Christianity, and this may have helped pave the way for a similar reading of other "stone" passages.[27] The particular rendering of Isa-

22. So rightly Dodd, *According to the Scriptures,* p. 43.

23. On the relationship of 1 Peter to the Pauline tradition, see the careful discussion of John H. Elliott, *1 Peter,* AB 37B (New York: Doubleday, 2000), pp. 20-40.

24. Even if our authors used anthologies of scriptural quotations or other traditional sources, this does not mean that they were not also familiar with the wider passages in Isaiah from which their citations were excerpted. The author of 1 Peter later cites Isa. 8:12-13 (1 Pet. 3:14-15), while Paul elsewhere appeals to Isa. 28:11-12 (1 Cor. 14:21); 28:22 (Rom. 9:28); 29:10 (Rom. 11:8); 29:14 (1 Cor 1:19); 29:16 (Rom. 9:20). Paul further employs the language of Isa. 8:22 in Rom. 2:9; 8:35; 2 Cor. 4:8; 6:4, and of Isa. 9:2 in 2 Cor. 4:6; on these passages, see Hays, *Echoes of Scripture in the Letters of Paul* (New Haven: Yale University Press, 1989), pp. 43, 152-53, 203 n. 23; Wilk, *Bedeutung,* pp. 269-74. Whether and to what extent Paul and the author of 1 Peter did indeed draw on the wider contexts of Isaiah 8 and 28-29 as they employed these citations of Isa. 8:14 and 28:16 remains to be shown, but the possibility that they did so cannot be excluded *a priori.*

25. See, e.g., Barnabas Lindars, *New Testament Apologetic* (London: SCM, 1961), pp. 169-88; Klyne R. Snodgrass, "I Peter II.1-10: Its Formation and Literary Affinities," *NTS* 24 (1977-78): 97-106; Albl, *Scripture Cannot Be Broken,* pp. 265-85.

26. Although *Tg. Isa.* 28:16 understands the "stone" in personal terms, as a "severe, mighty, and fearsome king," a *messianic* reference is unlikely (contrast *Tg. Isa.* 28:5-6), for this king sends Israel into exile (vv. 17-19). A later tradition (attributed to the sons of R. Hiyya, fl. ca. 200 CE) interprets Isa. 8:14 as referring to the time of the coming of the Son of David (*b. San.* 38a; cited in Str-B 2.139-40).

27. See M. Black, "The Christological Use of the Old Testament in the New Testament," *NTS* 18 (1971-72): 12-14. A messianic interpretation of Ps. 118:22 is attributed to Jesus by the evangelists (Mark 12:10-11; Matt. 21:42; Luke 20:17; cf. Acts 4:11). See further J. Ross Wagner,

iah 28:16 in the LXX, "the one who trusts *in it/him*" (ὁ πιστεύων ἐπ' αὐτῷ), would have facilitated a personal — and so eventually messianic — interpretation of this image, whether or not one imagines this to have been the intent of the translator.[28]

While Isaiah 28:16 apparently was not read messianically at Qumran, the building imagery in this verse did serve to articulate the self-identification of the *Yaḥad* as the eschatological community securely founded by God.[29] Similarly, a number of Qumran texts draw on Isaiah 8:11 to depict the community as an obedient remnant in the midst of unfaithful Israel, identifying the covenanters as "those who turn from walking in the way of the people."[30] Such community-centered strategies of reading find strong parallels in the interpretations of these Isaianic texts in both Romans and 1 Peter, as we will see.

More strikingly, Jewish tradition offers a clear precedent for the interpretive relationship established between Isaiah 8:14 and 28:16 in Romans 9:33 and in 1 Peter 2:6-8. Strong verbal and thematic links bind Isaiah 8 and 28–29 together already in the Hebrew text.[31] In Isaiah 28:11-16 we encounter once again the same cast of characters featured in 8:11-18: an unnamed "they" who call for fidelity to the Lord (28:11-12a; 8:11); their opponents, named "this people" (28:11; 8:11)/"the rulers of this people in Jerusalem" (28:14; cf. 8:14b), who, by setting themselves in opposition to the Lord, stum-

---

"Psalm 118 in Luke-Acts: Tracing a Narrative Thread," in *Early Christian Interpretation of the Scriptures of Israel: Investigations and Proposals,* ed. Craig A. Evans and James A. Sanders, JSNTSup 148 (Sheffield: Sheffield Academic, 1997), pp. 154-78, esp. 158-61. Note also the possible allusion in Luke 20:18 to Isa. 8:14 (with Dan. 2:34-45; cf. Josephus, *Ant.* 10.210).

28. Koch, "Beobachtungen," p. 179 n. 18, persuasively defends the originality of ἐπ' αὐτῷ to LXX Isaiah. The phrase stands as one of several links forged by the translator between Isaiah 28–29 and Isaiah 8. Cf. the similar addition to the Targum, where "in them" (באליון) identifies the prophecies of Isaiah as the object of trust.

29. 1QS 8.7-8 evokes Isa. 28:16 in speaking of "the council of the community" as "the tested wall, the precious cornerstone" that "will not be shaken." William L. Schutter, *Hermeneutic and Composition in 1 Peter,* WUNT 2.30 (Tübingen: Mohr Siebeck, 1989), p. 132 and n. 137, argues for an allusion to Isa. 8:14 in the preceding lines (1QS 8.5-6), but the evidence for this is negligible (*pace* Schutter, the idea finds no support in the careful study of Otto Betz, *Offenbarung und Schriftforschung in der Qumransekte,* WUNT 6 [Tübingen: Mohr Siebeck, 1960], pp. 158-63). For images of the community drawn from Isa. 28:16, see further 1QS 5.5; 1QHᵃ 14[6].26-27; 15[7].9. Cf. the allusion to Isa. 28:17 in 1QHᵃ 14[6].26; 16[8]21-22.

30. 1QSa 1.1-3; 4QFlor frgs. 1-2 1.14-16; 11QMelch 2.24; CD-A 8.16 = CD-B 19.29 (cf. CD-B 20.23-24).

31. See the fuller discussion in Wagner, *Heralds,* pp. 145-51; Snodgrass, "1 Peter II.1-10," p. 99.

ble and are broken (28:12b-15; 8:15);[32] and finally, the Lord, who promises to be a refuge for those who trust (28:16; 8:14a).[33] Moreover, Isaiah 29:22-23 portrays the repentance of the "house of Jacob" (29:22; 8:14, 17) as consisting in "sanctifying" and "fearing" the Lord (29:23), precisely the response called for in Isaiah 8:12-13.[34]

The Septuagint translator not only recognizes and preserves these connections; in some cases he also enhances them. Especially noteworthy is the translator's addition of the phrase ἐπ' αὐτῷ ("in it/him") to Isaiah 28:16 ("the one who trusts *in it/him*"), echoing two other texts he has joined together by means of a similar interpretive addition: Isaiah 8:14 ("if you trust *in him*") and Isaiah 8:17 ("I will trust *in him*"). In this way, the translator forges a strong link between the two stone sayings of Isaiah 8 and Isaiah 28, both of which now emphasize the necessity of trust as the proper response to God.

On balance, the evidence suggests that in selecting and linking together Isaiah 8:14 and 28:16, Paul and the author of 1 Peter draw to some extent on early Jewish and Christian tradition. Acknowledging this indebtedness to tradition is only the beginning of the story, however, for as the next stage of our investigation will reveal, each author creatively appropriates these texts for his own rhetorical and theological purposes.

Isaiah 8:14 in Romans 9:30–10:13

Romans 9:30–10:13 is bounded by the conflated citation of Isaiah 28:16/8:14 in Romans 9:33 and the re-citation of Isaiah 28:16b in Romans 10:11.[35] As already noted, Paul probably drew his citations from a text of LXX Isaiah revised unsystematically toward a Hebrew exemplar. Given the lack of firm evidence, one can only speculate how extensive these revisions were. One need not suppose with Koch that they radically altered the syntax of the entire sentence in Isaiah 8:14.[36] What traces we do find of such activity in the period before Aquila reveal sporadic and selective alterations toward a proto-

---

32. Isaiah 8:15 and 28:13 share the string of verbs וכשלו . . . ונשברו ונוקשו ונלכדו.

33. Note also Isa. 8:8 (שטף ועבר) and 28:15, 18 (שוט שוטף כי יעבר); Isa. 8:16 and 29:11 (the only occurrences of חתם in Isaiah).

34. The verbs ערץ and קדש appear in the *hiphil* in Isaiah only in 8:12-13 and 29:23.

35. On this passage, see Hays, *Echoes*, pp. 73-83; Wagner, *Heralds*, pp. 120-70. For further echoes of Isa. 8:14 in Romans, see *Heralds*, pp. 262-64 (Rom. 11:9) and 340 n. 129 (Rom. 14:13, 21).

36. Koch, *Schrift*, pp. 59-60.

Masoretic text rather than thoroughgoing recensions. The revision of Isaiah 28:16 attested in Romans 9:33 and 1 Peter 2:6, for example, leaves untouched both the LXX plus ἐπ' αὐτῷ and the distinctive septuagintal rendering οὐ μὴ καταισχυνθῇ in the latter half of the verse. A modest reworking of Isaiah 8:14 centered on the genitive constructions describing the stone would sufficiently explain the wording of the citations in Romans and 1 Peter.[37] Given Paul's practice elsewhere, it is quite conceivable that as he created this conflated citation, he himself further modified his *Vorlage*, omitting εἰς and replacing οὐδέ with καί. In what follows, I argue that the hypothesis that Paul knew Isaiah 8 in a form substantially like the LXX illuminates significant aspects of his argument in Romans 9:30–10:13.

In Romans 9:30-31, Paul begins to trace the cause of Israel's failure (for the most part — cf. 9:24; 11:1-7) to embrace the gospel. His opening sentence lays out the paradoxical state of affairs that has resulted from the mission to the nations: "Gentiles, who were not pursuing righteousness, have obtained righteousness — namely, the righteousness by faith" (9:30). By contrast, Israel, though pursuing "a law that leads to righteousness" (νόμον δικαιοσύνης),[38] has failed to catch up with, not "righteousness," as one would expect Paul to say, but "the *law*" itself (9:31). This is because they have run the race *as if* following the law were a matter of "works" (ὡς ἐξ ἔργων) rather than "faith" (ἐκ πίστεως, 9:32). Consequently, Israel "stumbled over the stumbling stone, just as it is written" (9:32-33a). What follows in 9:33 is a composite citation in A-B-A form, with a portion of Isaiah 8:14 spliced into the middle of Isaiah 28:16 (see p. 83). Paul's conflation attributes a dual character to the stone: it is both the cause of stumbling for those who do not pursue the law by faith and the ground of salvation for those who trust "in it/him." Who or what the "stone" is, Paul does not yet specify.

Just what Paul means by "stumbl[ing] over the stumbling stone" gradually comes into focus in Romans 10:1-13. The apostle begins with a fervent prayer for Israel's salvation (10:1). He laments that Israel, though zealous for God, remains ignorant of "God's righteousness" (10:2-3), that is, God's way of delivering his people, which is revealed in the gospel (cf. 1:16-17). Rather than "submit[ting] to God's righteousness" through pursuing the law "by faith," Israel stubbornly seeks to "establish its own righteousness" (10:3), in

---

37. Cf. Wilk, *Bedeutung*, p. 24 (cf. p. 209), who offers the following as a possible reconstruction of Paul's *Vorlage*: οὐκ εἰς λίθον προσκόμματος οὐδ' εἰς πέτραν σκανδάλου . . .

38. Cf. ἡ ἐντολὴ ἡ εἰς ζωήν, Rom. 7:10. On the difficult phrase νόμος δικαιοσύνης, see C. E. B. Cranfield, *A Critical and Exegetical Commentary on the Epistle to the Romans*, 2 vols., ICC (Edinburgh: T. & T. Clark, 1975-79), 2:507-8.

particular, the righteousness that is available only to commandment-keeping Jews, by acting as if observing the law were a matter of "works."[39] In contrast, Paul insists that the *telos* to which the law, pursued "by faith," has always led is none other than Christ, in whom is found "righteousness for everyone who trusts," Jew and Gentile alike (παντὶ τῷ πιστεύοντι, 10:4; cf. 1:16; 3:22, 29-30; 10:12).

Paul summons no less a personage than Moses himself (10:5, citing Lev. 18:5) to attest that the way of following the law has always been "by faith."[40] His promise that doing the law leads to "life" is then taken up by a personified "Righteousness-by-Faith," who radically redefines "doing" the law in light of its *telos* in Christ (10:4): it is responding to "the word of faith that we preach" by confessing that Jesus is Lord and trusting that God raised him from the dead (10:6-10, citing a version of Deut. 30:12-14 that Paul has modified with astonishing freedom).

The apostle grounds his appeal to respond to the "word of faith" in a re-citation of Isaiah 28:16b: "Everyone who trusts in it/him will not be ashamed" (Rom. 10:11). The word "everyone" represents a Pauline addition to the text that connects Isaiah 28:16 more closely with the following quotation from Joel 2:32: "Everyone who calls on the name of the Lord will be saved" (Rom. 10:13). By linking the citations in this way, Paul closely identifies the "it/him" of Isaiah 28:16 with the "Lord" of Joel 2:32. In context, both now clearly refer to Christ, though not in contradistinction to God. Rather, Paul's careful argument inscribes the human Jesus (10:9) into the identity of the God of Israel, the one God of all, Jew and Gentile alike.[41] There is thus in the argument of Romans 9:30-10:13 an irreducible polyvalence to the "stone" image. The stone is at once Christ, and God's righteousness revealed in Christ for the salvation of everyone who trusts, and the "word of faith" that proclaims this good news to Jew and Gentile alike.

---

39. Cf. E. P. Sanders, *Paul, the Law, and the Jewish People* (Philadelphia: Fortress, 1983), pp. 37-38. While Paul's focus here is the contrast between a way of life patterned on law observance and one shaped by trust in God's redemptive acts in Christ, Paul can also counterpose the gracious initiative of God in salvation, not to legal observance per se, but to human action of *any* kind (Rom. 9:10-13, 16; 11:6; cf. Rom. 4:1-8).

40. My reading of Rom. 10:5-13 follows Hays, *Echoes*, pp. 75-83. See further Wagner, *Heralds*, pp. 157-70.

41. Compare Paul's formulation in Rom. 10:12 with that in Rom. 3:29-30. See the perceptive treatment of this whole question by C. Kavin Rowe, "Romans 10:13: What Is the Name of the Lord?" *HBT* 22 (2000): 135-73.

Reflections on the Interpretation of Isaiah 8 in Romans

Paul's reading of Isaiah 8 coheres with his wider pattern of reading Isaianic oracles as prefigurations both of his own Gentile mission and of Israel's divided response to the gospel. Finding in Isaiah a fellow herald of "the message of Christ that we preach" (Rom. 10:8; cf. 10:16), Paul draws from the prophet's words the language of "faith/trust" that plays such a crucial role in his redefinition of the *telos* of the law.[42] Paul's radical recasting of Leviticus 18:5/Deuteronomy 30:12-14 to assert that only those who trust attain righteousness and salvation is grounded in the divine asseveration of Isaiah 28:16/8:14 and its reiteration that bookend the entire section: "the one who trusts in it/him will not be ashamed" (Rom. 9:33; 10:11). In Paul's hands, the phrase "in it/him" from Isaiah 28:16 focuses this trust on what God has done for the world in raising Christ from the dead and exalting him as Lord. At the same time, Paul's insertion of Isaiah 8:14 into his citation of Isaiah 28:16 serves to define "it/him" as a cause of division in Israel — an aspect of the stone's character to which Paul explicitly draws his hearers' attention through his introductory comment, "they stumbled over the stumbling stone" (Rom. 9:32). Isaiah thus attests that Christ is both the *telos* of the law resulting in righteousness for all who trust and a stumbling block for an Israel intent on pursuing the law that leads to righteousness as if doing so were a matter of "works."

However, the most striking feature of Paul's argument in Romans 9:30–10:13, his close association of "law" with "faith" rather than "works," finds support not in the actual words of his scriptural citations but in the wider context of LXX Isaiah 8, where we likewise meet an Israel divided by its response to God's promise of salvation. As we have seen, "this people" not only relies on foreign alliances (8:6) and foreign gods (8:19) for deliverance; they also "seal up" the law in order not to learn it (8:16). Their lack of trust in God goes hand in hand with their failure to understand and obey God's law as a divinely given help (8:20).[43] LXX Isaiah 8:11-18, read in context as a coherent whole, offers Paul a crucial scriptural warrant for attributing Israel's stumbling over the "stone" — interpreted as the message of God's righteousness revealed in Christ for the salvation of Jew and Gentile alike — to their failure to understand that the law is rightly pursued only "by faith."

---

42. Romans 9:30 marks the first appearance of this terminology since Rom. 6:8; together, πίστις and πιστεύειν occur thirteen times in Rom. 9:30–10:17.

43. Cf. the further charge in Isa. 28:10-13 that "this people" reject the prophetic oracles, leading them to fall and be broken (echoing Isa. 8:15).

Finally, it is of the greatest rhetorical and theological significance for Paul's argument that the speaker of these words of Scripture is none other than God himself.[44] This is not simply a matter of Paul appealing to Scripture to claim authority for his statements. What is at stake here, as throughout Romans, is the very integrity and reliability of the God who gave Israel a "law that leads to righteousness." Here, in his own voice, God assumes responsibility for placing the stumbling stone on the racecourse. It is "God's righteousness" to which Israel refuses to submit (10:3), for it is God who has appointed Christ the *telos* of the "law that leads to righteousness" (9:31; 10:4). The divinely determined outcome is "righteousness for everyone who trusts" (10:4) but frustration for Israel's attempt to establish "their own righteousness" (10:3).

Yet it is at just this point that the oracles of Isaiah 8 and 28-29 exert pressure on the direction that Paul's argument in Romans 9-11 will ultimately take. Faced with the rebellion of "this people," Isaiah resolves to wait for God and trust in God's purposes for his people (Isa. 8:17). Similarly, Paul responds to Israel's stumbling by turning to God in fervent prayer for the salvation of his kinsfolk.[45] Moreover, just as Isaiah's message to Israel is not ultimately one of stumbling and ruin but of salvation and restoration after judgment,[46] so Paul goes on to argue in Romans 11 that God, who is the primary agent responsible for the stumbling and even "hardening" of "the rest" of Israel, is also the one who has in the present time graciously chosen "a remnant" as a sign of future redemption for his elect people Israel (11:1-10). "The rest" have not "tripped" so as to "fall" (11:11; cf. 9:6), for God remains true to his promises in election and, in the end, will himself effect the salvation of "all Israel" (11:25-32).

---

44. Cf. Hans Hübner, *Gottes Ich und Israel: Zum Schriftgebrauch des Paulus in Römer 9-11* (Göttingen: Vandenhoeck & Ruprecht, 1984), p. 127: Paul's argument is grounded in "die Autorität des sich selbst mitteilenden Gottes, die für ihn selbstverständlich hinter der Schrift, freilich, hinter der Schrift als ganzer, steht."

45. Rom. 10:1; I owe this observation to Florian Wilk, *Bedeutung*, p. 222. Cf. also Rom. 9:1-3 and Isaiah's anguished cry, "How long, O Lord?" (Isa. 6:11).

46. LXX Isaiah 29 ends with a vision of redemption that recalls key terminology from Isa. 8:11-18 and 28:16:

> Therefore thus says the Lord regarding the house of Jacob (cf. 8:14, 17), whom he separated from Abraham: "Now Jacob will not be ashamed (cf. 28:16). . . . But when their children see my works, for my sake they will sanctify my name. And they will sanctify the holy one of Jacob and fear the God of Israel" (cf. 8:13). (Isa. 29:22-23)

Isaiah 8 in 1 Peter

The author of 1 Peter twice draws on LXX Isaiah 8, citing Isaiah 8:14 in 1 Peter 2:8 and Isaiah 8:12-13 in 1 Peter 3:14-15. We will consider each of these citations in some detail before reflecting on the author's interpretation of Isaiah 8 more broadly.[47]

Isaiah 8:14 in 1 Peter 2:4-10

First Peter 2:4-10 plays a key role in the development of the letter's argument.[48] The author's skillful interweaving of scriptural citations and allusions with his own interpretive comments establishes a firm theological foundation for the depiction of the recipients as God's elect people in the letter's opening section. At the same time, 2:4-10 provides crucial scriptural grounding for the repeated exhortations to patient and hope-filled witness in the midst of suffering that will be sounded throughout the remainder of the letter. The passage exhibits an overarching A-B-A'-B' structure. Its initial sentence states the theme: Christ's election and vindication by God (2:4, A) determines the identity and destiny of the elect community that God has called into being through Christ (2:5, B). Through his deft use of catchwords, the author anticipates the two carefully constructed scriptural arguments in 2:6-8 (A') and 2:9-10 (B') that anchor and elaborate the two halves of his thesis. Taken together, parts A-A' present Christ as the rejected and chosen "stone" who brings both salvation and judgment,[49] while sections B-B' address the recipients as an elect and holy people, "living stones" in a spiritual temple summoned to glorify the God who has mercifully called them from darkness to light.[50]

The rather odd sentence opening in 1 Peter 2:4, "as you come to him,"

---

47. As in the case of Paul, the author of 1 Peter probably knew Isaiah 8 in a slightly revised form that was nevertheless substantially similar to LXX Isaiah 8 (as indeed the citation of Isa. 8:12-13 in 1 Pet. 3:14-15 suggests). See further Karen H. Jobes, "The Septuagint Textual Tradition in 1 Peter," in *Septuagint Research,* ed. Krause and Wooden, pp. 311-33.

48. My reading of this passage is particularly indebted to the insightful expositions of John H. Elliott, *The Elect and the Holy,* NovTSup 12 (Leiden: Brill, 1966); idem, *1 Peter;* and Richard Bauckham, "James, 1 and 2 Peter, Jude," in *It Is Written: Scripture Citing Scripture,* ed. D. A. Carson and H. G. M. Williamson (Cambridge: Cambridge University Press, 1988), pp. 303-17.

49. Vv. 4, 6-8, citing Isa. 28:16; Ps. 117:22 LXX; Isa. 8:14.

50. Vv. 5, 9-10, conflating Isa. 43:20-21 with Exod. 19:6/23:22 and paraphrasing Hos. 2:23/1:6, 9-10.

(πρὸς ὃν προσερχόμενοι), echoes Psalm 33:6 LXX,[51] "come to him" (προσέλθατε πρὸς αὐτὸν).[52] In connection with the preceding sentence (2:3, which draws on the language of Ps. 33:9), it identifies the one whom they approach in worship and devotion, Jesus Christ, as "the Lord."[53] Anticipating the catena of citations that follows in 2:6-8, all of which contain the word "stone," the author describes Christ as a "living stone." He is the "living" stone because, although he was "rejected" by humans (Ps. 117:22 LXX/1 Pet. 2:7), he is "chosen and precious" before God (Isa. 28:16/1 Pet. 2:6), who vindicated him by raising him from the dead (1 Pet. 1:3).

In vv. 6-8, the author interweaves three scriptural citations (Isa. 28:16; Ps. 117:22; Isa. 8:14) with interpretive comments in order both to establish the identity of Christ as God's chosen one and to highlight the sharp division that God's work in Christ creates among human beings. The divine authority that undergirds the author's argument is emphasized by the citation formula that introduces all three quotations, "for it stands in scripture" (2:6), and by the first-person speech of God in the first citation (and so, by implication, in the remaining two as well). Beyond the catchword "stone," the three texts of the catena share a number of important themes. We have already observed the web of interconnections linking Isaiah 8 and 28 within LXX Isaiah. Psalm 117, like Isaiah 28, refers to the stone as the "cornerstone."[54] With Isaiah 8, Psalm 117 emphasizes "fearing" the Lord rather than humans.[55] And all three texts call for "trust" in the Lord as the proper response of the faithful.[56]

As we have seen, the citation of Isaiah 28:16 in 1 Peter 2:6 probably de-

---

51. Psalm citations from this point forward follow the LXX versification.

52. On the author's repeated evocation of Psalm 33 through citation and allusion, see most recently Sue Woan, "Psalms in 1 Peter," in *The Psalms in the New Testament,* ed. Steve Moyise and Maarten J. J. Menken (London: T. & T. Clark, 2004), pp. 213-29.

53. On the cultic connotations of προσέρχομαι, see BDAG 878. The potential for a christological wordplay in 2:3 (χρηστός/Χριστός) has long been noted (cf. the textual variant in P[72] et al., which testifies to the two words' similar, if not identical, pronunciation). Through the consistent use of the title "Lord" (κύριος) for Jesus (see esp. 1:3; 3:15), the author associates him in the closest possible way with the God of Israel — including making Jesus the referent of scriptural citations that originally had Israel's God in view (1:25; 2:3; 3:12, 15; cf. esp. 1:23 with 1:25) — yet without confusing the two (note the author's carefully worded formulations in 1:2, 3, 21; 4:11). We noted a strikingly similar theological move in Romans 10 (p. 88 above).

54. κεφαλὴν γωνίας, Ps. 117:22; ἀκρογωνιαῖος, Isa. 28:16.

55. Ps. 117:4, 6; Isa. 8:12-13.

56. ἀγαθὸν πεποιθέναι ἐπὶ κύριον, Ps. 117:8; ἐὰν ἐπ᾽ αὐτῷ πεποιθὼς ᾖς, Isa. 8:14 (cf. 8:17); ὁ πιστεύων ἐπ᾽ αὐτῷ, Isa. 28:16.

rives from a text of LXX Isaiah revised in part toward a proto-Masoretic Hebrew text (see p. 83).[57] The author has already directed his hearers' attention to the dominant theme of election by highlighting the terms "chosen" and "precious" from Isaiah 28:16a in his introductory remarks (ἐκλεκτὸν ἔντιμον, 2:4). He follows the citation with an interpretive comment (2:7a) that focuses on the promise of Isaiah 28:16, "the one who trusts (ὁ πιστεύων) in it/him will certainly not be ashamed." God's election of Jesus Christ provokes two responses that fundamentally divide humanity. "You . . . who trust" (ὑμῖν . . . τοῖς πιστεύουσιν) share in the "honor" bestowed by God on the "chosen and precious stone" (τιμή; cf. ἔντιμον, Isa. 28:16; 1 Pet. 2:4, 6). In contrast, "those who do not trust" (ἀπιστοῦσιν) find themselves actively opposed by God.[58] Citing Psalm 117:22, the author asserts that despite the rejection of Jesus by unbelievers, God has chosen him as the "cornerstone" (2:7b). Moreover, as Isaiah 8:14 attests, God has appointed him to be "a stone of stumbling and a rock of offense" (2:8a) for those who "disobey the word" (τῷ λόγῳ ἀπειθοῦντες, 2:8b), that is, the message of the gospel (cf. 1:25).[59] And yet God's sovereign purposes in election stand behind even their opposition and stumbling, "for which they were appointed."[60]

In vv. 5 and 9-10, the author incorporates the community into his christologically oriented reading of the stone texts. Christ is the "cornerstone" (2:6, 7) of the spiritual temple into which God is building them as "stones" (2:5).[61] Just as the Risen Christ is "the *living* stone" (2:4), so they too

57. The different order of the adjectives describing the stone in 1 Peter, ἀκρογωνιαῖον ἐκλεκτὸν ἔντιμον, may be due to the author's predilection for assonance (cf. 1:4, 19; 2:15, 21). It is hard to judge whether the omissions of πολυτελῆ and εἰς τὰ θεμέλια αὐτῆς are due to the author or to his *Vorlage* (see further Jobes, "Septuagint Textual Tradition," p. 322).

58. The language of Isa. 28:16 doubtless influenced the choice of ἀπιστεῖν, which occurs only here in 1 Peter; elsewhere the author uses ἀπειθεῖν (2:8; 3:1, 20; 4:17).

59. The stone is thus in the argument of this passage both "Christ" and "the gospel." Compare the similar polyvalence of the stone image in Romans above. The verb ἀπειθεῖν ("disobey," "rebel") provides a verbal connection to Isa. 8:11; it is unclear whether such a link was intentional, however, since the author uses this formula elsewhere to refer to unbelievers (3:1; 4:17; cf. 3:20). In contrast, the letter's recipients are characterized by "obedience to the truth" (1:22; cf. 1:2, 14).

60. The *inclusio* formed by τίθημι (2:6)/ἐτέθησαν (2:8) "marks the theme of election as the overarching theme" of the whole section; see Bauckham, "James, 1 and 2 Peter, Jude," p. 311. Earlier we noted a corresponding emphasis on divine election in Paul's use of Isa. 8:14 and 28:16 in Romans. Oss, "Interpretation of the 'Stone' Passages," pp. 193-94, similarly highlights this as a significant point of contact between the interpretations of the "stone" in Romans and in 1 Peter.

61. Cf. the interpretation of the building imagery of Isa. 28:16 in 1QS as a reference to

are "*living* stones" (2:5), because they have been "given new birth" through Christ's resurrection (1:3). And just as Christ is "chosen" (λίθον . . . ἐκλεκτόν, 2:4, 6), so also the community that trusts in him has been "chosen" (γένος ἐκλεκτόν, 2:9; cf. 1:1) to be God's own people, called to obedient service and joyful witness to God's mercies.

The author's christocentric and ecclesiocentric reading strategies intertwine, for he is convinced that the communities he addresses have come to share in the vocation and destiny of their Lord. The main argument of vv. 4-10 asserts that their gracious election as God's people rests securely on Christ's election by God (Isa. 28:16). At the same time, the undercurrent of conflict introduced through the citations of Psalm 117:22 and Isaiah 8:14 suggests an implicit corollary that will slowly rise to the surface as the letter progresses: sharing in Christ's election entails sharing also in his rejection and suffering at the hands of God's adversaries.[62] As the author's second citation of Isaiah 8 promises, however, Christ's exaltation as cornerstone provides a firm foundation for their own hope both for present help in suffering and for future vindication by God.

Isaiah 8:12-13 in 1 Peter 3:13-22

In 1 Peter 3:13-22, the author issues an earnest appeal for patient well-doing even in the face of unjust suffering. This exhortation is grounded in the extended citation of Psalm 33:13-17a that closes the previous section (3:10-12) promising "life," "good days," and the favor of the Lord for those who do good. Borrowing the language of the psalm, the author offers his hearers the general principle "Who is going to do evil to you if you are zealous for good?" (3:13).[63] At the same time, he gently alludes to the prospect of suffering "for the sake of righteousness" (3:14).[64] This possibility has, in fact, become an all-too-painful reality for some of his hearers (cf. 1:6; 4:12-19; 5:9-10). In the face of this formidable challenge to their faith, the author issues a strong command, appropriating the words of Isaiah 8:12-13 as his

---

God's establishing of the community as a new temple (see above, n. 29). See further Betz, *Offenbarung*, pp. 158-63.

62. See 2:18-25; 3:17-18; 4:12-19. This note was sounded already in 1:6-7.

63. τίς ὁ κακώσων ὑμᾶς echoes ποιοῦντας κακά (Ps. 33:17/1 Pet. 3:12). Compare "zealous for good" with Ps. 33:15/1 Pet. 3:11: "Let him do good; let him seek peace and pursue it."

64. First Peter 2:15 similarly qualifies the optimistic evaluation of government officials in 2:13-14; see also 2:18-25. "Righteousness" here refers particularly to the conduct arising from their devotion and obedience to Christ (3:16; cf. 2:24).

own: "Do not fear them, and do not be troubled. Rather, sanctify the Lord Christ . . ." (3:14-15).[65]

LXX Isaiah 8:12-13	1 Peter 3:14-15
12 . . . τὸν δὲ φόβον αὐτοῦ οὐ μὴ φοβηθῆτε οὐδὲ μὴ ταραχθῆτε· 13 κύριον αὐτὸν ἁγιάσατε	14 . . . τὸν δὲ φόβον αὐτῶν μὴ φοβηθῆτε μηδὲ ταραχθῆτε, 15 κύριον δὲ τὸν Χριστὸν ἁγιάσατε ἐν ταῖς καρδίαις ὑμῶν

The author follows the LXX fairly closely,[66] with the exception of one crucial interpolation: v. 15 explicitly identifies "the Lord" (Isa. 8:13) whom they are to revere as "Christ."[67] Despite the way the interpretive addition "in your hearts" strikes modern Western ears, this exclusive devotion to Christ is no private affair. These "Christians" cannot shrink back from publicly declaring that Jesus is Lord, even though it is this very confession that so incites their persecutors (1 Pet. 4:14, 16).[68] Rather, they must always be prepared to offer a respectful defense of the hope that fills them (3:15-16).

Secure in their identity as those "blessed" by God, they are to put away all fear. The command τὸν φόβον αὐτῶν μὴ φοβηθῆτε can be read as either "do not fear them [i.e., your persecutors]" or "do not fear what they fear."

65. It is possible that some hearers would not have immediately recognized this as a quotation; however, my interest centers here on *the author's* interpretation of Isaiah 8. An intertextual link that may have facilitated the author's move from Psalm 33 to Isaiah 8 is the common reference to the "fear" of the Lord in Isa. 8:13 and Ps. 33:12 (the verse that immediately precedes those cited in 1 Pet. 3:10-12; cf. Ps. 33:10a). Interestingly, a citation from Psalm 33 earlier introduced the complex of "stone" texts, including Isa. 8:14, in 1 Pet. 2:4-8.

66. First Peter 3:14 has αὐτῶν where the best LXX manuscripts read αὐτοῦ. Clearly, the plural suits the author's argument, but it is unclear whether the reading originates with him or with his *Vorlage* (αὐτῶν is attested by a significant number of LXX manuscripts). The simplification of the negatives to μή . . . μή is probably to be attributed to the author; the alteration does not appreciably weaken the force of the prohibitions. The omission of μηδὲ ταραχθῆτε in P[72] B L likely reflects haplography. See further Jobes, "Septuagint Textual Tradition," pp. 329-30.

67. For the "Lord" as Christ in 1 Peter, see n. 53 above. The reading θεόν (K L P etc.) may represent an assimilation to the context of Isaiah 8.

68. On the significance of the name "Christian" in 1 Peter, see David G. Horrell, "The Label Χριστιανός: 1 Peter 4:16 and the Formation of Christian Identity," *JBL* 126 (2007): 361-81.

Perhaps the ambiguity need not be resolved. It makes little difference whether the phrase refers to the gods (including Caesar) whom their opponents revere or to these local adversaries (perhaps including Caesar's representatives) themselves. Because Jesus is Lord, the dominant religious and political powers of this world are not ultimate.[69] God remains in control, even when his people suffer (3:17; cf. 4:19). Christians are to submit to the king and his governors and pay them due honor, but they must fear only God (2:17). Indeed, fearing God, they need fear no one else.

Those who revere Christ as Lord in the face of slanderous opposition will not, in the end, be ashamed; rather, their "good conduct in Christ" will bring shame upon their detractors (3:16).[70] The "Lord" whose "eyes are on the righteous" but whose "face is against evildoers" (Ps. 33:16-17/1 Pet. 3:12) is none other than the Lord Christ, who will surely deliver those who suffer "for the sake of righteousness" (3:14) from those who "do evil" to them (3:13). However obscure it may be in other respects, the following section of the letter (3:18-22) makes this point abundantly clear. Christ, the paradigmatic righteous sufferer, has died for their sins and reconciled them to God (3:18).[71] What is more, Christ has been raised from the dead and installed as Lord at God's right hand, with "angels and authorities and powers" in subjection to him (3:22). As God exalted Christ, so God will also vindicate those who honor Christ as Lord in the face of hostile opposition. They share Christ's sufferings now so that they may also share his joy on the day his glory is revealed.[72]

Reflections on the Interpretation of Isaiah 8 in 1 Peter

The author of 1 Peter deploys Isaiah 8 in close connection with a number of other scriptural texts: Isaiah 28, Psalm 117, Psalm 33. As we have seen, these passages are interconnected by a network of catchwords and by their shared

69. For a glimpse of the intrusion of these powers into early Christian communities in Pontus/Bithynia, see the well-known exchange of letters ca. 112 CE between the emperor Trajan and his governor Pliny (Pliny, *Ep.* 10.96-97).

70. There is perhaps in the phrase "so that they may be put to shame" (ἵνα . . . καταισχυνθῶσιν, 3:16) an inverted echo of the promise of Isa. 28:16, cited in 1 Pet. 2:6 (οὐ μὴ καταισχυνθῇ; cf. Ps. 33:6). So, similarly, Schutter, *Hermeneutic and Composition*, p. 150.

71. In so doing, Christ has made possible their imitation of his own patient well-doing in suffering, as the author has previously emphasized (2:21-25).

72. 1 Pet. 4:13. The leitmotiv of hope in eschatological vindication recurs throughout the letter (cf. 1:5, 7, 13; 5:1, 10).

promise of salvation for those who fear and trust in God alone. Two interrelated convictions shape the author's interpretation of these texts: first, that "the Spirit of Christ" testified beforehand to the prophets concerning "the sufferings of Christ and the glories that would follow"; second, that all this was for the sake of the communities that God is now calling into existence in Christ through the preaching of the gospel empowered by that same Spirit (1:10-12).[73] Reading Israel's Scriptures in light of what God has accomplished for the world in the death and resurrection of Christ, the author fashions for his predominantly Gentile Christian communities a new identity as the people of God, both by appropriating for them significant scriptural designations typically reserved for Israel and by allowing the words of Scripture to address their lives directly.[74]

In 1 Peter 2 and 3, the author imaginatively situates his communities in the world of Isaiah 8. He treats it as self-evident that this prophetic text about division within Israel speaks to their own conflicts with their pagan neighbors. In stark contrast to Paul's interpretation of Isaiah 8 in Romans, the author of 1 Peter does not address the question of Jews per se, whether inside the community or out. Neither does he make a connection, as LXX Isaiah 8 and Romans do, between "trust" and Israel's "law." Such concerns are apparently not pertinent to his hearers and their present crisis. Rather, Christ is the elect "stone" of Isaiah 8:14 that divides, not Israel, but all of humanity (1 Pet. 2:8). Yet the crisis point remains the same as in Isaiah's oracle: Will one rely on or repudiate God's promise to save those who trust in him? Those who disobey the gospel (a secondary referent of the "stone" metaphor) find Christ to be a "rock of offense" against which they stumble and fall. But like the small band of the faithful in Isaiah 8 who strenuously rebel against the ways of "this people" among whom they live,[75] the believers addressed in 1 Peter revere Christ alone as Lord and firmly resolve to fear only him (Isa. 8:12-13/1 Pet. 3:14-15). Their loyalty to Christ leads them to a patient endurance of suffering founded on the same unshakable hope in God that is expressed by the faithful in Isaiah's oracle (Isa. 8:17). They do not encounter

---

73. Cf. Paul's similar understanding of the purpose of the Scriptures: Rom. 4:23-25; 15:4; 16:25-27; 1 Cor. 9:10; 10:11.

74. That the recipients are Gentiles by background is suggested by 1:14, 18; 4:3-5. For the use of scriptural identity terms designating Israel, see, e.g., 1:1; 2:4-10; 4:17. Their new identity is further reinforced by the author's designation of outsiders as "the Gentiles" (see 2:12; 4:3). See further J. Ramsey Michaels, *1 Peter*, WBC 49 (Waco: Word, 1988), pp. xlv-lv.

75. Cf. the use of Isa. 8:11 as a self-designation in some of the Qumran texts (see n. 30 above).

Christ as a stumbling stone; for them, Christ is the firm foundation of their salvation, as the closely related Isaianic oracle declares: "the one who trusts in him will certainly not be put to shame" (Isa. 28:16/1 Pet. 2:6). The God who utters this promise of vindication sustains them in their present suffering, and he himself will soon "restore, support, strengthen, and establish them" firmly forever (5:10).[76]

Isaiah 8:17 and 18 in Hebrews 2:10-18

The author of the early Christian homily known as Hebrews cites Isaiah 8:17 and 18 in the service of a theological discourse whose theme is the solidarity of the eternal Son of God with human beings. The Son has come to share their humanity in order that they, together with him, might fulfill their exalted destiny (Heb. 2:5-18). The first phase of the discussion (2:5-9) offers an extended quotation and exposition of Psalm 8:5-7. As the homilist reads it, the psalm tells the story of Jesus, the humiliated and exalted "Son of Man." At the turning point of this drama of descent and ascent stands the cross. It is "on account of the suffering of death" that Jesus has been "crowned with glory and honor." Indeed, he was "made for a little while lower than the angels" for this very reason: "in order, by God's grace, to taste death for everyone" (2:9).

Just how Jesus' death is a death "for everyone" comes into focus in the second stage of the discourse (2:10-18). Exploiting the polyvalence of the terms "man/son of man" in Psalm 8, our author moves from the "Son" to the "many sons" whom God is leading to glory (2:10).[77] Two images capture the close connection between the "Son" and the "sons." First, Jesus is the "pioneer of salvation" who through death breaks the power of the devil and frees his children from their captivity to fear (2:10, 14-16). Second, he is the "merciful and faithful high priest" who atones for his people's sins and who helps them faithfully endure testing (2:11, 17-18). God has qualified Jesus to fulfill these roles in the economy of salvation in two ways: by making him "like [human beings] in every respect" (2:17) and by making him "perfect through

---

76. The verb θεμελιοῦν, "lay a foundation" (1 Pet. 5:10; cf. LXX Isa. 28:16), extended figuratively to mean "establish" (BDAG 449), evokes the building imagery used for the community in 1 Pet. 2:5.

77. Terminology drawn from Psalm 8 and from the author's interpretive comments in Heb. 2:5-9 recurs throughout Heb. 2:10-18: "son" (2:6, 10), "glory" (2:7, 9, 10), "all things" (2:8, 10), "suffering" (2:9, 10, 18), "death" (2:9, 14, 15).

sufferings" (2:10). The short catena of scriptural citations that stands at the center of this section of the discourse (2:12-13) plays a critical role in establishing both points.

The homilist places great rhetorical emphasis both on the solidarity of the Son with the community and on his faithful character as their pioneer and high priest by bringing Jesus forward, as it were, to speak in his own voice for the first time in the letter. God has previously addressed the Son through scriptural citations (1:5-13); now, in turn, the Son responds in the words of Scripture.[78] By means of brief citation formulas (λέγων . . . καὶ πάλιν . . . καὶ πάλιν), the author divides Jesus' words, drawn from Psalm 21:23 and Isaiah 8:17-18, into three short statements.[79] As a result, Jesus' twin avowals of a close familial bond with human beings ("brothers," Ps. 21:23 LXX/Heb. 2:12; "children," Isa. 8:18/Heb. 2:13b) now frame the central affirmation of his trust in God (Isa. 8:17/Heb. 2:13a).

LXX Isaiah 8:17-18	Hebrews 2:13
17 καὶ ἐρεῖ· μενῶ τὸν θεὸν τὸν ἀποστρέψαντα τὸ πρόσωπον αὐτοῦ ἀπὸ τοῦ οἴκου Ιακωβ καὶ πεποιθὼς ἔσομαι ἐπ' αὐτῷ.	καὶ πάλιν· ἐγὼ ἔσομαι πεποιθὼς ἐπ' αὐτῷ, καὶ πάλιν·
18 ἰδοὺ ἐγὼ καὶ τὰ παιδία ἃ μοι ἔδωκεν ὁ θεός, καὶ ἔσται εἰς σημεῖα καὶ τέρατα ἐν τῷ Ισραηλ παρὰ κυρίου σαβαωθ, ὃς κατοικεῖ ἐν τῷ ὄρει Σιων.	ἰδοὺ ἐγὼ καὶ τὰ παιδία ἃ μοι ἔδωκεν ὁ θεός.

Thematic and catchword connections bind the first and last statements of the catena tightly to the context of the larger argument in Hebrews 2. The

---

78. Cf. Harold W. Attridge, "The Psalms in Hebrews," in *Psalms in the New Testament,* ed. Moyise and Menken, pp. 208-9. Note also the report of Jesus' speech to the Father in the words of Ps. 39:7-9 LXX (Heb. 10:5-10). For a perceptive analysis of both of these passages, see Tomasz Lewicki, *"Weist nicht ab den Sprechenden!": Wort Gottes und Paraklese im Hebräerbrief,* PaThSt 41 (Paderborn: Schöningh, 2004), pp. 38-47.

79. Despite the fact that the last two utterances in the catena are contiguous sentences in their original context (Isa. 8:17-18a), the author of Hebrews employs three introductory formulas here in order to make three distinct points. Cf. his use of καὶ πάλιν in Heb. 10:30 to split his citation from Deut. 32:35-36 into two separate statements, giving to each part its own rhetorical weight.

author prepares for the citation of Psalm 21:23 by tracing the ties of kinship that bind the Son to the "sons." Alluding to Jesus' priestly role, the author affirms that "the one who sanctifies" and "those who are being sanctified" all have one Father (ἐξ ἑνὸς πάντες, 2:11).[80] Consequently, Jesus is "not ashamed to call them *brothers*" (2:11), which indeed he immediately does, taking on his own lips the words of Psalm 21:23: "I will proclaim your name to my *brothers;* in the midst of the assembly I will sing praise to you" (2:12). The citation offers scriptural authorization for the close familial bond the author has established between Jesus and the community. Jesus' resolve to confess God's name and to offer praise further establishes a pattern for relating to God "through him" that his brothers and sisters will be called to emulate (13:15-16).[81]

In the final statement of the catena, "Here am I and the children God has given me" (Isa. 8:18/Heb. 2:13b), the author finds an expression of the intimate flesh-and-blood relationship that binds Jesus to the community of faith. Having come to share (μετέχειν) in the same "blood and flesh" as these children, Jesus is able to experience death "for everyone" and, by destroying the terror of death, to free the "seed of Abraham" from slavery (2:14-16).[82] Because the "pioneer of their salvation" (2:10) fully participates in their humanity, the "many sons" partake of his glorious destiny: these "holy brothers" have become "sharers" (μέτοχοι) in a heavenly calling (3:1), "sharers" (μέτοχοι), indeed, in Christ himself (3:14). Moreover, as the homilist will later argue at length, it is through the once-for-all offering of his own body and blood that Jesus, the high priest who "became like his brothers in every respect" (2:17), sanctifies his people forever.[83]

If the first and last utterances of the catena establish the deep solidarity with his people that enables Jesus to represent them as their pioneer and high priest, the central affirmation, "I will trust in him," drawn from Isaiah

---

80. Although the identity of the "one" is ambiguous, in context it is most likely God; so Harold W. Attridge, *The Epistle to the Hebrews,* Hermeneia (Philadelphia: Fortress, 1989), pp. 88-89.

81. Similarly, just as Jesus is "not ashamed" to call them brothers (2:11; cf. 11:16), so they are later summoned to "bear his reproach" by identifying with him publicly (13:13; cf. 11:26).

82. The reference to the "seed of Abraham" (cf. Heb. 11:9, 18) further specifies the identity of the "children." While Isa. 41:8-9 offers the closest verbal parallel in the LXX to Heb. 2:16, the author's use of the phrase here may owe something to the earlier catena of scriptural citations in 2:12-13 as well. Psalm 21:24 refers to the "seed of Jacob" and "seed of Israel." Isaiah 8:17-18 similarly mentions the "house of Jacob" and "house of Israel."

83. Heb. 9:13-14; 10:10, 14, 20, 29; 13:12.

8:17, draws attention to the moral qualifications that enable him to fulfill these roles perfectly (2:13a).[84] For the author of Hebrews, Jesus is not pioneer of salvation and high priest simply by virtue of his intimate identification with humanity. Rather, having come to share their humanity, he had to be "made perfect" through his faithful, trusting obedience even in the face of suffering and death (2:10; cf. 7:28). Only as one who himself "suffered by being tested" (and while doing so remained "without sin," 4:15) has he become the "merciful and faithful (πιστός) high priest" who removes the sins of his people and helps them faithfully endure their own trials (2:17-18).

Jesus' trust in God, epitomized in the quotation from Isaiah 8:17, grounds the homilist's subsequent exhortation to the community to remain faithful to "the living God" (3:12). The author skillfully sandwiches the negative example of the wilderness rebellion (3:7–4:13) between two appeals to focus on the faithful character of Jesus, their high priest (3:1-6; 4:14–5:10). In stark contrast to the exodus generation, who were characterized by "unbelief" (ἀπιστία, 3:12, 19), lack of "trust" (πίστις, 4:2), and "disobedience" (ἀπειθεῖν/ἀπείθεια, 3:18; 4:6, 11), Jesus, like Moses, was "faithful (πιστός) to the one who appointed him" (3:2). As the Son who "learned obedience through what he suffered" and so "became perfect," Jesus has become "the source of eternal salvation for all who obey him" (5:8-9). Because the community has in Jesus not only a pattern of faithfulness but also a high priest who enables their own faithful obedience, the author calls them to persevere in trials with godly fear (4:1), emulating Jesus' reverent trust in God (cf. 5:7, εὐλάβεια). Their eyes fixed on the merciful and faithful "apostle and high priest of [their] confession" (3:1), the "great high priest who has gone through the heavens — Jesus, the Son of God" (4:14), they are to "hold fast their confession" (4:14; cf. 10:23), boldly coming to God's throne to find "mercy and grace" to help them in their time of need (4:16).

Reflections on the Interpretation of Isaiah 8 in Hebrews

Placed on the lips of Jesus himself, the words of Isaiah 8:17 and 18 play a pivotal role in the argument of Hebrews 2:10-18. The author employs these texts

---

84. The citation follows the LXX, except for the addition of ἐγώ and the consequent transposition of ἔσομαι and πεποιθώς. As both alterations lack support in the manuscript tradition of LXX Isaiah, they may well originate with the author of Hebrews. Wording identical to LXX Isa. 8:17 is found in Isa. 12:2 and 2 Kgdms. 22:3. In view of the quotation from Isa. 8:18 that immediately follows, it is likely that the homilist has Isa. 8:17 in mind here, though not necessarily to the exclusion of the other passages.

both to develop the notion of Jesus as the pioneer and high priest who shares fully the human "blood and flesh" of the "children" and to display Jesus' exemplary trust in God. The close integration of these excerpts from Isaiah 8 into the larger context of Hebrews suggests that this bold and creative interpretation of Isaiah 8:17-18 originated with the homilist himself. Nevertheless, one need not imagine that this novel reading of Isaiah 8 owes no debt to prior Christian traditions of interpretation.[85] In a significant number of instances, the author of Hebrews draws on passages used elsewhere in early Christian writings — particularly in the Pauline tradition — but selects different parts of these passages as the focus of his interpretation.[86] It is not unreasonable to suggest that such a creative transformation of tradition lies behind the author's appeal to Isaiah 8 as well.

In particular, the homilist's appropriation of Isaiah 8:17 and 18 as utterances of Jesus builds on the interpretation of Isaiah 8 attested in Romans and 1 Peter that identifies Christ as the "stone" and finds the community prefigured in the group of the faithful who "trust in him."[87] The author of Hebrews, whose high-priestly Christology emphasizes the solidarity of Jesus with the believing community, extends this earlier christocentric and ecclesiocentric trajectory of interpretation, taking Jesus to be the one speaking in Isaiah 8:17 as the representative voice of the community.[88] The author

85. Indeed, Isa. 8:17-18 falls in the midst of a section of Isaiah (6:1–9:7) that is a focal point for much early Christian messianic exegesis; see Dodd, *According to the Scriptures,* pp. 78-82; cf. J. Cecil McCullough, "Isaiah in Hebrews," in *Isaiah in the New Testament,* ed. Moyise and Menken, pp. 163-64.

86. In addition to his prominent use of Ps. 109:1 LXX (Heb. 1:3, 13, passim), widely employed in early Christianity to speak of Jesus' exaltation, the author of Hebrews alone in the NT cites Ps. 109:4 (Heb. 5:6, passim). Whereas other authors draw on Ps. 8:3 (Matt. 21:16) and Ps. 8:7 (1 Cor. 15:27; Eph. 1:22; Phil. 3:21; 1 Pet. 3:22), Hebrews alone includes the larger segment Ps. 8:5-7 (Heb. 2:5-9). Several verses from the first half of Psalm 21 LXX appear in the Gospel passion narratives, but Ps. 21:23 is found only in Heb. 2:12. While Paul, like the author of Hebrews, cites Hab. 2:4 (Gal. 3:11; Rom. 1:17; Heb. 10:38), the homilist quotes a larger block of text, Hab. 2:3-4, and develops a different point from the passage. Similarly, the author of Hebrews appeals to Deut. 32:35 (Heb. 10:30), a text also found in Rom. 12:19, but then goes on to cite Deut. 32:36, a verse that, despite the apostle's numerous quotations of and allusions to Deuteronomy 32, never appears in Paul's letters.

87. On the relationship of Hebrews to Pauline traditions and to 1 Peter, see L. D. Hurst, *The Epistle to the Hebrews: Its Background of Thought,* SNTSMS 65 (Cambridge: Cambridge University Press, 1990), pp. 107-33.

88. The author's close identification of Christ with the community opens the way for a no less striking interpretation of Moses' decision to "suffer mistreatment together with *the people of God*" as a willingness to embrace "reproach for the sake of *the Messiah*" (Heb. 11:24-26).

may have understood the voice in Isaiah 8:17 to be the prophet's and so regarded Isaiah and his children as prefigurations of Christ and the church.[89] At the same time, the ambiguity created by the rather curious introduction of the speaker in LXX Isaiah 8:17, "and he will say" (καὶ ἐρεῖ), may have allowed the author to attribute these statements to someone other than the prophet.[90] Richard Hays has pointed out that it would be possible to identify the speaker as "κύριος" (from 8:11) and thus — for an early Christian author — as Jesus.[91] This suggestion becomes even more attractive when one notices that in LXX Isaiah the speaker himself refers to "θεός" (8:17, 18) rather than "κύριος," thus allowing for a distinction between "Lord" and "God" in the context of 8:11-18.[92] The association of the phrase "I will trust in him" with David (2 Kgdms. 22:3)[93] might have further encouraged the identification of the speaker as Jesus, for in the citation of Psalm 21:23 to which he joins Isaiah 8:17, as well as in his later citation of Psalm 39:7-9 (Heb. 10:5-10), the author follows the widespread early Christian interpretive convention that discerns in the words of David the voice of Jesus the Messiah.[94] Whatever its origins, the author's interpretation of the prophetic oracle in Isaiah 8:17-18 as the speech of Jesus accords with his foundational hermeneutical conviction that the same God who spoke "through the prophets" has now spoken "through one who is a Son" (1:1-2).

For all of his exegetical innovations, however, the author's appeal to Isaiah 8:17-18 remains firmly rooted in the thematic center of LXX Isaiah 8:11-

---

89. Although Isaiah is not explicitly named among the heroes of faith in Hebrews 11 (contrast Sir. 48:20-25), the author apparently knows the tradition that he was martyred by being sawn in two (Heb. 11:37; so Origen, *Ep. Afr.* 9); see further William L. Lane, *Hebrews 9–13*, WBC 47B (Dallas: Word, 1991), p. 390.

90. See above, p. 80. So also J. van der Ploeg, "L'Exégèse de l'ancien testament dans l'Épître aux Hébreux," *RB* 54 (1947): 211; Friedrich Schröger, *Der Verfasser des Hebräerbriefes als Schriftausleger*, BU 4 (Regensburg: Friedrich Pustet, 1968), pp. 93-95.

91. Discussion in the Pauline Soteriology Group, Society of Biblical Literature Annual Meeting, San Diego, Calif., November 19, 2007.

92. In 8:11, 17, 18 1QIsaᵃ and MT attest יהוה in each instance, although a few Masoretic manuscripts read אלהים in v. 18.

93. Cf. A. Vanhoye, *Situation du Christ: Hébreux 1–2* (Paris: Cerf, 1969), pp. 343-44.

94. See Richard B. Hays, "Christ Prays the Psalms: Paul's Use of an Early Christian Exegetical Convention," in *The Future of Christology*, ed. Abraham J. Malherbe and Wayne A. Meeks (Minneapolis: Fortress, 1993), pp. 122-36; reprinted in Hays, *The Conversion of the Imagination: Paul as Interpreter of Israel's Scripture* (Grand Rapids: Eerdmans, 2005), pp. 101-18. Note also the christological interpretations given to the psalms in Hebrews: Pss. 2:7 (Heb. 1:5; 5:5); 21:23 (Heb. 2:12); 44:7-8 (Heb. 1:8-9); 101:26-28 (Heb. 1:10-12); 109:1, 4 (Heb. 1:13; 5:6, passim).

18, the call to "trust in him" sounded in 8:14 and resoundingly affirmed in 8:17. As he stands in the assembly of his brothers and sisters praising God, Jesus embodies the attitude of the small remnant of the faithful in Isaiah 8, who in the midst of a hostile society resolve to fear and to trust in God alone.[95] Not only does Jesus model for the community unwavering trust in God; he also frees them from fear. Through his victory over death, he has destroyed the power of the devil to enslave them through fear of death and so liberated them to fear none but God.[96] Jesus' solidarity with the community, expressed in the citation of Isaiah 8:18 as well as in the quotation of Psalm 21:23, implies that these "children" and "brothers" will emulate his attitude of trust. This expectation comes to explicit expression as the sermon approaches its hortatory climax. The language of trust, the notion of Jesus as "pioneer," and the terminology of kinship cluster together once more as the homilist calls the community to recognize that their own experience of suffering is a sign that they too are God's "sons" (12:1-11). As God's children, Jesus' brothers, they are to look to Jesus, "the pioneer and perfecter of faith" (12:2), and submit trustingly to the wise discipline of his — and their — loving Father.

Conclusion

Paul, the author of 1 Peter, and the homilist of Hebrews actualize the "meaning potential" of the Greek text of Isaiah 8 in the service of their own individual rhetorical, theological, and pastoral ends. Their encounters with the text of Greek Isaiah in various forms[97] are shaped by interpretive traditions and foundational theological convictions, some unique to early Christian

95. With Jesus as the speaker, the referent of "him" in Heb. 2:13a is clearly God, just as in Isa. 8:17; the homilist does not exploit the christological potential that κύριος (Isa. 8:13-14) affords to make Jesus the antecedent of ἐπ᾽ αὐτῷ. As we have seen, however, in their christological interpretations of Isa. 8:14, neither Paul nor the author of 1 Peter excludes God as the object of trust.

96. For the fear of God, see Heb. 10:27, 31; 12:21, 28; cf. 4:1. See further Patrick Gray, *Godly Fear: The Epistle to the Hebrews and Greco-Roman Critiques of Superstition,* SBLAB 16 (Atlanta: SBL, 2003).

97. We have seen that the textual character of the explicit citations varies, even within a single author. Some citations transmit the LXX (see n. 3 above) nearly verbatim (Isa. 8:12-13/1 Pet. 3:14-15; Isa. 8:17-18/Heb. 2:13); others reflect a distinctively septuagintal text that has been revised in part toward a proto-Masoretic form of the Hebrew text (Isa. 8:14 and 28:16/Rom. 9:33 and 1 Pet. 2:6, 8).

communities, some shared with other Second Commonwealth Jewish groups. Nevertheless, the ends to which our authors employ these citations from Isaiah 8 reflect, to one degree or another, the fact that they are drawing on *Greek* Isaiah and a tradition of interpretation that is embedded in, or that has grown up around, the LXX text. In reading Isaiah 8:14 together with Isaiah 28:16, both Paul and the author of 1 Peter follow the lead of the LXX translator, who has enhanced the verbal and thematic links between Isaiah 8 and 28-29 already found in the Hebrew text. Moreover, the distinctive plus "in it/him" (ἐπ' αὐτῷ) shared by LXX Isaiah 8:14 and 28:16 clearly facilitates these Christian interpreters' identification of the "stone" as Christ. Similarly, the LXX rendering of the divine name as κύριος in Isaiah 8:13 opens the door to a christological reinterpretation of the passage in 1 Peter, while the ambiguous speech formula καὶ ἐρεῖ in LXX Isaiah 8:17 paves the way for the author of Hebrews to appropriate the words that follow as utterances of Christ. Particularly striking is the way that Paul's sweeping redefinition of "doing" the law as trusting in God's saving act in Christ mirrors the distinctive shape of Isaiah 8:11-18 in the Septuagint, with its heightened emphasis on "trust" and its close connection between "trust" and "the law."

As much as these three early Christian authors differ from one another, their interpretations of Isaiah 8 nonetheless share a strong "family resemblance."[98] Each finds in the ancient oracle divine testimony to the sovereign pleasure of God in appointing Christ as Savior. Moreover, each employs this christocentric interpretation of Isaiah 8 with a sharp ecclesial focus, regarding the passage as a word directly addressed to the contemporary communities of faith that God has established in Christ.[99] In none of the texts we have examined do citations of Isaiah 8 serve as mere rhetorical ornamentation. On the contrary, in Romans, 1 Peter, and Hebrews alike it is evident that the author's intense and persistent engagement with Isaiah's oracles has profoundly shaped his understanding and articulation of the gospel and its claims on the lives of those to whom he writes. With their bold and creative reappropriations of Isaiah's words in the service of the early Chris-

---

98. For the notion of a "family resemblance" among Christian interpreters of Isaiah through the ages, see the masterful study of Brevard S. Childs, *The Struggle to Understand Isaiah as Christian Scripture* (Grand Rapids: Eerdmans, 2004).

99. On Paul's hermeneutic as both "christocentric" and "ecclesiotelic," see Richard B. Hays, "On the Rebound: A Response to Critiques of *Echoes of Scripture in the Letters of Paul*," in *Paul and the Scriptures of Israel*, ed. Craig A. Evans and James A. Sanders, JSNTSup 83 (Sheffield: JSOT, 1993), pp. 70-96; reprinted in Hays, *Conversion of the Imagination*, pp. 163-89.

tian mission, these three writers eloquently testify to the radical "conversion of the imagination" wrought in them by the God who raised Jesus
Christ from the dead.[100]

100. This expression is borrowed from Richard Hays's seminal essay "The Conversion
of the Imagination: Scripture and Eschatology in 1 Corinthians," *NTS* 45 (1999): 391-412; reprinted in Hays, *Conversion of the Imagination*, pp. 1-24.

Idolatry in the New Testament

Joel Marcus

Opposition to idolatry is central to the message of the Old Testament, and the theme continues to be important in intertestamental Judaism and the New Testament. In both of the latter, however, this anti-idolatrous attitude confronts the changed situation of the Greco-Roman world. The theme of idolatry in the New Testament, therefore, is a premier example of the reappropriation of Old Testament (and early Jewish) traditions and theology in the New Testament. I am happy to dedicate the expanded version of this study to my friend and colleague Richard Hays, foe of idolatry and lover of exegesis, from whom I have learned much about many things, including the appropriation and transformation of the Old Testament in the New.[1]

I. Continuities with the Old Testament and Jewish Traditions

In the Old Testament and later Jewish traditions, the first and second commandments are intimately interrelated: "You shall have no other gods before me" implies "You shall not make for yourself an idol" (Exod. 20:2-5). This is because, in the polytheistic and iconographic religious world of the ancient Near East, worship of deities other than the God of Israel necessarily involved veneration of their icons, and images were therefore tarred by their association with paganism; the Decalogue and its interpreters consequently sought to ensure the worship of Yahweh alone by forbidding not only depic-

---

1. This is an expanded version of an article published in *Int* 60 (2006): 152-64.

tions of foreign gods but also graven images of the true one.[2] At a later point, however, this interdict on images received a metaphysical justification: God is so transcendent and dynamic that freezing him in a finite and static form is a trivialization (see, e.g., Deut. 4:15-16 and Isa. 40:18-19).[3]

The word "icons" in the previous paragraph is used advisedly. Many pagans would have viewed the images of their gods as visible objects separate from the invisible divinities they represented but participating sacramentally in their numinous power.[4] The polemic against idol worship in the Old Testament, later Jewish literature, and the New Testament is therefore a caricature;[5] pagans did not characteristically worship the images per se[6] but the gods who, by their grace, might manifest themselves through them.[7] To be sure, different pagans doubtless understood the "special relationship" between the god and the image in different ways,[8] and the more superstitious among them may have identified the two;[9] there is, for example, abundant evidence of people

2. For this and many other points in this section, I have drawn on the excellent treatment in Terry Griffith, *Keep Yourselves from Idols: A New Look at 1 John,* JSNTSup 233 (London/New York: Sheffield Academic, 2002), pp. 28-57.

3. Cf. Moshe Halbertal and Avishai Margalit, *Idolatry* (Cambridge, Mass./London: Harvard University Press, 1992), pp. 37-38.

4. On ancient Near Eastern images, see Horst Dietrich Preuss, *Verspottung fremder Religionen im Alten Testament,* BWANT 92 (Stuttgart/Berlin/Köln/Mainz: Kohlhammer, 1971), p. 47, who emphasizes that the presence of the divinity in the image is not static and continuous but temporally limited and actualized by ritual activity.

5. Pertinent texts include Isa. 44:9-20; Jer. 10:1-6; Hab. 2:18-19; Pss. 115:4-8; 135:15-18; Wis. 15:7-19; Epistle of Jeremiah; *Apocalypse of Abraham* 1-8; Rom. 1:18-32. According to Griffith, *Keep Yourselves from Idols,* pp. 37-38, the OT polemic consists of five major elements: "(1) the equation of idols with the gods themselves; (2) an emphasis on their material and perishable nature; (3) their origin in the mind and skills of the artificer; (4) their lifelessness and their consequent ability only to disappoint those who put their trust in them; and (5) their unreal and consequently deceptive nature." All of these points probably would have been disputed by thoughtful pagans.

6. The fourth-century Greek rhetorician Libanius, for example, says that despite the beauty of the statue of Asclepius in Beroea, "no one [even of the Christians] was so shameless that he would dare to say that sacrifices were offered to this statue" (*Or.* 30.22-23, cited in Derek Newton, *Deity and Diet: The Dilemma of Sacrificial Food at Corinth,* JSNTSup 169 [Sheffield: Sheffield Academic, 1998], p. 150).

7. In an Egyptian text, for example, the god Hathor flies down from heaven to unite himself with his icon; see Preuss, *Verspottung,* p. 47.

8. For a fascinating comparison with the variety of attitudes toward images among contemporary residents of India, see Roger Hooker, *What Is Idolatry?* (London: Committee for Relations with People of Other Faiths, British Council of Churches, 1986), pp. 4-11.

9. For the term "special relationship" and the idea of "substitution," see Halbertal and

trying to get the gods to do things for them by manipulating their images.[10] But it is a distortion when the biblical, Jewish, and Christian traditions portray crass identification of the image with the god as the essence of paganism.

The distortion was probably often deliberate.[11] For the authors of the Hebrew Bible, later Jews, and early Christians, images of foreign divinities constituted a clear and present danger to monotheistic faith and, accordingly, were objects of abhorrence and calculated derision.[12] The Greek translation of the Old Testament most often refers to these proscribed images as εἴδωλα, a term whose etymology and subsequent usage convey the notion of things that appear to be something they are not.[13] Falsity and deceptiveness, therefore, are built into the Greek word from which the English term "idol"

Margalit, *Idolatry,* pp. 40-45, who point out that a similar sort of special relationship and even an approach to substitution is present in the OT itself in the attitude toward the holy vessels; the Ark of the Covenant, for example, "could bring life and death: it brought disaster upon the Philistines and killed thousands of Israel's people in Beth Shemesh" (1 Sam. 5:1–7:1).

10. For ancient Near Eastern examples, see Preuss, *Verspottung,* pp. 44-46, who points to processions of images, belief in their healing properties, and their wakening, clothing, and nourishment by priests. For the Greco-Roman world, see Newton, *Deity and Diet,* pp. 148-74, who cites among other passages Pausanias, *Descr.* 7.22.2-3, which mentions an image of Hermes at Pharae in Achaea to which worshipers sacrificed, burned incense, and directed questions. Pausanias also describes an incident in which abuse of the image of a divinized man led to the death of the abuser, whose sons subsequently prosecuted the statue for murder (6.11.2-9)! See also Plutarch, *Mor.* 379C-D: "There are some among the Greeks who have not learned nor habituated themselves to speak of the bronze, the painted, and the stone effigies as statues of the gods and dedications in their honour, but they call them gods . . ." (trans. Babbitt, LCL). Both Preuss and Newton suggest that the difference between these two approaches corresponds to that between the elite and the common people, but this distinction is probably too neat.

11. The rabbis, for example, were capable of a nonfetishistic view of Roman icons (see, e.g., *Exod. Rab.* 15:17), but they did not generally allow themselves this luxury (see, e.g., *b. 'Abod. Zar.* 20a); indeed, "in the Jewish tradition a positive description of idolatry is not only nonexistent, it is forbidden." See Halbertal and Margalit, *Idolatry,* pp. 7, 259.

12. See Griffith, *Keep Yourselves from Idols,* pp. 32-33, who cites the OT terms גלולים ("unclean things"), which is probably related to the word for dung, אלילים ("weak, worthless things"), and הבל ("breath, insubstantiality"). Other terms "emphasise the materiality and manufactured origins of idols."

13. "Plato's theory of knowledge uses the term εἴδωλον to describe the illusory phenomena or appearances that are the product of sense perception, in contrast to the immutable 'forms' or 'ideas' apprehended by the soul, which alone are the source of infallible knowledge. Because, philosophically, an εἴδωλον is at least one step removed from reality by virtue of being a copy of the true, and because it thus necessarily belongs to the realm of the transient and ambiguous, it is tainted with falsehood and deception." Griffith, *Keep Yourselves from Idols,* p. 29.

is derived. This linkage of idols with deceptiveness extends an attitude that is already present in the Old Testament and continues in later Judaism and early Christianity, in all of which the term "idol" applies not only to images of pagan gods but also to those gods themselves.[14] "The gods of the peoples are idols" (1 Chron. 16:26) because there is no real divinity but the God of Israel. This negative attitude toward pagan gods and images was well known; in the Greco-Roman world, Jews were alternately praised and condemned for their imageless worship and stubborn refusal to revere or even acknowledge the existence of other gods.[15] Correspondingly, polemic against idolatry occupies a prominent place in postbiblical Judaism.[16]

The subject of idolatry also rises to the surface in the New Testament, especially in the Pauline corpus. This concentration is not unexpected, since Paul's letters were addressed to Christian communities whose members, mostly from Gentile backgrounds, grew up worshiping pagan gods and venerating their images. As Paul puts it in 1 Thessalonians 1:9, however, they had now "turned to God from idols, to serve a living and true God." Despite the impression this passage leaves of a once-for-all separation, it was difficult for many pagan converts to Christianity to make a clean break from idolatry. Most ancient people lived and died in cramped quarters and rarely ate meat; their only real opportunity to assemble with friends and enjoy ample meat and wine was at the temples' religious festivals dedicated to the gods. In refusing to participate in such feasts, Jews and Christians were opting out of their world's main social events.[17] It is symptomatic of the difficulties this re-

14. Besides 1 Chron. 16:26, quoted below, see 1 Sam. 31:9; Jer. 14:22; Philo, *Spec.* 1.26; Josephus, *Ant.* 9.243; 10.50, 65; 1 Cor. 8:4; 1 Thess. 1:9; cf. Friedrich Büchsel, "Εἴδωλον, κτλ.," *TDNT* 2:377; Griffith, *Keep Yourselves from Idols*, p. 35.

15. See, e.g., Tacitus, *Hist.* 5.5; Juvenal, *Sat.* 5.14; Livy 102 (*Schol. Luc.* 2.593); Varro in Augustine, *Civ. Dei* 4.31.

16. For examples of the concern with idolatry in postbiblical Jewish literature, see the numerous entries under "idolatry," "idols," and "idol worship" in the subject indices of George W. E. Nickelsburg, *Jewish Literature between the Bible and the Mishnah* (Philadelphia: Fortress, 1981); and J. H. Charlesworth, *The Old Testament Pseudepigrapha* (Garden City: Doubleday, 1983). Concern over idolatry is particularly prominent in the *Sibylline Oracles, Joseph and Aseneth,* the *Testaments of the Twelve Patriarchs, Apocalypse of Abraham,* Philo's works, and the Qumran scrolls; for a survey of usages in these works and the Septuagint, see Griffith, *Keep Yourselves from Idols*, pp. 28-57. For a summary of the Jewish attitude, focusing mostly on rabbinic literature, see Peter J. Tomson, *Paul and the Jewish Law: Halakha in the Letters of the Apostle to the Gentiles,* CRINT 3/1 (Assen/Maastricht/Minneapolis: Van Gorcum/Fortress, 1990), pp. 151-86.

17. See R. MacMullen, *Paganism in the Roman Empire* (New Haven/London: Yale University Press, 1981), pp. 34-42.

fusal caused that while the New Testament books of Acts and Revelation tersely proscribe food that has been "sacrificed to idols" (Acts 15:20, 29; 21:25; Rev. 2:14, 20), Paul ends up giving the same issue a more nuanced treatment in 1 Corinthians 8 and 10 (see section IV below).

Questions related to idolatry, then, were still live ones in the New Testament period and beyond. This was true not only in the Christian sphere but also in the Jewish one; a famous story from the basic rabbinic law code, the *Mishnah,* for example, recounts the dilemma posed by the presence of a statue of the Greek goddess Aphrodite in the bathhouse frequented by the rabbinic sage Rabban Gamaliel.[18] Idolatry was not just a threat from without but also an enemy within. The fourth-century synagogue at Ḥamat Tiberias in the Lower Galilee, for example, pictures the Greek sun god Helios in the center of a mosaic floor featuring the signs of the Zodiac, which include a naked and uncircumcised male figure; Helios, moreover, holds a sphere representing the earth and a scepter, symbols that are explicitly proscribed in the Mishnah.[19] A rigorous rejection of idolatry, therefore, does not seem to have prevailed in all quarters,[20] and the rabbinic contention that the inclination to idolatry had been uprooted from Israel (e.g., *b. 'Abod. Zar.* 17ab; *Cant. Rab.* 7.8) probably represents wishful thinking rather than sociological reality.[21] Indeed, the author of one of the Dead Sea Scrolls inveighs passionately against fellow Jews who "set idols upon their hearts" (CD 20:9).[22]

Many of the writers of the New Testament share this fierce opposition to

18. *m. 'Abod. Zar.* 3:4; for a marvelous analysis of this story and the issues it raises, see M. Halbertal, "Coexisting with the Enemy: Jews and Pagans in the Mishnah," in *Tolerance and Intolerance in Early Judaism and Christianity,* ed. Graham N. Stanton and Guy G. Stroumsa (Cambridge: Cambridge University Press, 1998), pp. 159-72.

19. *m. 'Abod. Zar.* 3:1; see Lee L. Levine, *Judaism and Hellenism in Antiquity: Conflict or Confluence?* The Samuel and Althea Stroum Lectures in Jewish Studies (Seattle/London: University of Washington Press, 1998), p. 159.

20. For different attempts to deal with the contradiction between the textual and archaeological evidence, see Erwin R. Goodenough, *Jewish Symbols in the Greco-Roman Period: Abridged Edition* (Princeton: Princeton University Press, 1988), pp. 116-73; S. Schwartz, *Imperialism and Jewish Society, 200 B.C.E. to 640 C.E.* (Princeton/Oxford: Princeton University Press, 2001), passim; Steven Fine, *Art and Judaism in the Greco-Roman World* (Cambridge: Cambridge University Press, 2005), passim.

21. The rabbinic view, however, is still sometimes mirrored by both Jewish and Christian scholars; see, e.g., Louis Isaac Rabinowitz, "Idolatry," *EncJud* 8:1227-37; Edward M. Curtis, "Idol, Idolatry," *ABD* 3:380.

22. Translation from G. Vermès, *The Dead Sea Scrolls in English,* 3rd ed. (London: Penguin, 1987), p. 90.

idolatry. As in intertestamental Jewish texts (e.g., *Sib. Or.* 2.259; 3.36-38; *T. Levi* 17:11; *T. Jud.* 23:1) and later Christian literature strongly influenced by Judaism (e.g., *Did.* 3:4), idolatry appears in the New Testament in vice lists (Gal. 5:20; Col. 3:5; 1 Pet. 4:3; Rev. 21:8). Idolaters who are Christians are among those who will not inherit the dominion of God and are to be avoided (1 Cor. 5:10-11; 6:9). In Acts 15:20, 29; Romans 1:18-27; 1 Corinthians 10:7-8; and Revelation 2:14, 20, moreover, idolatry is associated in an especially close way with sexual immorality (πορνεία),[23] a linkage also found frequently in Jewish texts (see the next section). The Acts passage mentions "blood" as well — a concatenation reminiscent of the rabbinic position that a Jew should die rather than commit the three cardinal sins of idolatry, sexual immorality, and murder.[24]

II. Idolatry and Sexual Immorality

Although the reality was probably less sensational than its portrayal in Jewish and Christian polemic, Jews and Christians apparently did believe that pagan worship routinely involved sexual profligacy. As a general rabbinic opinion cited in *b. Ket.* 13b puts it, "Most of the idolaters are unrestrained in sexual matters." In *b. Sanh.* 63b, indeed, Rab Judah goes so far as to claim that the Israelites knew that the idols were nonentities but that they engaged in idolatry in order to allow themselves to have forbidden sexual relations. Here, then, the connection between idolatry and fornication is assumed to be so direct that the desire to indulge in the latter is the motivation for participation in the former.

Although this sort of attitude exaggerates the licentiousness of pagan worship, it is not a complete fantasy. For example, the most important Greek god outside of Greece in the Hellenistic age, the wine god Dionysus, was associated with dissipation of all sorts. His cult had to be severely restricted in Rome after "the great Bacchanalian scandal" of 186 BCE, in which initiates reportedly engaged in orgies and acts of murder, as described in lurid detail by Livy (39.8-13).[25] It flourished elsewhere, however, often as a mystery cult,

---

23. See also Gal. 5:19-20; Col. 3:5; cf. 1 Pet. 4:3.

24. See, e.g., *b. Sanh.* 74a; cf. G. F. Moore, *Judaism in the First Centuries of the Christian Era*, vol. 1 (New York: Schocken, 1971 [1927]), pp. 466-67.

25. On this scandal, see Hans-Josef Klauck, *The Religious Context of Early Christianity*, SNTW (Edinburgh: T. & T. Clark, 2000), pp. 114-15. D. Winston, *The Wisdom of Solomon: A New Translation with Introduction and Commentary*, AB 43 (New York: Doubleday, 1979),

and it may be connected with 2 Maccabees 6:2-5, where the pollution of the Jerusalem temple by the erection of a pagan altar is accompanied by drinking bouts and dalliance with prostitutes.[26] Popular suspicion that members of such cults indulged in free love probably helped encourage Jewish suspicion about the licentious nature of idolatry in general.[27]

But actual information about pagan cults was probably not the main factor in the persistent linkage of idolatry with fornication; after all, many non-Jews who themselves venerated images were also scandalized by the excesses of the Dionysus cult. A more important factor may have been sociological: intercourse with a Gentile might result in pregnancy and marriage, with the consequence that the Jewish partner might abandon his or her natal community and turn to "idolatry," that is, a Gentile way of life.[28] There may also have been an element of sheer vituperation, which was common in ancient polemic.[29] Idolatry and fornication were two of the worst sins that ancient Jews and Christians could imagine, so to them the fact that a person was an idolater may have been enough to imply that he or she was also a fornicator.

---

pp. 238-39, cites the Livy passage in explicating Wis. 12:3-4, which is closely linked with the polemic against idolatry in chapters 13-15. Similarly, Amos 7:9 LXX uses γέλως = laughter, a term frequently associated with Dionysus, to speak of Israel's idolatry.

26. Cf. 2 Macc. 6:7 and 14:33, which mention the Dionysus cult specifically, and see M. Hengel, *Judaism and Hellenism: Studies in Their Encounter in Palestine during the Early Hellenistic Period,* 2 vols. (Philadelphia: Fortress, 1974), 1:299 and 2:201-2, nn. 273-74.

27. Cf. Winston, *Wisdom of Solomon,* pp. 238-39, who points out that the LXX uses mystery terminology to translate various biblical verses that deal with the unchastity connected with idolatry (Num. 25:3, 5; Deut. 23:17; cf. Philo, *Spec.* 1.319-20). To what extent this image of licentious cults corresponded to reality is a more difficult question. The situation was probably similar to that with regard to modern-day descriptions of Tantric yoga, which tend to overemphasize the sensational and especially the sexual aspects of the practice.

28. See *b. Šabb.* 17b: "They decreed against [the Gentiles'] bread and oil on account of their wine, and against their wine on account of their daughters, and against their daughters on account of something else [i.e., idolatry]" (Soncino alt.). Cf. *b. Meg.* 25a, which speaks of "an Israelite who has intercourse with a Cuthean [= Gentile] woman and begets from her a son for idolatry," and *Jos. Asen.* 8:5-7, where Joseph says that "it is not fitting for a man who worships God, who will bless with his mouth the living God, . . . to kiss a strange woman who will bless with her mouth dead and mute idols . . ." (*OTP* alt.). Randall D. Chesnutt, "The Social Setting and Purpose of Joseph and Aseneth," *JSP* 2 (1988): 41-42 notes that here intimacy or intermarriage with a Gentile is forbidden and that this interdict is related to the danger of idolatry.

29. See L. T. Johnson, "The New Testament's Anti-Jewish Slander and the Conventions of Ancient Polemic," *JBL* 108 (1989): 419-41.

There are also deeper levels to the association between idolatry and sexual immorality. One is the idea that worship of images is the root of all other transgressions. In this regard, Paul's famous analysis of the genesis of evil in Romans 1:18-27 follows a trail blazed by a Hellenistic Jewish text, Wisdom 14:12-31, which describes idolatry as "the beginning of fornication" and "the beginning, cause, and end of every evil" (14:12, 27).[30] Idolatry is thus the primal sin, which leads ineluctably to all others, including, prominently, fornication — a connection that is especially close because both transgressions involve mistaking the creature for the Creator and bestowing upon the former the reverence and servitude that belong to the latter (see Rom. 1:25). Fornication, then, is a form of idolatry.[31] And conversely, idolatry is a form of fornication, since the two are intimately linked through the biblical metaphor of Israel as the bride of Yahweh and idolatry as adultery against him (most fully developed in Hosea 1–4 and Ezekiel 16 and 23).[32] This metaphor may be part of the background for the statement in Wisdom 14:12 that idolatry is the beginning of fornication, which is explicated by a list of diverse transgressions (14:13-27). "Fornication" here seems to become a broad term signifying any sort of unfaithfulness to God — a frequent nuance of "idolatry" as well.[33]

III. Idolatry and Money

The notion that idolatry either leads to or includes all other sins aids in the process of generalizing and transforming it into a metaphor. A New Testament example of such broadening is provided by Colossians 3:5, where a vice list consists of "fornication, impurity, passion, evil desire, and greed (which is idolatry)." This identification of idolatry with greed is not original to the New Testament author, and it may partly result from the biblical interpretation of the second commandment (Exod. 20:4) as a prohibition against constructing gods of silver and gold (Exod. 20:23). The deeper significance of

30. On the critique of idolatry in Wisdom 13-15, see Maurice Gilbert, *La critique des dieux dans le Livre de la Sagesse (Sg 13-15)*, AnBib 53 (Rome: Biblical Institute, 1973).

31. Cf. *b. Sanh.* 82a, which says that "he who is intimate with a heathen woman is as though he had entered into a marriage relationship with an idol," and *T. Reub.* 4:6, which says that fornication separates the soul from God and brings it near to idols.

32. For a full treatment of this metaphor, see Halbertal and Margalit, *Idolatry*, pp. 9-36.

33. See, e.g., *b. Šabb.* 105b, where the evil impulse, which causes human beings to revolt against God's will, is referred to as an idol.

this biblical juxtaposition is explained by the first-century Alexandrian Jewish philosopher Philo:[34]

> But apart from the literal prohibition, [God in Exod. 20:23] seems to me to suggest another thought of great value for the promotion of morality, and to condemn strongly the money-lovers who procure gold and silver coins from every side and treasure their hoard like a divine image in a sanctuary, believing it to be a source of blessing and happiness of every kind. And further, all the needy who are possessed by that grievous malady, the desire for money, though they have no wealth of their own on which they may bestow worship as its due, pay awe-struck homage to that of their neighbors, and come at early dawn to the houses of those who have abundance of it as though they were the grandest temples, there to make their prayers and beg for blessing from the masters as though they were gods. To such [God] says elsewhere, "You shall not follow idols and you shall not make molten gods" [Lev. 19:4], thus teaching them in a figure that it is not fitting to assign divine honors to wealth.[35]

Love of wealth, then, is a form of idolatry, because money-grubbers look not to God but to their own wealth or that of others for happiness and security. The same sort of analysis lies behind Jesus' assertion that "you cannot serve God and Mammon [= wealth]" (Matt. 6:24//Luke 16:13). The love of money sets up a competing loyalty that diverts people from their primary allegiance, which is to God. The early church may have left the word "Mammon" here untranslated, and thus sounding like a proper name, partly in order to bring out the implication that wealth quickly becomes an idol, an alternate lord who demands subservience in an almost personal way.[36] This connotation is already present in the verb δουλεύειν ("to serve"), which appears in the just-mentioned saying, "You cannot serve God and Mammon." This verb is most frequently used for the master-slave relationship and is also employed for allegiance to transcendent beings.[37] It is possible that 1 Timothy 6:10, which speaks of love of money being the root of all evil, is another New Testament reference to idolatry. Both the "root of all evil" ter-

---

34. On Philo's ideas about idolatry, see further Karl-Gustav Sandelin, "The Danger of Idolatry According to Philo of Alexandria," *Tem* 27 (1991): 109-50.

35. Philo, *Spec.* 1.23-25 (trans. Colson, LCL alt.)

36. See M. Hengel, *Property and Riches in the Early Church: Aspects of a Social History of Early Christianity* (Philadelphia: Fortress, 1974), p. 24.

37. See BDAG 259.

minology, which is similar to the phrasing of Wisdom 14:12, 27, and the picture of greed leading people astray from the faith are evocative of Jewish denunciations of idolatry.[38]

A further linkage of money with idolatry arose from the religious features of Roman coins in Jesus' time. Currency was minted by the state, and the state was personified by the emperor, who was believed to be divine, as is demonstrated by the pictures and inscriptions on coins from the time of Augustus on. Usage of such Roman coins was interpreted by some Jews as tantamount to acknowledging the emperor's idolatrous claim to divinity, and rigorists tried to abstain from being contaminated by them. Hippolytus, for example, reports that the Essenes refused to carry coins, "saying that they ought not either to carry, or behold, or fashion an image,"[39] and in rabbinic traditions R. Naḥum bar Simai is said to have been so holy that he never in his life looked at the effigy on a coin (b. Pes. 104a; b. 'Abod. Zar. 50a).[40] The issue was akin to that posed by the golden eagle erected by King Herod in the Jerusalem temple in 6 BCE, which was "both a divine symbol and the sign of the power of the king and the arms of the emperor"[41] and was therefore cut down by Jewish zealots who paid for their iconoclasm with their lives.[42] For a similar reason, Roman standards containing busts of the emperor caused riots when introduced into Jerusalem by Pontius Pilate in 26 CE.[43]

Like the eagle and the standards, the tribute coin about which the Pharisees and Herodians ask Jesus in Mark 12:13-14 could be viewed as a Trojan horse, an insidious means of planting blasphemous images in the heart of the holy city; the question, then, raises the issue of idolatry in a tacit but unmistakable manner.[44] This is especially true because the denarius requested

38. See, e.g., T. Jud. 19:1: "Love of money leads to idolatry, because once they are led astray by money, they designate as gods those who are not gods."

39. Hippolytus, Haer. 9.21 (trans. Macmahon, ANF 5:136).

40. For discussion of these passages, see Steven Fine, Art and Judaism in the Greco-Roman World (Cambridge: Cambridge University Press, 2005), pp. 114-15.

41. M. Hengel, The Zealots: Investigations into the Jewish Freedom Movement in the Period from Herod I until 70 A.D. (Edinburgh: T. & T. Clark, 1989 [1961]), p. 103.

42. Josephus, War 1.648-55; Ant. 17.149-63.

43. See Josephus, War 2.169-74; Ant. 18.55-59; cf. Hengel, Zealots, pp. 190-96; Raymond E. Brown, The Death of the Messiah: From Gethsemane to the Grave; A Commentary on the Passion Narratives in the Four Gospels, ABRL (New York: Doubleday, 1994), pp. 698-99.

44. Karl-Gustav Sandelin, "The Jesus-Tradition and Idolatry," NTS 42 (1996): 412-20 objects that this reconstruction "presupposes knowledge of the legend of the coin both in the mind of the author and in the mind of the implied reader or listener." But given the wide

by Jesus not only depicts the emperor as a high official of the Roman religion but also makes him an object of that religion. On its obverse the Emperor Tiberius's laurel-crowned head is surrounded by the inscription *TI[BERIVS] CAESAR DIVI AVG[VSTI] F[ILIUS] AVGVSTVS* ("Tiberius Caesar, son of the deified Augustus, [himself] Augustus"). This inscription continues on the reverse side of the coin, which reads *Pontif[ex] Maxim[us]* = "High Priest" and is accompanied by a picture of a seated woman representing Pax, the embodiment of the "peace" (i.e., military subjugation) of the empire.[45] Tiberius, then, is portrayed as the son of the deified Augustus, and himself Augustus, a term meaning "the one to be served with religious awe" and carrying its own implication of divinity, which is reinforced by the laurel crown on his head.[46] This coin was therefore not only an economic instrument and a symbol of the Jews' political subjection to Rome but also part of the developing ruler cult of the first century and hence would have been considered idolatrous by many Jews.[47]

Rejection of the coin and the tribute for which it was employed, however, would have carried the huge risk of being charged with subversion and an offense against the majesty of the emperor. Philostratus, for example, describes the conviction of a master for impiety "merely because he struck his own slave when the latter had on his person a silver drachma coined with the image of Tiberius."[48] If this report is to be believed, the image of the divine emperor on coins was considered sacrosanct, and even an indirect assault upon it could be met with severe penalties. In our passage, the Pharisees and

distribution of this particular coin, that presupposition does not seem problematic; see H. St J. Hart, "The Coin of 'Render Unto Caesar . . .' (a Note on Some Aspects of Mark 12:13-17; Matt. 22:15-22; Luke 20:20-26)," in *Jesus and the Politics of His Day*, ed. E. Bammel and C. F. D. Moule (Cambridge: Cambridge University Press, 1984), pp. 244-45, 248. The religious dimension of such coins was probably as familiar as the inscription "In God We Trust" is to modern Americans. Sandelin may be right that Jesus' response invokes the Shema (Deut. 6:4-9; 11:13-21; Num. 15:37-41) and other OT passages (e.g., Isa. 45:21), but this does not exclude a primary allusion to the coin inscription, which as he himself admits "would be a most natural presupposition for what Jesus says."

45. For photographs and analysis, see Hart, "Coin."

46. On the association of the laurel crown with the gods Apollo and Zeus, see Ovid, *Trist.* 3.1.35-48, 77-78; Pliny, *Nat.* 15.136; cf. C. Hünemörder, "Lorbeer," *DNP* 7:440-42; P. Bastien, *Le buste mónetaire des empereurs romains*, vol. 1 (Wetteren, Belgium: Éditions Numismatique Romaine, 1992), pp. 61-66.

47. See L. J. Kreitzer, *Striking New Images: Roman Imperial Coinage and the New Testament World*, JSNTSup 134 (Sheffield: Sheffield Academic, 1996), pp. 69-98.

48. Philostratus, *Vit. Apoll.* 1.15 (trans. Jones, LCL alt.).

Herodians are trying to incite Jesus to commit a much more flagrant offense with their "tempting" comment that Jesus does not "look at the face of human beings" — a probable reference to the bust of the emperor on the denarius. Jesus, then, is being invited to show his disdain for the emperor's countenance by refusing to pay the coin that bears his idolatrous image.

But this close connection between the denarius coin and the emperor's person and divinity makes Jesus' response at first seem puzzling. He asks whose inscription and image the denarius bears, and being told that they belong to Caesar (i.e., the emperor), declares: "Pay therefore to Caesar the things of Caesar, and the things of God to God" (12:16-17a). This response seems to gloss over the crucial fact that in Jesus' world the sphere of God and that of the emperor were not clearly demarcated from each other; the very inscription and image under discussion, as we have just seen, melded those two realms in a way that was intolerable for many Jews. The Jesus of the Gospels, however, appears to ignore this fusion, since the most natural way of reading Mark 12:16 is that the image and inscription relate to Caesar *rather than* to God.

This suppression of the crucial nexus between Caesar and the divine may be not just an evasion but a deliberate secularization of the emperor's image. Jesus' strategy would then be similar to that of Rabban Gamaliel, who resolves the Venus-in-the-bathhouse quandary by saying that "what is treated as a god is forbidden, but what is not treated as a god is permitted"; since bathers stand naked and urinate before Aphrodite's image, they obviously do not consider it to be divine.[49] Jesus would be carving out a secular space in which the emperor can be recognized and his benefits enjoyed without his being acknowledged as divine. His response would imply both a demythologizing of imperial propaganda — Caesar is *not* God — and a recognition of the right of his representatives to collect taxes. The state can be obeyed without acknowledging its claim to ultimacy; since Caesar is not really God, paying taxes to him is not really idolatry. In fact, withholding tribute in a militant manner might, paradoxically, ascribe to him a transcen-

---

49. See Halbertal, "Coexisting with the Enemy," pp. 166-67. Jesus' strategy of compartmentalization here is also similar to that of Josephus, who defends his people against the charge of disloyalty to the emperor by noting that while Moses forbade the making of statues, he "did not prohibit that good men be paid homage with other honors, secondary to God" (*Ap.* 2.76) — ignoring that the customary way of proving one's loyalty to the emperor was to acknowledge his divinity. Cf. John M. G. Barclay, "Snarling Sweetly: A Study of Josephus on Idolatry," in *Durham Essays on Idolatry,* ed. Stephen Barton (London/New York: Continuum, 2007).

dence he does not deserve by treating his request for taxes as a demand for supreme loyalty.

In the end, though, the import of "Pay therefore to Caesar the things of Caesar, and the things of God to God" remains somewhat ambiguous; one *could* interpret it in a revolutionary rather than a quietistic sense, as a call to tax revolt, since according to Israelite tradition *everything* belongs to God.[50] The clever ambiguity of Jesus' reply is probably part of the reason for his interrogators' amazement, with which the passage concludes (12:17b). He has succeeded in saying something that neither gives them a pretext for reporting him to the Romans nor undermines his integrity by endorsing the emperor's divine status.

A similarly ambiguous reply is recorded in the *Tosefta,* where R. Eliezer responds to a Roman ruler who questions him about a charge of sectarianism, perhaps meaning adherence to Christianity, by saying, "I have trust in the judge" (*t. Ḥul.* 2:24). As Daniel Boyarin points out, here Eliezer "answers the charge of Christianity, implicitly a charge of disloyalty to the Empire, by indicating his fealty to the Roman *hegemon* [= ruler]." The reply, however, is presented by the *Tosefta* as a double entendre. After recording it, the text comments: "The ruler thought that he was speaking of him, but he meant his father in heaven."[51] Here, then, as in our New Testament passage, a Jewish figure evades a charge of disloyalty to the empire by making a reply that can be taken as a recognition of the Roman ruler ("Pay therefore to Caesar the things of Caesar"/"I have trust in the judge") but can also be interpreted as undermining the ruler by implying his subordination to God ("and the things of God to God"/"I have trust in the Judge"). Boyarin sees R. Eliezer's "duplicitous" reply as the sort of trickster language commonly used by colonial subjects.[52]

If the Jesus of the Gospels uses similarly ambiguous, trickster language, he may not do so merely to save his own skin; unlike Eliezer, Jesus did end his life on a Roman cross. The deliberate ambiguity may rather be directed at

---

50. R. A. Horsley, *Hearing the Whole Story: The Politics of Plot in Mark's Gospel* (Louisville: Westminster John Knox, 2001), p. 43; cf. C. A. Evans, *Mark 8:27–16:20,* WBC (Nashville: Thomas Nelson, 2001), p. 347.

51. Daniel Boyarin, *Dying for God: Martyrdom and the Making of Christianity and Judaism,* Figurae (Stanford: Stanford University Press, 1999), pp. 27, 51, 56.

52. Cf. James C. Scott, *Domination and the Arts of Resistance: Hidden Transcripts* (New Haven/London: Yale University Press, 1990), passim. Boyarin contrasts Eliezer's ambiguous reply with *Mart. Pol.* 9:2, where Polycarp uses a bivalent but unambiguous phrase, "Away with the atheists," to denounce his accusers and thus ensure his martyrdom.

insiders as well as outsiders — which helps explain why it has occasioned such great debate in Christian history. Jesus does not lay down a hard-and-fast edict for relations with the ruling authorities; his concluding pronouncement instead leaves room for the discernment of his hearers as to when the claims of God and Caesar conflict and when they do not.[53] Early Christians knew of instances in which they did, and when that happened the choice was obvious (cf. Acts 5:29: "We must obey God rather than human beings"). Mark 12:17 itself, by the principle of end stress, implies that the demands of God trump those of Caesar. But the claims of these two rulers do not *always* clash, and when they do not, it is possible to be loyal to both.

IV. Food Sacrificed to Idols

In Paul's discussion of food sacrificed to idols, which begins in 1 Corinthians 8, the apostle seems at first to be occupying a similar middle ground. He agrees in principle with his Corinthian correspondent that idols (i.e., the gods behind pagan images) have no real existence and therefore that food offered to them is not being presented to a real, competing god. Presumably, then, such food may be eaten (8:4-6). The only qualification he states is that if a "weak brother" who does believe in idols sees Paul's correspondent eating idol food, he may be tempted to do something against his own conscience, and this would harm him morally (8:7, 10). The problem, then, is not the existence of the competing god but the weak brother's false belief in it; if the weak brother were not observing, it would presumably be acceptable for a Christian to eat idol food, even if this were done in the idol's temple.[54]

In 1 Corinthians 10:20, however, the argument takes a sudden and unexpected turn. While reiterating that idols have no real existence, Paul nevertheless rejects the corollary that it is permissible for Christians to take part in pagan sacrifices; those who do, he thunders, sacrifice to demons and not to God. This charge is rooted in a common Old Testament and Jewish association of idol worship with evil spirits,[55] but it seems to contradict what Paul said earlier. How can idols be both nonentities and mortally danger-

---

53. See J. Gnilka, *Das Evangelium nach Markus*, vol. 2, EKKNT 2 (Zürich/Neukirchen: Benziger/Neukirchener, 1978-79), pp. 153-54.

54. See Peter D. Gooch, *Dangerous Food: 1 Corinthians 8–10 in Its Context*, SCJ 5 (Waterloo, Ontario: Wilfrid Laurier University Press, 1993), p. 79.

55. See, e.g., Deut. 32:17; Pss. 95:5 LXX; 106:37; Isa. 65:11 LXX; Bar. 4:7; *1 En.* 19:1; *Jub.* 11:4-5; 22:17; *T. Job* 3:3.

ous?[56] And what has become of the implication of chapter 8 that idol food may be consumed so long as the eater acknowledges that "there is no idol in the world," but only the one God?[57] There is inconsistency, moreover, not only between 1 Corinthians 8 and 1 Corinthians 10 but also within 1 Corinthians 10. If participating in pagan sacrifices is drinking the cup of demons and partaking of their table (10:20-22), how can Paul go on to say that the issue has nothing to do with the Christian's conscience (10:25-30)?

Scholars have dealt with this tension in various manners.[58] The easiest solution is to posit that the different attitudes toward idolatry come from different letters, which have been amalgamated in our present 1 Corinthians.[59] But is it really inconceivable that Paul wrote all of 1 Corinthians 8 and 10 at the same time? Within this section, different aspects of the idol-food problem are being considered, and part of Paul's shifting attitude may reflect the shifting subject. He forbids actual participation in pagan cults (10:14-22) but is more tolerant about eating food that may have formed part of a pagan

56. As C. K. Barrett, *The First Epistle to the Corinthians*, HNTC (New York: Harper & Row, 1968), p. 236, points out, this contradiction may explain why some good ancient manuscripts (P[46] ℵ* A C* etc.) omit "or that an idol is anything" from 10:19, though it is also possible that the words have dropped out through a scribal error, since ἢ ὅτι εἴδωλον ("or that an idol") is both preceded and followed by τί ἐστιν ("is anything").

57. Wendell Lee Willis, *Idol Meat in Corinth: The Pauline Argument in 1 Corinthians 8 and 10*, SBLDS 68 (Chico, Calif.: Scholars Press, 1985), passim, argues that the Corinthians participated in meals such as those described in 1 Cor. 8:10 without any notion that they were committing idolatry, since the meals were social rather than cultic in character. As Gooch, *Dangerous Food*, pp. 81-82, 152-55, argues, however, such a distinction is implausible in an ancient context; summing up his survey of the archeological and literary data, Gooch says: "[T]he dissociation of temples and meals involving religious rites was not likely. The presence of a great number of dining rooms at the sanctuary of Demeter and Kore [in Corinth] was not coincidental: the cult and its rites centred on the provision of food. The literary evidence shows time and again that socially significant meals involved explicit religious rites. If such meals involved rites even when held in private homes, it seems most unlikely that there would not be some cultic acts in meals celebrated in cultic settings. Finally, social events and religious events could not be separated in the Greco-Roman world to the same extent as they can be in ours" (pp. 81-82).

58. See the survey in Gooch, *Dangerous Food*, pp. 47-59, 129-55.

59. Hans-Josef Klauck, *Herrenmahl und hellenistischer Kult: Eine religionsgeschichtliche Untersuchung zum ersten Korintherbrief*, NTAbh 15 (Münster: Aschendorff, 1982), p. 283, for example, argues that Letter A, which consists of 1 Cor. 9:1-18, 24-27; 10:1-22, represents the hard line that Paul originally took on the question of food sacrificed to idols, but that he had to rethink his position in view of the practical difficulties with which his Corinthian correspondents confronted him. This rethinking, according to Klauck, is visible in Letter B, which consists of 8:1-13; 9:19-23; 10:23–11:1.

sacrifice and was subsequently sold in the market (10:25) and/or served at an unbeliever's house (10:27-30).

There is still, to be sure, a tension between 8:4-13, which implies that idols have no real existence and therefore pose no threat, and 10:20, which asserts that pagans sacrifice to demons rather than to God.[60] An analysis of the rhetoric of this section of the letter, however, makes the transition from the one approach to the other seem less illogical. In chapter 8 Paul is leading up to the portrait of his own ministry in chapter 9, where he emphasizes his sacrifice of his own rights in the service of others, a pattern that Paul sees as a model for the church at large. In chapter 8, therefore, he emphasizes that even if one has a theoretical right to eat food that has been sacrificed to idols, one should relinquish that right in the interest of the weak brother. In chapter 10, however, the subject of idolatry that he has raised takes Paul back to biblical examples from the exodus period, and along with these Old Testament narratives comes the acute sense of idolatrous danger that Paul presumably imbibed with his mother's milk.

The more uncompromising parts of chapter 10 probably reveal Paul's reflexive feelings on the subject of idolatry, whereas elsewhere he tactically concedes more to the Corinthian point of view than he is really comfortable doing.[61] His attitude toward food sacrificed to idols is basically negative, but he tries out a more conciliatory argument in chapter 8 before pulling out the heavy artillery of scriptural condemnation in 10:1-22. This rhetorical variation is similar to that in 1 Corinthians 11:2-16, where Paul justifies his opposi-

---

60. C. Kavin Rowe, "New Testament Iconography? Situating Paul in the Absence of Material Evidence," in *Picturing the New Testament: Studies in Ancient Visual Images,* ed. Annette Weissenrieder et al. (Göttingen: Mohr Siebeck, 2005), p. 308 n. 81, attempts to defuse the tension by claiming that in 10:19b Paul is denying not that there is a spiritual reality behind the idol but that the material object itself is dangerous. But 10:19 (τί οὖν φημι; ὅτι εἰδωλόθυτόν τί ἐστιν ἢ ὅτι εἴδωλόν τί ἐστιν;) echoes 8:4 (Περὶ τῆς βρώσεως οὖν τῶν εἰδωλοθύτων, οἴδαμεν ὅτι οὐδὲν εἴδωλον ἐν κόσμῳ, καὶ ὅτι οὐδεὶς θεὸς εἰ μὴ εἷς). The implication of 10:19 that the εἴδωλον is nothing, therefore, is foreshadowed by Paul's agreement with the Corinthians in 8:4 that "there is no εἴδωλον in the world, and there is no God but one." Εἴδωλον in 8:4 cannot refer to the statue itself, which obviously *does* exist, but only to the putative spiritual reality behind it. Only in this way does the first part of the statement, that there is no εἴδωλον in the world, cohere with the second part, that there is only one God. On εἴδωλον as a term for the pagan gods behind their material representations, see section I above.

61. Gooch, *Dangerous Food,* p. 83. On "all of us possess knowledge" (8:1) and "no idol in the world really exists" (8:4) as Corinthian slogans, see Willis, *Idol Meat in Corinth,* pp. 67-71, 83-84.

tion to women praying bareheaded first by a biblical argument revolving around Genesis 2:22, then by a reference to Jewish traditions about lustful angels, and then by an argument from nature, before finally aborting the discussion with a curt appeal to prevailing practice in Christian communities. In 1 Corinthians 8–10 as in this later passage, Paul's vehemence and the twists and turns of the argument probably reveal that he himself is not completely easy with it; the sudden and somewhat contradictory changes in direction in 10:25-30 with regard to the word "conscience,"[62] for example, may suggest that his own conscience on the subject of idols is troubled.

This turmoil probably reflects a deep theological ambivalence. On the one hand, Paul wants to agree with his Corinthian interlocutors that idols have no real existence, since to say otherwise would be to acknowledge a rival to God about whom God and the believer need to feel concerned. On the other hand, simply to go along with the Corinthian claim that since idols do not really exist it is permissible to offer them worship is for Paul also a way of granting them undeserved recognition. Paul's dilemma is similar to that posed in *b. 'Abod. Zar.* 54b-55a, where rabbis respond to pagans who assert that God's "jealousy" of idols suggests that the latter exist. As Halbertal and Margalit comment on this passage: "It seems as though God has been placed in an untenable position: if he does not confront the idol this may be seen as a sign of his weakness, while if he is jealous of it this is seen as a sign of the idol's importance. Here the midrash grasps the internal contradiction within the feeling of jealousy itself."[63] Paul's shifting comments on idols in 1 Corinthians 8–10 seem to reveal a similar sort of theological "jealousy." On the one hand, he wants to agree with the Corinthians that the idols they are reverencing are nonentities, so the most that one should worry about is how such reverence looks in the eyes of outsiders. But on the other hand, the Corinthians' willingness to offer worship to other deities strikes him viscerally as a blow to the honor of God. In this sort of honor/shame scenario, the jealous God of the Old Testament suddenly pops out of the woodwork and demands a decisive choice:

---

62. 10:25: "Eat whatever is sold in the meat market without raising any question on the ground of conscience"; 10:27: "Eat whatever is set before you without raising any question on the ground of conscience"; 10:28: "Do not eat it, out of consideration for the one who informed you, and for the sake of conscience"; 10:29a: "I mean the other's conscience, not your own"; 10:29b: "Why should my liberty be subject to the judgment of someone else's conscience?" (NRSV).

63. Halbertal and Margalit, *Idolatry,* pp. 27-28.

What pagans sacrifice, they offer to demons and not to God. I do not want you to be partners with demons. You cannot drink the cup of the Lord and the cup of demons. You cannot partake of the table of the Lord and the table of demons. Shall we provoke the Lord to jealousy? (10:20-22 RSV)

There is a similar ambivalence in Luke's portrayal of Paul in Athens in Acts 17. On the one hand, Paul is revolted to see the city full of idols (17:16) and delivers a sermon in which he denounces the ignorance that supposes "that the deity is like gold, or silver, or stone, an image formed by human art and imagination" (17:29 NRSV alt.). On the other hand, he makes the inscription on one of those "idols" his point of departure for the positive aspect of the sermon, which implies that pagans are, through their worship of such images, actually searching for "the unknown god," whom Paul proceeds to unveil as the God of Israel, who has now raised Jesus from the dead (17:22-27). Paul's comment in 17:22 that the Athenians are δεισιδαιμονεστέρους (lit., "rather *daimonia*-fearing") perfectly captures the ambiguity of the speech. If δαιμόνια is taken in its usual Jewish and Christian sense, as a reference to spirits hostile to God, the adjective is negative (cf. the KJV translation "too superstitious"). But if it is taken in its classic Greco-Roman sense, as a reference to intermediate members of the divine hierarchy, as seems to be the case in Acts 17:18,[64] a positive nuance is possible (cf. the NRSV translation "extremely religious").

The Corinthians with whom Paul is corresponding, like the Athenians portrayed in the Areopagus speech, may have seen the δαιμόνια in this more positive sense, and in fact the δαιμόνια terminology in 1 Corinthians 10:20-22 may have originated with them.[65] The Corinthians may have agreed with

64. The Athenians here dub Paul "a proclaimer of ξένων δαιμονίων," which the NRSV translates as "foreign divinities." For the Athenians, then, Jesus and Resurrection (which they perhaps understand as a personification) are themselves δαιμόνια.

65. Paul never uses δαιμόνια elsewhere in his authentic correspondence, though it does appear in the Deutero-Pauline 1 Timothy (4:1). Paul speaks characteristically, rather, of ἀρχαὶ καὶ ἐξουσίαι = "principalities and powers" (Rom. 8:38; 1 Cor. 15:24; Col. 1:16; 2:10, 15; cf. Eph. 1:21; 3:10; 6:12; Tit. 3:1) or "the rulers of this age" (1 Cor. 2:6) when he wants to refer to demonic powers. Furthermore, the classic Hellenistic sense of "daimons" as intermediate members of the hierarchy of divine powers accords very well with the Corinthian theology echoed in 8:4-6. To be sure, the usual Greek term for the more positive association is δαίμων rather than the diminutive δαιμόνιον, but the latter does occur with a positive association in pagan and Jewish literature and the NT; see, e.g., Plato, *Symp.* 23 (202E), "Every δαιμόνιον is between a god and a mortal"; Josephus, *War* 1.69; and Acts 17:18 (see n. 64 above), which uses the plural (cf. BDAG 210 [1]).

Paul that taking part in pagan cults meant sacrificing to δαιμόνια, but they may have disputed the negative construction Paul puts on such worship; indeed, they may have interpreted it as an indirect way of worshiping God, the putative chairman of the divine board of which the δαιμόνια were subordinate members.[66] The jealousy that Paul posits between God and the demons would then reveal a needless touchiness: why worry about a being that has no independent existence and is really just a visible manifestation of the invisible God?

Paul and the Corinthians, then, seem to reach different conclusions based on their shared premise that God is one (8:6). For the Corinthians, this implies that pagan worship is not directed toward a different God but toward the same God in a different guise. For Paul in chapter 10, however, it implies that sacrificial service of entities other than the God of Israel, even if they are conceived as being part of the pantheon over which he presides, is worship not of God but of evil spirits, "demons" in the Jewish and Christian sense. Paul can agree, as he had in 8:4, that the idol is "nothing" (10:19), but this does not mean that it is innocuous.[67] And Paul would probably say that this is because "beings that by nature are not gods," even divine creations such as the beauties of nature or the sacred commandments of the Torah, transform themselves into instruments of bondage when they become objects of worship (see Gal. 4:8-10; Rom. 1:20-25). The world is God's world and the law is God's law, but neither the law nor the world *is* God, and those who reduce the dynamic fullness of the Godhead to the one or the other end up serving an inert image that cannot deliver the life it promises but instead robs both individual and community of integrity and freedom.

---

66. On this pyramid in Greco-Roman religion, see MacMullen, *Paganism in the Roman Empire*, 73-94. On the 1 Corinthians passage, see Johannes Woyke, *Götter, Götzen, Götterbilder: Aspekte einer paulinischen 'Theologie der Religionen,'* BZNW 132 (Berlin/New York: de Gruyter, 2005), p. 239. Cf. Halbertal and Margalit, *Idolatry*, p. 4, who say that one of the issues in disputes over idolatry is "whether worship must be exclusive to the figure at the head of the hierarchy" of divine powers.

67. See G. D. Fee, *The First Epistle to the Corinthians*, NICNT (Grand Rapids: Eerdmans, 1991), p. 471: "[A]n idol has no reality, in the sense that an idol does not in fact represent what might truly be called a 'god.' But what the Corinthians have failed to discern right along is that to say an idol is not a god does not mean that it does not represent supernatural powers." Cf. the famous section §50, "God and Nothingness," in Karl Barth, *Church Dogmatics* III/3, *The Doctrine of Creation* (Edinburgh: T. & T. Clark, 1960), pp. 289-368.

V. Christ Worship as Idolatry?

And what *is* the dynamic fullness of the Godhead, the antithesis to idolatry? To return to 1 Corinthians 8:4-6, Paul contrasts the many "gods" and many "lords" of paganism with the Christian confession that "for us there is one God, the Father, from whom are all things and for whom we exist, and one Lord, Jesus Christ, through whom are all things and through whom we exist" (NRSV). As opposed to pagan polytheism, then, Paul posits the one God of the Shema (Deut. 6:4) and classic Jewish belief. Yet this oneness is somehow compatible with the proclamation of Jesus as Lord, a synonym for God himself.[68]

Does that not mean, however, that Christians worship two Gods, the Father and Jesus, and thus violate the first commandment? And since, as noted at the beginning of this essay, the first commandment is inextricably intertwined with the second, does it not also imply that Christians themselves are idolaters — a charge that becomes common in medieval Jewish polemic against Christianity and is already implicit in some rabbinic traditions?[69]

Apparently, some Jews known to the authors of the New Testament did think that Christian reverence for Jesus as divine infringed the first commandment or the proclamation of God's oneness in the Shema (Deut. 6:4), which is closely related to the first commandment in the Old Testament and later Jewish and Christian traditions.[70] In the Gospel of John, for example, "the Jews" twice try to stone Jesus — the penalty for blasphemy (see Lev.

---

68. On κύριος as the translation for the Tetragrammaton in the Septuagint, see David B. Capes, *Old Testament Yahweh Texts in Paul's Christology*, WUNT 2.47 (Tübingen: Mohr Siebeck, 1992), pp. 37-43.

69. Whether or not Christianity is idolatry is a matter of controversy in medieval Judaism; see David Novak, *Jewish-Christian Dialogue: A Jewish Justification* (New York/Oxford: Oxford University Press, 1989), index s.v. "idolatry." Those who believe that it is base themselves partly on the church's use of images and partly on the perceived infringement of monotheism in the Trinity. The classic example of the latter concern is in Maimonides, *Mishneh Torah*, Avodah Zarah 1.3-4; for a qualified recent endorsement of Maimonides' position, see David Berger, "*Dabru Emet*: Some Reservations about a Jewish Statement on Christians and Christianity" (2002), http://www.bc.edu/research/cjl/meta-elements/sites/partners/ccjr/berger02.htm. For a rabbinic passage that links "two powers in heaven" heretics, who probably include Christians, with idolatry, see the discussion of *Sipre Zuta*, Shalaḥ 15:30 in A. F. Segal, *Two Powers in Heaven: Early Rabbinic Reports about Christianity and Gnosticism*, SJLA 25 (Leiden: Brill, 1977), pp. 89-97.

70. On the close connection between the Shema and the Decalogue, especially the first commandment, see Dale C. Allison Jr., *Resurrecting Jesus: The Earliest Christian Tradition and Its Interpreters* (London/New York: T. & T. Clark, 2005), pp. 152-60.

24:16) — for making himself, a mere man, equal to God (8:58-59; 10:31-33; cf. 5:18). In Mark 2:5-7, similarly, the scribes take offense at Jesus' pronouncement of forgiveness of sins to the paralytic, accusing him of blasphemy because no one "can forgive sins except One, that is, God" — a formulation that seems to be designed to recall the Shema.[71] Later in Mark, the high priest repeats the blasphemy charge because Jesus has prophesied for himself a position at God's right hand, thus implying his commensurateness with the deity (14:61-64).[72]

It seems likely, therefore, that Paul's juxtaposition of idol terminology with the "one God, one Lord" formula is not fortuitous but a deliberate recognition of the paradoxical and potentially scandalous nature of the Christian proclamation of Jesus' lordship. Paul would probably argue that Christians are not guilty of idolatry, because Jesus is not a divinity separate from the one God but the latter's cosmic agent in the creation and restoration of the world, like the Wisdom figure of the Old Testament or the Logos of Philo.[73] This solution to the "two powers in heaven" problem is similar to that in the Fourth Gospel, where Jesus reinterprets the Shema as being compatible with the coinherence of the Father and the Son, so that the two are "one" (John 10:30; 17:11, 22-23).[74]

Like Paul in 1 Corinthians 8, the conclusion of the First Epistle of John manages simultaneously, and with an apparently polemical intention, to proclaim the divinity of Jesus and to repudiate idolatry. Here, in the final verse of the letter, and in a way that does not at first seem to be anticipated by anything that has gone before, the author exhorts his readers: "Little chil-

---

71. See Joel Marcus, "Authority to Forgive Sins upon the Earth: The *Shema* in the Gospel of Mark," in *The Gospels and the Scriptures of Israel,* ed. C. A. Evans and W. Stegner, JSNTSup 104/SSEJC 3 (Sheffield: Sheffield Academic, 1994), pp. 196-211.

72. See Joel Marcus, "Mark 14:61: Are You the Messiah-Son-of-God?" *NovT* 31 (1989): 125-41.

73. On the influence of Wisdom and Logos theology on the NT, including Paul, see Larry W. Hurtado, *One God, One Lord: Early Christian Devotion and Ancient Jewish Monotheism* (Philadelphia/London: Fortress/SCM, 1988), pp. 42-48; Hurtado, *Lord Jesus Christ: Devotion to Jesus in Earliest Christianity* (Grand Rapids/Cambridge: Eerdmans, 2003), index s.v. "Logos" and "Wisdom"; Daniel Boyarin, *Border Lines: The Partition of Judaeo-Christianity,* Divinations (Philadelphia: University of Pennsylvania Press, 2004), pp. 89-147.

74. Cf. C. K. Barrett, "The Old Testament in the Fourth Gospel," *JTS* 48 (1947): 155-69. See also Mark 2:10, where Jesus' presumed infringement of the Shema is refuted by his pronouncement that "upon the earth the Son of Man has authority to forgive sins." God has the authority to forgive sins *in heaven,* but *upon the earth* it is the Son of Man, as God's designated agent, who can do so; cf. Marcus, "Authority to Forgive Sins."

dren, keep yourselves from idols" (1 John 5:21). The best clue to this cryptic exhortation seems to be the immediately preceding words, which refer to God's Son, Jesus Christ, as "the true God and eternal life." In the LXX, Hellenistic Jewish literature, and the New Testament, "the true God," on the one hand, and "idols" and related terms, on the other, are frequent antonyms.[75] With this background in mind, the author of 1 John seems to be asserting that Jesus is the true God, not an idol, and the verse may in part be meant to answer critics who claim that equation of Jesus with God is tantamount to idolatry.[76] Here, as in Paul's writings, the audacious assertion of the Godhead of Jesus and the simultaneous repudiation of idolatry have been anticipated by the strong linkage between Father and Son, who are so closely associated that to speak of the one is to speak of the other (cf. 1 John 2:22-24).

For 1 John as for Paul, worship of Jesus is not idolatry, because Jesus is "the true God and eternal life." These two terms are mutually illuminating. Jesus is not an idol, because he is not a static, frozen image of divinity, like the image worshiper's statue or even the iconoclast's Torah scroll; rather, he is a living, incarnate, ever-changing reality.[77] As Kavin Rowe has shown in an important essay, the Pauline literature seems to make this point explicit when it calls Jesus the εἰκών ("icon," "image") of the invisible God (Col. 1:15; cf. 2 Cor. 4:4), thus transferring to Christ a term and conceptuality that were ubiquitously used for pagan images (cf. Rom. 1:23).[78] As Rowe puts it, "The invisible God turns out to be visible precisely in his human image." And since Paul elsewhere uses εἰκών for the image of Christ and of God that is borne, at least *in nuce,* and as an eschatological pledge, by the believer (Rom. 8:29; 1 Cor. 11:7; 15:49; 2 Cor. 3:18), the implication would seem to be that Paul's addressees are to seek God's

75. See Griffith, *Keep Yourselves from Idols,* pp. 59-60, 80-81, citing 2 Chron. 15:3-16; Isa. 65:3-16; 3 Macc. 6:11-18; *Liv. Pro.* 21:8-11; *Jos. Asen.* 11:7-10; *Sib. Or.* 1:20-22; 3:43-47; Philo, *Legat.* 367; *Spec.* 1.332; *Prelim. Studies* 159-60; 1 Thess. 1:9.

76. Cf. Griffith, *Keep Yourselves from Idols,* p. 206, who claims that 1 John 5:21 is "an example of the reversal of Jewish polemic against Judaism" but does not, so far as I can see, link this reversal with Jewish charges that Jesus veneration is idolatry.

77. Cf. Dietrich Bonhoeffer, *Ethics* (New York: Macmillan, 1955), p. 85: "For indeed it is not written that God became an idea, a principle, a programme, a universally valid proposition or a law, but that God became man." It should be noted, however, that for many observant Jews, the Torah was and is not just "an idea, a principle, a programme, a universally valid proposition or a law" but a dynamic divine gift superbly adapted to the true good of humanity and capable of changing with the times. See Friedrich Avemarie, *Tora und Leben: Untersuchungen zur Heilsbedeutung der Tora in der frühen rabbinischen Literatur,* TSAJ 55 (Tübingen: Mohr Siebeck, 1996), passim.

78. Rowe, "New Testament Iconography," p. 302.

likeness not in the religious statuary that crowds their world but in the moveable icons that are their Christian brothers and sisters, "whom he . . . predestined to be conformed to the εἰκών of his Son" (Rom. 8:29).[79]

VI. Hermeneutical Problems

The foregoing survey poses two major hermeneutical problems.

The first is the question of scriptural consistency. Different New Testament figures seem to take up different attitudes toward pagan images. While Paul cannot seem to escape from the abhorrence of idolatry with which he grew up, Jesus himself, in the reply to the question about tribute, seems to take a *laissez-faire* attitude: the coin's assertion that Caesar is divine is simply ignored, and Caesar is treated as the secular reality that, Jesus implies, he ultimately is. Tribute can therefore be rendered unto Caesar, even at the price of momentarily overlooking his claim to be divine. This attitude forms a striking contrast, however, to that in the book of Revelation, which praises to the skies the martyrs who refuse to receive the sign of the Beast, without which they can neither buy nor sell, and are put to death for their refusal to acknowledge the Beast's idolatrous claims (13:11-18; 14:9). The sign, the number 666, is usually interpreted as a numerological code for "Nero Caesar" and a reference to the cult of Nero's successor, Domitian.[80] The martyrs of Revelation, then, like later Christians who refused to swear by the genius of the emperor,[81] but unlike the Jesus of the Gospels, withhold from the emperor a seemingly perfunctory act of allegiance, which in Revelation as in the Gospels is somehow connected with economic activity. As a result of this refusal, they lose their lives.

It is important, however, to be clear not only about the similarities but also about the differences between the two contexts in question. The emperor cult seems to have become more aggressive under Domitian, the probable emperor of Revelation, than it was under Augustus and Tiberius, the emperors in Jesus' time,[82] and Revelation seems to reflect a situation in

79. Cf. Rowe, "New Testament Iconography," p. 309.

80. See D. E. Aune, *Revelation*, 3 vols., WBC 52 (Nashville: Thomas Nelson, 1997-98), 2:760-80.

81. See, e.g., Pliny, *Ep.* 10.96; *Mart. Pol.* 8:3; 9:2; 10:1.

82. See Klauck, *Religious Context of Early Christianity*, pp. 309-10, and cf. Aune, *Revelation*, 2:780: "It is likely that the foundation of the provincial cult of Domitian at Ephesus late in the first century (involving the participation of the entire province of Asia) provided a cli-

which a public act of allegiance to the divine emperor is being demanded as a test of loyalty. The situation Jesus confronts lacks such a direct test; he is not being asked explicitly to swear by the genius of the emperor or to attest to the truth of the inscription on the coin that proclaims him a god but merely to relinquish the coin to the imperial tax collectors as a sign that he accepts Caesar's authority. Presumably, if he were asked to swear to Caesar's divinity, he would refuse to do so. Scripture, then, does not efface the difference between Revelation's fierce polemic against the Beast and the mild attitude of Jesus' saying about rendering unto Caesar, but it does help clarify the issue: to the extent that the ruling authority claims divine transcendence and demands worship, it must be strenuously resisted.

The second hermeneutical problem concerns the role of polemic. This is a more difficult question: to what extent is the biblical opposition to idolatry the reflection of an outmoded, dangerously exclusivist ideology? The Bible's polemic against idolatry does not seem at first to provide a promising model for interreligious dialogue. The attack on the pagan veneration of images, for example, like much of the Reformation's assault on Catholic "idolatry," carelessly or willfully misunderstands such veneration, which was not a substitute for the worship of the invisible God but a way of sacramentally getting in touch with divine powers that chose to make themselves visible and tangible at particular places on earth in order to lend a hand to struggling humanity.[83] Biblical interpreters who close their eyes to this more generous understanding of paganism run the risk of justifying Jules Isaac's term, "teaching of contempt."[84] Moreover, the biblical linkage of idolatry with fornication seems to express negativity not only about adherents of other religions but also about the human body and the created order that it represents, and to many modern readers may seem simply "over the top."

mate in which enormous pressure was placed on Christians to be loyal citizens and participate in the imperial cult."

83. On medieval understandings of icons, see Ernst Kitzinger, "The Cult of Images in the Age before Iconoclasm," *DOP* 8 (1954): 83-150; Michael Camille, *The Gothic Idol: Ideology and Image-Making in Medieval Art* (Cambridge: Cambridge University Press, 1989). On the iconoclasm of the Reformation, see Carlos M. N. Eire, *War Against the Idols: The Reformation of Worship from Erasmus to Calvin* (Cambridge: Cambridge University Press, 1986). For a comparison between the biblical and Reformation critiques of idolatry, see Halbertal and Margalit, *Idolatry,* pp. 40 and 259 n. 7.

84. Jules Isaac, *The Teaching of Contempt: Christian Roots of Anti-Semitism* (New York: Holt, Rinehart & Winston, 1964). Isaac uses this term with reference to Christian attitudes toward Judaism, but it could also be employed for Jewish and Christian attitudes toward the nonmonotheistic religions.

And yet Jewish and Christian polemic against idolatry is directed not only at outsiders but also at insiders, at members of "our" group who "set idols upon their hearts" (CD 20:9). And there is a recognition within the tradition that idolatry can assume forms that are not as obvious as genuflecting before a statue, forms that affect religious people as much as irreligious, such as lust for wealth, or even more, such as creating an idol out of one's own interpretation of the divine law. And even modern people who are not religious may acknowledge that the charm of bodies, the possibilities associated with wealth, and the capacity of the state to maintain public order, while good things in themselves, can get out of hand, threatening to twist existence into a frantic race to accumulate goods and power that do not ultimately satisfy but instead destroy human flourishing.

There are still times, then, when people of faith are called to stand up and say, "No!"[85] The Bible does not provide strict rules for determining when this should be. There are circumstances in which rendering unto Caesar, or Aphrodite, or the 401(k) may be the right and godly thing to do.[86] But there are also circumstances when an appropriate appreciation for the world's goods crosses the line to idolatry — and the Scriptures suggest that this happens with some frequency. The Bible does not provide an infallible template but parables and pointers. Discernment of the line between prudent use of the world in a spirit of Christian liberty, on the one hand, and idolatrous control by it, on the other, is the province of hard-nosed exegesis, open-eyed, prayerful theological reflection, and the mutual enlightenment and correction of the community of faith.

---

85. The second anathema of the Barmen Declaration by the Synod of the Confessing Church of Germany in May 1934 is a famous example of rejection of the deification of the state; for the text of Barmen, see http://www.ucc.org/faith/barmen.htm. Cf. the discussion of Barmen in Christopher Morse, *Not Every Spirit: A Dogmatics of Christian Disbelief* (Valley Forge: Trinity Press International, 1994), pp. 34-37, a book organized around the things that Christians down through the centuries have *refused* to believe.

86. The Song of Solomon and Prov. 5:15-19 are examples of biblical passages that express a positive attitude toward sexuality, and the OT is full of promises of abundance to those who walk in God's ways (e.g., Deut. 28:1-14; Isa. 30:23-26; cf. 2 Cor. 9:6-10). These are aspects of the "worldliness" of the OT that attracted Dietrich Bonhoeffer; see Bonhoeffer, *Letters and Papers from Prison* (New York: Touchstone, 1997 [1953]), index s.v. "world." For Bonhoeffer, to be sure, these scriptural promises always exist in a dialectical tension with the call of Christ to drop everything and follow him.

Healing in the Wings of His Garment:
The Synoptics and Malachi 4:2

Dale C. Allison Jr.

In the second edition of his book *The Faith of Jesus Christ,* Richard Hays has observed that the first edition's "account of the history of research focuses almost exclusively on twentieth-century studies." He acknowledges that were he to rewrite the book today, he would put more emphasis upon the history of interpretation, for "one of the important growing edges" of his current work "is the recognition that we have a great deal to learn by broadening the conversation to include the questions and insights of our predecessors who lived before the so-called 'Enlightenment.'"[1]

The sentiment deserves our wholehearted endorsement. The history of interpretation is invaluable for assessing our interpretive proposals — especially our novel proposals. I have indeed come to the view that if I construe a particular text in an essentially unprecedented way, so that I am a lone voice in exegetical history, then one of two things must be true: either the passage communicates its meaning so poorly that seemingly no one, over the course of two thousand years of intense reading and reflection, has seen the point before, until I came along, or I am wrong. In most instances, surely the latter is the case.

The history of interpretation does not just effectively curb our appetite for novel readings. It additionally serves us well because the guild sometimes suffers from what I have called "exegetical amnesia" (a phrase that

---

1. Richard B. Hays, *The Faith of Jesus Christ: The Narrative Substructure of Galatians 3:1–4:11,* 2nd ed. (Grand Rapids: Eerdmans, 2002), pp. xlvii-xlviii.

Richard, I am happy to note, has himself used).[2] Too many of us today have a naïve faith that anything of real importance said once will be said again and so not forgotten. We presume that all the good interpretations and hypotheses have been passed down from book to book and from generation to generation and so on to us. But it is not so. Sometimes plausible or interesting exegetical options drop out of the commentaries and become undeservedly forgotten. I have offered several examples of this phenomenon in previous publications,[3] and I should like to honor Richard by calling attention to yet another, in this case an ancient intertextual reading of a remarkable Synoptic phrase.

*   *   *

"The fringe of his garment" (τὸ κράσπεδον τοῦ ἱματίου αὐτοῦ) occurs only once in Mark, in 6:56, where it belongs to the third and climatic verse in a series:

- First, in Mark 3:10, sick people touch Jesus and are healed.
- Second, in 5:27, a woman touches his garment (τοῦ ἱματίου αὐτοῦ; vv. 28, 30: τῶν ἱματίων) and is healed.
- Third, in 6:56, people touch only the fringe of Jesus' garment (v. 56: τοῦ κρασπέδου τοῦ ἱματίου αὐτοῦ) and are nonetheless healed.[4]

This textual crescendo is unique to Mark. Luke has no parallel to Mark 6:53-56 and so has no comparable triad. Only twice does the Third Gospel tell of people touching Jesus for healing. The first time is in 6:19, which leaves Jesus' clothing out of account (cf. Mark 3:10). The second time is in 8:44, where the woman with a chronic hemorrhage touches Jesus' garment. This verse recalls Mark 6:56 and presumably depends partly upon it: "She came up behind him and touched the fringe of his garment" (τοῦ κρασπέδου τοῦ ἱματίου αὐτοῦ).

Matthew likewise fails to reproduce Mark's neat triadic scheme and is

---

2. See Dale C. Allison Jr., "Exegetical Amnesia in James," *ETL* 86 (2000): 162-66; "Forgetting the Past," *DRev* 120/421 (2002): 255-70; Hays, *Faith of Jesus Christ*, p. lii.

3. In addition to the articles in n. 2, see the first six chapters of Dale C. Allison Jr., *Studies in Matthew: Interpretation Past and Present* (Grand Rapids: Baker Academic, 2005).

4. See further J. T. Cummings, "The Tassel of His Cloak: Mark, Luke, Matthew — and Zechariah," in *Studia Biblica 1978, II: Papers on the Gospels*, ed. E. A. Livingstone (Sheffield: JSOT Press, 1980), pp. 47-61.

further like Luke in that he narrates only two occasions when people touch Jesus for healing. In both instances, individuals touch τὸ κράσπεδον of Jesus' garment:

- Matthew 9:20-21: ἥψατο τοῦ κρασπέδου τοῦ ἱματίου αὐτοῦ· ἔλεγεν γὰρ ἐν ἑαυτῇ· ἐὰν μόνον ἅψωμαι τοῦ ἱματίου αὐτοῦ σωθήσομαι (cf. Mark 5:27-28)
- Matthew 14:36: παρεκάλουν αὐτὸν ἵνα μόνον ἅψωνται τοῦ κρασπέδου τοῦ ἱματίου αὐτοῦ· καὶ ὅσοι ἥψαντο διεσώθησαν (cf. Mark 6:56).

It is not the concern of this essay to sort through the source-critical issues that arise from Mark 3:10; 5:27; and 6:56, and their Synoptic relatives.[5] I am interested only in investigating the possible meanings of the phrase τὸ κράσπεδον τοῦ ἱματίου αὐτοῦ. How are we to explain it? Why do the sick touch specifically Jesus' κράσπεδον?

The canonical evangelists have regrettably left us no editorial commentary, so we are here forced to play detective; and in a case such as this, it will be helpful to review, if only briefly, what our exegetical predecessors have made of the relevant verses:

(1) According to some commentators, those who touched nothing save the edge of Jesus' garment did so out of humility and respect. People who sought healing did not wish their sinful hands to defile his holy person. This was the interpretation of Remigius of Auxerre. Commenting on Matthew 9:20 and the woman with an issue of blood, Remigius wrote that her "humility must be praised, that she came not before his face, but from behind, and judged herself unworthy to touch the Lord's feet; indeed, she touched not his whole garment but only its hem."[6] Sometimes this woman's hesitance to touch Jesus is explicitly related to her uncleanness in the eyes of Torah (cf. Lev. 15:25-31). According to Chrysostom, the woman tried to touch Jesus surreptitiously because she knew herself to be ceremoniously impure and was ashamed.[7] Theophylact affirms that if the

5. I have attempted this briefly elsewhere: W. D. Davies and Dale C. Allison Jr., *A Critical and Exegetical Commentary on the Gospel according to Saint Matthew*, 3 vols., ICC (Edinburgh: T. & T. Clark, 1988, 1991, 1998), 2:129.

6. See Aquinas's *Catena* on Matthew ad loc. (trans. Newman, p. 348). Cf. Johann Albrecht Bengel, *Gnomon Novi Testamenti*, 2 vols. (Tübingen: Ludov. Frid. Fues, 1850), 1:74.

7. Chrysostom, *Hom. Matt.* 31.2 (PG 57:371). Cf. Origen, *Hom. Lev.* 4.8 (ed. Borret, SC 286-87, pp. 188, 190); Robert H. Gundry, *Matthew: A Commentary on His Handbook for a Mixed Church under Persecution*, 2nd ed. (Grand Rapids: Eerdmans, 1994), p. 173.

woman had openly come forward, law-observing Jews would have stopped her.[8]

(2) Other interpreters have surmised that Mark 6:56 and the similar verses where healing comes through the very edges of Jesus' garment serve to magnify his healing prowess. Does not the numinous potency of even the periphery of his clothing testify to his unprecedented powers? "What mighty influence must the grace and Spirit of Christ have in the soul, when even the border or hem of his garment produced such wonders in the bodies of those who touched!"[9] Jesus' healing virtue was so great that it "flowed from him to every part of his garment."[10] As Hilary of Poitiers wrote: "The power residing in his body added a health-giving quality to mortal things, and a divine efficacy went even unto the fringes of his garments. God was not divisible and able to be contained, as if he could be shut up in a body."[11]

(3) The Synoptic testimony that Jesus had tassels on his garment has become the occasion, above all in modern times, to remark that he must have been "a pious Jew."[12] He obediently displayed the tassels prescribed by Num-

---

8. Theophylact, *Comm. Matt.* ad loc. (PG 123:229D). So too Origen, *Comm. Matt.* frg. 182 (ed. Benz and Klostermann, GCS 41, p. 87); Cyril of Alexandria, *Comm. Luke* 45 (ed. Chabot, CSCO Scriptores Syri 4/1, p. 136). For questions regarding the woman's illness and its relationship to Levitical legislation — on both of which the Synoptic texts, as opposed to the commentators, are wholly silent — see Amy-Jill Levine, "Discharging Responsibility: Matthean Jesus, Biblical Law, and Hemorrhaging Woman," in *Treasures Old and New: Contributions to Matthean Studies,* ed. David R. Bauer and Mark Allan Powell (Atlanta: Scholars Press, 1996), pp. 379-97; and for criticism of Levine, note Craig S. Keener, *A Commentary on the Gospel of Matthew* (Grand Rapids/Cambridge, UK: Eerdmans, 1999), pp. 302-3, nn. 102-5. The story of the hemorrhaging woman eventually played a role in the ecclesiastical discussion of whether menstruating women should approach the Eucharist. Dionysius of Alexandria, *Ep. Basilides* β (ed. Feltoe, pp. 102-3) said that they should not, and this opinion eventually became the official ruling in both East and West. Contrast the use of our story in *Didasc.* 6.22 (ed. Funk, pp. 376-78) and Gregory the Great *apud* Bede, *H.E.* 1.27.8 (ed. Plummer, pp. 55-56).

9. Adam Clarke, *The Holy Bible, Containing the Old and New Testaments: The New Testament,* vol. 1, *Matthew to Romans* (London: Thomas Tegg & Son, 1836), p. 169. Cf. Origen, *Hom. Jer.* 17.5 (ed. Husson and Nautin, SC 238, p. 172).

10. Matthew Poole, *Annotations on the Holy Bible,* 3 vols. (London: Henry G. Bohn, 1846), 3:69.

11. Hilary of Poitiers, *Comm. Matt.* 9.7 (ed. Doignon, SC 254, p. 210).

12. So Ulrich Luz, *Matthew 8–20: A Commentary,* Hermeneia (Minneapolis: Fortress, 2001), p. 42. Cf. François Bovon, *Luke 1: A Commentary on the Gospel of Luke 1:1–9:50,* Hermeneia (Minneapolis: Fortress, 2002), p. 338. But this is not just an observation of modern exegetes; note already Remigius *apud* Aquinas, *Catena,* ad Matt. 9:20 (trans. Newman, p. 348).

bers 15:38-40 and Deuteronomy 22:12, so "in dress Jesus was not noncon-formist."[13] Perhaps this partly explains why some witnesses to the text of Luke 8:44 lack τοῦ κρασπέδου: there were those who wished to avoid an un-wanted inference about Jesus' faithful Jewish observance.[14]

(4) Ronald A. Brauner and Manfred Hutter have urged that grabbing the hem of a robe should be understood as an act of entreaty. In addition to two Akkadian texts, they cite 1 Samuel 15:27 ("As Samuel turned to go away, Saul laid hold upon the skirt of his robe, and it tore," RSV) and Zechariah 8:23 (see below), as well as the relevant gospel texts.[15] To these one may add *b. Ta'an.* 23b ("When the world needed rain, the rabbis would send the school children to him [Hanan ha-Nebha] and they would take hold of the hem of his garment [בשיפולי גלימיה] and say to him, Father, Father, give us rain") and perhaps *Ahikar* 77 (ed. Lindenberger, p. 174: "If a wicked person grasps the fringe of your garment . . .").[16]

(5) Jesus seems, in the Synoptic texts under review, to be the uncon-scious, involuntary source of a supernatural efflux, the carrier of a healing current that can, without his consent, flow via contact into ailing others.[17] This peculiar circumstance, in which the miracle seems to come automati-cally by nature and not by volition, has reminded many of Acts 19:12, where handkerchiefs or aprons, having once been in contact with Paul, heal the in-firm, a tale that has left many theologians feeling a bit uncomfortable. Begin-ning with Origen, many Christians have felt a similar discomfort when read-ing Mark 6:56 and its relatives, and they have been anxious to assure us that the healings Jesus worked had nothing to do with "magic."[18] Donald Hagner represents this apologetic tendency: the story of the woman with an issue of blood being healed "should not be thought of as quasi-magical. If healing

13. Alexander Balmain Bruce, "The Synoptic Gospels," in *The Expositor's Greek Testa-ment,* vol. 1 (New York: George H. Doran, n.d.), p. 154. Cf. Joseph Klausner, *Jesus: His Life, Times, and Teaching* (New York: Macmillan, 1925), p. 364.

14. D a d ff² l r¹ omit; so too Marcion *apud* Epiphanius, *Haer.* 42.11.6, 17 (ed. Holl, GCS, pp. 109, 130); cf. Tertullian, *Marc.* 4.20.8-13 (ed. Evans, OECT, pp. 366-70).

15. Ronald A. Brauner, "'To Grasp the Hem' and 1 Sam 15:27," *JANESCU* 6 (1974): 35-38; Manfred Hutter, "Ein altorientalischer Bittgestus," *ZNW* 75 (1984): 133-35. See also Francesco Vattioni, "Et tetigit fimbriam vestimenti eius (Mt. 9,20)," *Aug* 5 (1965): 533-38.

16. For Babylonian texts in which one seizes the garment of a god for the purpose of re-ceiving a blessing, see Ferris J. Stephens, "The Ancient Significance of ṢÎṢÎTH," *JBL* 50 (1931): 59-70.

17. See especially Friedrich Preisigke, *Die Gotteskraft der frühchristlichen Zeit,* PH 6 (Berlin/Leipzig: de Gruyter, 1922), pp. 1-5 (200-204).

18. Origen, *Comm. Matt.* frgs. 181-82 (ed. Benz and Klostermann, GCS 41, p. 87).

power could be experienced by touching a special person directly (e.g., Mark 3:10; Luke 6:19), then it could also extend to touching what had touched that person. If there is a slight hint of magic in this, the woman's strategy is at least commendable as a sign of deep faith in the power of Jesus."[19]

(6) In his commentary on Matthew 9:20, Joachim Gnilka cites as a parallel the eschatological prophecy of Zechariah 8:23: "In those days ten men from the nations of every tongue will take hold of the robe of a Jew, saying, 'Let us go with you, for we have heard that God is with you.'"[20] Although Gnilka does not claim that Matthew understood Jesus' ministry of healing to be a fulfillment of this prophetic oracle, which the evangelist nowhere cites, J. T. Cummings has made just this claim: the First Evangelist "perceived in the touching of the tassel of Jesus' cloak an allusion to the prophecy of Zech 8:23."[21] Long before Cummings, Jerome and Rupert of Deutz registered the same conviction.[22]

(7) Exegetical history offers several allegorical interpretations of our Synoptic phrase. Jerome identifies the hem of Jesus' garment with the least of Jesus' commandments and then cites Matthew 5:19, where those who fail to observe "the least of these commandments" will be "called least in the kingdom of heaven."[23] Augustine, asserting that the hem is the last and least of a garment, equates his Lord's hem with the Apostle Paul and then exhorts believers to imitate the first Gentile Christians who touched Paul and so became saved.[24] Chrysostom, following Origen, encourages hearers with the claim that they can touch more than the hem of Jesus' garment because they can touch and eat and be filled with his whole body, as that

---

19. Donald A. Hagner, *Matthew 1–13*, WBC 33A (Waco: Word, 1993), p. 249. Cf. Frederic Louis Godet, *A Commentary on the Gospel of St. Luke*, 2 vols. (Edinburgh: T. & T. Clark, n.d.), 1:391; Alexander Sand, *Das Evangelium nach Matthäus*, RNT (Regensburg: Friedrich Pustet, 1986), p. 201, and many others. Some, such as John Calvin, *Commentary on a Harmony of the Evangelists, Matthew, Mark, and Luke*, vol. 1 (Grand Rapids: Eerdmans, 1972), p. 207, have criticized the woman for her superstitious behavior. Others, such as Cornelius à Lapide, *The Great Commentary of Cornelius à Lapide*, 2nd ed., 6 vols. (London: John Hodges, 1874-87), 3:392-93, have defended her actions.

20. Joachim Gnilka, *Das Matthäusevangelium 1. Teil: Kommentar zu kap. 1,1-13,58*, HTKNT 1/1 (Freiburg/Basil/Vienna: Herder, 1986), 1:341.

21. Cummings, "Tassel," pp. 51-52.

22. Jerome, *Comm. Jonah* ad 4:10-11 (ed. Antin, SC 43, pp. 117-18); Rupert of Deutz, *Comm. Matt.* ad loc. (PL 168:1481D); cf. Albertus Magnus, *Super Mt. cap. I-XIV* ad loc. (ed. B. Schmidt, *Opera Omnia* 21/1, p. 436).

23. Jerome, *Comm. Matt.* 2.14.290 (ed. Bonnard, SC 242, p. 318).

24. Augustine, *Serm.* 63A.3 (trans. Hill, p. 178).

body is present now in the Eucharist.[25] The seventh-century commentary wrongly assigned to Jerome — *Expositio Evangelii secundum Marcum* (ed. Cahill, CCSL 82) — conflates Matthew 9:20 with Mark 5:27 and likens touching Jesus' fringe to "the cymbals and pomegranate-shaped decorations which hung from the hem of the high priest's tunic. A cymbal stands for confession and a pomegranate for unity."[26] Theophylact, in his remarks on Matthew 14:36, equates the border of Jesus' garment with the conclusion of the Messiah's earthly sojourn, the practical application being that Christians need to believe especially in the salvific events recorded in the passion narratives.[27]

I shall refrain, in the present context, from evaluating the exegetical history just introduced. My judgment, for what it is worth, is that something is perhaps to be said for most of the options, and more than one might be true at the same time.[28] My chief purpose herein, however, is to call attention to yet another exegetical tradition that has, for no good reason known to me, failed to find a home in the higher-critical commentaries of the last one hundred and fifty years.

I begin by citing the so-called *Testimony Book* falsely attributed to Epiphanius, a Greek work dated by its recent editor, Robert V. Hotchkiss, to the fourth century.[29] Section 7:30 of this collection of scriptural *testimonia* contains these words: "That the fringe (κράσπεδον) of his [Jesus'] garment would heal — Malachi says: 'to those who fear his name, the sun of righteousness rises having healing in his wings (πτέρυξιν)'" (Mal. 4:2).[30] What are we to make of this? Why is "healing in his wings" associated not with Jesus' therapeutic ministry in general but with people touching the κράσπεδον of his garment in particular?

The first relevant observation is that early Christian readers knew well the closing section of Malachi and commonly identified "the sun of righ-

25. Chrysostom, *Hom. Matt.* 50.3 (PG 57:507). For Origen, see *Catenae in Evangelia S. Matthaei et S. Marci ad Fidem Codd. Mss.*, ed. J. A. Cramer (Hildesheim: Georg Olms, 1967 [1842]), p. 119.

26. Translation from Michael Cahill, *The First Commentary on Mark: An Annotated Translation* (New York/Oxford: Oxford University Press, 1998), p. 57.

27. Theophylact, *Comm. Matt.* ad loc. (PG 123:304C).

28. I do, however, wonder how grabbing the edge of Jesus' garment can be a gesture of entreaty. The woman is plainly trying not to be noticed.

29. *A Pseudo-Epiphanius Testimony Book,* ed. and trans. Robert V. Hotchkiss, TT 4, ECLS 1 (Missoula, Mont.: SBL, 1974), p. 5.

30. Pseudo-Epiphanius, *Test.* 7:30 (ed. Hotchkiss, p. 38).

teousness" there foretold with their Savior, Jesus.[31] But there is almost certainly much more going on in Pseudo-Epiphanius. Matthew 9:20; 14:36; Mark 6:56; and Luke 8:44 recount that people touched precisely Jesus' κράσπεδον. As most exegetes now recognize, κράσπεδον probably refers in these places precisely to one of the decorative fringes or tassels that, by edict of the Torah, Jews attached to the four corners of the rectangular outer cloaks they typically wore (Num. 15:37-41; Deut. 22:12).[32] This is the meaning that the word has in Matthew 23:5 ("they make their phylacteries broad and their fringes long"), and of the five LXX occurrences of κράσπεδον, fully four appear in the pentateuchal legislation on fringes:

- Numbers 15:38: "Let them make tassels (κράσπεδα; MT: צִיצִת) for themselves upon the borders (πτερύγια; MT: כַּנְפֵי) of their garments (ἱματίων; MT: בִגְדֵיהֶם) throughout their generations."
- Numbers 15:38: "You will put a lace of blue upon the fringes (τὰ κράσπεδα; MT: צִיצִת) of the borders (πτερυγίων; MT: הַכָּנָף)."
- Numbers 15:39: "And it [the lace of blue] will be upon your fringes (τοῖς κρασπέδοις; MT: צִיצִת) and you will look upon them and you will remember all the commandments of the Lord to do them."
- Deuteronomy 22:12: "You will make fringes (κρασπέδων; MT: כְּנָפוֹת) on the four corners of your garments."[33]

31. For Jesus as Malachi's "sun of righteousness," see Melito of Sardis, *Bapt.* frg. VIIIB (ed. Perler, SC 123, p. 232); Origen, *Cels.* 6.79 (ed. Marcovich, p. 456); Eusebius, *Dem. ev.* 5.29 (ed. Heikel, GCS 23, p. 248); idem, *Ecl. proph.* (ed. Gaisford, p. 134); Ambrose, *Hex.* 4.1.2 (ed. Schenkl, CSEL 32.1, p. 111); Cyril of Alexandria, *XII Proph.* ad loc. (ed. Pusey, 2:621-22); Theodoret of Cyrus, *Eran. Dial.* 2 (ed. Ettlinger, p. 151), etc. The identification is still popularly known from the third stanza of the Christmas carol "Hark! The Herald Angels Sing" ("Hail the Sun of Righteousness! Light and life to all He brings, Ris'n with healing in His wings"), words by Charles Wesley (1739). Theodore of Mopsuestia, *Comm. XII proph.* ad loc. (PG 66:629C), in not applying Mal. 4:2 directly to Jesus, is atypical of Christian exegesis. For other uses of Malachi 3–4 in early Christian writings, see Matt. 11:3, 10 (cf. Mal. 3:1); 17:10-11 (cf. Mal. 4:5); Mark 1:2 (cf. Mal. 3:1); 9:11-12 (cf. Mal. 4:5); Luke 1:17 (cf. Mal. 4:5-6); *1 Clem.* 23:5 (cf. Mal. 3:1); *2 Clem.* 16:3 (cf. Mal. 4:1); *Ep. Diog.* 7:6 (cf. Mal. 3:2); *Liv. Proph. Mal.*, Dorothei rec. (ed. Schermann, p. 37), etc. If *T. Zeb.* 9:8 is not Christian, it attests to a messianic interpretation of Mal. 4:2 within Judaism, something otherwise hard to document. In its present context, however, it ties Mal. 4:2 to Jesus. Rabbinic literature gives Mal. 4:1-4 an eschatological but not a messianic sense.

32. See Edgar Haulotte, *Symbolique du vêtement selon la Bible* (Paris: Aubier, 1966), p. 65. For a helpful collection of rabbinic materials, see SB 4/1:277-92.

33. The one other use of κράσπεδον is in Zech. 8:23: "ten men from the nations of every tongue will take hold of the כְּנַף of a Jew."

DALE C. ALLISON JR.

Targum Onqelos, moreover, uses the loanword כרוספדין (=κράσπεδον) to render ציצת in Numbers 15:38 and Deuteronomy 22:12. One understands why the Curetonian Syriac for Matthew 14:36 translates the Greek κράσπεδον with תכלתא, a word that means the purple-blue thread used for tassels,[34] and why Shem Tob's Hebrew version of Matthew 9:20 uses ציצית.[35]

The importance of all these lexical facts for our purposes is this: according to Numbers 15:38, the ציצית are attached to the כנפים/ות, and, in the dictionaries, the first meaning of כנף is "wing" (cf. Exod. 19:4; 1 Kings 6:24; Ezek. 17:23; Mal. 4:2, etc.). Furthermore, Deuteronomy 22:12 MT uses כנף as though it were a synonym for ציצת. Jews, then, could think of the edges of their garments as being like the feathery edges of wings and speak of them accordingly (cf. 1 Sam. 15:27; 24:5-6; Zech. 8:23). Numbers 15:38 LXX naturally enough translates כנפ(י) with πτερύγια/ων, πτέρυξ being the standard Greek word for "wing."

With all of this in mind, we may return to the *Testimony Book* of Pseudo-Epiphanius. We are now in a position to understand why it connects Malachi's prophecy about "wings" of "healing" with people touching Jesus' tassels: those tassels were understood to be his "wings." "The sun of righteousness" (= Jesus) literally had healing "in his wings," that is, in his hanging fringes.

This explication of Pseudo-Epiphanius gains confirmation from a passage in Photius, the ninth-century lexicographer. In his *Bibliotheca*, we find the following: "'For,' it says, 'the sun of righteousness will arise upon you who fear my name, and healing will be in his wings.' The sun of righteousness is the Lord of good things, and the wings (πτέρυγας) are the tassels (κράσπεδα) of his garment."[36] This is exactly the equation that explains Pseudo-Epiphanius's proof-texting five centuries earlier.

That we are not dealing here with a striking coincidence between Pseudo-Epiphanius and Photius but rather with an interpretive tradition spanning several centuries is put beyond all doubt by a passage (of uncertain date and provenance) in Pseudo-Chrysostom, *De turture, seu de ecclesia sermo*: "Concerning the sun of righteousness, Isaiah [*sic*] cries out saying: In

---

34. The Syriac versions of Matt. 9:20; 14:36; Mark 6:56; and Luke 8:44 otherwise use ܓܢܒ or ܩܪܢܐ (= "corner") for κράσπεδον.

35. See George Howard, *Hebrew Gospel of Matthew* (Macon, Ga.: Mercer University Press, 1995), p. 39 (v.l. ציצת). In 14:36, Shem Tob uses כנף (Howard, p. 73). Cf. also perhaps the plural in some Sahidic mss. of Luke 8:44: this corresponds to the plural ציצית.

36. Photius, *Bib.* cod. 271 (ed. Bekker, p. 505b.3).

those days the sun of righteousness will rise, and healing will be in his wings (πτέρυξιν). For when Christ the sun of righteousness came, the woman with a flow of blood touched the wing (πτερυγίου) of his garment and the fountain of blood was dried up" (PG 55:600). Here πτέρυξ = "wing" has actually displaced the κράσπεδον of Matthew 9:20 = Luke 8:44 in order to make the link between the Synoptic event and Malachi's prophetic oracle all the plainer.

I have found yet a fourth old Greek text that finds in the healing properties of Jesus' tassels a fulfillment of Malachi 4:2 — a sermon on Mary, of uncertain date, attributed to Hesychius of Jerusalem.[37] Moreover, Ephraem the Syrian, although he fails explicitly to equate Jesus' tassels with the wings of Malachi, does, in his commentary on the *Diatessaron*, think of Malachi 4:2 as being fulfilled in Jesus' healing ministry.[38] Other commentators have done the same since.[39]

The secondary sources so far cited are all Greek, and I have not yet found the proposed exegetical link in any Latin writers, ancient or medieval. The intertextual reading is not, however, confined to old Greek texts. The following words are from Matthew Poole's seventeenth-century commentary on Malachi: "'Arise with healing in his wings.' . . . It may be (as some have observed from the word) an intimation of the healing virtue that from Christ went forth to such as in faith touched the hem of his garment, Matt. ix. 20, 21, and is as effectual for the healing of soul maladies and infirmities as of bodily diseases."[40]

One wishes that Poole had been more specific. His "some" leaves one frustrated. Yet at least one of his sources was certainly Hugo Grotius (1583-1645), with whose exegetical writings he was familiar.[41] Grotius, in his commentary on Matthew, asserts that ἥψατο τοῦ κρασπέδου τοῦ ἱματίου αὐτοῦ alludes to Malachi 4:2 (מרפא בכנפיה), and he observes not only that Deuteronomy 22:12 LXX selects κρασπέδων as the equivalent of כנפות but fur-

37. *Hom. I de sancta Maria deipara* 7 (ed. Aubineau, p. 202): "Malachi [prophesied]: 'The sun of righteousness will rise upon you who fear my name, and healing will be in his wings.' And [this concerns] the matter of the woman with an issue, who was healed after many years . . . who received healing by fastening on to the κρασπέδου."

38. Ephraem, *Comm. Diat.* 6.21b.

39. See, e.g., John Gill, *Gill's Commentary*, 6 vols. (Grand Rapids: Baker, 1980), 4:893.

40. Poole, *Annotations*, 2:1029.

41. Grotius is frequently quoted in Poole's *Synopsis criticorum aliorumque S. Scripturae interpretum*, 5 vols. (London: Typis J. Flesher & T. Roycroft, prostat Cornelium Bee, 1669-76).

ther that the Syriac for Matthew 14:36 translates κρασπέδου with כנפא.[42] In his *Synopsis criticorum,* Poole reproduces Grotius's comment.[43]

To what predecessor or predecessors Grotius himself was indebted for connecting Malachi 4:2 and Jesus' κράσπεδον we do not know — Photius is a possibility — just as we do not know whether Poole's words "some have observed" really tell us that he knew more than one commentary that associated Malachi 4:2 with Jesus' clothing. "Some" may instead be imprecise rhetoric; perhaps Poole's sole source was Grotius. Whatever the case, Grotius and Poole were not alone. A few other post-Reformation writers were familiar with the interpretation we are considering. Matthew Henry (1662-1714), in expounding Malachi 4:2, made this comment: "He shall arise 'with healing in his skirts'; so some read it, and they apply it to the story of the woman's touching 'the hem of the garment,' and being thereby 'made whole,' and his finding that 'virtue went out of him,' Mark v.28-30."[44] As Henry otherwise knew and often used Poole's magnificent commentary, it is quite possible that his imprecise "some" has simply been lifted from his predecessor. This is all the more plausible in that Henry, like Poole, illustrates the conduction of healing powers through Jesus' garment by recalling the precious oil that ran down the beard of Aaron onto his robes (Ps. 133:2).[45]

Henry was, in any case, not the last of the commentators to associate Jesus' healing tassels with Malachi 4:2. According to H. Elsley (1745-1833), the κράσπεδον of Matthew 9:20 is the "fringe peculiarly worn by the Jews, as [in] Deut. xxii. 12 where it appears in the LXX for כנפות. And this Hebrew word is also in Malach. iv. 2 to which passage this may refer."[46] Similar words, this time occasioned not by Matthew 9:20 but by Matthew 14:36, appear in the work of Christopher Wordsworth (1807-85): "Observe Christ's miraculous power, exerted here and on other occasions (ix. 20) by 'the skirts of his clothing' (Ps. cxxxiii. 2), in connexion with the prophecy (Malachi iv. 2), which

42. Hugo Grotius, *Opera omnia theologica,* vol. 2, pt. 1 (Amsterdam: Joannis Blaev, 1679), p. 103.

43. Poole, *Synopsis,* 4:274.

44. Matthew Henry, *Commentary on the Whole Bible,* vol. 4, *Jeremiah to Malachi* (New York: Revell, n.d.), ad loc.

45. But perhaps not too much weight should be put upon this last coincidence, because patristic and medieval commentaries also know this analogy; see, e.g., Albertus Magnus, *Enarrationes in Primam Partem Evang. Lucae (I-IX)* ad Luke 8:44 (ed. Borgnet, Opera Omnia 22, p. 583).

46. H. Elsley, *Annotations on the Four Gospels and the Acts of the Apostles* (Oxford: J. Vincent, 1844), p. 124.

speaks of 'healing in His wings'; the word 'wings' being used by the Hebrews to describe the 'fringes' of the garments."[47]

That, however, to judge from my researches, is the end of the line for the commentaries. I have not run across what we find in Grotius, Poole, Henry, Elsley, and Wordsworth in more recent exegetical work. To the extent of my knowledge, their interpretation has, in recent times, fallen completely out of favor, or rather seems to have dissipated altogether. The guild has forgotten it.

There is, however, one place where the construal of Malachi 4:2 known to Pseudo-Epiphanius and others after him lives on among us: it is in fact alive and well on the Internet. A good number of sites promote the claim that when people were healed by grabbing onto the tassels of Jesus' garment — or, as they often have it, the fringes of his *tallit,* or prayer shawl — the prophecy of Malachi 4:2 came to literal fulfillment.[48] Sometimes they even make the unsubstantiated claim that ancient Jews gave Malachi 4:2 messianic meaning and so expected the tassels of the Messiah to heal people.

Almost all of these sites appear to belong to Jewish Christians, to so-called "messianic Jews," who are so fond of upholding their faith and evangelizing fellow Jews by drawing correlations between prophecies in the Hebrew Bible and episodes in the New Testament. I do not know the source of their common exegesis of Malachi 4:2 — there must be one — but it seems unlikely that it is one of the obscure Byzantine texts I have cited or an old Protestant commentary that today collects dust rather than readers. It is far more plausible that we have here the independent recovery of an ancient reading. Speculating further, maybe a modern Jewish Christian, reading

---

47. Christopher Wordsworth, *The New Testament of Our Lord and Saviour Jesus Christ, in the Original Greek,* vol. 1, *The Four Gospels, and Acts of the Apostles,* new ed. (London: Rivingtons, 1864), p. 53.

48. See, e.g., "The Fringe on the Borders of a Garment," http://www.tyndale.cam.ac.uk/ Scriptures/www.innvista.com/scriptures/compare/fringe.htm; "The Hem of His Garment," www.rbooker.com/html/the_hem_of_his_garment.html; "Prayer Shawl and Bible Manners and Customs," http://www.hopeofisrael.net/tallis.htm; "The Prophetic Teaching of the Tzit-Tzit," http://ariyah.waytruthlife.com/tassels.htm; David M. Hargis, "The Talit: Garment of Glory," http://www.messianic.com/talit/talit.htm (section five; this includes the clever suggestion that the ταλιθα κουμ of Mark 5:41 misunderstands what Jesus originally said, which was טלית קומי = "Arise to My Talit"); Clarence H. Wagner Jr., "The Hem of the Garment," http://www.bridgesforpeace.com/modules.php?name=News&file=article&sid=1694. One can also order a video on this topic from the Web site of a certain Michael Rood, a self-described "messianic moreh"; see http://www.michaelrood.com/Merchant2/merchant .mvc?Screen=PROD&Store_Code=NMMJR&Product_Code=EP5-6&Category_Code=VT. These pages were accessed 12/22/2005.

some modern Hebrew New Testament, in which κράσπεδον in the Synoptics is rendered by כנף,[49] naturally made the link with the כנף of Malachi 4:2, especially as the end of Malachi has always been for most Christians a messianic portion of Scripture. However the association was initially made or whoever first made it, more than a few Jewish followers of Jesus have become enthusiastic proponents.

One issue remains. How old is the exegetical tradition that the messianic Jews have seemingly rediscovered on their own in recent times? The earliest witness to it is Pseudo-Epiphanius. This presumably takes us back to the fourth century, and maybe it would be wisest to stop there and say no more. I suspect, however, that this tradition is older; indeed, it seems plausible that some contributors to the Synoptic tradition, or first-century hearers of Matthew, Mark, or Luke, like others after them, already associated Jesus' healing fringe with Malachi 4:2.

Pseudo-Epiphanius's *Testimony Book* is a collection of proof texts, many of which were conventional. This fact is consistent with Pseudo-Epiphanius not being the first to correlate Malachi 4:2 with touching the edge of Jesus' garment for healing. Beyond that, the *Testimony Book* was, to my knowledge, not one of antiquity's best sellers, a circumstance that matters because there is no good reason to posit that the other Greek witnesses to our exegetical tradition are all derivative from it, directly and indirectly.

In line with this, it appears altogether reasonable that the link between the Synoptics and Malachi 4:2 was first made in a Jewish Christian environment, where someone familiar with Jewish customs could think of the κράσπεδα or the ציצית of a garment as "wings," as כנפים. This appears to be what happened two millennia later among modern messianic Jews.

Perhaps we may push the argument a stage further. The early stories about Jesus tend to be sparse; circumstantial details are occasional, adjectives less than abundant. There are, to be sure, exceptions, such as Mark's tale of a wild demoniac (5:1-20), which obviously reflects someone's delight in storytelling: "He lived among the tombs; and no one could restrain him any more, even with a chain; for he had often been restrained with shackles and chains, but the chains he wrenched apart, and the shackles he broke in pieces . . ." (vv. 3-4 NRSV). But this is an exception, and often stray details rather serve an intertextual end. The bread that Jesus multiplies in John 6 is barley bread (ἄρτους κριθίνους, v. 9) because it is barley bread that Elisha feeds to his

---

49. So, e.g., ספרי הברית החדשה (Jerusalem: United Bible Societies, 1983), ad Matt. 9:20; 14:36; Mark 6:56; Luke 8:44 (pp. 24, 42, 107, 174).

crowd in the very similar 2 Kings 4:42-44 (LXX: ἄρτους κριθίνους).[50] The multitude in Mark 6:30-44, which is like sheep without a shepherd, reclines upon the green grass because the text is establishing a typological correlation with Psalm 23, where the Lord, like a shepherd, supplies the needs of the psalmist who is seated upon the green grass.[51] Again, when Jesus is transfigured in Matthew, we read not only that his clothes became dazzlingly white (so Mark 9:3) but also that his face shone like the sun (Matt. 17:2), a feature that enhances his resemblance to Moses on Sinai.[52] Often the seemingly odd or superfluous specification is there in order to send thoughts back to the Old Testament. That is why Tertullian, in his polemic against Marcion, could espy so many small details common to the stories about Jesus and about Old Testament worthies, and why, centuries later, David Friedrich Strauss could do exactly the same thing, albeit for the very different end of showing the Gospels to be full of fiction inspired by old stories.[53]

And so one wonders about the specificity of τὸ κράσπεδον τοῦ ἱματίου. Although the phrase is attested in secular Greek,[54] it is not a Septuagintal construction, nor does it have any place in early Christian literature except for the Synoptics and writings that take up Matthew 9:20; 14:36; Mark 6:56; and/or Luke 8:44. Jewish tradition does not seem to attach healing properties to the tassels of garments;[55] and given, furthermore, that early Chris-

---

50. C. H. Dodd, *Historical Tradition in the Fourth Gospel* (Cambridge: Cambridge University Press, 1963), p. 206; Ernst Haenchen, *John 1: A Commentary on the Gospel of John, Chapters 1-6*, Hermeneia (Philadelphia: Fortress, 1984), pp. 271-72. Cf. Chrysostom, *Hom. John* 42 (PG 59:241): Andrew remarked upon the young lad with five barley loaves and two fishes because he knew the story about Elisha in 2 Kings 4:42-44.

51. Dale C. Allison Jr., "Psalm 23 in Early Christianity: A Suggestion," *IBS* 5 (1983): 132-37.

52. Dale C. Allison Jr., *The New Moses: A Matthean Typology* (Minneapolis: Fortress, 1993), pp. 243-48.

53. David Friedrich Strauss, *The Life of Jesus Critically Examined* (Philadelphia: Fortress, 1972), passim.

54. E.g., Plutarch, *Gracch.* 19.5.4 (ed. Perrin, LCL); Appianus, *BC* 1.2.16 (ed. White, LCL).

55. The story, told in *Num. Rab.* 115, of the fringes that stood up and slapped a man when he was about to sleep with a prostitute is hardly comparable to what we have in the Synoptics. Also irrelevant is 1 Sam. 24:1-7; see John F. Craghan, "Mari and Its Prophets," *BTB* 5 (1975): 42-44. The closest parallel I have found is in *PGM* 7.371-74 (ed. Preisendanz, 2:17): "In opposition to every beast, creature of the water, and robber: Attach a κράσπεδον to your ἱματίου and recite: 'Lōma Zath Aiōn . . . guard me, So-and-so, in the present hour, at once, at once, quickly, quickly.'" Unfortunately, this text is of uncertain date and provenance. The identification of Jesus' hem as a magical prophylactic in *Ques. Barth.* 4:18 (ed. Wilmart and

tians undeniably paid considerable attention to the last portion of Malachi, the specificity of τὸ κράσπεδον τοῦ ἱματίου may well be a sign that a contributor to the Synoptic tradition associated Jesus' tassels with Malachi 4:2.

I freely confess that these considerations fall woefully short of establishing a firm conclusion. At the same time, we undeniably have here an old exegetical tradition; and given our fragmentary knowledge, a first-century origin for it is really no less plausible than a second- or third-century genesis. Maybe indeed it is as old as the story it belongs to. Christian Jews of the first century had the same textual materials to hand — Malachi 4:2 and traditions about Jesus' κράσπεδον — as the messianic Jews of more recent times who have independently rediscovered the old reading of Malachi 4:2. So should not our critical commentaries at least note that Matthew 9:20; 14:36; Mark 6:56; and Luke 8:44 can and have sent some readers back to Malachi 4:2, to the prophecy that "the sun of righteousness will arise with healing in his wings"?

Tisserant, *RB* 10 [1913]: 330) — "And Bartholomew was afraid and said: 'Lord Jesus, give me a hem of your garment that I may venture to approach him,'" namely, Beliar — presumably depends wholly upon the Synoptic verses in which Jesus' tassels are instruments of healing.

See My Tears: A Lament for Jerusalem
(Luke 13:31-35; 19:41-44)

Bruce N. Fisk

And look, see my tears. They fill the whole night sky.

Bruce Cockburn[1]

Among Richard's published works, I suppose my favorite remains the first one I read: *Echoes of Scripture in the Letters of Paul.* I read *Echoes* a year or two after it was published. To smile my way through a monograph was a new experience for me. Here was someone who cared as much about clarity and artistry as he did about argument, someone for whom exegesis, theology, art, and life were intricately woven — or hopelessly tangled — threads in a tapestry. It wasn't long after I finished *Echoes* that I applied to study at Duke, where, to my delight, I found no discernible difference between the implied author of the book and the historical figure who graciously became my supervisor.

---

1. "The Whole Night Sky," written by Bruce Cockburn. © 1997 Golden Mountain Music Corp. (SOCAN). Used by permission. Early in my grad school career at Duke I attended a Bruce Cockburn concert. In Canada, Cockburn's fans fill grand halls; in the United States, he plays theaters, guitar stores, and clubs like the dim, graffiti-laden venue in Chapel Hill where I found a seat meters from the artist and next to my supervisor, Richard Hays — who, it turned out, shared my love for Cockburn's exquisite fingering and provocative lyrics. That was my first listen to "The Whole Night Sky," a lament for those times when we hang by fraying strands of faith and when all reality refracts through the lens of our own tears. I should add that Cockburn's role in the lifelong conversion of my imagination has been substantial; those with ears to hear will recognize more than a few Cockburn echoes in this essay.

*   *   *

According to Richard Hays, the Third Gospel affirms the continuity of the church with ethnic Israel. Luke's ecclesiology thus aligns closely with Paul's except for one substantive difference: Luke displays nothing of the anguished tension between Abrahamic promise of blessing and widespread Jewish unbelief — the tension that grips Paul's dialectic in Romans 9-11. As Richard explains, this tension is lacking because for Luke, Israel is now absorbed without remainder into the church:

> We find in Luke no speculative hope for the ultimate salvation of all Israel, no sense that the covenant faithfulness of God somehow requires an eschatological reconciliation of the Jewish people as a whole to the truth of the gospel.[2]

Then, like Paul recalling a household he once baptized (1 Cor. 1:16), Richard issues a slight retraction:

> Only in Luke's haunting image of Jesus weeping over Jerusalem (Luke 19:41-44) do we find an echo of Paul's agonized lament for his own people.[3]

Luke's depiction of the Holy City rising behind a wall of Jesus' tears is certainly haunting.

> 41As he drew near he saw the city and wept over it, 42saying, "You, if only you had recognized on this day the things that make for peace! But now they are hidden from you. 43For the days will come upon you when your enemies will set up siege works against you and encircle you and constrain you on every side, 44and they will raze you to the ground, you and your children within you, and they will not leave one of your stones on another, because you did not recognize the time of your visitation." (Luke 19:41-44)

Jesus' earlier lament over Jerusalem comes immediately to mind:[4]

---

2. Richard B. Hays, *The Moral Vision of the New Testament* (New York: HarperSanFrancisco, 1996), p. 421 (cf. 417-21). On Hays's discussion of Paul's persistent hope for Israel's future restoration through Christ, see idem, *Echoes of Scripture in the Letters of Paul* (New Haven: Yale University Press, 1989), pp. 67-70; *Moral Vision*, pp. 411-17; *The Conversion of the Imagination: Paul as Interpreter of Israel's Scripture* (Grand Rapids: Eerdmans, 2005), pp. 187-88.

3. Hays, *Moral Vision*, p. 421.

4. Recall also Jesus' poignant words to the "daughters of Jerusalem" (Luke 23:28-31), on

34Jerusalem, Jerusalem, the city that kills the prophets and stones those sent to her! So often have I sought to gather up your children as a hen gathers her brood under her wings, but you refused! 35See, your house is left to you. And I tell you, you will not see me until the time comes when you say, "Blessed is the one who comes in the name of the Lord." (Luke 13:34-35)

To feel the weight of these two oracles is to sense some of what Jesus felt as the city, and his death, loomed. Understandably, the two passages have fused in the Christian imagination, nowhere more strikingly than in the small Dominus Flevit chapel on the western slope of the Mount of Olives. Looking out across the Kidron Valley toward Jerusalem's Temple Mount, the chapel's "stained glass" window is, oddly, not stained but clear. What *should* be bits of leaded, colored glass is actually the city itself, with the Dome of the Rock and, behind it, the Church of the Holy Sepulchre strategically "etched" at the window's center. Beneath the altar that marks the spot where Jesus wept, a bronze mosaic medallion features a white hen spreading her wings over seven chicks. Circumscribing the mosaic is a Latin citation of Luke 13:34. Thanks to the brilliance of architect Antonio Barluzzi, the Lord weeps not for an idealization of Jerusalem — a tinted, fragmented Byzantine replica — but for the groaning, divided city we know today.

Together, these laments invite questions about Luke's eschatology, about Jesus' prophetic vision, and about the place of Jerusalem in both. Do they imply Lukan distress over the plight of Jacob's physical descendants? Does Luke foresee *only* judgment for Israel, or does he hold out hope also for her salvation? To return to Richard's observation, does Luke share Paul's *agony* over unbelieving Israel?[5] There was a time when I would settle for answers to historical questions like these. Today, in Richard's shadow, I want also to hear Luke's word for the church. How might Jesus' lament shape us into "a community that embodies the love of God as shown forth in Christ"?[6] How

---

which see below. We might also compare Jesus' sober (but not quite mournful) oracle of the city's destruction (Luke 21:6, 20-24) and, more remotely, his indictment of an "unbelieving and perverse generation" (Luke 9:41).

5. Richard's influential work on πίστις Χριστοῦ encourages us to seek correspondences between the narrative substructure of Paul's letters and the narrative genre of the Gospels. See Richard B. Hays, *The Faith of Jesus Christ: The Narrative Substructure of Galatians 3:1–4:11* (Grand Rapids: Eerdmans, 2002), p. 6 et passim; idem, "Is Paul's Gospel Narratable?" *JSNT* 27 (2004): 217-39.

6. Hays, *Echoes*, p. 191. Cf. also p. 178 and *Conversion of the Imagination*, p. 189.

might Jesus' burden for the ancient city convert our imaginations as we behold modern Jerusalem, drawn and quartered, occupied and militarized as it is? What *for us* lies behind the time-blurred panes of Dominus Flevit?

Sacred Geography

Before staring at a grown man weeping, we should consider the object of his lament: the Holy City itself, particularly as it appears and reappears in the Third Gospel. The prominence of Jerusalem in Luke is universally acknowledged.[7] The opening scene features an unlikely country priest chosen to ascend to Jerusalem to burn incense in its temple (1:9-10). Young Jesus twice journeys to the city (2:22, 42). His visionary ascent to the temple pinnacle not only forms the climax of Jesus' dialogue with the devil (4:9; contrast Matt. 4:5); it also provides "symbolic anticipation"[8] of the passion. At another narrative high point, Jesus converses with Moses and Elijah concerning (uniquely in Luke) the "exodus" that Jesus intends to accomplish in Jerusalem (9:31).[9] From there, almost immediately, Jesus sets out on a perilous quest to ascend the slopes of Zion (9:51).

A side glance at the other Gospels confirms the prominence of Jerusalem on Luke's sacred horizon. Unique to Luke are the following:

2:22	The infant Jesus is presented in Jerusalem.
2:25	Righteous Simeon waits in Jerusalem for Israel's consolation.
2:38	Anna the prophetess speaks to those awaiting Jerusalem's redemption.
2:41-45	Young Jesus stays in Jerusalem after the feast.

7. Lloyd Gaston, *No Stone on Another: Studies in the Significance of the Fall of Jerusalem in the Synoptic Gospels,* NovTSup 23 (Leiden: Brill, 1970), pp. 365-69; James D. G. Dunn, *Jesus Remembered* (Grand Rapids: Eerdmans, 2003), p. 790; Hans Conzelmann, *The Theology of St. Luke,* trans. G. Buswell (New York: Harper & Row, 1960), pp. 73-94; J. Bradley Chance, *Jerusalem, the Temple, and the New Age in Luke-Acts* (Macon, Ga.: Mercer University Press, 1988), pp. 1-4 et passim.

8. Joel B. Green, *The Gospel of Luke,* NICNT (Grand Rapids: Eerdmans, 1997), p. 195.

9. Jesus' ἔξοδος here likely refers to his death and resurrection *and* to their significance as Israel's rescue/salvation/liberation. See Hays, *Moral Vision,* p. 117; I. Howard Marshall, *The Gospel of Luke,* NIGTC (Grand Rapids: Eerdmans, 1978), pp. 384-85; David P. Moessner, *Lord of the Banquet: The Literary and Theological Significance of the Lukan Travel Narrative* (Minneapolis: Fortress, 1989), p. 262; Jack D. Kingsbury, *Conflict in Luke: Jesus, Authorities, Disciples* (Minneapolis: Augsburg Fortress, 1991), pp. 6, 55-60.

9:31	Jesus discusses the "exodus" he is about to accomplish at Jerusalem.
9:51	Jesus sets his face toward Jerusalem. (In Matt. 19:1 and Mark 10:1 Jesus departs to Judea and beyond the Jordan.)
9:53	Samaritans reject Jesus because his face is set toward Jerusalem.
10:30	Jesus tells of the man going down from Jerusalem to Jericho.
13:22	Jesus goes through villages as he journeys toward Jerusalem.
13:33	Jesus moves under compulsion to get to Jerusalem before he dies.
17:11	Jesus, on the way to Jerusalem, passes between Samaria and Galilee.
18:31-34	Jesus predicts his passion in Jerusalem. (Cf. Matt. 20:17-19 and Mark 10:32-34, but only Luke emphasizes prophetic fulfillment.)
19:11	Jesus tells a parable because he is near Jerusalem and people think the kingdom is about to appear.
19:28	Jesus goes up to Jerusalem. (Only Luke emphasizes Jerusalem as the sole destination.)
19:41-44	Jesus laments over the city and its coming destruction.
21:20	Jesus speaks of Jerusalem "surrounded by armies." (Cf. Matt. 24:15 and Mark 13:14, but only Luke mentions the city by name.)
21:24	Jesus warns that Jerusalem will be trampled by the Gentiles. (Cf. Matthew 24 and Mark 13.)
23:28	Jesus counsels the "daughters of Jerusalem" not to weep for him.
24:13-33	Cleopas thinks Jesus may be the only visitor to Jerusalem ignorant of recent events. The travelers return to Jerusalem and find other disciples.
24:47-52	Jesus' "great commission" begins with Jerusalem. (Matthew 28:16-20, set in Galilee, doesn't mention Jerusalem.) After the ascension, the disciples return to Jerusalem (cf. Acts 1:12).
Acts 1:4	Jesus orders his disciples to wait in Jerusalem.

Also noteworthy, if not unique to Luke, are the following passages:

4:9	Jesus' temptation on the pinnacle of the temple in Jerusalem appears last in the series, perhaps for emphasis. (Matthew lists it second and sets it in "the holy city.")
5:17	The Pharisees and teachers of the law come from villages in Galilee and Judea and from Jerusalem. (Crowds are not mentioned in Matt. 9:1-8 until the end; Mark 2:1-12 refers only to "many gathered at the door.")

6:17   Luke describes a great multitude of people from all Judea and Je-
        rusalem (and Tyre and Sidon). (Matthew 4:25 and Mark 3:7 men-
        tion Jerusalem after Galilee and, in Matthew, the Decapolis.)

All signs suggest that Luke sees Jerusalem as Jesus' theological ἀρχή and
τέλος. Jesus *has* to return to the city where he, like others before him, will
face hostility and rejection. He *has* to proclaim his teachings in the temple
(19:47), whose teachers long before held him spellbound (2:46). The proverb
Jesus once hurled at Nazareth (4:24) *has* to prove even more apt for Jerusalem (19:39, 47; 20:2, 19-20; 22:2). The Holy City *has* to reject one more
prophet and witness one more tragedy.[10]

The well-known logistical problems[11] posed by Luke's central "travel
narrative"[12] need not occupy us here. However contrived and poetic the
"journey" and however serpentine the path, Luke asks us to picture Israel's
greatest prophet inexorably drawn to the Holy City, like a moth to flame,
convinced not only *that* he will die a martyr's death but also that it will occur
in Jerusalem. Luke does not invest the city with new significance. On the
contrary, Luke's Jerusalem, the place of God's choosing,[13] does to Jesus precisely what it has done many times before.

10. It is, of course, *from Jerusalem* that the risen Jesus dispatches his disciples into the
world (Luke 24:47; Acts 1:8). Even with the transition from Jerusalem (via Samaria, Antioch,
and Ephesus) to Rome, Jerusalem remains historically and theologically strategic to Luke's
second volume. Intriguingly, Charles H. H. Scobie, "A Canonical Approach to Interpreting
Luke: The Journey Motif as a Hermeneutical Key," in *Reading Luke: Interpretation, Reflection, Formation,* ed. Craig Bartholomew, Joel Green, and Anthony Thiselton (Grand Rapids:
Zondervan, 2005), pp. 339-42, suggests that by including a second city, Luke locates Christian identity "between Jerusalem and Rome" (p. 341). Moessner, *Lord of the Banquet,* pp.
296-307, argues persuasively that Acts depicts Jesus' disciples imitating the journey and prophetic vocation of their "Moses."
11. Luke 10:38 occurs in a suburb of Jerusalem; 17:11 is set up north. Ποσάκις *(how often)*
in Luke 13:34 might imply multiple journeys to Jerusalem, paralleling Jesus' pilgrimages in
John (2:13; 7:10; 12:12; so, tentatively, Marshall, *Luke,* p. 575). Or it could simply inscribe Jesus'
unflagging passion, or repeated frustration, as he pondered the city's receptivity (on which
see Kim Huat Tan, *The Zion Traditions and the Aims of Jesus,* SNTSMS 91 [Cambridge: Cambridge University Press, 1997], pp. 104-5).
12. Most interpreters begin the section at 9:51 and end between 18:14 and 19:48. On the
geographical anomalies and "disturbingly stubborn disunity at the level of Luke's story," see
Moessner, *Lord of the Banquet,* pp. 14-44, 290-94 (quotation p. 31). Particularly helpful on
Luke's narrative strategies are Scobie, "Canonical Approach," and Frank J. Matera, "Jesus'
Journey to Jerusalem (Luke 9:51–19:46): A Conflict with Israel," *JSNT* 51 (1993): 57-77.
13. Cf. the Deuteronomic refrain: "the place the LORD your God shall choose" (Deut.

Where Prophets Go to Die (Luke 13:31-33)

> 31At that very hour some Pharisees approached, saying to him, "Go out from here because Herod wants to kill you." 32And he said to them, "Go and tell that fox, 'Look, today and tomorrow I am casting out demons and performing cures; on the third day my mission will finally be complete. 33Indeed, it is necessary for me to journey onward today and tomorrow and the next day, for it is not possible for a prophet to perish outside Jerusalem.'" (Luke 13:31-33)

On hearing that Antipas hopes to do to Jesus what he has done to John the Baptist, Jesus testily declares his mission *incomplete,* and therefore invulnerable, until such time as he arrives in Jerusalem (13:32-33). Fitzmyer paraphrases Jesus' reply: "it is not destined that Herod will kill me, but that Jerusalem will."[14] Jesus will not save his life by leaving Herod's territory; he will lose it.[15] He is not fleeing *from* Galilee; he is being pulled *toward* Jerusalem.

A few syntactical comments are in order. First, the absolute use of τελειοῦμαι (pres. pass.) in v. 32 may be intentionally vague, which makes it tricky to translate.[16] In line with Luke 9:51, 12:50, 13:33, and 18:31, I suggest "my mission will finally be complete."[17] A double entendre is in play: Jesus' journey and his life are simultaneously reaching their *telos.*[18] With the phrase δεῖ . . . πορεύεσθαι, v. 33 sounds a note of divine compulsion; the infinitive in final position allows for maximum resonance: *I am driven — today, tomorrow, the day after — forward.*[19] Even the seemingly innocuous

---

12:5, 11, 14; 14:23; 15:20; 16:6, 16; 17:10; 18:6; 26:2; 31:11; cf. 2 Chron. 7:12, 15-16; Ps. 78:68-69). The temple in Luke is as much a place to pray (18:10) and teach (19:45-48; 20:1, 19-20, 26, 45; 21:1, 37-38) as it is to sacrifice (1:9; 2:24).

14. Joseph A. Fitzmyer, *The Gospel according to Luke X–XXIV,* AB 28A (Garden City: Doubleday, 1985), p. 1032.

15. Similarly, Tan, *Zion Traditions,* p. 72.

16. "I shall be perfected" (KJV) is too literal, but neither "I finish my work" (NRSV) nor "I reach my goal" (NASB; cf. NIV, TNIV, Fitzmyer) seems weighty enough for the occasion.

17. Cf. John Nolland, *Luke 9:21–18:34,* WBC 35B (Nashville: Thomas Nelson, 1993), p. 740, who translates "I am finished." Though the verb is present tense, the context makes clear that a future moment is in view.

18. Cf. Tan, *Zion Traditions,* pp. 71, 77.

19. Πορεύομαι occurs frequently in Luke (49x, 25 of which are in the Gospel's central "journey" section) and Acts (39x). See most notably Luke 9:51 (αὐτὸς τὸ πρόσωπον ἐστήρισεν τοῦ πορεύεσθαι εἰς Ἰερουσαλήμ). On the technical force of this verb in Luke's narrative, see Scobie, "Canonical Approach," p. 333; Moessner, *Lord of the Banquet,* p. 116.

σήμερον καὶ αὔριον καὶ τῇ ἐχομένῃ *(today, tomorrow, the day after)* does more than refer to the near future; in biblical idiom it signals that Jesus moves in accord with the cadence of God's will.[20]

The final clause of v. 33, "for it is not possible for a prophet to perish outside Jerusalem," is transitional. The ὅτι *(because, for)* looks *back* to explain why Jesus can't possibly fall prey to Herod in the Galilee: prophets should die only in the capital. The clause also leans *forward*; its final word, "Jerusalem," prepares us for the apostrophe of vv. 34-35 introduced by the charged double vocative, "Jerusalem, Jerusalem."[21]

But where does it say that prophets[22] cannot *possibly*[23] die outside Jerusalem? Only a handful of biblical episodes fit the description:

- Uriah, son of Shemaiah, was slain by sword by King Jehoiakim for prophesying against "this city" (Jer. 26:20-23).
- Zechariah, son of Jehoiada, was stoned to death by order of King Joash "in the court of the house of the LORD" (2 Chron. 24:20-22).[24] (This is notable because one of the monumental tombs in the Kidron valley, dating to the first century BCE, was thought to be Zechariah's tomb. Luke 11:47-48 [cf. Matt. 23:29] may allude to this monument.)
- Jeremiah was *almost* killed in Jerusalem for prophesying against "this city" (Jer. 26:1-24; cf. vv. 6, 9, 11, 12, 15).

20. See Ben F. Meyer, *The Aims of Jesus* (London: SCM, 1979), p. 182, for the Semitic context of the phrase.

21. On the literary unity of Luke 13:31-35, see David L. Tiede, *Prophecy and History in Luke-Acts* (Philadelphia: Fortress, 1980), pp. 70-78; Nolland, *Luke*, pp. 738-39. Matthew has no parallel to Luke 13:33; his lament oracle (Matt. 23:37-39) is tied to its context not by the word "Jerusalem" but by the theme of murdered prophets (see Matt. 23:29-31, 34-35).

22. Προφήτης (anarthrous, singular, personal) denotes prophets *as a class*, not *the* prophet. Cf. H. W. Smyth, *Greek Grammar* (Cambridge: Harvard University Press, 1956) §1129.

23. Cf. BDAG s.v. ἐνδέχομαι. Something like "(completely un-)acceptable" is in view here. The Shepherd of Hermas (*Mand.* 11.12) describes something similarly "impossible" (οὐκ ἐνδέχεται) for a prophet: charging money for his oracles.

24. The death of this Zechariah is noted in Luke 11:51, but Luke seems to confuse him with the prophet Zechariah, son of Berechiah (Zech. 1:1), in Matt. 23:35, on which see W. D. Davies and Dale C. Allison Jr., *A Critical and Exegetical Commentary on the Gospel according to Saint Matthew,* 3 vols., ICC (Edinburgh: T. & T. Clark, 1997), 3:318-19, followed by David M. Moffitt, "Righteous Bloodshed, Matthew's Passion Narrative, and the Temple's Destruction: Lamentations as a Matthean Intertext," *JBL* 125 (2006): 307 n. 22.

Not only is the roll call of prophets martyred in Jerusalem surprisingly short, but there are obvious counterexamples.[25] Most glaringly, Moses — whose prophetic office, according to Luke, Jesus fulfills (Acts 3:20-23; 7:37; cf. Deut. 18:15, 18) — died across the Jordan in Moab (Deut. 34:5-6).[26] Likewise, John the Baptist died at Machaerus, a hilltop fortress in Perea (so Josephus, *Ant.* 18.119), or perhaps in Tiberias of the Galilee (Mark 6:21).

Simply put, rejected prophets were *not* routinely brought to Jerusalem for trial and execution. Nolland repairs this minor glitch by reading the verse ironically: "if you must reject those sent you by God, you should do it properly, by doing it at the heart of all Jewish affairs in Jerusalem."[27] More likely is Green's suggestion of synecdoche:

> Jerusalem . . . stands as a cipher for Israel as a whole; hence, not only must it be the ultimate destination of the prophet proclaiming a message of reform, but it is there, where the message of reform contrasts most sharply with accepted beliefs and practices, that resistance to the prophet will reach its acme.[28]

Such appeals to rhetoric and reason may be necessary, but they only confirm that Jesus' quest to reach *and die in* Jerusalem conforms to no known pattern. Nor is our dilemma fully resolved by invoking first-century oral traditions.[29] It would seem that Luke 13:33 functions for Luke less as factual claim than as unmarked metaphor for his entire narrative, a narrative whose trajectory begins with God's calling and deliverance (Acts 7:2, 36-37), continues through Israel's obduracy (Luke 11:49-51; 19:14, 42), and climaxes with Messiah's death in the city (Acts 3:13; 7:51-52). How — indeed, whether (accord-

---

25. E.g., 1 Kings 18:4, 13; 19:10, 14; Neh. 9:26; Jer. 2:30.

26. On the theological and exegetical problem of Moses dying outside the land, see W. D. Davies, *The Gospel and the Land: Early Christianity and Jewish Territorial Doctrine* (Sheffield: JSOT Press, 1994 [1974]), p. 104 n. 76, and the literature cited there. This contrast between Moses and Jesus cannot erase the numerous similarities the evangelists see between the two figures. Perhaps even in the details of their deaths there is symmetry, as Scobie ("Canonical Approach," p. 338) observes: "like Moses, Jesus' 'exodus' culminates in his death, apparently before reaching his goal."

27. Nolland, *Luke*, p. 741.

28. Green, *Luke*, p. 537.

29. As implied by Fitzmyer, *Luke*, p. 1032; Eduard Schweizer, *The Good News according to Luke*, trans. D. E. Green (Atlanta: John Knox, 1984), p. 230. Luke 11:47-48 likely means that we should presume the presence of local traditions, not least about the Kidron valley tombs. Some such oral embellishment convinced Josephus that among King Manasseh's many Jerusalem victims (2 Kings 21:16) were ranking prophets (*Ant.* 10.3.1).

ing to Luke) — Jerusalem's story continues beyond that point is one of the questions animating this essay.

Neither Lion nor Eagle (Luke 13:34)

> Jerusalem, Jerusalem, the city that kills the prophets and stones those sent to her! So often have I sought to gather up your children as a hen gathers her brood under her wings, but you refused! (Luke 13:34)

To deliver the oracle of vv. 34-35, Jesus turns toward the city. The apostrophe is linked to its context by the catchword "Jerusalem," the initial double vocative adding notes of solemnity, authority, and tragedy to what follows. The pendent nominative construction ("the [city] that kills the prophets and stones . . .") levels the charges at the same time that it builds suspense.[30] The oracle thus serves both as commentary on the previous exchange and as independent indictment: the prophet must die in Jerusalem (13:33), but it will not be of natural causes — he will be "killed" (cf. Luke 9:22; 11:47-49), and "Jerusalem" will be the killer.[31]

To argue that Jesus numbered himself with John the Baptist among Israel's prophets is to stand on solid ground. One need not venture beyond Luke's Gospel to learn that "prophet" as a designation for Jesus is deeply embedded in various strata of the tradition.[32] And if a prophet, then a potential

---

30. For the double vocative elsewhere in Luke, see Luke 6:46. In the LXX, see Gen. 22:1; 46:2; Exod. 3:4; Deut. 3:24; 9:26; Judg. 16:28; 1 Kgdms. 3:4, 6; 2 Kgdms. 19:(1), 5; 3 Kgdms. 13:2; 4 Kgdms. 2:12; 13:14; 1 Chron. 17:24; Pss. 129:3; 139:8; 140:8; Jer. 22:29; Amos 7:2, 5. "Jerusalem" is found in the vocative in 2 Chron. 20:17; Pss. 121:2; 147:1; Isa. 62:6; Jer. 4:14; 6:8; 13:27; 15:5. Roughly half of all LXX uses of "Jerusalem" in the vocative are in Jeremiah. Not in the vocative but noteworthy are the multiple woes to Jerusalem delivered by Jesus, son of Ananias, in Josephus, *War* 6.301, 304, 306, 309.

31. The juxtaposition of vv. 33 and 34 is likely Luke's doing; it simultaneously makes more and less sense than Matthew's placement of the lament at 23:37-39, at the conclusion of Jesus' woes against the Pharisees. More, because Matthew's sequence might imply that the Pharisees were responsible for executions. Less, because in Matthew Jesus is actually in Jerusalem when he addresses the city (cf. Matt. 21:1; 24:1). Matthew has likely inserted the lament into his context to bolster the charge that Israel's leaders repeatedly killed God's messengers (23:29-35).

32. Cf. Luke 4:24; 7:16, 39; 20:9-18; 22:64; 24:19. To sample the consensus on this point, see Dale C. Allison Jr., *Jesus of Nazareth: Millenarian Prophet* (Minneapolis: Fortress, 1998), pp. 65-67; A. E. Harvey, *Jesus and the Constraints of History* (Philadelphia: Westminster, 1982), pp. 57-59; Dunn, *Jesus Remembered*, pp. 655-64; Ben Witherington III, *Jesus the Seer:*

martyr. Meyer's assessment of Jesus' self-understanding, if speculative, can't be too far off:

> It is probable, owing to the nexus between "prophet" and "violent fate" in contemporary religious tradition . . . , that the prospect of a violent death belonged unthematically to [Jesus'] self-understanding from the start and that under the impact of the Baptist's execution, the deadly hostility of his critics, and the consequent threats to his life, this early became thematically conscious.[33]

Whether this particular oracle (Luke 13:34-35) goes back to the pre-Easter Jesus, however, is another matter.[34] The reference to death by stoning (λιθοβολέω) rather than crucifixion *may* support the dominical origins of the saying,[35] but surely the reason for the parallelism in 34a (ἡ ἀποκτείνουσα . . . καὶ λιθοβολοῦσα . . . , "that kills . . . and stones . . .") is to emphasize Israel's persistent abuse of God's emissaries, not to forecast a specific mode of execution. The charge is that Jerusalem's corporate rejection of her latest prophet corresponds to a long-standing pattern.[36] But whether or not the language belongs to Jesus,[37] the contours of the lament resonate with what

---

The Progress of Prophecy (Peabody: Hendrickson, 1999), pp. 246-92; N. T. Wright, *Jesus and the Victory of God* (Minneapolis: Fortress, 1996), p. 150 et passim. Such a claim, moreover, is unlikely to have been invented by the early church, because the epithet "prophet" was not sufficiently elevated and distinctive (Wright, *Jesus and the Victory of God,* p. 162; cf. 549).

33. Meyer, *Aims of Jesus,* p. 252.

34. The close parallel at Matt. 23:37-39 prompts Two-Source theorists (e.g., Tan, *Zion Traditions,* pp. 101-4; Marshall, *Luke,* p. 573; Nolland, *Luke,* p. 739) to assign this unit to Q. Lacking their enthusiasm, I note only that the placement of the oracle here, with Jesus still some distance from Jerusalem, should probably count against the authenticity of this setting, though not necessarily of the saying itself. Tan, *Zion Traditions,* pp. 121-24, concludes that Luke 13:34-35 is dominical but its original context cannot be known. On the problematic nature of both Matthew's and Luke's settings, see Robert J. Miller, "The Rejection of the Prophets in Q," *JBL* 107 (1988): 225-40, esp. p. 237. For Miller, Luke 13:34-35 is a saying of the risen Christ spoken by the Q prophets (pp. 233-40). Similarly, Gaston, *No Stone on Another,* p. 344; cf. 321-23; M. Eugene Boring, *Sayings of the Risen Jesus: Christian Prophecy in the Synoptic Tradition,* SNTSMS 46 (Cambridge: Cambridge University Press, 1982), p. 171.

35. See Tan, *Zion Traditions,* pp. 107-8; cf. Marshall, *Luke,* p. 575; Darrell L. Bock, *Luke 9:51–24:53,* BECNT (Grand Rapids: Baker, 1996), p. 1249; tentatively, Fitzmyer, *Luke,* p. 1035.

36. On stoning, see 2 Chron. 24:21 (cf. Luke 11:51); 1 Sam. 30:6; 1 Kings 12:18; 21:10-15. In the NT, see Matt. 21:35; 23:37; Acts 7:58-59; 14:5, 19; 2 Cor. 11:25; Heb. 11:37; 12:20. For Israel's routine rejection of the prophets, see Jer. 7:25-27; Zech. 1:4-6; 7:11-13; Wright, *Jesus and the Victory of God,* p. 579.

37. On challenges to the authenticity of Luke 13:34-35, Dunn, *Jesus Remembered,* p. 793,

we know about Jesus from elsewhere: he identified himself as one of God's authorized but rejected messengers and ranked his opponents in Jerusalem among those in line for imminent judgment. Nor was Jesus unique in this respect. The story of Zechariah whispers from the shadows.

> 17Now after the death of Jehoiada the officials of Judah came and did obeisance to the king; then the king listened to them. 18They abandoned the house of the LORD, the God [LXX: they abandoned the Lord God] of their ancestors, and served the sacred poles and the idols. And wrath came upon Judah and **Jerusalem** for this guilt of theirs. 19Yet **he sent prophets** among them to bring them back to the LORD; they testified against them, but they would not listen. 20Then the spirit of God took possession of Zechariah son of the priest Jehoiada; he stood above the people and said to them, "Thus says God: Why do you transgress the commandments of the LORD, so that you cannot prosper? Because you have forsaken the LORD, he has also forsaken you." 21But they conspired against him, and by command of the king **they stoned him to death** in the court of the house of the LORD. 22King Joash did not remember the kindness that Jehoiada, Zechariah's father, had shown him, but **killed** his son. As he was dying, he said, "May the LORD see and avenge!" (2 Chron. 24:17-22 NRSV)

The elements shared by Luke and the Chronicler are not sufficiently distinctive or explicit to warrant the claim of intentional allusion or intertextual echo,[38] yet there is enough symmetry to encourage readers to recall the Zechariah saga here, as Luke himself does in 11:51. Both Jesus and Zechariah were divinely commissioned ("sent") prophets who indicted Jerusalem for unfaithfulness, warned of pending judgment, and died (as prophets should) in Jerusalem. Not long after Zechariah's death, moreover, he was vindicated: a Syrian force attacked Jerusalem, the city's wealth was removed, and Joash, the perpetrator, was assassinated. Evidently, the city that would "stone" Jesus should expect similar judgment, and Jesus similar vindication.[39]

---

wryly observes: "The question whether Jesus was motivated by a sense of destiny in regard to his own role vis-à-vis Jerusalem cannot be answered simply by dismissing the clearest evidence in favour of a positive answer."

38. Richard's seven "tests" for discerning intertextual echoes are relevant here, on which see Hays, *Echoes*, pp. 29-32. See also my *Do You Not Remember? Scripture, Story, and Exegesis in the Rewritten Bible of Pseudo-Philo* (Sheffield: Sheffield Academic, 2001), pp. 78-82 et passim, and works cited on p. 78 n. 83.

39. We might thus add Zechariah to the list of prophets after which Jesus modeled his ministry, on which see Wright, *Jesus and the Victory of God*, p. 166.

Luke's evocative simile — Jesus brooding over Jerusalem like a hen over her young — recalls biblical images of YHWH sheltering Israel.[40] A less original thinker might have likened himself to a circling eagle (ἀετός; cf. Exod. 19:4) or pacing lion (λέων; cf. Lam. 3:10), but Jesus here acknowledges gentler, more maternal instincts. He longs to provide — to be — God's shelter for those who will receive it. He yearns to see Jerusalem's children safe under the Mercy.[41]

If the bird analogy is theologically presumptuous, it is nevertheless also historically plausible. This is precisely the sort of audacious innovation we should expect of a Jewish prophet who was convinced he spoke on God's behalf. The avian imagery should probably not be pressed, however, to infer that Jesus, like a hen sacrificing herself for her chicks, sought to take on himself the fate hanging over the city.[42] The image of a bird sheltering its young (e.g., Deut. 32:11; Isa. 31:5) is predominantly one of strength and protection, not of sacrifice or substitution. Whether or not Jesus imagined himself as the one who somehow carried upon himself the destiny of the many,[43] the rhetorical power of this oracle consists principally in the fact that Jesus' offer of protection, though maternal, inviting, and desperately needed, was brazenly spurned.

Dark Tomorrows[44] (Luke 13:35a)

See, your house is left to you. (Luke 13:35a)

Luke 13:34 ranks among the most poignant passages in all of Scripture. But where there is pathos, is there also hope? If judgment is imminent, will res-

---

40. E.g., Deut. 32:11; Ruth 2:12; Pss. 17:8; 36:7; 57:1; and additional references in Bock, *Luke*, p. 1249; Marshall, *Luke*, p. 575. No surviving compositions antedating Luke compare God specifically to a hen (ὄρνις).

41. On "gathering" imagery in the OT as indicative of God's restoration, see συνάγω in Jer. 31:8, 10; cf. references listed in Tan, *Zion Traditions*, p. 113.

42. As argued by Wright, *Jesus and the Victory of God*, pp. 571-72. Wright's call for a substitutionary reading (my label, not his) of the image gains in plausibility when clustered with other "riddles of the cross" (pp. 565-73; cf. Mark 12:28-34; Luke 7:36-50; 12:49-50; 20:9-19; 23:27-31).

43. So Hays, *Conversion of the Imagination*, p. 118; Wright, *Jesus and the Victory of God*, pp. 576, 587-88, 591, 593, et passim.

44. From "All Our Dark Tomorrows," written by Bruce Cockburn. © 2002 Golden Mountain Music Corp. (SOCAN). Used by permission.

toration follow? Can we expect, with old Simeon, not only the *falling* (πτῶσις) of many in Israel but also their *rising* (ἀνάστασις, 2:34)? Although the imagery of v. 35a is reminiscent of various Old Testament texts, streams of direct influence can be difficult to trace to the source.[45] The closest parallels are in Jeremiah:

Luke 13:35

your house is being left to you   ἀφίεται ὑμῖν ὁ οἶκος ὑμῶν

Matthew 23:38

your house is being left to you desolate   ἀφίεται ὑμῖν ὁ οἶκος ὑμῶν ἔρημος

Jeremiah 12:7

I have forsaken my house   ἐγκαταλέλοιπα τὸν οἶκόν μου

Jeremiah 22:5

this house shall become a desolation   εἰς ἐρήμωσιν ἔσται ὁ οἶκος οὗτος

Both Jeremiah texts probably left their mark on Luke's imagination, if not on his lexical choices. Jeremiah 12:7 pictures Israel abandoned by God for her unfaithfulness. Jeremiah's ἐγκαταλείπω *(forsake)* is stronger than Luke's ἀφίημι *(leave)* but the semantic space between them in this context is probably not great. It is unclear whether the "house" in 12:7 is the people[46] or their city and temple.[47] As for Jeremiah 22:5, the future form of εἰμί followed by εἰς matches nicely Luke's futuristic present ἀφίεται.[48] Matthew's ἔρημος, if original, strengthens the connection to Jeremiah 22:5. More striking than similarities in diction, however, are broader parallels between Luke 13 and Jeremiah 22, and between the figures of Jesus and the Weeping Prophet.

> 1Thus says the LORD: Go down to the house (τὸν οἶκον) of the king of Judah, and speak there this word, 2and say: Hear the word of the LORD, O

45. See also 1 Kings 9:8; Ps. 69:25 (68:26 LXX); Isa. 64:10-11 (9-10 LXX); Ezek. 10:18-19; 11:23; Hag. 1:9; Tob. 14:4 (BA); Bar. 4:12, 19. The addition of ἔρημος to some copies of Luke 13:35 (e.g., D, *f*[13]) is due to the influence of either Matt. 23:38 (where it has greater ms. support) or to the presence of the cognate ἐρήμωσις in Jer. 22:5. Cf. Fitzmyer, *Luke*, p. 1036; Marshall, *Luke*, p. 576; Robert H. Gundry, *Matthew: A Commentary on His Literary and Theological Art* (Grand Rapids: Eerdmans, 1982), p. 473.

46. William McKane, *A Critical and Exegetical Commentary on Jeremiah*, 2 vols., ICC (Edinburgh: T. & T. Clark, 1986), 1:269.

47. Robert P. Carroll, *Jeremiah: A Commentary* (Philadelphia: Westminster, 1986), p. 290.

48. Cf. M. Zerwick, *Biblical Greek* (Rome: Scripta Pontificii Instituti Biblici, 1963) §32.

King of Judah sitting on the throne of David — you, and your servants (ὁ
οἶκός σου), and your people who enter these gates. ₃Thus says the LORD:
Act with justice and righteousness, and deliver from the hand of the op-
pressor anyone who has been robbed. And do no wrong or violence to the
alien, the orphan, and the widow, or shed innocent blood in this place.
₄For if you will indeed obey this word, then through the gates of this
house shall enter kings (εἰσελεύσονται ἐν ταῖς πύλαις τοῦ οἴκου τούτου
βασιλεῖς) who sit on the throne of David, riding in chariots and on horses
(καθήμενοι ἐπὶ θρόνου Δαυιδ καὶ ἐπιβεβηκότες ἐφ᾽ ἁρμάτων καὶ ἵππων),
they, and their servants, and their people. ₅But if you will not heed these
words, I swear by myself, says the LORD, that this house shall become a
desolation (εἰς ἐρήμωσιν ἔσται ὁ οἶκος οὗτος). ₆For thus says the LORD
concerning the house (τοῦ οἴκου) of the king of Judah:

You are like Gilead to me,
    like the summit of Lebanon;
but I swear that I will make you a desert,
    an uninhabited city (ἐὰν μὴ θῶ σε εἰς ἔρημον πόλεις μὴ
        κατοικηθησομένας).
₇I will prepare destroyers against you,
    all with their weapons;
they shall cut down your choicest cedars
    and cast them into the fire.

₈And many nations will pass by this city, and all of them will say one to another, "Why has the LORD dealt in this way with that great city (τῇ πόλει τῇ
μεγάλῃ ταύτῃ)?" ₉ And they will answer, "Because they abandoned the covenant of the LORD their God, and worshiped other gods and served them."

₁₀Do not weep (μὴ κλαίετε) for him who is dead,
    nor bemoan him;
weep (κλαύσατε κλαυθμῷ) rather for him who goes away,
    for he shall return no more
    to see his native land. (Jer. 22:1-10 NRSV)

First and most obviously, Jesus shares Jeremiah's burden to warn Jerusalem of looming judgment. Jeremiah's indictment of the city (22:3 and elsewhere)[49] is full of specifics: injustice, corruption, violence, abuse of the vul-

49. Cf. Jer. 5:26-29; 6:13; 7:5-6; 22:17.

nerable. These consistently social, or "horizontal," vices can also be summarized (e.g., in 22:9) in strictly "vertical," theological terms: "they abandoned the covenant of the LORD their God, and worshiped other gods and served them." The "desolation" Jeremiah foresaw became reality in 586 BCE when Nebuchadnezzar's forces laid siege to Jerusalem, destroyed its temple, and led thousands into exile.[50] For Jesus to utter *any* lament over the city of Jerusalem would thus be to invite comparisons with the Weeping Prophet.[51] That Jesus was similarly eager to identify covenant faithfulness with social justice should come as no surprise.[52] That Jesus displayed similar indignation over rampant abuse of the poor and vulnerable[53] is one more way he demonstrated kinship with Israel's prophets.

Second, several contours of Luke 13:35 stand out in the twilight of Jeremiah's gloomy oracle. As noted above, Luke's "your house is left to you" (13:35) recalls Jeremiah's "this house shall become a desolation" (22:5). Luke's ambiguous ἀφίεται could imply God's (final) *abandonment,* or it could denote a more provisional *release* to Jerusalem's enemies, as described in Luke 21:20-24.[54] If we assume that the harsh tone of Jeremiah's ultimatum, including the threat of *desolation,* was known to the earliest Jewish Christian communities, Jesus' oracle would have sounded, paradoxically, more muted (*abandonment* rather than *desolation*) and more pressing (near present certainty rather than conditional future possibility) at the same time.

As for the referent of Jesus' "house," Francis Weinert has persuaded a number of scholars that since the abandoned "house" in Jeremiah 22 is the king's royal household (22:1-2), "your house" in Luke 13:35 refers not to the temple but to "Israel's Judean leadership, and those who fall under their au-

---

50. Jeremiah uses both oracle and narrative to describe the Babylonian captivity. See, e.g., 4:4-10, 20, 27; 5:17; 7:14-15, 34; 9:10-12; 24:1-10; 29:16-20; 32:28-32; 38:2; 39:1-10; 52:1-30.

51. Jeremiah (including Lamentations) and Baruch inspired more than a few Jews living around the time of the Second Temple's destruction, including, most notably, 2 Baruch, Josephus (*War* 5.391-95; cf. *Ant.*10.79, 112-42), and Matthew, on which see Moffitt, "Righteous Bloodshed," pp. 299-320.

52. Examples abound. In the immediate context, see Luke 13:15-16, 24-30; 14:3-5, 13-14, 21-23.

53. See, e.g., Luke 3:10-14; 6:24, 30-38; 16:25; 18:1-8; 19:8-9, 45-46; 20:46-47.

54. On the various ways ἀφίημι has been interpreted here, see Marshall, *Luke,* p. 576. Paul denies that God has *rejected* (ἀπωθέω) his people (Rom. 11:1). Luke's *left* (ἀφίημι) is considerably weaker. What it surely cannot mean, however, is *left in peace,* contra Francis D. Weinert, "Luke, the Temple, and Jesus' Saying about Jerusalem's Abandoned House," *CBQ* 44 (1982): 73 n. 16, who presses his thesis — that Luke has a more sympathetic view of the temple than many allow — too hard.

thority."[55] For others, the "abandoned house" is Jerusalem, not only because the city is the clear focus of Jesus' oracle, but also because the image of a forsaken, empty city is a common *topos* in Scripture.[56] Of course, a third possible referent for οἶκος is the temple.[57]

Against Weinert, we cannot assume that if Jeremiah inspired Luke's lexical choice, he also determined Luke's meaning. Given that Jesus addresses wayward Jerusalem in the second person (σου . . . ἠθελήσατε)[58] in v. 34, the pronoun ὑμῶν in v. 35a most naturally refers to Jerusalem, and thus the abandoned "house" to the temple. It is arguably circular to reason that when οἶκος refers to the temple, accompanying pronouns *must* refer to God.[59] Furthermore, the excerpt from Psalm 118:26a (117:26a LXX) in Luke 13:35b concludes with a clear reference to the temple: εὐλογήκαμεν ὑμᾶς ἐξ οἴκου κυρίου ("we have blessed you from the house of the Lord," v. 26b). Thus, the two halves of Luke 13:35 are inversely parallel to the two halves of Psalm 118:26: the "house" that rightfully belongs to YHWH, from which should be heard the blessings of God's people, is being abandoned "to you." God's glory is moving out.[60]

Luke 13:35		Psalm 118(117):26	
A.	See, your **house** is left to you.	B.	**Blessed is the one who comes in the name of the Lord.**
B.	And I tell you, you will not see me until the time comes when you say, "**Blessed is the one who comes in the name of the Lord.**"	A.	We have blessed you from the **house of the Lord.**

55. Weinert, "Luke, the Temple, and Jesus' Saying," p. 76. Similarly disinclined to see "your house" as a reference to the temple are Fitzmyer, *Luke*, pp. 1036-37; Bock, *Luke*, p. 1250.

56. E.g., Lamentations 1. See Moessner, *Lord of the Banquet*, p. 235 n. 133; Nolland, *Luke*, p. 742; Marshall, *Luke*, p. 576; Green, *Luke*, p. 539; and sources cited by Tan, *Zion Traditions*, p. 113 n. 77.

57. Cf. Jer. 7:10, 11, 14; 11:15; 23:11, etc. See Wright, *Jesus and the Victory of God*, p. 571 n. 120; Tan, *Zion Traditions*, pp. 113-15.

58. The shift from singular (σου) to plural (ἠθελήσατε) simply reflects the collective force of the singular Ἰερουσαλήμ.

59. Str-B 1.943-44, followed by Marshall, *Luke*, p. 576, challenged by Tan, *Zion Traditions*, p. 114. In Luke 11:51 it is the context, not the accompanying pronoun, that makes clear that the sanctuary is in view. In Isa. 64:11 (64:10 LXX) the temple is called "our . . . house" (ὁ οἶκος, τὸ ἅγιον ἡμῶν).

60. G. R. Beasley-Murray, *Jesus and the Kingdom of God* (Grand Rapids: Eerdmans, 1986), p. 305, is among those who find a close analogy in Ezekiel's vision of the Shekinah abandoning temple and city (Ezek. 10:1-22).

If, then, "your house" means the temple, we shall have to add this oracle to the list of things Jesus said and did that might be construed (rightly or wrongly) as anti-temple (Luke 21:6; Mark 14:58; 15:29; John 2:19; Acts 6:14; *Gos. Thom.* 71).[61] At the end of the day, however, the distinction between city and temple may be moot: a divinely abandoned Jerusalem includes its temple; a forsaken temple leaves the city without protection.

Finally, Jeremiah's oracle resolves into tears. The content and structure of Jeremiah 22:10 parallel closely another of Jesus' laments — his charge to the "daughters of Jerusalem" in Luke 23:28. The sequence in both is second-person prohibition + imperative + ground.

Jeremiah 22:10 (LXX)	Luke 23:28-29
μὴ κλαίετε τὸν τεθνηκότα μηδὲ θρηνεῖτε αὐτόν,	**μὴ κλαίετε** ἐπ' ἐμέ·
κλαύσατε κλαυθμῷ τὸν ἐκπορευόμενον,	πλὴν ἐφ' ἑαυτὰς **κλαίετε** καὶ ἐπὶ τὰ τέκνα ὑμῶν,
ὅτι οὐκ ἐπιστρέψει ἔτι καὶ οὐ μὴ ἴδῃ τὴν γῆν πατρίδος αὐτοῦ	**ὅτι** ἰδοὺ ἔρχονται ἡμέραι ἐν αἷς ἐροῦσιν· μακάριαι αἱ στεῖραι . . .
Stop weeping for the dead nor mourn for him;	**Stop weeping** for me;
weep greatly rather for the one who departs	**weep** rather for yourselves and for your children
because he will not return and will never again see his homeland	**because**, behold, days are coming when they will say, "blessed are the barren . . ."

These similarities do not amount to literary dependence, but they do provide further reason to imagine Jesus in the company of Jeremiah. If, as Richard would say, "we choose to hear a connection" between Jeremiah 22 and Luke 23, "we have performed a synthetic hermeneutical act"[62] that effectively deepens and intensifies Jesus' lament for a people living on the verge of one more exile.

---

61. See Wright, *Jesus and the Victory of God*, pp. 333-36, 526, and, on the temple incident (Luke 19:45-46 //), 415-25. E. P. Sanders, *Jesus and Judaism* (Philadelphia: Fortress, 1985), pp. 61, 70-76, famously took Jesus' action against the temple as the historical starting point in his quest for the historical Jesus. See also Davies, *Gospel and Land*, pp. 349 n. 45 and 350 n. 46. For an (unpersuasive) attempt to challenge the point, see Gaston, *No Stone on Another*, pp. 154, 161, 242, et passim.

62. Hays, *Echoes*, p. 24.

Nor is Jeremiah 22:8-10 the only time the prophet invites us to *see his tears:*

- 9:1 (8:23 MT): O that my head were a spring of water, and my eyes a fountain of tears, so that I might weep day and night for the slain of my poor people![63]
- 9:18 (17 MT): let them quickly raise a dirge over us, so that our eyes may run down with tears, and our eyelids flow with water.
- 13:17: But if you will not listen, my soul will weep in secret for your pride; my eyes will weep bitterly and run down with tears, because the LORD's flock has been taken captive.
- 14:17: You shall say to them this word: Let my eyes run down with tears night and day, and let them not cease, for the virgin daughter — my people — is struck down with a crushing blow, with a very grievous wound.
- Lamentations 2:18: Cry aloud to the Lord! O wall of daughter Zion! Let tears stream down like a torrent day and night! Give yourself no rest, your eyes no respite!

Each of these grim laments should come to mind when we "belàted rootless readers"[64] overhear Jesus bewailing the fate of Jerusalem and its daughters. Indeed, Jeremiah's woes likely helped Jesus himself find his prophetic voice. They supplied the chord chart, bass line, even a haunting riff or two, with which Jesus could perform, in the same venue, blues improvisations of his own.

Given these various notes of resonance with Jeremiah, we dare not forget that it was Jeremiah's prophetic mandate not only to kindle fires of coming judgment but also, eventually, to forecast rains of restoration. As long as God's covenants stand, Jeremiah reasoned, Jerusalem's woes could not last.[65] The prophet's warnings were not only ominous; they were also provisional. If only the king and his "house" would forswear corruption, then one Davidic monarch after another would enjoy a triumphal entry en route to the throne (Jer. 22:4); if injustice continued unchecked, however, the royal "house" (22:5) and the "great city" (22:8) would be left desolate.[66] The condi-

---

63. Translations in this series are from the NRSV.

64. Hays, *Echoes*, p. 43.

65. Jer. 33:25-26; cf. Jer. 1:10; 5:18; 16:14-15; 23:3-8; 29:10-14; 30-31; 32:36-44; 33; 52:31-34.

66. Jeremiah's image of a righteous Davidic king riding through Jerusalem's gates intensifies the irony of Jesus' royal ascent (Luke 19:28-40).

tional nature of Jeremiah's oracles — what Dale Allison calls "the contingency of prophecy"[67] — should encourage readers to ask whether Jesus (and Luke) could have shared Jeremiah's vision of judgment without also sharing his hope for restoration. If the permanent desolation of Jerusalem was unimaginable for Jeremiah, could it be otherwise for Jesus?[68]

Tears Can Sing and Joy Shed Tears[69] (Luke 13:35b, c, d)

Scholars debate whether or not our passage promises the restoration of Jerusalem's fortunes. Do alienation and judgment prevail, or does Jesus' tearful lament invert into a joyful shout, like Paul's, that all Israel will be saved (cf. Rom. 11:26)? The debate turns in part on how to construe the logic of v. 35.

a. ἰδοὺ ἀφίεται ὑμῖν ὁ οἶκος ὑμῶν.

b. λέγω [δὲ] ὑμῖν, οὐ μὴ ἴδητέ με

c. ἕως [ἥξει ὅτε] εἴπητε,

d. εὐλογημένος ὁ ἐρχόμενος ἐν ὀνόματι κυρίου.

a. See, your house is left to you.

b. [And] I tell you, you will not see me

c. until [the time comes when] you say,[70]

d. "Blessed is the one who comes in the name of the Lord."

If God's absence from Jerusalem's "house" (35a) coincides with Messiah's absence from Jerusalem (35b),[71] does the (re-)appearance of Messiah

---

67. Dale C. Allison Jr., *The End of the Ages Has Come* (Philadelphia: Fortress, 1985), pp. 157-59.

68. Cf. Nolland, *Luke*, p. 742, and see the discussion of contingency in Luke 13:35 below.

69. A line from "Hills Of Morning," written by Bruce Cockburn. © 1979 Golden Mountain Music Corp. (SOCAN), used by permission, in which people await the arrival in Jerusalem of the "glittering joker" (i.e., Jesus). On the integrity of vv. 34-35 (against claims by, e.g., Haenchen, Kloppenborg that v. 35b was not part of the original oracle), see Tan, *Zion Traditions*, p. 104. We noted earlier that the two halves of v. 35 share a common debt to Ps. 118:26. See also Dale C. Allison Jr., "Matt. 23:39 = Luke 13:35b as a Conditional Prophecy," *JSNT* 5 (1983): 76-77.

70. Matthew 23:39 has οὐ μή με ἴδητε ἀπ' ἄρτι ἕως ἄν ("from now on until"), since according to Matthew 21 Jesus is already in the city. The bracketed words in Luke [ἥξει ὅτε] ("the time comes when") are absent from P[45], P[75], ℵ, B, *f*[13], etc., and present in A, D, *f*[1], 𝔐, etc. Marshall, *Luke*, p. 577, cautiously supports their originality.

71. The parallelism between these two clauses probably counts as "external" evidence against the mildly adversative δέ that connects 35a and 35b in most manuscripts. (It is absent

(35c) herald the city's restoration? Will Jerusalem yet bless the Coming One?[72]

We can safely rule out the contention that the outburst in 35d is a begrudging, anguished concession uttered by the condemned.[73] The language of Psalm 118, including the verse cited here (and repeated in Luke 19:38), is entirely too animated and joyful. Also unsatisfactory is the suggestion that because Luke (unlike Matthew) has Jesus utter these words well *before* his arrival in Jerusalem, we are to see them fulfilled at the triumphal entry in the jubilant throng's invocation of them (19:38) — precisely as Jesus foretold — and in the people's delight in "the mighty works they had *seen*" (εἶδον, 19:37; cf. ἴδητε in 13:35).[74] Not only does the temporal sequence — Jerusalem "sees" Jesus (13:35b) *only after* her house is abandoned (13:35a) — tell against such an identification, but it would be utterly anticlimactic and "heavily ironical"[75] for Jesus to refer, in solemn, scriptural tones and at the pinnacle of his oracle, to a fleeting gesture performed only a few short days before he is executed. Luke implies as much when he juxtaposes the disciples' euphoric welcome with the Pharisees' cynical rebuke (19:39), followed immediately by Je-

---

in P[45] and the original hand of ℵ.) Likewise, the fact that Matthew's γάρ (23:39) makes "you will not see me until" *explanatory* reinforces the parallelism and may indirectly support the absence of an *adversative* conjunction in Luke.

72. On ἐρχόμενος ("Coming One") as a Messianic title in Psalm 118 (117 LXX) and Hab. 2:3, see Richard Hays, "Apocalyptic Hermeneutics: Habakkuk Proclaims 'The Righteous One,'" in *Conversion of the Imagination*, p. 125 n. 16. Psalm 118 is one of Luke's favorites. A marked citation of Ps. 118:22 appears in Luke 20:17 (and, unmarked, in 9:22; 17:25; and Acts 4:11); we hear echoes of Ps. 118:15 in Mary's Magnificat (Luke 1:51); and we find Ps. 118:26, unmarked, not only in our text (13:35) but also in Luke 19:38 and, allusively, in 7:19-20. On the significant shift in focus from "Coming One" (Ps. 118:26) to "rejected Stone" (118:22) in the course of Luke's narrative (occurring between Luke 19:38 and 20:17), see J. Ross Wagner, "Psalm 118 in Luke-Acts: Tracing a Narrative Thread," in *Early Christian Interpretation of the Scriptures of Israel: Investigations and Proposals*, ed. Craig A. Evans and James A. Sanders, JSNTSup 148 (Sheffield: Sheffield Academic, 1997), pp. 154-78.

73. Those who think Jerusalem's confession will be "too late" include Fitzmyer, *Luke*, p. 1036; T. W. Manson, *The Sayings of Jesus* (London: SCM, 1971), p. 128; Wright, *Jesus and the Victory of God*, p. 572. For rebuttals, see Beasley-Murray, *Jesus and the Kingdom*, pp. 305-6; Allison, "Conditional Prophecy," pp. 75-76; Tan, *Zion Traditions*, pp. 116-17.

74. Cf. Schweizer, *Luke*, p. 230; Luke T. Johnson, *The Gospel of Luke*, SP 3 (Collegeville, Minn.: Liturgical Press, 1991), pp. 219-21; Leander E. Keck, *Who Is Jesus? History in Perfect Tense* (Columbia: University of South Carolina Press, 2000), p. 119. This reading gains credence if the clause that includes εἶδον in Luke 19:37 (not in Matthew or Mark) is Luke's own contribution.

75. Marshall, *Luke*, p. 577. Similarly, Wright, *Jesus and the Victory of God*, p. 572, but whether he sees literary or historical irony here (or both) is unclear.

sus' second lament (19:41-44), which emphasizes Jerusalem's inability to *see* (ἐκρύβη ἀπὸ ὀφθαλμῶν σου). If, however, the brief swirl of enthusiasm accompanying the triumphal entry is for Luke ironic *non*-fulfillment of Jesus' oracle, there are reasons to think it nevertheless serves to preview coming eschatological attractions.[76]

Luke 13:35 anticipates a time when the city will not only "see" but also "bless" her Messiah, a time when Jerusalem's mourning will turn to laughter.[77] Does Luke see Israel's reconciliation as an unqualified certainty or a contingent possibility? Does Jesus lay out a sequence of assured future events, or does he lay down conditions that Jerusalem must meet? What logic, in other words, governs the relationship between 13:35b and 35c? Examples of both alternatives — unqualified certainty and contingent possibility — lie close at hand. In each of the following, the main clause contains a negative prediction or oath and the subordinate clause is introduced by ἕως.

Temporal-unqualified: X will not happen *until (at least until, only until)* Y happens.

Luke 9:27   τινες . . . οἳ οὐ μὴ γεύσωνται θανάτου ἕως ἂν ἴδωσιν (aor. subj.) τὴν βασιλείαν. Some will see the kingdom **before** they die (i.e., they will not die **at least until** they see the kingdom).

Luke 21:32   οὐ μὴ παρέλθῃ ἡ γενεὰ αὕτη ἕως ἂν πάντα γένηται (aor. subj.). These things will take place **before** this generation passes (i.e., this generation will live **at least until** it sees these things take place).

Luke 22:34   οὐ φωνήσει σήμερον ἀλέκτωρ ἕως[78] τρίς με ἀπαρνήσῃ (fut. ind.) εἰδέναι. A rooster will not crow today **until** you have denied that you know me three times (i.e., the rooster will remain silent **only until** you deny me three times); cf. Luke 22:16, 18; 24:49.

---

76. Thus Nolland, *Luke*, p. 742. Matthew's sequence (entry in ch. 21, lament in ch. 23) rules out such a reading.

77. Similarly, Robert C. Tannehill, "Israel in Luke-Acts: A Tragic Story," *JBL* 104 (1985): 84-85; Bock, *Luke*, p. 1251; Nolland, *Luke*, p. 742.

78. Textual variants (πρίν ἤ, ἕως ὅτου, ἕως οὗ) do not alter the sense. Luke 22:61 has πρίν.

Temporal-contingent: X will not happen *unless* Y happens.

Luke 12:59 οὐ μὴ ἐξέλθῃς ἐκεῖθεν, ἕως[79] καὶ τὸ ἔσχατον λεπτὸν ἀποδῷς (aor. subj.). You will not get out **until (before, unless, if . . . not)** you pay (i.e., **if** you pay the debt, **then** you will get out).

Acts 23:12 οἱ Ἰουδαῖοι ἀνεθεμάτισαν ἑαυτοὺς λέγοντες μήτε φαγεῖν μήτε πιεῖν ἕως οὗ ἀποκτείνωσιν (aor. subj.) τὸν Παῦλον. The Jews were bound not to eat or drink **until (before, unless, if . . . not)** they killed Paul (i.e., **if** they killed Paul, **then** they would eat); cf. Luke 15:4, 8; Acts 23:14, 21; Matt. 18:30; 2 Thess. 2:7.

If Luke 13:35b-c recounts an "unqualified" temporal sequence, the idea is that Jerusalem will one day witness the arrival of the Coming One, offer a blessing, and be restored. To paraphrase: "you will say 'blessed is the one . . . ', *and then* you will finally see me." On this reading, Jesus implies no imperative and issues no challenge. A strong case can be made, however, for reading Luke 13:35b-c as a "contingent" statement.[80] Not only is this a live grammatical possibility,[81] but it fits better in a context that has been consistently judgmental. A "contingent" promise works like a negative condition: "you will not see me *unless* you say." Jesus' word would be, like Peter's in Acts 3:19-21, a call for Jerusalem to repent and to embrace her Messiah *in order that* "times of refreshing" may come. On this reading, Israel's embrace of Messiah would be a necessary precondition of the consummation,[82] as Lloyd Gaston remarks:

---

79. Some manuscripts insert οὖ or ἄν after ἕως.

80. See especially Allison, "Conditional Prophecy," p. 78. The argument is reiterated in Allison, *End of the Ages*, pp. 155-60, summarized in Davies and Allison, *Matthew*, pp. 323-24, and followed by Tan, *Zion Traditions*, pp. 115-18; Green, *Luke*, p. 538.

81. On the functional equivalence of ἕως clauses and conditional relative clauses, see E. Burton, *Syntax of the Moods and Tenses in New Testament Greek* (Chicago: University of Chicago Press, 1900; reprint, Grand Rapids: Kregel, 1976) §329. Cf. BDF §§382-83; Smyth, *Greek Grammar* §§2422-29.

82. Strikingly reminiscent of Jesus' words and tone in Luke 13 is Josephus's mournful apostrophe over Jerusalem offered shortly before the Roman onslaught began (*War* 5.19-20): (1) Josephus addresses Jerusalem directly (ὦ τλημονεστάτη πόλις, "O most wretched city"); (2) Jerusalem's future devastation is assured; (3) the city can no longer be called "God's place" (θεοῦ . . . οὔτε ἧς ἔτι χῶρος); (4) the city's inhabitants are called "householders" (οἰκείων); (5) hope of "better things" ἀμείνων is imagined; (6) the orator confesses personal grief (τὰ πάθη, ὀλοφυρμός); (7) the future depends on whether or not Jerusalem appeases God (εἴγε ποτὲ τὸν πορθήσαντα θεὸν ἐξιλάσῃ).

By making the coming [of the Messiah] dependent on Israel's prior repentance and readiness to receive him, the saying is in this sense a threat. This threat expresses clearly the nature of all the threats to Israel in this gospel: it serves to call Israel to repentance, but God forbid that Israel should not repent and the threat become a reality.[83]

Strikingly, it is only with this final clause — this (contingent) offer of salvation — that we come face to face with Israel's Scripture. Not that the biblical precursor hasn't been hovering all along, like a hen over its brood. Each element of v. 34 — the "Jerusalem" doublet, the charge of "propheticide," the avian imagery — echoes Scripture (especially Jeremiah), and the metaphor of the abandoned "house" in v. 35 is densely allusive (especially, again, of Jeremiah). But only here as the oracle reaches its climax, with talk of eschatological reversal and the appearance of the Coming One, is there explicit citation.[84] By incrementally appropriating biblical language and imagery, the prophecy builds in a crescendo until stark condemnation finally gives way to urgent paraenesis and qualified hope.

Tears Spot the Dust[85] (Luke 19:41-44)

41As he drew near he saw the city and wept over it, 42saying, "You, if only you had recognized on this day the things that make for peace! But now they are hidden from you. 43For the days will come upon you when your enemies will set up siege works against you and encircle you and constrain you on every side, 44and they will raze you to the ground, you and your children within you, and they will not leave one of your stones on another, because you did not recognize the time of your visitation." (Luke 19:41-44)

Jesus utters his second lament *while approaching* (ὡς ἤγγισεν) Jerusalem. Evidently we should picture Jesus wending through the throngs on his way

83. Gaston, *No Stone on Another,* p. 347.

84. Hays, *Echoes,* p. 23, pictures a "spectrum of intertextual reference, moving from the explicit to the subliminal." For a helpful fourfold description of New Testament dependence on the Old (ranging from direct citation to allusions and echoes), see Richard Hays and Joel Green, "The Use of the Old Testament by New Testament Writers," in *Hearing the New Testament,* ed. Joel B. Green (Grand Rapids: Eerdmans, 1995), pp. 226-28.

85. "Postcards From Cambodia," written by Bruce Cockburn. © 2002 Golden Mountain Music Corp. (SOCAN), used by permission, laments the human cost of war.

down the Mount of Olives *and then* pausing to weep in the Kidron — not far from the prophets' tombs, perhaps? — before his final ascent.[86] The abrupt switch from jubilation (19:37-38) to lamentation (19:41), albeit punctuated by the Pharisees' rebuke (19:39-40), is starkly ironic. Fleeting winds of popularity cannot dispel gathering clouds. Each tear striking the hot dust is an omen of coming rains.

It was precisely this abrupt shift in Luke's account — from joy to lament, from accepting praise to assessing blame — that convinced Brent Kinman to examine the "triumphal entry" in Luke (19:28-44) through the lens of the Roman *parousia* (i.e., the celebratory welcome of dignitaries).[87] According to Kinman, Luke aimed to show that the response of the city's "leading men" (cf. 19:47) to Jesus' royal entry was woefully inadequate and grossly insulting. Someone acquainted with the Roman *parousia*, he contends, would feel this tension immediately.

Kinman's efforts may be judged a success to the extent that he has illuminated Jesus' royal status as "Son of David" (18:38) and king[88] and made sense of the animal's role (19:30-35) and the disciples' homage (19:36). And there is no question that chapter 19 as a whole is anticlimactic: Israel's long-awaited king is met not with citywide acclaim but with conflict, controversy, and rejection. But the Roman *parousia* may be less helpful as an interpretive context than Kinman suggests. Luke 19:42-44 does not read like a *response* to insult and reception.[89] This oracle is less at home among snubbed Roman

86. One would have expected Jesus to weep over Jerusalem *as the city first came into view, before* his descent into the Kidron. Luke's sequence (royal ride, then lament) makes for better theology than geography. Marcus Borg and John Crossan's idea, in *The Last Week* (New York: Harper SanFrancisco, 2006), pp. 2-5, that Jesus deliberately staged his procession on the city's east side so as to counter Pilate's military entrance from the west, is good theology but dubious history. Either way, Luke gives no thought to Pilate's theatrics here.

87. Brent Kinman, "Parousia, Jesus' 'A-Triumphal' Entry, and the Fate of Jerusalem (Luke 19:28-44)," *JBL* 118 (1999): 279-94.

88. Cf. "kingdom" in 19:11, 12, 15 and "king" in 19:38 (not in Mark 11:9). On the *royal* dimensions of Jesus' ride, see especially James A. Sanders, "A Hermeneutic Fabric: Psalm 118 in Luke's Entrance Narrative," in C. A. Evans and J. A. Sanders, *Luke and Scripture: The Function of Sacred Tradition in Luke-Acts* (Minneapolis: Fortress, 1993), pp. 141-48. The ascent is more than a retrospective reenactment. Jesus rides in anticipation of future coronation.

89. The nobleman/king of Luke 19:12 inflicts harsh judgment (19:27) on his unwilling subjects (19:14), not because they failed to *welcome him,* but because they sent a delegation to protest his rule *while he was away* (19:14). The slaughter of 19:27 prefigures the fall of Jerusalem (cf. 19:43-44), but the common denominator between 19:11-27 and 28-44 is not a royal *parousia.* It would have been easy for Luke to shape the parable such that the rebellious subjects displayed their hatred *upon his arrival.*

dignitaries than among rejected Israelite prophets including, once again, Jeremiah.[90]

Kinman may be right that some readers of Luke's Gospel would judge the reception Jesus received to be modest, even dishonorable, lacking as it did a welcome from the city's elite (19:47). But given Jesus' track record with religious leaders thus far (e.g., 11:15-16, 53-54; 13:14; 15:2; 16:14), readers would hardly be expecting a red-carpet welcome. Indeed, they might be struck more by the surprising warmth of the "multitude" (19:37) of urban disciples than by the predictable hostility of Jerusalem's aristocracy (19:39, 47).

Also problematic is Kinman's proposal that ἐν τῇ ἡμέρᾳ ταύτῃ ("on this day," 19:42) refers to the literal "day" Jesus entered the city and, further, that Jesus' indictment of Jerusalem was in direct response to the city's failure to welcome him properly on his arrival.[91] It is certainly true that Luke's narrative has been building toward "this (very) day" and that the advent of Israel's king should have prompted all to exclaim, "this is the day (αὐτὴ ἡ ἡμέρα) that the Lord has made" (Ps. 118:24).[92] But given Luke's use of ἡμέρα elsewhere,[93] it is not clear that "day" in 19:42 should be construed so narrowly. Moreover, Jerusalem's incomprehension is described as a *fait accompli* (note the second class condition; cf. 13:34-35); the rejection of the king began well before he appeared on the horizon.

Jesus' tears do not flow until he *sees* the city. As Luke tells it, Jesus saw two things: a people who had tragically spurned his offer of peace, and a city whose destruction was now assured. This was no piece of theater. Like Paul's anguished offer to go to hell to save his people (Rom. 9:3), Jesus' distress cannot be contained. How different this is from the dry-eyed composure of Mark Twain, who seems almost proud of his impassivity.

---

90. Kinman, "Parousia," p. 290, grants that 19:41-44 is "a rich *mélange* of OT language and imagery." The words of David Tiede, *Prophecy and History in Luke-Acts*, p. 78, cited by Nolland, *Luke 18:35–24:53*, WBC 35C (Dallas: Word, 1993), p. 931, are apt: "It is finally the sympathy of the suffering prophet, of Deuteronomy's Moses, of Jeremiah, Isaiah, and Hosea, caught up in the rage, anguish, frustration, and sorrow of God for Israel that constitutes the pathos of the story."

91. Kinman, "Parousia," p. 290.

92. According to the (properly tentative) reconstruction of J. Sanders ("Hermeneutic Fabric," p. 145), the recitation of Psalm 118 during annual enthronement ceremonies in the preexilic period included the singing of vv. 22-25 by "the chorus and perhaps all the people."

93. "That day" refers generically to a future unspecified time (6:23) or to the coming "day" of judgment (10:12; 17:31; 21:34). Luke can also refer to the future crisis with the plural, "those days" (21:23). Cleopas marvels that a stranger doesn't know what has happened "in these days" (24:18).

At last, away in the middle of the day, ancient bite of wall and crumbling arches began to line the way — we toiled up one more hill, and every pilgrim and every sinner swung his hat on high! Jerusalem!

Perched on its eternal hills, white and domed and solid, massed together and hooped with high gray walls, the venerable city gleamed in the sun. . . .

We dismounted and looked, without speaking a dozen sentences, across the wide intervening valley for an hour or more. . . .

I record it here as a notable but not discreditable fact that not even our pilgrims wept. I think there was no individual in the party whose brain was not teeming with thoughts and images and memories invoked by the grand history of the venerable city that lay before us, but still among them all was no "voice of them that wept."

There was no call for tears. Tears would have been out of place. The thoughts Jerusalem suggests are full of poetry, sublimity, and more than all, dignity. Such thoughts do not find their appropriate expression in the emotions of the nursery.[94]

Twain's Jerusalem was poetic and dignified; Jesus' was besieged and devastated. Twain's vision was clear; Jesus' tears filled the sky. Twain fell respectfully silent; Jesus sounded forth with prophetic audacity,[95] his cadence metered by the damning pronoun σύ.[96]

In contrast to Luke 13, Jesus' lament lacks entirely the self-conscious ἐγώ: he sheds no tears for himself, only for Jerusalem.[97] Also absent is any clear word about what will happen after the city falls; the horizon of Jesus' prophetic foresight is limited.[98] In what he does say, two lines stand out: 19:42a and 44b. The first of these is an incomplete second class condition: "if only you had recognized (εἰ ἔγνως) on this day the things that make for

---

94. Mark Twain, *The Innocents Abroad* (Hartford: American Publishing, 1869). Excerpt from ch. 52.

95. Cf. Ezek. 4:1-3; Isa. 29:3; Jer. 6:6, 15.

96. Σύ occurs twelve times in an oracle of sixty-two words.

97. Luke's Jesus anticipates his death (13:33-34; 14:27; 17:25; 18:31-33; 20:14-15, 17; 22:2, 15) without personal distress (Luke 23:28, 34, 43, 46; contrast Luke 22:40 with Matt. 26:37-38; Mark 14:33-34; John 12:27).

98. On the limitations of prophetic knowledge, see Scot McKnight, *A New Vision for Israel: The Teachings of Jesus in National Context* (Grand Rapids: Eerdmans, 1999), pp. 138-39; Meyer, *Aims of Jesus,* pp. 246-47. On how Luke-Acts creates space for the church between Jerusalem's desolation and the end (e.g., Luke 21:21-24; Acts 3:21), see Hays, *Moral Vision,* pp. 129-31; Davies, *Gospel and Land,* pp. 258-59.

peace (τὰ πρὸς εἰρήνην)." Readers must supply their own apodosis or, better yet, allow Jesus' voice to trail off.[99] The sentence's broken syntax mirrors the city's dashed hopes.

"Peace" is a loaded term for Luke, who deploys it fourteen times in his Gospel. It is the last word of Zechariah's prophecy (1:79); it is the promise of angels (2:14), the prayer of Simeon (2:29), and, most recently, the hope of crowds lining Jesus' path (19:38).[100] The word points to the city's deliverance (cf. παράκλησις in 2:25; σωτήριον in 2:30; λύτρωσις in 2:38; ἀπολύτρωσις in 21:28); its horrific converse is Roman devastation (19:43-44; 21:6, 20-24).[101]

A second key phrase (44b) matches the first: "you did not recognize (οὐκ ἔγνως) the time (καιρός, strategic moment) of your visitation (ἐπισκοπή)." Together these phrases (42a and 44b) frame the oracle and explain the coming destruction in terms of Jerusalem's "incomprehension" — not benign nonrecognition (cf. 2:50) but culpable obduracy, the penalty for which is the city's destruction.

The relentlessly negative tone of this oracle may mean that Jesus saw no further than 70 CE, though several considerations should be kept in mind. First, we are told that Jerusalem's failure to welcome God's messenger means that "now" (νῦν) the truth has been hidden from their sight (42b). This "hiding" is clearly God's doing.[102] In Luke, however, blindness and incomprehension may be partial (9:45; 18:34) and need not be permanent (24:25, 31, 45; Acts 9:8, 17). Recall that Jesus' first lament spoke (we argued, contingently) of Jerusalem's *future restored vision:* you will by no means *see* me unless and until you say . . . (13:35). If our two oracles are mutually illuminating, Jerusalem's present (νῦν) blindness need not be the final state of affairs.

Second, the second lament has a tight focus. So close is Jesus to Jerusalem's gates that he can see only two things: the city's lost chance for peace and the looming specter of war. Jerusalem's rejection of him (42a, 44b) is

99. On aposiopesis (including broken conditions) signaling "strong emotion," see BDF §482. Marshall, *Luke,* p. 831, argues for reading the v. l. (παρενέγκαι) in Luke 22:42 to produce a similarly fraught expression: "If you are willing to remove this cup from me."

100. See also 7:50; 8:48; 10:5, 6a-b; 11:21; 12:51; 14:32 (τὰ πρὸς εἰρήνην); 24:36. It appears seven times in Acts but only four times in Matthew, once in Mark, and six times in John.

101. We should not, however, reduce "peace" to homeland security, as if to imply that Jesus' goal was to craft a strategy for national resurgence and political autonomy. "Peace" certainly includes the absence of war, as the rest of the oracle makes clear, but the word is shorthand for much more: justice, reconciliation, prosperity, friendship, tranquility, safety, security, and redemption (cf. 13:34; Isa. 52:7-9).

102. Κρύπτω occurs in the "divine" passive (cf. ἀφίεται in Luke 13:35). For the equivalent in the active, see Luke 10:21.

now to be matched by God's rejection of the city (43-44a). The siege of Jerusalem (at least in this context[103]) will be clear vindication of Jesus as an authentic prophet of Israel. The oracle makes no attempt, however, to go beyond this moment of paradoxical vindication and destruction. Indeed, one might argue that for Jesus to tack something hopeful onto the end of this oracle would be to trivialize both the horrors of the siege[104] and the tragedy of the city's rejection of its prophet.

A final point is simply to recall offers of forgiveness later in Luke-Acts — most notably, in Jesus' cry from the cross: "Father, forgive them" (23:34).[105] Jesus' explicit appeal to the culpable yet forgivable ignorance (οὐ γὰρ οἴδασιν) of his executioners is an obvious point of contact with Luke 19:42a, 44b, as is Peter's temple sermon that highlights Jerusalem's "ignorance" (κατὰ ἄγνοιαν ἐπράξατε) alongside God's offer of forgiveness (εἰς τὸ ἐξαλειφθῆναι ὑμῶν τὰς ἁμαρτίας, Acts 3:17, 19; cf. 7:60; 13:27). Jesus' final words in Luke's Gospel (24:47) are also telling: to be proclaimed to all the nations is "repentance leading to forgiveness of sins" (μετάνοιαν εἰς ἄφεσιν ἁμαρτιῶν), "beginning from Jerusalem" (ἀρξάμενοι ἀπὸ Ἰερουσαλήμ).

These points do not prove that Luke anticipated the salvation of "all Israel," nor do they reveal how far Jesus could see beyond the devastation of Jerusalem. On the other hand, if we let Jesus' two laments interpret each other, and if we play both refrains in the key of Jeremiah, we may decide that Luke's tale of Jerusalem should not be reduced to one of refusal and utter abandonment. Indeed, Jesus' twofold lament in Luke may even whisper what Paul's Roman epistle proclaims — that Israel's rejection of her Messiah need not be final and that Jerusalem's *fullness* (πλήρωμα) and *acceptance* (πρόσλημψις) may yet follow her *defeat* (ἥττημα) and *rejection* (ἀποβολή, cf. Rom. 11:12, 15; Luke 13:35; 21:24).

---

103. I am not persuaded (yet) that talk of the "coming" of the "Son of Man" in Luke 21:27 // is apocalyptic code for the vindication of Jesus' messiahship in the events of 70 CE, as argued by N. T. Wright, *Jesus and the Victory of God*, pp. 510-19; McKnight, *New Vision*, p. 136. Cf. George B. Caird, *The Language and Imagery of the Bible* (London: Duckworth, 1980; reprint, Grand Rapids: Eerdmans, 1997), p. 266.

104. Several times during Josephus's grisly account of Jerusalem's destruction he offers moving lamentations: *War* 4.181, 323; 5.19-20, 391-93, 415-17, 420; 6.109-11, 300-307.

105. The authenticity of Luke 23:34a is, of course, suspect. It is absent in P75 ℵ1 B D* etc. For a cautious defense of authenticity, see Marshall, *Luke*, pp. 867-68. For forgiveness in Luke, see also 1:77; 3:3; 5:20-24; 7:47-50; 11:4; 12:10; 17:3-4; 24:47.

Waiting for a Miracle[106]

Like the Holy City of Herod and Pilate, today's Jerusalem still pulses with the cries of merchants and the prayers of holy men. Pilgrims, flush with foreign currency, still wrangle in the streets. Armed soldiers still patrol near the Temple Mount, and rumors of foreign incursion or homegrown uprising still circulate. Like Jesus descending the Mount of Olives, I cannot approach Jerusalem today without fighting back tears. She is no closer to blessing the Coming One than she was in Jesus' day, and the things that make for peace continue to elude her. Sustained confrontations are rare, but the chill of cold war hangs over the Muslim Quarter. Detained Palestinian youths wait while Israeli police check IDs. Armed vehicles crowd intersections. Riot barricades stand ready. Israeli flags fly proudly, provocatively, from Jewish settlements. And everywhere, guns. Ironically, the word heard most frequently on the streets of the city today, in both Hebrew and Arabic, is *peace. Shalom. Salaam.*

Not long ago I witnessed a Daewoo bulldozer flatten the home of a Palestinian family who simply lacked a building permit — a permit Jerusalem's bureaucracy makes it all but impossible for Palestinians to acquire.[107] I stared like a voyeur as the paterfamilias wept. On Jerusalem's outskirts I have watched armed Israelis compelling middle-aged Palestinian men to drop their pants on a public street to show they wore no explosives, and border police climbing out of jeeps to fire live rounds at young children whose only arsenal was the rubble at their feet. I have walked the "sterilized" streets of old Hebron, where Palestinians can no longer go, and listened to a former Israeli soldier describe how he used to torment civilians there.[108] In sight of Jerusalem I have stayed in homes whose rooftop water tanks must be refilled

106. Luke might appreciate Cockburn's question, "How come history takes such a long, long time when you're waiting for a miracle?" From "Waiting For A Miracle," written by Bruce Cockburn. © 1983 Golden Mountain Music Corp. (SOCAN). Used by permission.

107. Meir Margalit, *No Place Like Home: House Demolitions in East Jerusalem* (Jerusalem: ICAHD, 2007), pp. 21-27; Jeff Halper, *Obstacles to Peace: A Reframing of the Palestinian-Israeli Conflict,* 3rd ed. (Jerusalem: ICAHD, 2005), pp. 32-52.

108. "Sterilized" is Israeli military diction. For soldiers' stories, see "Breaking the Silence: Soldiers Speak Out about Their Service in Hebron" (from an exhibit sponsored by the group Breaking the Silence [Shovrim Shtika], Jerusalem, 2004, available at http://www.peacenow.org/news.asp?cid=76). See also the reports "Standing Idly By: Non-enforcement of the Law on Settlers, Hebron 26-28 July 2002" and "Ghost Town: Israel's Separation Policy and Forced Eviction of Palestinians from the Center of Hebron, May 2007" (both published by B'Tselem: The Israeli Information Center for Human Rights in the Occupied Territories, available at www.btselem.org/English/Hebron).

by hand when the Israeli authorities cut off electricity and ration water to ensure that settlers on nearby hilltops can water their lawns and fill their swimming pools.[109] Behind the Mount of Olives in Anata (home of Jeremiah), I have comforted a Palestinian forbidden to enter Jerusalem to visit his hospitalized daughter. I have smelled tear gas, felt percussion grenades, and looked on as soldiers battered nonviolent protestors whose crime was their stubborn presence on Israeli-confiscated Palestinian farmland. I have walked the course of the wall that knifes through Jerusalem, separating kin from kin, worker from job, farmer from olive grove, and people from sunset. And I've read the rage splashed across the wall's cold concrete canvas. My favorite graffiti is a hastily sprayed message in green paint: *Jesus wept for Jerusalem — we weep for Palestine.*

I do not excuse the suicide attacks and summary executions perpetrated by militant Palestinians, nor do I dispute charges of rampant corruption in the Palestinian Authority. But it is the asymmetry of the conflict that I find breathtaking. In one of history's peculiar ironies, Israel today plays the imperial role once filled by Rome, while the Palestinians mirror the part played by the Jews of ancient Galilee and Judea. We might (at some risk) compare yesterday's Jewish Zealots to today's Palestinian insurgents. Or Rome's legions to the modern IDF. The-state-of-Israel-*qua*-Rome justifies its incursions and human rights abuses in the name of security and economics, while perpetuating a caste system that extends full privileges to Jews and only a minority of Israeli Arabs.[110] Palestinian-militants-*qua*-Zealots justify targeting civilians in the name of honor, clan loyalty, and divine mandate, while shamelessly recruiting "peasants" whose harsh living conditions engender rage, despair, and shame. Tragically, eyes on both sides of the conflict seem blind to "the things that make for peace."

I would hesitate to wax political in a forum such as this (and may regret it) except that Richard himself pointed the way when he publicly objected to a decision by the esteemed Studiorum Novi Testamenti Societas to hold its 2000 annual meeting in Tel Aviv. According to the Society's minutes, Richard worried that the society would be "affording political legitimacy to the

109. See Hilal Elver, "Palestinian/Israeli Water Conflict and Implementation of International Water Law Principles," *HICLR* 28 (2005): 421-47. According to Elver (p. 427), Israel allocates ten times more water per capita to Jewish settlers than to West Bank Palestinians, while Palestinians pay up to six times more per unit of water.

110. On Israeli citizenship and Palestinian ID cards, see Gary Burge, *Whose Land? Whose Promise?* (Cleveland: Pilgrim, 2003), pp. 138-41. Burge's chapter 8 surveys the issues that define the occupation.

Israeli government at a time when it systematically denied to Palestinians basic human rights."[111]

Richard's moral critique of the state of Israel is not, *nota bene*, driven by theological supersessionism or Christian triumphalism. Indeed, his chapter on anti-Semitism and ethnic conflict in *Moral Vision* is an explicit repudiation of "the supersessionist illusion."[112] His critique is driven, rather, by the same passion for justice that burned within prophets like Jeremiah and Jesus. Nor does Richard adopt a two-covenant solution to the problem of Jewish-Christian relations. Instead he clings, together with Luke, Paul, and Jesus, to the audacious hope that one day Jerusalem's eyes will open to recognize and welcome the One whose coming Scripture has promised.[113] He is, I suppose, waiting for a miracle.

> The last act of the drama has not been played, and the mystery . . . is that its climax will be the reconciliation of all Israel. Such an account of the world makes sense only if the eschatological hope is literally real, only if we still expect God to act in the future. Paul (and Luke . . .) teach us to live with such an expectation and therefore to read Scripture as a continuous story within which we stand. The ending of that story remains open, but it stands under the promise of God's grace, God's assurance that he will not abandon his people.[114]

111. Minutes of the 53rd general meeting of the SNTS (Copenhagen, Aug 4-8, 1998), www.th.vu.nl/deboer/snts/53rdgm_mins.html.

112. Hays, *Moral Vision*, p. 436.

113. For a preview, see Luke 24:31-32, and on the opened eyes of the Emmaus road disciples, see Richard B. Hays, "Reading Scripture in Light of the Resurrection," in *The Art of Reading Scripture,* ed. Ellen F. Davis and Richard B. Hays (Grand Rapids: Eerdmans, 2003), pp. 229-32.

114. Hays, *Moral Vision*, p. 436.

"Managing the Audience": The Rhetoric of Authorial Intent and Audience Comprehension in the Narrative Epistemology of Polybius of Megalopolis, Diodorus Siculus, and Luke the Evangelist

David P. Moessner

> *If the reader has become part of the action, is caught up by the language, the question of what the passage "means" does not arise. Once the desired effect has been achieved, there is no need, or room, for interpretation.*
>
> — Jane Tompkins,
> "The Reader in History:
> The Changing Shape of Literary Response"[1]

In this influential essay of 1980, Professor Tompkins argues that "interpretation" is a modern, post-Renaissance endeavor and has very little to do with the ancients' notion of the impact of a literary performance upon an audience:

> The concept of language as a force acting on the world, rather than as a series of signs to be deciphered, accounts for the absence of specificity in ancient descriptions of literary response. . . . The text as an object of study or contemplation has no importance in this critical perspective, for literature is thought of as existing primarily in order to produce results and not as an end in itself. A literary work is not so much an object, therefore, as a unit of force whose power is exerted upon the world in a particular direction.[2]

---

1. In Jane P. Tompkins, ed., *Reader Response Criticism: From Formalism to Post-Structuralism* (Baltimore: Johns Hopkins University Press, 1980), pp. 201-32, quotation p. 203.

2. Tompkins, "Reader in History," pp. 203-4.

As a prime example she cites Aristotle's well-known "pity and fear," emotions "proper to tragedy" yet illustrating a force of impact rather than specific cognitive-affective understandings elicited by the form or structure of the tragedy itself. "In other words, it is not the *nature* of the impact that concerns him [Aristotle], but the degree."[3]

Tompkins's general observation is of course correct that in antiquity (as Robert Reid would put it) "words were a power loosed,"[4] that even during the critical cultural transition from orality to orality *and* literacy in the Greece of the fifth to fourth centuries, inscribed texts functioned primarily to impact an audience through oral performance and were not conceived as "objects" of scrutiny. Overall, her essay is a brilliant survey of the role of the audience throughout the entire history of literary criticism.

I would like to suggest, however — without denying Tompkins's lasting contribution — that she overstates the dichotomy between "effect" and "interpretation." It is simply not the case that ancient literature does not concern itself with specific content that may be rightly or wrongly interpreted. To be sure, the "degree" of impact is of paramount concern during the Hellenistic period as rhetoric flourishes into a distinct, self-conscious discipline.[5] Yet the "nature" of this impact, the specific content that the author wishes the audiences to comprehend, can be of primary concern to the author without lessening the potency that his or her words will effect in producing their overall impact.

We can even say that, contra Tompkins's conclusion, *narrative* (διήγησις) theory in the Hellenistic period had developed a rather sophisticated system of "arrangement" (οἰκονομία) to ensure audience comprehension. A triadic synergy of authorial purpose (τέλος/συντέλεια), realized through discrete forms of the text (ποίησις, σύνταξις), leading to audience approbation of the author's "understanding" or "thought" (ἐπιστήμη, διάνοια) on the subject matter presented is typical of *diēgētic* logic and discussions of the epistemology of narrative in the Hellenistic period. Particularly through the development of *diēgētic*-rhetorical strategies (ἐξεργασίαι) to insure clarity of understanding (σαφ-ῆ/ῶς; σαφήνεια) of an author's own

---

3. "Aristotle . . . judges the merit of poetic production in general on 'vividness of impression,' and 'concentrated effect,' and says that the end of the art is to be 'striking.'" Tompkins, "Reader in History," p. 203.

4. See Robert S. Reid, "When Words Were a Power Loosed: Audience Expectation and *Finished* Narrative Technique in the *Gospel of Mark*," *QJS* 80 (1994): 427-47.

5. See, e.g., Richard L. Enos, *Greek Rhetoric Before Aristotle* (Prospect Heights, Ill.: Waveland, 1993).

point of view, the question of "interpretation" is often not far removed in the oral-aural interaction. The Hellenistic composers Polybius of Megalopolis and Diodorus Siculus, to give but two examples, provide extensive discussions of their main *diēgētic* "methods of development" (ἐξεργασίαι) through which they will "manage" (οἰκονομέω) their audiences to understandings and evaluations of events that will conform and build to match their own ideological construals of the larger narrative whole. Given the limits of space, I will present only one aspect of each author's "methods of development." These, along with many other such examples of *diēgētic* rhetorical strategy in the Hellenistic period, form a significant backdrop for the suasive enterprise of the church's narrative Gospels in "proclaiming good news."

This glimpse into authorially designed interpretation is offered in honor of Professor Richard Hays, who through his pioneering work in the intertextuality of Jewish Scriptures in the letters of Paul has spearheaded nothing short of a Copernican revolution in assessing the importance of authorial intent in interpreting biblical texts. His demonstration of the decisive roles of intertextual citations and echoes of Scripture in the New Testament authors' interpretation of the Christ event is methodically overturning revered "standards" in the field of biblical interpretation. This brief essay is intended to express enduring gratitude to a most revered scholar as well as to a beloved colleague and friend.

I. "Synchronisms" as "Metaleptic Prompts" in Polybius's *Histories*

Polybius is the first (extant) composer of multivolume narrative (διήγησις) to appeal to his narrative organization as an "arrangement" (οἰκονομία) specifically designed to lead his audience to the "proper" (sc., authorially intended!) understanding of the events that he recounts. To be sure, Polybius does not refer to his narrative presentation of events as *mimēsis,* as Aristotle describes for the "representation" of the poet in tragedy and epic (*Poet.* 6, passim); nevertheless, this Greek historian will compose his narrative history like a well-constructed epic, as "converging to the same goal" (*Hist.* 1.3.4: πρὸς ἓν γίνεσθαι τέλος τὴν ἀναφορὰν ἁπάντων; cf. *Poet.* 23.26: πρὸς τὸ αὐτὸ συντείνουσαι τέλος). For it is his bold assertion that never before in the history of the world had events coalesced in this most unusual way to link the world as one and thus produce a "common history" (καθόλου πραγμάτων, 1.4.2).[6] For this rea-

6. See Adele C. Scafuro, "Universal History and the Genres of Greek Historiography"

son, Polybius contends, he must construct a narrative that reflects this unity through its own "economy" or "arrangement" (οἰκονομία):[7]

> 1.3.3-4 Previously the happenings of the world had been, so to speak, scattered, as they were held together by no unity of initiative, results, or place; but ever since this date history has conjoined to become an organic whole (σωματοειδῆ συμβαίνει γίνεσθαι τὴν ἱστορίαν), and the affairs of Italy and Africa have been interwoven (συμπλέκεσθαί τε τὰς . . . πράξεις) with those of Greece and Asia, all leading up to one result (τέλος).[8]

Because of this great unifying act, the narrative "economy" or "arrangement" must exhibit a plotted "continuity" (τὸ συνεχές)[9] that will adequately mirror this unprecedented interweaving through the orchestrations of "fate"/"Fortune" (τυχή). Even through forty long volumes, Polybius must create a narrative "road" that will lead all who take the journey to the proper comprehension of this unparalleled convergence of peoples and affairs. Rather than the tightly knit "necessary or probable causality" of the one-action plot of tragedy or epic, the unity of Polybius's composition will be established through a *continuity of narrative performance* (ὁ συνεχὴς λόγος)[10] that leads the audience to this "one result." A triadic synergy of interpretation thus undergirds and ensconces Polybius's enterprise: Polybius's goal

---

(Ph.D. diss., Yale University, 1983), pp. 102-15. Polybius refers to his work as τὸ καθόλου, in contrast to historians who concentrate on limited geographical areas of (a) specific nation(s), who thus write κατὰ μέρος (e.g., *Hist.* 1.4.2; 3.23.3; 5.31.3; 7.7.6; 8.2.11; 16.14.1; 29.12). Scafuro contends that Polybius's critique of Ephorus, Theopompus, Kallisthenes, and especially Timaeus as "universal historians" (bk. 12) extends only to the events that are contemporary with the time of their own writing; only on that basis can he attack their own lack of "autopsy" or shoddy interrogation of other αὐτόπται. In essence, then, Polybius is redefining the categorization of their "universal histories" (from the beginnings of recorded civilization to their own day) to the status of "monographs" of limited scope, whereas his own work, though concentrating on one period of history, is the true universal history since it weaves together the events that for the first time were truly "common" or universal to the peoples of the whole (known) world. Cf. "Universal History," p. 111: "Rather than invent a new name — one that represented the fact that its universality was 'horizontal' (synchronic) rather than 'vertical' (diachronic) — he kept the old names of *koinē historia* and *hē katholou.*"

7. See esp. *Hist.* 1.13.9.

8. Translations are my own, from the Greek text of the LCL, except where otherwise indicated.

9. Cf. *Hist.* 1.5.5: ὁ συνεχὴς λόγος ("the message/text that continues on . . . ," i.e., to its overall "goal"). See n. 13 below.

10. *Hist.*1.5.5; cf., e.g., 4.1.8; 6.2.1.

(authorial intent) to reflect the harmonious workings of "Fortune" for his audience will be represented through a continuity of narrative poetics (form of-/formal text) through which the audience will comprehend Fortune's one result (audience impact/understanding).

Undoubtedly, one of Polybius's greatest innovations in enhancing this overarching continuity of multiple volumes is his "synchronisms." Instead of the decorative bookends or mnemonic devices of his predecessors, Polybius's synchronistic conjunctions become aural aids in sounding the way to "follow" (παρακολουθέω) Polybius's "arrangement." Though the world is not yet united through Fortune's maneuverings (cf. bks. 7ff.), Polybius wants his auditors during these earlier periods to anticipate the new era after 218 BCE when the discrete affairs of individual nations will have issued in a "common result" (συντέλεια). Synchronisms are pressed into service as undisguised "listening stations" to lure Polybius's auditors to the author's way of hearing what would otherwise sound like totally coincidental occurrences. Thus, in Polybius's narrative development (ἐξεργασία), synchronisms are strategically planted rhetorical sounding boards to conduct Polybius's audience through his own tour of Fortune's grand performance of her multifarious maneuverings that converge in "one result" (τέλος).[11]

Polybius develops three types of synchronisms beyond his predecessors: *(i)* multiple "deaths" and "accessions"; *(ii)* a main event with auxiliary event(s) treated later in the narrative;[12] and *(iii)* a main event with auxiliary event(s) not treated later. Our scope permits only the last, the curious alignment of the "continuity of the narrative"[13] with ancillary events that will *not*

---

11. See especially Scafuro, "Universal History," pp. 155-204. On scope, setting, and purpose of Polybius's history writing, see, e.g., F. W. Walbank, *A Historical Commentary on Polybius*, 3 vols. (Oxford: Clarendon, 1957, 1967, 1974); Kenneth S. Sacks, *Polybius on the Writing of History* (Berkeley: University of California Press, 1981); Shaye J. D. Cohen, "Josephus, Jeremiah, and Polybius," *H&T* 21 (1982): 366-81.

12. As Scafuro, "Universal History," p. 178, observes, "[the reader] begins to think that the intrusive international events of the synchronism may subsequently have something to do with the narrative he is presently reading." Book 6 is an account of republican Rome's constitution that serves in the narrative as a bridge between the two poetics schemes (κατὰ μέρος vs. συμπλοκή) of books 1-5 and 7-40 respectively.

13. "Continuity of the narrative" (τὸ συνεχὲς [τῆς διηγήσεως]; cf. *Hist.* 1.5.5; 1.13.8; 3.2.6; 4.1.8; 6.2.1; 38.5.3) is tantamount to Aristotle's notion of "plot" (μῦθος/πράξεις) for tragedy and epic as the dynamic organization or "structuring of events" (ἡ τῶν πραγμάτων σύστασις, e.g., *Poet.* 6[1450a].15, 32) to produce a coherent story with a "beginning," "middle," and "end" issuing in a "new state of affairs" (μετάβασις/μεταβολή); see D. P. Moessner, "'Man-

be treated later in the narrative. What possible interest could Polybius have in certain happenings seemingly remote in space and geopolitical influence from the main engagements of Rome's rise to power?

> **1.6.1** "The Gauls Occupy Rome Nineteen Years after the Battle of Aegospotami, Sixteen Years before Leuctra, the Same Year as the Spartans Make the Peace Known as Antalcidas with the King of Persia, and the Year in which Dionysius the Elder Besieges Rhegium"

Polybius makes no secret of the reason for this synchronism, which comes so early in the whole work. The Gauls' occupation of Rome in 387-386 BCE marks the pre-beginning (πρώτη) of the crucial beginning point (ἡ ἀρχή) of Rome's ascendancy to world domination and thus of Polybius's whole enterprise (ἐπιβολή).[14] The Gauls' conquest of Rome (1.6.1) — in tandem with the rising and falling of other empires — throws down a gauntlet to the reader to make sense of Rome's rising "from the dead."

Rome's *sea crossing* to Sicily in 264 BCE marks the beginning (ἡ ἀρχή) of their world expansion, as well as the seminal incursion of the First Punic War (264-241). From this point on, according to Polybius, Rome's rise to power is inescapably orchestrated by Fortune in a fashion that defies all precedents:

> **1.5.1-5** I shall adopt as the beginning point (ἀρχή) of this book the first occasion on which the Romans crossed the sea from Italy. . . . The beginning point must be a period generally accepted and recognized, and one self-evident from the events themselves (καὶ τοῖς πράγμασι δυναμένην αὐτὴν ἐξ αὐτῆς θεωρεῖσθαι, 5.4), even if this means that I go back a little in time and recall by way of summary those events which happened between the earlier point and the beginning. For if the audience is ignorant or indeed in any doubt as to what are the set of events from which the work opens (τῆς γὰρ ἀρχῆς ἀγνοουμένης), it is impossible that what follows should find acceptance or credibility (οὐδὲ τῶν ἑξῆς οὐδὲν οἷον τε παραδοχῆς ἀξιωθῆναι καὶ πίστεως); but once we produce agreement on this [starting] point, then *the whole of the continuous message of the narrative* (πᾶς ὁ συνεχὴς λόγος) will be favorably received by those who will hear it (παρὰ τοῖς ἀκούουσιν).

---

aging' the Audience. Diodorus Siculus and Luke the Evangelist on Designing Authorial Intent," in *Luke and His Readers: Festschrift A. Denaux*, ed. R. Bieringer, G. Van Belle, J. Verheyden, BETL 182 (Leuven: University and Peeters Presses, 2005), pp. 61-80, esp. 69-75.

14. *Hist.* 1.5.1-5; 5.31.8-32.5.

No "reader" vaguely familiar with Rome's first foray outside Italy can dispute the landmark character of this crossing into Sicily for their later domination of the Mediterranean. Without the anchor of "cause" (αἰτία), the continuing chains of cause and effect will remain indecipherable to Polybius's readers. We notice how the historian's larger purpose is driven by this *audience understanding;* not only the organization of the whole work, which produces its "continuity," but also its "beginning" and "ending" points must be deemed worthy for the performance of the whole "by those who will hear it"!

By "beginning" at an even earlier event in Rome's history — at a point symbolic of the very antithesis of her rise to dominion, when Rome herself is under foreign domination — the historian can poignantly illustrate the paradoxical, even miraculous "turnaround" (περιπέτεια) of affairs guided by Fortune. Polybius intends his readers to "follow" (παρακολουθέω) a "synoptic" account of these earlier events to establish a pattern in their minds: there is a rhythm to the rise and fall of empires; but Rome can be seen to fit into this pattern only up to a point. When *historia's* workings would seem to indicate otherwise, Rome manages to break the pattern.

> **1.12.6-7, 1.13.6, 10-11** To follow out (παρακολουθῆσαι) this previous history — how and when the Romans after the disaster to Rome itself began their progress to better fortunes, and again how and when after conquering Italy they entered on the path of foreign enterprise — seems to me necessary for anyone who hopes to gain a proper general survey (συνόψεσθαι) of their present supremacy. . . . Now to recount all these events in detail is neither incumbent on me nor would it be useful to my audience (τοῖς ἀκούουσι). . . . I shall, however, attempt to narrate somewhat more carefully the first war between Rome and Carthage for the possession of Sicily; since it is not easy to name any war which lasted longer . . . with more battles, and greater "changes of fortune" (περιπέτεια).[15]

The chronology of 1.6.1 places Rome's singular character in bolder relief in comparison (σύγκρισις) with the actions and traits of other nations.[16]

15. Trans. Paton, LCL alt.

16. Scafuro, "Universal History," pp. 155-65, suggests that Polybius has formulated a response to Aristotle's arguments in *Poet.* 9 and 23. Aristotle lampoons historians like the later Timaeus who try to impute "marvelous" workings of Fortune/Fate by linking similar happenings in different parts of the world that have no putative relationship of cause and effect. "What is being likened [by Aristotle] is . . . the lack of unity in history and in 'improper' epic . . . due to the inclusion of events that are not causally related" (p. 164). Aristotle cites Herodotus, not Thucydides, as his standard for exemplifying events that occurred at the

Finally, by linking the rising (Sparta, Thebes, Syracuse) and falling (Athens, Persia, Sparta) of empires in 1.6.1 with the Gauls' capture of Rome, Polybius puts into play one of the chief "characters" of his "arrangement" so as to facilitate the larger plot of Rome's aspiration for universal empire (cf. 3.2.6[17]). Rome's subsequent defeats of the *Gauls*, in contrast to empires like Athens, which were never to recover from their fall, thus punctuate Fortune's maneuverings "against the odds." More than that, by linking the defeat of Athens by Sparta in the battle of Aegospotami with the later defeat of Sparta by Thebes in the battle of Leuctra — as well as synchronizing the further humiliation of Athens in the Peace of Antalcidas and the seizing of Rhegium by Dionysius of Syracuse in the same year as the conquest of Rome by the Gauls — Polybius would seem to suggest that Rome was a most wondrous exception to the usual pattern of rising and falling.

Hence, Polybius's audience is alerted early on that parallels in the plotted developments of nations "figure" the significance of Rome's development to world domination, but now especially by way of antithetical parallelisms that counter audience expectation. For Polybius is quick to narrate that, unlike other peoples, Rome made peace with its captors and, to Rome's surprise, was immediately granted sufficient freedom to set about conquering all of their indigenous neighbors (the Latins, Etruscans, Celts, Samnites), "attacking the rest of Italy not as if it were a foreign country, but as if it rightfully belonged to them (ὡς ὑπὲρ ἰδίων)" (1.6.6). Polybius attributes this success to their "valor," which in turn allowed them to become "veritable masters of the art of war" (1.6.6). There is no small suggestion that Fortune had a most propitious people to "work with," even if Fortune's role is more vaguely conceived in this prequel than in the main events themselves.[18]

Synchronisms like 1.6.1, then, provide *aural prompts* to "following" (παρακολουθῆσαι) "the continuous character of the narrative" (τὸν τρόπον συνεχοὺς . . . τῆς διηγήσεως, 1.13.9). Even more auspiciously, 1.6.1 announces the "starting point" (ἡ ἀρχή) of the entire narrative, which in turn serves as the hermeneutical key to unlocking the "assortment" of all subsequent affairs:

---

same time yet "do not converge to a common result" (οὐδὲν πρὸς τὸ αὐτὸ συντείνουσαι τέλος, *Poet.* 23.26).

17. ἔννοιαν σχεῖν τῆς τῶν ὅλων ἐπιβολῆς ("their [Rome's] conceiving the project of universal empire").

18. E.g., *Hist.* 1.6.8: Polybius describes this period of conquests after Gallic defeat as one "with extraordinary good fortune" (παραδόξως ἁπάντων ἐγκρατεῖς); cf. 1.6.4: "because of courage and the fortune of war" (διά τε τὴν ἀνδρείαν καὶ τὴν ἐν ταῖς μάχαις ἐπιτυχίαν).

5.32.1-5 For the ancients, saying that the beginning (ἡ ἀρχή) is half the whole, advised that in all matters the greatest care should be taken to make a good beginning (ὑπὲρ τοῦ καλῶς ἄρξασθαι). . . . One may indeed confidently affirm that the beginning (ἡ ἀρχή) is not merely half of the whole, but reaches as far as the end (πρὸς τὸ τέλος διατείνειν). For . . . how is it possible to sum up events properly without referring to their beginning (μὴ συναναφέροντα τὴν ἀρχήν), and understanding whence, how, and why the final situation of the events was brought about (πόθεν ἢ πῶς ἢ διὰ τί πρὸς τὰς ἐνεστώσας ἀφῖκται πράξεις)? So we should think that beginnings (αἱ ἀρχαί) do not only reach half way, but reach to the end, and both the readers (τοὺς λέγοντας) and the audience (τοὺς ἀκούοντας) of a general history should pay the greatest attention to them.[19]

Auditors should therefore not be surprised that in book 2 Polybius will begin weaving Roman engagement of the Carthaginians with the Romans' defeats of the Gauls, a foreshadowing of their later war with the Carthaginians, who will have to rely upon the Gauls as critical allies.[20]

To sum up, synchronisms function *noetically* and not simply empathically in configuring the author's signification of both parts and whole of his history narrative, or, as we have just seen, of Polybius's own grand sweep of Fortune's performances that converge in "one result" (τέλος/συντέλεια).

II. "Synchronic Links" as "Metonymic Prompts" in Diodorus Siculus's *Library of History*

In the same noetic vein as Polybius, Diodorus regards the instrument of history narrative (ἱστορία) as a mouthpiece for the interweavings of "Fate" and "Providence" of the whole inhabited world "as though the affairs of one city/ state" — hence Diodorus's epithet for *historia* as "mother-city (μητρ-ό-πολις) of philosophy as a whole" (1.2.2).[21] Moreover, "proper" historiography, Diodorus insists, must not only entail a "universal" scope of time and geography but must also be "arranged" to facilitate the historians' role as "ministers of divine Providence" (ὑπουργοὶ τῆς θείας προνοίας, 1.1.3) "to all hu-

19. Trans. Paton, LCL alt.
20. Cf. Scafuro, "Universal History," p. 187: "later Roman defeats of the Gauls become much more significant since the Gauls had once themselves captured Rome, and Rome is all the more wonderful in her rise to power for having started out so inauspiciously."
21. Cf. the contemporary discussion of a "global village"!

manity who love and seek the truth" (πασῶν εὐχρηστοτάτην συντάξαιτο τοῖς φιλαναγνωστοῦσιν, 1.3.6).[22]

But when Diodorus surveys past ensembles of the workings of Providence, he becomes convinced that the narrative arrangements themselves have not lived up to their task:

> 1.3.2 Most writers (οἱ πλεῖστοι) have recorded no more than isolated (αὐτοτελεῖς) wars waged by a single nation (ἔθνος) or a single state (πόλις), and but few have undertaken (ὀλίγοι δ᾽ . . . ἐπεχείρησαν), beginning with the earliest times (ἀρχαίων χρόνων ἀρξάμενοι) and coming down to their own day, to record the events connected with all peoples (τὰς κοινὰς πράξεις).[23]

What is missing are the interconnections among peoples and events both "vertically" through time and "horizontally" through the cause-effect nexuses of the interweavings of Providence. It is simply not the case à la Tompkins that Diodorus complains primarily about the *degree* of impact upon the audience or that the wrong emotions are vicariously experienced (πολυπειρία) by the readers of these earlier historians (cf. 5.1.2). Rather, insufficient knowledge is conveyed through the narrative connections themselves such that the cognitive impact is found wanting. It is extremely toilsome, he says, for any reader to learn why events have transpired in specific ways:

> 1.3.4-5 For this reason, because both the times of the events and the events themselves are strewn about in numerous accounts and in diverse history writers, attaining knowledge of them becomes difficult for the mind to coordinate and for the memory to retain (δυσπερίληπτος ἡ τούτων ἀνάληψις γίνεται καὶ δυσμνημόνευτος).
>
> Consequently, once we had examined the compositions of each of these other historians, we decided to compose a history according to a plan which would reward its readers with the greatest of benefits but, at the same time, inconvenience them the least (μὲν ὠφελῆσαι δυναμένην, ἐλάχιστα δὲ τοὺς ἀναγινώσκοντας ἐνοχλήσουσαν).

From first to last, the reader must be more illumined in the ways of Providence through the poetic paths created by the arrangement of the narrative itself:

22. *Library of History* translations are mine, from the Greek text of the LCL, unless otherwise specified.

23. Trans. Oldfather, LCL.

1.3.8 The account which keeps within the limits of a single narrative (ἡ δ' ἐν μιᾶς συντάξεως περιγραφῇ πραγματεία) and contains a connected account of events (τὸ τῶν πράξεων εἰρόμενον ἔχουσα) facilitates the reading and contains such recovery of the past (τὴν μὲν ἀνάγνωσιν ἑτοίμην παρέχεται) in a form that is perfectly easy to follow (τὴν δ' ἀνάληψιν ἔχει παντελῶς εὐπαρακολούθητον).[24]

Both the sheer chronological sweep and the wide swath of interconnections are impossible for *the reader to grasp* ("follow" [παρακολούθητος]) unless the two dimensions are fused through the emplotted continuity of the one narrative. It is this synoptic intercalating of happenings mimetic *of a larger force unfolding* that constitutes the "greater" benefit allegedly lacking in the other histories. Both form and content must inhere in order to cohere!

In contrast to the narratives of his precursors, then, Diodorus's history narrative will combine both linear chronological trajectories and lateral synchronological networks to "ensemble forth" the finely meshed workings of the "one global village."[25] "A history of this nature [i.e., Diodorus's] must be held to surpass all others to the same degree as the whole is more useful than the part (χρησιμώτερόν ἐστι τὸ πᾶν τοῦ μέρους) and continuity than discontinuity (τὸ συνεχὲς τοῦ διερρηγμένου)" (1.3.8).[26] Such entwinements and details make sense only when, as the primary aims of the narrative emplotment executed through the "mind"/"thought" of an author, they become "useful" for proper *interpretation,* as well as for emotive response.

One of the "methods of development" (ἐξεργασία) of this synchronic networking is Diodorus's "linking transitions" at the beginnings and endings of sequel volumes.[27] To make absolutely certain that his audience does not miss the emplotted significations of the "continuous thread of the narrative," Diodorus inserts at the beginning of each new book a summary capsulation of the previous volume, along with a listing of the main events that will develop out of this prior emplotment. More than that, because of the complex webbings of cause and effect, it is not unusual for him at the end of a volume

24. Trans. Oldfather, LCL alt.

25. Scafuro, "Universal History," pp. 116-54, 205-62, is one of the few to treat these critical epistemological aspects of the poetics of narrative historiography in any detail; see esp. her discussion on pp. 205-62.

26. Trans. Oldfather, LCL.

27. Diod. 2.1.1-3; 3.1.1-3; 4.1.5-7; 5.2.1; 6.1.1-3; [7-10]; 11.1.1; 12.2.2-3; 13.1.1-3; 14.2.4; 15.1.6; 16.1.3-6 (cf. 15.95.4!); 17.1.1-2; 18.1.5-6; 19.1.9-10; 20.2.3; [21-40]. Brackets indicate fragmentary books without extant linking passages.

to include "metonymic prompts." By such *aide-mémoire* Diodorus nudges the reader to recall that what the author-narrator had projected must take place has in fact developed through the linear and lateral connections configured throughout the sequel volume.

For instance, in declaring that he is on task by closing book 15 (15.95.4) with the events that led up to King Philip, Diodorus announces that book 16 will begin (ἄρξομαι) with Philip's accession to the throne and incorporate "all the achievements of this king to his death (τελευτή), including in its compass (συμπεριλαμβάνοντες) those other events as well which have occurred in the known portions of the world."[28] At the same time, Diodorus is echoing the beginning of book 15, where he had announced his scope as *beginning* with the war of the Persians against Evagoras in Cyprus and *ending* with the year preceding the reign of Philip, son of Amyntas (15.1.6).

Consequently, it is no surprise when at the beginning of the next volume, book 16 (16.1.3-6), Diodorus declares: "Now that I have reached the actions of Philip son of Amyntas, I shall endeavor to include the deeds performed by this king within the compass (περιλαβεῖν) of the present Book" (16.1.3). Even more telling, Diodorus proceeds to summarize the main achievements of Philip by previewing *the scope* and *culminating events* of this new book (e.g., "he took over the supremacy of all Hellas with the consent of the states" [16.1.4], resulting in "the greatest of the dominions in Europe" [16.1.3], and "left armies so numerous and powerful that his son Alexander had no need to apply for allies" [16.1.5], etc.).[29] The reader is thus clued in from the very beginning what to expect by way of "continuity" and "culmination" for that book. Hence, in order to meet audience expectations, book 16 must show through "the continuous thread of the narrative" (16.1.6) how and/or why Philip was able to accomplish all of this.[30]

28. Trans. Sherman, LCL.

29. Trans. Sherman, LCL.

30. At the conclusion of book 16 (16.95.1), Diodorus summons the line of 16.1.3 that "Philip . . . had made himself the greatest of the kings in Europe" before summing up the causes he purports to have illumined through his narration: more than any previous ruler, Philip excelled in an "adroitness and cordiality of diplomacy" (16.95.2). But this primary characterization stands in stark contrast to the Lacedaemonians, whose moral decline and unscrupulous diplomacy, portrayed in book 15, propelled them into an irreversible forfeiting of their hegemony. The moral point is clear enough. Not only has the continuity of books 15 and 16 driven home Diodorus's intended lesson, but also an overarching "moral" trajectory for Diodorus's "universal history" is once again reinforced through the more encompassing narrative vehicle. Predictably enough, book 17 begins, "In this Book, by writing down the continuing strands of the narrative (τὰς συνεχεῖς), we shall begin the events from the acces-

To sum up, Diodorus develops intricate interconnections for ensuring audience comprehension, including metonymic prompts to configure new events and circumstances into the more encompassing plot. Or as he himself boasts at the *archē* of book 17, "This is the best procedure, we maintain, that events be remembered, since the narrative is arranged by subject matter and adheres to the continuity from the beginnings to the very end (τὰς πράξεις εὐμνημονεύτους ἔσεσθαι κεφαλαιωδῶς τεθείσας καὶ συνεχὲς ἐχούσας ταῖς ἀρχαῖς τὸ τέλος)" (17.1.2)!

III. Luke's ἀρχή and ἀρχαί as Defining the "Continuity" of His Two-Volume Work

The Third Evangelist composes in the Hellenistic tradition of multivolume διήγησις with a clearly marked ἡ ἀρχή that elucidates and partitions the plot in ways that an audience can clearly follow. Moreover, like his predecessors Polybius and Diodorus, Luke directs his readers to that ἡ ἀρχή through certain "methods of plot development" (ἐξεργασίαι), including synchronisms and a linking *prooimion* in his sequel volume. As Luke confides in his opening *prooimion* to his whole work, his new narrative arrangement will produce a "clarity of understanding" (ἡ ἀσφάλεια) *greater* than that of the "many" who have already attempted such a narrative configuration (ἐπεχείρησαν ἀνατάξασθαι) of "events that have come to fruition" (Luke 1:1-4). Our scope permits only a brief sketch of his "synchronistic linking" of his two volumes through his secondary *prooimion*. Luke does employ a number synchronisms with poetic strategies similar to those of Polybius; these, however, must remain beyond the boundaries of the present essay.[31]

Luke draws attention to the ἀρχή of his work already in his preface

---

sion of Alexander as king, including the deeds of this king down to his death, and we shall write down also those events which took place together with them (τὰ ἅμα τούτοις συντελεσθέντα) in the known parts of the inhabited world" (17.1.2).

31. See David P. Moessner, "'Listening Posts' along the Way: 'Synchronisms' as Metaleptic Prompts to the 'Continuity of the Narrative' in Polybius' *Histories* and in Luke's Gospel-Acts. A Tribute to David E. Aune," in *The New Testament and Early Christian Literature in Greco-Roman Context: Studies in Honor of David E. Aune,* ed. John Fotopoulos, NovTSup 122 (Leiden: Brill, 2006), pp. 129-50. On the defining synchronism of Luke 3:19-20 as indicating the continuity by anticipating the "turning point" of the plot, see now David P. Moessner, "'How he was known in the breaking of the bread,'" *Sacra Scripta* 5 (2007): 221-38.

when he ties "eyewitnesses and attendants" to "the beginning" of "the message" (ὁ λόγος) that his narrative will unfold: οἱ ἀπ' ἀρχῆς αὐτόπται καὶ ὑπηρέται γενόμενοι τοῦ λόγου ("those who were from the beginning eyewitnesses and attendants of the message," 1:2). Implicit in this link between the authoritative accounts of events that he claims "were delivered over to us" and his own composing is the reliability of this ἀρχή as the proper "beginning point" to inform and sustain his "narrative continuity." By relating the rest of the narrative to this seminal event, Luke intends to anchor his audience to an occurrence of importance that will effect maximum benefit for them in "securing a firmer grasp" of all of the events (ἵνα ἐπιγνῷς περὶ ὧν κατηχήθης λόγων τὴν ἀσφάλειαν, 1:4; cf. 1:3).

That Luke ties great significance to this ἀρχή in its epistemological impact to clarify and bring coherence is evident in his "linking transition" performed by his sequel *prooimion*.

1. *Like Diodorus, Luke in the prooimion to his second volume summarizes the content of the first — "all that Jesus began to do and to teach . . . until the day in which he was taken up" (Acts 1:1-2) — and then announces the outline of events that will follow — ". . . you [eleven apostles] shall receive power when the Holy Spirit comes upon you and you shall be my witnesses in Jerusalem . . . and to the end of the earth" (1:7-8). In so doing, Luke establishes "the continuity" of the two-volume work.*

Now "witnesses" (μάρτυρες) replaces "the from the beginning eyewitnesses and attendants" of Luke 1:2, while "power" from the Holy Spirit reminds Luke's auditors of the empowering event of Jesus' baptism at the beginning of his calling, Luke 3:21-22, when "the Holy Spirit descended upon him in the physical form as a dove." Does the *empowerment of the Holy Spirit for witness* constitute the "continuous thread of the narrative," to use Polybius's and Diodorus's designation of the plotted "economy" or "arrangement" of their multivolumes?

The *diēgētic*-rhetorical devices that Luke employs argue for an unequivocal "yes."

First, "until the day in which he was taken up" (Acts 1:2) is laced with the command Jesus gives "through the Holy Spirit to the apostles whom he had chosen." This lateral connector not only points the audience back to the first volume (Luke 6), where Jesus "selected twelve whom he called apostles" (6:13), but also points them forward to Pentecost (Acts 2), where the "exalted Jesus" "pours forth" the Holy Spirit according to the "promise of the Father" to these apostles and a larger group of "witnesses" (2:32-33; cf. 10:41; 13:31 — μάρτυρες αὐτοῦ πρὸς τὸν λαόν).

Second, and more immediately, of course, this *metaleptic* prompt of Acts 1:2 directs Luke's audience back to the end of volume one where Jesus at table with the apostles actually charges the eleven to "stay in this city [Jerusalem] until you are clothed with *power* from on high" (Luke 24:49b). Now, however, the linking preface of Acts reconfigures this concluding one-day event of volume one in a most unconventional way. By a striking rhetorical ploy, Luke augments this command into the climax of a forty-day period of resurrection appearances in which Jesus' instruction to the apostles concerning the kingdom of God recharacterizes the charge to "await the Spirit." Jesus in fact "interrupts" and takes over the voice of the narrator to break into the scene directly: "And while eating with them he commanded them not to depart from Jerusalem but to await the promise of the Father which (narrator speaking) you heard from *me!*" (Jesus speaking). The *prooemial* voice of the narrator is overtaken by the voice of the leading character of volume one. All that "Jesus began to do and to teach" thus continues on now, already, in the linking preface. Jesus' own teaching voice binds the two volumes and addresses the audience directly as he continues "to do and to teach." The "end" of the Gospel volume must now be viewed as a telescoped summary of the beginning of the second, sequel volume.

Third, the particular content of what Jesus now utters is also quite unexpected: ". . . which you heard from me. Because/for (ὅτι) John baptized with water but you shall be baptized with the Holy Spirit not after these many days" (Acts 1:5). Where did the apostles hear these words from Jesus? Are these words echoing Jesus' final command in Luke 24:49? If so, there is nothing explicit there about John the Baptist's baptism. Or are these words also resonating earlier words during the time of "all that Jesus began to do and to teach" (cf. Acts 1:1b)? Although it is not clear whether the ὅτι of Acts 1:5 should be translated *(i)* causally, "because", or *(ii)* epexegetically, "for"/ "namely," or *(iii)* as the ὅτι *recitativum* introducing direct speech, what will become certain is that Jesus' words project both forward and backward in the "narrative continuity." In fact, not only do Jesus' words function metaleptically to transfer the audience back both to the "end" of volume one and even further back to "the beginning" of Jesus' ministry with "the baptism of John"; these words also project forward to the middle of Acts, anticipating the initiative of God through the Holy Spirit as "God Himself bears witness" among the Gentiles as the witness continues to develop.[32]

---

32. Acts 15:8: "God bore witness (ἐμαρτύρησεν) to them [the Gentiles/Cornelius] by giving them the Holy Spirit just as He had given to us [Peter and Jewish believers]."

2. *Within the linking prologue (Acts 1:1-8), Jesus' direct speech (Acts 1:4b-5) functions as the linchpin of the two-volume "continuity of the narrative." By this synchronistic overlap, Luke configures the ongoing narrative as the continuing work of Jesus through the power of the Spirit, which Jesus grants to his "witnesses."*

First, Jesus' words in Acts 1:5 echo John the Baptist's words in Luke 3:16: "I myself am baptizing you with water, but one is coming who is mightier than I . . . , he will baptize you with Holy Spirit and fire." John's words come just before the narrator summarizes the Baptist's entire calling as the one who, fulfilling the role of the prophet called in Isaiah 40, "proclaims good news" (εὐηγγελίζετο, Luke 3:18; cf. Isa. 40:9 LXX, ὁ εὐαγγελιζόμενος). But hardly do these words stick before the narrator flashes forward quickly to John's imprisonment by Herod (3:19-20).

Second, then, John's word of contrast between two baptisms in Luke 3:16 introduces Jesus' own "anointing" by the Holy Spirit (cf. Acts 10:38, ὡς ἔχρισεν αὐτὸν ὁ θεὸς πνεύματι ἁγίῳ καὶ δυνάμει). As the clanging doors of the prison gates are still reverberating in the audience's ears (Luke 3:20), they see the Holy Spirit alight upon Jesus "as a dove" and hear the voice from heaven proclaim Jesus to be "My beloved Son, in you I take pleasure" (3:21-22).

Third, Jesus' words in the linking *prooimion* (Acts 1:5) resound even more distinctly through Peter's utterance in Acts 11:16. Reporting back in Jerusalem about his experiences with Cornelius, Peter declares to "the circumcision" who were critical of his behavior in Caesarea that when "the Holy Spirit" began to "fall" upon Cornelius and his household, "I remembered the word of the Lord how he had said, 'John baptized with water, but you shall be baptized with Holy Spirit'" (11:15-16). This "word" can be none other than the *prooemial* voice of Acts 1:5, which Peter restates verbatim, minus the adverbial phrase "not after these many days."

Now, curiously, this "word of the Lord" invokes another "beginning," namely, the command to the apostles to be "witnesses" even "to the nations" (Acts 1:8). This "witness" "begins" at Pentecost when hundreds of Jews representing "every nation under heaven" "hear in their own tongues the marvels of the works of God" through the testimony of Galilean Jews who, "filled with the Holy Spirit, began to speak other languages just as the Spirit was giving them to utter" (2:4-12). Peter himself draws the comparison: "As I began to speak the Holy Spirit fell upon them just as also the Spirit had fallen upon us 'at the beginning'" (ἐν ἀρχῇ, 11:15). What ravels this knot even more tightly in Luke's emplotment is the ground of the criticism by believers of "the circumcision" against Peter: "You entered to lodge in the household of an uncircumcised man and ate with them" (εἰσῆλθες πρὸς ἄνδρας ἀκροβυστίαν ἔχοντας καὶ συνέφαγες αὐτοῖς, 11:3)! Curious again, then, that in his "sermon" to Cornelius's household, Peter had related the incident when the apostles and larger circle of witnesses were at table with the resurrected Jesus, how Jesus had declared that "God had chosen" not all the people of Israel but them only as "witnesses, . . . those who had eaten and drunk with him after he had risen from the dead" (Acts 10:41→Acts 1:4-5). Now ironically, while being chided by fellow believers of the circumcision for eating and drinking with "unclean" Gentiles, Peter refers back to his eating and drinking with Jesus in Acts 1:4-5, which, as we have seen, in turn recasts Jesus' appearance and charge to the apostles *at table* in Luke 24:36-49. "Witness" at table to Jesus' eating and drinking functions, therefore, as a *sine qua non* for "witness" to the "unclean" peoples of "the nations" (cf. Luke 24:47 — εἰς . . . τὰ ἔθνη).

Fourth, by delineating a secondary ἀρχή, Luke, like Polybius and Diodorus, fuses his sequel volume more closely to the continuity of the larger narrative as determined by the ἀρχή of the whole work. In the middle of Acts, Peter is justifying his lodging and witness among the Gentiles to his critics in Jerusalem through the very event that the *prooemial* voice of Jesus had announced would bind all that "he had begun to do and to teach" to all that his *witnesses* would continue to do and to teach. Peter's reference to the linking prologue and the empowerment of the Spirit and its reference, in turn, back to *the beginning* of Jesus' calling in volume one is made even clearer at an earlier point in the speech to Cornelius. "You yourselves know that event which happened throughout the whole of Judea, *beginning* (ἀρξάμενος) from Galilee with *the baptism of John* which John proclaimed; even Jesus of Nazareth whom God anointed with Holy Spirit and power; . . . and we ourselves are *witnesses* of all those things which he did in the region of the Jews and in Jerusalem" (Acts 10:37-39). "Witness" again harks back to "the beginning," and it becomes even more certain that "the baptism of John" functions as a metonym for "the beginning" (ἡ ἀρχή) of Jesus' anointed calling and thus as *the* ἀρχή for the two volumes.

Finally, when Peter presents his report at the apostolic assembly in Acts 15, he now looks back to that period known as "from those days of beginnings" (ἀφ᾽ ἡμερῶν ἀρχαίων [pl.], 15:7) as the time when God chose him to speak the gospel to *the nations/Gentiles* (τὰ ἔθνη). The echo of Acts 1:8 as well as the voice from heaven "not to call what God has cleansed unclean" (11:9b) reverberate here as one (15:7-9). But more than that, God's choosing Peter and the twelve from those days characterized by decisive beginning events re-sounds the "beginning" of Peter's witness to Jesus' eating and drinking with "unclean tax collectors and sinners," "beginning from Galilee" through the whole region of the Jews and up to Jerusalem (cf. 10:37, 39).

The secondary "beginning" of Pentecost in fact inheres with the replacement of Judas by Matthias to reconstitute the twelve as Jesus' foundational appointment of twelve witnesses (i.e., "to receive the place of this apostolic service from which Judas had departed to go to his own place," Acts 1:25). The Spirit's falling upon the twelve witnesses at the beginning of Pentecost is made possible only when the first beginning is brought to its proper, that is, scriptural fulfillment, "as it stands written . . . [LXX Pss. 68:26; 108:8]. It is necessary that one of those men who traveled with us from the whole time the Lord Jesus went in and out among us, *beginning from the baptism of John until the day he was taken up* (ἀρξάμενος ἀπὸ τοῦ βαπτίσματος Ἰωάννου ἕως τῆς ἡμέρας ἧς ἀνελήμφθη), one of those must become together with us a *witness* to his resurrection (δεῖ . . . μάρτυρα τῆς ἀναστάσεως αὐτοῦ σὺν ἡμῖν γενέσθαι ἕνα τούτων)" (Acts 1:20-22). "From the baptism of John" thus coordinates *the beginning* of Jesus' calling and witness with the calling and witness of the apostles to function as a semaphore for the ἀρχή of the two volumes. Like Polybius and Diodorus, the secondary ἀρχή derives its significance from the primary ἀρχή, when Jesus himself was "anointed with the Holy Spirit and power." In this way, then, the ἀρχή of Jesus becomes a prerequisite of *witness* for those appointed *to witness* to the coming of the Holy Spirit upon the "unclean Gentiles" (cf. Luke 3:22; Acts 10:38; 11:15-18; 15:7-9). "Witness to the resurrection" therefore entails witness to the whole time Jesus "went in and out among [them], beginning from the baptism of John," including therefore also Jesus' "eating and drinking with tax collectors and sinners" (Luke 5:30; 7:34; 15:2) and "entering into the house of a sinner to lodge with him" (Luke 19:7), and "those who ate and drank with him after he had risen from the dead" (Acts 10:41).

Conclusion

We can summarize our conclusions:

1. Through his secondary linking *prooimion* in the beginning of the second "volume," Luke intends to write one continuous *work* (τὸ ἔργον). The "continuity of the narrative" of conventional Hellenistic multivolume narratives of events (e.g., Polybius, Diodorus Siculus) is methodically established through both retrospect and prospect in Acts 1:1-8. The organic unity of

both volumes is the "acting and teaching" of Jesus of Nazareth enacted through authenticated "witness." The unity "from Galilee . . . to the end of the earth" is therefore a narrative unity established by the Hellenistic poetics of emplotment through *diēgētic*-rhetorical "methods of development," and not simply a unity created by theme (e.g., "witness," "acts of the Holy Spirit," geographic movement, etc.) or a unity of a "movement" founded by a famous person and continued by the "followers." Rather, the unity of witness harks back to multiple citations, emplotments, and allusions to the story of Israel in the Jewish Scriptures, which forms "those events come to fruition" that God himself had attended (Luke 1:1).

2. "Authenticated witness" is established through the coming of the eschatological Spirit upon the "witness," whether it be Jesus of Nazareth at his calling/baptism or upon the twelve apostles and the larger group of women and men "who had come up to Jerusalem from Galilee with him to become witnesses to the people (λαός)" (Acts 13:31). This emplotted "movement of empowered witness" forms the material unity of the "continuity of the narrative."

3. The ἀρχή and the ἀρχαί coordinate the movement of the plot through partitioning, synchronistic overlapping, and metaleptic referencing of various parts that, in their dynamic interrelationships, form the organic narrative whole. The ἀρχή and the ἀρχαί "manage" the audience at key hermeneutical junctures to the coming, fulfilled empowerment of the Holy Spirit. This standard Hellenistic convention of "the beginning" thus establishes the formal unity of the narrative and characterizes audience comprehension, contra Tompkins, as fundamentally an *interpretive* one.

Finally, it is my hope that the charismatic character of Luke's two-volume enterprise may catalyze future enrichment with Professor Hays's own rich description of the charismatic texture of Paul's exegesis. That Luke fundamentally misunderstood Paul may possibly still be true, but the focus of both writers on the hermeneutical role of the Spirit in characterizing the "events brought to fruition" in Jesus, Israel's Christ, may well point in the opposite direction.

"In Our Own Languages": Pentecost, Babel, and the Shaping of Christian Community in Acts 2:1-13

Joel B. Green

Not least on account of the phenomenological questions it raises, and their important ramifications for ecclesial communities, the interpretation of Acts 2:1-13 has been especially controversial. "No episode narrated in Acts has received more attention than this one," writes Robert Wall.[1] Specifically at issue is the significance of the outpouring of the Holy Spirit and its expression in the miracle of languages. Almost thirty years ago, I. H. Marshall pushed the conversation in the right direction when he urged: "It has been objected that probably most of the crowd would speak Aramaic or Greek, the two languages which the disciples also would speak, and that therefore the miracle of tongues was unnecessary. But this difficulty must surely have been obvious to Luke also. What was significant was that the various *vernacular* languages of these peoples were being spoken."[2] This emphasis on the vernacular identifies a crucial theological concern that has not been adequately explored in the study of Luke's Pentecost account, and it is the purpose of this essay to pursue the matter more fully.

My examination of the Lukan account of the outpouring of the Spirit and its immediate sequelae in Acts 2:1-13 will focus on three issues intricately interwoven in this episode: first, the phenomenon of "speaking in other languages" as inspired, doxological speech drawing its raw material from Scripture; second, geographical orientation; and finally, the importance of

---

1. Robert W. Wall, *Acts*, NIB 10 (Nashville: Abingdon, 2002), p. 53.

2. I. Howard Marshall, *The Acts of the Apostles: An Introduction and Commentary*, TNTC 5 (Grand Rapids: Eerdmans, 1980), p. 70, emphasis original.

"speaking in other languages" in identity and identity formation. Attending both to issues of intertextuality and to the larger context of the Pentecost event in Acts, I will urge that Luke's account constitutes a profoundly theological and political statement displacing Babel- and Jerusalem- and Rome-centered visions of a unified world in favor of an altogether different sort of community. Unity is found at Pentecost, but not by reviving a pre-Babel homogeneity. With the outpouring of the Spirit, koinonia is possible not by the dissolution of multiple languages but rather by embodiment in a people generated by the Spirit, gathered in the name of Jesus Christ.

"Speaking in Other Languages"

What requires explanation within Luke's narrative in Acts 2:1-13, and has also been a source of puzzlement and controversy to Luke's readers, is the phenomenon of "speaking in other languages" (λαλεῖν ἑτέραις γλώσσαις). Indeed, the extraordinary, baffling character of these events is underscored by otherwise redundant references to the reactions of the onlookers — συνεχύθη in v. 6, ἐξίσταντο δὲ καὶ ἐθαύμαζον in v. 7, and ἐξίσταντο δέ . . . καὶ διηπόρουν in v. 12. "Astonished" and "amazed" (συγχέω, ἐξίστημι, and θαυμάζω) are typical responses to the miraculous or numinous in the Lukan narrative,[3] sometimes as a precursor to faith. The use of συγχέω is reminiscent of the Babel story (Gen. 11:7, 9 LXX; see also σύγχυσις in Gen. 11:9). It shares conceptual affinity with the term Luke introduces in v. 12, διαπορέω, used elsewhere in the Lukan narrative in contexts where further explanation is both required and invited.[4] In fact, this need is explicitly stated: "What does this mean?" (v. 12).[5] Such reactions indicate the anomalous nature of the phenomena witnessed. Evidently, these events are not self-interpreting; even when the language spoken can be understood, interpretation is necessary. A hermeneut is needed.

Not all greet the events of this Pentecost with inquisitiveness, however. Responding with sneering and ridicule, some exhibit the division within Israel presaged by Simeon (Luke 2:34) and John (Luke 3:15-17): "But others said sarcastically, 'They have been filled with new wine!'" (Acts 2:13). The disci-

---

3. Συγχέω (see also 9:22; 19:32; 21:27, 31), ἐξίστημι (see also Luke 2:47; 8:56; 24:22; Acts 2:12; 8:9, 11, 13; 9:21; 10:45; 12:16), and θαυμάζω (see also Luke 1:21, 63; 2:18, etc.; Acts 3:12; 4:13; 7:31; 13:41) are close semantic kin.

4. Cf. Luke 9:7; Acts 5:24; 10:17.

5. On the form, cf. 17:20.

ples of Jesus are thus presented with two motivations to speak — one to address the puzzlement of those gathered, the other to respond to the negative challenge of those who have spoken acrimoniously.

The spectacle Luke records has been subjected to a startling array of analyses,[6] though what he describes seems relatively straightforward.[7] Luke presents the Spirit as an actor who works to enable speech, specifically "inspired speech" (ἀποφθέγγομαι),[8] which the Spirit "gives." As vv. 5-11 make clear, "other" languages bespeak the extent of the language miracle; it is not only Spirit-inspired discourse but speech using languages other than those familiar to the speakers. Luke's account also makes clear that the content of these Spirit-inspired utterances is praise to God. That is, in v. 4, people who have been filled with the Spirit are enabled by that same Spirit to speak in languages previously unknown to them,[9] and what they speak turns out to be "the great things of God" (v. 11).

6. Though dated, a helpful entry point into the discussion is Watson E. Mills, ed., *Speaking in Tongues: A Guide to Research on Glossolalia* (Grand Rapids: Eerdmans, 1986); Mills gathers exegetical, historical, theological, psychological, and sociocultural perspectives. For glossolalia in the NT and Hellenistic world, see Christopher Forbes, *Prophecy and Inspired Speech in Early Christianity and Its Hellenistic Environment* (Tübingen: Mohr Siebeck, 1995; Peabody, Mass.: Hendrickson, 1997), pp. 44-187. The work of Gerald Hovenden, *Speaking in Tongues: The New Testament Evidence in Context,* JPTSup 22 (London: Continuum, 2002), pp. 77-94, surveys various interpretations of the phenomenon in Acts 2 but is oriented primarily around urging that Luke had no theological agenda in introducing what, therefore, must have been a historical event.

7. Luke uses four phrases — λαλεῖν ἑτέραις γλώσσαις (v. 4), τῇ ἰδίᾳ διαλέκτῳ λαλούντων αὐτῶν (v. 6), τῇ ἰδίᾳ διαλέκτῳ ἡμῶν (v. 8), and λαλούντων αὐτῶν ταῖς ἡμετέραις γλώσσαις (v. 11) — with reference to the same phenomenon. Linguistic differences among these phrases — e.g., διάλεκτος for γλῶσσα — do not signal differences of substance, as the parallel between vv. 8 and 11 makes clear. That Luke portrays glossolalia as xenolalia (speaking in real, unlearned human languages) is widely acknowledged (e.g., Philip Schaff, "The Pentecostal and the Corinthian Glossolalia," *JBL* 50 [1931]: xxvii-xxxii; Philip F. Esler, "Glossolalia and the Admission of Gentiles into the Early Christian Community," *BTB* 22 [1992]: 136-42; Mark J. Cartledge, "The Nature and Function of New Testament Glossolalia," *EvQ* 72 [2000]: 135-50), though some (e.g., Schaff and Esler), using Paul's portrait of glossolalia in 1 Corinthians 12–14 as the benchmark, insist that Luke is in error.

8. Ἀποφθέγγομαι appears in the NT only in Acts 2:4, 14; 26:25; in the LXX it is used with reference to fortune-telling (e.g., Mic. 5:11 [12 Eng.]; Zech. 10:2) and prophetic speech (1 Chron. 25:1; Ezek. 13:9, 19) — cf. *A Greek-English Lexicon of the Septuagint,* ed. J. Lust et al., 2 vols. (Stuttgart: Deutsche Bibelgesellschaft, 1992-96), 1:58; Gerhard Schneider, "ἀποφθέγγομαι," *EDNT* 1:147.

9. In the history of interpretation, some have found in this narrative unit a miracle of "hearing" rather than of "speaking"; see, e.g., Jenny Everts, "Tongues or Languages? Contex-

What astonishes the Jerusalemites is their recognition both that those doing the speaking are Galileans and that these Galileans are speaking in languages that, far from representing the vernacular of Galilee, are native to their own homelands. Subsequent to the military exploits of Alexander the Great in the latter fourth century BCE, all of these persons would have trafficked in Greek, and likely would also have known Aramaic. It would not have been unusual, though, for expatriates to maintain their own, native languages, especially given that multinational cities like Jerusalem generally included areas or districts where immigrants could find (and refresh) languages and customs familiar to their homelands.[10] Although the language practices current in the first century CE are not always certain for the peoples mentioned by Luke, the terminology Luke employs to describe what is heard by these Jerusalemites is sufficiently elastic to allow for a variety of phenomena, including not only distinctive languages but also the use of idiomatic expressions of style and even accent. In some cases, such as Pamphylia and Crete, we should think of aberrant Greek dialects, while for Egypt and Phrygia, for example, we may think of a distinct language.[11] That is, bystanders, who might just as easily have understood these words of

---

tual Consistency in the Translation of Acts 2," *JPT* 2 (1994): 74-75. But Luke makes no suggestion that the Spirit fell on the crowd, enabling them miraculously to hear; rather, the crowd gathers subsequently, in response to the outpouring of the Spirit.

Robert Zerhusen, "An Overlooked Judean Diglossia in Acts 2?" *BTB* 25 (1995): 118-30 argues that the language problem is grounded in the fact that Jesus' followers prophesied in a language other than Hebrew — that is, that they used Low language rather than High in a context where anyone claiming to speak with religious authority would have used High language; see also the synopsis of Zerhusen's argument in David Crystal, "Why Did the Crowd Think St. Peter Was Drunk? An Exercise in Applied Sociolinguistics," *NBf* 79 (1998): 72-76. This ingenious argument has almost nothing to commend it in the Lukan text. Most importantly, Jesus' followers make no claim to speak with religious authority; they are praising God, and, it so happens, they are doing so in languages that others can understand.

10. Cf. Wayne A. Meeks, *The First Urban Christians: The Social World of the Apostle Paul* (New Haven: Yale University Press, 1983), p. 29; Richard L. Rohrbaugh, "The Pre-Industrial City in Luke-Acts: Urban Social Relations," in *The Social World of Luke-Acts: Models for Interpretation*, ed. Jerome H. Neyrey (Peabody, Mass.: Hendrickson, 1991), pp. 129-37.

11. For διάλεκτος, see LSJ 401. The *OCD* provides readily accessible summaries for many of the regions Luke lists: a western Middle Iranian language was spoken in Parthia (1117), Elamite in Elam (515), Egyptian in Egypt (512), Latin in Rome (817-20), and so on; it is less clear, however, regarding patterns of usage over time. Colin J. Hemer, *The Book of Acts in the Setting of Hellenistic History*, ed. Conrad H. Gempf, WUNT 49 (Tübingen: Mohr Siebeck, 1989), p. 205, summarizes data regarding Phrygian and the Pamphylian dialect.

praise had they been expressed in Greek or Aramaic, nonetheless testify to hearing in their own native tongues "the great things of God." In this way, the scene Luke paints anticipates the nature of things to come — a world-wide mission enabled by the Holy Spirit,[12] resulting in the worship of God in locales far removed from the socioreligious center of the Jewish world, Jerusalem and its temple.

What those gathered hear is prophetic speech insofar as it is enabled by the Holy Spirit, but not primarily a form of missionary proclamation, articulated in their own native languages — as though they could not understand the good news were it preached in Aramaic or Greek (as indeed it will be in 2:14-36).[13] Luke regards all sorts of speech acts as "prophetic," including (as in this case) prayer and praise, provided that they are inspired speech.[14] What Luke envisages in this scene, then, is similar to what we read in the Lukan birth narratives: being filled with the Spirit leads to praise (Luke 1:46-55, 67-79; 2:25-32).[15] The phrase "great things of God" appears to be borrowed from the Psalms, where it is found in the context of doxology (see Pss. 106:2; 145:4, 12); elsewhere too God's mighty acts figure prominently in

12. This is emphasized recently by Ju Hur, *A Dynamic Reading of the Holy Spirit in Luke-Acts,* JSNTSup 211 (Sheffield: Sheffield Academic, 2001), pp. 223-26; cf. also Giuseppe Betori, "Luke 24:47: Jerusalem and the Beginning of the Preaching to the Pagans in the Acts of the Apostles," in *Luke and Acts,* ed. Gerald O'Collins and Gilberto Marconi (New York: Paulist, 1993), pp. 115-16.

13. Contra Robert P. Menzies, *Empowered for Witness: The Spirit in Luke-Acts,* JPTSup 6 (Sheffield: Sheffield Academic, 1994), p. 177. See Max Turner, *Power from on High: The Spirit in Israel's Restoration and Witness in Luke-Acts,* JPTSup 9 (Sheffield: Sheffield Academic, 1996), pp. 271-72; Jacques Dupont, "The First Christian Pentecost," in *The Salvation of the Gentiles: Essays on the Acts of the Apostles* (New York: Paulist, 1979), pp. 49-50. Luke does not present Acts 2:1-13 as an occasion of missionary proclamation; we can recognize a rhetorical distinction between what the Galileans utter here and what Peter preaches in 2:14-36. Missionary proclamation begins in v. 14, with Peter's address (at which point there is no suggestion that he is speaking in an unknown language); prior to that, those filled with the Spirit are extolling God.

14. So rightly Forbes, *Prophecy and Inspired Speech,* p. 51.

15. See Leo O'Reilly, *Word and Sign in the Acts of the Apostles: A Study in Lucan Theology,* AnGr 243 (Rome: Pontifical Biblical Institute, 1987), pp. 54-57. The one exception is Luke 1:41-45 (Elizabeth, filled with the Spirit, blesses Mary), but this provides no analogue to the present scene. Note that Spirit-inspired utterances in the birth narratives extol God *and* are said in the presence of others. In terms of the Lukan narrative, those utterances serve primarily as hermeneutical asides to Luke's own audience — situating the events he narrates within the history of God's dealings with Israel. In the current scene, it is true that "devout Jews . . . hear them expressing the great things of God," but the content of these utterances is not specified and so they cannot function as hermeneutical asides for Luke's audience.

praise (e.g., Exodus 15; Judges 5; 1 Samuel 2). In Acts 10:46, speaking in other languages is clearly bundled with doxology; and in light of the collocation of prophesying with "blessing" the Lord in Luke 1:67, we may be justified in imagining that the prophetic speech in Acts 19:6 too is doxological. Finally, we read in Luke 1:49 that Mary lifts her voice in praise: "The Mighty One has done great things for me!" Of course, as in Acts 16:25, for Luke to refer to words of praise (vertical speech, directed to God) does not deny that these words might be heard by and influence those persons nearby; however, it is only in 2:14 that, on behalf of Jesus' followers, Peter more specifically addresses those gathered (horizontal speech).

Any hint of intertextuality in 2:11 is of special interest, since in other episodes of "inspired speech" (ἀποφθέγγομαι) Luke refers to manifestly comprehensible speech concerned with scriptural interpretation (Acts 2:14; 26:25). Peter's Pentecostal address (2:14-41) is identified as Spirit-inspired speech,[16] consisting above all of scriptural citation and explication (especially Joel 2:28-32; Pss. 16:8-11; 110:1, but also 1 Kings 2:10; Ps. 132:11; Isa. 32:15; 57:19; Deut. 32:5, etc.), with the scriptural message comprehended in terms of its actualization in the ministry, death, resurrection, and exaltation of Jesus. We also find the verb in the context of Paul's speech before Herod Agrippa II and Porcius Festus, where Festus's outburst, "You have lost your mind!" is countered by Paul's claim to inspired, sober speech (26:24-25). The basis of Festus's interruption is not Paul's ecstatic or hysterical speech (which one might expect, given Festus's characterization of Paul) but rather Paul's exposition of Scripture as witness to Jesus. As Joseph Fitzmyer observes: "Festus protests first over Paul's erudition, his strange way of arguing, and his allusions to Moses and the prophets. Festus has difficulty in following all this argumentation and especially in admitting such a thing as resurrection."[17] That is, lacking the conceptual categories to make sense of Paul's argument, Festus presumes that Paul is the one lacking in cognitive equipment. Read in relation to these other texts where the verb ἀποφθέγγομαι is found in Acts, Luke's reference to inspired speech con-

---

16. Cf. Jacob Jervell, *Die Apostelgeschichte: Übersetzt und erklärt,* KEK 3 (Göttingen: Vandenhoeck & Ruprecht, 1998), pp. 141-42.

17. Joseph A. Fitzmyer, *The Acts of the Apostles,* AB 31 (New York: Doubleday, 1998), p. 763. With reference to Acts 2:1-13, Keith Warrington, *Discovering the Holy Spirit in the New Testament* (Peabody, Mass.: Hendrickson, 2005), p. 54, urges similarly that the charge of drunken babbling aimed at Jesus' followers is not the consequence of their speaking in other languages, since in cosmopolitan Jerusalem a multiplicity of languages would be expected; instead, the *content* of their speech attracted ridicule.

cerning "the great things of God" in 2:11 is best understood as charismatic interpretation of Scripture.[18] It is not surprising, then, that in both Acts 2 and Acts 26, the consequence of Spirit-inspired speech is a charge against the speakers that they have lost their mental capacities. In neither case is this due to maniacal or ecstatic behavior but rather to the alien quality of their proclamation, writing as it does the death and resurrection of Jesus into the story of Israel as that story's culmination. "The great things of God," accordingly, find their center and meaning in the exaltation of Jesus of Nazareth.

"Other Languages" and Social Geography

It is one thing for any group of people to manifest doxological outbursts, and quite another for them to do so in regional languages they have not learned. To add to the prodigious character of this event, Luke notes that the Jerusalemites recognize the speakers as Galileans. This may result from the distinctive speech patterns of Galileans;[19] in any case, it is important to note that for the sophisticates of a city like Jerusalem, and the Holy City at that, Galileans were regarded as "boorish dolts" — that is, as outlanders devoid of intellectual accomplishment who inhabited a region far from the center of religious power and purity.[20]

As a pilgrim feast, Passover would have attracted huge crowds to Jerusalem, both from Palestine and from the Jewish Diaspora. Luke's use of κατοικέω in 2:5 apparently includes both those present in Jerusalem for the festival (see 2:9) and those from Palestine and the Jewish Diaspora who had relocated to the city (see 2:14).[21] Emphasis thus falls on Jerusalem as a multinational city representative of the world of Jews and proselytes outside Jeru-

18. The role of the Spirit in inspired interpretation of Scripture is well known in the literature of Second Temple Judaism (e.g., Josephus, at Qumran, in Sirach, in Philo) — cf. John R. Levison, *The Spirit in First Century Judaism*, AGJU 29 (Leiden: Brill, 1997), pp. 254-59.

19. F. F. Bruce, *The Acts of the Apostles: The Greek Text with Introduction and Commentary*, 3rd ed. (Grand Rapids: Eerdmans, 1990), p. 116.

20. Bruce J. Malina and Jerome H. Neyrey, "Conflict in Luke-Acts: Labelling and Deviance Theory," in *The Social World of Luke-Acts: Models for Interpretation*, ed. Jerome H. Neyrey (Peabody, Mass.: Hendrickson, 1991), p. 104. See Matt. 4:15; Acts 4:13.

21. Κατοικέω occurs in the Third Gospel twice (11:26; 13:4), twenty times in Acts. "Temporary lodging" is not its typical sense for Luke (see esp. Acts 1:19; 4:16; 9:22; 13:27).

salem. This is not because Luke holds the Jewish people collectively responsible for Jesus' death. It is not in this way that these Jerusalemites are "representative," as is made clear in 13:27-29, when in an address to Jews in Pisidian Antioch Paul says that "the residents of Jerusalem and their leaders . . . asked Pilate to have Jesus killed."[22] Rather, Luke's characterization of Jerusalem contains the coordinates of a universal, missionary geography.[23]

Recognition of the place of Luke's list of nations in relation to the Table of Nations tradition supports this suggestion, since a partial list of the nations might stand in symbolically for the whole.[24] Of course, his picture is hyperbolic: "every nation" does not find its way into the list of peoples in vv. 9-11. Nevertheless, "under heaven" (see the parallel "from heaven" in v. 2) portends the divine outlook, of which these nations are illustrative.

Luke's list of nations takes a decidedly Jerusalem-oriented perspective on the Jewish Diaspora and anticipates in interesting ways the missionary activity of Jesus' witnesses yet to be narrated in Acts.[25] The resulting map distributes the nations listed in vv. 9-11 along lines determined by the four points of the compass, reminding us that cartography is a science invested with ideology; mapping is a human enterprise that incorporates heavy doses

---

22. Contra Jack T. Sanders, *The Jews in Luke-Acts* (Philadelphia: Fortress, 1987), pp. 233-35. See the more nuanced view of Frank J. Matera, "Responsibility for the Death of Jesus according to the Acts of the Apostles," *JSNT* 39 (1990): 77-93.

23. Cf. Eberhard Güting, "Der geographische Horizont der sogenannten Völkerliste des Lukas (Acta 2:9-11)," *ZNW* 66 (1975): 149-69.

24. See Philip S. Alexander, "Geography and the Bible (Early Jewish)," *ABD* 2:980-85; James M. Scott, "Luke's Geographical Horizon," in *The Book of Acts in Its Graeco-Roman Setting*, ed. David W. J. Gill and Conrad Gempf, A1CS 2 (Grand Rapids/Carlisle: Eerdmans/Paternoster, 1994), pp. 527-28. Calling attention to the analogue in *Rudiments of Paulus Alexandrinus* (fourth c. BCE), some have urged that Luke's list is comprehensive because it gives one nation for each of the twelve signs of the zodiac; see esp. Stefan Weinstock, "The Geographical Catalogue in Acts ii,9-11," *JRS* 38 (1948): 43-46 — followed by, e.g., Gerd Lüdemann, *Early Christianity according to the Traditions in Acts: A Commentary* (Minneapolis: Fortress, 1989), pp. 40-41. Cf., however, Bruce M. Metzger, "Ancient Astrological Geography and Acts 2:9-11," in *Apostolic History and the Gospel: Biblical and Historical Essays Presented to F. F. Bruce on His 60th Birthday*, ed. W. Ward Gasque and Ralph P. Martin (Grand Rapids: Eerdmans, 1970), pp. 123-33; Güting, "Geographische Horizont," p. 151.

25. Cf. Ezek. 5:5; *Jub.* 8:19; *1 En.* 26:1. See Richard Bauckham, "James and the Jerusalem Church," in *The Book of Acts in Its Palestinian Setting*, ed. Richard Bauckham, A1CS 4 (Grand Rapids: Eerdmans, 1995), pp. 417-27; Loveday C. A. Alexander, "'In Journeyings Often': Voyaging in the Acts of the Apostles and in Greek Romance," in *Luke's Literary Achievement: Collected Essays*, ed. Christopher M. Tuckett, JSNTSup 116 (Sheffield: Sheffield Academic, 1995), pp. 30-31.

of social, political, and religious agenda.[26] Interestingly, within Acts, once Philip and Paul appear on the scene, the map configured by vv. 9-11 is unmade, or remade; the result is a new way of organizing social space so as to include Samaria and Ethiopia, Macedonia and Achaia. The narrative of Acts often demands a map, but it is a map that evolves with the narrative itself, moving away from a Jerusalem-centered perspective and casting such persons as Philip and Paul as persons who advance beyond the boundaries of "the known world." Of course, such locales as Paul visits, say Corinth or Athens, are prominent on *some* maps of the Empire — maps of economic or banking centers, for example — but apparently not within the structuring of space determined by the sacredness of Jerusalem and its temple for Jews scattered throughout the Mediterranean as this is conceived in vv. 9-11.

Luke's "map" thus locates those gathered in Jerusalem at the "center of the world," so it is not surprising to see him characterize them further as "pious (εὐλαβεῖς) Jews" (v. 5). Εὐλαβής is always a positive quality for Luke, referring essentially to persons who are blameless before the law and in tune with the will of God.[27] The identification of residents of Jerusalem and those present for the pilgrim feast as "Jews" may seem redundant, but it serves Luke's purpose — a purpose that becomes all the more clear when the pattern of Acts 2 is juxtaposed with the beginnings of Jesus' ministry:

Jesus in Luke 3:21–4:30	Disciples in Acts 2
Baptized/anointed with the Spirit	Filled with the Spirit
Genealogy	Table of Nations
Testing in the wilderness	————————
First public sermon	First public sermon

As Jesus' genealogy portended the universal significance of his mission, so the catalog of nations throws the net of the good news over all the lands to which the Jewish people had scattered and from which they had gathered. Anticipated here is an interpretation of the Pentecost event as the reconstitution of Israel, from whom a light to the nations would shine forth — an interpretation that will be made explicit in Peter's address, beginning in 2:14.

26. On geography as social space, see, e.g., Edward W. Soja, *Postmodern Geographies: The Reassertion of Space in Critical Social Theory* (London: Verso, 1989); Benno Werlen, *Society, Action, and Space: An Alternative Human Geography* (London: Routledge, 1993).

27. Cf. Luke 2:25 (Simeon); Acts 8:2 ("devout" men buried Stephen [on burying a corpse as a mark of piety, see Josephus, *Ap.* 2.29 §211; Tob. 1:16-2:10]); 22:12 (Ananias).

"Other Languages," Babel, and Identity Formation

The interrelation of the Table of Nations material with the Babel episode in Genesis 10–11 and the clear echoes of the Table of Nations tradition in Acts 2:5-11 are enough to suggest the possibility of reflection on the Babel tradition in Luke's narrative. This possibility receives further support from linguistic parallels[28] and from the centrality in each scene of the divine enabling of languages. Nevertheless, scholars remain divided on the presence of the Babel story in the background of Luke's scene, differing especially on the possible utility of the Babel scene in Luke's account.

Those who find an allusion to Babel in Acts 2 regard Luke as portraying a kind of "reversal of Babel,"[29] and those who deny the influence of Babel in the Lukan narrative typically do so by arguing that in fact Pentecost does not so much reverse the confusion of languages as make use of it for missionary purposes.[30] (I have already urged that Spirit-inspired speech in this pericope is *doxological* rather than *missiological* in primary aim, however.) The discussion, then, has heretofore been funded by an erroneous presumption — namely, that within the biblical narrative of salvation history Babel required reversal. Given the romantic belief, popular from the early Dark Ages to the Renaissance, that the language spoken in the garden of Eden was the original and perfect language, and that all subsequent languages were its degenerative descendants from the catastrophes of the fall

---

28. The data was summarized long ago by J. G. Davies, "Pentecost and Glossolalia," *JTS,* n.s., 3 (1952): 228-29. See the use of φωνή (Gen. 11:1, 7; Acts 2:6), οὐρανός (Gen. 11:4; Acts 2:2), πῦρ (Gen. 11:3; Acts 2:3), γλῶσσα (Gen. 11:7; Acts 2:4), and συγχέω (Gen. 11:7; Acts 2:6; cf. σύγχυσις in Gen. 11:9); as well as the contrast between the plan to "make for ourselves a name" and the proclamation of "the mighty acts of God." See also Hee-Seong Kim, *Die Geisttaufe des Messias: Eine kompositionsgeschichtliche Untersuchung zu einem Leitmotiv des lukanishen Doppelwerks: Ein Beitrag zur Theologie und Intention des Lukas* (Bern: Peter Lang, 1993), pp. 158-60.

29. E.g., the Venerable Bede, *Commentary on the Acts of the Apostles,* trans., with introduction and notes, Lawrence T. Martin, CS 117 (Kalamazoo, Mich.: Cistercian, 1989), p. 29; Bruce, *Acts,* p. 59; idem, "The Holy Spirit in the Acts of the Apostles," *Int* 27 (1973): 171; Stanley Hauerwas, "The Church as God's New Language," in *Scriptural Authority and Narrative Interpretation,* ed. Garrett Green (Philadelphia: Fortress, 1987), pp. 179-98; Geoffrey W. Grogan, "The Significance of Pentecost in the History of Salvation," *SBET* 4 (1986): 97-107; John Michael Penney, *The Missionary Emphasis of Lukan Pneumatology,* JPTSup 12 (Sheffield: Sheffield Academic, 1997), p. 83.

30. E.g., I. Howard Marshall, "The Significance of Pentecost," *SJT* 30 (1977): 366; Andrew T. Lincoln, "Theology and History in the Interpretation of Luke's Pentecost," *ExpTim* 96 (1985): 204-9.

and Babel,[31] the idea that Babel needed to be overturned is easy to understand. Indeed, since the British jurist Sir William Jones observed in the late eighteenth century the marked similarity between such diverse languages as Greek, Celtic, and Sanskrit, linguists have largely assumed that most of the 144 so-called Indo-European languages derive from a single ancient tongue, fueling the ongoing search for an original (if not an original, perfect) language.[32] Earlier commentators (e.g., von Rad) took Genesis 11:1 to mean that all of humanity had one language and one vocabulary, whereas Victor Hamilton has more recently suggested that the Genesis account proposes the existence of a single *lingua franca*.[33]

In fact, however, the Genesis account does not present the confusion of languages as merely a punitive response on the part of God. Rather, the confusion of languages comprised a divine intervention effecting what had apparently been God's purpose from the outset. Humanity was to fill the whole earth according to Genesis 1:28, and this mandate was reiterated after the flood (Gen. 9:1, 7); indeed, according to the Genesis record, from Noah's sons "the nations spread abroad on the earth" (10:32). "Scattering," then, is integral to the human vocation — a vocation explicitly countered by the unity of language and idolatrous purpose represented by the building project undertaken on the plain of Shinar: "Let us . . . not be scattered" (11:4). Here is another point of contact between the narratives of Acts and Genesis. According to Genesis 1:28 (also 9:1, 7), the human family is "to increase and to multiply" (αὐξάνω and πληθύνω), and after the flood the people are "scattered" (διασπείρω, 10:32). In Acts, the word of God "increased" and the number of disciples "multiplied" (αὐξάνω and πληθύνω in Acts 6:7; 12:24; αὐξάνω alone in 19:20; πληθύνω alone in 9:31), and the "scattering" (διασπείρω) of witnesses is a precursor to proclamation of the word to the end of the earth (8:1, 4; 11:19).

31. See Umberto Eco, *The Search for the Perfect Language,* TM (Oxford: Blackwell, 1995).

32. For example, combining contemporary computational methods from evolutionary biology with the older technique of glottochronology, Russell D. Gray and Quentin D. Atkinson recently concluded that a proto-Indo-European language was spoken more than 8,000 years ago by Neolithic farmers in Anatolia; see Gray and Atkinson, "Language-Tree Divergence Times Support the Anatolian Theory of Indo-European Origin," *Nature* 426 (2003): 435-39.

33. Gerhard von Rad, *Genesis: A Commentary,* rev. ed., OTL (Philadelphia: Westminster, 1972), p. 148; Victor P. Hamilton, *The Book of Genesis: Chapters 1-17,* NICOT (Grand Rapids: Eerdmans, 1990), p. 350.

The unity of language reported in Genesis 11 is only the first of four ways in which the narrator indicates that these human efforts ran counter to the divine will. Second, the articulation of the people's plan, "Let us make a name for ourselves . . ." (11:4), belies their hubris. Third, the plan's "Let us" form is reminiscent of God's speech concerning humanity — both in creation ("Let us make humankind," 1:26) and in response to this building project ("Let us go down," 11:7); hence, this human-initiated plan is cast in language that parodies God's own plan, pitting human counsel against divine. Fourth, the Babel account opens with a reference to "one language" — a metaphor for the subjugation and assimilation of conquered peoples by a dominant nation. This is the finding of Christoph Uehlinger, whose examination of Assyrian royal inscriptions has identified a recurring pattern: "one speech," building, naming, and world empire. Of special interest is the identification of the motif of "one speech" with oppressively instituted conformity.[34] For an illustration of the power of language as an implement of cultural assimilation, one need look no further than the nineteenth-century production of the *Oxford English Dictionary*, a gargantuan task for which the impetus came not only from the modernist impulse to classify and define but also from colonial concerns. In his narration of the making of the famed *OED*, Simon Winchester observes with tongue in cheek, "God . . . naturally approved the spread of the [English] language as an essential imperial device."[35]

Against the backdrop of Uehlinger's work, we may read the phrase "one language" in Genesis 11:1 as metonymic for conquest and domination; indeed, even prior to Uehlinger's work the history of interpretation evidences such a reading.[36] Recently, for example, G. D. Cloete and D. J. Smit have re-

---

34. See Christoph Uehlinger, *Weltreich und "eine Rede": Eine neue Deutung der sogenannten Turmbauerzählung (Gen. 11,1-9)*, OBO 101 (Freiburg: Universitätsverlag, 1990). See also David Smith, "What Hope after Babel? Diversity and Community in Gen 11:1-9, Exod 1:1-14, Zeph 3:1-13 and Acts 2:1-3," *HBT* 18 (1996): 169-91.

35. Simon Winchester, *The Professor and the Madman: A Tale of Murder, Insanity, and the Making of the* Oxford English Dictionary (New York: HarperCollins, 1998), p. 78.

36. It might be objected, as Terence E. Fretheim observes, that "the text offers no sign of this building project as an imperial enterprise." "In fact," Fretheim goes on to urge, "the discourse and motivation are remarkably democratic . . ."; see Fretheim, *Genesis, NIB* 1 (Nashville: Abingdon, 1994), p. 411. Such a view might gain support from the unmistakable images of oppression characteristic of the exodus story, compared with the apparent dearth of such images here. But one of the pillars of interpretive theory is that in any given utterance, most of the discourse meaning remains unverbalized yet is presumptively shared between the model speaker/author and the model audience; see, e.g., John Lyons, *Linguistic Semantics: An Introduction* (Cambridge: Cambridge University Press, 1995), pp. 234-342; Peter Grundy,

minded us that South African apartheid found in Genesis 11 a divine mandate and blessing for an oppressively constituted conformity.[37] Reaching further into the past, Pieter Brueghel's striking rendition "The Tower of Babel" (1563) juxtaposes the ascending tower as a failed architectural enterprise with scenes of political subjugation: the gargantuan tower overshadowing the peasant village, a tower that itself seems to suffer the scars and bloodshed of battle, warships anchored off the coast, and the obeisance of common folk to royalty (presumably Nimrod) in the painting's foreground.[38] Pushing back further still, Augustine observed that the city of the Tower of Babel, Babylon, founded by Nimrod, was the head of all other cities of the kingdom (*Civ.* 16.4), while Chrysostom found in Genesis 11 evidence of humanity's inclination always to long and reach for more and more (*Hom. Gen.* 30.5). For Josephus, Nimrod opposed the scattering to which God had called the people, transforming their situation "little by little . . . into a tyranny, holding that the only way to detach persons from the fear of God was by making them continuously dependent upon his own power."[39]

As Israel had itself experienced in the aftermath of the conquest of Palestine by Alexander, "one language" — in this case, Greek — was (and is) a potent weapon in the imperial arsenal; integration into a single linguistic community is a product of political domination. It is not for nothing that scenes of persecution from and struggle with foreign rule in 2 Maccabees are peppered with references to Jews speaking "in the language of their ancestors" (7:8, 21, 27; 12:37; 15:29; cf. 4 Macc. 12:7; 16:15). In the face of powerful

---

Doing Pragmatics (London: Edward Arnold, 1995). In his study of *Weltreich und "eine Rede,"* Uehlinger has shown that the shared social world (or presupposition pool) would "fill in the gaps" of the significance of "one language" with images of imperialism and dominance. Contra Fretheim, moreover, rather than representing the speech of democracy, the words "Let us" point to the age-old practice whereby those in power speak for all. That images of domination are central to the portrayal of Israel's life in Egypt is only to be expected, given the importance for Israel's self-understanding (and for the biblical narrative more generally) of the exodus story — a significance not shared by the Babel account.

37. G. D. Cloete and D. J. Smit, "'Its Name Was Called Babel . . .,'" *JTSA* 86 (1994): 81-87.

38. See http://www.ibiblio.org/wm/paint/auth/bruegel/babel.jpg, accessed November 13, 2007.

39. Josephus, *Ant.* 1.4.1-4 §§109-21, quotation 1.4.2 §114 (trans. Thackeray, LCL alt.). Philo's interpretation of Babel resembles a collage of allegorical referents and is focused on wickedness within the person and the mob-like wickedness of a people (i.e., the lack of order). He reads the phrase "the earth was all one lip and one voice" as "a consonance of evil deeds great and innumerable," including "the injuries which cities and nations and countries inflict and retaliate" (*Conf.* 5 §15, trans. Colson, LCL).

imperial forces, maintaining one's native or ancestral tongue is an instrument of resistance precisely because it is a badge of (minority) identity. Thus, although the building project of Genesis 11 is thwarted by Yahweh, to be sure, his scattering the people over all the face of the earth is not so much a curse against the human family as an intervention in reaffirmation of the divine purpose in creation and opposition to coercive human subjugation.

This general perspective on "one language" is supported by recent work in sociolinguistics and linguistic anthropology. If contemporary linguists have adopted a descriptive posture vis-à-vis language in use, they also recognize the importance of linguistic prejudice as a powerful social force. As R. A. Hudson observes: "A good deal of evidence shows that people use language in order to locate themselves in a multi-dimensional social space."[40] Language and dialect communicate information about speakers, including their affiliations and social status (whether actual or projected). Thus, language use is a symbol of group membership and may become the site of struggle over the cultural and political values mediated by means of language. Pierre Bourdieu presses further, as do students of political resistance, observing that the adoption, extension, and maintenance of official language are bound up with the genesis and social uses of the state. Language use functions like a market overseen by agents of regulation and imposition, who are empowered to examine and sanction those who depart from the established norm. Conversely, one of the ways that dominated people fashion their own identity apart from alien rule is through dialect and other tactics of language use that construct subgroups within the larger whole.[41]

What do such considerations have to do with Acts 2:1-13? The ongoing maintenance of native tongues by regional populations long assimilated through Greek, then Roman, occupation is itself symptomatic of the persistent cultivation of regional identities in the face of imperial forces. Against the backdrop of these regional identities, Spirit-inspired doxological speech, engaging scriptural interpretation in the vernacular languages of those gathered at Pentecost, redefines social space in telling ways. That is, divinely en-

40. R. A. Hudson, *Sociolinguistics*, CTL (Cambridge: Cambridge University Press, 1980), p. 195.

41. Pierre Bourdieu, *Language and Symbolic Power*, ed. John B. Thompson (Cambridge, Mass.: Harvard University Press, 1991). Cf. James C. Scott, *Domination and the Arts of Resistance: Hidden Transcripts* (New Haven/London: Yale University Press, 1990); idem, *Weapons of the Weak: Everyday Forms of Peasant Resistance* (New Haven/London: Yale University Press, 1985); Michel de Certeau, *The Practice of Everyday Life* (Berkeley: University of California Press, 1984).

abled, charismatic doxology in the vernacular of those gathered from the four winds in Jerusalem at Pentecost undermines the imperial vision of Alexander the Great and, more recently, that of Rome. The basis of unity among these persons was not to be identified with the cultural and linguistic assimilation that energizes colonial impulses in any age. Luke's Pentecost is thus the scene of resistance to a world centered in Rome, or Jerusalem.

Derrida rightly has it that God "deconstructs" false unity in Genesis 11,[42] but Acts provides no invitation to return to a single language as a divine promise or blessing. Had Luke presented such a "reversal," this might have suggested the centrality of Jerusalem as the gathering place of the unity of humanity. Pentecost, however, leads away from Jerusalem, to a missionary movement scattered to "the end of the earth"; it decenters (or, at least, portends the decentering of) Jerusalem as the locus of divine worship. Pentecost constitutes, rather, a criticism of an ethics of election focused on the privileged place of those who claim by birth to be descendants of Abraham (see already Luke 3:7-14), but also at least an implicit critique of Rome, whose imperial destiny (so it was said) was to "form one body under the name of Romans."[43]

The countervision provided in Acts 2 taken as a whole furthers Luke's presentation of the social arrangement of the believers in the form of an egalitarian community marked by unpretentiousness and the democratization of the experience of the Holy Spirit. Repeatedly, Luke emphasizes the unity of the community — both in anticipation and as a consequence of the outpouring of the Spirit — and highlights the importance of "each" person within that community.[44] In an interesting wordplay, for example, the "division" (διαμερίζω) of tongues, like flames of fire, that alighted on each of them (v. 3) prepares for and leads to the "division" (διαμερίζω) of the community's property and possessions according to the need of each person (v. 45). In Luke's summary representation of the community in 2:42-47, considerations typical in an agonistic, status-conscious world like that of the ancient Mediterranean are undermined. No accommodation is allotted status-

---

42. Jacques Derrida, "Des tours de Babel," *Semeia* 54 (1991): 7.

43. See François Bovon, "Israël, l'Église et les nations dans l'œuvre double de Luc," in *L'Œvre de Luc: Études d'exégèse et de théologie*, LD 130 (Paris: Cerf, 1987), pp. 244-51; the citation is from Tacitus, *Ann.* 11.24 (trans. Jackson, LCL).

44. Cf. Richard P. Thompson, "Believers and Religious Leaders in Jerusalem: Contrasting Portraits of Jews in Acts 1–7," in *Literary Studies in Luke-Acts: Essays in Honor of Joseph B. Tyson*, ed. Richard P. Thompson and Thomas E. Phillips (Macon, Ga.: Mercer University Press, 1998), pp. 334-35.

based factionalism or tribalism in the economy ushered in by the outpouring of the Holy Spirit.[45] Even if Palestinian and Diaspora Judaisms are in focus among those who experience the outpouring of the Spirit and its results in Acts 2, the connotations of a worldwide experience of salvation are nonetheless transparent. Indeed, Jesus' parting words to his followers had been that this — a mission in Jerusalem, Judea, Samaria, and to the end of the earth — was the purpose of the Spirit's outpouring (1:8; cf. Luke 24:47-49).

Conclusion

The story continues beyond 2:1-13, of course, with Luke's portrayal of Peter's interpretation of the coming of the Spirit as the restoration of Israel (2:14-41) and subsequent summary report of the nature of the community of believers (2:42-47). In 2:1-13, though, a primary emphasis has already surfaced — namely, the generation of unity among diverse peoples through means other than dispensing with distinctions among those peoples. Unity is found, but not by reviving a pre-Babel (imperious) homogeneity. Indeed, Pentecost does not reverse Babel but parodies it — that is, Luke's intertextuality maps distinction in the midst of marked similarity.[46] Multiple languages continue to be spoken, and apparently all are appropriate for giving voice to "the great things of God." With the outpouring of the Spirit, koinonia is possible not as a consequence of the presence of a single, all-pervasive, repressive language, not by the dissolution of multiple languages, nor, indeed, by the dissolution of all social and national distinctives in the formation of cultural uniformity. Koinonia is rather the consequence of the generative activity of the Spirit who is poured out by Jesus, of the capacity of these persons both to grasp that the promise of God's mighty work is actualized in Jesus and to write themselves into that story of God's great acts, and then of the location of a new rallying point of identity: "in the name of Jesus Christ" (2:38).

45. Cf. Helen Schüngel-Straumann, "*Ruach, Pneuma* and Pentecost," *TD* 38 (1991): 334.
46. This understanding of "parody" is borrowed from Linda Hutcheon, *A Poetics of Postmodernism: History, Theory, Fiction* (New York/London: Routledge, 1988), pp. 124-40.

Saul/Paul: Onomastics, Typology, and Christian Scripture

Stephen B. Chapman

"I myself am an Israelite, a descendent of Abraham, a member of the tribe of Benjamin. God has not rejected his people whom he foreknew," writes Paul in Romans 11:1-2.[1] The thrust of this declaration, reinforced by other remarks in Paul's letters and certain features of his portrayal in Acts,[2] has long been difficult to square with the traditional interpretation of Paul's Damascus road experience as a "conversion," a term that usually refers to a change *of* religions rather than a change of conviction *within* a religion.[3] Yet if Paul

1. Scripture quotations are from the NRSV.

2. Cf. Acts 21:37–22:3; 23:6; 26:4-5; Rom. 9:1-5; 2 Cor. 11:22-28; Gal. 1:13-14; 2:15; Phil. 3:2-11.

3. The problematic use of the term "conversion" is forcefully characterized by Krister Stendahl, *Paul among Jews and Gentiles* (London: SCM, 1977), pp. 7-23. His position has been adopted by, among others, John Knox, *Chapters in a Life of Paul,* rev. ed. (Macon, Ga.: Mercer University Press, 1987); and Heikki Räisänen, "Paul's Conversion and the Development of His View of the Law," *NTS* 33 (1987): 404-19. In contrast to the established tradition of Christian interpretation, Stendahl calls attention to the lack of any indications in the NT of a guilty pre-"conversion" conscience on Paul's part and the absence of any post-"conversion" renunciation of his Jewish faith, noting that both features have long been associated with religious conversion from the perspective of Western Christian culture. According to Stendahl, the accounts of Paul's personal transformation in Acts instead exhibit striking similarities to prophetic call narratives in the OT, leading to Stendahl's judgment that it is preferable to speak of Paul's "call" rather than his "conversion." For an argument that Paul did experience repentance and forgiveness in his "conversion," even though he did not use this exact language to describe it, see Ben Witherington III, *The Paul Quest: The Renewed Search for the Jew of Tarsus* (Downers Grove, Ill.: InterVarsity, 1998), pp. 77-78. However that issue may be resolved, I find Stendahl's other point — the lack of any renunciation of Paul's Jewish faith — the stronger of the two, since such renunciation was apparently a dis-

did not "convert" to Christianity from Judaism but became a Christian Jew, then a number of widespread Christian theological assumptions concerning the relationship between the two Testaments of the Christian Bible, as well as contemporary relations between Judaism and Christianity, must be reappraised. Paul the "convert" remains a preeminent warrant and symbol for supersessionism within Christian theology.

To be sure, the account of Paul's Damascus road experience in Acts 9:1-19 (cf. its later retellings in 22:6-16; 26:12-18) is highly dramatic and entails a sudden, radical transformation of his life. A heavenly light unexpectedly shoots toward Paul while he is journeying to Damascus, and he falls to the ground in what is revealed to be an encounter with the resurrected Jesus, who then speaks to him. As a consequence of this encounter, Paul loses his sight, until a Christian disciple named Ananias restores it. However, as Romans 11:1-2 and other passages indicate, Paul still worships the God of Israel and identifies himself as a Jew.[4] According to the book of Acts, he has

---

tinctive characteristic of Jewish and Christian conversions already in antiquity; see A. D. Nock, *Conversion: The Old and the New in Religion from Alexander the Great to Augustine of Hippo* (Oxford: Clarendon, 1933). For a defense of "conversion" as an appropriate conceptuality regardless of Stendahl's objections, see Alan F. Segal, *Paul the Convert: The Apostolate and Apostasy of Saul the Pharisee* (New Haven: Yale University Press, 1990), pp. 5-6. Segal agrees with Stendahl about both guilt and renunciation being missing from descriptions of Paul's path to Christian conviction but nevertheless maintains that Paul's change was so radical that it can be fairly termed a "conversion" as well as a "call." Observe, however, the important rejoinder of Larry W. Hurtado, "Convert, Apostate, or Apostle to the Nations: The 'Conversion' of Paul in Recent Scholarship," *SR* 22 (1995): 283 that Segal's use of "conversion" is tainted by his assumption of a Gentile Christian community antedating Paul, who is then supposed to have "joined" it. Hurtado argues persuasively that better evidence leads to a view of Paul as himself the founder of Gentile Christianity. So if the appropriateness of the "conversion" model for Segal depends on an understanding of the term as "moving from one sect or denomination to another within the same religion" (Segal, *Paul*, p. 6), then his definition is at fatal variance with the reality he is attempting to describe. Although Hurtado sees other difficulties with Segal's position as well, in the end he agrees with Segal in opting for both "conversion" and "call" as a combined characterization of Paul's Damascus road experience.

4. Stendahl, *Paul*, pp. 1-7. Stendahl's critique of the traditional view is important and in my judgment correct, but his constructive alternative fails to characterize Paul's transformation adequately. Treating Acts 9:1-19 as a "call narrative" on analogy with prophetic call narratives in the OT does not take sufficient account of the radical quality of Paul's religious reorientation. The deeper problem with Stendahl's argument does not have to do with how "conversion" should be understood psychologically or sociologically but with Pauline passages such as Phil. 3:2-11, in which Paul insists on his Jewishness but emphatically devalues it in comparison with his later Christian experience and understanding.

Timothy circumcised (16:3); he conducts his ministry in close connection with the institution of the synagogue (e.g., 17:2; 18:4, 19); he observes vows (e.g., 18:18) and purification rites (e.g., 21:17-26);[5] and to the very end of the book Paul defends himself from the charge of undermining or opposing Jews and Jewish tradition (28:17-20).

More accurately, then, rather than being an instance of a "conversion" genre, Acts 9 is literarily a reversal narrative.[6] The would-be destroyer of the church is himself threatened with destruction.[7] As "Saul," he is the scourge of Christians, the peerless persecutor (8:3), who suddenly becomes the target of almost hostile divine attention, a confrontation in which the persecutor is overpowered, foiled, and turned into a consummate advocate. An important feature of this reversal in Acts 9 is the text's emphasis on the *name* of Jesus. Paul is later viewed in Acts as having once persecuted Jesus' "name" (26:9). In Acts 9 itself, however, after falling to the ground on the way to Damascus, "Saul" does not know who is calling out *his* name until the voice replies, "I am Jesus, whom you are persecuting" (9:5). Then "the Lord Jesus" (9:17)[8] tells Ananias to give assistance to Saul because "he is an instrument whom I have chosen to bring my *name* before Gentiles and kings and before the people of Israel; I myself will show him how much he must suffer for the sake of my *name*" (9:15-16). Likewise, when Saul begins to preach the gospel, it is Jesus' name that he invokes and emphasizes (9:20-21, 27-28).

A curious aspect of this narrative of reversal, in which names are so important, is that no notice is given of the well-known name change from Saul to Paul. Beginning with his introduction in Acts 7:58, Paul is known in the narrative exclusively as "Saul," and he continues to be called "Saul" throughout the Damascus road account. For symmetry, one might well expect Saul to lose his own name as he is overpowered by the name of Jesus, and to receive in turn a new name emblematic of his newfound Christian identity. Many popular accounts of Paul's "conversion" make exactly that move, treating the name "Paul"

5. Johan Christiaan Beker, *Heirs of Paul: Paul's Legacy in the New Testament and in the Church Today* (Minneapolis: Fortress, 1991). Beker argues against the idea that these actions can be dismissed as strategic compromises on Paul's part.

6. Jürgen Becker, *Paul: Apostle to the Gentiles*, trans. O. C. Dean Jr. (Louisville: Westminster John Knox, 1993), p. 61.

7. Cf. the similar sense of reversal in 1 Cor. 15:8-10; Gal. 1:13-24; Phil. 3:2-11.

8. On the importance of "Lord" for Lukan Christology and theology, see C. Kavin Rowe, *Early Narrative Christology: The Lord in the Gospel of Luke*, BZNW 139 (Berlin/New York: de Gruyter, 2006), esp. pp. 146-57.

as Saul's postconversion name.[9] Even some less careful scholarly treatments fall into this pattern,[10] which can already be found among early church theologians.[11] But Jesus calls Paul "Saul" on the Damascus road (9:4), Jesus plainly refers to Paul as "Saul" in instructing Ananias (9:11), and Ananias greets Paul with the words "Brother Saul" (9:17). Even after Saul's baptism he is consistently called "Saul" (9:22, 24). Acts introduces a new name for Saul only later in the narrative, and not in the context of the Damascus road.

Paul appears as "Saul" until Acts 13:9,[12] at which point he is described as having *two* names ("But Saul, also known as Paul . . ."). Thus, despite a well-established tendency in the exegetical literature to view the two names as historically sequential,[13] they are not narratively depicted as constituting a name *change* at all but as simultaneous name alternatives. Yet from Acts 13:9 onward, the name "Paul" is used exclusively, with "Saul" appearing only in the recounted dialogue of Paul's two later retellings of his Damascus road experience — in Jesus' question, "Saul, Saul, why are you persecuting me?" (22:7; 26:14), and in Ananias's pronouncement, "Brother Saul, regain your sight!" (22:13). Apart from these formulaic vocatives, which would understandably have been more resistant to alteration in the transmission of the tradition, the present narrative consistently refers to "Saul" prior to Acts 13:9 and "Paul" thereafter.

9. See the comments of Michael Compton, "From Saul to Paul: Patristic Interpretation of the Names of the Apostle," in *In Dominico Eloquio/In Lordly Eloquence: Essays on Patristic Exegesis in Honor of Robert Louis Wilken,* ed. Paul M. Blowers et al. (Grand Rapids: Eerdmans, 2002), p. 52.

10. E.g., Michael Grant, *Saint Paul* (New York: Scribner, 1976), p. 104: "The reason why Paul possessed the faith to believe and convey to others his belief . . . was because of his certainty that Jesus Christ had appeared to him in a vision: an experience which converted him from Saul, a savage opponent of Christianity, to Paul, its passionate follower." Here the two names are used to refer to Paul's identity before and after his Damascus road experience, which the text itself does not do. It is no accident that Grant employs the two names in this manner to bolster the "conversion" model of Paul's transformation. The lack of a new name in Acts 9 actually points away from the "conversion" model and toward greater continuity in Paul's life, pre- and post-Damascus.

11. See Compton, "Saul to Paul," p. 54.

12. As Compton, "Saul to Paul," p. 51 n. 4, correctly notes, several Western manuscripts of Acts introduce the name Paul in Acts 12:25. But Bruce M. Metzger, *A Textual Commentary on the Greek New Testament,* 2nd ed. (New York: United Bible Societies, 1994), p. 350, judges this feature of Acts 12:25 to be a "scribal anticipation" of Acts 13:9, paralleling the introduction in the same verse of John, "whose other name was Mark."

13. For the classic exegetical treatment of Paul's name, see G. A. Harrer, "Saul Who Also Is Called Paul," *HTR* 33 (1940): 19-33. The name "Saul" appears nowhere else in the NT.

The question to be explored in this essay is why. After evaluating the historical and literary possibilities, and proposing an answer, the theological impact of that answer will be considered for the relationship between the Old and New Testaments, and between Jews and Christians.

I. What's in a Name?

Sean McDonough has newly catalogued the main suggestions for an explanation of the shift from "Saul" to "Paul" in Acts.[14] Three proposals have been particularly conspicuous in biblical scholarship. Although interest in the topic extends back to the theologians of the early church, commentators have most recently tended to emphasize the vulgar associations of the Greek term σαῦλος that the writer of Acts — or Paul himself — might have wanted to minimize or eliminate.[15] Others have proposed that Saul took the name "Paul" as a way of honoring the Cyprian proconsul Sergius Paulus (Acts 13:7).[16] Certainly it bears noting that the name "Paul" is first introduced for Saul in connection with his successful effort in preventing the Jewish false prophet Bar-Jesus from turning Sergius Paulus away from the Christian faith (13:8). Still other writers have proposed that Saul took a new non-Jewish name in order to symbolize his post-"conversion" commitment to share the gospel among the Gentiles. However, there are significant problems with all three suggestions.

With regard to the first theory, the one emphasizing the unsavory connotations of σαῦλος, a major difficulty arises immediately upon closer examination. While the Greek name Σαῦλος is indeed used in the received text of Acts, the undeclined form Σαούλ also appears in the vocatives of Acts 9, 22, and 26, suggesting that a Semitic form of the name predates the Greek

---

14. Sean M. McDonough, "Small Change: Saul to Paul, Again," *JBL* 125 (2006): 390-91.

15. T. J. Leary, "Paul's Improper Name," *NTS* 38 (1992): 467-69. Leary posits that it would have been useful for Paul to employ a Roman name when dealing with Gentiles, especially those in authority, and argues from the wordplay regarding the name Onesimus in Philemon 11 that Paul himself had an evident concern for the meaning of names (p. 468). Leary describes σαῦλος as a widely known Greek term for "the loose and wanton gait of prostitutes." With such arguments, it is clear that Leary thinks concern about this term originates with the historical Paul rather than the author of Luke-Acts.

16. Compton, "Saul to Paul," pp. 57-58, points out the appearance of this idea already in Origen and Jerome. The view is also maintained by Stendahl, *Paul,* p. 11, among other modern writers.

form (cf. 26:14). This possibility gains support from the evidence of the Chester Beatty papyri (P[45]), the earliest extant witnesses to the text of Acts, throughout which the Semitic form Σαούλ is used exclusively.[17] For this reason, the spelling Σαῦλος looks to be a secondary modification of the Semitic form, made so that it could be declined in Greek and also mirror the sound and spelling of Παῦλος.[18] If this is the case, then the vulgar associations of the Greek term σαῦλος would likely not have been an issue, either for the historical Paul or for the writer of Acts, because the name Σαούλ was already dissimilar enough to prevent such associations from arising. (It would have helped that Σαούλ is a Semitic word, only transliterated into Greek and obviously foreign, whereas σαῦλος is a Greek term, with connotations at home in the Greek language.) Furthermore, this theory does not explain why the name "Saul" is used in Acts at all (especially since it is entirely absent from the Pauline letters) and why the shift in names from "Saul" to "Paul" occurs specifically in Acts 13.[19]

The second theory, that the shift from "Saul" to "Paul" occurs in relation to the appearance in the narrative of Sergius Paulus, possesses two funda-

---

17. Harrer, "Saul," pp. 24-25. This form is identical to that found in the septuagintal tradition for King Saul.

18. Jerome Murphy-O'Connor, *Paul: A Critical Life* (Oxford: Clarendon, 1996), p. 42, rejects the idea that the Semitic name Σαούλ (with the omicron) is original, since Σαῦλος also appears in Josephus as a proper name and therefore cannot represent a later harmonizing move only within the development of the text of Acts. However, Harrer, "Saul," p. 25, rightly views the form Σαούλος (the Semitic form with a Greek ending) as standard in Josephus, where it occurs some two hundred times. He concedes the presence of a single instance of the form Σαῦλος in Josephus's writings (*War* 2:418) but judges it to be a copyist's error, because the same referent, Saul, the relative of Agrippa II, is referred to as Σαούλος in both *Antiquities of the Jews* (20:214) and *Jewish War* (2:556, 558). In Harrer's view, Josephus normally added case endings directly onto the Semitic base Σαούλ; it was only on analogy with Παῦλος that Σαούλ in Acts lost its omicron, becoming Σαῦλος. Despite this overwhelming evidence, even if Murphy-O'Connor were somehow still correct, the presence of Σαῦλος as a name in Josephus's writings would then represent a different kind of setback for the notion that the vulgar associations of σαῦλος required the avoidance of a similar-sounding name — for if Σαῦλος is used without such a worry in Josephus, why should the same name not also be employed in Acts? Murphy-O'Connor, *Paul*, p. 42, acknowledges the force of this argument.

19. Leary, "Paul's Improper Name," p. 469, admits that Acts uses "Saul" up to Acts 13:9 but argues that Acts 13:9 is simply the earliest point in the narrative at which the author could have shifted names. But with this move, Leary now inconsistently appears to imply that it was the author of Acts rather than the historical Paul who wanted to avoid the unpleasant connotations of σαῦλος.

mental weaknesses. First, the notion that Saul himself took on Sergius Paulus's name depends on the likelihood that Παῦλος was either a Greek version of a well-attested Latin name, *Paul(l)us,* or a *supernomen* — a vernacular nickname used alongside one's official name. As a Roman citizen, Paul was required by law to hold three names (i.e., the *tria nomina*): the *praenomen,* or given name; the *nomen,* or ancestral name; and the *cognomen,* or family name. In the eastern part of the Roman Empire, however, it had become common by Paul's time for Roman citizens to adopt an additional name for informal use. This *supernomen* gradually gained quasi-official status, often being treated as a "fourth" name in inscriptions, following the *cognomen* and the connecting formula ὁ καί in Greek or *qui et* in Latin[20] (or sometimes preceding the connecting formula, with the *cognomen* placed afterward). This onomastic formula matches precisely the notice given in Acts 13:9: Σαῦλος δέ, ὁ καὶ Παῦλος.[21] Because the *supernomen* could appear either before or after the connecting formula, either "Saul" or "Paul" in this notice could have been the apostle's *supernomen;* several factors, however, point to "Saul" as the more likely.[22] This finding would mean correspondingly that "Paul" was probably the apostle's *cognomen.*[23]

The theory that Saul took the name "Paul" from Sergius Paulus relies

---

20. Harrer, "Saul," p. 21.

21. Credit for this original insight should be given to Harrer, "Saul," p. 22. He has been followed by many others; e.g., Murphy-O'Connor, *Paul,* p. 43. For discussion of an intriguing inscriptional example of the same onomastic formula and further bibliographic resources, see Colin J. Hemer, "The Name of Paul," *TynBul* 36 (1985): 179-83.

22. Harrer, "Saul," pp. 32-33, argues that "Saul" was likely the apostle's *supernomen,* since it could not function as a Roman name, at least not in its undeclined form; and he raises cogent objections to the argument that *Paul(l)us* was the *supernomen.* Moreover, according to Harrer, it was unheard of for one Roman to adopt another's *supernomen.* A variation of Harrer's view is found in Becker, *Paul,* p. 37: "In addition to their Semitic name, diaspora Jews normally bore a second, similar-sounding Roman-Hellenistic given name. Similar onomastic pairs included, for example, Joshua and Jason, Silas and Silvanus. In the Hellenistic world Paul used this second name exclusively." Cf. the comparable judgments of F. F. Bruce, *Paul: Apostle of the Free Spirit* (Exeter: Paternoster, 1977), p. 38; A. N. Sherwin-White, *Roman Society and Roman Law in the New Testament* (Oxford: Clarendon, 1963), pp. 153-54. On the other side, Murphy-O'Connor, *Paul,* p. 43, believes that "Paul" was the apostle's *supernomen,* but he does not go on to address the remaining problem of Paul's *tria nomina.*

23. Although *Paul(l)us* is attested as a *praenomen* in this period, its use as a *cognomen* was much more common. Its employment with the connecting formula also suggests that it was Paul's *cognomen* rather than his *praenomen.* Leary, "Paul's Improper Name," p. 467, agrees that "Paul" was probably the apostle's *cognomen;* likewise, Hemer, "Name of Paul," p. 183, considers "Paul" the *cognomen* and thus "his ordinary name in the Gentile world."

upon the custom for slaves and foreigners, upon gaining their freedom, to adopt the *praenomen* and *nomen* of the Roman citizen who had been their patron. In the present case, inscriptional evidence indicates that the Cyprian proconsul's full name was *L. Sergius Paul(l)us;* Saul therefore would have adopted *L. Sergius* as the first two parts of his new name, and the procedure would not have involved the *cognomen Paul(l)us* at all.[24] The difficulty is compounded by the odd idea that Saul would have taken Sergius Paulus's name in such a fashion in the first place, since Saul was already a free Roman citizen. Much more likely is that Saul got his *cognomen* the way most people did — by inheriting it from his parents.[25]

For all these reasons, the possibility that Paul himself changed his name because of his encounter with Sergius Paulus is remote. It is of course possible that the historical Paul decided as a consequence of this meeting to rely more upon his Gentile name in his work among Gentiles[26] or that the writer of Acts was prompted to introduce Saul's other name in Acts 13:9 because of the similarity of the name of Sergius Paulus. But these guesses manufacture dimensions to the narrative that are not in literary evidence. The narrative in Acts 13:1-12 neither describes Saul as being particularly affected by the proconsul nor suggests that Saul's other name was part of a "missionary strategy."

The second weakness in the theory of a causal relation between the figure of Sergius Paulus and the appearance of Saul's other name "Paul" is suggested by the structure of the narrative itself. Saul and Barnabas are confronted in Acts 13:1-12 by Bar-Jesus, a Jewish false prophet, who also

---

24. Harrer, "Saul," p. 29. The other possibility would be to argue that Luke did not accurately know the proconsul's name, but this idea seems unlikely since the name has survived in inscriptional form.

25. Paul's parents or forebears, however, likely gained the name *Paul(l)us* through manumission or the bestowal of citizenship, the two best-attested ways in antiquity to gain a Roman name; see further Hemer, "Name of Paul," p. 179. It remains problematic that *Paul(l)us* is unattested as a Latin *nomen.* Murphy-O'Connor, *Paul*, p. 42, also worries that the name *Paul(l)us* would have been too exalted a *cognomen* for an ordinary Jewish family on the edge of the empire, but I would like to see evidence for this kind of concern in antiquity. It seems more likely to me that names were to a certain degree "shared" as a way of honoring their better-known holders. Murphy-O'Connor allows that *Paul(l)us* might have been an invented *cognomen* in the case of Paul's family, chosen perhaps for its similarity to Saul.

26. Witherington, *Paul Quest*, p. 72, proposes viewing the name "change" as a "missionary strategy" on Paul's part, in order to encourage his Gentile audience to identify with him through his adoption of a Gentile name. The idea of such a strategy is not out of the question (e.g., Acts 16:3; 21:24; cf. 1 Cor. 9:19-23), but the narrative gives no explicit indication at this point that it is operative.

possesses the Greek name Elymas. In response, the narrative reports Saul's other name, as if to portray a double-named threat being challenged and overcome by a double-named rescuer. The notice of the apostle's two names is thus a literary device, not a historical renaming; "Paul" is not a new name but simply a name up to now unreported. That this motif of prophet versus prophet is fundamental to the narrative is reinforced by the temporary blindness of Elymas (13:11). At one time, Saul too was a Jewish leader working against the Christian gospel who lost his sight because of it. Now Saul not only sees; he can also inflict such blindness. A close reading of the Acts 13 narrative suggests that literary reasons were responsible for the report of the apostle's two names being placed where it is and not any historical speculations about the relationship between Sergius Paulus and Saul.

It may still be the case that the name of Sergius Paulus served as a prompt for the notice of Saul's other name to appear in the narrative where it now does. Moreover, the idea that Saul's two names have a different resonance and utility, depending on whether the context is Jewish or Gentile may also be a factor, albeit again at a literary level. However, insufficient evidence exists to claim that the "literary" Paul approached the matter of his Jewishness differently after his visit to Cyprus.[27] What can be said is only that the Acts narrative consistently uses "Paul" for "Saul" after Acts 13:9. So neither the theory that there was an effort made to avoid the connotations of σαῦλος nor the idea that the name of Sergius Paulus was somehow responsible for Saul's alternative name — whether these theories are teased out historically or literarily — offers an explanation for why the shift from "Saul" to "Paul" occurs specifically in Acts 13.

The third theory mentioned by McDonough, concerning the apostle's post-"conversion" commitment to share the gospel among the Gentiles, has greater explanatory potential, but here again there is a need to avoid an unwarranted historicism and frame the issue more literarily. I do want to argue that the shift from "Saul" to "Paul" is literarily constructed in a manner that pertains to Jewish-Gentile relations as they figure in Acts, especially Paul's speech in Acts 13. But before delineating that aspect of Paul's portrayal, it is first necessary to comment in more detail on McDonough's own proposal regarding Paul's name. McDonough's proposal revives a suggestion first made by Augustine and attempts to strengthen it by exploring intertextual

---

27. Even in the most Jewish of contexts following Acts 13:9 (for example, his defense "in the Hebrew language" addressed to "brothers and fathers," Acts 21:40–22:1), Paul is known as "Paul."

echoes between the story of Saul/Paul in Acts and the story of Saul in the Old Testament book of 1 Samuel.

Augustine had drawn attention to the meaning of the Latin term *paulus,* "little" or "small," arguing that the historical Saul of Tarsus himself chose a new name to symbolize his new, profound sense of Christian humility. "When he was Saul, he was proud, exalted; when he was Paul, he was lowly and little," Augustine wrote, citing 1 Corinthians 15:9 and Ephesians 3:8 for support.[28] With this interpretation Augustine not only viewed the selection of the name "Paul" as symbolic to a doubtful extent; he also problematically assumed the name to have been the result of Saul's own free choice, rather than a family name that he inherited.[29] As Murphy-O'Connor notes, it is not at all uncommon for names in general to possess inert adjectival meanings, and the proper name *Paul(l)us* was widely used in the Roman world.[30] Nevertheless, McDonough essentially attempts a revival of Augustine's argument in which additional literary factors are adduced for support.[31]

His central exegetical observation is helpful, however. McDonough perceives that not only does Paul go on in Acts 13 to offer a speech in the synagogue in Pisidian Antioch (13:16-41); Paul even mentions "Saul son of Kish" in his retelling of salvation history within the speech (Acts 13:21). Although no direct relationship between the two Sauls is made explicit, the similarity of the names and the rarity of the mention of Saul son of Kish establish an allusive link between the two stories. As McDonough rightly notes, the reference in Acts 13 to the Old Testament figure of Saul is the only one in the entire New Testament, implying a suggestive literary relationship between the *appearance* of Saul son of Kish within Paul's salvation-historical address and the coincident *disappearance* of "Saul" as an identity for Paul within Acts.

Such a striking literary phenomenon constitutes some sort of appeal from the New Testament to the Old. But for what purpose? McDonough briefly observes the ironic parallelism between the Old Testament figure of Saul as David's nemesis and the New Testament figure of Saul as the persecutor of the Son of David: "Such a name [Saul] might seem ill-fitting, given Paul's activities on behalf of David's descendant."[32] But he locates the more

---

28. As cited in Compton, "Saul to Paul," p. 58.

29. See Compton, "Saul to Paul," p. 59; Harrer, "Saul," p. 22 n. 12.

30. Murphy-O'Connor, *Paul,* p. 44.

31. Cf. the similar move in Philippe Lefebvre, *Livres de Samuel et récits de résurrection: le messie ressuscité "selon les Écritures,"* LD 196 (Paris: Cerf, 2004), p. 482.

32. McDonough, "Small Change," p. 390.

significant link between the two Saul stories in Augustine's suggestion about the meaning of "small" for *paulus*.

Whereas Saul son of Kish is described as physically prepossessing (1 Sam. 9:2; 10:23), a feature that is at first celebrated but then subverted by the Samuel narrative (e.g., chs. 15-17), David is by contrast characterized as young/small (16:1-13; 17:12-15, 33, 38-40, 42, 55-58),[33] something presented initially as a difficulty but then portrayed in the narrative as an unexpected spiritual advantage. McDonough thinks that the literary shift in names from Saul to Paul in Acts 13 draws upon these remembered contours of the Old Testament Saul story in order to illustrate "Paul's transformation from the proud 'big man' who persecuted the church . . . to the servant of 'little' David's messianic offspring."[34] Yet this literarily bolstered Augustinian reading is flawed.

Is it to be imagined that the historical *Paul* chose a new name because he wanted to think of himself as "little," since he was now serving Jesus, who was a descendant of David — who was also "little"? Such a speculative piling up of associations seems a stretch. McDonough argues instead that the historical *writer of Acts* wanted to depict Paul as "little" in contrast to the Old Testament analogue of his other name. But if so, the writer might have offered clearer and more consistent clues to such a depiction. Nowhere in the Acts narrative is Paul described as "little," or even physically characterized at all.[35]

To the extent that one attempts to make inferences about Paul's physical appearance from the narrative, his portrait in Acts emphasizes the heroic,

33. See, however, the protest lodged against this common interpretation by Antony F. Campbell, SJ, *1 Samuel*, FOTL 7 (Grand Rapids/Cambridge: Eerdmans, 2003), pp. 164, 171, 188-89. Campbell maintains that while the text describes David as the youngest of Jesse's sons, it "says nothing about his size or age." While he is right to question the popular image of David as a mere shepherd boy, a romantic image that goes beyond the language of the biblical text, certain scenes in the narrative still imply more about David's small size and youth than Campbell is willing to concede (e.g., 1 Samuel 17).

34. McDonough, "Small Change," p. 391.

35. For further discussion, see Abraham J. Malherbe, "A Physical Description of Paul," in *Christians among Jews and Gentiles: Essays in Honor of Krister Stendahl on His Sixty-fifth Birthday*, ed. George W. E. Nickelsburg and George W. MacRae (Philadelphia: Fortress, 1986), pp. 170-75. Already in the *Acts of Paul and Thecla*, however, the apostle is described as being "small of stature"; cf. Murphy-O'Connor, *Paul*, p. 44. On the subsequent literary tradition that Paul was short, see David L. Jeffrey and Camille R. La Bossière, "Paul," in *A Dictionary of Biblical Tradition in English Literature*, ed. David L. Jeffrey (Grand Rapids: Eerdmans, 1992), pp. 588-93.

miraculous aspects of his ministry (19:11-20), as well as his exceptional endurance in the face of persistent persecution and suffering (e.g., 20:17-24). Among other misfortunes, Paul survives shipwreck (27:13-44) and snakebite (28:3-6). His survival could thus imply a person who is at least fairly hale and hardy, if not also big and strong. There is no evidence for a large/small physical contrast at the heart of the story of Paul in Acts besides the meaning for Paul's name that McDonough wants to import.[36] Similarly, if the contrast is conceived as more metaphorical in nature — about Paul's character, his modesty and humility — then certain passages in Acts and the Pauline letters could be called upon for support,[37] but symbolic "smallness" is not explicitly thematized by the Acts narrative either.[38]

In the end, all three theories mentioned by McDonough, as well as his own proposal, share a historicist tendency to reconstruct some reason for an actual name change, although they exhibit ambiguity at points about whether the historical Paul changed his name or the writer of Luke-Acts described it as being changed for some historically oriented reason. The argument of this essay is rather that no name *change* was made at all, at the level of either the historical Paul or the Acts narrative's composition. The apostle did not "change" his name, nor did the author of Luke-Acts think that he had done so. In fact, the author of Acts possibly did not introduce Saul's other name at the time of his Damascus road encounter precisely because the author knew that a change of name had not occurred.

Instead, the narrative literarily constructs a *shift* of names. To misconstrue this evidence by inappropriately historicizing it is to miss its literary and theological significance. It is therefore important to return for further clarification to the question posed at the outset of this essay. Rather than asking the historically oriented question of why Paul's name "changed," this essay proceeds by inquiring why there is a *literary shift* between Paul's two names within Acts and why that shift occurs in Acts 13, when it might well have been expected in Acts 9.

---

36. It is true that soon after he gains Christian convictions, Paul is lowered through the Damascus wall in a basket in order to escape a threat to his life (Acts 9:25), but ancient baskets could be capacious. Paul's physical portrait in Acts has also often been read through the lens of 2 Cor. 10:10, but this move may obscure potential differences between the portrayal of Paul in Acts and his (self-)characterization in the letters.

37. One could begin with the motif of "weakness" in Paul's theology; see Stendahl, *Paul*, pp. 40-52.

38. For an example of how this can be done literarily, see 1 Sam. 15:17.

II. Saul of Kish/Saul of Tarsus

McDonough's passing reference to the relationship between Saul and David possesses greater promise than he himself develops for an explanation of why the name shift to "Paul" does not occur in Acts until chapter 13. More obvious in the Samuel narrative than the motif of Saul's physical size is the theme of his spiritual failure. Chosen by God and anointed king, Saul is nevertheless rejected by God in favor of David. This central theological difficulty animates the story: how can one who is chosen then be rejected? The figure of Saul in Samuel is thus a narrative cipher for the troubling theological mystery of the rejected within the economy of God.

Historically, the present shape of the Samuel narrative has likely been molded according to the Deuteronomistic understanding of blessing as conditional upon obedience (e.g., Deut. 4:25-31; 6:16-25; 8:11-20, etc.), which in turn reflects Israel's historical experience of the exile.[39] In the recent move to explore the exile's political, sociological, and cultural dimensions, scholars now sometimes overlook that the exile confronted Israel with a theological dilemma of enormous magnitude: how could the God who had promised to care for Israel "forever" (e.g., 2 Sam. 7:12-16; Psalm 125) abandon it so summarily?

The canonical responses to this question maintained that certain aspects of Israel's preexilic existence had unfolded counter to God's purpose, so that Israel itself was responsible for God's withdrawal of blessing. In this same vein, an analogy between a rejected Saul and a rejected Israel in exile is evident within the editorial shaping of the Samuel narrative. Ultimately, the references to Saul's height and to the unreliability of human appearances (e.g., 1 Sam. 16:7), which are certainly of considerable narrative importance, serve to deepen and to complicate this larger topic of election — and not the other way around, as McDonough's theory implies.

Within Acts, the single mention of Saul son of Kish shares the same thematic emphasis on election. In Acts 13:21-22 four items of information are conveyed along with the basic reference to Saul: (1) that God "gave" Saul to Israel in response to Israel's request for a king (κἀκεῖθεν ᾐτήσαντο βασιλέα καὶ ἔδωκεν αὐτοῖς ὁ θεὸς τὸν Σαοὺλ υἱὸν Κίς); (2) that Saul was a Benjaminite (ἄνδρα ἐκ φυλῆς Βενιαμίν); (3) that Saul reigned for the considerable (but also temporally circumscribed) period of forty years (ἔτη

---

39. Ralph W. Klein, *Israel in Exile: A Theological Interpretation,* OBT (Philadelphia: Fortress, 1979), pp. 29-30, 41-43.

τεσσεράκοντα); and (4) that God "removed" Saul from the kingship in favor of David (καὶ μεταστήσας αὐτὸν ἤγειρεν τὸν Δαυὶδ αὐτοῖς εἰς βασιλέα). Moreover, the genealogical connection between David and Jesus is then made explicit (τούτου ὁ θεὸς ἀπὸ τοῦ σπέρματος κατ᾽ ἐπαγγελίαν ἤγαγεν τῷ Ἰσραὴλ σωτῆρα Ἰησοῦν, 13:23). At the center of the speech's allusion to Saul son of Kish is thus the stubborn memory of his removal by God, despite the lack of any conditionality as to his being chosen and anointed.

Within the context of the speech in Acts 13, the example of Saul of Kish also possesses a figurative dimension. Paul's speech is directed to an audience of Jews and godfearers in Pisidian Antioch (13:16, 26). The aim of his retelling of salvation history is to explain how the life and resurrection of Jesus fulfill the promises of God to Israel's ancestors (13:32-33). In Jesus, the age-old intentions of God have been fulfilled and the words of Israel's ancient Scriptures realized. But Paul's speech also concludes by framing this messianic fulfillment as a challenge to those listening: "Beware," he stresses, "that what the prophets said does not happen to you," and he goes on to quote Habakkuk 1:5 to the effect that some will refuse to believe God's work even once it is communicated to them (Acts 13:41).

Within the body of the speech, Jesus' crucifixion functions somewhat ominously as an example of how "the residents of Jerusalem and their leaders" were unable to recognize Jesus for who he was or to "understand the words of the prophets that are read every sabbath" (13:27). By condemning Jesus, the Jewish leadership in Jerusalem had ironically fulfilled the prophetic words of Habakkuk even as they rejected the "message of salvation" (13:26) that had been proclaimed by Israel's prophets. So a dangerous precedent of sorts had been established for Jewish hearers of the gospel, Paul insinuates. Would his hearers now accept "the good news that what God promised to our ancestors he has fulfilled for us, their children, by raising Jesus" (13:32-33)? Or would the Jews of Pisidian Antioch follow the Jews of Jerusalem in becoming scoffers of God's work and thus fulfill the prophets' curses instead of the prophets' benedictions?

The reference to Saul son of Kish in Acts 13:21 specifies a further possibility within the conceptual world evoked by the overarching sweep of Paul's speech. God "gave" (ἔδωκεν) Saul but then "removed" (μεταστήσας) him. The idea of "removal" from leadership, from being a particular bearer and conduit of God's blessing, serves in this context as both a rhetorical warning to Paul's audience and an adumbration of the narrative conclusion to the chapter. Despite the approval of "many Jews and devout converts to Judaism" immediately after Paul's speech (13:42-43), "the Jews" are said to contradict

Paul on the following Sabbath (13:45), leading Paul, together with his companion Barnabas, to effect the momentous consequences that were previously introduced: "It was necessary that the word of God should be spoken first to you. Since you reject it and judge yourselves to be unworthy of eternal life, we are now turning to the Gentiles" (13:46).

For the larger scheme of Acts, this particular pronouncement has performative force. The possibility of the inclusion of the Gentiles into the reign of God has been raised within the book in a variety of ways already (e.g., Acts 8; 10:1–11:18), but Acts 13 is presented as a literal turning point (ἰδοὺ στρεφόμεθα εἰς τὰ ἔθνη) within the trajectory of salvation history.[40] Although the consequences of this "turn" do not entail a rejection of the Jewish people — Paul and Barnabas still go to the Jewish synagogue when they arrive in Iconium, their next destination after Antioch (14:1) — the message of Paul and Barnabas is noticeably directed toward Gentile hearers in Lystra (14:15-17), and the inclusion of the Gentiles is treated as an accomplished fact (14:27) by the time they return to Antioch.

This new ecclesial reality then receives communal scrutiny and ratification through the deliberations of a representative church assembly in Jerusalem (Acts 15). Significantly, the conclusion reached by the assembly is a "both/and" rather than an "either/or": the gospel will continue to be proclaimed to Gentiles as well as to the Jews (15:19). Yet such a resolution sits somewhat uneasily with the "turn" metaphor introduced by Paul's speech in Acts 13:46 — and, for that matter, with the speech's reference to Saul son of Kish, the "removed" king.[41] In its narrative context, the mention of Saul in

---

40. For a treatment of Acts 13:46 and other passages in Acts that express a similar "turn," see Robert C. Tannehill, "Rejection by Jews and Turning to Gentiles: The Pattern of Paul's Mission in Acts," in *Luke-Acts and the Jewish People*, ed. Joseph B. Tyson (Minneapolis: Augsburg, 1988), pp. 83-101. Tannehill provides good coverage of the exegetical ground, but note the appropriate criticism of his contemporary reflections in Marion L. Soards, *The Speeches in Acts: Their Content, Context, and Concerns* (Louisville: Westminster John Knox, 1994), p. 207 n. 51. That the "turn" of Acts 13:46 does not entail the wholesale rejection of the Jews is a point made persuasively by Tannehill and also Robert L. Brawley, "Paul in Acts: Lucan Apology and Reconciliation," in *Luke-Acts: New Perspectives from the Society of Biblical Literature Seminar*, ed. Charles H. Talbert (New York: Crossroad, 1984), esp. p. 131.

41. Nor is this association apparently restricted to Acts. According to Michael P. Knowles, "Scripture, History, Messiah: Scriptural Fulfillment and the Fullness of Time in Matthew's Gospel," in *Hearing the Old Testament in the New Testament*, ed. Stanley E. Porter, MNTS (Grand Rapids: Eerdmans, 2006), p. 79, the words of Samuel in 1 Sam. 15:28, "The LORD has torn the kingdom of Israel from you this very day, and has given it to a neighbor of yours, who is better than you," are echoed in Matt. 21:43.

Paul's speech provides a biblical precedent for God's turn away from, not all Jews, but those who would reject eternal life (13:46). Through Paul the Lord Jesus is winnowing the faithful remnant of Israel and incorporating Gentiles into that remnant as a means of forming one holy people.

In this broader narrative framework, Paul's own name shift reflexively takes on a similar connotation. His alternate name of Saul not only subtly evokes the Old Testament story of Israel's rejected king; it also lends greater prominence to the explicit mention of Saul son of Kish when it occurs in Acts 13.[42] Like Saul son of Kish, Saul of Tarsus at first stands aside from the actions of others, staying behind with their gear.[43] Saul son of Kish characteristically engages in "rash" or "thoughtless" actions (ἄγνοιαν μεγάλην, 1 Sam. 14:24 LXX),[44] even as Saul of Tarsus is said to be "still breathing threats and murder" (ἔτι ἐμπνέων ἀπειλῆς καὶ φόνου, Acts 9:1). Like Saul son of Kish, Saul of Tarsus can also be filled with the Spirit and employ prophetic gifts.[45] Yet, as if emboldened by his observance of Stephen's death, Saul of Tarsus becomes a leading persecutor of Christians: "ravaging the church by entering house after house; dragging off both men and women, he committed them to prison" (8:3). Such actions recall how Saul son of Kish relentlessly pursues David throughout the second half of 1 Samuel in a jealous effort to kill him. Saul of Tarsus is therefore associated with violence and killing, just as was Saul son of Kish.[46]

42. Konrad Huber, "Die Könige Israels: Saul, David, und Salomo," in *Alttestamentliche Gestalten im Neuen Testament: Beiträge zur Biblischen Theologie,* ed. Markus Öhler (Darmstadt: Wissenschaftliche Buchgesellschaft, 1999), p. 166.

43. See Acts 7:58; 22:19-20; cf. 1 Sam. 10:22. Note the contrast with David in 1 Sam. 17:22.

44. For indications also in the Hebrew text that Saul's impassioned actions characteristically outpace appropriate critical judgment, see 1 Samuel 11; 13:11-12; 14:24-30, 36-46; 15:19-21. Marsha C. White, "Saul and Jonathan in 1 Samuel 13 and 14," in *Saul in Story and Tradition,* ed. Carl S. Ehrlich and Marsha C. White, FAT 47 (Tübingen: Mohr Siebeck, 2006), pp. 128-35, has argued against this reading, but her interpretation is based upon a hypothetically reconstructed earlier text.

45. On the relationship in Acts between Paul's ministry and the Holy Spirit, see especially Acts 19:1-7. Paul's miraculous actions (e.g., Acts 14:8-18; 16:16-18; 19:11-20) can be placed firmly within the OT prophetic tradition, as can his confrontations with false prophets (e.g., Acts 13:4-12) and the basically proclamatory nature of his ministry. Paul's use of prophetic Scripture and the features of Acts 9:1-9 suggestive of prophetic call narratives confirm this association. See further Stendahl, *Paul,* pp. 9-10. For a full treatment, see Karl Olav Sandnes, *Paul — One of the Prophets?* WUNT 2.43 (Tübingen: Mohr Siebeck, 1991).

46. See Acts 8:1; 9:1, 13-14; 22:4, 19-20; 26:9-11; cf. 1 Tim. 1:13; for Saul son of Kish, see, e.g., 1 Sam. 14:43-46; 19:1-17; 22:16-19; 23:15. On Paul's "zeal" in persecution, see T. L. Donaldson, "Zealot and Convert: The Origin of Paul's Christ-Torah Antithesis," *CBQ* 51

The Acts narrative draws this analogy even tighter by interpreting Saul of Tarsus's persecution of Christians as Saul's persecution of Jesus himself. "Saul, Saul why do you persecute *me*?" asks the heavenly voice on the Damascus road (9:4). "I am Jesus, whom you are persecuting," responds the voice to Saul's question about its identity (9:5). Thus, Saul son of Kish, the antagonist of David son of Jesse, is a clear harbinger of Saul of Tarsus, the antagonist of Jesus, Son of David. Moreover, Jesus' question to Saul of Tarsus in Acts 9:4 is somewhat reminiscent of David's question to Saul son of Kish in 1 Samuel 26:18: "Why does my lord pursue his servant?"[47] Saul of Tarsus, by his participation in the death of Christians, can more broadly be said to mirror Saul son of Kish in his murderous rages. It is therefore no accident that Paul's speech in Acts 13 also stresses how the life and work of Jesus fulfilled the Davidic promise (Acts 13:23; cf. 13:34)[48] — an otherwise unusual emphasis in Acts as well as in Paul's letters.[49] Already in the Lukan birth narrative the Davidic dimension of Jesus' identity was introduced (Luke 1:32-33, 69, 70). This motif at the beginning of Luke is matched by a similar emphasis at the beginning of Acts (Acts 2:25-36). The antipathy of Saul of Tarsus toward Jewish Christians is therefore portrayed in Acts as not only hostility toward Jesus but hostility toward Jesus precisely in his identity as the Son of David.

Within the second half of the 1 Samuel narrative, the central question driving the plot is that of *how* David will eventually replace Saul. Although God rejects Saul at the end of 1 Samuel 15 and David is (privately) anointed in 1 Samuel 16, God does not intervene directly to bring about an immediate transition in Israel's political leadership. At the same time that the narrative offers hints of God's providential guidance with respect to the events it de-

---

(1989): 655-82. For an interesting exploration of the association between Saul of Tarsus and violence/killing/murder, see Richard V. Peace, *Conversion in the New Testament: Paul and the Twelve* (Grand Rapids/Cambridge: Eerdmans, 1999), pp. 50-51.

47. Lefebvre, *Livres*, p. 482. See in 1 Sam. 26:18 the Greek verb καταδιώκω; in Acts 9:4, the Greek verb διώκω. However, 1 Sam. 26:18 lacks the arresting double vocative of Acts 9:4.

48. See F. F. Bruce, "Paul's Use of the Old Testament in Acts," in *Tradition and Interpretation in the New Testament: Essays in Honor of E. Earle Ellis for His 60th Birthday*, ed. Gerald F. Hawthorne and Otto Betz (Grand Rapids/Tübingen: Eerdmans/Mohr Siebeck, 1987), p. 72: "This text, then, forms the climax of the first part of the homily — both because, as Paul goes on to announce, Jesus has come in fulfilment of God's promise to David, and also perhaps because, like David, so great David's greater Son is the man of God's choosing — preeminently so." Now see also Mark L. Strauss, *The Davidic Messiah in Luke-Acts: The Promise and Its Fulfillment in Lukan Christology*, JSNTSup 110 (Sheffield: Sheffield Academic, 1995), esp. p. 174. Cf. Acts 15:16-18.

49. See, however, Rom. 1:3; cf. 2 Tim. 2:8. For discussion, see Bruce, *Paul*, p. 55.

scribes, the specific actions needed to effect a change in the kingship are apparently left largely to the participants in the drama to accomplish. Although the eventual accession of David seems certain, narrative suspense is generated through the question of how exactly the change of kings is to be achieved. As the reader comes gradually to intuit, and as David ultimately realizes himself (especially with Abigail's assistance; see 1 Sam. 25:23-35), Saul must die. Yet his death can occur only in the course of a "natural" unfolding of events and not as something cynically orchestrated or bloodily forced, lest the curse of blood guilt afflict David's future reign.

The peculiar tragedy of Saul son of Kish emerges most clearly from this vantage point: Saul cannot change, although he is given many opportunities to do so.[50] He cannot become the kind of person who is able to do full justice to the expectations and responsibilities of the kingly office in which he finds himself. Here the emphasis upon his physical stature becomes a way of expressing both his inappropriate trust in human strength (i.e., because it symbolizes a corresponding lack of faith in God's power; e.g., 1 Sam. 14:52) and his apparently innate predisposition to govern at cross-purposes with God (e.g., 1 Sam. 15:17; 16:7).

The difficult-to-interpret but repeated episodes of Saul's prophetic activities (1 Sam. 10:9-13; 19:18-24) point in the same direction by registering the proverbial mystification of the people regarding his character and role: "Is Saul also among the prophets?" In other words, despite the *appearance* of prophetic activity on Saul's part, something about that activity does not ring true to its observers. Although he engages in prophetic behavior, Saul's personal identity otherwise appears to be unreformed. The ultimate motif of the narrative in this regard is that of his madness, described as the consequence of "an evil spirit from God" that torments Saul repeatedly (e.g., 1 Sam. 16:14-23; 18:10-11). Saul's inability to recognize David at key points in the narrative may also be an indication of his mental deterioration.[51]

---

50. God even gives Saul "another heart" (1 Sam. 10:9) — thus an admission that he is in need of one — but for some unexplained reason this new heart is inadequate to the task. By contrast, David is preeminently the man after God's "own heart" in the narrative (e.g., 1 Sam. 13:14, etc.). For a discussion of the category "tragedy" in relation to 1 Samuel, see E. M. Good, *Irony in the Old Testament,* 2nd ed., BLS 3 (Sheffield: Almond, 1981), pp. 56-80; David M. Gunn, *The Fate of King Saul,* JSOTSup 14 (Sheffield: Dept. of Biblical Studies, University of Sheffield, 1980).

51. See 1 Sam. 24:16; 26:17. On this possibility already at 1 Sam. 17:55, see Robert Polzin, *Samuel and the Deuteronomist: A Literary Study of the Deuteronomic History,* ISBL (Bloomington/Indianapolis: Indiana University Press, 1989), p. 162.

All these aspects of the Samuel narrative combine to underscore the tragic impossibility of Saul. His final suicide is at once a culmination and an unsettling admission of his still mystifying incorrigibility. Remarkably, the narrative steadfastly resists any recourse to moralism, refusing to blame Saul cheaply for personal defects and deficiencies that were never fully in his power to overcome. Instead, the book of Samuel affirms Saul's nobility, courage, and original election (e.g., 1 Sam. 14:47-48; 2 Sam. 1:19-27), as well as his abiding status as "the Lord's anointed" even *after* his rejection (e.g., 1 Sam. 24:5-15; 26:6-16, 22-24), although that very election increasingly puts Saul at war with himself and in the end destroys him.

By contrast, the shift of names in Acts from Saul to Paul represents a fundamentally different solution to the theological problem of election. Like Saul son of Kish, Saul of Tarsus can be considered "chosen" because he is a member of God's chosen people, the Jews.[52] The language of election appears in specific relation to Saul of Tarsus in Acts 9:15 (cf. 22:14), where he is described as a "chosen" instrument within God's plan to reach the Gentiles. Like Saul son of Kish, Saul of Tarsus attempts to promote the welfare of God and his people. Yet the result is again that of a Saul at cross-purposes with God:

> Indeed, I myself was convinced that I ought to do many things against the name of Jesus of Nazareth. And that is what I did in Jerusalem; with authority received from the chief priests, I not only locked up many of the saints in prison, but I also cast my vote against them when they were being condemned to death. By punishing them often in all the synagogues I tried to force them to blaspheme; and since I was so furiously enraged at them, I pursued them even to foreign cities. (26:9-11)

With this sketch of his life prior to the Damascus road, Paul describes the exact opposite of what would later become his Christian witness to the Gentiles. In this regard he personally "embodies the contradiction as well as the affirmation of the gospel."[53] Whereas Saul once worked against the name of Jesus, it is his own name that would eventually be attenuated in the narrative. Whereas he once traveled "even to foreign cities" in anger, trying to destroy Christians (22:4-5; 26:10-11), he would later journey throughout the

---

52. Interestingly, the Pauline letters indicate that Paul is of the tribe of Benjamin, even as was Saul son of Kish (Rom. 11:1; Phil. 3:5; cf. 1 Sam. 9:1-2).

53. Karl Löning, *Die Saulustradition in der Apostelgeschichte,* NTAbh, n.F., 9 (Münster: Aschendorff, 1973), p. 165 (my translation).

Roman world in order to *increase* the number of Christians by bearing witness to love, patience, and forgiveness.[54] And whereas Saul of Tarsus was at first driven by a madlike, almost demonic compulsion (8:3; 9:1; 26:11), he would subsequently be commissioned to work against "the power of Satan" (Acts 26:18),[55] and his theology become characterized by a reliance on the Holy Spirit.[56]

In this manner Acts opens up an existential possibility that is mysteriously unavailable within the narrative world of Samuel: Saul of Tarsus *can* be transformed; *his* personal identity can and does change radically. Indeed, the identity of Saul of Tarsus alters so fundamentally that his former friends turn into antagonists and his prior antagonists become friends (e.g., 9:21-27; 26:21). In Acts this personal transformation is depicted as the result of a direct and miraculous intervention of the Lord Jesus in Saul of Tarsus's life (9:1-19). Jesus does for Saul of Tarsus what Saul of Tarsus could not do for himself — and thus, by retrospective analogy, what mysteriously neither Saul son of Kish *could* do for himself nor what God *would* do for him. By contrast, Jesus introduces a possibility of personal change that overcomes Paul's limitations and reorients his capacities.

This personal transformation neither negates Paul's individual character nor erases his distinctive traits,[57] but it does radically reorient his allegiance, his perspective, and his activity.[58] Characteristic of Paul's Christian

54. See G. Walter Hansen, "Paul's Conversion and His Ethic of Freedom in Galatians," in *The Road from Damascus: The Impact of Paul's Conversion on His Life, Thought, and Ministry*, ed. Richard N. Longenecker, MNTS (Grand Rapids: Eerdmans, 1997), p. 232. Cf. Brawley, "Paul in Acts," pp. 138-39, on the "benefit of others" as a feature of Paul's portrait in Acts.

55. Peace, *Conversion*, p. 51, points to the interesting association between "Satan" and murder in John 8:44, speculating that it may form the necessary background for understanding Acts 26:18.

56. See Acts 9:17; 20:20-23; Rom. 15:18-19; 1 Cor. 2:4-5; 2 Cor. 12:12. Cf. Gordon D. Fee, "Paul's Conversion as Key to His Understanding of the Spirit," in *Road from Damascus*, ed. Longenecker, pp. 166-83. It always needs to be borne in mind, however, that in the Pauline letters the Spirit is never explicitly mentioned in conjunction with Paul's Damascus road experience (see 1 Cor. 15:8-10; Gal. 1:13-16; Phil. 3:4-11; 1 Tim. 1:12-16).

57. To this extent, descriptions of Paul's life as exhibiting "total change" are overstated and inaccurate, *contra* Grant, *Paul*, p. 197. Grant is correct, however, in maintaining that Paul's example stands for *genuine* change, in contrast to the apparent rarity of such change generally within Hellenistic culture.

58. One area of continuity may actually be Paul's focus on the Gentiles. If the reference in Gal. 5:11 is taken literally, it would seem to refer to a time prior to his Damascus road experience when Paul "preached circumcision" or urged Gentiles to convert to Judaism. See

faith from now on will be this radical quality of personal transformation (e.g., 1 Cor. 1:26-31; Phil. 3:4-16).[59] Such transformation has already been described in Acts as presently available, not only for Saul of Tarsus, but for all Jews:

> And all the prophets, as many as have spoken, from Samuel and those after him, also predicted these days. You are the descendants of the prophets and of the covenant that God gave to your ancestors, saying to Abraham, "And in your descendants all the families of the earth shall be blessed." When God raised up his servant, he sent him first to you, to bless you by turning each of you from your wicked ways. (Acts 3:24-26)[60]

Once again, here the Samuel tradition serves as a reference point not simply for Israel's prophetic tradition but for a genuinely new religious possibility: fundamental amendment of life.[61] In the post-Pauline passage 1 Timothy 1:12-17, Paul's personal transformation is set forth as exemplary for all Christians (including Jewish Christians).[62]

According to a classic study by A. D. Nock, early Christianity distinguished itself from the many competing religions of the Hellenistic world not by presenting more stringent moral demands than they did but by offering a source of power to meet those demands that went beyond what individuals otherwise considered themselves capable of:

> Christianity did not only give a motive. It claimed to give power to satisfy its requirements. It claimed that the baptized Christian received grace which, if he made reasonable effort, would enable him to live as he should. This is a point of cardinal importance.[63]

Early Christians believed, as they saw preeminently in Jesus and in Paul's own life, that "for God all things are possible" (Matt. 19:26//Mark 10:27).

Terence L. Donaldson, "Israelite, Convert, Apostle to the Gentiles: The Origin of Paul's Gentile Mission," in *Road from Damascus*, ed. Longenecker, pp. 81-82.

59. Richard N. Longenecker, "A Realized Hope, a New Commitment, and a Developed Proclamation: Paul and Jesus," in *Road from Damascus*, ed. Longenecker, p. 40.

60. Cf. Acts 13:39.

61. The Samuel reference in Acts 3:24 thus anticipates the mention of Samuel in Acts 13:20.

62. On the paradigmatic quality of Paul's personal transformation, see further Becker, *Paul*, pp. 74-75.

63. Nock, *Conversion*, p. 220.

III. At the Heart of the Hermeneutic

The argument of this essay is not that the writer of Acts invented the name "Saul" for Paul[64] or that the tradition of the apostle's two names is unhistorical. Colin Hemer offers the most sensible historical conclusion to questions regarding the name of the historical Paul: "Paul was both Hebrew and Roman by birth, and operated under either name (Saul or Paul) according to context."[65] The argument here is instead that the writer of Acts constructed a literary "shift" of names where a "change" did not exist. Even if Paul began at a certain point in his life primarily to employ the name "Paul" when previously he had usually used "Saul," this phenomenon would still not necessarily constitute a name "change." Instead, the writer of Acts took what were most likely simultaneously functioning names for the apostle and rendered them as sequential in order to emphasize the inclusion of Gentiles, pioneered by Paul, that is of crucial significance for the narrative. Particularly noteworthy in this literary move is that the writer drew in a variety of ways upon the Old Testament in order to shape his narrative, so that the theological turn to the Gentiles is made on the basis of Israel's own Scripture.

The Acts narrative might have been expected to use "Paul" as Saul's new name immediately after his Damascus road experience but does not. Instead, the name "Paul" first appears in Acts 13, where reference to Saul son of Kish is also made in the retelling of salvation history and the inclusion of the Gentiles is announced. The narrative of Acts *delays* using the "new" name of Paul, so that both names function as linked salvation-historical signs.[66] In the context of Acts 13, the reference to Saul son of Kish establishes an unsettling analogy with Saul of Tarsus and simultaneously becomes a trope for Jewish rejecters of the gospel. Saul son of Kish is thus a type for those Jews who oppose the gospel of Jesus, Son of David, just as Saul of Tarsus had done in his life before being confronted with the resurrected Jesus on the road to

64. See the reasons against this possibility given in Murphy-O'Connor, *Paul,* p. 43.
65. Hemer, "Name of Paul," p. 182.
66. Chrysostom offered an interesting alternative narrative explanation: when Saul began to proclaim the gospel in areas in which he had been previously known only by name and not by sight, the people would not have been able to recognize him if he had used another name. "For this reason [the Holy Spirit] allowed him for a time to keep the earlier name, so that [the change] might become clear to all the believers" (cited in Compton, "Saul to Paul," p. 67). Thus, Chrysostom's view still involved a name "change," but it registered the odd fact of the delay as well as retained both narrative coherence and a theological focus in its reading of the text.

Damascus. The shift to the name "Paul," by contrast, gives expression to the opening of a "door of faith for the Gentiles" (14:27) and to escaping the religious futility represented by Saul son of Kish. Paul's name is thus more expressive of the inclusion of the Gentiles within salvation history than of his own personal spiritual transformation, which has only a derivative relation to the larger issue. The symbolic dimension of Paul's name does not emerge from historically reconstructed details, however, but from the literary artistry of the text. The narrative's strategic introduction of the name "Paul" heightens the figurative aspect of both the name "Saul" and the figure of Saul/Paul himself.[67]

When the relationship between the two Testaments has been explored in the past, such exploration has often focused on the identification of citations of the Old Testament in the New.[68] Yet treatments emphasizing "citations" have frequently missed the kind of typological relationship identified in this essay. Thus, Joseph Fitzmyer admits the presence of Old Testament *allusions* in Luke-Acts but still places such an emphasis on quotation that he considers its absence in Acts 9 to be significant.[69] In fact, Fitzmyer mentions the lack of quotation from the Old Testament historical books generally in Luke-Acts as if that phenomenon indicated the absence of their influence.[70] He then uses the predominance of explicit quotations from the prophetic books (and prophetically interpreted passages from the Pentateuch and the Psalms) to argue that Luke-Acts unfolds according to a prophecy-fulfillment hermeneutic, citing Luke 1:1 (ἀνατάξασθαι διήγησιν περὶ τῶν πεπληρο-

---

67. In this way, Acts might be said to "rewrite" the OT story of Saul. On the possibility that Luke-Acts was written as an intentional continuation of OT narrative — in other words, as Scripture, see Gregory E. Sterling, *Historiography and Self-Definition: Josephos, Luke-Acts, and Apologetic Historiography,* NovTSup 64 (Leiden/New York: Brill, 1991). However, the trope of rewriting can also be misleading in this case. It remains highly significant that Luke did not attempt to rewrite OT narrative by altering the narrative itself; instead, Israel's Scripture was allowed to stand as it was.

68. The case of Brevard S. Childs is instructive on this point. Childs first proposed that a biblical theology take its cues from the use of the Old Testament by the New; see his *Biblical Theology in Crisis* (Philadelphia: Westminster, 1970), pp. 114-16. More recently, however, he rejected this approach as confusing a compositional feature of the New Testament with theological reflection on both Testaments as two intact scriptural collections; see Childs, *Biblical Theology of the Old and New Testaments* (Minneapolis: Fortress, 1992), p. 76.

69. Joseph Fitzmyer, "The Use of the Old Testament in Luke-Acts," in *Society of Biblical Literature 1992 Seminar Papers,* ed. Eugene H. Lovering Jr. (Atlanta: Scholars Press, 1992), p. 531.

70. Fitzmyer, "Use of the Old Testament," p. 532.

φορημένων ἐν ἡμῖν πραγμάτων). Yet crucial for Luke-Acts is the goal of presenting the story of Christ as fulfilled "events" (πράγματα) rather than words.[71] By giving typological allusions short shrift, Fitzmyer misconstrues the central thrust of Luke-Acts as a whole.[72]

This methodological problem goes well beyond the accurate identification of any one citation.[73] As numerous scholars have observed, a better model for Luke-Acts is the view that it proceeds on the basis of *analogy*.[74] Old Testament citations and allusions are used in order to establish continuity with the past rather than as proof texts for the purpose of prophecy fulfillment — as is more the case, for example, in the Gospel of Matthew.[75] A

71. Cf. Fitzmyer, "Use of the Old Testament," pp. 535-36.

72. See Soards, *Speeches in Acts,* p. 201, with his references to the literature on such methodological issues. For a further description of the problem(s), see Stanley E. Porter, "The Use of the Old Testament in the New Testament: A Brief Comment on Method and Terminology," in *Early Christian Interpretation of the Scriptures of Israel: Investigations and Proposals,* ed. Craig A. Evans and James A. Sanders, JSNTSup 148/SSEJC 5 (Sheffield: Sheffield Academic, 1997), pp. 79-96. This entire discussion has been decisively altered by the treatment of metalepsis/transumption in Richard B. Hays, *Echoes of Scripture in the Letters of Paul* (New Haven/London: Yale University Press, 1989), pp. 14-21; see also his "seven tests," pp. 29-32, and his subsequent presentation of them in Hays, *The Conversion of the Imagination: Paul as Interpreter of Israel's Scripture* (Grand Rapids: Eerdmans, 2005), pp. 34-45. From the side of Hebrew Bible/OT scholarship, Benjamin D. Sommer has also made a significant contribution to the discussion that deserves to be better known in NT scholarship; see Sommer, *A Prophet Reads Scripture: Allusion in Isaiah 40–66* (Stanford: Stanford University Press, 1998), pp. 10-18, 20-31. Sommer stresses how a single allusion can evoke an entire text and how the "alluding text" is transformed by association with the text to which the allusion is made (p. 12).

73. Also important for adjudicating such questions is the fact that scriptural quotations in Acts decline noticeably in frequency and prominence after Acts 13. See Fitzmyer, "Use of the Old Testament," p. 536.

74. Soards, *Speeches in Acts,* p. 183: "Through the principle of analogy Luke weaves speeches into the narrative of Acts and creates *emphasis* so that the speeches articulate a distinct worldview" (emphasis original). But analogy not only functions between the speeches and the Acts narrative; it is also employed to establish a relationship between the OT events described in the speeches and the narrative world of Acts. In this way citations and allusions to the OT provide continuity between the past, the present, and the future (p. 201). This continuity is theo- and ecclesiocentric in nature, that is, grounded in a belief in divine constancy and God's faithfulness to the covenant people. Cf. Brian S. Rosner, "Acts and Biblical History," in *The Book of Acts and Its Ancient Literary Setting,* ed. Bruce W. Winter and Andrew D. Clarke (Grand Rapids/Carlisle: Eerdmans/Paternoster, 1993), p. 82.

75. Soards, *Speeches in Acts,* pp. 201-3. This is not to say that a prophecy-fulfillment theme is completely absent from Luke-Acts, only that it is not the only or even necessarily the chief way in which the OT is employed within the narrative.

prophecy-fulfillment model is too restrictive to illuminate fully the literary dynamics of Luke-Acts and overlooks a host of typological associations in which Old Testament figures and motifs are not used to indicate the fulfillment of prophecy but have a different primary purpose.[76] History in Luke-Acts has instead become primarily hermeneutical: God may be reliably understood today on the basis of divine actions in the past.[77] Moreover, God's word to Israel remains standing as a true word; it is not rejected or written over from scratch but *continued* in light of the fullness of history.

Thus, the reference to Old Testament Saul in Acts 13 is part of a broader hermeneutical strategy according to which "prominent personalities from Israel's history" are allusively deployed,[78] offering authoritative hermeneutical guidance for understanding the contemporary work of God. This figural dimension of history is woven into the fabric of the New Testament, yet it has been ignored or dismissed in much historical-critical scholarship at the cost of hearing the entirety of the New Testament's message. Such figuration is not a radical departure from the Old Testament but a continuation of the figurative aspect of Old Testament tradition itself, as seen, for example, in the way Saul son of Kish already represents Israel's exilic experience in 1 Samuel. In other words, the customary distinction between typological reading and plain sense reading is a false binary, whether applied to the New Testament or the Old. A plain sense reading must itself be open to the typological dimensions of the text! The figure of Saul/Paul, therefore, rather than serving as an emblem of supersessionism, as has tended to be the case throughout the history of Christian biblical interpretation, can illustrate instead how a typological approach to Scripture respects the continuity as well as the discontinuity between the two Testaments, and between Judaism and Christianity.[79]

Of course, figural interpretation sometimes substitutes a Christian sensibility for the Old Testament text in such a way that the Old Testament's own theological message is domesticated or obliterated and Jewish understandings of Scripture are summarily dismissed. There needs to be an aware-

---

76. For a statement of the difficulties confronting the prophecy-fulfillment approach, see Charles H. Talbert, "Promise and Fulfillment in Lucan Theology," in Talbert, *Luke-Acts*, pp. 91-103.

77. Soards, *Speeches in Acts*, p. 203.

78. Soards, *Speeches in Acts*, p. 203.

79. Lefebvre, *Livres*, pp. 482-83: "Without a doubt the destiny of Saul of Tarsus recapitulates the entire heritage of Saul and David, leading to its fulfillment in himself" (my translation).

ness that Christian figural reading of the Old Testament operates to a certain extent "retrospectively"[80] — otherwise the Old Testament is at risk of losing its own witness within the shape of the Christian Bible, with the concomitant result that Judaism will be disinherited and devalued. Yet such reading cannot be *only* retrospective. There must also be an ontic dimension to Christian figural reading, which has traditionally been grounded and expressed in the doctrine of the Trinity.[81] Typological interpretation therefore needs greater attention today as a particular species of the figural — and here the term "typological" is not as important as the kind of figuration it represents.[82] In typology, not only is history respected, but the Old Testament retains its canonical status as Christian Scripture, as Richard Hays argues is the case within Paul's letters:

80. Pontifical Biblical Commission, *The Jewish People and Their Sacred Scriptures in the Christian Bible* (Vatican City: Libreria Editrice Vaticana, 2002). For a brief explanation of how the PBC statement attempts to counteract some serious problems in Christian biblical interpretation, see Philip A. Cunningham, *Sharing the Scriptures: The Word Set Free,* vol. 1 (New York/Mahwah, N.J.: Stimulus, 2003), pp. 78-79.

81. Denis Farkasfalvy, "The Pontifical Biblical Commission's Document on Jews and Christians and Their Scriptures: Attempt at an Evaluation," *Communio* 29 (2002): 715-37, esp. pp. 729-30. One way out of the present impasse between retrospective and nonretrospective reading may be the move toward a bidirectional approach modeled on the multisense interpretation of the early and medieval church; see Childs, *Biblical Theology,* pp. 84-85, 723-25. Henri de Lubac appeared to mean something similar in his description of "Christian dialectic"; see his *Scripture in the Tradition,* trans. L. O'Neill (New York: Herder & Herder/Crossroad, 2000 [1967]), pp. 173-82. Yet de Lubac retained the Old Testament for Christian theology only as it was "transfigured" in the New; on its own it was "abrogated" and "dead" (pp. 174-75).

82. The term "typology" has received criticism from Andrew Louth, *Discerning the Mystery: An Essay on the Nature of Theology* (Oxford: Oxford University Press, 1983), pp. 118-19. Louth maintains that the word was used as a modern strategy to retain certain traditional readings while also unfairly dismissing "allegory," and that the one kind of interpretation cannot fully be distinguished from the other. For a similar view, see de Lubac, *Scripture in the Tradition,* pp. 159-72. However, even if the term "typology" is a modern one, the language of "type" is already found in the NT (Rom. 5:14). Moreover, as Louth admits, de Lubac himself made a distinction between merely verbal/symbolic allegory *(allegoria verbi)* and historically based, authentically Christian allegory *(allegoria facti).* I would argue that in the details of de Lubac's treatment, his account of "Christian allegory" often approximated what others have meant by "typology." Cf. Marcellino D'Ambrosio, "Henri de Lubac and the Recovery of the Traditional Hermeneutic" (Ph.D. diss., Catholic University of America, 1991), pp. 285-86. Without meaning to denigrate or dismiss allegory, I am attempting to call attention to "typology" as a subset of allegorical or figural interpretation that remains crucial for biblical theology.

Typology is before all else a trope, an act of imaginative correlation. If one pole of the typological correlation annihilates the other, the metaphorical tension disappears, and the trope collapses. The viability of the Israel/church typology depends, for Paul's purposes, on maintaining the separate integrity of both poles. The church discovers its true identity only in relation to the sacred story of Israel, and the sacred story of Israel discovers its full significance — so Paul passionately believed — only in relation to God's unfolding design for salvation of the Gentiles in the church.[83]

To understand the New Testament, then, the two Testaments must be read together in a way that is alert to typological resonances as well as to history, even while such reading privileges the literary-canonical account of history in the Bible over against the speculative conceits of extra-narratival, historical reconstruction.[84]

Ironically, later Greek and Latin biblical translations obscured the very analogy that Acts had worked so hard to establish by differentiating the spelling of the name of New Testament Saul from Old Testament Saul.[85] This phenomenon poses a further question about how English Bible translations render proper names and whether certain inner-biblical echoes are dampened or misheard because their analogical relationship to each other is concealed. Examples can be found in the use of "Jacob" in the Old Testament but "James" in the New, and within the New Testament itself, the differentiation between "Judas" and "Jude," although the two names are identical in Greek.[86] The most important example, however, is that between "Joshua" or "Yehoshua" or "Jeshua" in the Old Testament and "Jesus" in the New.

Manfred Görg has reflected deeply upon this last example, which is well known but only rarely anymore considered worthy of comment.[87] For

83. Hays, *Echoes*, pp. 100-101.

84. Of interest here is the recent work of some French biblical scholars; in addition to Lefebvre, *Livres*, see, e.g., Paul Beauchamp, *L'un et l'autre Testament: Essai de lecture*, 2 vols. (Paris: Éditions du Seuil, 1976, 1990); Raymond Kuntzmann, ed., *Typologie biblique: De quelques figures vives*, LD (Paris: Cerf, 2002). There remains a danger with this typological approach — just as there is for allegory or any kind of figurative mode of interpretation. See John Kelman Sutherland Reid, *The Authority of Scripture: A Study of the Reformation and Post-Reformation Understanding of the Bible* (London: Methuen, 1957), p. 259: "Typology errs when the reality of the type is imperiled in order to supply a *figura* of the antitype."

85. See Harrer, "Saul," pp. 25-26.

86. For these examples, see Stendahl, *Paul*, pp. 100-101.

87. Manfred Görg, *In Abraham's Bosom: Christianity without the New Testament*, trans. L. M. Maloney (Collegeville, Minn.: Liturgical Press/Michael Glazier, 1999), pp. 76-89. Early

Görg, the danger of ignoring the linguistic relationship between these names is the danger of overlooking Jesus' forerunners in the Old Testament, of treating him as so unprecedented and unique that he is no longer conceived in a way that is Jewish, and then of thinking that the Christian gospel flatly supplants Judaism.[88] By contrast, recognizing the similarity between the names means that the name of Jesus in the New Testament is not a tradition-free nominal marker but instead bears content from the Old Testament even *prior* to any information about Jesus' own life and work being provided by the New:

> Does the name "Jesus" not have a theological content from the outset, on the basis of its bestowal and its background? It is all too obvious, and there is scarcely any reason to think otherwise, that the name Jesus could be more than a personal name chosen at random. Of course the infancy narrative indicates that the name Jesus had a special meaning, but here — and exegetes are unanimous on this point — there is already an interpretation present: "She will bear a son, and you are to name him Jesus, for he will save his people from their sins" (Matt 1:21). The name therefore means salvation, liberation, concern for humanity as only the God of Israel can give these things. The play on the semantics of the name at the same time avoids any explicit calling to mind of the prominent bearers of this name in the Old Testament. Instead, the Christian tradition in the Gospels has made way for a different group of predecessors by causing, in the transfiguration story, early Judaism's living "prophetic figures," Moses and Elijah, to appear with Jesus. Even if this line of tradition can be accented with good reason, this need not and should not mean that other typological connections suggested by the Old Testament cannot be valid as well.[89]

So although the New Testament does not develop the implicit analogy between Jesus and Joshua/Yehoshua/Jeshua suggested by their similar names, the names themselves open up space for contemporary intertextual reflection and symbolic cross-fertilization between the Testaments. It follows that

---

church authors, by contrast, thought the parallels between Joshua and Jesus compelled further exploration; see G. W. H. Lampe, *A Patristic Greek Lexicon* (Oxford: Clarendon, 1961), p. 672.

88. For a recent wide-ranging exploration of this problem, see Amy-Jill Levine, *The Misunderstood Jew: The Church and the Scandal of the Jewish Jesus* (San Francisco: Harper, 2006).

89. Görg, *Bosom*, pp. 77-78.

the traditional rule about typology — that it should be used only where there is an explicit New Testament warrant for it — cannot be maintained on the basis of the New Testament itself. Both Testaments provide implicit warrants for typological associations, independent of explicit development or even authorial intent.

After further exploring the literary/theological dimensions of the identities of both Joshua, Moses' successor, and Jeshua, Israel's high priest after the exile, Görg returns to the significance of the onomastic similarity between their names and the name of Jesus for the relationship between the two Testaments and for Christian biblical theology. Joshua and Jeshua have no literary "echo" within the New Testament, Görg maintains,[90] and yet he cannot imagine that their memory was not bound up in some way with perceptions about Jesus' name, and thus Jesus' identity:

> the Old Testament itself creates relationships that we could not at all anticipate from the New Testament, that were given but that achieved no recognition in the New Testament. This is what I mean in speaking of the paradigmatic deposit that is tangible in the Old Testament and points beyond it. Not every reliable and enduring truth, not even every such truth about Jesus, that is named in the Old Testament need have been uttered *expressis verbis* and exclusively in the New Testament. . . .
>
> One could say that there remains a remnant, and a none too modest remnant, that is not addressed at all in the New Testament, but that can be seen, so to speak, as a "holy remnant" in the Old Testament.[91]

In other words, *the Old Testament contributes something to the Christian witness of Holy Scripture that the New Testament itself does not contain.*

Thus, reflection on biblical names like "Saul" in Acts, rather than being a question of obscure linguistic and historical interest, points instead to the heart of the relation between the two Testaments in biblical theology. This relation must be one in which both Testaments retain their respective theological witnesses rather than one in which the New Testament becomes the Christian voice of the Old and the Old Testament is considered to have nothing to offer Christian theology independently of the New. A typological hermeneutic will emphasize the common ground shared by Christians and Jews, in contrast to the entrenched tradition of supersessionist Christian theology. This essay has arrived at such a hermeneutic through a

90. Görg neglects to mention Heb. 4:8 as the possible exception that proves the rule.
91. Görg, *Bosom*, pp. 88-89.

typologically alert literary analysis of the shift from "Saul" to "Paul" in the Acts narrative.[92]

No one in biblical scholarship is doing more than Richard Hays to show how the New Testament is understood rightly only when read in light of the Old.[93] I hope he will welcome this essay from an Old Testament colleague just as committed to reading the Old Testament in the direction of the New. I have been privileged over many years to know Richard as my professor, adviser, mentor, colleague, friend, and musical partner-in-crime. My life has been incomparably enriched through classes and conversations with him, the reading of his superbly crafted written work, his wise presence on the Duke faculty, and, thanks to his generosity, the occasional sharing of a Duke basketball game. *Ad multos annos!*

92. I would like to thank my colleagues Douglas Campbell and C. Kavin Rowe for their help in thinking through some of the issues discussed in this essay. I am also grateful for the assistance of Tommy Givens in preparing the manuscript for publication.

93. Cf. The Scripture Project, "Nine Theses on the Interpretation of Scripture," in *The Art of Reading Scripture*, ed. Ellen F. Davis and Richard B. Hays (Grand Rapids: Eerdmans, 2003), p. 2: "[A]gainst the assumption that Jesus can be understood exclusively in light of Christian theology's later confessional traditions, we affirm that our interpretation of Jesus must return repeatedly to the Old Testament to situate him in direct continuity with Israel's hopes and Israel's understanding of God."

The Book of Acts and the Cultural
Explication of the Identity of God

C. Kavin Rowe

I. Introduction

New Testament scholars are not accustomed to reading Karl Barth for help with their historical and exegetical work. Yet at one point at least, it is Barth above all others in our time who has seen clearly a central theological point without which many of the historical dynamics involved in "Christian origins" are virtually unintelligible: God is the measure of all things.[1] To speak properly of God in Barth's sense is to speak not of the grandest object within our horizon but of the reality that constitutes the total horizon of all human life and thought. God is not derivative of human culture (à la Feuerbach, Freud, et al.) but generative.

The hermeneutical corollary of Barth's insight is of momentous consequence and can be stated simply: what we think about God will determine what we think about everything else.[2] To speak of "God" is to invoke the context for all understanding, that to which all life and thought are related; to the extent that we live and think at all, therefore, we do so in light of our understanding — whether explicit or implicit — of God. Theology, that is, is never merely ideation. It is always and inherently a total way of life.

---

1. This theme is central to Barth's theology; it is difficult, therefore, to know where to point the reader. But see, e.g., Karl Barth, *Church Dogmatics* (ET Edinburgh: T. & T. Clark, 1958), II/1 §26, esp. pp. 76, 117; §28, esp. pp. 312-13; §31, p. 562; III/1 §§40-41, esp. pp. 5-7, 11-13.

2. Cf., e.g., Barth's statement in *Dogmatics in Outline,* trans. G. T. Thomson (New York: Harper & Row, 1959), p. 50: "[E]verything that is said about creation depends absolutely upon this Subject."

The early Christians were not Barthians. Yet to see that the contour of their life derived from their understanding of God is to penetrate to the core of the conflict that surrounded their birth and growth. From 1 Thessalonians (1:9) through Pliny's famous epistle (10.96) to the persecution under Decius and beyond, the clash of the gods was that which ultimately determined the shape of the collision between (emerging) Christianity and paganism.[3] There were of course confusion, diversity, difference, and complex interaction between paganism and Christianity. But the conflict as a whole and the instantiation of a new culture — for that is what it was[4] — are utterly inconceivable apart from the clash between the exclusivity of the Christian God and the wider mode of pagan religiousness.[5] To put it slightly differently: once one grasps the primary — *sensu stricto* — importance of God for a total way of life, the conflict becomes intelligible. Converting to the God of the Christians was not merely an adjustment of this or that aspect of an otherwise unaltered basic cultural pattern; rather, worshiping the God of the Christians simultaneously involved an extraction or removal from constitutive aspects of pagan culture (e.g., sacrifice to the gods) and a concomitant cultural profile that rendered Christians identifiable as a "group" by outsiders.[6] Yet the practices that created this cultural profile were themselves de-

3. There has long been phenomenological difficulty in identifying "paganism" as a single, unitary thing. Yet linguistic alternatives prove to create more problems than they solve; traditional usage is thus best retained so long as it is not understood to describe a monolithic religion, culture, power structure, etc. For a brief and lucid statement of the problem, see Robin Lane Fox, *Pagans and Christians* (New York: Alfred A. Knopf, 1987), p. 33.

4. See, e.g., Ramsay MacMullen, *Paganism in the Roman Empire* (New Haven: Yale University Press, 1981), p. 88; Frances M. Young, *Biblical Exegesis and the Formation of Christian Culture* (Cambridge: Cambridge University Press, 1997), pp. 50, 70, 286-91.

5. Lane Fox is again concise on the problem of speaking of paganism as a single "religion" — it is, he argues, more like a pattern of religiousness. Still, this pattern displays enough of a common core and broad similarity that we can speak of it in something of a holistic way; see Lane Fox, *Pagans and Christians,* pp. 31-38, 90, etc. In addition, I take it now for granted that "religion" in pagan antiquity was a public and political affair, that the attempt to privatize beliefs or piety perpetuates a modern mistake in the study of antiquity, and that these matters have been amply demonstrated in recent study; see, e.g., Simon R. F. Price, *Rituals and Power: The Roman Imperial Cult in Asia Minor* (Cambridge: Cambridge University Press, 1984), pp. 15-16, 234-48; Robert Louis Wilken, *The Christians as the Romans Saw Them,* 2nd ed. (New Haven: Yale University Press, 2003), p. x. Cf. n. 95 below.

6. This is not necessarily to say, however, that in the early periods "Christian" is the word that would have been used. In many cases the Jewish Christian missionaries (Paul, etc.) would simply have been "Jews" to the outsiders (as in Acts 16:20, for example). It is also noteworthy that Tertullus presents Paul to Felix as a ringleader of a Jewish sect (αἵρεσις), the

pendent upon the identity of God. Christian ecclesial life, in other words, was the cultural explication of God's identity.

Taken as a whole, the narrative of the Acts of the Apostles is a rich exposition of this cultural explication of divine identity. In the book of Acts, the expansion of God's εὐαγγέλιον is coterminous with the creation of a people whom, in Luke's terms, God has taken out of the Gentiles for his name's sake (Acts 15:14: ὁ θεὸς ἐπεσκέψατο λαβεῖν ἐξ ἐθνῶν λαὸν τῷ ὀνόματι αὐτοῦ).[7] The revelation of God in Christ, that is, necessarily entails the formation of a people who bear witness to God's name.[8] In this way, volume two of Luke's overall literary project displays the narrative outworking of the claim of volume one that the salvation of God comes through Jesus Christ as an apocalypse to the Gentiles (Luke 2:30-32; Acts 13:47; cf. Isa. 42:6; 49:9).

Space does not permit an elucidation of these matters from the entirety of Acts; that task belongs to a much larger project.[9] We shall therefore focus

---

Nazarenes (24:5). Yet once Gentiles are in the picture, the word Χριστιανοί is doubtless there soon, too: there is a community of Jews and Gentiles that behaves socially like Jews in some very important ways (one God, no sacrifice to pagan gods, etc.) but differs visibly from other Jews in some very important ways (the absence, for the most part, of dietary restrictions, no circumcision, no rigorous Sabbath keeping, the claim to follow Jesus as the Messiah, etc.). Acts 11:26; 26:28; 1 Pet. 4:16 all suggest that Χριστιανός was first coined by outsiders. On this important issue, see David G. Horrell, "The Label Χριστιανός: 1 Peter 4:16 and the Formation of Christian Identity," *JBL* 126 (2007): 361-81.

7. For the OT echoes in this phrasing, see Nils A. Dahl, "A People for His Name (Acts xv. 14)," *NTS* 4 (1957-58): 319-27. Though Dahl settles on Zech. 2:15 LXX (2:11 Eng.) as the "most interesting parallel" to Acts 15:14, he also notes that "[t]he number of similar [LXX] texts indicates that Acts xv. 14 is modelled upon the general pattern rather than upon any individual passage" (p. 323). In my judgment, Dahl is correct to say that Luke's formulation in Acts 15:14 depends upon a larger reading of the OT (including Zech. 2:14-17) in which "the conversion of Gentiles is seen as a fulfilment of God's promises to Israel: Luke ii. 29-32; Acts ii. 39; iii. 25; xiii. 47, etc." (p. 327). As these remarks indicate, my way of putting the issue of the formation of a people (main text, above) hardly intends to say that Acts is unconcerned with Judaism and Jewish traditions; Luke is very much concerned with Judaism. Recent and extensive studies confirm this fact (see, e.g., the work of Joseph Tyson). By comparison, only scant attention has been given to Luke's concern with Gentiles/paganism. In fact, I know of only two recent attempts, the first of which is quite brief. See Hans-Josef Klauck, *Magic and Paganism in Early Christianity: The World of the Acts of the Apostles* (Edinburgh: T. & T. Clark, 1999); Christoph W. Stenschke, *Luke's Portrait of Gentiles Prior to Their Coming to Faith,* WUNT 2.108 (Tübingen: Mohr Siebeck, 1999).

8. In theological terms: theology proper is distinct but never separate from ecclesiology. God's revelation and the formation of a people are in fact one theological movement.

9. In which I am presently engaged. The study is provisionally entitled "The Apocalypse to the Gentiles and the Culture of God: Reading Acts in the Graeco-Roman World."

upon two instances in which the reconfiguration of divine identity necessitated by the witness of the early missionaries results in a clash between the expansion of the gospel and essential assumptions of religiocultural life in the ancient Mediterranean world: the accounts of Christian mission in Lystra (Acts 14:8-19) and in Philippi (Acts 16:16-24). These two scenes are exegetically advantageous because they exhibit *in nuce* the potential volatility inherent in much early Christian interaction with pagan culture. In so doing, they allow us to draw out something of the necessary interconnection between theology and politics.

Before moving to the exegesis, however, a brief word about interpretive method is in order.[10] The exegesis below proceeds on two simple assumptions: first, that word meaning is contextually dependent, and, second, that a text is most fruitfully interpreted with at least some understanding of the "cultural encyclopedia" relevant to the text's genesis.[11] Thus, on the one hand, my treatment of these two passages should not be read as two separate diachronic studies of Luke's historical accuracy, skill in creating "Lokalkolorit," etc.[12] To the contrary, in each case the entire narrative of Acts is assumed as the wider interpretive context in which exegetical understanding is to be had. On the other hand, this literary reading is resolutely historical, in the sense that the narrative of Acts is situated within the Mediterranean culture of its early auditors. With these clarifications in mind, we may turn now to the exegesis.

10. For a thorough account of the present state of method in the study of Acts, see Todd Penner, "Madness in the Method? The Acts of the Apostles in Current Study," *CBR* 2 (2004): 223-93.

11. The language of "cultural encyclopedia" derives from Umberto Eco and refers to the wider cultural knowledge (tacit and explicit) assumed by the author and embedded in a text by virtue of its origin within a particular time in history. So, for example, in contrast to the cultural encyclopedia that is now relevant to modern democracies, Luke has no idea of that which many people now claim is necessary, namely, the separation of religion and politics; this crisp distinction is simply not part of his knowledge base. To access Luke's cultural encyclopedia is immediately to become aware of the inextricable unity of religion and politics in one form of life.

12. For an excellent study of Luke's accuracy in local description, see Peter Lampe, "Acta 19 im Spiegel der ephesischen Inschriften," *BZ* 36 (1992): 59-76.

II. Acts 14: Paul and Barnabas as Hermes and Zeus

To all but a few of the highly educated, the gods were indeed a potential presence whom a miracle might reveal.[13]

After escaping a second straight round of persecution (first in Pisidian Antioch, then in Iconium), Paul and Barnabas make their way through Derbe, Lystra, and the surrounding countryside preaching the gospel (εὐαγγελιζόμενοι ἦσαν, 14:7). In the Roman colony of Lystra, Paul dramatically heals a cripple who has been listening to him preach (14:9a), whom Paul recognizes as having the πίστις to be healed (τοῦ σωθῆναι, 14:9bc).[14] The effect upon the crowds is immediate and overwhelming: they respond with religious acclamation and prepare to make a sacrificial offering to Paul and Barnabas as Hermes and Zeus (14:11-13). The apostles,[15] delayed by their inability to understand Lycaonian,[16] finally rush forth to protest this pagan worship and to call for its abandonment on the basis of a reconfiguration of divine identity (14:14-18). As a result, after the arrival of some Jews from Antioch and Iconium, the crowds are persuaded to stone Paul (14:19).[17]

Though it is perhaps startling to moderns, it is hardly surprising that in the ancient world a display of power would occasion the acclamation οἱ θεοὶ ὁμοιωθέντες ἀνθρώποις κατέβησαν πρὸς ἡμᾶς (14:11). Not only was great theological importance attached to miracles,[18] but Greco-Roman religious sensibilities had long been under the "spell of Homer,"[19] in which the ap-

---

13. Lane Fox, *Pagans and Christians*, p. 140.

14. The parallels with Peter's act of healing in Acts 3:1-10 and Jesus' in Luke 5:17-26 have long been observed, as has the connection to Jesus' programmatic reading of Isaiah 61 in the synagogue in Nazareth (Luke 4:18-19). Cf. Luke 7:22.

15. Acts 14:4, 14, the only time Paul and Barnabas are called ἀπόστολοι in Acts.

16. Many scholars note that this detail helps explain why the sacrificial act progressed as far as it did without the apostles' interference. See, e.g., Henry J. Cadbury, *The Book of Acts in History* (Eugene, Ore.: Wipf & Stock, 2004), p. 22.

17. There is a marked emphasis upon the ὄχλοι. The word occurs five times in ten verses (14:11, 13, 14, 18, 19).

18. Ramsay MacMullen, *Christianizing the Roman Empire: A.D. 100-400* (New Haven: Yale University Press, 1984), pp. 25-42, for example, has argued strongly for the importance of Christian "wonder-working" as a major factor in the story of how Christianity won the battle of religions in the empire (cf. his *Paganism in the Roman Empire*, pp. 96-97).

19. The phrase "spell of Homer" is taken from Walter Burkert's treatment of that theme in his classic study *Greek Religion* (Cambridge, Mass.: Harvard University Press, 1985), pp. 119-25. Burkert speaks of a "common Homeric literary culture" from the eighth century on-

pearance of the gods in human form was to be expected: "gods in the guise of strangers from afar put on all manner of shapes, and visit the cities."[20] This was no less true in various hamlets or in the interior of Asia Minor than it was in Greece itself: "Even in wretched Olbia, on the Black Sea, the wandering orator Dio (c. 100 A.D.) flattered his audience on their passion for Homer and his poems."[21]

Philosophers, of course, from Xenophanes and Plato to the time of the New Testament and beyond were critical of Homer's anthropomorphism of the gods, crudely interpreted.[22] Only through sophisticated demythologization of the inherited mythology could Aristotle, for example, make the views of the "forefathers and of the earliest thinkers . . . intelligible."[23] Among intellectuals, this criticism naturally gained considerable currency. Luke's contemporary Josephus, for example, praises "the severe censure" of the Homeric tales by the "leading thinkers" among the "admired sages of Greece."[24]

Yet if we take our measure from material remains and from the views presupposed by the critics' criticism — as well as from the kind of data we see in Pausanias's vivid descriptions of local piety, for example — we find that "far into the second and third centuries A.D., this piety of the majority

---

ward (p. 8). The judgment about the importance of Homer's influence is ubiquitous among classicists. See, e.g., Lane Fox, *Pagans and Christians*, p. 110; A. D. Nock, "Religious Attitudes of the Ancient Greeks," in Nock, *Essays on Religion and the Ancient World*, ed. Z. Stewart, 2 vols. (Oxford: Clarendon, 1972), 2:534-50 (esp. pp. 543, 550); Simon R. F. Price, *Religions of the Ancient Greeks* (Cambridge: Cambridge University Press, 1999), p. 6.

20. Homer, *Od.* 17.485-86 (trans. Murray, LCL). Cf. Lane Fox, *Pagans and Christians*, p. 119: "Greek votive reliefs of all periods owe a large debt to sightings of their gods." For this theme in the apocryphal Acts, see Rosa Söder, *Die apokryphen Apostelgeschichten und die romanhafte Literatur der Antike* (Stuttgart: Kohlhammer, 1969 [1932]), pp. 95-98.

21. Lane Fox, *Pagans and Christians*, p. 110. For a concise treatment of the excerpts from Homer (and other ancient material) that circulated in the ancient world, see Henry Chadwick, "Florilegium," *RAC* 7:1131-60.

22. For a helpful starting point, see Price's chapter "Greek Thinkers" in *Religions of the Ancient Greeks*. Harold W. Attridge, "The Philosophical Critique of Religion under the Early Empire," *ANRW* 2.16.1:45-78, provides a significant overview of the discussion during the time of the NT. See also Daniel Babut, *La religion des philosophes grecs: de Thalès aux Stoïciens* (Paris: Presses Universitaires de France, 1974), who discerns a broad unity in the focus of the critique despite considerable historical development and points of material disagreement within such a focus (esp. pp. 204-5).

23. Aristotle, *Metaph.* 12.8.18 (1074B; trans. Tredennick, LCL). Aristotle here holds that the mythology of gods "human in shape or . . . like certain other animals" was developed "to influence the vulgar and as a constitutional and utilitarian expedient."

24. Josephus, *Ap.* 2.239-42 §§33-34 (trans. Thackeray, LCL alt.).

survived the wit of poets and philosophers."[25] Alexander of Abonuteichos, to take but one outstanding case from the mid-second century CE, began his career by

> addressing the people from a high altar, . . . [congratulating] the city be-cause it was at once to receive the god [Asclepius] in visible presence. The assembly — for almost the whole city, including women, old men, and youths, had come running — marveled, prayed and worshiped. Uttering a few meaningless words like Hebrew or Phoenician, he dazed the people, who did not know what he was saying save only that he everywhere brought in Apollo and Asclepius.[26]

After Alexander displayed his divine powers by producing a small snake he had secretly prepared for the occasion, the people "at once raised a shout [and] welcomed the god."[27]

Lucian is no doubt having a bit of fun here, but in point of fact the cult in Abonuteichos — geographically considered, a sure misfire for economic gain — was enormously successful and did center on Alexander and his pet snake. From around 150 to the mid-170s, "people flocked to this distant point where Providence seemed to have broken afresh into the world. Its god gave personal advice to Romans of the highest rank and sent an oracle to the Emperor himself."[28] If behind Lucian's satire, therefore, we glimpse a philo-sophically trained (Pythagorean) and religiously nimble Alexander, we must also see that his skillful charlatanry was well calculated to fit a vast believing public.

Nor is it any surprise that in Lystra the local priest of Zeus and the crowds instantly prepared to sacrifice to Paul and Barnabas (θύειν, Acts

---

25. Lane Fox, *Pagans and Christians*, p. 115. One of the outstanding merits of Lane Fox's study is that, in terms of historical perception, he refuses simply to adopt the more sophisti-cated philosophical perspectives that are frequently the viewpoint of the literary sources and instead attempts to correlate more closely the views presupposed by those sources with other types of evidence (inscriptions, statues, etc.). Cf. the insightful remarks of MacMullen, *Pa-ganism in the Roman Empire*, esp. pp. 77-79. On Socratic criticism as the cause of an Athe-nian "religious crisis," see the judicious discussion by Robert Parker, *Athenian Religion: A History* (Oxford: Clarendon, 1996), esp. pp. 199-217, who notes that Socrates' criticism of the gods was taken to be socially dangerous only because of its (perceived) necessary link to a moral relativism (esp. p. 212).

26. Lucian, *Alex.* 13 (trans. Harmon, LCL alt.).

27. *Alex.* 14 (trans. Harmon, LCL).

28. Lane Fox, *Pagans and Christians*, p. 242. Lane Fox's concise discussion situates the cult within the overall "normal" cultic practice of the empire (pp. 241-50).

14:13, 18), inasmuch as to worship the gods in antiquity was to sacrifice. Ovid's *Metamorphoses,* to cite a work obviously germane to Acts 14, opens its treatment of transformation with Jupiter's (Zeus's) account of his descent from Olympus "as a god disguised in human form *(deus humana ... imagine).*" After appearing at his destination, Jupiter reports, "I gave a sign that a god had come, and the common folk began to worship me."[29] Ovid's tale is significant, not simply because he was still the most influential poet of Rome when it was composed (ca. 8 CE), but because it reflects, with Acts 14:8-18, a common *topos,* a standard way of thinking about the appearance of the gods and the human response to them (cf. Acts 10:25-26 and 28:1-10). Indeed, if we read on in the *Metamorphoses* to book 8, we find the delightful account of the visit of Jupiter and Mercury (Hermes) — *specie mortali* — to the Phrygian countryside, where they are (finally[30]) received hospitably by the old couple Baucis and Philemon, who eventually ask to serve as priests for the gods (i.e., to guard their temple, to preside over the sacrifices, etc., 8.707-8). The similarity to Luke's account of Paul and Barnabas in Lystra is striking, and it is not without good reason that Acts scholars have frequently drawn attention to this passage in the *Metamorphoses* as a possible basis for Luke's story.[31] Prima facie, one might easily think the Lystrans' eagerness to honor Paul and Barnabas makes excellent sense in light of their religious prehistory: Hermes and Zeus had been sighted in the interior of Asia Minor before.

Whether or not Luke knew the story in Ovid's *Metamorphoses* or a local tradition is largely indeterminable.[32] The syncretistic Jew Artapanus (second c. BCE), for example, tells of Egyptians who accorded Moses divine hon-

---

29. Ovid, *Metam.* 1.200-220 (trans. Miller, LCL).

30. They are first unrecognized in their human form and rejected: "To a thousand homes they came, seeking a place for rest; a thousand homes were barred against them" (*Metam.* 8.628-29, trans. Miller, LCL).

31. Luke Timothy Johnson, for example, remarks that "Luke may well be playing off a literary motif concerning the hospitality shown to the gods Zeus and Hermes by residents of Phrygia.... These folk do not want to miss the chance to be the next Baucis and Philemon!" Johnson, *The Acts of the Apostles,* SP 5 (Collegeville, Minn.: Liturgical Press, 1992), p. 251; see also his earlier remark: "It is difficult to avoid the suspicion that Luke's account plays off such a tradition" (p. 248). Cf., e.g., C. K. Barrett, *A Critical and Exegetical Commentary on the Acts of the Apostles,* 2 vols., ICC (Edinburgh: T. & T. Clark, 1994-98), 1:677; Klauck, *Magic and Paganism,* p. 59.

32. Cf. Cilliers Breytenbach, "Zeus und der lebendige Gott: Anmerkungen zu Apostelgeschichte 14.11-17," *NTS* 39 (1993): 396-413, who argues that both Ovid and Luke draw upon local traditions (p. 403).

ors and designated him "Hermes" in response to his hermeneutical skill.[33] And Horace, too, suggests that Augustus was Mercury in human shape.[34] But that Luke shares with Ovid and other Greco-Romans a basic understanding of the religious patterns that surround the appearance of the gods can hardly be denied. In this, as in other areas of his portrayal of paganism (see below), Luke is simply a man of his time. As Robin Lane Fox puts it, "Acts' author believed this response was natural."[35]

Where Luke's historical situatedness is forgotten, the critical theological edge of this carefully sketched scene is badly blunted. Ernst Haenchen, for example, asks with respect to the pagan response to Barnabas and Paul, "But is it really conceivable?" His answer is clearly that it is not:

> [T]hat the priest of Zeus would immediately believe that the two wonder-workers were Zeus and Hermes, and hasten up with oxen and garlands, is highly improbable. . . . It is not only the priest's credulity, moreover, but that of the people which is unconvincing. The healing of the cripple was admittedly a great miracle. But surely not so great as to persuade the Lycaonians that their very gods stood in their midst.[36]

But this reading is, at best, to replace ancient religious practice with its philosophical critique, or already to adopt unawares the perspective of Paul and Barnabas. At worst, it is no less than a radical modernizing of the text, in the sense that it dismisses fundamental aspects of pagan religion as mere silliness.[37]

33. See the text in Carl Holladay, *Fragments from Hellenistic Jewish Authors*, vol. 1, *Historians* (Chico, Calif.: Scholars Press, 1983), pp. 210-11, frg. 3 lines 10-13 (*apud* Eusebius, *Praep. ev.* 9.27.6; Eusebius quotes at this point from Alexander Polyhistor). Because of his theological "synchronism," whether Artapanus was Jewish or pagan has been a point of contention, but the consensus now is that he was a Jew (see Holladay, *Fragments,* pp. 189-90).

34. Horace, *Carm.* 1.2 lines 40-45 (sive mutate iuvenem figura ales in terris imitaris almae filius Maiae patiens vocari Caesaris ultor). Noted also in A. D. Nock, *Conversion* (Oxford: Clarendon, 1933), p. 237.

35. Lane Fox, *Pagans and Christians,* p. 100.

36. Ernst Haenchen, *The Acts of the Apostles: A Commentary,* trans. B. Noble and G. Shinn, rev. R. McL. Wilson (Philadelphia: Westminster, 1971 [ET from 14th German ed. of 1965]), p. 432.

37. Klauck, *Magic and Paganism,* p. 57, remarks: "Apparitions of gods on earth in human form are a stable element of hellenistic piety — assertions to the contrary in some commentaries are nothing more than a sign that their authors have never read the 'Bible of the Greeks,' Homer's epics." Klauck does not mention whom he has in mind, and it is difficult to believe that Haenchen never read Homer, but Klauck's general point is sound.

By contrast, to become aware of the normalcy — indeed, the religious propriety — of the pagan reaction is to become aware of the requisite back-ground against which Luke's scene derives its critical force. For Luke's call through the mouths of Paul and Barnabas is not simply an admonition to tweak a rite or halt a ceremony. It contains, rather, a summons that simulta-neously involves the destruction of an entire mode of being "religious."

It is true, of course, that in a certain respect Paul and Barnabas appear "as genuine philosophers who reject such attempts at deification"[38] and in this way evince a joining of hands with pagan philosophical criticism.[39] Yet simply to note this connection is to reduce the import of the passage to a sin-gle point of contact with a small minority in the wider culture.

With few exceptions, principal philosophical critique was directed more against superstition (see, e.g., Plutarch's περὶ δεισιδαιμονίας[40]) and overly lit-eral interpretation of myth than it was against cultic practice.[41] In spite of the manifest theological problems exposed by his lucid dialogue on the na-ture of the gods, for example, Cicero believed firmly in the necessity of tradi-tional cultic practice (*Nat. d.* 1.2.4) and was himself — despite *De divinatione* — a member of the College of Augurs (*Nat. d.* 1.6.14).[42] So too the same Plu-

---

38. Johnson, *Acts*, p. 251. Cf. Nock, *Essays*, 2:549.

39. By the first century CE, this "refusal of divine honors" had become a highly complex, grand-scale political maneuver — specifically in relation to the Roman emperor — and var-ied as to its interpretation within the different parts of the empire. See, e.g., M. P. Charlesworth, "The Refusal of Divine Honours: An Augustan Formula," *PBSR* 15 (1939): 1-10; or Price, *Rituals and Power*, pp. 72-77. Pseudo-Callisthenes' *Alexander Romance (The Life of Alexander of Macedon)* is frequently cited in relation to Acts (so Johnson, *Acts*, p. 249); see, e.g., 2.22: "I beg off from honors equal to the gods. For I am a mortal man and I fear such cere-monies. For they bring danger to the soul" (trans. Haight). But it should be acknowledged that even in this work Alexander does not always refuse the honors (e.g., 2.14) and that the third-century date and the weak historical core of the work make it difficult to relate to Acts.

40. On the complex associations surrounding this term and its cognates, which also occur in Acts 17:22 and 25:19, see P. J. Koets, *Δεισιδαιμονία: A Contribution to the Knowledge of the Religious Terminology in Greek* (Purmerend: J. Muusses, 1929).

41. Certain types of Cynics are the primary exceptions (e.g., Diogenes of Sinope and, if Eusebius is accurate, Oenomaus of Gadara). There were of course accusations leveled at Epicurus along these lines (recall, e.g., the linkage of Epicureans with Christians and atheists in Lucian, *Alex.* 38), but we must remember that Philodemus's *On Piety* defended Epicurus with respect to traditional religious practice, claiming even that he was initiated into the Eleusinian Mysteries. On this point in general, see Attridge, "Philosophical Critique"; Price, *Religions of the Ancient Greeks*, pp. 135-37.

42. See too, of course, his *On the Laws* — modeled on Plato's similarly titled work — in which he argues for the necessity of religious practice for the good of Roman society; indeed,

tarch who in his earlier years could rant against the impiety of the superstitious could later become a priest at Delphi with no sense of discontinuity.
And the Stoics, despite Zeno's criticism of building temples to gods, "attend
the mysteries in temples, go up to the Acropolis, do reverence to statues
(προσκυνοῦσι . . . τὰ ἔδη), and place wreaths upon the shrines."[43] Even Epicureans, though considered by some to be atheists,[44] sacrificed to the gods.[45]

Luke's criticism, however, goes much deeper and aims at the very foundations that support the edifice of pagan religiousness in the effort to break the
entire structure with a single biblical word — μάταια.[46] Accompanied by prophetic action — the rending of their clothes[47] — Paul and Barnabas characterize the whole scene as worthless, futile, or vain.[48] Though εἰκόνες/ἀγάλματα/
ξόανα would hardly be excluded, the passage gives no indication that they are
directly in view. At this point, images are not in themselves the problem.
Rather, the critique reaches further, toward the entire religious complex of pagan deities and cultic sacrifice. Luke is not interested in philosophical reform
or in demythologizing but in ἐπιστροφή, a conversion to a way of life incompatible with traditional pagan cults (cf. Acts 15:3, τὴν ἐπιστροφὴν τῶν ἐθνῶν;
26:20, καὶ τοῖς ἔθνεσιν ἀπήγγελλον μετανοεῖν καὶ ἐπιστρέφειν ἐπὶ τὸν θεόν).[49]

---

the "rites shall ever be preserved and continuously handed down in families, and . . . they
must be continued forever" (*Leg.* 2.19.47, trans. Keyes, LCL). On Plato as the "first political
thinker to argue that matters of belief can be criminal offences," see Price, *Religions of the
Ancient Greeks,* pp. 133-34.

43. Plutarch, *Mor.* 1034B (trans. Cherniss, LCL).

44. See, e.g., Cicero, *Nat. d.* 2.30.76; Lucian, *Alex.* 38.

45. Plutarch, *Mor.* 1034C; cf. Cicero, *Nat. d.* 1.30.85, 123; 3.1.3.

46. The relevant occurrences are plentiful. See, e.g., (LXX) Lev. 17:7; Amos 2:4; Isa. 32:6;
Jer. 10:3, 15; Ezek. 8:10. See also BDAG 621.

47. Though it may well be that "Halb nackt mit zerrissenen Kleidern (vgl. *Appian,* Bell
Civ I, 66,300) man kaum noch für einen Gott gehalten werden [kann]" (Rudolf Pesch, *Die
Apostelgeschichte,* 2 vols. [Neukirchen-Vluyn: Neukirchener, 1986], 2:58), the more likely
point for the narrative audience is similar to what one sees in the OT or, better, in Matt.
26:65//Mark 14:63 when the high priest tears his clothes at the perceived blasphemy. Cf.,
from a later period, *m. Sanh.* 7:5.

48. Reading diachronically, the crowd in Lystra would hardly have heard μάταια with
its larger biblical resonance (false god). Yet at the level of the narrative audience, Luke shapes
the auditor's perception by the use of this theologically freighted word from the LXX.

49. Of course, pagans too could speak of ἐπιστροφή (Plato, *Resp.* 7.517C ff. of the task of
educating the soul) or *conversio* (Cicero, *Nat. d.* 1.37.77 of the philosophers' attempt with the
masses), but the point here is that such "turning" was compatible with traditional cultic
practice, whereas for Luke it clearly is not, and the ultimate object toward which one is to
turn is clearly different.

Turn, say Paul and Barnabas, from these backward acclamations (the honor of mere humans as θεοί) and lifeless practices (sacrifice), to the living God.[50]

The criticism thus has both a deconstructive and a constructive dimension. On the one hand, where the pagan action would bring the human and divine almost entirely together, there is in the cry (κράζοντες) of Paul and Barnabas the explicit emphasis upon ἄνθρωποι in their sheer humanness, as it were, as an attempt to open a space between human beings and God. Καὶ ἡμεῖς . . . ἐσμεν ἄνθρωποι is emphatic and, indeed, reminds the reader/auditor of Peter's similar exclamation when confronted by a prostrate Cornelius: καὶ ἐγὼ αὐτὸς ἄνθρωπός εἰμι! (10:26).[51] In both cases, the speakers move to establish a common humanity with their audience and hence to drive an ontological wedge between themselves and the divine. In Acts 14:15 this attempt is further strengthened with the use of ὁμοιοπαθεῖς . . . ὑμῖν, particularly as it counterbalances ἡμεῖς . . . ἐσμεν. Ἡμεῖς ὁμοιοπαθεῖς ἐσμεν ὑμῖν ἄνθρωποι: "we" are just like "you" — human beings through and through. Ὁμοιοπαθεῖς would of course, to the ear of the philosophically trained auditor, seal the deconstructive case: a true θεός is one without πάθος.[52] Paul and Barnabas are human.

On the other hand, the message is not simply cease and desist. Rather, as Luke Johnson notes, the religious impulse of the crowds is received even as the official machinery is shut off. In this way, the reception of the pagan impulse involves an essential reinterpretation as to its *telos* — the living God. Barrett is correct that θεὸς ζῶν is "almost a proper name";[53] the potency of the name comes through in the utter contrast between death and life, the turning away from τούτων τῶν ματαίων toward θεὸν ζῶντα, the source of life itself: ἐποίησεν τὸν οὐρανὸν καὶ τὴν γῆν καὶ τὴν θάλασσαν καὶ πάντα τὰ ἐν αὐτοῖς (v. 15).[54] To be the "living" God is to be Creator, to possess the life-giving power to do good and to bring rain and sustenance (v. 17).

---

50. Barrett, *Acts*, 1:680, is right to note of ἐπιστρέφειν that "the verb has so fully taken on the sense of proclamation that it means almost *to command: telling you to turn.*" The relationship to 1 Thess. 1:9 has often been discussed; see, e.g., Ulrich Wilckens, *Die Missionsreden der Apostelgeschichte* (Neukirchen: Neukirchener Verlag, 1961), esp. pp. 86-87.

51. On this point, see C. Kavin Rowe, "Luke-Acts and the Imperial Cult: A Way through the Conundrum?" *JSNT* 27 (2005): 279-300, esp. p. 290. Cf. Barrett, *Acts*, 1:665, who notes that the "denial that apostles and evangelists are anything other than human" is a Lukan theme.

52. Cf. Josephus's criticism in *Ap.* 2.251 §35.

53. Barrett, *Acts*, 1:680.

54. Cf. Breytenbach, "Zeus und der lebendige Gott," p. 397, who notes the OT and early Jewish link between ὁ θεὸς ζῶν and his status as Creator.

The pagan religious impulse is thus redirected toward the living God by a sweeping criticism and the unveiling of the true divine reality behind the gifts that sustain life in the natural world. Zeus was of course seen as the giver of good things — ἐπιδιδόναι γὰρ δὴ ἀγαθὰ αὐτὸν ἀνθρώποις[55] — and, in particular, as the rain god (Ζεὺς ῾Υέτιος/῎Ομβριος, etc.). In fact, these two functions could easily be linked, as Pausanias reports: "there is on Parnes another altar, and on it they make sacrifice, calling Zeus sometimes Rain-god (ὄμβριον), sometimes Averter of Ills (ἀπήμιον)."[56] In light of these well-known functions of Zeus,[57] the radical nature of the apostles' reinterpretation emerges in that it does not, in the manner of Aristobulus, for example, consist of a simple substitution of numinous realities — "that which you call Zeus is really the God of Israel."[58] It thus has no affinity with ancient pluralism (in which, e.g., divine names can be only incidental to divine realities[59]). Instead, it involves both a demolition of the pagan model *in toto* (worshiping Zeus is futile) and a call for a new construction of divine identity. Cilliers Breytenbach puts well the implicit theological ground: the God whom they preach is not only "der lebendige Gott" but "auch der *einzige* lebendige

55. Pausanias, *Descr.* 8.9.2, here of Zeus in Mantineia.

56. *Descr.* 1.32.2 (trans. Jones, LCL). "Averter of ills" can be read as the obverse of one who brings good. See ἀπήμιος and its cognates in LSJ (188; cf. ἀπήμων as "kindly" or "propitious" in *Od.* 7.266). For the ancient altar on Parnes, see Parker, *Athenian Religion*, pp. 30-31. Breytenbach, "Zeus und der lebendige Gott," pp. 399-403, provides an excellent summary of the relevant material for Zeus and Hermes in relation to Lystra in particular.

57. See the relevant material in Arthur Bernard Cook's monumental study *Zeus: A Study in Ancient Religion*, 3 vols. (Cambridge: Cambridge University Press, 1914-40).

58. In citing the opening lines of Aratus's *Phaenomena*, Aristobulus simply substitutes θεός for Ζεύς/Δίς: "we have signified [that the power of θεός permeates all things] by removing the divine names Δίς and Ζεύς used throughout the verses; for their inherent meaning relates to θεός . . ." (*apud* Eusebius, *Praep. ev.* 13.12). For the text and translation of Aristobulus, see Carl R. Holladay, *Fragments from Hellenistic Jewish Authors*, vol. 3, *Aristobulus* (Atlanta: Scholars Press, 1995), pp. 171-73. Such theological moves were of course routine in the ancient Mediterranean world. To take only two of many possible examples, we may think of the closing hymn to Apollo in the first book of Statius, *Thebaid*, in which Apollo is asked for his blessings "whether 'tis right to call thee rosy Titan . . . or Osiris . . . or Mithras" (1.696-720, trans. Mozley, LCL); or, in a more philosophical vein, of Pseudo-Aristotle: "God being one has many names" (*Mund.* 401A). See also the discussion below in section III.

59. "Dis pater Veiovis Manes, sive vos quo alio nomine fas est nominare," ran an ancient Roman prayer; preserved in Macrobius, *Sat.* 3.9.10; cited in P. W. van der Horst, "The Unknown God," in *Knowledge of God in the Graeco-Roman World*, ed. R. van den Broek et al. (Leiden: Brill, 1998), p. 39. Modern religious relativism (in which, e.g., divine names reflect only the social location of the religious person) is of course also nowhere in sight.

Gott."[60] At least as Luke would have it, the *telos* of the pagan religious impulse is not in need of a different or additional name; rather, the impulse itself requires a fundamentally new direction, from dead worship to the living God.

With such a message, it is no great wonder that the crowds, having barely (μόλις) been put off, are subsequently persuaded to attack (14:18-19).[61] This end to the episode in Lystra articulates narratively something of the offense caused by a collision of divine identity and the practices it entails. Contrary to much received scholarly wisdom, in Acts the gospel does not routinely meet with exuberant acceptance among the Gentiles (cf., e.g., 14:2 and the careful ὅσοι formulation of 13:48).[62] It may well be that God ἐν ταῖς παρῳχημέναις γενεαῖς εἴασεν πάντα τὰ ἔθνη πορεύεσθαι ταῖς ὁδοῖς αὐτῶν (v. 16), but simply by its mention, the phrase intimates that the time has now come for Gentiles to turn away from their foolish ὁδοί toward the living

60. Breytenbach, "Zeus und der lebendige Gott," p. 397. For a list of the allusions to the OT in 14:15-18, see esp. Gustav Stählin, *Die Apostelgeschichte*, NTD 5 (Göttingen: Vandenhoeck & Ruprecht, 1962), pp. 193-94, who lists nine principal areas — with about twenty texts — that demonstrate the OT theological roots of Paul's exclamation.

61. Taking the pl. λιθάσαντες in v. 19 to include the crowds (in light of πείσαντες — what else would be its purpose?). So, rightly, Jacob Jervell, *Die Apostelgeschichte: Übersetzt und erklärt*, KEK 3 (Göttingen: Vandenhoeck & Ruprecht, 1998), p. 379 n. 607; Gerhard Schneider, *Die Apostelgeschichte*, 2 vols., HTKNT (Freiburg: Herder, 1980-82), 2:162. Contra Klauck, *Magic and Paganism*, pp. 60-61, who thinks *(a)* that Luke includes only the Jews from Iconium, and *(b)* that Luke needs correction — Paul would not have survived a Jewish stoning — so that a Gentile mob is in view. If one takes λιθάσαντες to include the crowds, Klauck's problem simply disappears.

62. So, rightly, Pesch, *Apostelgeschichte*, 2:59-60. Johnson, *Acts*, p. 251, forces the passage in a positive direction when he writes that this scene shows how God "is opening a door of faith for the Gentiles." Johnson is correct that the Gentiles are not simply condemned for their idolatry. In an important sense, they are open to divine visitation. However, to read the passage as something of a commendation of the Gentile impulse toward idolatry ("Luke portrays these rustics as having precisely the conditions for genuine faith," p. 251) goes too far and makes unintelligible the concluding evangelistic disaster. If God is opening a door for the Gentiles in Lystra (see μαθηταί in 14:22), it would seem to be on the basis of Paul's preaching (14:7) rather than this healing in particular (indeed, as Haenchen, *Acts*, p. 431, noted, the mention of πίστιν τοῦ σωθῆναι in 14:9 presupposes Paul's preaching). Moreover, the exhortation in 14:22 to the disciples in Lystra, Iconium, and Antioch seems to point to some level of persecution in these locations (παρακαλοῦντες ἐμμένειν τῇ πίστει καὶ ὅτι διὰ πολλῶν θλίψεων δεῖ ἡμᾶς εἰσελθεῖν εἰς τὴν βασιλείαν τοῦ θεοῦ). That "much suffering/many tribulations" could be the life of the disciples in Lystra is of course narratively compelling in light of the proximity of 14:22 to the Lystra story, though it could easily pertain also to the missionaries' prior experience in Pisidian Antioch and Iconium (13:50–14:6).

God.[63] If idolatry is at least as much "an error about the management of society (a political error)" as it is an error of the mind,[64] it should occasion no surprise that those who would be affected by the destabilizing power of its theological critique should attempt to drive the bearer of the message out of their community.

III. Acts 16: Paul and the Pythian Spirit

[S]treet prophets were strongly in evidence. We hear much about prophetic women, "pythonesses," as they were popularly known.[65]

After Paul's escape from Lystra, Luke narrates swiftly the passage through Derbe and Paul's eventual journey to the apostolic council (14:19–15:5). Upon approval from James and the council, Paul resumes his Mediterranean mission, and soon thereafter, in response to a vision, travels to the Roman colony of Philippi with his fellow missionaries (note the change to "we" in v. 10). In Philippi, after the conversion of Lydia (16:14-15), the missionaries are "opposed" (ὑπαντῆσαι) by a certain παιδίσκη with a πνεῦμα πύθωνα, whose oracles bring her masters (κύριοι) much economic benefit. Subsequent to their initial meeting, the mantic girl follows the missionaries around, crying (ἔκραζεν), "these men are slaves τοῦ θεοῦ τοῦ ὑψίστου, who proclaim to you ὁδὸν σωτηρίας" (16:17).[66] Paul, who is greatly annoyed, exorcises the spirit in the name of Jesus Christ (16:18), and in turn, the girl's masters — with the ὄχλος and στρατηγοί (vv. 22-23) — see that Paul is removed from their midst. For our purposes, we may focus upon four aspects of the scene in Philippi.

First, recalling that ὕψιστος was "a term . . . vague enough to suit any god

63. Jacob Jervell, *The Theology of the Acts of the Apostles* (Cambridge: Cambridge University Press, 1996), p. 19, takes v. 16 as a statement about God's absence from the history of Gentiles. Perhaps this is to go too far, but the narrative contrast with the description of God's continuous activity in Israel is certainly striking.

64. Moshe Halbertal and Avishai Margalit, *Idolatry*, trans. Naomi Goldblum (Cambridge, Mass.: Harvard University Press, 1992), p. 163.

65. Lane Fox, *Pagans and Christians*, p. 208.

66. Cf. Luke 8:28, where the Gerasene demoniac cries out in a great voice (ἀνακράξας . . . φωνῇ μεγάλῃ), "What have you to do with me, Jesus, Son τοῦ θεοῦ τοῦ ὑψίστου?" In this pericope Luke speaks both of demons (pl., δαιμόνια) and of an unclean spirit (sg., τὸ πνεῦμα τὸ ἀκάθαρτον). These two different ways of speaking are presumably unified in the single name "Legion," which stands for the man's possession by many demons.

treated as the supreme being"[67] helps disclose the narrative force of v. 17's initial ambiguity. Within the world of the story there exists the linguistic and chronological space — Paul was followed for "many days" (πολλὰς ἡμέρας) — for the pagan misidentification of the God of Israel with the highest god in the (local) pantheon.[68] Indeed, if Stephen Mitchell is right, there are "good grounds for thinking that the place where this confrontation occurred was a sanctuary of Theos Hypsistos. . . . [T]he cult of Theos Hypsistos is well attested epigraphically in cities of Aegean and Propontic Thrace around the middle of the first century AD."[69] In any case, such fusion and interchangeability of the divine were of course commonplaces in Greco-Roman antiquity, at both the popular and the philosophical levels. As Celsus would later put it, "I think . . . that it makes no difference whether we call Zeus the Most High (ὕψιστον), or Zen, or Adonai, or Sabaoth, or Ammon like the Egyptians, or Papaeus like the Scythians."[70]

This is hardly to say, of course, that the proclamation (καταγγέλλω[71]) presupposed by the narrative was itself polytheistic, as if Christian auditors/readers of Acts would be unaware of the specific identity of the Most High

67. Nock, *Essays,* 1:425. See Cook for Zeus; Barrett, *Acts,* 2:786 for other literature.

68. So, rightly, e.g., Barrett, *Acts,* 2:786.

69. See Stephen Mitchell, "The Cult of Theos Hypsistos between Pagans, Jews, and Christians," in *Pagan Monotheism in Late Antiquity,* ed. Polymnia Athanassiadi and Michael Frede (Oxford: Clarendon, 1999), p. 110; cf. 115-21. A cultic site has yet to be found in Philippi in particular. Mitchell's suggestion depends upon *(a)* a coordination of Luke's use of προσευχή (Acts 16:13, 16) with the terminology of other known Theos Hypsistos "shrines," *(b)* the possibility that Lydia — as a god-fearer — would have already been involved in the worship of Theos Hypsistos, and *(c)* the widespread finds mentioned in the main text of this essay. Mitchell notes that the cult of Theos Hypsistos "from the Hellenistic period until the fifth century was found in town and country across the entire eastern Mediterranean and the Near East" (pp. 125-26). See too the concise treatment by Paul R. Trebilco, *Jewish Communities in Asia Minor,* SNTSMS 69 (Cambridge: Cambridge University Press, 1991), pp. 127-44 (esp. 143 for this context).

70. *Apud* Origen, *Cels.* 5.41 (trans. Chadwick). The identification of Jupiter/Zeus ὕψιστος with the God of the Jews was of course present already in Varro (see the collection of texts in Menaham Stern, *Greek and Latin Authors on Jews and Judaism,* 3 vols. [Jerusalem: Israel Academy of Sciences and Humanities, 1974-84], 1:210-11) and continued through late antiquity. See, e.g., Damascius, *Isid.* 141 (*apud* Photius, *Bibliotheca*): "[Isidorus wrote] that on this mountain there is a most holy sanctuary of Zeus the Highest [ὕψιστος] to whom Abraham the father of the old Hebrews consecrated himself" (trans. Stern, 2:674). One does not have to argue that the populus was consciously aware of the Platonic or Stoic philosophical pressure toward one supreme being — refracted differently through different (local) gods — to note the intermingling of divine names (Zeus Sarapis/Attis/Dionysius, etc.).

71. For Luke's use of καταγγέλλω, see esp. Acts 4:2; 13:38; 16:21(!); 17:3, 18, 23; 26:23.

God. Rather, it is to point out that the reader can realistically imagine that the Gentile audience of Paul and his companions (ἡμεῖς, v. 17) would have heard the mantic's cry as a polytheistic interpretation of Christian proclamation — that is, these are the prophets of the Most High (ὁ ὕψιστος Ζεύς) who provide healing (σωτηρία).[72] Indeed, as Klauck suggests, this conscription of God's identity by local religious tradition may well be the (implied) reason for Paul's annoyance (v. 18).[73]

The ambiguity in the phrase τοῦ θεοῦ τοῦ ὑψίστου, however, lasts only until the exorcism, at which time the identity of the Most High receives christological specification: ὁ θεὸς ὁ ὕψιστος is not Ζεὺς ὕψιστος (or any other "supreme being") but the God who works σωτηρία through the name of Jesus Christ (cf. Acts 4:12!). Moreover, prior to this specification, it is not clear within the world of the story that Paul's proclamation necessarily entails an attack upon pagan religiousness. But the explicit appearance of the name Jesus Christ involves a simultaneous confrontation with a pagan πνεῦμα and the economic practices that depend upon pneumatic presence. That the citizens of Philippi find the implications of this confrontation threatening is made clear by the ensuing events, in which the power of Jesus Christ is interpreted narratively as a force of subversion for the religio-economic habits of the polis (16:19-24).

Second, though some scholars note the possible meaning of πύθων as "ventriloquist,"[74] such a reading makes little sense here.[75] However much the double accusative may surprise us,[76] it seems clear that the meaning is something like "a pythian/pythonic spirit."[77] The description is not of linguistic

---

72. On the noneschatological meaning of σωτηρία for pagans, Nock, *Conversion*, p. 9, is concise.

73. Klauck, *Magic and Paganism*, p. 69.

74. Werner Foerster, "πύθων," *TDNT* 6:917-20.

75. See too the still-relevant critique of ventriloquism in general as a way to explain the phenomena of divination, prophecy, etc. in E. R. Dodds, *The Greeks and the Irrational* (Berkeley: University of California Press, 1951), pp. 71-72, with notes.

76. Barrett, *Acts*, 2:785.

77. The girl, that is, has "a spirit, a pythian/pythonic one," taking the accusatives in apposition. Though a larger resonance with the official priestess (πυθία or πυθιάς) in Delphi or its mythological prehistory could well be intended (see Beverly Roberts Gaventa, *The Acts of the Apostles*, ANTC [Nashville: Abingdon, 2003], p. 238), "official" cultic religion is not primarily in view here. In the first instance, πύθων is used at this point, rather, in a more general sense of one of the many and various fortunetellers of the ancient world (see, e.g., the tale of the nameless but influential wanderer in Plutarch, *Def. orac.* 421A-E, or Lucian, *Alex.* 9, which mentions traveling mantics [μαντεύεσθαι] as if they were a commonplace; and Dio

trickery but of the animating spirit that is the source of the oracles (μαντευομένη, v. 16).[78] It is this spirit of divination — in Plutarch's language, the δαίμων[79] — that is the immediate target of Paul's exorcism. This emerges clearly in v. 18, where Luke is careful to differentiate the spirit (σοι) from the girl (ἀπ' αὐτῆς) through Paul's direct address to the πνεῦμα: "I charge *you* in the name of Jesus Christ to come out from *her.*"

Thus it is, third, that the intense anger of the masters is narratively intelligible. It is not that Paul has announced the nature of a ventriloquist's linguistic trick to the wider public in order to enlighten their minds, but rather that he has destroyed the means by which the oracles were produced. The display of power through the evocation of the name Jesus Christ has removed *dynamically* — rather than simply epistemologically — the economic benefit derived from the possession of the girl. The masters own the παιδίσκη, not the πνεῦμα. The πνεῦμα has gone out (ἐξῆλθεν).[80] Indeed, the text may even suggest that this display of Jesus Christ's superior power is visible to the masters: they see (ἰδόντες) that the hope of their gain has gone out (ἐξῆλθεν).[81]

Finally, it is this dynamic character of the exorcism that is at bottom what is so fundamentally disruptive in Philippi. If Cicero is right, there had long been philosophical criticism of μαντική (*Div.* 1.4ff.; *Nat. d.* 2.3.9), at least

---

Chrysostom, *Disc.* 1.56, who contrasts a true mantic with the οἱ πολλοὶ τῶν λεγομένων ἐνθέων ἀνδρῶν καὶ γυναικῶν — the many men and women who are only *said* to be inspired). Cf. too the plural "pythons" in Pseudo-Clement, *Hom.* 9.16.3: ὅτι καὶ πύθωνες μαντεύονται ἀλλ᾽ ὑφ᾽ ἡμῶν ὡς δαίμονες ὁρκιζόμενοι φυγαδεύονται ("for even pythons prophesy, but they are cast out by us as demons, and put to flight"). Klauck, *Magic and Paganism*, pp. 65-66, takes πύθων as a proper name, "a spirit, Python." This is an attractive translation in view of the emphasis upon the πνεῦμα in v. 18; yet in light of Lukan style, it is probably better to retain the adjectival sense (see BDF §242).

78. On μαντεία, κτλ. as oracle, etc., see LSJ 1079-80. We may also note that μαντεύεσθαι is used only here in the NT and thus never of Christian prophets. Luke's usage follows that of the LXX, where μαντεύεσθαι, κτλ. are uniformly employed in a critical sense and not of Israel's prophets.

79. See *Def. orac.* 417 et passim.

80. Cf. Plutarch, *Pyth. orac.* 402B-C, who notes the worry about the πυθία that "the spirit [πνεῦμα] has been completely quenched and her powers have forsaken her" (trans. Babbitt, LCL), or *Def. orac.* 418D, where Cleombrotus speaks, for the moment, for those who believe that the defection of the oracles should be attributed to the departure of the δαίμονες (cf. also, e.g., *Def. orac.* 438C-D).

81. Of course, it is entirely possible that 16:19 simply means that the masters become aware that the oracles will stop. But in light of the "form" of exorcism stories in general, it would not be out of character for there to be a demonstration of the spirit's departure.

in its more official forms.[82] Yet Paul's action is hardly the type of intellectual stroke that can be parried by the piety of the masses. To the contrary, the vanquishing of the pythonic spirit is a tear in the basic fabric of pagan popular religion in that it demonstrates publicly the weakness of the pagan πνεῦμα in the face of the missionaries and their message. Inasmuch as such religious life was woven together with material gain,[83] such a tear means the unraveling of mantic-based economics as well (v. 19). If it is anywhere near true that "prophetic persons were to be found everywhere, in the cities, the countryside, in every cultural zone of the Empire,"[84] the economic effect could well be considerable. In this sense, the masters of the παιδίσκη perceive rightly that the power of the name Jesus Christ extends beyond one mantic; Paul and Silas are in fact "disturbing the city" (v. 20).

Verse 21 thus encapsulates the juxtaposition of perspectives present in the conflict: καὶ καταγγέλλουσιν ἔθη ἃ οὐκ ἔξεστιν ἡμῖν παραδέχεσθαι οὐδὲ ποιεῖν ῾Ρωμαίοις οὖσιν. Of course, if we read from Luke's perspective and take οὐκ ἔξεστιν in v. 21 in a strictly legal sense, the charges are untrue and incapable of substantiation, as we know from the magistrates' decision to release Paul and Silas in peace (16:36, *prior* to their knowledge that Paul and Silas are Roman citizens). The missionaries are not calling for riotous insurrection (στάσις). Yet read from within the perspective of the characters who utter the charges, it must be admitted that, despite their motivation (v. 19), they have witnessed in Paul's exorcism the inherently destabilizing power of Jesus Christ for the pagan way of life. The recognition of the supe-

82. Cicero mentions Xenophanes. See also Dodds, *The Greeks and the Irrational*, p. 190, who makes reference to Cicero's note, along with other evidence.

83. In addition to this passage itself, see, e.g., Cicero, *Div.* 2.132-33, who mentions diviners who "prophesy for money" and "beg a coin": "I [Ennius] do not recognize fortunetellers, or those who prophesy for money, or necromancers, or mediums, whom your friend Appius makes it a practice to consult . . . for they are not diviners either by knowledge or skill. . . . From those to whom they promise wealth they beg a coin . . ." (trans. Falconer, LCL); and Plato, *Resp.* 2.364B-C, who knows of nonprofessional diviners that are the equivalent of door-to-door religious salesmen.

84. Lane Fox, *Pagans and Christians*, p. 207. Cf. Ramsay MacMullen, *Enemies of the Roman Order: Treason, Unrest, and Alienation in the Empire* (Cambridge, Mass.: Harvard University Press, 1966), p. 128: "In the Roman empire, a universal confidence that the future could be known either through rites of official priests on public occasions, or privately, produced an infinitely combustible audience for predictions." At the level of more official oracles, scholars have long noted that Plutarch's *De defectu oraculorum* is not the final word on the subject. Business in Delphi may have slowed, but it was booming in Abonuteichos. See, e.g., MacMullen, *Paganism in the Roman Empire*, pp. 61-62 and 175-76 n. 55.

rior power of Jesus Christ is simultaneously the invalidation of the power claims of other πνεύματα. As Ramsay MacMullen has rightly noted, "the unique force of Christian wonder-working . . . lies in the fact that *it destroyed belief as well as creating it* — that is, if you credited it, you had then to credit the view that went with it, denying the character of god to all other divine powers whatsoever."[85] To adopt the ἔθη advocated by these missionaries, as in fact happens in the Philippian pericopae both preceding and following (Lydia and the jailer), would thus be to accept (παραδέχεσθαι) and to embody (ποιεῖν) a set of convictions that run counter to (οὐκ ἔξεστιν) the religious life of the polis. In this way, too, the ὄχλος and στρατηγοί — doubtless encouraged by the Ἰουδαῖοι/Ῥωμαῖοι contrast[86] — are given credible motive in the logic of the narrative to join in the attack (vv. 22-23). Harbingers of economic and/or religious disaster rarely elicit affection. Given such a confrontational display of power, it is hardly surprising that after their beating and imprisonment, the missionaries are finally asked to leave the city (vv. 22-24, 39).

IV. Conclusion

In an article that attempted to explore Luke's "common ground with paganism," F. G. Downing concluded that in Acts "only the persistent literalists are under attack."[87] At a glance, one can see how Luke's criticism of "literalist" views of statues and images (Acts 17:24-25, 29) — if taken in isolation — could generate such a conclusion. Upon a closer reading of the evidence, however, Downing's proposal can be seen to fall far short of the mark.

As the scenes in the Roman colonies of Lystra and Philippi illustrate, the apocalypse of God to the Gentiles does not merely offer a professor's remonstrance to the simple-minded but, much more radically, exposes the profound incommensurability between different theological frameworks and the resultant overall construal of human existence. This is no less true in Iconium, Thessalonica, Athens, Ephesus, and elsewhere. The particular nar-

---

85. MacMullen, *Christianizing the Roman Empire*, pp. 108-9, emphasis original.

86. For a compendium of ancient attitudes toward Jews, see Stern, *Greek and Latin Authors*. Roman citizenship is obviously an important aspect of this passage (cf. 16:37-38), particularly because of Philippi's status as a *colonia*, but the issues involved, regrettably, cannot be treated here.

87. F. G. Downing, "Common Ground with Paganism in Luke and Josephus," *NTS* 28 (1982): 557.

rative segments vary in intensity, of course,[88] but seen as a whole, the picture is one of collision between Christian mission and constitutive aspects of pagan culture. Gods and goddesses are challenged, important rulers and authorities intervene, magicians and spirits are vanquished, money and jobs are lost, books are burned, riots break out, missionaries are persecuted and/ or flee, and the world is turned upside down. Acts is thus not a book of minor cultural remodeling but rather a narrative exposition of another way of life. In Martha Nussbaum's terms, Luke attempts to "unwrite" the culture-forming stories of paganism by offering a different narrative that construes the entirety of reality in light of the God of Israel's act in Jesus.[89]

To unwrite culture-forming stories is not so much to criticize the various cultural details that exist in the foreground of life — particular forms of speech, patterns of behavior, etc. — as it is to redo the *background* of life against and because of which all of these particular details are intelligible. Such unwriting in its theological sense, that is, pertains to the entirety of life inasmuch as it attempts to rearticulate the comprehensive context in which the various aspects of life make sense.[90] To rearticulate the background of life is to re-create the world in which one lives; it requires, therefore, nothing less than a new way of being. Precisely in this way, the shift involved in coming to inhabit another comprehensive or background story is the move toward an alternative culture.[91]

88. Many scholars, for example, would see Paul's speech in Athens as a placid, philosophical discussion. This view, however, overlooks the significance of the Socratic echoes and the role of the Areopagus as the Athenian tribunal. On this latter point in particular, see the excellent article of Timothy D. Barnes, "An Apostle on Trial," *JTS* 20 (1969): 407-19.

89. Martha Nussbaum, "Narrative Emotions: Beckett's Genealogy of Love," *Ethics* 98 (1988): 225-54. Cf. διήγησις in Luke 1:1. Nussbaum's essay is focused upon (culturally constructed) "emotions" rather than theology per se. Yet her way of articulating the profound impact of alternative narratives provides a helpful language for thinking about the interface between the early Christians and pagans.

90. On the importance of the distinction between the "background" and "foreground" of life, see Charles Taylor, *Philosophical Arguments* (Cambridge, Mass.: Harvard University Press, 1995), esp. pp. 132-33.

91. After two millennia of Christian influence upon the Western imagination, it can be difficult to grasp again what it would be like to have an entire theological horizon fundamentally undone, and yet this is precisely what we must attempt to do if we are to understand the cultural dynamics of the early Christian encounters with pagan culture. Paradoxically perhaps, in recent history it was Nietzsche who famously put clearly the issue of a totally and radically different pattern of life on the basis of a theological vision undone: "'Whither is God' [cried the madman]. 'I shall tell you. We have killed him — you and I. All of us are his murderers. But how have we done this? How were we able to drink up the sea? *Who gave us the sponge to wipe*

Such unwriting does not mean that Luke's theological vision is developed in an effort to engineer directly a political coup, as the depiction of Paul — echoing that of Jesus himself — makes plain.[92] Yet because of the structuring role of "God" for all of human life, the concrete explication of God's identity positions followers of the Way resolutely against the grain of pagan culture. Indeed, for Gentiles there is a "taking out" (λαβεῖν ἐξ, Acts 15:14). To embrace the theological vision of Acts is in principle at once to abandon traditional cultic practice; it is not to add yet another name to the high god atop the pyramid of powers but is to reject all other claims to ultimate divine power.[93] The early Christians thus differed substantially from pagan philosophy — the closest pagan analogue to early Christianity, as Nock saw long ago — and from pagan polytheism. Where the former could offer "a life with a scheme,"[94] it did not require a rejection of traditional cultic practices, even in the face of sophisticated theological criticism of those practices. Where the latter could absorb virtually countless divine beings, it was not structurally open to one that demanded the denial of the rest.

These differences point to a crucial aspect in the attempt to trace the cultural profile of God's identity, namely, the myth of pagan tolerance. It is true, of course, that philosophy had the intellectual space for criticism of a "superstitious" understanding of religious practice and that polytheism had substantial theological space for other gods. It is superficial and anachronistic, however, to assume that such space was roomy enough to accommodate a challenge that would potentially abolish entire sets of practices that held together the fabric of pagan life.[95] The ideals of modern Western liberalism

---

away the entire horizon? What did we do when we unchained this earth from its sun? Whither is it moving now? Whither are we moving now? Away from all suns? Are we not plunging continually? Backward, sideward, forward, in all directions? Is there any up or down left? Are we not straying as through an infinite nothing? Do we not feel the breath of empty space? Has it not become colder? Is not night and more night coming on all the while? Must not lanterns be lit in the morning?'" Friedrich Nietzsche, *The Gay Science* §125, trans. Walter Kaufmann, *The Portable Nietzsche*, ed. Kaufmann (New York: Viking, 1954), p. 95, emphasis mine.

92. Paul is falsely accused of στάσις by the rhetorician Tertullus (Acts 24:5; cf. 23:10). Jesus, too, in contrast to Barabbas (Luke 23:18, 25), is not guilty of στάσις or perverting the people (23:14-15, 20, 22); he is, rather, δίκαιος, as the centurion at the cross confirms (23:47; cf. esp. 22:52). See further Rowe, "Luke-Acts and the Imperial Cult," pp. 287-88, with notes.

93. On the pyramid of divine powers, see MacMullen, *Paganism in the Roman Empire*, pp. 73-94.

94. Nock, *Conversion*, p. 167.

95. Cf. Seneca, *Ep.* 90, who wrote of philosophy: "From her side religion never departs, nor duty, nor justice, nor any of the whole company of virtues which cling together in close-

have all too often been read back into antiquity.[96] As a leading ancient historian has recently put it:

> "Polytheism" . . . is often seen as a tolerant and open religious system. It is associated with amateur priests, who lacked authority, and with an absence of dogma, orthodoxy and heresy. Already having many gods, it is attributed the capacity to accommodate even more at any time. This romantic view of Greek religious liberalism has little to commend it. The absence of dogmas did not entail that anything was permitted, nor was the pluralism of gods open-ended.[97]

Luke would agree. To follow the Way of God is to be confronted by the cultural limits of ancient pluralism. That such limits are, in the narrative of Acts, frequently enforced with violence only serves to indicate the depth of the conflict. God is the measure of all things: theology is a total way of life. This both historic paganism and the book of Acts seemed to sense, the one as threat and the other as promise.

---

united fellowship" (trans. Gummere, LCL). "Religion" as a separate or private sphere of life — distinct from politics, for example — is of course a modern construct: see, e.g., Lane Fox, *Pagans and Christians*, p. 82: "Civic cults . . . were only some of the many times for regulated worship in a pagan city. If we look beyond them, we can appreciate the gods' role on every level of social life and their pervasive presence . . . in early Christians' existence"; Nock, *Conversion*, p. 272: "Religion in Greece and Rome was not a distinct and separate aspect of life, but something which ran through all its phases"; and Young, *Biblical Exegesis*, p. 50: "Ancient religion was indistinguishable from culture."

96. For the philosophical issue here, see Taylor's chapter entitled "The Politics of Recognition," in *Philosophical Arguments*, pp. 225-56.

97. Price, *Religions of the Ancient Greeks*, p. 67. Cf. Parker, *Athenian Religion*, who writes that "no Greek surely would have supposed that an impious opinion should be permitted to circulate out of respect for freedom of speech" (p. 209) and that, with respect to Athenian polytheism in particular, "we are dealing not with principled tolerance but with a failure to live up to intolerant principles" (p. 210).

"They Bear Witness to Me": The Psalms in the Passion Narrative of the Gospel of John

Marianne Meye Thompson

Like so many early Christian authors, John quotes the Old Testament as a witness to Jesus by demonstrating how specific aspects of his ministry, and particularly his suffering and death, were foreshadowed or foretold there. But John introduces Old Testament quotations differently in the first and second parts of the Gospel, and it is particularly the quotations in the second part that fit John's apologetic agenda. In the first part of the Gospel (1:1–12:16), John introduces Old Testament quotations with the phrase "as it is written";[1] in the second part of the Gospel (12:17–19:42), he uses some variation of the formula "that the scripture might be fulfilled" (with a form of the verb πληρόω).[2]

Those texts cited in the second part of the Gospel focus specifically on Jesus' rejection or death. In 12:38-40, where John first introduces an Old Testament citation with explicit reference to fulfillment of a biblical text, he accounts for Jesus' rejection by his contemporaries with twin quotations from Isaiah: "Lord, who has believed our report, and to whom has the arm of the Lord been revealed?" (Isa. 53:1), and "He has blinded their eyes and hardened their heart, lest they should see with their eyes and perceive with their

---

1. With the verb γράφειν; 6:31, 45; 8:17; 10:34; 12:14; so also 15:25. But see 12:38, "that the word spoken by the prophet Isaiah might be fulfilled," which is at a turning point in the Gospel. Scripture quotations not otherwise identified are from the RSV.

2. John 13:18; 15:25; 17:12; 19:24, 36, 37. The quotation formula at 19:28 uses the verb τελειόω. There are no explicit quotations from Scripture in chs. 20-21; the only reference to "Scripture" is found in 20:9: "for as yet they did not understand the scripture, that he must rise from the dead" (NRSV).

heart, and turn for me to heal them" (Isa. 6:10).[3] These two quotations sum-marize the first part of the Gospel, typically called the Book of Signs; the rest of the quotations in the second part of the Gospel belong to the so-called Book of the Passion.[4] But since the scriptural quotations in John 12:38-40 share the same introductory formula with the rest of the quotations in chapters 13-19 — where Jesus' last meal with his disciples, his arrest, trial, and crucifixion are actually narrated — they too adumbrate the significance of Scripture in connection with the events of Jesus' passion.

With respect to the function of scriptural citations in John, Craig Evans comments:

> Whereas in the first half of the Gospel Jesus performs his many "signs" and conducts his ministry "just as it is written," in the second half of the Gospel Jesus' rejection and crucifixion take place "in order that Scripture be fulfilled." Far from proving that Jesus was not Israel's Messiah (as is implied by such a statement as, "We have heard from the Law that the Messiah remains forever" [12.34]), his rejection and death fulfilled Scripture and so proved that he really was the Messiah.[5]

While Evans's comment can scarcely be gainsaid, it can be sharpened, particularly with reference to the quotations in the second part of the Gospel. First, taken together, the scriptures cited in 12:38–19:42 bear witness, as Evans hints, to Jesus' rejection, as do the quotations from Isaiah that summarize the predominantly negative response to Jesus' signs. The belief that Scripture testifies to Jesus' identity as Israel's Messiah lies behind those texts, but the actual quotations foreground the negative response to him. It is Israel's unbelief, the rejection of Jesus by "his own" (1:11), that particularly troubles the evangelist and demands a scriptural explanation.[6]

---

3. On the function of these dual quotations from Isaiah, see Martin Hengel, "The Old Testament in the Fourth Gospel," in *The Gospels and the Scriptures of Israel*, ed. Craig A. Evans and W. Richard Stegner, JSNTSup 104 (Sheffield: Sheffield Academic, 1994), pp. 392-93.

4. These terms come from C. H. Dodd, *The Interpretation of the Fourth Gospel* (Cambridge: Cambridge University Press, 1953); Raymond E. Brown and others modified them somewhat, so that Book of Signs and Book of Glory are today more common, although, in my view, less apt.

5. Craig A. Evans, *Word and Glory: On the Exegetical and Theological Background of John's Prologue*, JSNTSup 89 (Sheffield: JSOT Press, 1993), p. 176.

6. See here also Bruce G. Schuchard, *Scripture within Scripture: The Interrelationship of*

Second, with few exceptions,[7] the passages that John cites in the second part of the Gospel, after the summary quotations from Isaiah in chapter 12, come from the Psalms. In appropriating the witness of these psalms, John has stamped them with his own peculiar interpretation. To be specific, while these psalms figure in the passion narratives of the other Gospels, John favors portions of these "royal lament psalms" to portray Jesus as the King who was maltreated, pursued, or deserted by his contemporaries.[8] Although the Psalms were traditionally thought to have been written by David, as the later assignment to various aspects of David's life also suggests, John never notes that these quotations come from the Psalms (cf. Luke 20:42; 24:44; Acts 1:20), nor does he make reference to David, their alleged author, as do other New Testament authors (Matt. 22:43; Mark 12:36; Luke 20:42; Acts 2:25; 4:25; Rom. 4:6; 11:9).[9] For John, these passages are important, first, because they are *Scripture,* and, second, because these scriptures foreshadow the destiny of the Messiah, the eschatological King of Israel.[10] David's fate and experiences portend the path of the Messiah — and the particular experiences that are held up for reflection are those in which the speaker experiences hostility or enmity of one sort or another. In these psalms, John finds prefigured the one who "came to his own home" but was not received by his own (1:11). Although the true King of Israel (1:49), he was denied and betrayed by his disciples (13:18), "handed over" by and to the Jewish authorities (18:30, 35,

---

Form and Function in the Explicit Old Testament Citations in the Gospel of John, SBLDS 133 (Atlanta: Scholars Press, 1992), ch. 7, "His Own People Received Him Not," pp. 85-90; John Painter, "Scripture and Unbelief in John 12:36b-43," in *The Gospels and the Scriptures of Israel,* ed. Evans and Stegner, pp. 430-31.

7. In addition to the introductory quotations from Isaiah at John 12:38-40, John quotes Zech. 12:10 at 19:37. The problem of identifying the OT quotation in 19:36 will be taken up below.

8. On the point that the psalms in the passion narratives are invoked not to present the "paradigmatic righteous sufferer" but rather the suffering and death of Jesus, the King of the Jews, see Martin Hengel, *The Atonement: The Origins of the Doctrine in the New Testament* (Philadelphia: Fortress, 1981), pp. 40-41; Donald H. Juel, *Messianic Exegesis: Christological Interpretation of the Old Testament in Early Christianity* (Philadelphia: Fortress, 1988), pp. 102-3; Margaret Daly-Denton, *David in the Fourth Gospel: The Johannine Reception of the Psalms* (Leiden: Brill, 2000), pp. 238-39.

9. Daly-Denton, *David in the Fourth Gospel,* p. 318, comments: "It is important to remember that Davidic 'authorship' of the psalms was a 'given' so obvious that it did not require reiteration every time a psalm was cited."

10. As A. T. Hanson, "John's Use of Scripture," in *The Gospels and the Scriptures of Israel,* ed. Evans and Stegner, p. 363, rightly notes, Jesus' "Davidic origin is not emphasized, and it would probably be more accurate to say that the Davidic ruler is a type of Christ."

36; 19:11, 16), and crucified by Gentiles. This is the shape of Jesus' fate, and John finds it prefigured in the Scriptures.[11]

In his seminal discussion "Christ Prays the Psalms," Richard Hays suggests that the church appropriated the Davidic psalms in the context of the passion narrative because it saw both the sufferings and the vindication of Israel, embodied in the sufferings and the vindication of its king, to have been accomplished in an eschatologically definitive way in the death and resurrection of Jesus. Thus, Hays notes, "the movement of the royal lament psalms from suffering to triumph is correlated hermeneutically with the story of Jesus' death and resurrection."[12] But for John, it is not so much the movement from suffering to triumph as the contrast between persecution by human beings and vindication by God that determines John's choice and quotation of the psalms. In John's use, these psalms might more aptly be titled "psalms of the rejected king." In his monumental tome *The Death of the Messiah,* Raymond Brown discusses the possibility that the Old Testament provided the raw stuff from which the passion narratives of the Gospels were constructed. Speaking in particular of Psalm 22, he notes that, at most, such an Old Testament reference led early Christians to do three things: (1) concentrate on certain details in the passion narrative (such as the piercing of Jesus' feet and hands); (2) dramatize the mocking hostility toward Jesus from those around the cross; and (3) highlight the reversal in Jesus' abandoned death and subsequent victory.[13] It is the third point that is missing in John: Jesus is not abandoned — at least not by God — in his death, and the movement is not from abandonment to victory. Jesus is mocked and rejected by his contemporaries, but he is never abandoned by God, even when on the cross.

In exploring more fully John's use of the Psalms, we will begin with a comparison of the use of the Psalms in the passion narratives of the Synoptic Gospels with that in John. Such a review can be cursory at best, but it will

11. See also Andrew T. Lincoln, *Truth on Trial: The Lawsuit Motif in the Fourth Gospel* (Peabody, Mass.: Hendrickson, 2000), p. 54.

12. Richard B. Hays, "Christ Prays the Psalms: Israel's Psalter as Matrix of Early Christology," in *The Conversion of the Imagination: Paul as Interpreter of Israel's Scripture* (Grand Rapids: Eerdmans, 2005), pp. 101-18, quotation p. 111; reprinted from *The Future of Christology,* ed. Abraham J. Malherbe and Wayne A. Meeks (Minneapolis: Augsburg Fortress, 1993), pp. 122-36.

13. Raymond E. Brown, *The Death of the Messiah: From Gethsemane to the Grave; A Commentary on the Passion Narratives in the Four Gospels,* ABRL (New York: Doubleday, 1994), p. 1462.

serve to show both that John uses different portions of the Psalms and that he uses them somewhat differently than do the other Gospels. Following this review, we shall look more closely at each of the psalms used by John in the passion narrative, showing the purposes for which John appropriates them. Finally, we shall consider how John's reading and citations of the Psalms might serve to shape our own readings of the Scriptures as witnesses to Christ.

The Use of the Psalms in the Passion Narratives

A number of psalms are thought to play a role in the passion narratives of the Synoptic Gospels. Here we shall discuss briefly the comparative use among the Gospels of (only) those psalms quoted or alluded to in the Gospel of John.[14] Undoubtedly, the most important of the psalms in the passion narratives is Psalm 22, which is used differently by the different evangelists. Perhaps best known of the "last words" of Christ is the quotation, uttered by the dying Jesus in Matthew (27:46) and Mark (15:34), of Psalm 22:1: "My God, my God, why hast thou forsaken me?" Neither in Luke nor in John does Jesus speak these words. The difference may be explained in part by noting the import of those final words in Matthew and Mark, on the one hand, and Jesus' final words in Luke and then in John. In Luke, Jesus' last words are a prayer, "Into thy hands I commit my Spirit" (23:46), taken from Psalm 31:5; in John, the confident declaration "It is finished" (19:30). Hence, the so-called cry of dereliction found in Matthew and Mark has given way to Jesus' statement of trust in God in Luke and to Jesus' summation of his mission in John. The apparent sense of abandonment expressed by Jesus (in Matthew and Mark) gives way to rather different sentiments in the other two Gospels. One might note that in the case of John, the absence of the quotation of Psalm 22:1 fits with the fact that the entire scene of Jesus' agony and prayer in Gethsemane fails to find a place in the narrative of Jesus' passion (but see John 12:27). In John, there is no prayer in the garden, no struggle to know or do the will of God, because Jesus is the one who always does

14. The psalms cited by John in the passion narrative include Psalms 22, 34, 41, and 69. In each, the speaker finds himself in some peril or distress, surrounded or pursued by his foes, and pleads to God for deliverance. For a list of other possible allusions to the Psalms in the Gospel passion narrative, see the discussion in Brown, *Death of the Messiah*, pp. 1451-65, and the bibliography cited there. As a rule, references to the Psalms here follow the English versification; where relevant, the differences in the LXX and MT are noted.

the will of the Father (4:34; 5:30; 6:38-39; 8:28); he finishes that work on the cross.[15]

Matthew also uses a near quotation of Psalm 22:8 ("He committed his cause to the LORD; let him deliver him, let him rescue him, for he delights in him!") to provide the substance of the taunts hurled against Jesus on the cross: "He trusts in God; let God deliver him now, if he desires him; for he said, 'I am the Son of God'" (Matt. 27:43).[16] While the words are taken from the psalm, Matthew neither refers to the source of the quotation nor indicates any connection between the voicing of the taunts here and their utterance in the psalm. Mark (15:30-31) and Luke (23:35) record taunts against Jesus, calling on him to save himself if indeed he is the Messiah, but the echoes of the psalm are far fainter. It is difficult to tell whether either evangelist has this portion of Psalm 22 in view at all. The taunt from Psalm 22 is absent from John.

Finally, the incident of casting lots for Jesus' garments, which appears in all four Gospels (Matt. 27:35; Mark 15:24; Luke 23:34; John 19:24), is tied to Psalm 22. But John alone quotes Psalm 22:18 — "they divide my garments among them"[17] — at this point, noting that this event "was to fulfill the scripture." The Synoptic evangelists neither quote the psalm explicitly nor indicate any correlation between what happened to Jesus' garments and the incident recounted in the psalm. John does both and thus demonstrates that the soldiers' stake in Jesus' clothing fulfilled the scripture. What happened to Jesus at the hands of those who put him to death was written about in the psalm.

Only John makes use of Psalm 34:20, in John 19:36.[18] Here the soldiers

---

15. Similarly, the final words of Jesus in Luke seal Jesus' submission expressed in his prayer "not my will, but thine, be done" (22:42). Luke's account of Gethsemane is more compact than either Matthew's or Mark's. Jesus' prayer in Luke is somewhat closer to the Lord's Prayer, "Thy will be done," and is framed by the admonition to his disciples, "Pray that you may not enter into temptation" (22:40, 46).

16. In Matthew's account, those at the cross taunt Jesus as "King of Israel" (27:42; so also Mark 15:32).

17. John's citation matches that of the LXX exactly. Whereas the MT (22:19) has an imperfect (יחלקו בגדי להם), which is rendered "they divide my garments among them" by English translations, the LXX (21:19), followed by John, has an aorist, rendered by most translations "they divided my garments among them."

18. The reference is contested; I shall argue below that John intends a primary reference to this psalm rather than to Exod. 12:46. So also, among others, C. H. Dodd, *Historical Tradition in the Fourth Gospel* (Cambridge: Cambridge University Press, 1963), pp. 42-44, 131; John A. T. Robinson, *The Priority of John*, ed. J. F. Coakley (London: Meyer Stone, 1985), p. 153.

had come to break Jesus' legs in order to hasten his death before the onset of Passover. The incident is not in the other Gospels; hence, neither is there an allusion to this psalm. Similarly, only John quotes Psalm 41:9, "he . . . has lifted his heel against me," noting that even Judas' treachery could be explained by the fact that "the scripture may be fulfilled" (13:18). Although the other Gospels report Judas' betrayal of Jesus, none link it to the citation of a psalm. Finally, John alone cites Psalm 69 (69:4 = John 15:25; 69:9 = John 2:17; 69:21 = John 19:28). While the other Gospels report that Jesus was offered a sponge with vinegar (Matt. 27:48; Mark 15:36; Luke 23:36), only John reports that Jesus said "I thirst" and that this incident was in fulfillment of Scripture (John 19:28).[19]

In summary, we note that there are telling differences in the usage of these psalms in the Synoptic Gospels and in John. First, the Synoptics use Scripture more allusively. For example, while the Synoptic Gospels report that the soldiers cast lots for Jesus' garments, John alone notes that the incident fulfilled the scripture. Again, while the Synoptics note that Jesus was offered vinegar to drink, John alone sets the incident in the context of Jesus' acknowledgment of his thirst, which John reports took place in order "to fulfil the scripture." To be sure, the Synoptics do sometimes place words of the Psalms directly in Jesus' mouth. Psalm 22:1 ("My God, my God, why hast thou forsaken me?") is attributed to Jesus in both Matthew and Mark, and Psalm 31:5 ("Into thy hands I commit my spirit") to Jesus in Luke. But curiously, the Synoptics do not introduce these as citations of Scripture, as John does regularly, nor do they note that the words spoken or the incidents narrated fulfill Scripture or are spoken of in Scripture (John 13:18; 15:25; 19:24, 28, 36; less directly, 2:17). In other words, the Synoptics do not make the scriptural source of the quotation or allusion explicit, whereas John does. It is particularly important in John's account of Jesus' crucifixion that what happened to him be understood as foretold in the Scriptures. Since the Scriptures bear witness to him as Messiah (1:45-49; 5:39, 46), they must also witness that the peculiar shape of this King's fate is also found written in the pages of Scripture.

What is further noteworthy in John's use of these Psalms is not only what he takes up and quotes but also what he omits. The absence of Psalm 22:1 ("My God, my God, why hast thou forsaken me?") from the Fourth Gospel is often noted. Like the other Gospels, John does not use portions of the Psalms that express human failure, folly, or sin, but neither does

---

19. It is also possible that Ps. 22:15 is in view here.

John quote that portion of Psalm 22 that gives the impression of God's absence or distance — which would not fit with John's portrayal of Jesus as the Righteous One who is never alone because God is with him (John 8:29; 16:32). God did not abandon Jesus on the cross, nor did Jesus experience a sense of being forsaken by God. Instead, virtually every line of quotation from the Psalms in John emphasizes the malice of the speaker's enemies, who betray, hate, seek to destroy, and falsely accuse Jesus. The scriptures cited are used to vindicate Jesus as Messiah and to account for the hostility against him by his numerous enemies, since the fate he suffered was not that commonly anticipated for God's Messiah. Jesus' fate follows the path described in the Psalms, which, not incidentally, is the path of David, king of Israel.[20]

John makes more extensive use of the Psalms in the passion narrative: he cites or alludes to more Psalms (22, 34, 41, 69 [3x]) than do any of the other Gospels; he uses them to account for specific aspects of Jesus' destiny, from his betrayal by Judas to his crucifixion (the bulk of the quotations) to his subsequent resurrection (69:9 in 2:17); and he emphasizes the point that what happened to Jesus fulfilled the Scriptures. This last point is particularly important and is underscored by John's repeated use of the statement "This took place in order to fulfil the scripture," or some variation thereof. In other words, for John the status of the citations as Scripture, and Jesus' fulfillment of them — precisely in his persecution and death — is of utmost significance.[21] What happened to Jesus was mysteriously written beforehand in the Scriptures of Israel: the fate of Israel's Messiah was actually found lodged in

---

20. In "Reading Scripture in Light of the Resurrection," in *The Art of Reading Scripture,* ed. Ellen F. Davis and Richard B. Hays (Grand Rapids: Eerdmans, 2003), p. 223, Richard Hays writes: "[A] reading of Psalm 69 after the passion and resurrection of Jesus would disclose that the psalm is to be read as a poetic prefiguration of the suffering and vindication of Jesus the Messiah, whose voice 'David' anticipated." In his actual choice of quotations, we might add, John stresses the means by which Jesus experienced that suffering, namely, through the hostile actions of his enemies.

21. One might note here the emphasis in John on "scripture." The term is used 12x in John; 4x in Matthew, 3x in Mark, 4x in Luke. Except for 5:39, John always uses the singular (γραφή) rather than the plural, likely because "scripture" denotes for him a particular verse. However, the point has often been made to the contrary, namely, that John is more interested in the fulfillment of Scripture as such than in the fulfillment of individual passages; see, e.g., Johannes Beutler, SJ, "The Use of 'Scripture' in the Gospel of John," in *Exploring the Gospel of John: In Honor of D. Moody Smith,* ed. R. Alan Culpepper and C. Clifton Black (Louisville: Westminster John Knox, 1996), pp. 147-48. Beutler notes a number of other interpreters who make the same point.

the pages of these texts.[22] The Scriptures, in other words, bear witness not only to Jesus as King but also to the kind of King that Jesus was, and the kind of followers one would expect him to have: "If the world hates you, know that it has hated me before it hated you" (John 15:18; cf. the citation of Ps. 69:4 in 15:25). We turn, then, to a closer look at John's use of the Psalms in his passion narrative.

The Psalms and the Death of Jesus in John

John's quotation of the Psalms in connection with the death of Jesus begins with the account of Jesus' last meal with his disciples. While not explicitly connected with Jesus' crucifixion, these quotations do read the Psalms as predicting or explaining Jesus' impending fate. Hence, John 13:18 quotes Psalm 41:9 ("He who ate my bread has lifted his heel against me") to account for the treachery of Judas.[23] Like David's, Jesus' foes could be found among his intimate friends. Similarly, a statement later in the Farewell Discourses, "they hated me without a cause" (15:25; cf. 15:18), quotes Psalm 69:4 with reference to Jesus.[24]

Psalm 69 supplies other quotations that present Jesus as the rejected or hunted King. The rest of Psalm 69:4 — "many are those who would destroy me, my enemies who accuse me falsely" (NRSV) — may be echoed particularly in Jesus' word interpreting his cleansing of the temple: "Destroy this

22. To the contrary, one might note, Justin Martyr argues that the passage had to apply to Jesus alone because Psalm 22 (Psalm 21, according to Justin) reads, "They pierced my hands and my feet," on which Justin comments to Trypho: "no one in your nation who has been called King or Christ has ever had his hands or feet pierced while alive, or has died in this mysterious fashion — to wit, by the cross — save this Jesus alone" (*Dial.* 97, ed. Roberts and Donaldson, *ANF* 1:248). For Justin, it is not the commonality with but rather the distinction from David's suffering that demands that this psalm be applied to Christ.

23. On the form and origin of the quotation, see Maarten Menken, *Old Testament Quotations in the Fourth Gospel: Studies in Textual Form,* CBET 15 (Kampen: Kok Pharos, 1996), pp. 123-38. Schuchard, *Scripture within Scripture,* pp. 114-16, shows the parallels between the accounts of Ahithophel's betrayal of David in 2 Samuel and Judas' betrayal of Jesus in John; Jewish interpretative traditions regarding Ahithophel are discussed by Daly-Denton in *David in the Fourth Gospel,* pp. 194-96. On the quotation of the OT here, see also J. Ramsey Michaels, "Betrayal and the Betrayer: The Uses of Scripture in John 13:18-19," in *The Gospels and the Scriptures of Israel,* ed. Evans and Stegner, pp. 459-74.

24. Psalm 69:4 also speaks of the psalmist's enemies who judge him unjustly (68:5 LXX: pursue unjustly, οἱ ἐκδιώκοντές με ἀδίκως; for the theme of just judgment in John, see 5:30; 7:24, 51; 8:15-16, 26).

temple, and in three days I will raise it up" (2:19). Set early in the narrative of John's Gospel, the cleansing of the temple foreshadows both the death and the resurrection of Jesus. Whereas Psalm 69 speaks of "many" who seek to "destroy me," so in the Gospel of John Jesus speaks of those who destroy the temple — an allusive prediction to his death by crucifixion. John thus adapts Psalm 69:9, "Zeal for thy house has consumed me," by changing the aorist κατέφαγεν ("has consumed," 68:10 LXX) to the future middle καταφάγεται ("will consume") on the apparent assumption that Jesus is the speaker in the psalm. From the use of this psalm in John 2, it is clear that Jesus will be consumed by forces hostile to him, even as the temple will be destroyed. In the Gospel of John, the Jewish Sanhedrin acknowledges that unless they are able to curb reaction to Jesus' ministry, the Romans will come and destroy their holy place (11:48-52). Little does Caiaphas realize, in his related prophecy, that not only will the Romans destroy the temple in Jerusalem; they will also crucify the one in whom God's glory dwells (1:14), and who will be raised up as an indestructible temple of God's presence.

Only the Fourth Gospel links the cleansing of the temple with a word about its destruction and rebuilding (2:19).[25] To be sure, Matthew, Mark, and Luke indicate that Jesus predicted the temple's destruction (Matt. 24:1-2; Mark 13:1-2; Luke 21:5-6), and these sayings are raised at Jesus' trial as charges against him (Matt. 26:59-61; 27:40; Mark 14:55-59; 15:29; cf. Acts 6:14). But John's is the only account to join the action in the temple with a statement concerning its destruction and rebuilding ("I will raise it up"). This point is significant for understanding Jesus as Messiah in John because in biblical texts it is the king, and particularly David the king, who desires to build a temple for God (2 Sam. 7:12-14; 1 Kings 5:3-5; 1 Chron. 22:10-11; 2 Chron. 2:1-5, 12; 6:7-10; Zech. 6:12-13).[26]

---

25. Alan R. Kerr, *The Temple of Jesus' Body: The Temple Theme in the Gospel of John*, JSNTSup 220 (Sheffield: Sheffield Academic, 2002), p. 84, summarizes eight possible readings of Ps. 69:9 in its context in John and concludes that in spite of the uncertainties of interpretation, it is clear that the psalmist suffered for his zeal, that he was ostracized, insulted, and alienated from his own family. One might also note the remainder of Ps. 69:9, "and the insults of those who insult thee have fallen on me," which makes explicit the reciprocity between God and the rejected king (John 15:24). Psalm 69:9 is quoted by Paul in Rom. 15:3; cf. Hays, "Christ Prays the Psalms," pp. 102 and 105. As Hays further notes, C. H. Dodd took Psalm 69 to be among those OT texts used by the early church in the development of Christology; see Dodd, *According to the Scriptures: The Sub-structure of New Testament Theology* (London: Nisbet, 1952), pp. 57-60.

26. David's role as the one who desires to build the temple is emphasized by the Chronicler. For further discussion of David as the founder of temple and cult in the OT narratives,

Although in John the account of the temple's cleansing does not follow upon the triumphal entry, with its acclamation of Jesus as "King of Israel" (John 12:13), the promise to "raise up" a temple recalls the hopes for a new and glorious temple and portends the arrival of the messianic age. The new temple that Jesus will build, however, is the temple of his risen body, a temple that shall never be destroyed and that will manifest God's glory in the world even as did the incarnate Word. In a nutshell, then, the Johannine account of Jesus' cleansing of the temple presents Jesus, the Messiah, the King of Israel (see 1:17; 1:41, 45, 49), as raising up an indestructible temple in which God's presence dwells precisely because this temple is holy and undefiled. That is to say, the hostility toward Jesus that leads to his death — his "destruction" — does not hinder his messianic mission or impugn his identity as Messiah.

The final reference to Psalm 69 is found in John 19:28-29, "After this Jesus, knowing that all was now finished (τετέλεσται), said (to fulfill the scripture [ἵνα τελειωθῇ ἡ γραφή]), 'I thirst.' A bowl full of vinegar stood there; so they put a sponge full of the vinegar on hyssop and held it to his mouth."[27] Because of the references to thirst and vinegar, this is often — and probably rightly — taken as an allusion to Psalm 69:21, "They gave me poison for food, and for my thirst they gave me vinegar to drink." In that psalm, these appear to be the hostile actions of the king's foes. In the Gospel, the psalm explains the actions of the Roman soldiers, as does the quotation from Zechariah, "They shall look on him whom they have pierced" (12:10), at 19:37.

---

see Daly-Denton, *David in the Fourth Gospel,* pp. 72-79; Kenneth E. Pomykala, *The Davidic Dynasty Tradition in Early Judaism: Its History and Significance for Messianism,* EJL 7 (Atlanta: Scholars Press, 1995), pp. 69-111. The image of the king as builder of the temple, and particularly of David as the one who desires to build the temple for God, is underscored in later strands of interpretation. For example, at 2 Sam. 7:11, where the MT reads "the LORD declares to you that the LORD will make you a house" (והגיד לך יהוה כי בית יעשה לך יהוה), the LXX reads "the Lord will tell you that you will build a house for him" (2 Kgdms. 7:11 LXX). In *Ant.* 7.334, Josephus retells the story of David's building an altar at the threshing floor of Araunah (2 Sam. 24:18-25; 1 Chron. 21:21-28), adding that David intended "to build a temple to God there." Furthermore, in some later Jewish texts a new temple is associated with the messianic age (4QFlor [4Q174]). Here it is not the son of David who builds a house for God but rather God who raises up the temple. Later, the Targums bear witness to the view that the Messiah would build the temple of the Lord (*Tg. 1 Chr.* 17:12-13; *Tg. Zech.* 6:12; *Tg. Isa.* 53:5).

27. Martin Hengel, "Old Testament in the Fourth Gospel," p. 393, argues that the evangelist's unique use of τελειοῦν at the point of Jesus' death marks "an increase over the previous formulaic πληροῦν" because it is linked with the "ultimate fulfillment" of all prophecy in the death of Jesus.

That quotation may have been prompted by the repeated concern in Zechariah 12 for "the house of David," as well as by the reference in Psalm 22 to the "company of evildoers" who "encircle me" and who "have pierced my hands and feet" (22:16). It is precisely as the King that Jesus is pierced.

This leads directly, then, to the (disputed) reference in John 19:36, "For these things took place that the scripture might be fulfilled, 'Not a bone of him shall be broken' (ὀστοῦν οὐ συντριβήσεται αὐτοῦ)." John does not specify which "scripture might be fulfilled," and commentators have suggested a reference either to Exodus 12:46, in which case Jesus is presented as the Passover Lamb, or to Psalm 34:20, in which case Jesus is presented primarily as the Righteous One vindicated by God; or to both. Although scholarly consensus seems to have preferred an allusion to Exodus 12:46, the Greek favors a primary reference to Psalm 34, for several reasons. First, the passive form of the verb (συντριβήσεται) in John's quotation corresponds better to the psalm (κύριος φυλάσσει πάντα τὰ ὀστᾶ αὐτῶν, ἓν ἐξ αὐτῶν οὐ συντριβήσεται, 33:21 LXX) than to the text in Exodus, which contains the imperative form of the verb (ὀστοῦν οὐ συντρίψετε ἀπ᾽ αὐτοῦ). Furthermore, whereas Exodus 12:46 gives a command to the Israelites regarding the celebration of Passover — they are not to break the bones of the Passover lamb — the psalm expresses a promise, as does its use in John: God shall guard his righteous one. In this sense, then, a quotation of the psalm fits better into the context of the passion narrative, where God's protection of the righteous, especially one regarded as Messiah, might well be understood to be threatened. In addition, since quotations from other psalms play an important role in both the Johannine passion narratives and in the passion narratives of the other Gospels, it seems more likely that John intends, first and foremost, an allusion to the promise of the psalm.[28] Indeed, there is no explicit reference to the Passover in 19:31-37. Although the rightful King has been pierced, not a bone of him shall be broken by those "who hate the righteous" (Ps. 34:19-21).[29] The context of the quota-

---

28. The argument that the intended reference is Exod. 12:46 hinges to a large extent on the argument that John wishes to present Jesus as the Passover Lamb, an argument that I consider less than persuasive, although it is widely accepted. The main problem, in a nutshell, is that in those places where John speaks of a lamb (1:29, 36), he does not mention Passover, and where Passover is in view (as it is in chapters 2, 6, and the passion narrative), there is no explicit reference to a lamb. John exploits the Passover connection especially in chapter 6, where Jesus is likened to the manna from heaven that God provides for the wilderness pilgrimage, and not to the Passover lamb whose blood secured Israel's release from Egypt.

29. Elsewhere in the NT, the Righteous One appears as a designation of Jesus (Acts 3:14;

tion in Psalm 34, with its note of hostility toward the righteous, provides further suggestive evidence that this is the passage that John has in view.[30]

One objection to the view that John quotes Psalm 34:20 here is that God has not rescued the righteous from "all their afflictions." Jesus, after all, dies on the cross. His bones may not be broken, but nearly everything else is. Still, it is difficult to believe that John would have thought that Jesus was somehow deserted by God, since the Gospel includes several assertions to the contrary. It is on the cross that God glorifies Jesus, on the cross that Jesus' work of making God known is finished. As Jesus elsewhere says, "he who sent me is with me; he has not left me alone, for I always do what is pleasing to him" (8:29; 16:32). These assertions are no less true of his death on the cross. The fact that his bones were not broken would have demonstrated that he was the Righteous One, chosen and vindicated by God — over against all other authorities, Jewish or Roman, who opposed him.

While the Psalms seem, on the one hand, to play a rather grim role in foretelling Jesus' path toward death, they also serve, on the other hand, as a witness to Jesus' identity as the elect one, the anointed, of God. On John's reading, the Psalms present Jesus, not as a desperate King seeking protection from his enemies and rescue by a seemingly absent God, but as a righteous King vindicated by God against those who falsely accuse and pursue him. Even as David, God's anointed, encountered hostility on the road to kingship, so Jesus — in his rejection and crucifixion — was prefigured in David's struggles with his contemporaries. In other words, when John himself "searches the scriptures" to see what witness they might bear to Jesus, he indeed finds that they testify to Jesus as the Messiah (e.g., 1:45-46), precisely because they portend the opposition that he encountered as King.

7:52; 22:14; 1 Pet. 3:18; 1 John 2:1). In *1 Enoch*, "the Righteous One" designates the eschatological deliverer (e.g., *1 En.* 38:2-3; 39:6; 53:6), also called the Son of Man. The substantive is not used in John to refer to Jesus, although the adjective is used with reference to his judgment (5:30; 7:24). For a discussion of "the Righteous One" as a standard epithet for the Messiah in early Jewish Christian circles, see Richard B. Hays, "Apocalyptic Hermeneutics: Habakkuk Proclaims 'The Righteous One,'" in *The Conversion of the Imagination*, pp. 119-42; reprinted from *The New Testament and Apocalyptic*, ed. J. Marcus and M. L. Soards (Sheffield: JSOT Press, 1988), pp. 191-215.

30. Günter Reim, *Studien zum alttestamentlichen Hintergrund des Johannesevangelium*, SNTSMS 22 (Cambridge: Cambridge University Press, 1974), p. 265, suggests that John never uses typology proper, but John's use of the Psalms argues against his contention. On this point, see Hanson, "John's Use of Scripture," pp. 362-65.

The Witness of the Scriptures

One could easily imagine a catena of psalms that would yield quite a different portrait of the King — honored, revered, and victorious. Indeed, the frequently quoted Psalm 110 portrays a king seated in a position of honor at the right hand of God. Yet this psalm, cited in the Synoptic Gospels and other New Testament texts (Matt. 22:44; Mark 12:36; Luke 20:42-43; Acts 2:34-35; Heb. 1:13; 5:6, 10), is not cited in John.[31] To state the obvious, John reads Jesus in light of the witness of the Psalms, but he also reads the Psalms in light of the concrete shape of Jesus' life and ministry,[32] anticipating the fate of Jesus' disciples as well as Jesus himself. Still, it is possible to read the Psalms and to be aware of Jesus' fate without reading the two as mutually illuminating, or at least not in the particular way that John finds them to be. As Andrew Lincoln points out, in the Gospel of John, Scripture, properly understood, bears witness to Jesus (5:38-39); but unless one is taught by God (6:45), reads Scripture in light of the resurrection of Jesus (2:17, 22), and is guided by the teaching of the Spirit of truth (14:26; 16:13-14), one hears the Scripture not as a witness to the identity of Jesus as the life-giving Word of God but as an accusing witness, a judge.[33] In short, one can "search [the Scriptures]" and learn that "no prophet is to rise from Galilee" (7:52), or one can search the Scriptures and hear the witness they bear to Jesus (5:39).

Those who hear (or read) the Scriptures so as to discern the testimony that they bear to Jesus do so not because they are particularly adept exegetes but because they participate in the realities spoken of and enacted by Jesus.[34]

---

31. Psalm 110 is perhaps alluded to elsewhere; notably, in Jesus' response to the high priest's question whether he is the Messiah ("You will see the Son of man seated at the right hand . . . ," Matt. 26:64; Mark 14:62; Luke 22:69), and elsewhere in the NT in references to Jesus' being seated — in the heavenly places, at the right hand, etc. — as in Rom. 8:34; Eph. 1:20; Col. 3:1; Heb. 1:3; Rev. 3:21. In the Johannine trial narratives, only Pilate asks Jesus about his identity as king (18:33-37); Jesus' response — "My kingship is not of this world" — may reflect the early Christian view of Jesus' enthronement at the "right hand of God" in the "heavenly places."

32. Hanson's argument that John inserts teaching, conversations, and incidents into the Gospel "that have no basis in his historical tradition if he believes he has justification in Scripture for doing so" ("John's Use of Scripture," pp. 370-72, quotation p. 370) surely overstates the case and misrepresents John's use of the OT. The shape of Jesus' life and fate constrain John's use of the texts.

33. Lincoln, *Truth on Trial*, pp. 54-56.

34. In what follows I am indebted to Markus Bockmuehl's discussion in *Seeing the Word: Refocusing New Testament Study*, STI (Grand Rapids: Baker Academic, 2006), pp. 70-72.

Alasdair MacIntyre put it this way: "What the reader . . . has to learn about him or herself is that it is only the self as transformed through and by the reading of the texts which will be capable of reading the texts aright."[35] The implied readers of the Gospel have adopted the stance of faith to which Jesus calls disciples and have undergone the "birth from above" of which he spoke to Nicodemus. They participate in those very same realities that are spoken of in the text: they have been born anew by the Spirit of God, who brings Jesus' word to remembrance (14:26), bears witness to Jesus (15:26), and guides into all truth (16:13). The Spirit thus works to grant fuller understanding of the truth of Jesus' identity (cf., e.g., 1 John 4:1-2, where appeals to Spirit-inspired prophecies ground divergent testimonies to the person of Jesus). Those who live out of the realities of faith promised by Jesus in the Gospel, who believe that "Jesus is the Messiah, the Son of God," read the Scriptures as pointing to him as the King of Israel. Given their faith in Jesus as Messiah, King of Israel, it is hard to imagine how any other reading of these psalms could make sense.

But this portrait of the implied reader of John's Gospel can easily be taken as cloyingly triumphalistic: those who read the Scriptures as pointing to Jesus understand that Jesus can be found in them. All others are left out of the discussion of Jesus' identity and the role of Scripture in bearing witness to him: those who are not taught by God do not understand Scripture; hence, if one does not read as John dictates, one is not taught by God. Can such hermeneutics ever engender more than dogmatic sectarianism?

Several aspects of John's reading of the Scriptures call for a second look and might well prompt one to read with humility. When read as John reads, Scripture highlights the recalcitrance of human beings, even God's own people, toward God. John reads the Psalms as prefiguring the hostility that Jesus, the King of Israel, would encounter, even as David, the king of Israel, had encountered similar hostility. In each case, God's anointed one was not welcomed by God's people. John's account makes it clear that God's presence among human beings is often mysterious and indeed often met not with crowns of acclamation but rather with a cross of rejection. Similarly, those sent by God encounter rejection. John finds this point reinforced in the Scriptures, as the citations from Isaiah at John 12:38-40 and others demonstrate. In John, there is no triumphalistic understanding with respect to God's work or presence in the world: indeed, the one through whom the

---

35. Alasdair MacIntyre, *Three Rival Versions of Moral Enquiry* (Notre Dame: University of Notre Dame Press, 1990), p. 82.

world was created was present in that world but was not recognized or welcomed (1:10-11).

It is easy enough to limit the implicit warnings in such texts to "others" in the "past"; but John's appropriation of the Psalms to apply to Jesus shows that the original meaning has been appropriated so as to testify not to the past but to his present. Even as David was resisted and Jesus was rejected, so Jesus' followers will be "hated" (15:18). That too is one of the realities in which the readers of the Gospel participate and that shapes their reading of the Psalms. Those who read the Psalms as pointing to Jesus will hear also the subtle warning that their own lives may be similarly marked by struggle and alienation. Reading the descriptions of the hostility directed against David as opposition aimed at Jesus and his followers allows one to reread such passages as continuing to characterize Jesus' followers today. But again, one might well ask whether the Scriptures do not warn also against an unwitting identification with those who persecute the righteous, who then as now are prone to reject the word and work of God, rather than with the persecuted. To read the Scriptures as bearing witness to Jesus, whose road to kingship was surely not the one expected by his contemporaries, might then also mean to read them as warnings against a self-satisfied assumption that one always hears them rightly. Indeed, when the life, death, and resurrection of Jesus become the prism through which the Old Testament is read, it is not only the anticipation of glory at the right hand but also the vicissitudes of human life that constrain our reading of them.

John invites his readers to read the Psalms as instruction in "following Jesus" (1:43; 21:19, 22). Jesus' first invitation to "Follow me" (1:43) leads to the promise that those who do so will "see heaven opened, and the angels ascending and descending upon the Son of man" (1:51). The imperative "Follow me" appears again at the end of the Gospel, where it follows Jesus' word about Peter's destiny: "you will stretch out your hands, and someone else will fasten a belt around you and take you where you do not wish to go" — a prediction of Peter's martyrdom (21:18-19 NRSV). Whereas in the first instance Jesus promises that following him will lead to a vision of heavenly realities, he later warns that it can also lead to an experience of worldly rejection. Jesus tells his disciples that they should not be surprised at this, since those who hated him will hate them as well (15:18). He also speaks of an hour when "whoever kills you will think he is offering service to God" (16:2). The various testimonies that John adduces from the Psalms explain these odd realities: even as God's anointed encountered obstacles in his path, so too God's Messiah and his followers encounter a similarly uneven highway. To read the

Scriptures as testifying to Jesus will mean to read them as adumbrating the difficult path that he walked, and the sometimes equally challenging road that his disciples would also follow.[36] This too stands within that truth into which the Spirit guides Jesus' disciples.

36. See the same point made by Hays with respect to Paul's quotations of the Psalms in "Christ Prays the Psalms," p. 117.

John and *Thomas* in Context:
An Exercise in Canonical Criticism

Luke Timothy Johnson

The connection between canon formation and community identity is clearer in the case of Christianity than in some other religious traditions,[1] because the selection of certain books for the Christian canon involved as well the explicit rejection of other books and other teachings as heretical. Although the core of the Christian collection had gathered organically through a process of exchange and use,[2] the crisis posed by Gnosticism demanded a more explicit selection. Whatever the antecedents of this complex religious sensibility,[3] we meet its Christian version in the second century, and the sources are filled with the noise of battle.

Claims about proper teaching, authoritative books, and a visible succession of reliable teachers point to a deeper and more fundamental conflict concerning the true nature of the Christian religion. Teachers such as Valentinus and Ptolemy saw Jesus primarily as a revealer of transformative knowledge to secretly designated teachers, and located this *gnosis* in books other than those commonly read in public worship. Although certainty is not possible on this point, they appear to have claimed as well that such re-

1. See William A. Graham, *Beyond the Written Word: Oral Aspects of Scripture in the History of Religion* (Cambridge: Cambridge University Press, 1987); Jonathan Z. Smith, "Sacred Persistence: Toward a Redescription of Canon," in *Imagining Religion* (Chicago: University of Chicago Press, 1987), pp. 36-52.

2. See Luke Timothy Johnson, *The Writings of the New Testament: An Interpretation*, 2nd rev. ed., with Todd Penner (Minneapolis: Fortress, 1999), pp. 595-619.

3. For the range of options, see Ugo Bianchi, ed., *Le Origini dello Gnosticismo*, SHR 12 (Leiden: Brill, 1967).

vealed knowledge was not merely supplementary to the exoteric tradition but rather supplanted it. The esoteric tradition was the original Christianity that had been obscured by the "apostolic men" and their organizational, sacramental, and all-too-accessible catholicism.[4] On the other side, Tertullian and Irenaeus claimed that the original Christianity was the public one: Jesus' teachings to the apostles were handed on by their episcopal successors. Not an esoteric code but a public profession of faith provided the key to the Scriptures. Not secret books but the apostolic writings shaped authentic Christian identity. Real Christianity, furthermore, was not a small and separate band of *illuminati* but an *ecclesia mixta,* an assembly of righteous and sinners, wise and stupid, perfect and fallible, all together.[5]

My summary is dazzlingly oversimplified. Gnosticism, we have come to understand, was less "one thing" than a bewildering variety of things.[6] The Nag Hammadi Library discovered in 1945[7] shows us — almost for the first time — what Gnostics had to say for themselves,[8] and we begin to appreciate how tidy Irenaeus had made things. Because, as an heir to the Greek philosophical tradition, he thought in terms of schools (αἱρέσεις) with doctrines, he transmuted his opponents into such neat categories as well.[9] The collec-

---

4. The polemical edge is found especially in the *Gospel of Philip* 51.29-52.24; 55.21-35; 56.16-20; *Gospel of Mary* 10; and the *Testimony of Truth.*

5. The classic argument, which also provides the strategy for all subsequent ecclesial self-definition, is laid out by Irenaeus in *Against Heresies* (*Haer.* 1.10, 3.1-5).

6. For a classic exposition of Gnosticism as a unified yet diverse phenomenon in the history of religions, see Kurt Rudolph, *Gnosis: The Nature and History of Gnosticism,* trans. and ed. R. McL. Wilson (San Francisco: HarperSanFrancisco, 1987); for a recent discussion of the role Gnosticism played in the canonization process, see Pheme Perkins, "Gnosticism and the Christian Bible," in *The Canon Debate,* ed. L. M. McDonald and J. A. Sanders (Peabody, Mass.: Hendrickson, 2002), pp. 355-71.

7. For an account of the discovery, see James M. Robinson, "The Discovery of the Nag Hammadi Codices," *BA* 42 (1979): 206-24. I will be using the translations of the compositions found in Robinson, ed., *The Nag Hammadi Library in English* (San Francisco: HarperSanFrancisco, 1977), hereafter *NHLE;* see also Bentley Layton, *The Gnostic Scriptures: A New Translation with Annotations and Introductions* (Garden City, N.Y.: Doubleday, 1987).

8. The Coptic manuscript of the Gnostic composition *Pistis Sophia* came to the British Museum after the death of its owner in 1774 and was published in 1851. Together with the apocryphal acts of the apostles and Ptolemy's *Letter to Flora,* it was the only primary source available to the great historian Adolf Harnack when he wrote his *History of Dogma* in 1886-89 (New York: Dover, 1961 [ET from 3rd German ed.]) and, dependent completely on patristic literature, characterized Gnosticism as "the acute hellenization of Christianity."

9. Note the way in which Irenaeus approached the "schools" (αἱρέσεις) through their founders, characteristic doctrines, and moral corollaries (*Haer.* 1.11-31), in

tion of codices discovered in Egypt reveals how sprawling, unwieldy, and various were the writings that could be grouped together within leather bindings. So disparate are the manifestations of this ancient dualistic tendency that some have argued for dispensing with the term "Gnosticism" altogether.[10]

For that matter, pressure toward canonization was applied not only by the Gnostics' expansionist tendencies but also by the canonical contraction proposed by Marcion,[11] and the supplanting of the fourfold Gospel by Tatian's *Diatesseron*.[12] It is nevertheless fair to say that both tendencies were sponsored by a profound dualism that sought salvation of the spirit apart from or beyond the realm of the body, whether individual or corporate.[13] And while ecclesiastical power struggles may have played some role,[14] the very nature of the Christian religion was seriously in negotiation: the heresiologists saw themselves as defending the "truth of the gospel" against distortion,[15] while their opponents undoubtedly viewed their version of Christianity as "the Gospel of Truth."[16]

One benefit of the Nag Hammadi discoveries has been the liberation of historians from all-encompassing explanations. The past decades have seen the patient sorting through of the diversity of writings found in that collection, together with a willingness to allow the diversity to stand on its own

---

much the same way that Diogenes Laertius would lay out the various "schools" (αἱρέσεις) of Greek philosophy in *Lives of Eminent Philosophers*.

10. Michael Allen Williams, *Rethinking Gnosticism: An Argument for Dismantling a Dubious Category* (Princeton: Princeton University Press, 1996).

11. The best source for Marcion is Tertullian, who discusses him in *Praescr.* 7.3; 30.1-2; 41-43; *Carn. Chr.* 1-8; *Res.* 2, 4, 14 and 54; *An.* 21, and throughout *Adversus Marcionem libri quinti.* For a recent discussion of the role Marcion may have played in canon formation, see John Barton, "Marcion Revisited," in *Canon Debate,* ed. McDonald and Sanders, pp. 341-54.

12. For the position that Irenaeus's categorizing of Tatian as a Valentinian (*Haer.* 1.28.1) is erroneous, see now Emily J. Hunt, *Christianity in the Second Century: The Case of Tatian* (London: Routledge, 2003).

13. For a survey of the varieties of dualism in second-century Christianity, see Peter Brown, *The Body and Society: Men, Women, and Sexual Renunciation in Early Christianity* (New York: Columbia University Press, 1988).

14. Given the Gnostic sensibility, it is difficult to imagine how it could have mustered a significant challenge at the institutional level, but the character of Valentinianism in particular threatened the institution through its subtle reinterpretation.

15. Paul uses the phrase ἡ ἀλήθεια τοῦ εὐαγγελίου in Gal. 2:5 and 2:14.

16. In *Haer.* 3.11.9, Irenaeus refers to a "comparatively recent writing" produced by the Valentinians called "The Gospel of Truth," which are the first words of the theological reflection now designated with that title in the Nag Hammadi collection (I, 3 and XII, 2).

terms and to challenge our assumed codes of interpretation. Scholarship has progressed by regression to the reexamination of little things, leaving grand theories for a later day.[17] But such regression is also a delight, for it allows our imaginations room to play. In such a spirit of playfulness, I want in this essay to engage in a thought experiment, and ask a "what if" question. What if the *Gospel of Thomas (GT)* from the Nag Hammadi collection had in fact been accepted into the New Testament canon? How would it have been read and understood? How would the rest of the canon have been affected? What difference would its inclusion have made for the shaping of readers' identity? In the present essay, I cannot engage all of these questions, but can only work my way toward them in a preliminary fashion.

I do not intend to argue that the *GT* should have been included or excluded, nor am I explicitly asking why it was excluded, although my conclusions touch on that question. Rather, I want to test the effect of canonical placement on a specific writing, asking how placement among other writings might affect its reading. The most basic objection to the exercise is obvious: we cannot know how ancient readers' interpretation would have been affected, even if they went through the compositions precisely in the order of their present arrangement. All that we are able to say is how we, as present-day readers, find our reading of the text to be affected by its placement in a selection of other compositions.[18] The exercise I propose is artificial, but it does enable us to pose a serious question: how might anthologization control polyvalence in texts?

I begin with two premises concerning the New Testament itself. The first is that the writings included in the canon are irreducibly diverse, both literarily and thematically. When I speak about implied points of consonance among them, I agree that these occur within a framework of diversity and, on some points, disagreement.[19] The second is that the New Testament does not provide its own interpretation. It is not perspicuous. If it were, the battle over its meaning would not have been so fierce or lengthy. As Elaine

17. See, e.g., Bentley Layton, ed., *The Rediscovery of Gnosticism: Proceedings of the International Conference on Gnosticism at Yale, New Haven, Connecticut, March 28-31, 1978,* 2 vols., SHR 41 (Leiden: Brill, 1980).

18. In this regard, we are like theologians who read a Gospel in the context of the Bible as a whole rather than in the imagined context of its original audience, or students of Shakespeare who consider one of his plays as a textual composition within the complete works rather than as a drama performed before an Elizabethan audience.

19. See Luke Timothy Johnson, "Koinonia: Diversity and Unity in Early Christianity," *TD* 46 (1999): 303-13.

Pagels's studies of the Gnostic interpreters of John and Paul have shown, the texts of the New Testament can be read within quite distinct interpretive codes.[20] Our accustomed reading appears "obvious" to us only because what Irenaeus calls the *regula fidei* of orthodox confession has been so deeply ingrained in us.

Nevertheless, I argue in this essay, the orthodox *regula fidei* is not by any means arbitrary. It does correspond to the strongest signals provided by the compositions themselves and by the way in which the compositions fit together in the collection. I make this case by carrying out the same exercise on the Gospel of John and the *Gospel of Thomas,* asking about the space between that which is "different" and that which is "deviant."

Elaine Pagels's Comparison of John and *Thomas*

In a recent book, Elaine Pagels also carries out a comparison between the Fourth Gospel and the *Gospel of Thomas,* apparently led by a supposition similar to my own: "For if Matthew, Mark, and Luke had been joined with the Gospel of Thomas instead of with John, for example, or had *both* John and Thomas been included in the New Testament canon, Christians probably would have read the first three gospels quite differently."[21] In fact, however, her project is different from my own in a number of ways.

Pagels clearly has a personal stake in rendering the *GT* as attractively as possible, for her analysis is preceded by what can only be called a personal narrative of Gnostic discovery. As a teenager she belonged to an evangelical group that gave her a feeling of inclusion — a group that loved the Gospel of John. She did not appreciate then the "disturbing undercurrents" of that Gospel (and evangelical Christianity) that led to judging and excluding others (pp. 30-31). Then, she learned Greek and read ancient literature, and saw there a "different religious sensibility." This discovery of a wider world of spirituality led her "to look for the 'real Christianity' — believing, as Christians traditionally have, that I might find it by immersing myself in the earliest Christian sources" (p. 31). Her personal quest was rewarded by the dis-

---

20. Elaine Pagels, *The Gnostic Paul: Gnostic Exegesis of the Pauline Letters* (Philadelphia: Fortress, 1975); *The Johannine Gospel in Gnostic Exegesis: Heracleon's Commentary on John* (Nashville: Abingdon, 1973).

21. Elaine Pagels, *Beyond Belief: The Secret Gospel of Thomas* (New York: Vintage, 2004), p. 38, emphasis original. Subsequent page references to this volume will be placed in parentheses within the text.

covery of Gnostic texts at Harvard that showed diversity within ancient Christianity that "later, 'official' versions of Christian history had suppressed so effectively that only now, in the Harvard graduate school, did we hear about them." More than that, she was "surprised to find in some of them unexpected spiritual power," naming specifically a passage from the *GT* (p. 32). The upshot of her study is that she "began to understand the political concerns that shaped the early Christian movement" (p. 33).[22]

Any number of observations might be made about this narrative, but three elements in particular stand out. First, Pagels has effectively equated John with evangelical Christianity and evangelical Christianity with exclusionary tendencies. As a master of the soft argument of suggestion, she knows that a further inference follows: canonical Christianity also is all about exclusion rather than inclusion. Second, she suggests that "real Christianity" is to be found in the "earliest sources," once more suggesting that these are not the writings found in the canon. Third, she neatly suggests a connection between the ancient "suppression" of writings with "unexpected spiritual power" and her earlier experience of an exclusionary form of "canonical" Christianity centered in the Gospel of John. Before any analysis at all, in short, she has made John stand for exclusion and *Thomas* stand for inclusion.

The perspective established by her preliminary narrative continues through several premises that are, once more, not explicitly stated but instead suggested. The first is that the Fourth Gospel (FG) and the *GT* are roughly contemporaneous.[23] In fact, "Thomas Christians" are prior to "Johannine Christians," because — and here is the second premise — the FG is written expressly against those "Thomas Christians," so their positions were known to the author of the Fourth Gospel (pp. 34-38).[24] Indeed, John

22. Here she touches on the theme that she developed in *The Gnostic Gospels* (New York: Random House, 1979).

23. Pagels does not engage in a close analysis of the layers of the *GT*. Her notes suggest that she accepts the early dating of at least the material parallel to Q — referring to Stevan Davies, *The Gospel of Thomas and Christian Wisdom* (New York: Seabury, 1983), Stephen J. Patterson, *The Gospel of Thomas and Jesus* (Sonoma, Calif.: Polebridge, 1993), and Richard Valantasis, *The Gospel of Thomas* (London: Routledge, 1997) — although it is by no means clear that even if one accepts that the materials paralleling the Synoptics are as early as the hypothetical Q, the materials that give the *GT* its distinctive character are as early as the Gospel of John. In any case, the entire practice of determining redactional layers must be closely scrutinized because of the tendency toward circularity; see Christopher M. Tuckett, "Q and Thomas: Evidence of a Primitive 'Wisdom Gospel'? A Response to H. Koester," *ETL* 67 (1991): 346-60.

24. Pagels suggests that the author of John may well have met some of these "Thomas Christians" in person (p. 58).

20 is an indirect attack on them through the negative portrayal of "Doubting Thomas" (p. 58).[25] The final premise is that the FG controls the reading of the other canonical Gospels, specifically with respect to belief in the divinity of Jesus, which, again by suggestion, is the key to the tendency toward the exclusion of other spiritualities.[26]

Building on these premises, Pagels first compares John to the Synoptics on two points only: the sequence and meaning of the temple incident, and the claim to divinity. The focus on these two points of contrast tends to minimize the many other points that John and the Synoptics have in common. Second, Pagels compares John to *Thomas* also on two points: the focus on creation rather than the end time, and Jesus' private revelation to his followers.[27] Third, she makes the major point of difference between John and *Thomas* the same as the one between John and the Synoptics: John thinks that God can be approached only through Jesus, whereas *Thomas* thinks that each person can find the divine within. The effect of this is to suggest (again) that John is exclusively responsible for the divinity of Christ within the New Testament[28] and for the tendency toward exclusion in Christianity.

25. She refers to Gregory J. Riley, *Resurrection Reconsidered: Thomas and John in Controversy* (Minneapolis: Fortress, 1995).

26. "[M]ost Christians came to read these earlier gospels through John's lens, and thus to find in all of them evidence of John's conviction that Jesus is 'Lord and God'" (p. 38).

27. Pagels distorts the evidence on this point. She states that "John and Thomas give similar accounts of what Jesus taught privately. Unlike Matthew, Mark, and Luke, who say that Jesus warned of the coming 'end of time,' both John and Thomas say that he directed his disciples instead toward the beginning of time — to the creation account of Genesis 1 — and identify Jesus with the divine light that came into being 'in the beginning'" (p. 40). But John makes clear what Jesus' private revelation to the disciples was (John 13–17), and it is not in the least connected to the prologue of the Gospel that declares Jesus to be the light coming into the world (John 1:1-3). Pagels confuses, deliberately or not, the evangelist's perspective on Jesus with the content of Jesus' private revelation to the disciples.

28. On pp. 44-45, she acknowledges the high Christology of Philippians 2 and rejects the notion of an evolution from a lower to a higher Christology within early Christianity, but her failure to deal with the NT language as a whole (Hebrews, etc.) and her systematic downplaying of elements suggesting Jesus' divinity in the Synoptics have the effect of isolating John as the NT writing that makes Jesus' divinity most explicit. For a better accounting of the data, see Larry W. Hurtado, *Lord Jesus Christ: Devotion to Jesus in Earliest Christianity* (Grand Rapids: Eerdmans, 2003).

A More Adequate Comparison

Pagels's treatment of John and *Thomas* is less a serious engagement with the two compositions than a slapdash and highly selective characterization. A more adequate analysis needs to encompass at least five tasks: (1) to compare the FG and the *GT* with the one thing they both certainly have in common, namely, the Synoptic tradition;[29] (2) to discuss each one's distinctive material in relation to what they share; (3) to consider in each the compositional or redactional controls that might direct the reader toward one mode of construal or another; (4) to examine the kinds of controls for reading provided by anthological placement; and (5) to ask how each writing might have been read if it had been placed within the other collection.

The Gospel of John

John and the Synoptic Material

I propose that Pagels has it exactly backward. The other Gospels are not dominated by John. Rather, the New Testament is dominated by the Synoptic Gospels and Paul, and in more than a purely quantitative way. Together, they provide the interpretive grid for the understanding of other writings. Scholars have long recognized how the second volume of Luke-Acts places Paul in the context of the larger mission and tends to domesticate his more radical tendencies.[30] Less frequently noted is the way that Acts also connects

---

29. In contrast to Pagels, I find more convincing the scholarship that sees in the *GT* signs of dependence on the Synoptic tradition as such rather than on a form of the sayings tradition prior to the Synoptics; see, e.g., R. McL. Wilson, *Studies in the Gospel of Thomas* (London: Mowbray, 1960); Bertil Gärtner, *The Theology of the Gospel of Thomas,* trans. E. Sharpe (London: Collins, 1961); F. M. Strickert, "The Pronouncement Sayings in the Gospel of Thomas and the Synoptics" (Ph.D. diss., University of Iowa, 1988); Wolfgang Schrage, *Das Verhältnis des Thomas-Evangeliums zur synoptischen Tradition und zu koptischen Evangelien-übersetzungen,* BZNW 29 (Berlin: Töpelmann, 1964). A particularly discerning analysis is provided by John P. Meier, *A Marginal Jew: Rethinking the Historical Jesus,* 3 vols. (New York: Doubleday, 1991-2001), 1:123-39. This case is heightened by the fact that other Nag Hammadi writings show clear knowledge and use of the canonical writings; see Christopher M. Tuckett, *Nag Hammadi and the Gospel Tradition,* ed. J. Riches (Edinburgh: T. & T. Clark, 1986).

30. Thus, for F. C. Baur, the portrait of Paul in Acts represented the harmonizing tendencies of "early Catholicism" and made Paul appear in partnership with Peter rather than opposed to him; see *Paul the Apostle of Jesus Christ: His Life and Works, His Epistles and*

Paul to the story of Jesus recounted in Luke's Gospel. Acts not only continues the story told by the Gospel; it also recapitulates that story through the speeches of Peter and Paul, which rehearse the story of Jesus in accord with the basic Synoptic pattern.[31]

The connection between Paul and the Synoptic story of Jesus is not, however, due entirely to Acts; recent study of the narrative substructure of Pauline theology has shown the importance of the story of Jesus in Paul's letters.[32] By means of allusion and application, Paul repeatedly points his readers to a narrative pattern concerning Jesus that provides the content for his cryptic phrases νοῦς Χριστοῦ (1 Cor. 2:16) and ὁ νόμος τοῦ Χριστοῦ (Gal. 6:2): the faith of the human Jesus has become exemplar both for the obedience of his followers toward God and for their mutual dispositions of love.[33]

The simple juxtaposition of verses can illustrate the deep narrative consonance between Paul and the Synoptic tradition. Paul tells the Galatians: "Bear one another's burdens, and so fulfill the law of Christ (ὁ νόμος τοῦ Χριστοῦ = 'Pattern of the Messiah')" (Gal. 6:2).[34] Jesus tells his disciples in Mark: "For the Son of man also came not to be served but to serve, and to give his life as a ransom for many" (Mark 10:45). For Paul, the most critical part of Jesus' story is its ending, Jesus' obedient death on the cross (see especially Phil. 2:6-11), which Paul understands as the "obedience of [Jesus']

Teachings (Peabody, Mass.: Hendrickson, 2003 [1873]), pp. 1-14. Baur considered Acts to have distorted the historical Paul in the same way that John distorted the historical Jesus. W. Ward Gasque, A History of the Criticism of the Acts of the Apostles (Grand Rapids: Eerdmans, 1975), p. 40, notes: "The Book of Acts, according to Baur, stands in the same basic relationship to the epistles of Paul as the Gospel of John stands in relation to the synoptics."

31. For the argument concerning Acts, see Luke Timothy Johnson, The Gospel of Luke, SP 3 (Collegeville, Minn.: Liturgical Press, 1991); The Acts of the Apostles, SP 5 (Collegeville, Minn.: Liturgical Press, 1992). For literature on the speeches of Acts, see Luke Timothy Johnson, Septuagintal Midrash in the Speeches of Acts, Pere Marquette Lecture 33 (Milwaukee: Marquette University Press, 2002).

32. The fundamental insight here was offered by the friend and colleague to whom this essay is dedicated, Richard B. Hays, The Faith of Jesus Christ: An Investigation of the Narrative Substructure of Galatians 3:1–4:11, SBLDS 56 (Chico, Calif.: Scholars Press, 1983). I have expressed my admiration for this contribution in a foreword to the second edition (Grand Rapids: Eerdmans, 2002).

33. Hays's insights have borne fruit in subsequent contributions to an understanding of Paul's theology; see especially A. Katherine Grieb, The Story of Romans: A Narrative Defense of God's Righteousness (Louisville: Westminster John Knox, 2002); Thomas Stegman, The Character of Jesus: The Linchpin to Paul's Argument in 2 Corinthians, AnBib 158 (Rome: Pontifical Biblical Institute, 2005).

34. Scripture quotations are from the RSV.

faith" (Rom. 3:21-26; 5:12-21).[35] In the Synoptics, likewise, the passion and death of Jesus dominates the account of healings and teachings: Jesus is above all the suffering Son of man. In Paul, the pattern of Christian existence replicates Christ's self-emptying by looking to the interests of others (Phil. 2:1-5). In the Synoptics, the path of discipleship consists of following in the way of suffering first traversed by Jesus (Mark 8:34-37). The connections are most obvious between Paul and Mark,[36] but although Matthew and Luke work variations on the pattern, and to some extent obscure it by the addition of other material, it remains for them the basic framework for telling the story of Jesus. And it is against this massive narrative background that we must consider what is different in the Fourth Gospel.

How John Is Different

It was surely not by accident that John was the Gospel most admired by Gnostic teachers. The first full-scale commentary on John, indeed, seems to have been that of Heracleon, a disciple of Valentinus.[37] In ways both interesting and important, John appears among the earliest Gospels as an alternative to the Synoptics, not only in the obvious points of divergence concerning the length and location of Jesus' ministry, but also in the overall depiction of Jesus and his disciples, a depiction that would make the FG more appealing than the other canonical gospels to a Gnostic sensibility.[38]

In the FG, Jesus is above all the revealer.[39] His self-referential mono-

35. Luke Timothy Johnson, "Romans 3:21-26 and the Faith of Jesus," *CBQ* 44 (1982): 77-90; I develop this thesis further in *Reading Romans: A Literary and Theological Commentary* (New York: Crossroad, 1996).

36. The point here is not a literary dependence of Mark on Paul but rather a deep consonance in their respective perceptions of the character of Jesus. For the technical discussion of "affinities with Pauline teaching," see Vincent Taylor, *The Gospel according to Mark*, 2nd ed. (London: Macmillan, 1966), pp. 125-29. For the argument concerning the convergence of NT witnesses on the question of Jesus' human character and the nature of discipleship, see Luke Timothy Johnson, *Living Jesus: Learning the Heart of the Gospel* (San Francisco: HarperSanFrancisco, 1999).

37. We are able to reconstruct substantial portions of Heracleon's commentary because of the generous citation (and refutation) of it in Origen's *Commentary on John*.

38. John's Gospel does not have a direct literary connection to the Synoptic Gospels, but it is in touch with a substantial amount of the traditions used by the Synoptics. For a review of the data, see Johnson, *Writings of the New Testament*, pp. 528-32.

39. See especially Rudolf Bultmann, *The Gospel of John: A Commentary*, trans. G. R. Beasley-Murray, R. W. N. Hoare, and J. K. Riches (Philadelphia: Westminster, 1971 [1964]);

logues both reveal and establish the distance between himself ("the Man from above") and his opponents ("those from below"). He can be designated simply as "the Word," and Käsemann gets at least part of the truth when he terms John's Christology a "naïve docetism."[40] Jesus reveals as Father one whom the world does not know (1:10). The world, indeed, is a place of darkness that can neither overcome the light nor grasp it (1:5).[41] As there is an absolute distance between Jesus and the world, defined by place of origin, so is there also between Jesus' followers and the world: the world hates them as it hated him (15:18-21).[42]

There is a different sense of time in John's Gospel: temporal distinctions seem to collapse into the figure of Jesus. The ancient Scriptures speak of him (5:39), Abraham sees his day (8:56), and Isaiah beheld his glory (12:41). The struggles of his followers are anticipated by the conflicts experienced by Jesus (9:22; 12:42). And there is little future eschatology. Judgment is now, in response to the presence of Jesus (3:19-21) and in the continuation of his presence through the Spirit among his disciples (16:8-15).

The disciples in John are those who have received the light that comes from God. They have "beheld his glory" and on that basis can be called, simply, "children of God" (1:12-14). After the dramatic close of his public ministry, Jesus draws his disciples to himself and delivers to them the secret, nonironic revelation of who he is, where he has come from, and where he is going (13:1-17, 36) that he made available to the public only through veiled signs and ironic disputation.[43] As for John's understanding of "church," it would seem ideally fitted to the antihierarchical impulses of many Gnostics. Jesus' followers are simply "friends," equally joined to the vine (15:1-27). The in-

---

Theology of the New Testament, trans. K. Grobel, 2 vols. (New York: Scribner, 1951, 1955), 2:49-69.

40. The phrase was used by Ernst Käsemann in his 1966 Shaffer Lectures at Yale University, published as *The Testament of Jesus according to John 17,* trans. G. Krodel (Philadelphia: Fortress, 1968), p. 26.

41. For the (perhaps intentional) ambiguity in καὶ ἡ σκοτία αὐτὸ οὐ κατέλαβεν, see Raymond E. Brown, *The Gospel according to John,* 2 vols., AB 29 (Garden City, N.Y.: Doubleday, 1966), 1:7-8.

42. The classic study is Wayne A. Meeks, "The Man from Heaven in Johannine Sectarianism," *JBL* 91 (1972): 44-72.

43. Pagels is right to emphasize the distinctive character of Jesus' private revelations in John, but she mischaracterizes the content when she suggests (again!) that Jesus revealed teachings about the beginning (*Beyond Belief,* p. 40). For a more adequate account, see Fernando F. Segovia, *The Farewell of the Word: The Johannine Call to Abide* (Minneapolis: Fortress, 1991).

dwelling of Father and Son is shared by all who are "not of the world" (17:16-21). The FG has no trace of public institution or visible authority structure.

Finally, the FG singles out among the disciples a shadowy figure designated as "the disciple whom Jesus loved," who offers intriguing possibilities for Gnostic interpretation. He is the one who leans on Jesus' breast at the supper to receive intimate knowledge (13:23). He witnesses the mysterious outpouring of blood and water (19:26-37). He outruns Peter to the empty tomb and is the first to believe (20:1-10). And throughout, he remains anonymous! He is the ideal source for a tradition of secret teaching beside the hierarchical structure of the visible church.

So obvious are these elements of the FG that in the early third century the Roman presbyter Gaius reputedly rejected John's Gospel and the book of Revelation because he considered them to be the work of the Gnostic teacher Cerinthus.[44] Precisely the possibility of understanding John within a Gnostic framework, furthermore, may even have divided Johannine Christians. The Johannine letters place particular stress on the coming of Christ in the flesh and his expiatory death, arguably in response to a possible reading of the Johannine tradition.[45]

Compositional Controls on John

The elements that make John so markedly different are held in control by both internal composition and canonical placement, which I consider in turn. By compositional controls, I mean other elements within the Gospel itself that serve to mitigate the tendency toward the Gnostic that I have identified.

The "naïve docetism" of the FG is countered by explicit affirmations of Jesus' humanity. The Word *does* "become flesh," after all (1:14), and John stresses the fleshly character of Jesus' existence: his fatigue (4:6), indecision (7:1-10), and human anguish (11:33-35; 12:27). In this Gospel, Jesus' interactions with other humans are real, complex, and perilous (6:60-71; 8:12-59). In the end, he truly dies, with his side pierced by a lance, and his blood spilled (19:34-37). John did not really need to provide explicit resurrection accounts, for throughout the narrative, Jesus is "the resurrection and the life" (11:25), yet, if anything, his accounts are even more palpable than the Synoptics: linens and kerchiefs are left in the tomb (20:6-7), a woman clings to him

---

44. Eusebius, *Hist. eccl.* 2.26.6.

45. See the argument of Raymond E. Brown, *The Community of the Beloved Disciple* (New York: Paulist, 1979).

outside the tomb (20:17), a hand is placed in his side (20:27), and fish are fried on the seashore (21:9). Jesus is the true bread "come down from heaven," but his flesh is also to be "munched" (τρώγειν) by believers (6:58).

Further, as I have suggested, John's emphasis is on a realized eschatology: Jesus is judge in his earthly manifestation (5:22). But the FG contains clear affirmations of traditional, future eschatology as well. The two strands appear together in the fifth chapter. In 5:25 Jesus declares, "Truly, truly, I say to you, the hour is coming, and now is, when the dead will hear the voice of the Son of God, and those who hear will live," but then also in 5:28-29, "Do not marvel at this; for the hour is coming when all who are in the tombs will hear his voice and come forth, those who have done good, to the resurrection of life, and those who have done evil, to the resurrection of judgment."

In the same way, statements that could be taken to indicate a cosmological enmity between God and the world, or Jesus and the world, or the disciples and the world, are mitigated by statements such as this: "God so loved the world that he gave his only Son, that whoever believes in him should not perish but have eternal life. For God sent the Son into the world, not to condemn the world, but that the world might be saved through him" (3:16-17). And although this Gospel undoubtedly positions Jesus and his followers against "the Jews," it also asserts continuity between the world of Torah and the revelation made through Jesus (1:16-18).

The FG also affirms the world through the use of a realistic narrative for communicating its understanding of Jesus. Narrative by its very nature implicitly affirms the value of bodies and of time. John's narrative, moreover, is unmistakably grounded in the realities of first-century Palestinian life.[46] And although the Gospel betrays no interest in the institutional aspects of the church, it is surely connected to the sacramental life of believers, with no suggestion that the visible forms of water and bread and light are unworthy to bear divine significance.[47]

Finally, the possibility of making the beloved disciple the source for secret revelations derived from the bosom of Jesus is dramatically undercut by the "second ending" of the Gospel in John 21.[48] The epilogue weaves to-

46. See Brown, *Gospel according to John,* pp. xlii-xliii.

47. See Bruce Vawter, "The Johannine Sacramentary," *TS* 17 (1956): 151-66; Brown, *Gospel according to John,* pp. cxi-cxiv.

48. Scholars today are virtually unanimous in regarding John 21 as a later addition to the Gospel; for a contrary (and, as always, refreshingly independent) view that also captures the point of the epilogue, see Paul S. Minear, "The Original Functions of John 21," *JBL* 102 (1983): 85-98.

gether the futures of Peter and John. John will not live until Jesus' return as the community had expected (21:21-23), and Peter will experience martyrdom (21:18-19). But it also clearly assigns authority to Peter rather than John: "Do you love me more than these . . . Lord, you know that I love you. . . . [Then] feed my sheep" (21:15-17). Peter is not only restored to discipleship; he is established as leader of the church. He is also the model for discipleship: Peter wants to *know,* but he is told simply, "Follow me" (21:22).

In short, John's Gospel contains a tension between an outlook that could easily be read as Gnostic and an outlook that more obviously conforms to the dominant Synoptic/Pauline pattern. If we also attend to John's placement in the New Testament canon, we see how elements that might seem secondary when the Gospel is read in isolation are given greater controlling authority.

Canonical Controls on John

In the majority of Greek New Testament manuscripts, John's Gospel is placed after Matthew, Mark, and Luke, immediately preceding the Acts of the Apostles. The sequence is not universal, as we learn from our only sources for such information, early canonical lists, and manuscripts containing most of the New Testament collection,[49] but the position after the Synoptics and before Acts is the normal position in the largest number of even the earliest witnesses.[50] The sequence is broken when Acts is located differently, as it is in a number of lists and at least two important manuscripts.[51]

---

49. For the data, I am using the lists provided by Lee Martin McDonald in *The Canon Debate,* pp. 591-97, and Carl R. Holladay, *A Critical Introduction to the New Testament: Interpreting the Message and Meaning of Jesus Christ,* 2 vol. ed. (Nashville: Abingdon, 2005), 2:871-81; I have profited from Professor Holladay's guidance in this matter.

50. Acts appears after the four Gospels in the canonical lists of Eusebius, Cyril of Jerusalem, Athanasius, Gregory of Nazienzen, the African Canons, Amphilochius, Rufinus, Gelasius, Junilius, Cassiodorus, the Syrian Catalogue, and the Synods of Laodicea and Carthage. Among codices, it appears after the Gospels in Vaticanus (but before James rather than Paul) and Alexandrinus. Among translations, it takes the same position in the Peshitta and the Vulgate.

51. Acts appears at the end of the canonical list in the Apostolic Canons, as it does also in Codex Claromontanus, which is also distinctive in having the "apostolic Gospels" Matthew and John precede Luke and Mark. Acts is found after Paul's letters in the Cheltenham Canon, Epiphanius, and Codex Sinaiticus. In the lists of Jerome, Augustine, Innocent, and Isidore, Acts comes after James and before Revelation, and in Eucherius is listed after Hebrews and before James. Perhaps the oddest sequence is found in the Muratorian Canon, in which Acts follows both John's Gospel and the letters of John.

For the purposes of this thought experiment, I will take the sequence that eventually became universal as available to many, perhaps even most, readers from the fourth century on.[52]

The effect of such placement is to homologize the FG even more to the Synoptic/Pauline pattern. John's version follows a threefold repetition of the Synoptic story, so that the pattern of ministry/death/resurrection is already firmly imprinted in the readers' minds and hence all the more easily discerned within John's multiple variations. The way that John alters Synoptic traditions therefore seems less impressive than the fact that he reinforces the Synoptic pattern.

The location of John between Luke and Acts also provides the reader with a narrative rather than a transformative/revelational code. Notice the way readers' identification of the figure of John is affected. In the Synoptics, John appears as one of the sons of Zebedee, part of an inner group (Peter, James, John) who are privy to Jesus' most intimate moments.[53] In Luke, the Gospel immediately preceding the FG, there is a mention of John that is lacking in Matthew and Mark: when Jesus sends two disciples to prepare the Last Supper, only Luke identifies the two as Peter and John (Luke 22:8).

Readers progressing from Luke to the FG would therefore instinctively identify the beloved disciple (first so named at that Last Supper, John 13:23) as John the son of Zebedee. And the pairing with Peter, as we have seen, is firmly fixed by John's epilogue (see 21:2): both are witnesses and believers, both beloved of and lovers of Jesus. But John is second to Peter in authority.

When readers turn to the *next* canonical writing, the Acts of the Apostles, which picks up the Gospel story after the resurrection, they find Peter and John first in the list of apostles who are waiting for the Holy Spirit (Acts 1:13). Throughout the first eight chapters of Acts, furthermore, John is constantly associated with Peter. They are the only apostles named as leaders of the Jerusalem community (Acts 3:1, 3, 4, 11; 4:13, 19; 8:14, 17). But John is entirely silent. It is Peter who speaks, decrees, strikes dead, and rebukes, with John as his silent partner. In Acts, John is mentioned only once more, at the death of his brother James (Acts 12:2).

What John's epilogue suggests, then, the narrative of Acts confirms: John is associated with and subordinate to Peter. Despite the remarkable dif-

---

52. Even when the precise sequence is not found, the presence of Acts in the list serves to move John toward the Synoptic/Pauline narrative pattern, though in a less impressive fashion.

53. See Mark 1:19, 29; 3:17; 5:37; 9:2, 38; 10:35, 41; 13:3; 14:33.

ferences found in the Gospel of John, it is firmly rooted in the same narrative framework shared by the Synoptic Gospels. What Acts did to domesticate the dangerous Paul by placing him in the larger context of apostolic Christianity it did also for John, helping to reduce its dangerous potential for deviance to an interesting degree of difference.[54]

The Gospel of Thomas

The *Gospel of Thomas* is perfect for this experiment in canonical criticism for three reasons. First, even more obviously than the FG, it makes use of a considerable amount of Synoptic discourse material, arguably in a form earlier than that found in the Synoptics — the comparison to the hypothetical Q is a natural one.[55] Second, the *GT,* like the Gospel of John, contains a mixture of tendencies that enable the composition to be read with different emphases; scholars debate whether and in what sense the *GT* should be considered a "Gnostic" writing.[56] Third, again like John, the *GT* is placed within something like a canonical collection, or at least an anthology. In the Nag Hammadi Library, it is found in Codex II, preceded by the *Apocryphon of John* and followed by the *Gospel of Philip.*[57]

The *Gospel of Thomas* opens in this fashion: "These are the secret sayings which the living Jesus spoke and which Didymos Judas Thomas wrote down."[58] The remainder of the composition consists of 114 sayings of Jesus,

54. In *The Canonical Function of Acts: A Comparative Analysis* (Collegeville, Minn.: Liturgical Press, 2002), pp. 41-78, David E. Smith shows how Irenaeus used the narrative of Acts to establish the narrative (historical) context for his argument concerning apostolic succession and the unity of primitive belief.

55. See, e.g., John S. Kloppenborg et al., *Q-Thomas Reader* (Sonoma, Calif.: Polebridge, 1990); Patterson, *Gospel of Thomas and Jesus;* Valantasis, *Gospel of Thomas.*

56. See the discussions respectively in Gärtner, *Theology of the Gospel of Thomas,* and Valantasis, *Gospel of Thomas.*

57. It has even been suggested that the sequence of compositions in Nag Hammadi Codex II (where the *GT* is placed) represents something of a "counter-canon" that imitates features of the NT; see Michael A. Williams, "Interpreting the Nag Hammadi Library as 'Collection(s)' in the History of 'Gnosticism(s),'" in *Les Textes de Nag Hammadi et le problème de leur classification: Actes du colloque tenue à Québec du 15 au 19 Septembre 1993,* ed. L. Painchaud and A. Pasquier, BCNH.E 3 (Quebec: Les presses de l'Université de Laval, 1995), pp. 17-28. I am not making so strong a claim.

58. I am using the translation of the *GT* in the *Nag Hammadi Library in English.* Small variations are found in the translation provided by Elaine Pagels as an appendix to *Beyond*

regularly introduced by "Jesus said." Occasional entries begin with "they said," with Jesus responding to statements or queries made by one or another disciple, among whom are named Peter, Matthew, and Thomas (#13), Mary (#21), and Salome (#61).[59] A handful of sayings have the bare elements of a *chreia*, in that they are introduced by the briefest of biographical settings: some babies nursing (#22), a Samaritan carrying a lamb (#60), a person asking Jesus to divide an inheritance (#72), a woman crying from the crowd (#79), Jesus shown a gold coin (#100). Otherwise, the *GT* is a set of discrete sayings. Not even these miniature *chreiai* establish any sort of narrative character, for they appear atomistically among other discrete sayings. In contrast to both John and the Synoptics, Jesus neither performs mighty deeds nor undergoes suffering and death. It is difficult to say, therefore, whether the sayings of the "living Jesus" are meant to come from his resurrection state or during his ministry — or even whether it would matter. In this composition, Jesus appears as pure revealer.

In contrast to both John and the Synoptic Gospels, furthermore, the *GT* lacks any citations from Torah. Biblical figures, in fact, appear only allusively: Adam is mentioned twice (## 46 and 85), while John the Baptist (#46) and James the Just (#12) are mentioned once. There are single references to "the Jews" (#43), "the Pharisees and the scribes" (#39), "the Pharisees" (#102), the "prophets" of Israel (#52), "the Sabbath" (#27), and "circumcision" (#53). If we add the "Samaritan carrying a lamb on his way to Judea" (#60), we have everything the *GT* contains concerning the symbolic world of Judaism.

Because of the lack of narrative or contextual framework, and because of the way the sayings appear as discrete utterances, it is difficult to find either thematic or formal unity within the *Gospel of Thomas*. The understanding of any single saying seems to depend on knowledge of the overall interpretive code. Although this code was surely available to the composition's ancient readers, it is not to us. We must draw our best guesses from the clues provided by the juxtaposition of sayings, by the dissonances among traditional and redactional elements, and by the *GT*'s placement within the anthology.

Belief, pp. 227-42, based in turn on Marvin Meyer, *The Gospel of Thomas: The Hidden Sayings of Jesus* (San Francisco: HarperSanFrancisco, 1992).

59. James the Just has no voice but is identified as the one to whom disciples should turn as a leader after Jesus leaves (#12); for James elsewhere in the Nag Hammadi collection, see the *First Apocalypse of James*, in *NHLE*, pp. 242-48; the *Second Apocalypse of James*, pp. 249-55; the *Apocryphon of James*, pp. 29-36.

The Gospel of Thomas and Synoptic Material

Some 31 of the *GT*'s 114 sayings strikingly resemble ones found in the Synoptics, supporting the notion that this composition has roots in a primitive Gospel tradition. Ten of these sayings take the form of parables,[60] and the rest are *chreiai*/aphorisms.[61] The principle used for choosing the particular sayings is not entirely clear, but the motif of division and selection is certainly strong: Jesus came to cast fire (#10), to cause division and not peace (#16). He is a prophet rejected in his own country (#31), and has no place to lay his head (#86). He is also the pearl of great price (#76) and the treasure of the field (#109), who invites followers to "come unto me" (#90). To do this, a person must hate mother and father and — in a note otherwise absent — "take up his cross in My way" (#55).

Even these hauntingly familiar sayings, however, have some distinctive twists in the *GT*. We may be startled to discover that at the end of the parable of the great banquet, which otherwise forms a neat parallel to Luke 14:16-24, Jesus says, "Businessmen and merchants will not enter the Places of My Father" (#64). For the most part, however, these discrete sayings not only resemble those found in the Synoptics; they could easily slip back into the narrative framework provided by the Synoptics and make perfectly good sense there.

Other sayings in the *GT* are clearly related to the Synoptic tradition but show significant signs of redactional reworking. Some of the longer sayings, for example, appear to be conflations. Their elements appear in the Synoptics, and even a reader sympathetic to the *GT* would think that they make more sense in the Synoptic narratives. In sayings such as *GT* ## 91 and 92, in fact, Synoptic and Johannine material seems to have been conflated into a single (and not altogether intelligible) statement. Likewise, sayings with a Synoptic basis are given a distinctive addition: in response to a question about tribute to Caesar, Jesus says, "Give Caesar what belongs to Caesar, give God what belongs to God, and give Me what is Mine" (#100; compare Mark 12:17//).

Similarly, the statement "Do not let your left hand know what your right hand is doing" is familiar from Matthew 6:3, where it is used with reference to almsgiving. In *GT* #62, however, the saying forms the conclusion to quite another sort of statement: "It is to those who are worthy of My mysteries that I tell My mysteries. Do not let your left hand know what your right hand is

---

60. *GT* ## 9, 20, 57, 63, 64, 65, 76, 96, 107, 109.
61. *GT* ## 6, 10, 16, 26, 31, 32, 33, 34, 35, 39, 45, 54, 55, 72, 79, 86, 90, 95, 99, 100, 101.

doing." In Matthew 10:34-36 and Luke 12:49-53, Jesus declares that he has come to bring division on the earth and that households will be divided because of him, "three . . . against two and two against three, the father against the son, and the son against the father." But in *GT* #16, the saying concludes: "And they will stand solitary."

Perhaps the most dramatic example of the distinctive twist the *GT* gives to Synoptic material is found in ## 63-72. It is helpful to begin with the Synoptic parallel. In Luke 12:13, while Jesus is on his fateful journey to Jerusalem, "one of the multitude said to him, 'Teacher, bid my brother divide the inheritance with me.'" And Jesus responds, "Man, who made me a judge or divider over you?" Then he says, "Take heed, and beware of all covetousness; for a man's life does not consist in the abundance of his possessions" (Luke 12:13-15). It is at this point that Luke has Jesus tell the parable of the rich fool (12:16-21): the man was so rich that he needed to build extra silos, and he was a fool because he identified his life with those possessions. In Luke this is a moral tale that illustrates Jesus' saying about covetousness, as the conclusion neatly states: "So is he who lays up treasure for himself, and is not rich toward God" (Luke 12:21).[62]

The redaction in the *GT* is drastic. First, *Thomas* separates the parable of the rich fool entirely from its Synoptic framing. The parable itself has the same form as in Luke but concludes with the declaration "Let him who has ears hear" (#63). This is followed immediately by the parable of the great banquet, which, as noted above, ends with the statement that businessmen and merchants will not enter the places of the Father (#64). There follows in the *GT* a third parable, that of the wicked husbandmen, who kill the heir of the vineyard (#65), again with the portentous ending "Let him who has ears hear." The *GT* in this section appears to present a series of oblique, coded messages against worldly wealth and involvement.

Then what has happened to Luke's introduction? It is found in *GT* #72, completely severed from the parable of the rich fool. It reads:

> A man said to Him, "Tell my brothers to divide my father's possessions with me." He said to him, "O man, who has made Me a divider?" He turned to His disciples and said to them, "I am not a divider, am I?"

In Luke's version, the response is ethical: "Beware of all covetousness." In the *GT,* the saying concerns Jesus' identity: "I am not a divider, am I?" While the

---

62. For full discussion of the Lukan parable in context, see Johnson, *Gospel of Luke,* pp. 197-202.

precise significance of this remains uncertain, other sayings in the *GT* may provide a partial code for its solving. In *GT* #61, Jesus says to Salome: "I am He who exists from the Undivided. I was given some of the things of My father." Salome responds, "I am Your disciple." Jesus then says to her, "Therefore I say, if he is undivided, he will be filled with light, but if he is divided, he will be filled with darkness."

My review of the contents of the *GT* up to this point may lead one to think that it is much closer to the Synoptics than John's Gospel is. That case could, perhaps, be made with respect to the materials I have cited thus far. It is when we turn to the sayings unique to the *GT* that its sharp differences become more apparent.

How the Gospel of Thomas Is Different

Among the sayings unique to the *GT* are some that remain simply ambiguous, particularly if they are read in isolation. I noted above that *GT* #55 contains the Synoptic version of hating father and mother. In *GT* #101, however, the saying is repeated with an intriguing variation. In this instance there is no mention of taking up the cross as Jesus did or of being worthy of his father. Instead, we find this:

> Jesus said, "Whoever does not hate his father and his mother as I do cannot become a disciple to Me. And whoever does not love his father and his mother as I do cannot become a disciple to Me. For My mother gave me falsehood, but My true Mother gave me life."

Connected to this saying must also be the short aphorism of *GT* #105: "He who knows the father and the mother will be called the son of a harlot." But who are the "father and mother" in this set of sayings? Surely, not the biological parents of the disciples. Another example is *GT* #104, which has a superficial resemblance to the controversy story about fasting in Mark 2:18-20//, but in which everything is reworked:

> They said to Jesus, "Come, let us pray today and let us fast." Jesus said, "What is the sin that I have committed, or wherein have I been defeated? But when the bridegroom leaves the bridal chamber, then let them fast and pray."

There are certainly echoes here of the tradition concerning fasting and the bridegroom in Mark 2:19//, but that tradition contains no mention of a "bridal chamber." If we had only the saying in the *GT,* we could not know what is meant by "leaving the bridal chamber," although we note that there is a pertinent statement in *GT* #75: "Many are standing at the door, but it is the solitary who will enter the bridal chamber."

Even odder — from the perspective of one coming from the Synoptic tradition — is the parable in *GT* #97. It is found only in this composition, and defies interpretation:

> Jesus said, "The Kingdom of the Father is like a certain woman who was carrying a jar full of meal. While she was walking on the road, still some distance from home, the handle of the jar broke and the meal emptied out behind her on the road. She did not realize it; she had noticed no accident. When she reached her house, she set the jar down and found it empty."

Because it has no narrative context, the parable seems prosaic in the extreme: what can be meant by broken jars and emptiness, and how does it explicate the kingdom? Nothing within the *GT* — and certainly nothing in the canonical Gospel tradition — offers anything approaching a code for construal.

There are finally the elements in the *GT* that are obviously Gnostic, or at the very least, intensely ascetical, in orientation. Not only are there as many sayings of this sort in the *Gospel of Thomas* as there are of the Synoptic variety, but they dominate the *GT* because of their placement and because they thematically control the other strands.

Compositional Controls on the Gospel of Thomas

The strangeness and ambiguity in most of the other statements of the *Gospel of Thomas* are provided their thematic context by the distinctive Gnostic sayings. In response to a question as to how they as children might enter the kingdom, for example, Jesus responds:

> When you make the two one, and when you make the inside like the outside and the outside like the inside, and the above like the below, and when you make the male and the female one and the same, so that the male not be male nor the female female; and when you fashion eyes in place of an eye, and a hand in place of a hand, and a foot in place of a foot, and a likeness in place of a likeness; then will you enter the Kingdom. (*GT* #22)

Again, in *GT ## 49-50*, we find:

> Blessed are the solitary and elect, for you will find the Kingdom. For you are from it, and to it you will return. . . . If they say to you, "Where did you come from?," say to them, "We came from the light, the place where the light came into being on its own accord and established itself and became manifest through their image." If they say to you, "Is it you?," say, "We are its children, and we are the elect of the Living Father." If they ask you, "What is the sign of your Father in you?" say to them, "It is movement and repose."

Such sayings cohere with the following aphorisms and provide them with a context. After speaking of divisions in households, as we saw, *GT #16* concludes, "And they will stand solitary." In *GT #23*, Jesus says, "I shall choose you, one out of a thousand, and two out of ten thousand, and they shall stand as a single one." And *GT #42* in its entirety reads: "Jesus said, 'Become passers-by.'"

Likewise, this series of sayings: "Whoever has come to understand the world has found (only) a corpse, and whoever has found a corpse is superior to the world" (*GT #56*), which connects to the conclusion of saying #60, "You, too, look for a place for yourselves within Repose, lest you become a corpse and be eaten," and saying #80, "He who has recognized the world has found the body, but he who has found the body is superior to the world," and saying #87, "Wretched is the body that is dependent upon a body, and wretched is the soul that is dependent on these two," and saying #110, "Whoever finds the world and becomes rich, let him renounce the world," and saying #112, "Woe to the flesh that depends on the soul; woe to the soul that depends on the flesh."

Finally, very much along the same lines are these two statements, which cohere perfectly with the ones just cited:

> Jesus said, "The heavens and the earth will be rolled up in your presence. And the one who lives from the Living One will not see death." Does not Jesus say, "Whoever finds himself is superior to the world"? (*GT #111*)

and

> Jesus said, "It is I who am the light which is above them all. It is I who am the All. From Me did the All come forth, and unto me did the All extend. Split a piece of wood, and I am there. Lift up the stone, and you will find Me there." (*GT #77*)

Such sayings point readers to a distinctive Gnostic sensibility, combining hostility to the material world, the claim to origins in the light, the coincidence of opposites, the secret revelation, removal from society, and the identity of revealer and revelation, of teacher and disciple:

> Jesus said to His disciples, "Compare me to someone and tell Me whom I am like." Simon Peter said to Him, "You are like a righteous angel." Matthew said to Him, "You are like a wise philosopher." Thomas said to Him, "Master, my mouth is wholly incapable of saying whom You are like." Jesus said, "I am not your master. Because you have drunk, you have become intoxicated from the bubbling spring which I have measured out." (*GT* #13)

As in John's Gospel, then, the *Gospel of Thomas* contains an ambiguous combination of materials and perspectives. In John, the narrative that ends in the suffering, death, and resurrection of Jesus pulls the ambiguities toward the clarity of the Synoptic pattern and serves to highlight those elements in the Gospel that counter its more transformative tendencies. In the *GT,* the opposite is true. There is no suffering, death, and resurrection of Jesus. The literary form of discrete *logia* reinforces the image of Jesus as pure revealer. And the elements that are shared with the Synoptics are consistently redacted in the direction of the dominant Gnosticizing code found in the sayings unique to *Thomas.*

Canonical Controls on the Gospel of Thomas

In the case of John, it is abundantly clear that placement among the Synoptics and especially Acts tends to moderate what might be deviant in John and make it appear as an interesting difference. Does the placement of the *GT* in Codex II of the Nag Hammadi Library serve to reinforce or to soften its Gnostic tendencies? The evidence is overwhelming that canonical placement in this case serves to make the *GT* more rather than less different from the Synoptic tradition.

The document immediately preceding the *GT* is the *Apocryphon of John,*[63] which contains secret revelations of Jesus to John, the son of Zebedee, and which provides one of the most elaborate expositions of Gnos-

---

63. The composition actually occurs in three places: a short recension (III, 1) and two copies of a long recension (II, 1; IV, 1). The multiple versions suggest the importance of the composition for its readers.

tic myth in the Nag Hammadi Library.[64] Jesus discourses on the origin of the world and the way to escape from it. If we want to know why the *GT* speaks of the world as a corpse, the *Apocryphon of John* offers the reader some clues. The process of cosmogony begins with the error of Sophia (the female acting without the consent of the Male), who begets the creator god Yaltabaoth (9-12). Adam inhabits "the tomb of the newly-formed body with which the robbers had clothed the man" (21).

The composition that immediately follows the *GT* is the *Gospel of Philip* (in II, 3).[65] Like the *GT,* the *Gospel of Philip* consists in discourse rather than in narrative. It presents a series of theological and ethical observations, not as coming from Jesus, but from an authoritative teacher. Many of the statements remain obscure to us, since we do not possess the complete code for their interpretation. My point is simply that some of these obscurities are clearly and directly connected to elements that we also found obscure in the *GT.* The notion that the world is a corpse, for example, is confirmed by the *Gospel of Philip* 73.19-75.10. More impressive is the way in which the *Gospel of Philip* provides an interpretive context for the two references to a "bridal chamber" in the *GT* (## 75 and 104). The bridal chamber, it turns out, is one of the most dominant themes of the *Gospel of Philip.*[66] We read, for example:

> A horse sires a horse, a man begets a man, a god brings forth a god. Compare the bridegroom and the bride. Their children were conceived in the bridal chamber. No Jew was ever born to Greek parents as long as the world has existed. And, as a Christian people, we ourselves do not descend from the Jews. There was another people and these blessed ones are referred to as "the chosen people of the living God" and "the true man" and "the Son of man" and "the seed of the Son of man." In the world it is called "this true people." Where they are, there are the sons of the bridal chamber. (*Gospel of Philip* 75.25-76.5)

Placement between the *Apocryphon of John* and the *Gospel of Philip* serves to strengthen precisely those elements that make the *GT* less like the Synoptic Gospels and more like the other Nag Hammadi literature. On either side of the *Apocryphon of John* and the *Gospel of Philip,* furthermore, are writings of an even more thoroughgoing Gnostic outlook: the *Apocryphon* is preceded

---

64. It is the version in II, 1 that immediately precedes the *GT;* see *NHLE,* pp. 98-116.

65. See *NHLE,* pp. 131-51.

66. See *Gospel of Philip* 65.1-25; 67.1-30; 69.1-14; 69.25-35; 70.35-71.15; 82.1-25; 84.21-35; 86.5-15.

by the *Tripartite Tractate* (I, 5),[67] and *Philip* is followed by the *Hypostasis of the Archons* (II, 4).[68] The elements in the *GT* that resemble the Synoptic Gospels are virtually smothered by an overwhelming context of Gnosticism. If we reach even further into the Nag Hammadi anthology, we find other clues for construing some of the cryptic sayings of the *Gospel of Thomas*. I noted above the strange story of the woman with the broken jar that she discovered to be empty (*GT #97*). An additional part of the code is provided by the *Gospel of Truth* 26.4-27:

> When the Word came into the midst, . . . a great disturbance took place among the jars because some had been emptied, others filled; that is, some had been supplied, others poured out, some had been purified, still others broken up. All the spaces were shaken and disturbed, because they had no order nor stability. Error was upset, not knowing what to do; it was grieved, in mourning, afflicting itself because it knew nothing. When knowledge drew near it — this is the downfall of error and all its emanations — error is empty, having nothing inside.

The canonical placement of the *GT* works to reinforce those elements in it that differ from the Synoptics, just as the canonical placement of the FG works to reinforce those elements in it that it shares with the Synoptic tradition.

Trading Places

A final playful question can be posed, though not adequately answered. What would happen if the writings were switched? How would John work if it were placed where the *GT* now resides within the Nag Hammadi collection? How would the *GT* look if it were placed in the New Testament between Luke and Acts?

John might be made to work, since it contains so much that could fit within an understanding of Jesus as revealer and of discipleship in opposition to the world. But it would be difficult. What would the reader do with the countering statements in John concerning God's love for the world, or with the authority given to Peter? Above all, what would readers do with the narrative form (with its implications concerning materiality), and with the positive interaction with Judaism and the symbolic world of Torah?

67. *NHLE*, pp. 54-97.
68. *NHLE*, pp. 152-60.

It is even more difficult to think of the *GT* as placed between Luke and Acts. To be sure, the forty-day period between the resurrection and ascension would provide a fine opportunity for Jesus' secret revelations to Didymos Thomas. But although Thomas appears in the Synoptic lists of the Twelve (Matt. 10:3; Mark 3:18; Acts 1:13), he is a lesser figure, and is known as Didymos (the Twin) only because of John. And it is only in *that* Gospel that Thomas plays any significant narrative or revelatory role.

Readers who came to the *GT* from the perspective of the Pauline/Synoptic pattern would surely recognize some of Jesus' sayings, although their form might occasionally jar. Other sayings, however, would be totally bewildering. Not only does the *GT* put more violent twists than normal on the Synoptic material; it frames the Synoptic sayings within other statements utterly incongruous with the Synoptic outlook. The image of Jesus in the *GT* would be difficult to comprehend within the present New Testament anthology. There is no real grounding in Judaism; there are no signs and wonders; above all, there is no passion, death, and resurrection. Every element in the Pauline/Synoptic narrative pattern — which defines Jesus in terms of what he does for others — is lost.[69] Instead, we find a mystical identity between teacher and disciple. There is no community among Jesus' followers, or even the basis for one. There are only the individual readers who are blessed precisely because they are passers-by and solitary.

Finally, a great deal of the *GT* would remain utterly unintelligible to the reader who knew only the New Testament anthology, for the only clues for its interpretation are scattered through its home collection. What would the New Testament reader make of the empty jars and the bridal chamber, of the world as a corpse, and of the Jesus who declares, "lift up the stone, and you will find Me there" (*GT* #77)? Nothing. It is hard enough for us, and we now at least have the portions of the Gnostic code made available in the Nag Hammadi codices.

In the case of John in the New Testament canon, and in the case of the *Gospel of Thomas* in the Nag Hammadi library, it appears that birds of a feather did truly flock together.

---

69. See Luke Timothy Johnson, "Does a Theology of the Canonical Gospels Make Sense?" in *The Nature of New Testament Theology: Essays in Honour of Robert Morgan*, ed. C. Rowland and C. Tuckett (Oxford: Blackwell, 2006), pp. 93-108.

The Historical Figure of Jesus in 1 John

D. Moody Smith

In recent years the Gospel of John has gained increasing credibility in Jesus research. It figures as a significant historical source in John P. Meier's definitive *A Marginal Jew*, as well as Paula Fredriksen's *Jesus of Nazareth*.[1] There is now a John, Jesus, and History Group in the Society of Biblical Literature. Brill's compendious *Handbook of the Study of the Historical Jesus* will contain an article on Jesus tradition in the Gospel of John.[2] Given this resurgence of interest in the historical value of the Fourth Gospel, one thinks also of the First Epistle, in which the historical figure of Jesus plays an important role.[3]

In anticipating this article, I assumed that the subject of Jesus in 1 John would have been treated already, in articles if not monographs. Yet a survey of the bibliographies of recent scholarly commentaries on the Johannine Epistles (R. E. Brown, Rudolf Schnackenburg, Georg Strecker, and John Painter)

1. John P. Meier, *A Marginal Jew: Rethinking the Historical Jesus*, 4 vols. (New York: Doubleday, 1991-); Paula Fredriksen, *Jesus of Nazareth, King of the Jews* (New York: Knopf, 2000).

2. D. Moody Smith, "Jesus Tradition in the Gospel of John," in *Handbook of the Study of the Historical Jesus*, 4 vols. (Leiden: Brill, forthcoming).

3. The term "the historical figure of Jesus" is adopted from E. P. Sanders, *The Historical Figure of Jesus* (London: Penguin, 1993), because it is, in my view, more suitable and less ambiguous than "the historical Jesus." The author of 1 John did not write with the historical Jesus, as moderns may reconstruct or construe him, in view. But he did have in view a historical figure, as much as his conception of him may have differed from any modern reconstruction or construal.

turned up few works with Jesus Christ in the title, much less the historical Jesus, or the historical figure of Jesus.[4]

Of course, every serious commentator must address the question of the meaning of "beginning" (ἀρχή) in 1 John 1:1 and thereafter. In verse 1 the subject is not "Word" (λόγος), as in the opening of the Gospel, but "that which was from the beginning" (as RSV translates ὃ ἦν ἀπ' ἀρχῆς). NRSV translates "We declare to you what was from the beginning," but in doing so obscures the fact that "beginning" (ἀρχή) stands at the very beginning of the document.

Interestingly enough, both RSV and NRSV capitalize "Word" in the prologue of the Gospel, but not in the Epistle. Nor does either capitalize "life," which becomes the subject (1 John 1:2) and is clearly the equivalent of "that which was from the beginning" (1:1). Neither is taken to be a christological title. Yet both are (in 1:1-2) said to have been seen, looked at, heard, and touched (ψηλαφάω occurs in the Epistle only in 1:1; cf. Luke 24:39; John 20:25). Apparently, "from the beginning" signifies the beginning of the community's proclamation of Jesus, which constituted it as church (a term that does not appear in the Johannine Epistles until 3 John 6), but also the historical appearance of Jesus himself.

In his justly famous article "Was von Anfang war," in the 1954 Bultmann *Festschrift*, Hans Conzelmann keenly observed that while in 1 John the vocabulary, particularly the theological vocabulary, is quite similar to the Gospel's, a *Verschiebung* (shift) of meaning has occurred.[5] In 1 John ἀρχή no longer means just the primordial beginning, as in the Gospel, but has in view

---

4. In chronological order, Raymond E. Brown, *The Epistles of John*, AB 30 (Garden City, N.Y.: Doubleday, 1982), pp. 131-46; Rudolf Schnackenburg, *The Johannine Epistles*, trans. Reginald and Ilse Fuller (New York: Crossroad, 1992), pp. 303-16, esp. 309-13; Georg Strecker, *The Johannine Letters*, trans. Linda M. Maloney, ed. Harold Attridge, Hermeneia (Minneapolis: Fortress, 1996), pp. xxi-xxvi; John Painter, *1, 2, and 3 John*, SP 18 (Collegeville, Minn.: Liturgical Press, 2002), pp. 108-13.

Quite recently, however, there has been an important article bearing directly on the subject: Theo K. Heckel, "Die Historisierung der johanneischen Theologie im Ersten Johannesbrief," *NTS* 50 (2004): 425-43. Obviously, Heckel's article is different from mine, but it is grounded in the same interest and insight. See also my "John's Quest for Jesus," in *Neotestamentica et Philonica: Studies in Honor of Peder Borgen*, ed. David E. Aune, Torrey Seland, and Jarl Henning Ulrichsen, NovTSup 106 (Leiden: Brill, 2003), pp. 233-53, esp. 246-53, where the position developed in this paper is first advanced.

5. Hans Conzelmann, "'Was von Anfang war,'" in *Neutestamentliche Studien für Rudolf Bultmann*, ed. W. Eltester, BZNW 21 (Berlin: Töpelmann, 1954), pp. 194-201, esp. the formulation on p. 201.

already the appearance of Jesus and the beginning of the proclamation about him, which now must be defended in the face of erroneous teaching. The Johannine letters are thus in effect "Johannine Pastorals" in their emphasis on right doctrine and their incipient distinction between orthodoxy and heresy (terms that, at least in my view, are no longer anachronistic). In his brief article, Conzelmann is obviously more concerned with the Johannine trajectory's moving forward toward early Catholicism than with its backward reference to Jesus, which he acknowledges but does not emphasize. That backward reference is closely related also to the identity of the author, and his relationship to the evangelist, as well as to Jesus himself. In this article I want to prescind from the authorship question in order to examine simply the role of the historical figure of Jesus in 1 John, primarily by looking at the occurrences and meaning of ἀρχή.

Jesus the Beginning

Is ἀρχή, despite its importance for church tradition and doctrine, pregnant with 1 John's conception of the historical figure of Jesus, together with his fundamental importance for distinguishing true teaching from false? The word occurs eight times in 1 John and twice in 2 John — taken together, more than in any other New Testament book. There are eight occurrences also in the Gospel of John, but it is a document about six times as long as 1 John and 2 John combined. Obviously, ἀρχή is very important in the Epistles. Do the occurrences in 1 John and 2 John all point back to Jesus, even if they are not in each instance simply identical with Jesus? (The one obvious exception is 1 John 3:8, where it is the devil who has sinned "from the beginning.") Significantly, in John 15:27 Jesus says to his disciples: "You also are bearing witness [or testifying], because you are [or have been] with me from the beginning." Here ἀπ᾽ ἀρχῆς ("from the beginning") refers to Jesus' ministry, as it clearly does in 16:4: "I did not say these things to you from the beginning (ἐξ ἀρχῆς), because I was with you." Here ἀρχή is virtually a technical term referring to Jesus' historic manifestation and ministry, and this should be borne in mind as we examine instances of its occurrence in 1 John.

In 1 John 1:1 "what was from the beginning" (NRSV), or "that which was from the beginning" (RSV), is, of course, neuter gender. Is the antecedent really then the message about the Son rather than the Son himself? Obviously, neuter implies the message, but seeing, hearing, and touching (1:1-2) imply the messenger as well. The life that was made manifest (1:2) was more than the message. It is the bearer and embodiment of the message. The simple language of 1 John is replete with ambiguities, sometimes inherent in the Greek. Here is a striking example. Although neuter gender implies the message, the one who embodies the message, and is the message, is clearly also in view.

In 1:5 the message described is the message heard "from him." From whom? From the Father or from his Son Jesus Christ (1:3)? The two are even more closely related, or even identified, in 1 John than in the Gospel. Therefore, in 1 John there is often a question of which, the Father or the Son, is the antecedent. This is a perennial and difficult problem, but as a kind of exegetical experiment I am going to choose "Jesus," the Son, wherever possible and see how that works out. In 1:5 the message proclaimed is about God, and God would seem to be distinguished from the source of the message ("from him"). So the "we" of 1:1-4 proclaim a message about God that they have heard from Jesus (1:5). It is Jesus' message. This works well, however, only as far as 1:7. "He is in the light" (1:7) might be Jesus, except for the immediately following reference to "the blood of Jesus his Son." So it may be — at this point seems to be — God. But can God be "in the light," when just previously (1:5) he is said to be light? Moreover, in 1:7 "we," now including the readers as well as the writer, are to walk in the light. Later, in 2:6, their walking in the light is clearly to be an imitation of someone else's walking in the light. That would necessarily be Jesus rather than the Father. Meanwhile, "Jesus Christ the righteous," the advocate with the Father, has already been mentioned (2:1) and therefore becomes the implied subject, whose commandment or words are to be kept (2:3-5) and whose walking is to be emulated by believers (2:6), who are implicitly his followers.

Actually, "follow" is used frequently of the disciples' relation to Jesus in the Gospel of John (1:37-43), as in all the Gospels. (Discipleship is "followship.") But it does not occur in the Epistle. In fact, in the New Testament aside from the Gospels, "to follow" (ἀκολουθεῖν), does not occur in the sense of "following as disciples" except in Revelation (14:4; cf. 14:13 and 19:14). Yet the concept of following, if not the term, is central to 1 John 2:6.

In 2:7 ἀρχή appears again as one reads of the commandment that is not new but old, the one "that you have had from the beginning." This is obviously a play on the new commandment of John 13:34. Jesus there gives his disciples a new commandment, with no reference to an old one. In 1 John the commandment is first old, but then new (2:8). In the Gospel this is, of course, the famous love commandment. It is not yet repeated in 1 John, but from the discussion of hatred and love that follows (2:9-11), it is clear that the love commandment is in view. Moreover, in 2 John 5 the commandment we "have had from the beginning (ἀρχή)" is explicitly said to be "that we should love one another." So the love commandment is that old commandment "that you have had from the beginning."

In 2:12-14 the writer addresses little children, fathers, and young men, with reasons given for addressing each. In the case of fathers only (who are of course the eldest), it is "because you know him who was from the beginning" (ἀπ᾽ ἀρχῆς, 2:13, 14). In the context of 1:1, where ἀρχή clearly means the beginning of the tradition, the one (masc. sing.) who is from the beginning is Jesus rather than God. It is the fathers, who are the oldest group named, who would be in a position chronologically to know the one man who was from the beginning, namely, Jesus. (This is said twice.) Presumably, the young men, or even the young children, would have been in as good a position to know God the Father, but not Jesus. Only the fathers go back that far.

Twice in 2:24 "what you have heard from the beginning" obviously refers to what has been proclaimed (1:5) rather than the historical figure of Jesus himself. It is the message from or about Jesus. But in any event, the message originates with Jesus. In 3:11 this message (ἀγγελία) heard from the beginning is the love command, "that we should love one another." The same is true of 2 John 5–6. There the play on old and new leads to the repetition of the love commandment (John 13:34), "that we love one another" (v. 5). Following Jesus' commandments (plural) is to love (v. 6). As in the Fourth Gospel, his commandments boil down to the one, love commandment. (As we have observed, the actual reference to the love commandment does not occur in 1 John 2:8-11, but the repetition here in 2 John 5–6 confirms that it is in view. Indeed, this is true of 3:11, except that it is called the message rather than the commandment.)

It is certainly arguable, and I think correctly so, that everywhere in 1 John (except 3:8) ἀρχή implies, if it does not denote, Jesus. With the possible exception of Hebrews (2:14-18; 4:14–5:10), in no New Testament book besides the Gospels are the reality and character of the historical figure of Jesus as a human being more important than in the Johannine Epistles, particularly 1 John.

From "Isness" to "Wasness"

The historical figure of Jesus is, of course, central to the Gospel of John. Otherwise, why was a gospel written, and not a theological treatise like the Gospel of Truth?[6] Yet on the question of the role of the Jesus of the past, the historical figure of Jesus, there is a curious difference between the Gospel and the Epistles. In the Gospel the emphasis falls upon the accessibility of Jesus in the present time, that is, the time following his death and resurrection appearances. There are numerous indications of this, but none more central or explicit than the so-called Paraclete sayings (14:15-17, 25-26; 15:26-27; 16:7-15). Through the ministry of the Παράκλητος, the one "called to the side of," the Advocate (NRSV) or Counselor (RSV), Jesus' presence is felt among his disciples, and he continues to guide them.

Jesus has taught his disciples to love one another (13:34), and that this love should have no limits, even as Jesus' love has been limitless. Such love entails the willingness to lay down one's life for one's friends (15:12-13). This is what Jesus teaches his disciples. Obviously, the Spirit will guide them in how to implement obedience to Jesus' command. Perhaps the crisis situation that produced the Gospel resulted in the distillation of Jesus' teaching to this one command. The disciples' obedience to Jesus replicates Jesus' obedience to the Father: "As the Father has sent me, so I send you" (20:21; cf. 17:18).

This narrowing of the content and focus of Jesus' teaching, unique in its simplicity and consistency, is not, however, paralleled in simplicity by the Fourth Gospel's presentation of his ministry. John's account is episodic, broken, with startling omissions that are recognized by the author or final editor (20:30; 21:25). It does not have the narrative force or compelling power of Mark's. Perhaps it was never completed and therefore was supplemented and published by a later editor. Yet John may well be right about some significant historical data, even as his narrative differs from the Synoptics: Jesus, as a follower of the Baptist, himself conducted a baptizing ministry for a time (3:22, 26; 4:1-2); his ministry lasted more than one year rather than less; he was never formally tried before the Sanhedrin (Mark 14:53-65; cf. John 18:12-23); he was crucified on the eve of Passover rather than the day after; therefore, the Last Supper was not a Passover meal. John sometimes cries out to be supplemented from the other Gospels, but it is

---

6. Ernst Käsemann once addressed this problem eloquently: "But if John felt himself under constraint to compose a Gospel rather than letters or a collection of sayings, Bultmann's argument is revealed as very one-sided. For it seems to me that if one has absolutely no interest in the historical Jesus, then one does not write a Gospel, but, on the contrary, finds the Gospel form inadequate." See the English-language collection of Käsemann's essays, *New Testament Questions of Today*, trans. W. J. Montague (Philadelphia: Fortress, 1969), p. 41. The essay appeared originally in the second volume of Käsemann's *Exegetische Versuche und Besinnungen* (Göttingen: Vandenhoeck & Ruprecht, 1964); see p. 47.

less than clear that this was the evangelist's intention. He wrote a parallel, but competing, account.

Obviously, the Epistles (1 John particularly, and also 2 John) look to the same historical figure of Jesus. His historicity, that he was really human, is of fundamental importance, as are his teaching and his death (1 John 1:7; 2:2; 5:6-8). They presuppose the gospel narrative, apparently the Gospel of John, although no details of John's narrative apart from the crucifixion are required to make sense of the Epistles. More important, however, is the Epistles' emphasis that Jesus' teaching is encapsulated in the command to love, an emphasis that fits the portrayal of the Gospel of John far better than any other Gospel. With good reason, Gospel and Epistles have been regarded as the work of the same author. Probably they are not. But they share theological and ethical axioms. God's love is fundamental and prior. The proper response to God's love is (the disciples') love for one another.

Yet while the evangelist emphasizes the present accessibility of Jesus, particularly through the Paraclete, the Holy Spirit, the author of 1 John has recognized the danger in any appeal to the authority and authorization of the Spirit alone (1 John 4:1-3). The importance of Jesus as a real human being is, moreover, underscored by the condemnation of christological heresy in 4:1-3. Who is from God (or "of God") and who is not? Obviously, the crucial criterion is confessing that Jesus has come in the flesh, which means as a real human being. Denial of the humanity of Jesus is the heresy that has divided the community (cf. also 2:18-25), and such denial cannot legitimately claim the support of the Spirit (4:1-3). Interest in the historical figure of Jesus is not academic. The interest is not in history per se but in doctrine, but the doctrine depends on the historical reality of a human being. Right doctrine is an overriding criterion. But that doctrine is not given in the present. It derives from Jesus, the ἀρχή, what he taught and who he was. Thus, in 1 John there is a surprising point of contrast with the Gospel. While the Gospel presents the "isness" of Jesus, particularly by way of reassuring the disciples that they have not been left alone in a hostile world, 1 John, somewhat by way of contrast, emphasizes his "wasness." Certainly, the author of the Epistle does not want to imply that believers have been left alone to fend for themselves. The Spirit continues to be the source of reassurance (3:24). Yet the Spirit is no longer identified with the Paraclete (cf. 2:1, "Advocate"), as in the Gospel. Rather, the identity of Jesus as a figure of the past is emphasized. His pastness is crucially important.

Thus, 1 John makes clear what the Word's becoming flesh (John 1:14) means. The Epistle is more explicit on this point than the Gospel, although it is a proper interpretation of the Gospel, for which the humanity of Jesus is a basic ingredient.[7] Rarely is Jesus spoken of as the son of Joseph in the Synoptic Gospels, but Philip introduces him to Nathanael as Jesus son of Joseph from Nazareth in John (1:45). After Jesus has referred to himself as the bread from heaven (6:41), the Jews, who are apparently his fellow Galileans, say, "Is not this Jesus, the son of Joseph, whose father and mother we know? How does he now say, 'I have come down from heaven'?" (6:42). Jesus is a human being whose natural origins are known. His claims, taken literally, are inconceivable, and therefore presumably false. But they are not to be taken literally. They must be demythologized, as the evangelist has demythologized the myth of the descending and ascending redeemer. For Gospel as for Epistle, the humanity and historical reality of Jesus are basic. At the risk of seeming a bit precious, however, one might say that as the Gospel of John makes explicit what is only implicit in the Synoptics, so 1 John makes unmistakably explicit what is already found, but not as prominently and unambiguously, in the Fourth Gospel, namely, the humanity of Jesus.

The Disappearance of the Jews

Conzelmann observed that there are real and significant differences between 1 John and the Gospel, but he was not the first to note them.[8] Most striking in my observation, however, is the difference in those cast as Jesus' opponents. In the Gospel they are "outsiders," "the Jews" or "the Pharisees" (and in the passion narrative "the Jews" or "the chief priests"). At the same time, of course, Jesus is also a Jew (cf. 4:9).[9] But at many points "the Jews"

---

7. See Marianne Meye Thompson, *The Humanity of Jesus in the Fourth Gospel* (Philadelphia: Fortress, 1988), reissued as *The Incarnate Word: Perspectives on Jesus in the Fourth Gospel* (Peabody, Mass.: Hendrickson, 1993).

8. See, e.g., C. H. Dodd, *The Johannine Epistles,* MNTC (London: Hodder & Stoughton, 1946), pp. liii-liv. Dodd noted differences in eschatology, the concept of the atonement, and the work of the Spirit, which were much debated at the time but have since been widely acknowledged as suggesting a later time and a different author, perhaps of more conservative tendencies, especially in relation to the Fourth Evangelist.

9. "The Jews" in quotation marks indicates that I am using the evangelist's nomenclature without prejudice to the question of who is meant by the author. It is important to note that not "all Jews" is meant, but the people so designated were Jews, as of course was Jesus, as well as his disciples. The fundamental work remains J. Louis Martyn, *History and Theology in the Fourth Gospel,* 3rd ed. (Louisville: Westminster John Knox, 2003), of which the original edition appeared in 1968. In subsequent editions (2nd ed. 1979), Martyn has taken account of criticism but has not altered his basic views.

identify themselves as such by rejecting Jesus. The polemic between "the Jews" and Jesus at times becomes exceedingly acrimonious.

In 1 John (and 2 John), however, the opponents are "insiders," not Christ-deniers but Christ-confessors. Baldly put, they are not Jewish but Christian. Moreover, we would never suspect from the Johannine Epistles alone that Jesus himself was Jewish, much less that his opponents were. In 1 John the opponents, who have separated from the community (2:18-19), are heretics. They get it wrong about Jesus, even though they may profess to be his followers (2:22-23). They have departed from what the community has heard from the beginning (2:24). They deny the fleshly reality of Jesus (4:1-3; cf. 2 John 7).

It is usually thought that 1 John is later than the Gospel of John and presupposes it, and the Gospel's precedence fits with the change in opponents as one moves from Gospel to Epistles.[10] Jesus' contemporaries and countrymen were Jews, as was Jesus himself. It is not necessary to decide whether Jesus was Torah observant, although he seems to have been. He differs with other Jews, particularly scribes and Pharisees, over matters of interpretation, but not over the centrality of the law for Judaism and of obedience to it. In the Gospel of John, Jesus can speak to the Jews of "your law," as if it were of no concern to him or his followers. Yet he presumes that he is on the side of Moses, or put better, that Moses is on his side, and that Scripture cannot be broken (10:35). It is not the case that older traditions are abandoned in John's Gospel because of Jesus, but they are reinterpreted. To put matters simply, in the Gospel Jesus is deeply embedded in Judaism even as he appears to stand out from it. This is quite different from the First Epistle, which, moreover, contains only one scriptural reference, the case of Cain's murder of Abel his brother (1 John 3:11-17, esp. 12-15; cf. Gen. 4:1-16).

Probably the author of 1 John realized that Jesus was Jewish, but this seems to have been of little theological importance for him. For the author of the Gospel, however, Jesus' Jewish milieu was of central importance, and the Gospel is replete with Scripture and Jewish tradition, even if they have been subjected to distinctive and radical reinterpretation.[11]

In the Gospel the beginning (ἀρχή) can mean the period of Jesus' minis-

---

10. See Brown, *Epistles of John*, pp. 32-35.

11. See my essay "John," in *Early Christian Thought in Its Jewish Context*, ed. John Barclay and John Sweet (Cambridge: Cambridge University Press, 1996), pp. 96-111, in which I argue that John shares common scriptural and theological ground with normative or common Judaism but has subjected everything to radical reinterpretation unacceptable to other Jews.

try, or even the beginning of his ministry (15:27; 16:4), but whichever, that beginning is not necessarily definitive, that is, in its revelatory or normative value. Accordingly, the disciples, when left alone without Jesus after his death or departure, can expect the Holy Spirit, the Παράκλητος, who will teach them, remind them, and guide them into all the truth (14:26; 16:13). Probably the Gospel itself is to be regarded as the literary deposit of the work of the Spirit-Paraclete.[12]

Here is an important difference from the Epistles, particularly 1 and 2 John. In them, the beginning, the ἀρχή — Jesus in his true humanity (flesh, 1 John 4:2) and teaching, which the disciples have had from the beginning (2:7; 3:11) — has a uniquely normative role. The author is, to use the words of another Epistle, contending for "the faith once for all entrusted to the saints" (Jude 3). Jude, like the Johannine author, was also confronted by those who claimed to be disciples but taught false doctrine (v. 4). The similarity across the board with the Pauline Pastorals is clear (cf. 1 Tim. 4:1-5; 6:20-21). The distinctiveness of the Johannine Pastorals lies, however, in the basis or norm to which they appeal: the beginning, that which was from the beginning, the old commandment (to love one another) — finally, Jesus Christ come in the flesh. The norm is Jesus, the one who was from the beginning, who set the movement on its course and gave it direction and meaning. As the passage of time carries the community farther and farther from Jesus, its source, Jesus becomes more and more important.

As we have already observed, according to the majority view, the First Epistle presupposes the Fourth Gospel or something very much like it. Yet what 1 John actually presupposes is the theology of the Gospel (with the differences to which we have referred), and particularly the narrowly focused teaching of Jesus himself, which is thoroughly commensurate with it. Does 1 John presuppose the narrative of events in the Gospel?

There is an unambiguous answer to this question: Except for the crucifixion, it does not. Yet none of the other writings in the New Testament reflect knowledge of the Gospels' narratives per se. At most they reveal knowledge of Gospel traditions (e.g., 1 Cor. 7:10-11; 11:23-26; Heb. 5:7-8; 13:11-12). Yet Christian readers have readily seen in them the natural continuation of the Gospels' story. The same may be true of the relationship between the Gospel of John and the Johannine Epistles, except that the Epistles have an

---

12. The definitive study remains George Johnston, *The Spirit-Paraclete in the Gospel of John*, SNTSMS 12 (Cambridge: Cambridge University Press, 1970), which has been reissued (2005) in paperback.

obvious literary and historical connection with the Gospel (with the Revelation to John standing, so to speak, to one side), even though they are probably not the work of the same author.[13] The closest analogy may be the relation of the Epistle of James (or the *Didache*) with the Gospel of Matthew. Yet in that case the similarities are not nearly as close, and while the possibility of some relationship at the level of Jesus tradition certainly exists, obviously James (or the *Didache)* does not depend on Matthew in the way that the Johannine Epistles depend on the Gospel of John.

The Second and Third Epistles are so brief that their lack of evidence of knowledge of the Fourth Gospel's narrative is scarcely significant, but 1 John is a different matter. It is worth asking why 1 John, if its author knew the Gospel, does not seem to reflect greater knowledge of the Fourth Gospel's narrative(s). The answer may be that the Epistle is rather narrowly focused because of the conflict that has emerged within the Johannine community. For in 1 John it is the teaching, not the deeds embodied in narrative, that is important. Schismatics, claiming the authorization of the Spirit, have espoused a docetic Christology. (Quite possibly they accepted the signs of Jesus but misconstrued the teaching.) It is a very significant early Christian document, but it might never have been written apart from this conflict. Therefore, its focus is quite narrow.

The nature of 1 John's conflict distinguishes it from the Gospel, where the antidocetic element is less obvious, in fact, to the extent that its existence continues to be the subject of debate.[14] On the other hand, the conflict between Jesus' followers and (other) Jews has left heavy tracks in this Gospel. And although the content and nature of that conflict is anachronistically portrayed in the Gospel as a conflict about Christology, it was doubtless rooted in Jesus himself and the Palestinian-Jewish setting of his ministry. At the very least, this is the Johannine community's perception, and the *sine qua non* of its existence. This conflict with "the Jews" moves the Gospel's narrative forward, in the sense that it is the motivating force. Since that conflict has disappeared and is no longer the setting or motivating force of

13. On the existence of a Johannine community or school, see R. Alan Culpepper, *The Johannine School,* SBLDS 26 (Missoula, Mont.: Scholars Press, 1975), esp. pp. 261-99. More briefly, D. Moody Smith, *Johannine Christianity* (Columbia: University of South Carolina Press, 1984), pp. 1-36, esp. 9-22. This essay appeared originally in *NTS* 21 (1976): 222-48.

14. The leading exponent of the antidocetic character of the Gospel of John is Udo Schnelle, *Antidocetic Christology in the Gospel of John: An Investigation of the Place of the Fourth Gospel in the Johannine School,* trans. Linda M. Maloney (Minneapolis: Fortress, 1992).

1 John, there is no reason for the Epistle to take up or reflect aspects of the Gospel's narrative. Jesus seems to have been wrenched from his Jewish context and placed in an altogether Christian context, indeed, one defined by intense, presumably bitter, controversy about the nature and meaning of Jesus himself. Yet the intelligibility of Jesus, who is the object of the faith of the community, in which 1 John was written, requires something like the Gospel's presentation, which we know only in narrative form.

The Composition and Narrative of the Fourth Gospel

Our present, canonical version of John betrays marks of the process of its composition, including hints that it was edited or emended (6:52-58; the possible reversal of chapters 5 and 6 in its original form; the addition of chapters 15-16[17]; the addition of chapter 21). Moreover, the long discourses and conversations in which Jesus is a participant are entirely unique to John, whether in form or in content. They illuminate the narrative but usually are not required by it. Theories about whether or in what form such materials antedated the composition of the Gospel are not lacking. The same may be said of its narrative framework (e.g., was there a Gospel of Signs?). Necessity is the mother of invention. The nature of the material itself — not the tendency to multiply entities beyond necessity, thus inviting the application of Occam's razor — leads to the formation of hypotheses about the composition and order of the Fourth Gospel.

First John, with its recurring references to "the beginning" (ἀρχή), presumes a living tradition, and tradition history, about the historical figure of Jesus. (Otherwise, it is entirely fraudulent, which, although possible, is unlikely because it is an unsatisfying historical hypothesis.) Given the existence of such a historical tradition, one may ask in what form it likely existed. Individual stories? Individual discourses or sermons? An extended passion narrative? Were each and all of these separate units? Quite possibly. In the Gospel of John, unified as its individual parts may be, we see signs of its composite character. If the research of the past century has taught us anything, it is that there were in the beginning such discrete entities, formed and transmitted for use in Christian communities. Critical orthodoxy has seen in Mark, an anonymous genius of the late sixties or early seventies, the author who first put it all together in written form, but only after forty or so years. Mark was indeed a genius. (In fact, a distinguished Duke colleague, whose field is English literature, characterizes Mark as the most original narrative writer in history.)[15] The evangelists Matthew and Luke took up his narrative and expanded it. John did not. He may have known Mark, but to try to explain John as a new edition of Mark is an unlikely and largely hypothetical enterprise. But that John without relying on Mark produced (or was in the process of producing) a narrative broadly similar to Mark's, but with many differences and departures, should not surprise us. John was an independent Gospel.[16] More than likely, then, the author of 1 John knew it, although quite possibly in some precanonical form.

We remember our own lives in narrative form, as well as the lives of friends and family. Jesus gathered his own family of disciples (cf. Mark 3:31-35), who doubtless shared memories of him. Is not memory a universal human trait, indeed, one not confined to humans? Perhaps narrative memory is a distinctively human property. Be that as it may, is it more reasonable to believe that the memory of Jesus was from the beginning fragmented, with no narrative context, or that a narrative context would have been ingredient to any memory? The latter was the case at least in the passion narrative. As far as our present case is concerned, it is not possible to develop here a theory about the relation of tradition, narrative, and memory. But given the existence of 1 John, given the existence of the Gospel of John, given the close contact (if not agreement) between them, and furthermore the Epistles' insistence on the importance of "the beginning," it is reasonable to suppose that the letter writer knew a preexistent Johannine tradition in narrative form and that he therefore knew a document approximating the Fourth Gospel of the New Testament.

Conclusion: Jewishness or Docetism?

There is a continuum running from the Judaism that the Gospel of John presupposes through the Johannine Epistles, 1 John in particular. The Gospel of

---

15. Reynolds Price, *Three Gospels* (New York: Scribner, 1996), p. 17: "Yet a strong argument can easily be made that Mark . . . is the most original narrative writer in history, an apparently effortless sovereign of all the skills and arts of durably convincing storytelling. He is, above all, the first great master of ideal narrative distance — he stands his reader in the ideal position before his subject: the reader sees precisely enough at any moment to induce in him or her a further hunger to see more; and to the very end, that hunger is never surfeited, perhaps never sated."

16. See D. Moody Smith, *John among the Gospels,* 2nd ed. (Columbia: University of South Carolina Press, 2001), ch. 8 (pp. 195-241).

John itself represents a stage in which the circle of Jesus' disciples has moved away from its Jewish milieu in an unfriendly separation. So in it Jesus is distinguished from "the Jews," although he is still sometimes presented as a Jew (4:9). The First Epistle does not represent the next stage but presupposes at least an intervening stage after the Gospel, represented by the schismatics, in which the historical figure of Jesus has been transposed into an object of faith without discernible Jewish roots, who at the same time becomes more (or less) than human. Seemingly, the non-Jewish Jesus has become a nonhuman Jesus. Jesus' humanity is integrally related to his Jewishness. In the Epistles, 1 John and 2 John particularly, the denial of Jesus' true humanity, docetism, is strongly resisted, but without any reference to his Jewishness. One might say that in the Fourth Gospel that Jewishness is already departing. Among the schismatics whom the Epistle writer resists, it is gone, together with his humanity. The Epistle writer insists upon Jesus' humanity, but not his Jewishness.

Perhaps John 21 reflects a rapprochement with the Jewishness of Jesus, represented by Peter, without which his humanity would be in jeopardy. Johannine Christianity, in moving away from a Jewish Jesus, was moving toward docetism. That was a movement that 1 John (and 2 John) tried to stop, whether successfully or not we do not know. Is it possible that in a reconciliation with Petrine Christianity, which included Mark and the Synoptic Gospels, the Jewishness and humanity of Jesus were rescued? (John 21:25 implies its author's acknowledgement of other Gospels.) With that reconciliation accomplished, John would join a fourfold Gospel canon, but Johannine Christianity per se would disappear.[17]

*   *   *

Such reflections on the gospel narrative and its historical as well as literary dimensions form a fitting tribute to the character and significance of Richard Hays's exegetical and theological work, beginning with his dissertation, *The Faith of Jesus Christ: The Narrative Substructure of Galatians 3:1–4:11*. As Luke Timothy Johnson observes in the foreword to the 2002 reissue of the book, Hays "offers . . . the daring thesis that what appears explicitly in Paul's arguments is really directed by what seldom appears explicitly and directly

---

17. See the seminal suggestions of Raymond E. Brown, "Phase Four: After the Epistles — Johannine Dissolution," in *The Community of the Beloved Disciple* (New York: Paulist, 1979), pp. 145-64, esp. 161-62.

but is always present implicitly, namely the story of Jesus the Messiah." In appendix 2 of the 2002 edition, Hays reiterates his position: "Paul's theology must be understood as the explication and defense of a *story*. The narrative structure of the gospel story depicts Jesus as the divinely commissioned protagonist who gives himself up to death on a cross in order to liberate humanity from bondage (Gal. 1:4; 2:20; 3:13-14; 4:4-7)."[18]

---

18. For Johnson's comment, see p. xi in his foreword; for Hays's statement, see p. 274 in Appendix 2, "Πίστις and Pauline Christology: What Is at Stake?" in *The Faith of Jesus Christ: The Narrative Substructure of Galatians 3:1–4:11* (Grand Rapids: Eerdmans, 2002); emphasis original.

Did Paul's Theology Develop?

E. P. Sanders

Introduction

The question, Did Paul's theology develop? is often seen as part of the large and frequently debated question, Was Paul's theology coherent, consistent, or systematic? If his theology developed, it was not a complete *system* at the outset, and also a few *inconsistencies* may have appeared in the course of time. Thus, I wish to consider these three words (adding comments about one or two others) as an introduction to the present study of development. The three words are frequently taken to have the same meaning, but in fact they are distinct. The definitions of the words that I offer below are common and also those that I have always accepted. Others may define the words differently, though making them all synonymous is extremely confusing. My principal goal, however, is to clarify my own usage.

Paul's theology would be *systematic* if all parts of it could be fitted into a hierarchical outline that contained several main principles, each with subdivisions that follow from the main points. The word "systematics" is a synonym for "taxonomy" and refers to a scientific classification according to similarities and differences. In biology, for example, it is used for the classification of life forms. Every family of plants or animals includes a number of genera with some common characteristics. Each genus includes a number of species with some common characteristics. Et cetera. All life forms stand in a definable relationship to others, and each life form can be fitted into a pre-existing *system* of classification (though there are some complications).

A systematic theology proceeds from first principles, often those that are outlined in a creed. In the *Institutes of the Christian Religion,* for example, John Calvin began with the knowledge of God and worked his way systematically through the main headings of Christianity, progressing from God to the fall of Adam to salvation through Christ, and so on.

Paul did not write *a* systematic theology, since he wrote occasional letters relating to specific issues. Some people have tried to systematize Paul's thoughts by arranging them in some sort of creedal order. These efforts seem to me to be unsuccessful. They are certainly diverse, and it is notable that one person's systematization does not agree with that of another. Most Pauline scholars have difficulties with all of them. Thus, if Paul had a full system, we have not yet discovered it. (We shall return to systematic theology below, when discussing coherence.)

Consistency is most simply achieved by repetition. If one says the same thing about topic X every time one says anything about it, one will be perfectly consistent. It is easily possible to be entirely consistent but unsystematic. Consistent statements about topic X do not have to stand in a hierarchical or logical relationship to consistent statements about topics Y or Z.

Once a writer *varies* what he or she says about topic X, the reader may raise the question of consistency. And scholars do precisely that. We examine the consistency of one another's works, and we point out inconsistencies with glee. This enterprise is often worthwhile. On the other hand, consistency in *creative* religious thinking is much less important than *insight,* as well as less important than consistency in scholarly argument. Academics tend to overvalue simple consistency in the works of a religious genius. Simple consistency (such as defining the right policy in Iraq over a period of years by saying "stay the course," while the situation changed) is accurately called "the hobgoblin of little minds, adored by little statesmen and philosophers and divines."[1] It is at best a minor virtue and more often a serious fault. Things change, and people need to be able to adapt themselves to new information and circumstances. I think that we should be tolerant of little inconsistencies and try to explain major inconsistencies if we find them. Perfect consistency is inhuman, if one takes into account the span of a few decades, and we should not expect it.

My view is that Paul was on the whole consistent in his approach to similar questions. The only potential major inconsistency of which I know is a

---

1. Ralph Waldo Emerson, "Self-Reliance" (1841), in *Century Readings for a Course in American Literature,* ed. Fred Lewis Pattee, 3rd ed. (New York: Century, 1926), pp. 294-306, quotation p. 297.

conflict that appears in two chapters of the same letter. In 1 Corinthians 11:5 he states that women should cover their heads when they pray or prophesy in church, while in 1 Corinthians 14:33-34 he writes that women should not speak in church at all. If these two statements were written by Paul and refer to the same situation, they are badly inconsistent. No woman could obey both at the same time. (Inconsistency on a practical issue is much easier to identify than inconsistency on a theoretical one.) The question of women in church is such a striking case that many scholars look for a special explanation: one of the statements was inserted by someone else into Paul's letter, or his mind actually shifted to a different case, for example, a specific woman whom he wished to squelch. I have no solution to this problem, which I note only to clarify what it means to be "inconsistent."

There are several topics about which Paul makes *diverse* statements. The Jewish law is the most famous of these, but variety also marks Paul's descriptions of the human plight (e.g., transgression, bondage to Sin and the Flesh,[2] slavery under τὰ στοιχεῖα τοῦ κόσμου).[3] Although these different formulations allow the question of consistency to arise, I have never written that they are inconsistent. In *Paul and Palestinian Judaism,* I explained that the varying descriptions of the human plight sprang from Paul's "thinking backwards," meaning that he thought from solution to problem rather than the reverse.[4] Thus, they make sense as different statements of a consistent view: all people are in a situation that requires salvation through Christ. For Paul's statements on the law, I employed the same suggestion (thinking backwards),[5] though later I offered a second one: the questions to which each statement responds were different, a situation for which I used the phrase "different questions, different answers."[6]

---

2. English translations commonly capitalize the word "spirit" when it refers to the power of God; I have capitalized "sin" and "flesh" when, in my judgment, Paul uses them to refer to the opposing power.

3. On the human plight, see *Paul and Palestinian Judaism* (London/Philadelphia: SCM/Fortress, 1977), pp. 474-75 and n. 2; p. 509; hereafter cited as *P&PJ*. On the law, see immediately below.

4. Paul's thought ran "backwards": *P&PJ*, pp. 442-47, 474-75 (this explains diversity in describing the human plight), 481-82, 497, 499, 510, 555; see also *Paul, the Law, and the Jewish People* (Philadelphia: Fortress, 1983; London: SCM, 1985), p. 68; hereafter cited as *PLJP*. I have returned to this topic in "God Gave the Law to Condemn: Providence in Paul and Josephus," to appear in *The Impartial God,* ed. Robert Foster and Calvin Roetzel (Sheffield: Sheffield Phoenix).

5. *P&PJ*, pp. 474-97.

6. *PLJP*, part I. This answer was hinted at in *P&PJ*, p. 497.

In any case, I have not described Paul as committing frequent and gross inconsistencies, though I have often been accused of holding this position, I think because people often confuse "system" with "consistency." I *have* maintained that Paul's theology was not systematic.

Coherence means "clinging together." Probably all systematic arrangements are also "coherent," but it is possible to have coherence without hierarchical or logical arrangement. This is what I think of Paul: coherent, unsystematic, not notably inconsistent. My own image of Paul's thought is a circle containing two main principles: (1) The God of Israel is God of the whole world; he called the Jewish people, brought them out of bondage, and gave them the law; but all the creation is his. (2) In recent days, God sent his Son, Jesus Christ, to save the whole world from the wrath to come, without regard to whether or not people are Jewish.[7] Around the outside of this circle can be grouped diverse statements on such topics as the law and the human plight. Each statement, I think, relates to some part of Paul's two main principles — all of them cohere with main aspects of his thought — but they do not relate *systematically* to each other.

Is the tension between "particularity" (God is the God of Israel, and Jews are his chosen people) and "universality" (God is God of the entire created order and wills to save it without requiring people to be Jewish) a tension that is extreme enough to be called a *contradiction*? Well, the effort to hold the two principles together is certainly at the heart of Paul's two most difficult theological problems: God's intention in giving the law, whether to save or to condemn (Gal. 3:22; Romans 7; Rom. 11:32); and the significance of the election (Romans 9–11). I have written about both of these issues, and I have no desire to re-present those views here.[8] I wish only to note that these are serious clashes or, at a minimum, tensions in his thought, which are better understood once one sees that he carried two main principles in his

7. Before someone else points out that this statement of Paul's main principles is inconsistent with the lists in *P&PJ*, pp. 441-42, and *PLJP*, p. 5 (which themselves are not identical), I should say that I regard them merely as diverse formulations of the same overall position, with only a little development!

8. *PLJP*, pp. 70-81 (Romans 7), 192-96 (the salvation of Israel). The tension that is created when one believes both that God is God of the whole world and that he chose Israel can be seen in non-Christian Jewish sources as well. In Paul's thought, the solution to this tension is that God sent Christ to save the whole world without regard to the prior election of Israel. This, however, produces another tension between God's purpose in sending Christ (to save everyone) and the thus-far imperfect results (not everyone has accepted him). This tension is clear in Romans 11, where discussion moves from the olive tree (only those with faith will be saved) to the coming of the Redeemer (God will have mercy on all).

head. Positive statements about the election of Israel (as in Rom. 9:4-5; 11:28-29) relate to the first main principle (the God of the whole world chose Israel), while negative implications (as in the olive tree metaphor in Rom. 11:17-24) relate to the principle that Christ came to save all who have faith in him, whether they are Jewish or not.

The present point is that virtually all of Paul's theological thoughts relate in some way or other to these two principles. Once one lists the implications that arise from these principles, however, one does not have an outline that can be arranged hierarchically, in a list graded in accordance with importance or in a list that puts the various thoughts in a logical sequence. What we have, rather, are *insights*. The insights that spring so freely from Paul's head are not random thoughts but are coherent with main ideas.[9]

I wish now to give two examples that show the unsystematic nature of Paul's coherent thought. First, I would not know where to put, in a systematic outline, the view that Sin, Law, and Flesh go together as enslaving factors (Rom. 6:20–7:6), or that Christians are now "dead" to them, having died with Christ (Rom. 6:5-11; 7:6). Do these follow from the statement that the law is holy, righteous, and good (Rom. 7:12)? Do they lead to it? I do not think that they are incoherent, since they relate to main principles. Moreover (as indicated above), these and other statements about the law are not inconsistent, since they answer different questions. How may I be saved by Christ? Answer: by faith, not by obeying the law. If I am not in Christ, but under some other system (whether paganism, astrology, or the Jewish law), what is my status? Answer: bondage. If I want a good guide to behavior, how can one describe it — apart from saying, "live by the Spirit"? Answer: read the commandments, especially "love your neighbor."

I see that all of the negative statements about the law relate to the view that *salvation comes from Christ, and all other lordships or domains are to be rejected.* I also see that this principle is "in tension" or in conflict with the principle that the same God who sent Christ also gave the law — and created flesh! Thus, I see principles, I see conclusions from them, and I see tension between them; but I do not see a system.

Second example: A scholar who wishes to systematize Paul must find different headings in his or her outline for "righteousness by faith" and "being one person with Christ." Perhaps "righteousness" is preliminary to membership in the body of Christ. Or maybe it is the result of life in Christ. I think

---

9. E.g., *P&PJ*, p. 518: Paul "thought, . . . he thought on the basis of theological convictions, and consequently . . . he thought coherently."

that the more fruitful path is to see these statements as different formulations, from different semantic fields, which both point to the same reality.[10] The two "cohere," or stick together, with one of his main principles, but they are not discrete points on a systematic outline, where one follows from the other. Thus: I regard Paul as a coherent thinker, but not a systematic theologian. His letters are much more interesting, exciting, and in fact glorious than that.[11]

Although I wish not to footnote each of the scholars who has objected to my view that Paul was a coherent but not systematic thinker,[12] or who has misrepresented it, I shall offer as an extreme example a recent book by Douglas Campbell, which in many ways I like very much, but which confuses various terms, including the three I listed above and also others, among them "rationality." At various points in his book *The Quest for Paul's Gospel,*[13] Campbell describes his search: it is for an "intelligible Pauline Gospel" (p. 9), or for "coherence, objectivity, and rationality," as well as "intelligibility" (p. 12). He opposes postmodernism, which is "self-referentially incoherent," because he is a Christian and because he favors "rationality," "order," and "intelligibility" (p. 13).

At this point in the book, I was feeling downright hostile toward those postmoderns, whoever they are, who oppose Reason, which I hold as sacred. Then I reached Campbell's most sustained statement: "Others view [Paul] as an ad hoc thinker with no inner consistency or system at all (i.e. he is making it up as he goes along), or as someone who is simply confused and intellectually inadequate, at least at certain points." Campbell classifies Heikki Räisänen and myself in this camp (with partial support from others), which

10. "Righteousness by faith and participation in Christ ultimately amount to the same thing" (*P&PJ*, p. 506). Cf. p. 519: "The fact that Paul utilizes terms which we now identify as having different backgrounds does not do away with the claim that he thought coherently." For the entire discussion, see pp. 441, 487, 495, 501-8, 519-20.

11. The systematic theologies that I have read, which I find to be much less interesting and gripping than Paul's letters, were written by John Calvin, Karl Barth (I have read only a few volumes of his *Church Dogmatics*), Emil Brunner, and Paul Tillich. Moving beyond theology, the systematician whom I most admire is John Locke, whose treatises on epistemology and philosophy of government unfold with a logical clarity that is marvelous to behold.

12. "I view Paul as a *coherent* thinker, despite the unsystematic nature of his thought and the variations in formulation" (*P&PJ*, p. 433); "In taking the position that Paul was a coherent, but not systematic, thinker, we are taking the position most common among exegetes, and it needs little defence" (*P&PJ*, p. 518, with n. 1, where other scholars are cited). Note also the search for the "center" of Paul's theology, pp. 434-42.

13. Douglas A. Campbell, *The Quest for Paul's Gospel: A Suggested Strategy* (London: T. & T. Clark, 2005).

he dubs "anti-theological," although (he continues) we could just as well be called "anti-rational or anti-systematic." In the footnote, he claims that we ignore Paul's "overt attempted rationality" (pp. 29-30 and n. 2).

I find all of this to be terribly confused, since Campbell simply equates coherence, consistency, rationality, intelligibility, and system, though each of these words has a meaning of its own, and it is possible to be one or more of them but not another. It is simply bewildering that he describes my view of Paul as anti-rational and anti-theological. This is entirely untrue as a characterization of my view of Paul, and it seems possible that he has read only right-wing caricatures of my work, not the books themselves.

I think that Paul was a splendid creative theologian. He was a mystic (2 Cor. 12:1-10), but the numerous arguments in his letters operate entirely in the realm of reasoned (rational) argument, and they are all intelligible — in fact, I think that I have explained them, which proves that I find them quite comprehensible! There are major discussions in *Paul and Palestinian Judaism* and *Paul, the Law, and the Jewish People* of Paul's various arguments — each intelligible, each rational, though the forms of argumentation are diverse and many are unfamiliar today, since Paul often argued as would any great Jewish exegete of the ancient world. But that does not make them unintelligible, incoherent, or irrational. With regard to my having a view of Paul as anti-theological: the main topic of my work on Paul is his theology — Christology, theology proper (his ideas about God), faith, dying with Christ, his conception of sin, and so on.

On p. 139 Campbell claims that Professor Räisänen and I present Paul's discussions of the law as "confused." I pointed out above that I noted the variations in Paul's descriptions of the human plight but never called them "inconsistent." In general, I have not accused Paul of major and gross inconsistencies, and I certainly have never regarded him as confused.[14] His princi-

---

14. I am extremely grateful to Carol Shoun for finding "inconsistent" and "inconsistency" in *PLJP,* which I shall briefly review. In most cases these words refer to inconsistency (in the sense of "diversity") of *statement* or formulation (p. 35) or lack of harmony in argumentation (p. 35): Paul's arguments in favor of a given position were quite varied, without any noticeable change in the position itself — one of the main points of the book. Other statements on consistency are these: There is a (minor) inconsistency within Romans 5 (p. 36). In Romans 7, Paul's argument that God gave the law for life is inconsistent with the argument that he gave it in order to condemn, for example in Galatians 3 (p. 79). Romans 1:18–2:29 does not give a consistent description of Jews and Gentiles (p. 125). There are "*diverse* explanations of the function of the law," but "those who argue in favor of mere inconsistency" are wrong (p. 147).

If I had anticipated the furor that would be kicked up by the publication of Heikki

pal arguments on the law are, as noted above, diverse, since they deal with diverse issues. They appear confused only when a systematician wishes to make them all the same or to put them all equally under one heading of a systematic outline.

When, in 1975, I wrote, "I view Paul as a *coherent* thinker, despite the unsystematic nature of his thought and the variations in formulation,"[15] I could not have imagined that the words "unsystematic" and "variations" would be taken to mean "wildly inconsistent and confused," "wholly irrational," or "incoherent." I thought that all readers would know what systematic theology is and thus what "unsystematic" means. I presented Paul as having a definite "pattern of religion," which he often expressed in theological terms and which can be summarized as "participationist eschatology."[16] I also maintained that his theology has a "center" (see n. 12). If I found him to be unintelligible, incoherent, irrational, and nontheological, I could never have proposed that he had a theology that could be described and *summarized,* or that it had a center. How can one summarize an incoherent jumble? Or find its center?

As it turns out, Campbell's own view of Paul's theology is not all that different from mine: he prefers to expand my "participationist eschatology" into "PPME," standing for "pneumatologically participatory martyrological eschatology" (p. 42). The two additional words do point to main elements in the participatory scheme, though the title may be too complicated to catch on. In any case, if my summary term is usable, surely I did not argue or imply that it stands for thought that is incoherent, irrational, and unintelligible.

One of my major explanatory devices, by which I tried to unravel a lot of the statements that others have found to be confusing, was that Paul's

---

Räisänen's fine book *Paul and the Law,* WUNT 29 (Tübingen: Mohr, 1983), published the same year as *PLJP,* I would have written some of those lines slightly differently. But it is a fact that Paul was not perfectly consistent: no one is, and perfection is an unreasonable expectation. I also regard it as a fact that most of his inconsistencies are minor or are on the surface: different formulations, different explanations, or different argumentation, all referring to a small set of consistently held principles. The major complication is the "tension" between two of his main principles (see at n. 8 above). Carol Shoun's labors have given me the opportunity to see that my wording has not been perfectly consistent but that my view of Paul has been consistently maintained. For the main argument of the book on this point — "diversity" within "coherence" — see pp. 5-6, 144-48; on "consistency," see also pp. 71-81.

15. N. 12 above. It is noteworthy that the heading of pp. 518-20 is "Coherence, relevance and sources."

16. *P&PJ,* pp. 433 (his theology was an expression of his religion), 549 ("participationist eschatology").

thought ran backwards, from solution to problem (n. 4 above). Campbell accepts this sort of thinking, though without a footnote, calling it "a retrospective approach" that "'works backwards,' formulating its account of 'the problem' only after it has experienced 'the solution' in Christ."[17] Thus, we agree about one of the major aspects of Paul's thought, as well as about appropriate words to summarize it. It is not clear why my Paul is anti-rational and anti-theological, while Campbell's Paul is rational and theological.

Development (Growth)

The present paper is a "thought" piece, based not on the study of secondary literature but on analyzing the thinking of the man who wrote the letters with which I have lived for decades. The topic is usually called "development," though "growth" is probably better, for reasons that will appear. Development (to stay with the usual term) in and of itself is not necessarily systematic or unsystematic, consistent or inconsistent, coherent or incoherent. The sorts of development that I now see in Paul constitute "organic growth," the elaboration in later letters of ideas that are no more than incipient in early letters. They are thus coherent parts of Paul's thought.

I must begin by confessing that in my earliest book on Paul (completed thirty-three years ago, about the same period of time as that between Paul's conversion and Romans) I wrote, "I do not see any signs of major theological 'development' in Paul's thought, but there are certainly alterations in the way in which he expressed himself. . . ."[18] The twenty-eight-line footnote that follows that statement gives some information about efforts to find development. It concludes thus:

> My own view is that chronological change would be interesting and important if it could be definitely established. There are some changes which are obvious: thus the discussion of the law in Romans is more developed and more nuanced than the discussion in Galatians (a point which I owe to W. D. Davies). It does not necessarily follow that Paul changed what he *thought*, although he may have done so. It seems safest to take such changes as developments in *presentation* and *argument*. I do not know of any decisive evidence that Paul changed what he thought during the pe-

17. Campbell, *Quest*, p. 142.
18. *P&PJ*, p. 432.

riod of the surviving correspondence, although the possibility that he did so cannot be excluded; and the variations in argument in the letters will always provide grounds for speculations on this score.[19]

Two things occur to me about the thought of the young man who wrote that statement and the footnote: (1) He was not entirely comfortable with ruling out development but did not see how to proceed with a study of it. (2) He defined "development" as requiring "change," and "change" as meaning "retraction." Another line in the footnote states that 2 Corinthians 5 and Philippians 1:22-24 are not "a development away from the expectation of a future resurrection," since that expectation is later repeated in Romans. That is, Paul did not *retract* his earliest view. I now would define "development" and "change" as not requiring retraction or deletion of what Paul had previously thought. If we are looking for change in that sense, we shall not find it; but Paul could develop his thought, in the sense of "growing it," without renouncing previous views.

In the early 1990s, I offered a graduate seminar that looked at the question of development, focusing on eschatology. Thereafter, in all my seminars on Paul, we read the letters in chronological order and traced variations. In about the middle of this process, Gregory Tatum presented a splendid dissertation on development in Paul's thought, which has recently appeared in print; his work confirmed my suspicion that Paul's thought grew and developed.[20]

In other words, I am an adaptive human, and I have had new experiences, including reading Paul's letters through several dozen times since I wrote those lines and supervising enterprising and intelligent doctoral students. Paul tells us to imitate him, and I am doing my best: my thought has developed, and I now think that we can use the word "development" for Paul's theology.

In this sense, the answer to the question of development now seems completely obvious: Of course Paul's thought developed. How could it not? He was an intelligent and reactive human, who worked in an unprecedented environment. The latter days had arrived, and it was time for Jews to persuade Gentiles to turn to the God of Israel in order to share in the blessings of the messianic age. During his travels on behalf of this new vocation, Paul

---

19. *P&PJ*, pp. 432-33 n. 9, emphasis original.

20. Gregory Tatum, OP, *New Chapters in the Life of Paul: The Relative Chronology of His Career*, CBQMS 41 (Washington, D.C.: Catholic Biblical Association of America, 2007).

met and conversed with a variety of other humans, and he faced a series of new challenges. Only a dullard would repeat time after time what he had previously thought or refuse to think back through some of his opinions as issues and objections arose during his ministry. Adaptation must have been his watchword.

The most important consideration, however, is not the obvious but theoretical necessity for Paul's thought to develop during his tumultuous ministry, but rather the simple fact that his letters show him to have been a man of great variety and adaptability. As problems shifted, and as his understanding of them advanced, he made adjustments.

There is, of course, an alternative answer to the question, the one that I preferred in my callow youth. I shall repeat the question and vary the answer. Did Paul's theological thinking develop? Many have answered, Obviously not. I shall now outline one of the principal ways in which scholars reject the idea of development.

In chapter 3 of Philippians Paul depicts his conversion as involving a rejection of righteousness by the law. Some hold that this passage proves that the slogan "righteousness is by faith, not by works of law" in fact goes back to the time of his conversion. Even when not uttered, this "doctrine" is believed to have determined everything that he wrote from 1 Thessalonians to the end of Romans.

Turning to one of my favorite older commentators on Paul, I shall give an example of a similar argument that implicitly denies the possibility of development. I greatly admire all the work of J. B. Lightfoot and wish that there were more people like him. But on this topic — whether or not at the time of conversion Paul worked out the theology of Galatians and Romans — I believe that he erred. In discussing Paul's trip to Arabia shortly after the revelation that changed his life (Gal. 1:15-17), Lightfoot correctly points out that in ancient literature "Arabia" can mean either the Arabian peninsula (what we now call Saudi Arabia), the Sinai desert, or the area immediately south of Damascus (Coele Syria,[21] including some of the cities of the Decapolis). We could add to Lightfoot's evidence for the third use of "Arabia" the fact that Josephus sometimes used "Arabia" and "Coele Syria" interchangeably.[22] At

---

21. "Coele Syria" is now unfamiliar as a geographical term. It Latinizes κοίλη Συρία, or "the hollow of Syria," the northern extension of the Great Rift Valley, which begins in lower Africa and runs north approximately to Damascus. The Great Rift includes the Jordan valley and the Dead Sea, all below sea level.

22. Compare Josephus, *War* 1.89-90 with *War* 1.103; see also *War* 1.124-25.

any rate, Lightfoot chose not the area close at hand but the Sinai desert as the "Arabia" to which Paul went, commenting:

> Standing on the threshold of the new covenant, he was anxious to look upon the birthplace of the old: that . . . he might ponder over the transient glories of the "ministration of death," and apprehend its real purpose in relation to the more glorious covenant which was now to supplant it.[23]

The passage that Lightfoot used to explain Paul's theological reflection immediately after his call to be an apostle was not Philippians 3 but rather its mate (in subject matter), 2 Corinthians 3 ("ministration of death"). The argument is basically the same as the one I sketched above: shortly after his conversion Paul sat down and worked out the theology that appears thirty or so years later. This view clearly runs counter to the possibility of development.

There are a couple of curiosities about Lightfoot's choice of the Sinai desert. One is that he did not consider the amount of money that would be required to mount an expedition to Sinai: camels, donkeys, guards, guides, water, and food. Paul could simply have walked from Damascus to the "Arabia" east of the Jordan Valley. Lightfoot had a practical turn of mind, but I suppose that in writing on Galatians he was immersed in its theology. The second curious point is that Lightfoot did not consider the sequence of the letters. This is odd for a man who had written more than once on chronology and chronographers.

I have by no means done justice to arguments that can be offered against development, but I think that the most important ones hinge on interpreting Paul's conversion or call as he himself interpreted it in hindsight. Second Corinthians 3, to be sure, is not explicitly autobiographical, but it is not much of a stretch to connect it with Paul's discussion of his conversion in Philippians 3. The danger of the procedure is simply that hindsight can be misleading. The lens of more recent experience often influences how we see the past. A second objection is that it is impossible to see how Paul is applying "justification by faith," or his conception of the two "ministries," to the issues of 1 Thessalonians or 1 Corinthians. We are offered a systematization of Paul's thought that does not aid, and may hinder, exegesis.

We of course cannot directly refute the accuracy of Paul's own hindsight about the theological significance of his conversion. What we can do, how-

---

23. J. B. Lightfoot, *Saint Paul's Epistle to the Galatians* (London: Macmillan, 1892), p. 88.

ever, is simply to ask whether we can arrange Paul's letters in at least their approximate chronological order; and, if we can, to ask whether we find the *sort of adaptation and variety* that can reasonably be called "development" or "growth."

The entire discussion depends on topics that I cannot address in detail here: which letters in the Pauline corpus are "authentic," and in what sequence they were written. When, in my seminars, we read the letters in their probable chronological order, we adopted the following sequence: 1 Thessalonians, 1 Corinthians, 2 Corinthians 10-13, 2 Corinthians 1-9, Galatians, Philippians, and Romans (leaving Philemon out of account, as not bearing on the main topics of Paul's theology).[24] Studying the letters in this sequence was eye opening about how themes started and grew. I strongly recommend reading works — not just Paul's letters — in their chronological order.[25]

In his dissertation (and now his book), Gregory Tatum makes an interesting and even compelling case in favor of a somewhat more complicated chronological order: 1 Thessalonians, 1 Corinthians, 2 Corinthians 10-13, Galatians, Philippians, 2 Corinthians 1-9, Romans. Putting Galatians and Philippians before 2 Corinthians 1-9, rather than after all of 2 Corinthians, makes little difference to the study of the topics that I shall discuss.[26] Since explaining and utilizing the arrangement would occupy space, and this essay is already long, I shall stay with the simplified list that I first presented, putting Galatians and Philippians after all of 2 Corinthians. Other parts of the sequence are not very controversial: 1 Thessalonians first and Romans last. Galatians' relationship to the Corinthian correspondence has always been the hard problem, and I refer the reader to Tatum's book (see n. 20) for a full discussion. Now I shall turn to some cases where I see development in the sense of growth.

24. If one includes Colossians and Ephesians among the authentic Pauline letters, of course, the question of "development" changes markedly.

25. I regard my failure to think chronologically as the principal weakness in the Pauline section of *P&PJ*. I still view the emphasis on coherence (despite variety) and lack of system as correct, but it would have helped if I had seen that the variety is sometimes explicable as organic growth.

26. But see further n. 35 below.

Topics

1. Eschatology

We shall start with eschatology, which has often been discussed in connection with development. The passages on the resurrection of believers and the return of the Lord show Paul at his adaptive best, and there is certainly *variety*. Is it the kind of variety that may best be called "growth"?

In 1 Thessalonians we learn that Paul had told his converts to turn to the God of Israel and to await his Son from heaven (1 Thess. 1:9-10; 4:13-18). The Thessalonians were doing that when, apparently, one or more of them died. This was troubling, since the survivors were afraid that the dead would miss out on the return of the Lord. When Paul heard from his converts, he simply revised his prediction by saying that "the dead in Christ will rise first," before those who are still alive (4:15-17).[27] That is an extremely simple addition to his original message and hardly qualifies as "development." We assume that as a Pharisee he had always believed in the future resurrection, and it was natural to apply this view to his converts when the need arose.

Paul wrote 1 Thessalonians from Athens (see 3:1). From Athens he went to Corinth, where he founded a church. He doubtless told the Corinthians what he had written to the Thessalonians. I paraphrase: "The Lord will return while most of you are alive, but if some die they will rise first to greet him in the air." He left Corinth and traveled to Syria and Jerusalem, staying for an unknown period. Next he walked back to Ephesus.[28] This entire trip took at least two years, but probably longer. While in Ephesus he heard from the Corinthians. They did not like the idea of the resurrection of dead bodies. They knew what happened to corpses, and the idea that decaying body parts would go whizzing through the air to greet the Lord was probably offensive.[29]

Besides, they were presumably Greek in culture, and so they probably already believed in the immortality of the inner person, the ψυχή. Why not just say that at death the ψυχή will go to be with the Lord instead of down to Hades or to the Isles of the Blessed? Paul objected. He had seen the risen Lord, and the Lord had had a *body*. So, turning to the Greek translation of

---

27. Scripture quotations not otherwise identified are from the NRSV.

28. Acts 18:18–19:1.

29. In 1 Corinthians 15, the focus is on whether or not a body is raised; Paul's solution, a spiritual body that is not flesh and blood, is calculated to meet an objection to the resurrection of a fleshly body.

Genesis, he pointed out that Adam became a living ψυχή (Gen. 2:7), which Paul took to mean a *normal body* (as translators correctly have it), not an immortal "soul" or "inner person," which is the usual meaning of ψυχή. If the first Adam had a *psychic* (that is, normal) body, the second or last Adam must have a supernormal body, a *spiritual body* (1 Cor. 15:44-49).[30]

But then, Paul thought, in *some ways* the Corinthians were right in objecting to the resurrection of physical remains. And so he now insisted that "flesh and blood cannot inherit the kingdom of God" (1 Cor. 15:50). When this sentence was read to his church, the members (I imagine) stood and cheered. Paul would not divide the human into parts (ψυχή, or soul, and body), and he felt that he had to defend the word "body" in describing the entity that would be raised, but he granted the Corinthians' main point: it would not be a body of flesh and blood. Rather, everyone would be transformed: both the dead and the living would be changed in an instant ("in the twinkling of an eye," 15:52), and all would ascend as transformed, spiritual bodies.

In comparison with 1 Thessalonians, this is at least adaptation. To avoid the word "development," we could say that Paul was simply thinking more specifically and concretely in response to a difficult question than he had thought when he wrote to the Thessalonians. It appears in any case that, when he founded the church at Corinth, he had not said that at the resurrection the *body* that would be raised would be *spiritual*, not flesh and blood. I think that probably this shift in the definition of "body" was new, but we cannot exclude the possibility that it was new only to the Corinthians, not to Paul.

In 2 Corinthians — written after Paul had been to Corinth again — we find further variations. First, the transformation from flesh and blood to spiritual body will not come "in the twinkling of an eye" (which is what he wrote in 1 Corinthians) but rather is already underway: "all of us . . . *are being* transformed into the same image [that is, into Christ's image] from one degree of glory to another" (2 Cor. 3:18). Moreover, "our outer nature is wasting away, [while] our inner nature is being renewed day by day" (4:16).

Not only does Paul put the transformation in the present tense rather than in the future tense, but he also takes a step toward distinguishing the in-

---

30. "Must have": Paul remembered Gen. 2:7 as calling Adam "the *first* man, Adam" (1 Cor. 15:45). By the standard rules of Jewish exegesis, this implied that there would be a "second Adam" or a "last Adam," who would have to be different from the first Adam. Since the first Adam's body was a ψυχή, it was natural that the last Adam's body was πνεῦμα, thus "a spiritual body."

ner person from the outer person. In 2 Corinthians 4:16, *only the inner* is being renewed. This is, of course, required by the tense of the verb: he could not say that in the present the outer person is becoming a spiritual body, not of flesh and blood.

This division of the human into inner and outer, which he had refused to make in 1 Corinthians 15, is repeated in 2 Corinthians 5:1-5, where "we" — the inner, true selves — live in "tents" — temporary, outer coverings. Paul's inner person groans, wanting to be out of the tent. And yet not so, since that would mean that the inner person has a disembodied existence. Rather, the tent will be swallowed by a heavenly dwelling: the mortal swallowed by the immortal. Here Paul returns to one of the themes of 1 Corinthians 15. (He had given the proof text for "swallowing" in 1 Cor. 15:54.) In 2 Corinthians 5:4 apparently both the inner person and the tent are swallowed by life. Nevertheless, in 2 Corinthians 5:2-4 Paul can distinguish the inner person from its clothing, which we would not have expected on the basis of 1 Corinthians 15. Thus, there are bits of anthropological dualism, as well as "realized eschatology," in 2 Corinthians 3–5.

More famously, when in Philippians Paul is contemplating the possibility of his own death, he thinks that when he dies his true self will go to be with the Lord (1:23), presumably leaving his body behind until the general resurrection. This is clearly a case of anthropological dualism. Thus, 2 Corinthians and Philippians contain substantial alterations of 1 Thessalonians and 1 Corinthians.

In 1974-75 these variations or alterations did not appear to me to be "development," but rather merely varying formulations, because Paul did not *retract* the original view that in the very near future the Lord would return. In 2 Corinthians 4:14, in the midst of statements of realized eschatology, he still wrote that "the Lord will raise us . . . with Jesus." Similarly, in Philippians 3:20-21 he repeated that "we are expecting a Savior" from heaven (as in 1 Thessalonians) and that he "will transform the body of our humiliation" so that it will be like "the body of his glory," as in 1 Corinthians 15. Finally, the "swallowing" motif is the same in 2 Corinthians 5 as in 1 Corinthians 15. Thus, if "develop" means "retract," then clearly Paul's thought did not develop. His thought shifts in some verses of 2 Corinthians and in Philippians 1 but returns to a previous point in Philippians 3.

I would now say that "development" can and often does occur without retraction: thought can grow. As the Lord delayed, it seemed increasingly unsatisfactory — not only to Paul's converts, but finally to Paul himself — to think of the dead in Christ as lying in the grave, decaying, for month after month, year after year until the resurrection. When thinking of his own death, Paul himself wanted there to be an inner true self that could be with the Lord immediately after death.

Though not apostles, we are all free, and so we can choose whether to call this development of variety in Paul development or growth of his thought. I am now inclined to do so. Circumstances cause his thought to enlarge and become more complicated.

2. Inner Spiritual Life

The delay of the Lord's return, combined with the suffering of converts, led to a considerable development in Paul's thought about the inner spiritual life of the person. First Thessalonians, which is his earliest surviving letter by three or four years or more, is tough-minded when it comes to suffering. The Thessalonians in Christ were being persecuted. The persecution, to be sure, was probably closer to harassment than slaughter, but harassment can be difficult to endure. Paul is less sympathetic than one might wish. I paraphrase 1 Thessalonians: "Christ suffered and I suffer. I told you in advance that those in Christ suffer, so why are you complaining? Suck it up! Hang in there and wait! It won't last long. I have worried about you. Are you being blameless while waiting? If not, perfect yourselves, be blameless, shape up!"[31] He did, of course, offer some consolation: they loved one another (4:9), though he thought it worthwhile to urge them to try harder (4:10). And they had the Spirit (4:8), though he had to tell them not to quench it (5:19).

Possession of the Spirit is one of the unvarying aspects of Paul's view of the Christian life. The role of the Spirit is not, however, developed in 1 Thessalonians. Paul does not, for example, prove that his converts have the Spirit by reminding them of their spiritual gifts, nor does he contrast their present life, during which they possess the Spirit, with their former life "in the Flesh." One closes the letter thinking that the great apostle provided somewhat cold comfort to people who were hurting and who may have been doubting. Of course he urged them to hang on and praised them for doing

---

31. For "perfection" or "blamelessness," see 1 Thess. 3:13 ("holiness," "blameless"); 5:23 ("undamaged," ὁλόκληρον, in spirit and "blameless" in body); 4:7 (not impure); cf. Paul's own purity and blamelessness, 2:10.

so adequately, but the principal message is to be blameless and steadfast until the Lord's return and to endure suffering without wavering.

Next letter: One of the most obvious aspects of 1 Corinthians is the long section on spiritual gifts, chapters 12–14. Were I to lapse into fantasy, I would suggest that while he traveled from Athens to Corinth (after writing 1 Thessalonians) Paul determined to emphasize the value of having spiritual gifts. The enjoyment of such gifts would help his converts-to-be to remain true during persecution if the Lord still delayed his appearance. Or maybe the Corinthians were just inclined to enthusiasm, no matter what Paul chose to emphasize. In any case, when he heard reports of their life a few years later, he felt that he had to rebuke them for speaking in tongues so much and so loudly, especially since sometimes more than one person spoke at once (1 Corinthians 12–14).

After he sent the letter, he apparently continued to worry about his church in Corinth, and so he changed his travel plans and went there before revisiting Macedonia (2 Cor. 1:15-16).[32] The result was what we now call "the unhappy visit." The church was not obedient to Paul; some preferred other apostles, or perhaps only one other apostle (2 Corinthians 11). Paul left Corinth, hurt and angry. He wrote a harsh letter and sent Titus (2 Cor. 7:5-8). The combination worked. Titus subsequently found him in Macedonia and told him that all was well. Paul wrote a letter expressing his pleasure and relief. It is in the letter of relief (2 Corinthians 1–7 or 1–9) that he puts in the present tense the beginnings of the transformation into the glorious body of Christ (3:18 and 4:16, which I quoted earlier). In this letter there is another clear shift into realized eschatology: "If anyone is in Christ, there is a new creation: everything old has passed away; see, everything has become new" (5:17).

The reason for this considerable change in Paul's presentation of his view is, of course, unknown. I think of two possibilities: (1) The Corinthians felt scrunched by his rebuke over the handling of spiritual gifts; this encouraged him, after Titus had achieved a reconciliation, to go overboard in moving aspects of salvation into the present (or even the past); or (2) he was simply so happy that the Corinthians had returned to him that he got carried away by enthusiasm and moved the future new age and the coming transformation into the present.

32. In all of the discussions of the Corinthian correspondence, I am assuming arrangements of the material and travel that I cannot explain here. Among other things, I am one of the numerous scholars who read 2 Corinthians 10–13 as the "harsh letter," which was actually written before the letter of relief, 2 Corinthians 1–9 or 1–7.

This way of stating the present life of the Christian — we already live in the new creation; the old has gone; transformation into the glory of Christ is underway — had a very short life: these *formulations* did not survive 2 Corinthians. In the last part of Romans 8 the "already" and the "not yet" are re-established in their usual order. In the present, Christians have only the "first fruits of the Spirit" (as in 1 Thessalonians), while they wait for the final delivery from bondage to decay (Rom. 8:18-25). The transformation — "glory" (8:18), "the redemption of our bodies" (8:23) — lies ahead (as in 1 Corinthians 15).

Well, again, someone may say, Paul does not retract the view of 1 Thessalonians and 1 Corinthians: Christians now have the Spirit; they must wait; they will be transformed in the future. These views are repeated in the last verses of Romans 8. All true.

But although the language of present "transformation" and "new creation" does not appear after 2 Corinthians 3–5,[33] things are not the same in Romans as in 1 Thessalonians. The present life in Romans has changed in a different way: Paul's converts have died to Sin, etc. To see this, we need to press on to the third exploration, which is closely linked to this one.

3. Suffering, Imitation, and Sharing

"Imitation" is one of the largest and in some ways most consistent points in Paul's letters.[34] The language of "imitating" or being "imitators," to be sure, is not frequent (1 Thess. 1:6; 2:14; 1 Cor. 4:16; 11:1; Phil. 3:17 [συμμιμηταί]), but the theme is widespread. Paul constantly uses the first person ("I" or "we") with an implied exhortation to do things the way he does, and he does things the way Christ did. He wishes that with regard to sex his converts would be as he is: celibate (1 Cor. 7:7). He wishes that the other apostles would be more like him and much less like themselves. They preach wisdom; he and God are against human wisdom (1 Corinthians 3). The implication is that the Corinthians should, like Paul, be against human wisdom. And so on, almost forever.

While imitation covers a lot of points, the most explicit are suffering

---

33. The phrase "new creation" appears in Gal. 6:15, but not in the sense that it is already present.

34. There are now several excellent treatments of "imitation" in Paul's letters, including a Duke doctoral dissertation by Dustin Ellington: "'Imitate Me': Participation in Christ and Paul's Vocational Model for the Church in 1-2 Corinthians" (2004).

(both examples of the word "imitators" in 1 Thessalonians) and giving offense to no one (1 Cor. 11:1). I wish to focus on suffering. In 1 Thessalonians, this is imitation plain and simple: as we saw above, Christ suffered, Paul suffers, and his converts suffer; their comfort is that they are in good company. In Paul's letters, suffering is usually not punishment for sins (except when people have been bad! as in 1 Cor. 11:29-32) but rather imitation of Christ. But being Christlike is also eschatological: our mortal bodies will become like his glorious body (1 Cor. 15:43, 49). When aspects of eschatology move into the present in 2 Corinthians, becoming like Christ moves into the present, and mere imitation becomes carrying *his* suffering and death in our own bodies. At first this seems to be true only of Paul, who always carries in his body "the death of Jesus." In life, he is "always being given up to death for Jesus' sake, so that the life of Jesus may be made visible in [his own] mortal flesh" (2 Cor. 4:10-11). But this theme will expand (or grow) to include all Christians, as we shall see.

When I submitted this essay to the editors, Ross Wagner made a suggestion about the emphasis on suffering in 2 Corinthians 1–7 that I wish to incorporate: When Paul speaks of the suffering of Christ and Christian afflictions in 2 Corinthians 1:3-7, he offers as an example of affliction his own suffering in Asia, presumably in Ephesus (1:8-11). He even compares his experience, Wagner notes, to "a resurrection from the dead." "It seems to me," Wagner continues, "that this illuminates (though it does not exhaust the meaning of) his later statement in 2 Cor. 4 about being given over to death so that the life of Jesus may be manifest in his body." Though Paul routinely suffered affliction, and saw it as part of the Christian life, this major trauma "could have been instrumental in leading him to a new way of thinking about suffering."

Wagner's comments led me back to the thought to which I referred just above, that a lot of Paul's theology is autobiographical, and suffering is a major theme that allows him to draw lines from his own life to Christ's and to his converts. Wagner has put his finger on a vital point: Paul saw his sufferings in connection with those of Christ, and those of his converts in connection with the sufferings of both Christ and himself. And *obviously* — now that Wagner has made the observation — one should see a correlation between Paul's own dramatic affliction in Asia and what he wrote to the Corinthians, probably no more than a few months later.

Let us now connect suffering (co-suffering with Christ) with eschatology and realized eschatology (being transformed into Christ's image). As I noted earlier, the *language* of present, ongoing transformation and new creation does not continue after 2 Corinthians. But in Galatians we find another way of stating a change that takes place in the past or present. Paul himself has been "crucified with Christ" in the past tense (Gal. 2:19). Dying with Christ may be seen as building on the thought of suffering with him.[35]

The formulation of Galatians — sharing the death of Christ — has legs (as we now say): it will continue as he goes forward. In Romans, Paul extends it to Christians in general. In Romans 6, we find that all Christians have died with Christ (6:5). They should consider themselves "dead to Sin" (6:11). Only a few verses later, they are definitely "freed from Sin" (6:22). Paul and other Christians are no longer "living in the Flesh" (7:5). The possibility of condemnation for those in Christ has now disappeared; they are free from the law of Sin and Death (8:1-2). Paul repeats that Christians, in the present, are not in the Flesh but in the Spirit (8:9). The verbal formulations are different, but these claims are every bit as dramatic as present transformation and new creation in 2 Corinthians.

The concluding verses of Romans 8, as I pointed out above, return to the expected Pauline theme of the "already" and the "not yet." After saying that Christians have died with Christ and now share his life, at least in part, Paul reverts to the thought of suffering in order to share his *future* glory (Rom. 8:17-18), except that now suffering is *with* him, rather than in imitation of him. Christians have only the first fruits of the Spirit, and their bodies have not yet been redeemed (8:23).

Nevertheless, in a few giddy chapters in Romans Paul does something very similar to what he did in 2 Corinthians 3–5: he moves substantial aspects of salvation into the present. Christians share Christ's death, and so they partially, at least, share his new life: in Romans 6:5 the resurrection is future, but in 6:11 Christians are already "dead to Sin and alive to God in Christ Jesus." Christlikeness does not come all at once, at the resurrection (as in 1 Corinthians 15), but rather begins with baptism (Rom. 6:4). This is an

---

35. If we were strictly following Tatum's arrangement, we would say that "dying with Christ" in Galatians comes before "sharing his sufferings" in 2 Corinthians 1–7. After this essay was submitted, Tatum's work appeared in print, which gave me the first opportunity in a few years to read it. Now that I have done so, I must say that his arrangement is superior. See *New Chapters in the Life of Paul*, pp. 60-62, for the argument that Gal. 2:19-20 preceded 2 Cor. 5:14-15, which means that it also preceded the passages in 2 Corinthians 3 and 4 to which I referred. Cf. Tatum, pp. 87-88, on the relationship between 2 Cor. 4:10 and Philippians; p. 92 on the relationship between 2 Cor. 4:10 and 2 Cor. 13:4 and 1:5. For the purpose of this essay, the general point is that these passages are related and that they are a development of the theme of "imitating" Christ's sufferings in 1 Thessalonians.

advance on imitating the suffering of Christ in the present and awaiting new life in the future.

There were probably several features of Paul's interaction with his converts and opponents that were driving his thought. As far as I can now see, the most important was the need for *spiritual enrichment* in the present life while waiting, often in suffering, for the return of the Lord. The theme of merely imitating the suffering of Christ and Paul grew: it became sharing Christ's suffering or participating in his death. In the later letters, some form of "new life" is a present reality. As Christians shared Christ's death, so they also shared something of his life, even before the resurrection.

I would list as the second driving force the probability that the Corinthians were pushing Paul toward more realization in the present of the promises of the future. (He probably wrote Romans from Corinth.) Pressures created by the passage of time and the delay of Christ's return, plus interaction with his most inquiring converts, probably converged to yield the formulas of Romans 6 and 8: Christians have died with Christ; they live in the Spirit, not in the Flesh; they are freed from Sin and have new life in the present. These pressures were felt by Paul's converts, who needed a view of their present spiritual life that was richer than seeing it as a period of hanging on despite persecution. Paul himself felt them, as his discussions of his own suffering in 2 Corinthians 1 and of his death in Philippians 1 show.

Suffering was a constant issue; Paul needed to account for it theologically and to give it a positive value. It would not do to treat suffering for being Christian as punishment of transgression.[36] In the early to mid-50s, in addition to the admonition to hang on despite suffering, Paul had on hand the theme of imitation and the idea that, in partial compensation during this life, Christians possessed the Spirit. By the early 60s he could say (to repeat) that all Christians shared the sufferings and death of Christ; that all Christians lived in the Spirit and not in the Flesh; that therefore they had died to Sin and had new life in the present. This gives suffering a very positive role. It is not just imitation; it is co-suffering with Christ, representing dying with him. Here, it seems to me, are very powerful tools to help Christians endure until the Lord returns. These tools respond to the problems created by suffering and eschatology: there is more to the Christian life than suffering and waiting for a bliss that is

---

36. In Judaism, during the persecutions by Antiochus IV Epiphanes and Hadrian, when the people most loyal to God suffered most, the interpretation of suffering also had to develop. See briefly my *Judaism: Practice and Belief* (London: SCM; Philadelphia: Trinity Press International, corrected ed., 1994), pp. 273-74; more fully, "R. Akiba's View of Suffering," *JQR*, n.s., 63 (1973): 332-51.

constantly delayed. I think that if this theology had been available to Paul when he wrote 1 Thessalonians, he would have used it. I believe that it developed and grew from his concern for the spiritual life of Christians (including himself) as they suffered and waited while the Lord tarried.

Conclusion

There are four further brief points — or appendixes — regarding the development of Paul's theology. One is a general rumination about Paul; the other three are specific comments on questions of development.

First, a reminder about Paul himself, whom we have been discussing as a theologian: he was also a human and a missionary. Discussions of Paul's theology often make him too bookish or academic. He spent years of his life on the road, carrying (presumably on pack animals) his tent, clothing, and tools — not many scrolls, if any. He carried the Bible safely tucked away in his head, where it belongs.[37] As an apostle, he often supported himself by plying his trade. He was *busy*, traveling, working with his hands, winning people for Christ, shepherding or coping with his converts, responding to questions and problems. And he was very human; he knew not only fighting without but also fears within (2 Cor. 7:5). Paul the completely confident academic and systematic theologian — sitting at his desk, studying the Bible, working out a system, perfect and consistent in all its parts, unchanging over a period of thirty years, no matter how many new experiences he and his churches had — is an almost inhuman character, either a thinking machine or the fourth person of the Trinity. The real Paul knew anger, joy, depression, triumph, and anguish; he reacted, he overreacted, he repented, he apologized, he flattered and cajoled, he rebuked and threatened, he argued this way and that way: he did everything he could think of in order to win some. *Naturally* his mind matured, his thinking grew.

The second addendum is that the Body of Christ discussion in 1 Corinthians 12 appears to be based not on the idea of being one person with Christ but rather simply on a metaphor or, better, an analogy. Each person has a role in the church, though a different one, on analogy with the feet, hands, and private parts of an ordinary body. Once Paul had the idea of the body of

---

37. I have discussed the degree to which Paul had memorized the Bible in "Paul Between Judaism and Hellenism," in *St. Paul Among the Philosophers,* ed. Linda Martin Alcoff and John D. Caputo (Bloomington: Indiana University Press, forthcoming).

Christ, however, it was easy to use it to serve the mystical, or participationist, side of his thought. While I do not find participationism in 1 Corinthians 12–14, it does appear in 10:14-22, where participation in the cup and the loaf prohibits unions with demons. We also have a touch of participationist Christology — or Christ-mysticism, as Schweitzer called it — in the passage on the use of prostitutes in 1 Corinthians 6:15-17 ("your bodies are members of Christ").[38] This is the earliest hint in the direction of the more strongly participationist language of Galatians, Philippians, and Romans.

The third additional comment has to do with righteousness by faith and being in Christ. It has often been recognized that the so-called "doctrine" of righteousness by faith — it would better be called a "formulation" — is polemical and was introduced when circumcision was at issue. I would add to this that the form of words seems to originate in Paul's proof texts from Genesis 15:6 and 18:18, which he apparently used in order to refute the argument of his opponents in Galatia, who probably appealed to Genesis 17. (Paul's argument is, in effect, "Since Abraham was righteous by faith, as is proved by selected passages in Genesis, righteousness does not require circumcision — despite Genesis 17.") The limitation of the formulation is so clear and has such a precise origin — the debates about circumcision in Jerusalem (Titus) and Galatia — that in the 1970s it seemed easy to me to maintain that "being in Christ" is actually much closer to being the center of Paul's soteriological thinking than is "righteousness by faith," though, I argued, ultimately the two formulations point to the *same* reality.[39] Then one can also note that the word "faith" — which is ubiquitous in the letters — often leads to formulations other than "righteousness" to indicate the new status: we are children of God through faith, one person with Christ through faith, and so on (Gal. 3:26-29).[40] These other formulations are clearly more important in Paul's letters than the word "righteousness."

But now I should observe that being one person with Christ is also ab-

---

38. "Christianity is a Christ-Mysticism, that is to say, a 'belonging together' with Christ as our Lord, grasped in thought and realised in experience"; Albert Schweitzer, *The Mysticism of Paul the Apostle* (ET London: Adam & Charles Black, 1921), p. 378 (often reprinted). I accepted the heart of Schweitzer's view; but, since the term "mysticism" was widely misperceived, I substituted "participationism" and called Paul's theology "participationist eschatology": see *P&PJ*, p. 434 and n. 19, p. 440 and n. 49, pp. 453-63, 549, and elsewhere. "Participation" has the advantage of being a Pauline word (κοινωνία/κοινωνός), as in 1 Cor. 10:16, 18, 20; 2 Cor. 1:7, where it is used in the sense of "belonging together" or "sharing."

39. *P&PJ*, p. 506; see further above, n. 10.

40. *P&PJ*, p. 504.

sent from 1 Thessalonians. Not only that, "faith" in 1 Thessalonians is mostly steadfastness, holding on despite suffering, as in 3:2-3: "we sent Timothy . . . to strengthen and encourage you for the sake of your faith, so that no one would be shaken by these persecutions." Being one person with Christ as the result of faith is at least as remote from 1 Thessalonians as is being righteous by faith. In 1 Thessalonians, Christians — that is, "faithers" (οἱ πιστεύοντες, πᾶς ὁ πιστεύων, etc.) — believe in the God of Israel, renounce idols, believe in Christ and trust that he will return to save them from wrath; in this faith they hold on and live blamelessly. Perhaps I may repeat: I am sure that they would have appreciated being told that by faith they became one person with Christ. But we do not get that full statement until the end of Galatians 3.

Participation in the cup and loaf appears (as noted above) in 1 Corinthians 10:14-22, and participation in Christ is in 1 Corinthians 6:15-17, but we still do not find the formula "You are one person with Christ." We should not retroject either "life in Christ Jesus" or "righteousness by faith" into 1 Thessalonians on the ground that Paul must have had a completely worked-out theology, one that is now found in Galatians and Romans, when he wrote the letter.

The fourth appended thought is that participation in Christ is required by the argument of Galatians 3:15-29: Christ is the only heir of Abraham; only those who are in Christ can be coheirs. Although this is not the earliest sign of participationist thought, the argument may have helped push Paul further along that road, and it may partially account for the predominance of participationism in Romans 6–8.

Thus, I see growth and development all around. I think that the years of Paul's last "missionary journey" were extraordinarily fruitful for the development of his theology. The delay of Christ's return, the problem of suffering, the theme of imitation, the reality of κοινωνία (1 Corinthians 10), the need for spiritual enrichment while waiting for the return of the Lord, the growing Christ-mysticism (one person in Christ) — a lot of things came together during this last period of Paul's apostolic endeavors.

One of the results is a degree of warmth and richness in describing the present Christian life that was not available to Paul when he wrote to encourage the Thessalonians to hang on. Imitation has become sharing. Having the Spirit, or having spiritual gifts, has grown into living *in* the Spirit, not in the Flesh, and this development may also have helped lead to the conception of being one person with Christ. As we saw, this theme begins in the first person: "it is no longer I who live, but it is Christ who lives in me" (Gal.

2:20). But all Christians are or may be like Paul, who is like Christ. All may be Sons of God, as Christ is Son of God (Gal. 3:26; Rom. 8:16).

When circumstances, his own needs, and his converts pushed him to it, his active, creative, responsive brain spewed forth ideas and formulations, and his readers must be grateful to those doubtless often puzzled souls of Corinth and Galatia who pressed him until he came up with the ideas and the words that guide Christian life to this very day.

Summary

1 Thessalonians, 1 Corinthians		Later Letters
Having the Spirit: having a few gifts	grows to include	Living in the Spirit and not in the Flesh
Faith: being steadfast, confident	grows to include	Dying with Christ; becoming one person with Christ[41]
Present Christian life: enduring suffering while being blameless	grows to include	Being enriched by spiritual gifts; transformation beginning in the present
Imitation: suffering as he did	grows to include	Sharing Christ's suffering and death
Transformation: new life in the future	grows to include	New life in the present as well as in the future
Body of Christ: having various roles in the church	grows to include	Being one person with Christ

41. In the later letters, putting one's faith in Christ is parallel to "dying" with Christ and thus *becoming* "one person" with him (as in Gal. 2:20; 3:25-29). In the terminology of *P&PJ*, this is "getting in" or "transferring" (e.g., pp. 463-72). "*Being* one person with Christ," earlier in the essay and in the last line of this summary, refers to the resultant status — "being in."

ΕΚ ΠΙΣΤΕΩΣ: A Key to the Meaning of ΠΙΣΤΙΣ ΧΡΙΣΤΟΥ

James D. G. Dunn

Dear Richard,

I wanted very much to contribute to your *Festschrift*, primarily to say thank you for the quality and character of your scholarship and contribution to our appreciation of the biblical text both in the classroom and in daily living. But also to see whether we could carry our earlier discussion a little way forward in a positive direction. For in thinking about a possible topic for your *Festschrift*, my mind kept going back to our memorable debate on πίστις Χριστοῦ at the 1991 SBL meeting in Kansas[1] — and not simply because the scheduling of the discussion on the last morning meant that I had to re-schedule my flights back home, costing me $75 for the privilege and a night in a crummy airport motel! More to the point is that your earlier contribution on the phrase, in *The Faith of Jesus Christ*,[2] has proved so influential. Not, of course, that you were the first to argue that πίστις Χριστοῦ is best rendered as a reference to Jesus' own faith or faithfulness.[3] But your exposition proved to be something of a watershed, so that from the early '80s on-

---

1. Richard B. Hays, "ΠΙΣΤΙΣ and Pauline Christology: What Is at Stake?" and J. D. G. Dunn, "Once More, ΠΙΣΤΙΣ ΧΡΙΣΤΟΥ," in *Pauline Theology*, vol. 4, *Looking Back, Pressing On*, ed. E. E. Johnson and D. M. Hay (Atlanta: Scholars Press, 1997), pp. 35-60 and 61-81.

2. Richard B. Hays, *The Faith of Jesus Christ: An Investigation of the Narrative Substructure of Galatians 3:1–4:11*, SBLDS 56 (Chico, Calif.: Scholars Press, 1983).

3. You refer, e.g., to George Howard, "On the 'Faith of Christ,'" *HTR* 60 (1967): 459-65; D. W. B. Robinson, "'Faith of Jesus Christ' — A New Testament Debate," *RTR* 29 (1970): 71-81; others in the opening of my "Once More" essay (pp. 61-62), reprinted in your *Faith of Jesus Christ*, 2nd ed. (n. 8 below), pp. 249-50.

ward more and more recruits gathered round your flag. And not just the rank and file, but heavyweights like Lee Keck[4] and Lou Martyn,[5] and on this side of the pond, Morna Hooker[6] (though German-language scholarship remains mostly unpersuaded[7]). So much so that a strong strand of English-language New Testament writing now seems to take it more or less for granted that that is how the phrase should be rendered.

I was delighted that your *Faith of Jesus Christ* has come out in a second edition, and thought it a particularly generous act that you should have included both the essays on πίστις Χριστοῦ from the Kansas meeting, mine as well as yours, as appendices in that new edition.[8] It was this more than anything else, together with the reflections prompted by your introduction to the second edition, that prompted me to the thought that you might welcome a small attempt to join you in "moving the discussion forward," even in your own *Festschrift*.

I

Let me begin by welcoming the three emphases you bring out in the first section of your new introduction.

A. The Central Thesis

I am glad you have made the point that your book *(The Faith of Jesus Christ)* is "about the narrative elements that undergird Paul's thought," and is not just a discussion of the phrase πίστις Χριστοῦ.[9] It has been a somewhat unfortunate consequence of the attention given to this phrase that the main thrust of your thesis has been relatively overlooked. But you are right: Paul's

---

4. Most recently, Leander E. Keck, *Romans,* ANTC (Nashville: Abingdon, 2005).

5. Especially J. Louis Martyn, *Galatians,* AB 33A (New York: Doubleday, 1997).

6. Morna D. Hooker, "ΠΙΣΤΙΣ ΧΡΙΣΤΟΥ," *NTS* 35 (1989): 321-42, though with only passing reference to your *Faith of Jesus Christ* (326 n. 2).

7. For example, the most recent full-blown study of Paul, by Udo Schnelle, *Apostle Paul: His Life and Theology* (ET Grand Rapids: Baker Academic, 2005 [2003]), notes it only in passing (p. 523).

8. Richard B. Hays, *The Faith of Jesus Christ: The Narrative Substructure of Galatians 3:1–4:11,* 2nd ed. (Grand Rapids: Eerdmans, 2002), pp. 249-71 and 272-97.

9. *Faith of Jesus Christ,* p. xxiii.

argument in Galatians, as in his theology generally, presupposes a story about Jesus Christ. The point is disputed, of course, but in my view the allusions in Paul's letters to Jesus' life and the character of his mission[10] (not to mention his death, resurrection, and parousia) are sufficiently clear evidence that Paul knew of Jesus' mission as a story. And the allusions to Jesus' teaching are sufficiently coordinated with the allusions to the character of his mission[11] for us to make the appropriate deduction that Paul knew the Jesus tradition in some correlation with the story of Jesus' mission.

This we might have deduced anyway from the character of the Synoptic material, with its integration of individual narratives and blocks of teaching in a story framework. For the likelihood is that this was (one of) the way(s) that the earliest teachers and communities maintained and celebrated the Jesus tradition as they had received it. That is, we should not assume that Mark was the first to give a narrative framework to the tradition he transcribed. Just as we should avoid the tendency of form-critical analysis of the Gospel traditions to assume that the Jesus tradition was retained in the earliest days only as scattered aphorisms and isolated tales.[12] On the contrary, in the oral tradition period (including the whole of Paul's mission) it is quite probable that the local church teachers would have retained the church's deposit of Jesus tradition within (and by means of) some kind (or varieties) of narrative structure. Given not least that Mark almost certainly derived his use of "gospel" from Paul,[13] it is not a great jump of historical imagination to deduce that there were mini-oral "gospel" structures, in part at least, prior to the writing of Mark's Gospel (cf. Acts 10:36-41).

Like our mutual friend Tom Wright, I am very happy to push the argument about the narrative framework of Paul's theology back to include the larger story of God and his purpose for his people and his creation.[14] Indeed, in my most recent work on Romans I have found it more than helpful to see the structure of the main section (1:18–11:36) as a threefold telling of the

10. I may refer simply to my *Theology of Paul the Apostle* (Grand Rapids/Edinburgh: Eerdmans/T. & T. Clark, 1998), particularly pp. 185-95.

11. E.g., Gal. 5:14 with 6:2; 1 Cor. 11:1-2; Rom. 13:8-10 with 15:1-3.

12. See further my *Jesus Remembered* (Grand Rapids: Eerdmans, 2003), pp. 238-53; also *A New Perspective on Jesus* (Grand Rapids: Baker, 2005), pp. 124-25.

13. Wherever he derived the term "gospel" from, it was Paul who introduced the noun as a technical term into Christian vocabulary; see my *Theology of Paul*, pp. 164-69.

14. N. T. Wright, *The Climax of the Covenant: Christ and the Law in Pauline Theology* (Edinburgh: T. & T. Clark, 1991); also *Paul: Fresh Perspectives* (London: SPCK, 2005), pp. 7-13.

story of God's righteousness: the story of God's impartial judgment on all humankind, Jew first but also Gentile (1:18–5:11); the cosmic story of the entrance, machinations, and overcoming of the powers of Sin and Death, not by Torah but by Spirit (5:12–8:39); and the story of Israel, from call to completion (9:1–11:36).[15] As you know, it is this continuity of story, in Galatians as well as Romans, that makes me highly dubious of Lou Martyn's "relegation" of such an emphasis to the Teachers in Galatia.[16] Of course, the story of Israel itself has an apocalyptic dimension; the classic apocalypses are Jewish writings, particular "takes," shocking in their innovativeness, of the older versions of the story. But in taking an apocalyptic perspective on that story, Paul did not abandon the story: Galatians 4:1-2 in particular already foreshadows the fuller retelling of the story of Israel in Romans 9–11.

Incidentally, the three stories of Romans 1–11, which are all stories of God's righteousness, help explain the apparent incongruity between the story told in terms of continuity and the story in terms of apocalyptic disruption. For the story told as the story of Israel is all about continuity. Whereas the story told in terms of the overcoming of the cosmic powers of Sin and Death by the irruption of Jesus' death and resurrection does indeed highlight the apocalyptic character of the transition. And the story told in terms of salvation for all, Gentile as well as Jew, could be regarded as a kind of bridge between the two. What should be noted, however, is that the stories of Israel and of the larger creation do not provide a definitive or final answer to the powers of Sin and Death; these cosmic powers reigned despite creation, despite the call of and promise to Abraham, despite the giving of the law. Only with the mission of Jesus, his death and resurrection, and the bestowal of the eschatological Spirit, were these powers decisively broken and their final defeat ensured. So by setting out the three different versions of the story of God's righteousness consecutively, Romans avoids or removes the confusion made possible by their entanglement in Galatians (a confusion illustrated by Martyn's thesis). The point is that Paul could and did hold the stories of continuity and apocalyptic disruption together, as both valid and important ways of understanding the working out of God's saving purpose.

So I remain grateful to you for bringing out the narrative substructure of Paul's theology. Where I am less happy, however, is in the degree to which

15. J. D. G. Dunn, "Paul's Letter to Rome: Reason and Rationale," in *Logos — Logik — Lyrik: Engagierte exegetische Studien zum biblischen Reden Gottes; Festschrift für Klaus Haacker,* ed. V. A. Lehnert and U. Rüsen-Weinhold (Leipzig: Evangelischen Verlagsanstalt, 2007), pp. 185-200.

16. You refer to the discussion in your introduction, p. xxxix.

you think that πίστις Χριστοῦ is a necessary or integral part of that narrative, as a summary reference to Jesus' faithfulness in giving himself up to the cross. It is almost as though the narrative would be lost to sight without πίστις Χριστοῦ. But of course, that is not the case. The fact that Jesus was a Jew was an important part of the gospel story for Paul (Rom. 15:8; Gal. 4:4-5). His living out what he taught in the love command was taken for granted by Paul (Rom. 15:1-3; Gal. 6:2).[17] Paul speaks of Christ's "obedience" to the death of the cross more than once (Rom. 5:19; Phil. 2:8). What I don't find is that Paul made a point of stressing Jesus' "faithfulness" as such, apart from the disputed πίστις Χριστοῦ phrases. Were it as important as you imply, I would have expected to see the theme signaled in discussions where it could be referred to simply as "his πίστις," or in contrast with human (or Israel's) ἀπιστία.

More striking is the contrast with Paul's use of πίστις with reference to the larger story of *God's* faithfulness. Paul echoes Israel's confidence in God as "faithful" in several contexts: "God is faithful (πιστός)" (1 Cor. 1:9; 10:13; 1 Thess. 5:24),[18] a pattern that Paul seeks to emulate in his own dealings with his converts (2 Cor. 1:18). This divine faithfulness is a theme running through Romans, particularly signaled in 3:1-8, where Paul interweaves the thought of God's πίστις with his "truth" (both from the Hebrew root אמן) and his "righteousness" (overlapping into the sense of "covenant faithfulness"), and worked through in Romans 9–11 in terms of God's "word," "call," and "mercy."[19] Because the theme is so prominent and so richly varied in Romans, it becomes plausible to read one of the πίστις references in the thematic statement of Romans 1:17 ("from faith/God's faithfulness to faith") as a reference to God's faithfulness, as you agree.[20]

The point I am making here is this: if you load so much of the weight of Christ's exemplary and willing self-sacrifice onto the disputed phrase πίστις Χριστοῦ, there is a danger (because the reference of the phrase is disputed) that the Pauline theme of Christ's ready submission to his role as servant and

---

17. Romans 15:2 is the only passage in which Paul speaks of "the neighbor" (πλησίον) apart from the two references to Lev. 19:18: "you shall love your neighbor as yourself" (Rom. 13:9-10 and Gal. 5:14), so it is most probable that he had in mind Jesus' teaching that uniquely (for his time) prioritized Lev. 19:18 (Mark 12:29-31); see my *Jesus Remembered*, pp. 584-86.

18. If "the Lord" in 2 Thess. 3:3 (also 2 Tim. 2:13) is Christ, the reference is not to Christ's faithfulness in his mission but to his faithfulness to those who believe in him.

19. The point is often missed, but see my *Romans*, WBC 38 (Dallas: Word, 1988), pp. 132-33, 135-36, 847.

20. My *Romans*, p. 44.

JAMES D. G. DUNN

to death will be diminished (the absence of other references to Christ's "faith-fulness" suggests the relative unimportance of the theme), not enhanced.[21]

B. Participation in Christ

I am grateful to you also for highlighting this feature of Paul's gospel. For, like you, I fear that an overemphasis on the forensic category of justification in Paul's thought has been at the expense of what is equally if not more important in Paul's soteriology, what can be summed up as the whole "in Christ" motif that pervades his theology far more completely in comparison with the imagery of justification. Philippians 3:7-11 in particular well illustrates how Paul could hold both emphases in an integrated wholeness that seems to have escaped many of his modern interpreters![22] Indeed, I find here another case where Paul was able to hold together (and evidently thought it important to do so) what later commentators have insisted must be held apart (continuity/apocalyptic, justification/participation) with an insensitivity of exposition that has only muddied the scholarly debate and confused the faithful.

Where I again begin to demur is in your attempt to hitch your "faithful-ness of Christ" interpretation of πίστις Χριστοῦ to this central "participation in Christ" theme. Certainly, it follows at once that "'the faithfulness of Jesus Christ' refers . . . to his gracious, self-sacrificial death on a cross";[23] though, here again, I confess that I find this emphasis more clearly and more power-fully drawn in passages like Romans 5:6-11, 2 Corinthians 5:16-21, and Philippians 2:6-11, and again wonder why Paul did not include reference to Christ's faithfulness in such passages. Similarly, I note that there is only one πίστις Χριστοῦ that really integrates into the participation in Christ (or

21. Here I should perhaps draw your attention to Philip Esler's *Conflict and Identity in Romans* (Minneapolis: Fortress, 2003), with his typically robust response to your suggestion that some opposition to the subjective genitive reading of πίστις Χριστοῦ "may be rooted in an implicitly docetic Christology" (your "ΠΙΣΤΙΣ and Pauline Christology," p. 55; reprint p. 293); in *tu quoque* fashion, Esler warns of the proto-Arian direction that the subjective genitive reading may take and notes "the residual legacy of liberal Christianity [in North America], . . . which stressed Jesus as the model of Christian life" (pp. 157-59, quotation p. 159).

22. See my *New Perspective on Paul*, WUNT 185 (Tübingen: Mohr Siebeck, 2005), ch. 22. See also 1 Cor. 1:30 and 2 Cor. 5:21; Gal. 2:17; 3:14.

23. *Faith of Jesus Christ*, p. xxx.

Christ in us) theme, that is, Galatians 2:20. And the attempt to draw in the important theme of God's faithfulness is unable to cite any πίστις Χριστοῦ reference. All of which raises for me the question whether so much can or should be rested on a phrase that is at best allusive and undeveloped (in the "faithfulness of Christ" interpretation) in its usage.

C. The Poetic Character of Paul's Language

Once again I resonate in sympathy with what you say. Your work on allusion and echo in Paul's letters has served as a master class for a generation of fellow scholars and students. Far too often the powerful streams of theological reflection and pastoral counsel flowing from Paul's letters have been constricted within one or another dogmatic channel and siphoned off to water strange growths to feed a narrow sectarianism. Appreciation of the richness of metaphor, of the resonance of allusion, of the depths of insight coming to varied expression, with no one image capable of expressing the whole, is essential if the Word is not to be stifled by the words. And I have nothing in principle against reading πίστις Χριστοῦ with as rich and varied a meaning as it can possibly contain. It is just that I am still to be convinced that Paul himself *intended* a reference to "Christ's faithfulness" when he used the phrase πίστις Χριστοῦ. To which subject I now turn.

II

As you will probably recall, the problem I have always had with your πίστις Χριστοῦ interpretation is that it has to draw in so many of the other πίστις references in the contexts of Galatians and Romans in order to maintain its credibility. The point being, of course, that it is difficult to envisage Paul switching the reference of his πίστις usages back and forth from one sense (Christ's "faithfulness") to another (believers' "faith") in the same passage without giving his readers a clear signal of that change. It is because I find other πίστις references within the πίστις Χριστοῦ passages so clearly referring to believers' "faith," and do *not* find any signal given by Paul that the πίστις of the πίστις Χριστοῦ is to be understood differently, that I find myself unable to follow you. You will immediately reply, of course, that the attached Χριστοῦ is itself sufficient indication that the πίστις in the πίστις Χριστοῦ references is to be read differently from at least some of the other πίστις references. But in working with these passages on several further occasions since our debate, it has seemed to me again and again that *all* the other πίστις references have to be subsumed within your "faithfulness of Christ" interpretation of the πίστις Χριστοῦ references, or else Paul's argument becomes less and less coherent. And the cost is that Paul's insistence that his gospel is for all who *believe* diminishes in these πίστις passages. I do not think it good exegesis to enlarge Paul's emphasis on the self-sacrifice of Christ at the expense of his emphasis on the offer of the gospel to faith alone.

A. The Importance of ἐκ πίστεως

In my further reflections on πίστις Χριστοῦ in Paul, I have been more and more impressed by the importance of his use of the phrase ἐκ πίστεως. (1) It is the most common of Paul's prepositional πίστις terms (21 times).[24] (2) It is clearly a key phrase in Paul's understanding of his central theme on God's saving righteousness (Rom. 1:17; Gal. 2:16) and appears intensively in the passages in which πίστις Χριστοῦ features most strongly (Romans 3–4; Galatians 3).[25] (3) Most important of all, it evidently has a defining character, defining or identifying individuals (or conduct) by their character as ἐκ πίστεως:

Rom. 1:17	"the righteous ἐκ πίστεως shall live"
Rom. 3:26	"the one who is ἐκ πίστεως Ἰησοῦ"
Rom. 3:30	God justifies ἐκ πίστεως
Rom. 4:16	"the promise is . . . ἐκ πίστεως"
Rom. 4:16	"the one [who is] ἐκ πίστεως of Abraham"
Rom. 5:1	"having been justified ἐκ πίστεως"
Rom. 9:30	"the righteousness that is ἐκ πίστεως"
Rom. 9:32	a pursuit of the law of righteousness "not ἐκ πίστεως"
Rom. 10:6	"the righteousness that is ἐκ πίστεως"
Rom. 14:23	"everything that is not ἐκ πίστεως is sin"
Gal. 2:16	". . . justified ἐκ πίστεως Χριστοῦ"
Gal. 3:7	"those [who are] ἐκ πίστεως"

24. Rom. 1:17 (2x); 3:26, 30; 4:16 (2x); 5:1; 9:30, 32; 10:6; 14:23 (2x); Gal. 2:16; 3:7, 8, 9, 11, 12, 22, 24; 5:5.

25. The nearly as frequent διὰ πίστεως is not so concentrated — Rom. 1:12; 3:22, 25, 30, 31; 2 Cor. 5:7; Gal. 2:16; 3:14, 26; Eph. 2:8; 3:12, 17; Phil. 3:9; Col. 2:12; 1 Thess. 3:7; 2 Tim. 3:15 — including διὰ πίστεως Χριστοῦ (Rom. 3:22; Gal. 2:16; Phil. 3:9).

Gal. 3:8   "God justifies ἐκ πίστεως"

Gal. 3:9   "those [who are] ἐκ πίστεως"

Gal. 3:11   "the righteous ἐκ πίστεως shall live"

Gal. 3:12   "the law is not ἐκ πίστεως"

Gal. 3:22   "the promise is ἐκ πίστεως Ἰησοῦ Χριστοῦ"

Gal. 3:24   ". . . justified ἐκ πίστεως"

Gal. 5:5   "we await the hope of righteousness ἐκ πίστεως"

(4) The defining role of ἐκ πίστεως is particularly clear when it is set in antithesis to ἐκ νόμου or similar phrases:

Rom. 4:14   "if the heirs are ἐκ νόμου . . ." (cf. 4:16)

Rom. 4:16   "the promise is to all the seed, not to the one ἐκ τοῦ νόμου only, but also to the one ἐκ πίστεως of Abraham"

Rom. 9:32   "not ἐκ πίστεως but as though ἐξ ἔργων"

Rom. 10:5   "the righteousness that is ἐκ [τοῦ] νόμου" (cf. 10:6)

Gal. 2:16   ". . . justified ἐκ πίστεως Χριστοῦ and not ἐξ ἔργων νόμου"

Gal. 3:10   "as many as are ἐξ ἔργων νόμου" (cf. 3:9, 11)

Gal. 3:18   the inheritance is not ἐκ νόμου

Phil. 3:9   "not having my own righteousness that is ἐκ νόμου but that which is διὰ πίστεως Χριστοῦ"

Clearly, Paul was setting two self-understandings or self-definitions in contrast: those who defined themselves "out of the law," that is, by their submission to the law and daily obedience to its commands; and those who defined themselves "out of πίστις." The latter could be understood as "by reference to Christ's faithfulness," though it is much harder to see how Christ's faithfulness could provide a defining character to converts' daily living in the same way as the law with its extensive coverage of so many aspects of life. In contrast, to understand the phrase as "out of faith" carries with it the implication that a trustful commitment to the self-giving Christ can provide a pattern for daily living. This is precisely the claim that Paul makes in the phrases "the obedience of faith" (Rom. 1:5) and "the law of faith" (3:27), with the slight elaboration of the latter in 3:31: "faith" is a way of living obediently before God, and conduct ἐκ πίστεως fulfills the law more than mere outward obedience. In other words, "out of faith" answers to the alternative "out of the law" in a more direct way than "out of (Christ's) faithfulness" ever can, since the latter requires a further elaboration and teasing out before the contrast becomes obvious.

In short, "those ἐκ πίστεως" seems to be one of Paul's defining phrases, and as such is most obviously to be taken as the noun-phrase equivalent to οἱ πιστεύοντες ("those who believe")[26] or οἱ πιστεύσαντες ("those who believed/became believers").[27]

B. Setting the Phrase in Context

Now, of course, the identifying phrase alone is not sufficiently explicit as to what the defining πίστις character is to which reference is being made by the phrase ἐκ πίστεως. As the data stands in all its baldness, the phrase could refer to "the faithfulness of Christ/Jesus," as most obviously in Romans 3:26; or it could refer to those identified by (their) faith (in Christ/Jesus). I think we are agreed that the genitive phrase in Greek is open equally to an objective or a subjective reading: Philippians 3:8-9 being a good example of such an objective genitive ("the knowledge of Christ Jesus my Lord") in close proximity to a πίστις Χριστοῦ reference. Everything depends on the context in which ἐκ πίστεως appears: how does the context indicate Paul understood the ἐκ πίστεως phrase or wanted it to be read? what was the defining characteristic of the Christian and of the righteousness to which the Christian could lay claim through Christ?[28]

The contrast between "those ἐκ πίστεως" and "those ἐκ νόμου" also highlights a further problem with the "out of Christ's faithfulness" interpretation. It is so compressed as to require a substantial unfolding of its meaning. Of course Paul could use shorthand; he does not explain what he means by "the righteousness of God" in Romans 1:17, for example. But in such cases we could expect some help from the context to indicate how the phrase should be unpacked, and it is the contexts that point ineluctably, I think, to a πίστις = human response to the gospel/promise/act of God in Christ.

As note 24 shows, Paul's most intense usage of the phrase ἐκ πίστεως follows his initial usage in Galatians 2:16. Galatians 3:6-9 clearly defines Christians[29] by reference to Abraham's believing:

26. Rom. 3:22; 1 Cor. 14:22; 1 Thess. 1:7; 2:10, 13.
27. 2 Thess. 1:10.
28. See also Moisés Silva, "Faith Versus Works of Law in Galatians," in *Justification and Variegated Nomism*, vol. 2, *The Paradoxes of Paul*, ed. D. A. Carson et al., WUNT 2.181 (Tübingen: Mohr Siebeck, 2004), pp. 227-36.
29. I use the term "Christian" as shorthand, even though its usage is somewhat anachronistic for Paul — which is why the defining ἐκ πίστεως is so important.

₆Just as (καθώς) "Abraham believed God, and it was reckoned to him for righteousness" [Gen. 15:6]. ₇Know then that those ἐκ πίστεως, they are Abraham's sons. ₈And scripture, foreseeing that God would justify the nations ἐκ πίστεως, preached the gospel beforehand to Abraham, "In you shall all the nations be blessed" [Gen. 12:3; 18:18]. ₉Consequently, those ἐκ πίστεως are blessed with faithful Abraham.

It seems to me that an inescapable conclusion to be drawn from Galatians 3:6-7 is that "those ἐκ πίστεως" can be reckoned as Abraham's sons precisely and only because they *believe* as Abraham believed.[30] That is to say, "those ἐκ πίστεως" is a way of saying "those who have believed as Abraham believed." Which must mean that ἐκ πίστεως refers to the Galatians' own πίστις. Their defining feature, that which causes them to stand out from other Gentiles (and nonbelieving Jews) is their *faith*.[31] The parallel that Paul draws between Abraham's *believing*, which resulted in his being reckoned righteous, and God's justifying the nations ἐκ πίστεως (3:6-8) could hardly be clearer:

> Abraham had faith in God and it was reckoned to him for
> righteousness (δικαιοσύνη);
> God would "righteous" (δικαιοῦν) the nations from faith.

Paul clearly sees the several Genesis references cited as all of a piece (Gen. 12:3; 15:6; 18:18), as his argument in 3:6-14 shows. It is the fact that Abraham proves faith to be the crucial factor (not works of the law) that makes it possible for Paul to push the argument of 3:6-14 as he does; it is "through this (the same) faith" that the blessing of Abraham comes to Gentiles in Christ Jesus.[32]

---

30. Here I have to say that I find your treatment of Gal. 3:6-9 in *Faith of Jesus Christ*, pp. 168-73, among the least convincing in your exegesis. Martyn, *Galatians*, p. 299, also maintains that πίστις in 3:7 includes a reference to "the faith of Christ enacted in his death"; but there is nothing to show that the "faith" in view is different from Abraham's believing, and it is noticeable that Martyn does not attempt to press this fuller meaning on πίστις in 3:8 (p. 300). Bruce W. Longenecker, *The Triumph of Abraham's God: The Transformation of Identity in Galatians* (Edinburgh: T. & T. Clark, 1998), pp. 95-115, equally avoids the crucial nexus of 3:6-8.

31. As Tom Schreiner, *Paul: Apostle of God's Glory in Christ* (Downers Grove, Ill.: InterVarsity, 2001), p. 215, notes: "Galatians 3:6-9 eliminates any reference to the faithfulness of Christ."

32. The "in Christ Jesus" introduces the second strand of Paul's argument (3:15-29); but it should be clear enough that this second strand complements the first (3:1-14) rather than subsuming it. I regard your concession that πίστις does refer to "human believing" in 3:7-9,

An unavoidable corollary, in my view, is that the sequence of πίστις references in 3:11-12 has to be understood in the same way. It is surely improbable that anyone reading the quotation of Habakkuk 2:4 in 3:11 in context could or would read it as a reference to the Messiah's faith. Was it in any degree necessary or integral to the argument to maintain that *Jesus* was justified by faith (3:11b explains 3:11a)?[33] On the contrary, the most obvious way to read the quotation of Habakkuk 2:4 is as defining either "the righteous" or the conduct of the righteous in terms of πίστις. And what πίστις could that be, given the immediately preceding exposition of Genesis 15:6, other than "faith," like the faith of Abraham, the faith that God counts for righteousness? Likewise, to describe the law as "not ἐκ πίστεως" is to say that the law has a different character and function — a (way of) life characterized by doing what the law commands rather than by trusting as Abraham trusted.

These conclusions also carry with them the preceding references to πίστις in Galatians 3:2 and 5, which can probably be counted part of the ἐκ πίστεως motif: did the Spirit come to you "from (ἐξ) works of the law or from hearing with faith (ἐξ ἀκοῆς πίστεως)?" For the καθώς at the beginning of 3:6 clearly links the sequence of πίστις references together (3:2-9); Abraham's believing God's promise was his ἀκοὴ πίστεως. That is precisely why the parallel and precedent of Abraham can be drawn in so directly: the Galatians had believed, just as (καθώς) Abraham believed; Abraham and the Galatians were defined (in relation to the gospel — 3:8) precisely as being "those ἐκ πίστεως."[34]

The subsequent fuller exposition of Romans surely confirms this line of interpretation. (1) The argument of Romans 4 is a variation on and a more developed form of the argument in Galatians 3. One difference is the infrequency of the ἐκ πίστεως phrase. But the sequence of thought is obviously the same, with the ἐκ πίστεως of 4:16 fully equivalent to the repeated empha-

---

14, and 26 ("ΠΙΣΤΙΣ and Pauline Christology," pp. 58-59; reprint p. 296) as destructive of your case to a degree that you have not recognized.

33. To assume that your questionable exposition of Hab. 2:4 in Rom. 1:17 can simply be carried over into the earlier citation in Gal. 3:11 (*Faith of Jesus Christ*, p. 178) is at best a highly questionable procedure. And to maintain further that the ἐκ πίστεως references in Gal. 3:7-9 are a pre-reflection of the at best strained interpretation of Hab. 2:4 in Gal. 3:11 (p. 171) is a case of special pleading. It seems to me that your thesis forces you to such dubious exegesis simply because your thesis would fall without it. And to derive *all* of Paul's ἐκ πίστεως references from Hab. 2:4 ("ΠΙΣΤΙΣ and Pauline Christology," p. 57; reprint p. 295) surely does far too little justice to the range and contexts of Paul's use of the phrase.

34. See also Silva, "Faith Versus Works of Law," pp. 234-36.

sis on believing (πιστεύειν) as Abraham believed (4:3, 11, 17, 18, 24): the promise is ἐκ πίστεως (4:16), to those who believe as Abraham believed; because they believe as Abraham believed, they are Abraham's seed (4:13, 16), they are "ἐκ πίστεως of Abraham" (4:16).

(2) As in Galatians, the clarification of πίστις by reference to Abraham's faith in Romans 4 carries with it the immediately preceding references. The πίστις references of Romans 3:28 and 30 cannot be understood other than as references to "faith," and these carry with them the reference to the νόμος of πίστις in 3:27 and to the establishing of the law διὰ πίστεως.

(3) Pushing out beyond the immediate reference to Abraham's faith, "the righteousness that is ἐκ πίστεως" (Rom. 10:6) is elaborated in a sequence of obviously interchangeable πίστις and πιστεύω references (10:8, 9, 10, 11, 14, 16), climaxing in the conclusion "So πίστις comes from hearing (ἐξ ἀκοῆς)" (10:17), where the πίστις clearly encapsulates the believing that is the outcome of the preaching (10:14). This must equally carry with it the πίστις references in the preceding paragraph: "the righteousness that is ἐκ πίστεως" (9:30, the same phrase as 10:6), and the pursuit "not ἐκ πίστεως" (9:32), the latter contrasted with the believing (ὁ πιστεύων) of which Isaiah spoke (9:33). Here again, "he who is ἐκ πίστεως" is another way of saying "he who believes (ὁ πιστεύων)."

(4) In Romans we also find the same idea of conduct that, like the law (or "works of the law"), is *not* ἐκ πίστεως (Rom. 14:23). Here again, the context makes it clear beyond dispute that πίστις means "faith": Paul's concern is that those who are "weak in faith" (14:1) will act in a way that is contrary to their faith (14:14, 20), that is, their conduct will not be ἐκ πίστεως, will not arise out of their faith and as an expression of their faith.

Of course, it does not necessarily follow that Paul used the phrase ἐκ πίστεως with consistently the same reference. But when it is so consistently used to define the character of those who have responded to the gospel, or more precisely, the character of their response and consequent lifestyle, I find it very difficult to argue that in the other πίστις passages Paul intended a different reference.

C. What Then of the *πίστις Χριστοῦ* phrases?

It is when we realize that the reference of πίστις in Galatians 3:2-14 and Romans 3:27–5:1 is so consistently to "faith," believing as Abraham believed, that it becomes difficult to maintain the argument that the πίστις Χριστοῦ phrases could have a different reference, especially since the πίστις Χριστοῦ phrases include the ἐκ πίστεως Χριστοῦ phrases, all of them closely related to the larger exposition of πίστις to be understood as the same as the πίστις of Abraham.

What signal, for example, does Paul provide that the resumption of talk of ἐκ πίστεως (here ἐκ πίστεως Ἰησοῦ Χριστοῦ) in Galatians 3:22 should be understood differently from the succession of ἐκ πίστεως references in 3:7-12, all so clearly referring to faith like Abraham's faith? Likewise the reading of ἐκ πίστεως in 3:24, especially as it resumes the argument of 3:7: the sons of Abraham are those who are ἐκ πίστεως, who believe as Abraham believed. Would Paul have expected the Galatians to read διὰ τῆς πίστεως ἐν Χριστῷ Ἰησοῦ (3:26) as "through the faithfulness of Christ in Christ Jesus"? I think not.[35] Likewise, "the coming of πίστις" (3:23-25) is best understood as the fulfillment of the promise to Abraham, when "God would justify the nations from faith" (3:8) and fulfill the blessing of Abraham to the nations "through faith" (3:14); it is the coming of the era of faith, the human response that is the necessary complement to the coming of the seed (3:19). By taking the two comings as identical — the coming of the seed = the coming of (Christ's) faith(fulness)[36] — you lose the other side of the relationship prefigured by Abraham.

Similarly with the first of Paul's διὰ πίστεως Ἰησοῦ Χριστοῦ and ἐκ πίστεως Χριστοῦ references in Galatians 2:16. When Paul goes on to use ἐκ πίστεως so consistently to refer to "faith" in the following paragraph, and to do so without indicating that he is using the phrase in any way differently from Galatians 2:16, the implication must be that he is using the phrase ἐκ πίστεως consistently to refer to faith, the faith that is so different from "works of the law," as in 3:2, 5, and 10-12. The fact that he repeats the point three times —

> . . . a person is justified not from works of the law but only
>   through faith,
> and we have believed in Christ Jesus

---

35. "[T]he constitutive writings of Christianity (including the Pauline Corpus) give so much prominence to human faith, that their authors would surely expect readers to understand πίστις in this sense [the act of believing] unless contextual factors excluded such a meaning. . . . In conspicuous contrast, we cannot find even one *unambiguous* reference to the πίστις that belongs to Christ." Silva, "Faith Versus Works of Law," pp. 230-31, emphasis original.

36. As still in *Faith of Jesus Christ*, p. xxxi.

in order that we might be justified ἐκ πίστεως Χριστοῦ and not
   from works of the law,
because from works of the law shall no one be justified —

should not surprise us. Repetition is a commonplace as a means of emphasis, and Paul's writing probably reflects the way a speaker would emphasize his point — by repeating it with the sort of variations we find in 2:16.

The same applies to the διὰ/ἐκ πίστεως ᾿Ιησοῦ (Χριστοῦ) references in Romans (3:22, 26). Romans 3:30 so clearly refers to God's justifying "from faith" and "through faith," and the following exposition of Genesis 15:6, as in Galatians 3, so clearly and explicitly works with the thought of Abraham's faith, that it takes some exegetical boldness to argue that the 3:22 and 26 occurrences have a different reference — especially one that has to be so unpacked before its meaning becomes clear, whereas "faith in Christ" simply picks up the early motif of "faith" as what constitutes both the gospel and those who have responded to the gospel (1:5, 8, 12, 17).[37] Similarly, Lee Keck's interpretation (πίστις Χριστοῦ as meaning "the faithfulness of Christ")[38] leaves me puzzled about the sequence of Paul's thought from chapter 3 to chapter 4. Was Paul's exposition of Abraham's *faith* not in implicit opposition to the traditional exposition of Abraham's *faithfulness* in offering up Isaac?[39] But Keck doesn't really address the point. And while I have some idea of what Paul might mean in the phrase "living by faith," I am still wondering what Keck means when he talks about Christians "living by Jesus' faithfulness."[40]

In many ways the most persuasive argument for πίστις Χριστοῦ as referring to "faith in Christ" is that it ensures that Paul's πίστις phrases can and should be taken consistently as referring to the act of believing, of hearing and responding to the gospel with the commitment to Christ as Lord for which the gospel calls. To lose so many πίστις references on that front would

37. See now also Francis Watson, *Paul and the Hermeneutics of Faith* (London: T. & T. Clark, 2004), pp. 73-76: "'Through faith of Jesus Christ' indicates that the earlier 'by faith' is to be understood in some unspecified relation to Jesus Christ, but it can hardly indicate that Jesus is himself the subject of that faith or faithfulness. . . . It is striking that this passage [Rom. 3:22] interprets Jesus' death not as the outcome of his own faithfulness but as God's saving action" (pp. 74-75). Robert Jewett, *Romans*, Hermeneia (Minneapolis: Fortress, 2006), pp. 276-78: "'Faith' is used here [Rom. 3:22] to denote a group's assent to and participation in the gospel of Christ crucified and resurrected . . ." (p. 278).

38. Keck, *Romans*, pp. 104-5, 110.

39. See my *Romans*, pp. 200-201.

40. Keck, *Romans*, p. 113; contrast my comments on Rom. 14:23 above.

be to leave the fewer πιστεύειν references more or less without a noun equivalent, and undermine to a large extent what has usually been regarded as one of the central emphases of Paul's gospel — justification by faith alone, by faith in Christ.

In short, despite the neatness of seeing πίστις Χριστοῦ as a summary of the story of Jesus, and the weight of support that has gathered round that exposition, I remain unconvinced that Paul so intended the phrase. The story of Jesus as an important factor in the background (and sometimes foreground) of Paul's theology is independent of the significance of πίστις Χριστοῦ. And the exegetical maneuvers required to establish that reference in Galatians 2–3 and Romans 3 strain the logic of Paul's exposition far too much for me to find them convincing. In contrast, to find πίστις Χριστοῦ as a concise expression of the call of Paul's gospel for faith in Christ fits far more snugly into the lines of exposition that are such a strong feature of Galatians 2:15–3:29 and Romans 3:21–5:1. Sorry Richard.

Ad multos annos,
Jimmy

An Echo of Scripture in Paul, and Its Implications

Douglas A. Campbell

It is an honor and a pleasure to offer this short essay in celebration of the life and work (to date!) of Richard Hays, a scholar who has had a significant and — perhaps most importantly — highly constructive influence on a generation of New Testament interpreters, among whom I count myself as one untimely born. I will take a brief suggestion from his earlier work here and argue that, as is so often the case, broader and significant implications lie within it.

Richard Hays suggested some time ago that Romans 1:17 is informed by Psalm 98:2-3 (97:2-3 LXX).[1] On first considering this claim, I rejected it as unlikely.[2] I have since, however, reversed that judgment and now hold the suggestion to be both probable and highly significant. To note the issue of

---

1. Richard B. Hays, *Echoes of Scripture in the Letters of Paul* (New Haven: Yale University Press, 1989), pp. 36-37. Others have since noted some sort of connection, apparently independently of Hays: cf. C. E. B. Cranfield, *A Critical and Exegetical Commentary on the Epistle to the Romans*, 2 vols., ICC (London: T. & T. Clark, 2004 [1975]), 1:96 (parenthetically and without further comment); Robert Jewett, *Romans*, Hermeneia (Minneapolis: Fortress, 2007), p. 143, who cites Klaus Haacker, *Der Brief des Paulus an die Römer*, THKNT 6 (Leipzig: Evangelische Verlagsanstalt, 1999), p. 41; also Robert Morgan, *Romans*, NTG (Sheffield: Sheffield Academic, 1995), pp. 20-21, who is cited by A. Katherine Grieb, *The Story of Romans: A Narrative Defense of God's Righteousness* (Louisville: Westminster John Knox, 2002), p. 11 n. 21. Mark Seifrid cites this text as central to the broader debate but never connects it with Rom. 1:16-17; see *Christ, Our Righteousness: Paul's Theology of Justification*, NSBT 9 (Downers Grove, Ill.: InterVarsity, 2000), pp. 38-40.

2. One of the mistakes in *The Rhetoric of Righteousness in Romans 3:21-26*, JSNTSup 65 (Sheffield: JSOT Press, 1992).

significance briefly: if this intertext lies behind 1:17, then it enfolds — or at least directly informs — Paul's first use of δικαιοσύνη θεοῦ in Romans. This Old Testament text might then provide us with critical insight into the meaning of that important but much-contested phrase in Paul, perhaps rather as Habakkuk 2:4 arguably informs the apostle's use elsewhere in Romans of πίστις.[3] But in order to generate this significance, the suggestion must of course first prove true. Hence, our subsequent discussion will unfold in two stages.

First we must revisit the specific question of the echo itself that was posed initially by Hays: does Romans 1:17 demonstrably echo Psalm 98? Many have not detected this connection in the past. But if we conclude that it is likely, then we will have to explore the further semantic consequences of this realization — the broader echo chamber of the initial sounding, so to speak — since these have been largely overlooked. And I will suggest, in a move beyond Hays's initial work, that this echo generates a broad and rich resonance through Romans in terms of the ancient discourse of kingship. It is *this* particular chord that Paul is sounding with the strategic phrase δικαιοσύνη θεοῦ, mediated by the text of Psalm 98, which is a psalm of divine kingship. Δικαιοσύνη θεοῦ denotes for Paul nothing less than the decisive saving act of deliverance by the divine King of his royal appointed representative — that is, the resurrection and enthronement of Jesus (the) Christ.

The first stage in this demonstration — the detection of the initial echo — can be dealt with relatively quickly. However, the second — its orchestration in terms of the discourse of kingship — is more complex and controversial and will take us a little longer.

An Echo of Scripture in Romans 1:17

The detection of scriptural echoes is a delicate matter.[4] But an accumulation of various indicators suggests to me that Hays was absolutely right to assert

---

3. See Rom. 1:17; 3:5, 21, 22, 25, 26; 10:3 (2x); 1 Cor. 1:30; 2 Cor. 5:21; Phil. 3:9. Literature on this debate is voluminous; an excellent introductory survey and bibliography is supplied by John Reumann in his series of entries "Righteousness (Early Judaism)," "Righteousness (Greco-Roman World)," and "Righteousness (NT)," *ABD* 5:736-73. The suggestion concerning πίστις was made by Richard Hays as well, in *The Faith of Jesus Christ: The Narrative Substructure of Galatians 3:1–4:11,* 2nd ed. (Grand Rapids: Eerdmans, 2002 [1983]).

4. Hays's own initial treatment of the methodological issues in *Echoes* (esp. pp. 29-32) is difficult to better; his criteria for detecting an echo are presented again and revised in his

that Paul is echoing the opening verses of Psalm 98 in Romans 1:16-17 — an echo that encloses the critical phrase in which we are currently interested. The psalm reads (Ps 97:2-3 in the LXX, the version of the OT that Paul generally uses[5]):

ἐγνώρισεν κύριος τὸ σωτήριον αὐτοῦ ἐναντίον τῶν ἐθνῶν.
ἀπεκάλυψεν τὴν δικαιοσύνην αὐτοῦ.
ἐμνήσθη τοῦ ἐλέους αὐτοῦ τῷ Ιακωβ καὶ τῆς ἀληθείας αὐτοῦ τῷ
    οἴκῳ Ισραηλ.
εἴδοσαν πάντα τὰ πέρατα τῆς γῆς τὸ σωτήριον τοῦ θεοῦ ἡμῶν.

Paul then writes in Romans 1:16-17:

Οὐ γὰρ ἐπαισχύνομαι τὸ εὐαγγέλιον,
δύναμις γὰρ θεοῦ ἐστιν εἰς σωτηρίαν παντὶ τῷ πιστεύοντι,
Ἰουδαίῳ τε πρῶτον καὶ Ἕλληνι.
δικαιοσύνη γὰρ θεοῦ ἐν αὐτῷ ἀποκαλύπτεται
ἐκ πίστεως εἰς πίστιν, καθὼς γέγραπται κτλ.

There are three distinguishable indicators that underpin this judgment: phraseological, lexicographical, and thematic. There is, first, an echo of a clause (i.e., of a potentially self-sufficient phrase) and not merely of isolated words here; compare δικαιοσύνη γὰρ θεοῦ . . . ἀποκαλύπτεται in the target text with ἀπεκάλυψεν τὴν δικαιοσύνην αὐτοῦ from the source text. Although these syntagms are not precisely the same, they are essentially so — the same substantive, δικαιοισύνη, with a genitive denoting the same subject, God (θεοῦ/αὐτοῦ), being developed by the same verb, ἀποκαλύπτω, although in different tenses and voices. It is worth noting, moreover, that this basic clause and association in the two texts is *unequalled in its proximity, whether elsewhere in Paul or in the LXX.*[6] Second, this essentially phraseological echo

---

"'Who Has Believed Our Message?' Paul's Reading of Isaiah," in *The Conversion of the Imagination: Paul as Interpreter of Israel's Scripture* (Grand Rapids: Eerdmans, 2005), pp. 25-49. Some helpful recent refinements are undertaken by Leroy Huizenga, in dialogue in particular with the semiotic theories of Umberto Eco and Stefan Alkier; see especially "Dictionaries, Encyclopedias, and the Model Reader," ch. 1 in "The Akedah in Matthew" (Ph.D. diss., Duke University, 2006), pp. 43-101.

5. Dietrich-Alex Koch's conclusion in 1986, which still seems plausible; see *Die Schrift als Zeuge des Evangeliums: Untersuchungen zur Verwendung und zum Verständnis der Schrift bei Paulus* (Tübingen: Mohr, 1986).

6. Intriguingly, the Hebrew texts Isa. 56:1 and CD 20:20 are close to this clause, as

is accompanied in both texts by a parallel to δικαιοισύνη constructed with "salvation," the word σωτηρία occurring once in Romans 1:16, and its cognate twice in Psalm 98.[7] So a close lexical association seems to confirm the initial syntagmatic echo.[8] But, third, a series of broader thematic similarities is apparent as well. Both texts discuss an antithesis between Jews and pagans ('Ιουδαῖος vs. "Ελλην in Romans; τὰ ἔθνη vs. Ιακωβ/οἶκος Ισραηλ in the Psalm), in relation to which God is acting.[9] Moreover, in both texts God is acting to make something known, this point being made in Psalm 98 by further verbs of knowledge and of sight.[10] Finally, the aorist tenses in the psalm corroborate Paul's later temporal emphases in Romans 3:21-26 that the divine saving event has taken place "now," in the sense of the immediate past and the present, as against the future. God *has* acted. So the unusual temporality of the two texts — which is a crucial argumentative point in Romans for Paul — is identical as well.

In my view, this is an impressive accumulation of evidence, the force of which is difficult to deny. Phraseological, lexical, and three thematic echoes all reinforce one another in suggesting a connection, and more general considerations seem only to enhance these implications.[11] In view of all this evidence,

---

Haacker notes (*An die Römer*, p. 41), but the LXX blunts the echo of Isaiah in the Greek, translating צדקה with ἔλεος, and Paul's reproduction of a clause from Qumran directly is of course unlikely. Romans 3:21-22 is also a partial exception to this claim, although there the verb has changed to a synonym, φανερόω.

7. Strictly speaking, the LXX uses the neuter τὸ σωτήριον at this point.

8. This correlation is very significant, because it limits the relevant background texts to those that speak of *iustitia salutifera*. Moreover, this particular action occurs (as Morgan points out in *Romans*, pp. 20-21) primarily in the Psalter, although there is a significant cluster of such instances in Isaiah.

9. This emphasis is apparent in the context preceding Rom. 1:16-17 as well, where Paul has been speaking of his apostolic commission (to) "Ελλησίν τε καὶ βαρβάροις, σοφοῖς τε καὶ ἀνοήτοις.

10. And there is even a hint of priority of action toward Judaism in Psalm 98, as God is said to have remembered his mercy and fidelity to Israel, something the pagan nations there "see." This arguably echoes the overt statement of Jewish priority in Romans 1:16b — 'Ιουδαίῳ τε πρῶτον καὶ "Ελληνι — although I would not want to press this point. (I supply an additional explanation for this phrase in my extensive study of Justification questions in Paul, *The Deliverance of God: An Apocalyptic Rereading of Justification in Paul* [Grand Rapids: Eerdmans, forthcoming 2009], ch. 19.)

11. It is widely conceded that Paul quotes and alludes to Scripture repeatedly through Romans. Within this practice, it is also evident that he makes extensive use of texts from the Psalms (cf. esp. 3:10-18 and 20a in the immediate setting). And the later 3:21-22, which is so closely constructed to 1:17, is little more than a pastiche of scriptural texts — except, that is,

some relationship between Psalm 98:2-3 and Romans 1:16-17 looks almost certain. Hays's initial perception was therefore, in my opinion, profoundly right. We will need to consider in due course why Paul does not mark this quotation explicitly, as he does his other key intertexts in Romans;[12] this particular scriptural usage is allusive rather than overt. But I will suggest an explanation for this reticence shortly. It is important for now to investigate the semantic implications of this intertextual linkage further — the moment at which previous exploration of this connection has tended to falter. And here we enter the second, more complex phase in our intertextual exploration.

Paul and the Ancient Discourse of Kingship

Psalm 98 is a psalm of divine kingship,[13] and contains (as we will see in more detail shortly) terminology and thematology characteristic of that ancient Jewish discourse — a discourse that interwove in turn with broader conceptions of kingship, both divine and human, throughout the ancient Near East. The discourse of kingship had profoundly ancient roots but was also very much alive — sometimes in new variations — in Paul's day. And this raises the possibility that the phrase δικαιοσύνη θεοῦ is operating within that broader discourse and is colored by its distinctive concerns. Our investigation of this possibility will unfold in an analysis of five subordinate questions:

1. the general contours of the ancient discourse of kingship
2. the meaning(s) of "right" actions by a king
3. the presence (or absence) of this discourse in Romans
4. the probable particular meaning of δικαιοσύνη θεοῦ in Romans 1:17
5. the implications for the construal of δικαιοσύνη θεοῦ in relation to the covenant

---

at *this* point, where the disclosure of the δικαιοσύνη θεοῦ is stated, so the lacuna has now been addressed. Admittedly, this last argument may be a little opaque in the present setting, but it is, I would suggest, ultimately quite significant. If 3:21-22 is elsewhere demonstrably a pastiche of intertexts, then we might expect some intertext to emerge here as well, as indeed Ps. 98:2-3 does. For detailed development of this argument, see my *Deliverance of God*, ch. 15.

12. That is, with a quotation formula — usually γέγραπται.

13. Hays does not develop this point, referring rather to lament and exile (which are not to be excluded from the interpretation either of Paul or of Romans but do not seem so directly relevant here); cf. *Echoes*, p. 38. Seifrid is sensitive to this connotation but, as noted above, does not connect it directly to the key texts and phrases in Romans; cf. *Christ, Our Righteousness*, p. 39.

In navigating these last questions, we will be drawing upon certain recent scholarly advances in relation to Jesus' messiahship, resurrection, and lordship, some of which have recently been pressed through Romans, although in a rather preliminary way.

1. The Ancient Discourse of Kingship

Psalm 98 is part of a widespread ancient discourse concerning kingship and its particular ascription by pious Jews to their God.[14] (It is one of the classic expositions of this discourse as identified by Gunkel and Begrich in 1933. They pointed in particular to Psalms 47, 93, and 96-99,[15] texts that all name God explicitly at a certain point as "king" — see here v. 6.) Psalm 98 is typically theocentric throughout, speaking primarily of acts by God on his people's behalf in terms thought appropriate for the divine ruler — acts of salvation, deliverance, order, and judgment. These acts are accomplished by God's "right hand" or "holy arm." The people then respond with rejoicing and thanksgiving, and this response is typically hyperbolic; it is literally orchestrated, and other facets of creation join in as well (presumably because they are also ruled by God the King) — the sea and its contents, the world and all who dwell in it, the rivers, and the mountains. Significantly, because the scope of the divine King's rule is cosmic, these acts are visible to and indeed affect the pagan nations in addition to Israel.

Numerous other texts, both within and outside the Jewish scriptural tradition, freight this discourse in various ways.[16] But the complex data can be

---

14. Keith W. Whitelam provides an excellent summary and bibliography in "King and Kingship," *ABD* 4:40-48; see also J. H. Eaton, *Kingship and the Psalms* (London: SCM, 1976); James Luther Mays, *The Lord Reigns: A Theological Handbook to the Psalms* (Louisville: Westminster John Knox, 1994); J. Richard Middleton, *The Liberating Image: The* Imago Dei *in Genesis 1* (Grand Rapids: Brazos, 2005). A brief account more directly relevant to our concerns here is Richard Bauckham, *God Crucified: Monotheism and Christology in the New Testament* (Carlisle: Paternoster, 1998), pp. 9-13.

15. Denoting them "Enthronement Psalms" (as noted by Whitelam, "King and Kingship," p. 43). Significantly, S. Mowinckel had earlier worked with a much more extensive range of texts, so the Enthronement Psalms provide a very minimalist data pool. Mowinckel includes Psalms 8, 15, 24, 29, 33, 46, 48, 50, 66a, 75, 76, 81, 82, 84, 87, 114, 118, 132, 149, and Exod. 15:1-18; and the data can arguably be broadened still further.

16. And the Hellenistic and Roman data should not be ignored; cf. esp. Aristotle, *Pol.* 3.14-18; 5.10-11; Seneca, *De clementia;* Dio Chrysostom, *Discourses* 1-4 (cf. also *Discourse* 62); see E. R. Goodenough, "The Political Philosophy of Hellenistic Kingship," *YCS* 1 (1928): 55-

simplified (as is necessary here) by the recognition that much of it is characterized by a root metaphor concerning God — the metaphor precisely of God as a king.[17] The content of that image was generated largely by historical, human kingship, although presumably in the form of ideal types. God the King and the ideal human king were images that mutually interpreted one another, and this draws other illuminating texts into the elaboration of the discourse (especially Psalms 2, 45, 72, 89, and 110).[18]

We learn from these texts (supported by studies of ancient iconography, etc.) that ancient kings, and ancient gods conceived of as kings, had a fundamental duty of care in relation to their people.[19] This could unfold in two basic ways.

First, if a king's people were in some sort of difficulty, then it was the monarch's duty to resolve that difficulty. If they were oppressed or invaded, then the king was obliged to deliver or defend them. But this function was often narrated in the ancient Near East in cosmic terms (partly no doubt to underwrite the need for a king in the first place). Indeed, it was frequently in the first instance the divine king's duty to establish cosmic order, slaying or controlling the monsters of chaos that threatened the cosmos with instability or dissolution.[20] Alternatively, it was the chaotic waters bordering the

---

102; Bruno Blumenfeld, *The Political Paul: Justice, Democracy, and Kingship in a Hellenistic Framework,* JSNTSup 210 (Sheffield: Sheffield Academic, 2001).

17. Drawing here on the term and method of George Lakoff; see especially Lakoff, *Moral Politics: How Liberals and Conservatives Think,* 2nd ed. (Chicago: University of Chicago Press, 2001 [1996]); see also his earlier classic study (with Mark Johnson) *Metaphors We Live By,* 2nd ed. (Chicago: University of Chicago Press, 2003 [1980]). His work is discussed in more detail in my *Deliverance of God,* esp. chs. 1 and 7. Root metaphors have been applied to Paul's thought previously by John L. White, although in a rather different way from here; see *The Apostle of God: Paul and the Promise of Abraham* (Peabody, Mass.: Hendrickson, 1999), pp. 3-59.

18. Strong boundaries in the evidence should not be drawn between Jewish, ancient Near Eastern, and more recent Hellenistic and Roman discourses.

19. Cf. the later medieval and aristocratic notions of both *royaume* and *noblesse oblige;* cf. also, most importantly, Psalm 72, where this duty is often spelled out explicitly. Whitelam, "King and Kingship," p. 42, states more discursively (in relation specifically to human kingship) that "[t]he justification of kingship with its centralized social structure was based upon a guarantee of order, security, prosperity, fertility, etc., in return for loyalty and subservience."

20. The need to control the forces of chaos was widespread in the ancient Near East, although in different local forms: see, for example, the Egyptian ideology of the pharaoh as the Lord of *ma'at,* as against the Babylonian epic *Enuma Elish,* where Marduk establishes a right to rule by defeating the sea monster Tiamat. Ugaritic material evidences similar notions as well. (For references, see Whitelam, "King and Kingship," p. 45.)

world that needed to be controlled (and so on). Cosmic and more recognizably political activities thus intertwine throughout this discourse — and entirely deliberately. However, all of these actions, whether concretely political or more mythical and ritual, revolve around the basic notion of a ruler acting to save his people from disorder and oppression and to establish them in (relative) freedom and safety, whether that ruler is divine, human, or an alliance of the two.

Complementing this principal type of saving and ordering activity is the second broad duty incumbent on the divine and human monarchs, namely, sustaining a condition of peace and prosperity. Once order has been established, or reestablished, it is the duty of the divine monarch and/or the divinely appointed monarch to preserve it. It is worth noting that the "being" of kings, whether divine or human, consequently seems inseparable from their activity. Kings are what they do; character and activity are correlative notions in this relation. We can now note some further common elements in this discourse that are relevant to our unfolding concerns.

As has already been intimated, an important alliance generally holds between the divine king and an appointed earthly representative, who is also a king, although in a derivative sense. Numerous variations on this basic dynamic are observable, including the strand in the Old Testament that rejects this relationship altogether ("no king for Israel but God"). Yet even in this radical variant, divine kingship is effected through appointed earthly agents or representatives who act with authority that they receive by way of delegation from the divine ruler, often as they are inspired by the divine Spirit. Usually, however, such figures are royal and part of a divinely ratified dynasty, "the Lord" establishing "the lord." (This alliance cries out for an ideological analysis, but this is not our present concern.) The earthly king, then, is usually involved in the fulfillment of his duties in both sacral and overtly political and military activities, although these interpenetrate in ancient societies. The establishment and preservation of cosmic and political order are his responsibility, so cultic and political capacities are developed to carry out his duties in those respective spheres. Accordingly, there is an important observable relationship between palace and temple (not to mention the military), one that influences much of the Old Testament.[21] David and Solomon dominate the kingly ideals as they are presented by the Old Testament, Da-

---

21. The celebration of the human king as the "son of God" at an annual enthronement festival in ancient Israel has been much debated. Fortunately, this question does not have to be decided here.

vid acting overtly more as a deliverer of his people, the one who creates order, and Solomon as the establisher of a suitably impressive cultus over which he presides (cf. esp. 1 Kings 3:1-2; 5-6; 7:13-51; 8-9), thereby sustaining that order and prosperity. But he is also of course the archetypally wise ruler (cf. 1 Kings 2:6, 9; 3:9, 12, 16-28; 4:29-34; 5:7, 12; 10:23-24). The key symbols of scepter, crown, and throne — especially this last — are plainly evident in much of this material.[22]

2. "Right" Actions by a King

We must now ask the critical question in the present relation: what is a "right" action by a divine king or his appointed human representative? It can be seen almost immediately that the answer depends very much on the particular setting of a given action within the broader discourse. A "right" action may be a dramatic act of intervention that saves or reorders — a fundamentally liberative action, which presumably will have a corresponding oppressive effect on any opposing, hostile forces that are defeated. Alternatively, it may be an ongoing act that sustains peace and/or prosperity or an act that judges a given situation accurately in terms of the ethical rectitude of parties contending at law, thereby maintaining social order.[23]

Furthermore, because the ancient king combines in his person executive and judiciary functions, right actions can be described using terms drawn from either of these fields, although here the most important semantic crossover is probably the deployment of more strictly forensic terminology in relation to executive activity, the language of the law court being used to describe what a modern person would view as an executive political action. Hence, if a right action by a king is described using forensic terminology and imagery such as a "verdict" or "judgment," we might nevertheless be speaking of an essentially performative, oppressive or liberative event (and these two acts often go together), as against a more strictly retributive procedure (i.e., also performative, but with an indicative dimension predicated on appropriate retribution). A military victory, a proclamation of the Jubilee, and an arbitration of a difficult civil case can all be described as "judgments"

---

22. See Whitelam, "King and Kingship," p. 42, although arguably he overlooks the emphatically gender-coded symbolism of multiple beautiful wives and concubines as well; cf. esp. 2 Sam. 16:20-22 and 1 Kings 2:13-25.

23. All of these actions are widely attested, in relation to both God and human kings, in the OT.

by the king, and certainly all of these ideally ought to be "right" as well, but they are "right" in very different senses.[24] (Such language is still detectable in modern political discourse, although not as frequently, so an election result might be characterized as a "judgment," not meaning by this a retributive action.) The immediate context must therefore tell us what kind of activity is in view at any given moment. The language of "rightness" is often deployed in the Old Testament, and in the specific setting of kingship, in all of these specific senses.

Excursus: the relationship between right action and kingship in the Psalter

The densest concentration of δικαιοσύνη terminology in the setting of kingship — most frequently, denoting a liberating act — is in the Psalter: cf. especially (LXX) Pss. 44:5, 8; 47:11; 49:6; 71:1, 2, 3, 7; 88:15, 17; 95:13; 96:2, 6; 97:2 (Paul's allusion in Rom. 1:17), 9; 98:4; 117:19. The liberative notion of δικαιοσύνη occurs in many other psalms as well, so this semantic field overlaps with the discourse of kingship but is not coterminous with it. For God's liberating righteousness, cf. in addition (LXX) Pss. 5:9; 7:18; 9:9; 21:32; 30:2; 34:24, 28; 35:7, 11; 39:10, 11; 50:16; 68:28; 70:2, 15, 16, 18, 24; 84:11, 12, 14; 87:13; 102:17; 110:3; 111:3, 9; 118:7, 40, 62, 75 [?], 106, 123, 138 [?], 142 [2x], 160, 164; 142:1 (this reference also being especially significant for Paul), 11; 144:7. But this is hardly a problem for my case here. It simply suggests that this perception of the character of God was widespread (and maybe also that the discourse of divine kingship was more widespread than is often recognized — perhaps either tacitly or as a hidden transcript).

In sum, about 80 of the 336 instances of δικαιοσύνη in the LXX occur in the Psalter — around 25 percent. Approximately 50 of those 80 instances describe God, and then almost invariably in a liberative, salvific sense. Half a dozen of those instances, and several more important instances describing the human king in the same terms, also occur in texts that are indisputable enthronement psalms or texts denoting some other aspect of ancient kingship. This is where the lexical and thematological fields overlap especially clearly. Psalm 98 (97 LXX) operates within that intersection.

The correlation with various salvific terms is also worth noting, because it reinforces these claims. Δικαιοσύνη occurs in close relation to salvific terms in the LXX almost entirely in the Psalter and Isaiah. See the strong connections between liberation, salvation, and δικαιοσύνη in Pss. (LXX) 16:1, 15; 39:10, 11, 17 (cf. also vv. 14, 18); 50:16 (a psalm traditionally linked to David and his repentance for his adultery with Bath-

---

24. I distinguish these in a more detailed discussion elsewhere in terms of forensic-nonretributive and forensic-retributive actions. In the former, the rectitude of the parties being judged is irrelevant; the action is usually grounded in the right action, and hence character, of the primary actor — God or the king. In the latter, the rectitude of those being judged is relevant and needs to be assessed accurately by God or the king, so that the resulting judgment rightly reflects that prior ethical calculus. For more discussion, see my *Deliverance of God*, ch. 16.

sheba); 70:2, 15, 16, 18, 24; 71:1-4 (a psalm of ideal human kingship); 84:8, 11-14 (a psalm oriented more toward the land); 97:1b-2, 9 (the psalm that launched this entire investigation; cf. also v. 3); 117:14, 19, 21; 118:40-41, 121-23, 169-76.

The links with both salvation and kingship are, however, perhaps even more overt in Isaiah: see (LXX) 39:8 (where King Hezekiah is grateful for δικαιοσύνη — prosperity — in his day); overt royal instances of God triumphing through a rehearsal of the ancient combat myth in 51:5-11; 59, esp. vv. 14, 17; 62 (cf. esp. vv. 1, 2); 63:1-6, 8-9 — here the liberative sense of δικαιοσύνη (the related thematology of "father" is also prominent in 63:7-64:11). But the *maintenance* of prosperity, in part through "due process," is apparent in 60:17, 18, and intermingled with the liberative sense in 61:8, 11 (cf. the closely related Amos 5:7, 24; also 5:12, 15; 6:12).

Most importantly for our discussion here, δικαιοσύνη not infrequently denotes a liberating or delivering act — an action when it is "right" for either God the King or his appointed king to set someone free. Previously, some interpreters have referred to this particular subset of the data of δικαιοσύνη in the Old Testament as *iustitia salutifera*, because of the frequent occurrence of notions of salvation in context (and these have of course assisted our recognition of this usage as fundamentally liberative).[25] But possibly we now have a better explanation of just why the term functions in this way on occasion. It is "right" in certain circumstances for the king to act to deliver, especially if a client or his people are in some sort of difficulty. It is his duty to set them free — to save them. Similarly, God the King can act in such terms to deliver his appointed human king, provided that this king has done nothing heinously wrong (or, alternatively, that he has repented sufficiently of any such sins). Again, in these circumstances, it is "right" for God to act to save.[26]

It might be objected here that this ancient discourse is not especially significant for the New Testament — after all, by the first century CE Israel had not been ruled by one of her Davidic kings for a very long time. However, vigorous New Testament debates unfolding along various axes suggest that

25. This data was emphasized in a classic early study by Hermann Cremer, *Die paulinische Rechtfertigungslehre im Zusammenhange ihrer geschichtlichen Voraussetzungen* (Gütersloh: Bertelsmann, 1899). A useful brief overview is supplied by J. J. Scullion, "God's ṣedeq-ṣĕdāqâ: Saving Action" in "Righteousness (OT)," *ABD* 5:731-34.

26. The conviction seems to be widespread in the OT that God "cares" and hence can be appealed to directly for help in all sorts of difficult circumstances, irrespective of any claim on that help that might be generated by the appellant's ethical state. Sometimes that putative basis for a claim is introduced, but often it is not, and at times it is even directly disavowed in a repentant mode.

although the specifics of the discourse are far from clear, its presence is both significant and undeniable. The current discussions of the relevance of the Roman Imperial cult and Augustan ideology to the New Testament (especially to Paul), and the widespread data — especially in the Synoptic Gospels — concerning the "kingdom of God" (or its close equivalent), suggest this conclusion almost immediately.[27] This discourse was still very much in play — in all its subtle local variations — in the New Testament era.

With these broader observations in place, we can turn to consider an important contextual question in relation to Paul. Is a discourse of divine kingship operative in Romans?

3. Divine Kingship in Romans and the Early Church

This specific query touches on several important debates that are currently unfolding within New Testament studies.

Essentially since the seminal work of Wilhelm Bousset,[28] theological development in the early church has been viewed by many interpreters panoramically as a slow progression from limited, theologically primitive, Jewish, particular notions to a liberated, theologically mature, Hellenistic, universal gospel, perhaps best exemplified by John. And this famous paradigm has greatly influenced the reconstruction of almost every New Testament question, figure, and text, whether Jesus, the pre-Pauline church, Paul himself, or the figures that wrote after him like the authors of the Gospels. There have consequently been strong methodological tendencies to detach Paul's understanding of Jesus from "early," "low," and Jewish christological categories like Messiah and to interpret it instead in terms of "later," "higher" (although not necessarily "high/the highest"!), and Hellenistic categories,

---

27. Many other debates could be added to these two — for example, the stilling of the storm pericopes, which arguably present Jesus as the Divine Warrior; the triumphal entry; and so on. Wright gives an especially vigorous account of the presence of royal thematology in Jesus' life in *Jesus and the Victory of God* (Minneapolis: Fortress, 1996), esp. chs. 6-13 (pp. 198-653); the relevant data is listed in an appendix, "'Kingdom of God' in Early Christian Literature," pp. 663-70. An interesting application to a Pauline text of thematology especially associated with the Divine Warrior is Timothy G. Gombis, "Ephesians 2 as a Narrative of Divine Warfare," *JSNT* 26 (2004): 403-18.

28. Wilhelm Bousset, *Kyrios Christos: A History of the Belief in Christ from the Beginnings of Christianity to Irenaeus*, trans. J. E. Steely (Nashville: Abingdon, 1970 [1913; ET from 4th German ed. of 1965]).

within which stratum the apostle's use of "Lord" is generally included. This is often combined with emphases on a spiritual rather than a bodily resurrection and a supposed disinterest in the teaching and life of the historical Jesus. (I would add that this agenda also integrates in certain useful ways with the predominant Protestant way of construing Paul's soteriology, which emphasizes individualism, liberation from the crabbed constraints of the law, and the atoning death of Christ — i.e., Justification.)[29] All of these concerns have of course influenced the interpretation of Paul's most discursive letter, Romans, leading to a certain myopia at key points that we must try briefly in what follows to redress.[30]

Various scholars have for some time been attempting to roll back the broad agenda of Bousset, and with some success.[31] To point to one particularly useful representative in the present relation, N. T. Wright has vigorously reemphasized the Jewishness and messiahship of Jesus, his bodily resurrection, and his exalted lordship (which ought to be understood, furthermore, in a thoroughly Jewish sense). He is in the process of pressing these emphases through the thought of Paul, the argument of Romans, and the general theological development of the early church.[32] It is of course not necessary to endorse all the details of Wright's various claims and arguments

29. For a more detailed description of this soteriology and its various theological and social legitimations, see my *Deliverance of God,* esp. chs. 1, 6, and 9.

30. An accessible overview of this and related trends can be found in Larry W. Hurtado, *Lord Jesus Christ: Devotion to Jesus in Earliest Christianity* (Grand Rapids: Eerdmans, 2003), pp. 1-29. For more detailed engagements, see the following note.

31. Among others, see especially Bauckham, *God Crucified;* J. F. Fitzmyer, "The Semitic Background of the NT *Kyrios*-Title," in *The Semitic Background of the New Testament* (Grand Rapids: Eerdmans, 1997), pp. 115-42; idem, "New Testament *Kyrios* and *Maranatha* and Their Aramaic Background," in *To Advance the Gospel: New Testament Studies,* 2nd ed. (Grand Rapids: Eerdmans, 1998 [1981]), pp. 218-235; Martin Hengel, "Christological Titles in Early Christianity," in *The Messiah: Developments in Earliest Judaism and Christianity,* ed. James H. Charlesworth (Minneapolis: Fortress, 1992), pp. 425-48; idem, "'Sit at my right hand!' The Enthronement of Christ at the Right Hand of God and Psalm 110:1," in *Studies in Early Christology* (Edinburgh: T. & T. Clark, 1995), pp. 119-225; Larry W. Hurtado, *One God, One Lord: Early Christian Devotion and Ancient Jewish Monotheism,* 2nd ed. (London: T. & T. Clark, 1998 [1988]); idem, *Lord Jesus Christ,* passim; C. Kavin Rowe, "Romans 10:13: What Is the Name of the Lord?" *HBT* 22 (2000): 135-73. (For N. T. Wright, see the following note.)

32. Wright's principal treatments are *The Climax of the Covenant: Christ and the Law in Pauline Theology* (Edinburgh: T. & T. Clark, 1991); *The New Testament and the People of God* (London: SPCK, 1992); *Jesus and the Victory of God; Romans,* NIB 10 (Nashville: Abingdon, 2002), pp. 393-770; and *The Resurrection of the Son of God* (Minneapolis: Fortress, 2003). He references numerous shorter studies, many on Romans, in these major works.

— which are numerous — in order to find these basic corrections to Bousset's paradigm plausible.[33] (Indeed, arguably they participate in a new paradigm that is gathering momentum within New Testament studies, at least in certain quarters.) But his principal corrections are of great moment for our present discussion.

If interpreters approach Paul and Romans with ears freshly attuned to the importance and integration of Jesus' messiahship, resurrection, and exaltation to lordship, then the textual surface of the letter begins to shift in some interesting new directions. Initially, it becomes apparent that these themes have simply been underemphasized by much previous interpretation. So, for example, resurrection is a much more prominent theme in Romans than most commentators seem to have realized, as is Jesus' Davidic descent. But following these realizations it rapidly begins to emerge that the various recovered motifs are not just isolated points of emphasis for Paul — spots where his authentic Jewishness is gratifyingly apparent, and/or his continuity with the thinking of the early church. Rather, they are tightly integrated concerns that fulfill important argumentative and theological roles (and sensitivities to narrative and intertextuality are vital here — further evidence of the importance of the work of Richard Hays!). I would suggest, however, that while Wright and others have begun the resulting process of reinterpretation,[34] the addition of one or two more insights can bring still greater clarity and cogency to our reappropriation of the letter's argument.

I recommend that these recovered emphases be correlated in a significant interplay with the ancient discourse of kingship, which in Romans is now focused on — and in a real sense *realized by* — Jesus Christ. Indeed, an entire theological complex constructed in these terms is discernible within Romans, although subtly. This integrated program is signaled *in nuce* by Paul's famous opening statements in 1:1b-4 (a text we begin to recognize as programmatic for much of the rest of Romans):[35]

---

33. Arguably, there are insensitivities in certain aspects of his work, not to mention occasional gaps; for a slightly different account of the resurrection, for example, cf. Dale C. Allison Jr., *Resurrecting Jesus: The Earliest Christian Tradition and Its Interpreters* (London/New York: T. & T. Clark, 2005). I am assuming here, however, that his basic claims are plausible.

34. The work of Daniel Kirk is also of significance in this relation; see J. R. Daniel Kirk, *Unlocking Romans: Resurrection and the Justification of God* (Grand Rapids: Eerdmans, 2008).

35. Wright makes this point clearly: "The Christology of 1:3-4 is by no means an isolated statement attached loosely to the front of the letter but not relevant to its contents. It is the careful, weighted, programmatic statement of what will turn out to be Paul's subtext throughout the whole epistle (see also 9:5; and 15:12, the final scriptural quotation of the main body of

Paul, a servant of Jesus Christ, called to be an apostle, set apart for the gospel of God, 2which he promised beforehand through his prophets in the holy scriptures, 3the gospel concerning his Son, who was descended from David according to the flesh 4and was declared to be Son of God with power according to the Spirit of holiness by resurrection from the dead, Jesus Christ our Lord. (NRSV)

Christ's messiahship and lordship are here affirmed by his resurrection from the dead, which functions, furthermore, as a *heavenly enthronement*. This enthronement is effected by the Spirit of sanctification, who in the Old Testament sanctifies the cult and the people of God, and anoints the king. And, equally importantly, this event is widely attested by the Jewish Scriptures — both Torah and Prophets. Moreover, it is an explanation of Jesus' sonship. He is the Son of God because, as for any divinely appointed king, God has now become his Father. So he is the King of Israel not only by descent, as a "son of David," but by royal enthronement; his "coronation" has taken place. As a sanctifying act, this must somehow implicitly effect the broader reconciliation of God with creation and his people, presumably overcoming the oppressive and even chaotic forces that seek to disrupt that relationship. Order should be established and prosperity realized and preserved. So, entirely predictably, the appointed ambassadors of that reconciliation, like Paul, are sent out to establish the appropriate submission and fidelity to this ruler in the rest of the world by way of their delegation ("apostleship") and proclamation ("gospel") — so vv. 1b and 5-6.

This is an essentially narrative account — a story — rich with theological import that links Jesus' messiahship, resurrection, and lordship. And clearly, numerous Old Testament texts that speak of divine and human kingship will resonate with it. Scholars debate many further aspects within these broad assertions, but most of those debates do not concern us at this point.[36]

---

the letter)"; later he also points to 5:12-21 and "all the elements of chaps. 6-8 that follow from it" (*Romans*, pp. 413, 415-19, quoting pp. 417 and 418). Robert Jewett, *Romans*, pp. 96-98, 103-8, provides a nuanced analysis in full dialogue with the extensive secondary discussion.

36. It is not, for example, immediately apparent how "high" this Christology is. Paul's use of "lord" here could be divine, entirely human, or roaming somewhere in between. But this question is best addressed in relation to Rom. 10:9-13 (see esp. Rowe, "What Is the Name of the Lord?"). And it ought to be asked in due course whether this material represents Paul's thought exhaustively, or is presupposed by him in relation to his auditors. It must suffice here to indicate that I view it as a shared basis for discussion, Paul's own position pushing rather radically beyond it, although in continuity with it; for further justification of this claim see my *Deliverance of God,* esp. ch. 19.

What matters here is more limited — namely, the implicit evidence that this basic narrative is mobilized by Paul through a great deal of the rest of Romans. We can note five points of conspicuous emergence (followed by two further, supplementary pieces of evidence).

1. In Romans 5:1-11 God *reconciles* a hostile world to himself through the Christ event (see esp. vv. 10-11), Paul here describing the divine act in quite distinctive language that resonates with the language of diplomatic, political, and royal circles (and invariably so whenever a delegate is involved, as indicated by the presence of πρεσβευ- language).[37] There is, moreover, a complementary use of royal "access" language in v. 2, in relation to which this reconciliation takes place. Then, in 5:14, an emphatic use of the terminology of government begins, Paul speaking repeatedly of what are in effect two kingdoms, with two "rules," respective services, and even enslavements, and a military relationship of hostility and/or victory (these emphases continuing through subsequent chapters in the letter).[38]

2. In Romans 8 the thematology of heavenly enthronement and glorification of Christ signaled in 1:2-4 reemerges. In 8:15-17 those who cry "Abba Father" receive "sonship" or "adoption" (υἱοθεσία), become "children of God," "and if children, also heirs — heirs of God and fellow heirs with Christ. . . ." Paul affirms here (and in Gal. 4:6) this cry's appropriateness for Christians, who participate in the "firstborn," namely, Jesus (cf. Rom. 8:29-30). His resurrection, understood also as a heavenly enthronement (cf. esp. 8:34: . . . ἐν δεξιᾷ τοῦ θεοῦ), explains the access that Christians now have "in him" to the inheritance that he has received, their status as children of God, like him, and the consequent appropriateness of their cry to a God now characterized as "Father." And such father-son language and affirmations, in the context of adoption, inheritance, and glorification, seem best explained by texts like Psalm 89 and the broader dis-

---

37. Jewett surveys the "reconciliation debate" in Paul in *Romans*, pp. 364-66, noting that detailed studies by F. Hahn, M. Hengel, and C. Breytenbach support the reading being suggested here. Jewett also discusses "access" on pp. 347-50, although without linking the two debates.

38. So, for example, Paul uses the verb [συμ]βασιλεύω a total of only ten times, but six of those are in this section of Romans: cf. 5:14, 17 [2x], 21 [2x]; 6:12 (also 1 Cor. 4:8 [3x] and 15:25, where the royal connotations of this term are explicit). In 8:15 and 21 he uses δουλεία, and elsewhere only in (the closely similar) Gal. 4:24 and 5:1. In 8:37 he speaks of ὑπερνικάω, a hapax legomenon. And so on.

course of divine kingship.[39] The preserved Aramaism in Romans 8:15 is meanwhile a marker of this christological tradition's antiquity within the early church. We seem to be in touch here, then, with an early explanation of the resurrection — as the heavenly enthronement and glorification of Jesus, and as his consequent affirmation as Messiah and Lord, who will rule the cosmos on behalf of his divine Father.

3. Kavin Rowe has pointed out that Paul's repeated affirmations of lordship in Romans 10:9-13 draw on important Old Testament intertexts and are rooted in the entirely Jewish monotheistic veneration of Yahweh as the only true God. Moreover, the affirmation of Jesus' lordship, which is included unavoidably here by Paul in this central Jewish confession, is confirmed by his resurrection — a connection illuminated best by the interpretation of the resurrection as the enthronement of the Messiah, Jesus, *as* Lord.[40] (Paul's unusual reference to "the Christ" in 9:5 is also now comprehensible in part as an anticipation of his later use of this narrative.)[41]

4. Although it is often overlooked, Romans 15:12 effects the closure of the main letter body by affirming Jesus' Davidic lineage through a citation of Isaiah 11:10 (cf. also 42:4 LXX, which is closely accompanied by the divine King's δικαιοσύνη in v. 6). With this reference to "the root of Jesse," which resumes the Davidic claims of 1:3, Paul not only concludes his substantive discussion but fashions a messianic inclusio around most of the letter's discursive material.[42]

---

39. αὐτὸς ἐπικαλέσεταί με Πατήρ μου εἶ σύ, θεός μου καὶ ἀντιλήμπτωρ τῆς σωτηρίας μου· κἀγὼ πρωτότοκον θήσομαι αὐτόν, ὑψηλὸν παρὰ τοῖς βασιλεῦσιν τῆς γῆς (Ps. 89:26-27 [88:27-28 LXX]). Note also the use of δικαιοσύνη to describe benevolent and salvific acts of God in vv. 14 and 16 (15 and 17 LXX), in parallel with κρίμα, ἔλεος, εὐδοκία, καύχημα and ἀλήθεια. It may also be legitimate to detect an influence from Psalm 110 at this point in the reference to God's right hand — another royal enthronement psalm, of course, and one much used by the early church. Cf. Donald H. Juel, *Messianic Exegesis: Christological Interpretation of the Old Testament in Early Christianity,* new ed. (Minneapolis: Augsburg Fortress, 1998 [1988]), pp. 135-50.

40. Rowe, "What Is the Name of the Lord?"

41. Indeed, this subsection of Romans is arguably replete with various messianic and royal connotations, most notably perhaps of wisdom. For more details, see my *Deliverance of God,* ch. 19.

42. The discourse's connotations are arguably detectable to an even more significant degree if the contexts of the three other texts quoted are explored — so Ps. 18:49 (certainly) and Deut. 32:43 (a book that generally assumes the kingship of God); Ps. 117:1 seems too brief to set up any such resonances. For some elaboration of these claims, see Hays, *Echoes,* pp. 70-73;

5. Although almost entirely unnoticed, Romans 16:20 — ὁ δὲ θεὸς τῆς εἰρήνης συντρίψει τὸν σατανᾶν ὑπὸ τοὺς πόδας ὑμῶν ἐν τάχει — *echoes both 1 Corinthians 15:25-27 and underlying messianic readings of Psalms 8 and 110 (8:6 and 110:1).*

Both Psalms 8 and 110, when applied to Christ, speak of his messianic enthronement, implicitly through the resurrection, followed by a further process of subjugation in relation to all Christ's enemies, which will be consummated at his second coming "so that God might be all in all" (1 Cor. 15:28b; and this royal reading resumes the language of Gen. 3:15, along with the surrounding narrative[43]). Hence, not only does 16:20 echo the royal discourse, but it even seems to deploy that discourse — via Psalm 8 — opposite the Adamic thematology that is so important to Paul in much of Romans.[44]

These five texts all develop the clues that are supplied by Paul in Romans 1:2-4. We can see in each of these other places a narrative of Jesus' heavenly enthronement informing Paul's argument — a narrative that de-

---

see also his "Christ Prays the Psalms: Paul's Use of an Early Christian Exegetical Convention," in *The Future of Christology: Essays in Honor of Leander E. Keck*, ed. A. J. Malherbe and W. A. Meeks (Minneapolis: Fortress, 1993), pp. 122-36, esp. 134-35; Wright, *Romans*, pp. 733, 744-49, esp. 748.

43. There are no direct linguistic signals of a connection between Rom. 16:20 and Gen. 3:15; hence, the echo, if it exists, must be fundamentally narrative. Nevertheless, Dunn suggests that Gen. 3:15 was a staple of Jewish hope, citing Ps. 91:13; *T. Sim.* 6:6; *T. Levi* 18:12 (to which we should add *T. Zeb.* 9:8); Luke 10:18-19 (a text that includes a note of joy, like Rom. 16:19-20); supported by *TDNT* 5:81, Michel, Käsemann, Stuhlmacher (*Der Brief an die Römer* [Göttingen: Vandenhoeck & Ruprecht, 1989], p. 223), and Cranfield (*Romans*, 2:905).

44. Wright, like Dunn, points rather to Ps. 91:13, which is actually a markedly less apposite intertext. (In particular, there is no connection with 1 Cor. 15:25-27.) Somewhat curiously, he nevertheless detects the Adamic allusion, routing that through Luke 10:17-19 (cf. Rev. 12:10-11). The strongest intertextual echo in this subsection for Wright is the evocation of the Jesus saying recorded in Matt. 10:16 by 16:19b, which does not disturb the set of resonances being suggested in v. 20 (*Romans*, pp. 764-65). These connections are all clearer in 1 Cor. 15:25-27, and are further affirmed and explained by Eph. 1:20-22 and Hebrews 1–2 (see esp. 1:13; 2:6-8a). See A. C. Thiselton, *The First Epistle to the Corinthians: A Commentary on the Greek Text*, NIGTC (Grand Rapids/Carlisle: Eerdmans/Paternoster, 2000), pp. 1230-36. Hays also puts these points succinctly, introducing Mark 12:35-37 into the mix for good measure! See Hays, *First Corinthians*, IBC (Louisville: John Knox, 1997), pp. 265-66. The future tense of the verb inclines me to suspect that Psalm 110 is to the fore in the echo in v. 20, but probably only marginally. Moreover, Satan is presumably one of the enemies who will eventually be placed under the feet of God.

scribes Jesus as Son, Christ, "firstborn," and Lord, because of his enthrone-ment by the resurrection. At this point he has entered his inheritance (and in Paul's view this now also opens up that inheritance for all who indwell him, whether Jew or pagan). But this description of the Christ event rotates around the resurrection and interprets it in terms of the discourse of divine and human kingship.

If it is granted that these five texts are points of conspicuous emergence, where a robust narrative Christology developed in terms of ancient kingship protrudes into Paul's argument, it seems plausible to detect other points where such a discourse is operative in Romans, if not so overtly. At least two further texts are worth noting.

6. Paul cites Psalm 143:2 (142:2 LXX), suitably modified, rather pregnantly in 3:20a: διότι ἐξ ἔργων νόμου οὐ δικαιωθήσεται πᾶσα σὰρξ ἐνώπιον αὐτοῦ. This quotation is of course interesting in and of itself, but, as sev-eral scholars have noted, Psalm 143 speaks repeatedly of God's δικαιοσύνη (cf. esp. vv. 1 and 11), and this contextual material can hardly be coincidental when Paul is about to resume that motif emphatically in Romans 3:21, 22, 25, and 26.[45] It seems, then, that the rest of the psalm is implicit within Paul's allusion — at least, in some sense. Perhaps less ob-vious is the way the psalm echoes many of the key themes in the dis-course of divine kingship. It does not itself function within that dis-course, but it does articulate an element that functions within it, and this seems entirely deliberate.

    Psalm 143 is a prayer for help grounded overtly in the goodness of God and his works that also specifically disavows help from God in re-sponse to the supplicant's piety. That is, this psalm *specifically repudiates retributive activity by God,* acknowledging that this would result in con-demnation rather than assistance. So the psalmist observes (quite rightly in the view of much of the Christian tradition) that no one is en-titled to help from God couched in such terms, because "no one living is righteous before you." The ground for any divine assistance must there-fore be the divine character, which must in turn be compassionate and should result in liberative — and corresponding oppressive! (cf. vv. 3 and 12) — actions. Such behavior is directly compatible with either the

---

45. Classic studies are Richard B. Hays, "Psalm 143 and the Logic of Romans 3," *JBL* 99 (1980): 107-15; William S. Campbell, "Romans iii as a Key to the Structure and Thought of the Letter," *NovT* 23 (1981): 22-40.

divine or the human king rescuing one of his charges, as he ought to, merely by virtue of his own duty of care. This dyad of intertextual echoes in Romans 1–3 thereby reproduces the much broader pattern of such echoes in the Psalter itself. Both are informed by a basic perception concerning the goodness of God.

7. Finally, we should note that in 1:17b a messianic reading of Habakkuk 2:4 (that is now probably most frequently associated with the advocacy of Richard Hays, and that I find entirely plausible[46]) foregrounds Christ's resurrection and eternal life in relation to the gospel as it is disclosed by the δικαιοσύνη of God: "the righteous one, through fidelity, will live." The letter's auditors are thereby prompted to find some connection between the gospel (i.e., the announcement of the divine King's good news through his appointed representative), Jesus' resurrection, and God's δικαιοσύνη.

4. The Meaning of δικαιοσύνη θεοῦ in Romans 1:17, in Relation to Psalm 98:2

We should recall now the insight that catalyzed this investigation — Richard Hays's observation that the phrase δικαιοσύνη θεοῦ and its immediate development in Romans 1:17 echoes Psalm 98. If we supplement that insight by the additional observations that Psalm 98 is a psalm of divine kingship and that Romans itself develops the ancient discourse of kingship in relation to Christ explicitly from its outset, and repeatedly (contra Bousset et al.) throughout its body, then the conclusion seems to follow ineluctably that the phrase δικαιοσύνη θεοῦ is best interpreted in the light of that discourse as well. Such a reading fits Paul's local argument perfectly, resumes the opening concerns of 1:2-4 neatly, and integrates with the contextual hints we receive from the specific lexical data elsewhere in Paul.[47] And in the light of this broader frame, we can now invest this phrase with the meaning appropriate to its particular function within that broader discourse — here in relation to a decisive saving and delivering act of power by God, the divine King,[48] on

46. The suggestion is made in *Faith of Jesus Christ* (pp. 132-41; cf. also the introduction to the second edition, p. xxxvii). A few interpreters from an earlier generation of scholars had made this connection, but Hays would be the most prominent current advocate of the reading.

47. See especially my *Deliverance of God*, ch. 17.

48. And this sets up another resonance with 1:4, which also speaks of δύναμις.

behalf of his royal representative, Jesus. That is, Christ is not being judged by God here (or oppressed); he is being resurrected! So δικαιοσύνη θεοῦ must mean in 1:17 "the deliverance of God," or something closely equivalent.[49] This is the specific content of the righteous act that God has just undertaken on behalf of his messianic agent, Christ — the act of resurrection, empowerment, and heavenly enthronement after his oppression and execution by evil opposing powers. It is "right" for God to act in this way on behalf of his chosen Son, who has been unfairly executed. It remains, then, only to ask why the psalm is present allusively rather than overtly.

I suggest that it is precisely the allusive activation of this broader discourse, and the critical enthronement narrative within it, that seems to underlie Paul's subtle use of the actual text of Psalm 98 in Romans 1:17. The words of Psalm 98:2-3 are *mediating* this construct — a discourse composed of scriptural texts, which now operates at one remove from those texts, as a distinguishable theological entity. Hence, the detection of this particular scriptural text plays no overt rhetorical role in the broader argument; the Roman Christian auditors are not supposed to be impressed by Paul's citation here of an authoritative Jewish text (as they are by his citation of Hab. 2:4 in 1:17b). They are merely meant to understand what he is talking about in more general terms, and they should be able to do so insofar as they inhabit this Jewish Christian discourse concerning Jesus' resurrection and kingship. Paul is merely using the words of Psalm 98:2-3 to say here what he wants to say (and presumably in a way that other Christians have already formulated and so can recognize) — that God the King has acted to save his messianic Son.[50]

An explanation of the similar reticence of Paul with respect to this discourse in the rest of Romans is hinted at here as well, although it cannot be developed fully in this essay. As the detailed argumentative analysis of Romans continues to unfold, it becomes apparent that the ancient discourse of kingship is not so much elaborated as presupposed. Paul does not seem intent to describe or to justify it so much as to interact with and exploit it in support of various contingent goals in relation to the Christians at Rome. It seems to be traditional theology that the Roman Christians share with both

49. That is, "the salvation of God" or "the redemption of God." At this point my recommendations overlap with an insightful study by Peter Leithart, "Justification as Verdict and Deliverance: A Biblical Perspective," *ProEccl* 16 (2007): 56-72.

50. This rhetorical qualification should serve to meet some of Stanley's concerns with Hays's methodology as expressed in Christopher Stanley, *Arguing with Scripture: The Rhetoric of Quotations in the Letters of Paul* (London/New York: T. & T. Clark, 2004).

Paul and the Jerusalem church — an integrated, Jewish, and perhaps surprisingly "high" christological narrative that smoothly links Jesus' messiahship, sonship, resurrection, and exalted heavenly lordship. Paul then builds from this shared theology toward his more specific rhetorical points in Romans.

And with these realizations in explanation of the discourse's subtle quality, it remains only to note the possible covenantal resonances of the phrase, because these have recently been proposed by many as the invariable central content of δικαιοσύνη θεοῦ (not least by N. T. Wright). This phrase means for many nothing more nor less than "the covenant faithfulness of God."[51]

5. The Relationship to the Covenant

If the phrase δικαιοσύνη θεοῦ is located within the broader discourse of divine kingship, then covenantal associations are clearly not far away, and any such reading is not far from the truth. The earthly king was ratified at times by a particular covenant, and the divine King could structure his relationships with Israel directly in terms of a covenant, as the book of Deuteronomy perhaps most overtly attests.[52] It is certainly fair, then, to detect a covenantal strand within this discourse and hence possibly also in relation to this phrase, which operates within it. Indeed, there is something profoundly right about any such assertion, because it grasps and emphasizes that *God's fidelity is intrinsic to any act of salvation;* for God to save implies necessarily

---

51. Wright, esp. *Romans,* pp. 397-406, 413, 464-78. Hays himself endorses this reading at times as well — see, for example, "Justification," *ABD* 3:1129-33, although he tends to speak of Christ's death and resurrection in the same breath, which links up with my recommendations here. Somewhat curiously, J. D. G. Dunn, although on the opposite side of many questions from Wright and Hays, concurs on this issue; see his *Romans 1-8,* WBC 38 (Dallas: Word, 1988), pp. 40-42.

52. Moshe Weinfeld suggests that it is modeled on an Assyrian suzerainty treaty and hence fundamentally covenantal; see Weinfeld, *Deuteronomy 1-11* (New York: Doubleday, 1991). So construed, it is also arguably generous, although it remains conditional. (The royal covenant evident elsewhere in the OT looks unconditional.) This potential concession to contractual theology in certain covenantal forms is further cause for caution with the interpretation of δικαιοσύνη θεοῦ in this sense; cf. the elegant analysis and warnings of J. B. Torrance: "Covenant and Contract: A Study of the Theological Background of Worship in Seventeenth-Century Scotland," *SJT* 23 (1970): 51-76; "The Contribution of McLeod Campbell to Scottish Theology," *SJT* 26 (1973): 295-311; "Preface to the New Edition of John McLeod Campbell," in *The Nature of the Atonement,* by John McLeod Campbell (Edinburgh: Handsel, 1996 [1886]), pp. 1-16.

and immediately that God has, in that act, acted faithfully.[53] However, broader covenantal associations — that is, in terms of a more elaborate arrangement — are not always central and hence determinative or invariable. They may or may not be present in an act by a divine or human king in the Old Testament, which can take various more specific senses depending on its context, as we have seen, and are not always directly linked to a *covenant* (as in fact Psalm 98 demonstrated earlier). Covenantal connotations are consequently *possible* but not *necessary* semantic resonances of the phrase δικαιοσύνη θεοῦ, and we would need contextual information to activate them in Paul.

That is, δικαιοσύνη θεοῦ *might* denote a righteous act by the divine King in fidelity to his covenant with Israel — an act of covenant faithfulness (so perhaps an act that is πιστός or in terms of ἀλήθεια). However, it might denote a dramatically liberating act on behalf of Israel (σωτηρία/σωτήριον) that might — or might not — then be syntactically elaborated as — among other things — an act of covenant faithfulness. Or it might denote a saving act undertaken without reference to the covenant, or even in defiance of Israel's repeated violations of the covenant, and so be rooted merely in God's benevolence (ἔλεος). It might, moreover, denote an oppressive act against enemies — a righteous action — that has nothing to do with a covenant with them (a κρίμα). Alternatively, it might denote a retributive act that has nothing to do with a covenant but is oriented by the perception of an innocent person or group being accused or the guilty being acquitted (again a κρίμα, although here of a different sort). And so on.[54]

It is not surprising, then, that the phrase δικαιοσύνη θεοῦ or its close equivalent is sometimes found in the same textual locations as covenantal notions in the Old Testament (and the same considerations apply to links with creation). Both are elements within the discourse of divine kingship,[55] and so the phrase may possess legitimate covenantal resonances. In any later usage,

---

53. The order of this set of predications must be noted carefully. We know that God is faithful *because* he has acted to save. Hence, we do not *ground* that act of salvation *on* his faithfulness, as if these two dispositions could be prioritized, humanly speaking, and the latter made the basis of the former. Rather, we grasp two complementary aspects of God's personhood, which is now disclosed definitively in Christ. Some of the important salvation-historical implications implicit here are sketched in my *Quest*, pp. 63-68.

54. That is, many further semantic variations are conceivable. The phrase might denote a right but wrathful action by God against Israel. Or it might denote a judgment or a posture within a trial between God and Israel — a more retributive scenario.

55. And similar observations apply to any resonances with Roman imperial ideology.

however, these have to be established explicitly and not merely assumed. The covenant was not a central, standard, or invariable element in the discourse of divine kingship and hence in the phrase δικαιοσύνη θεοῦ. We must let Romans itself tell us how this complex discourse is being activated.

In the immediate location of 1:16-17, and its particular allusion to Psalm 98, I see nothing that activates such specific resonances explicitly. The phrase seems there, rather, to be oriented in a fundamentally *christocentric* direction. It speaks not of the covenant with Israel — although it has implications for that! — so much as of the inauguration of the age to come by way of Christ's enthroning resurrection. It therefore speaks of a liberating act that has implications for all of humanity (Israel of course included). Romans 3:21-22 and 23-26 confirm these suspicions rather strongly, as the claims of those later, related texts point ahead to universal arguments in Romans 4–8.[56] The "right" act of God in relation to Christ, resurrecting him from the dead and enthroning him on high, has implications for all of creation — something that Israel is implicit in without exhausting its implications. (And indeed here we perhaps need to emphasize precisely the *eschatological* nature of this "right" act, in continuity with Ernst Käsemann's classic study;[57] a new creation has been inaugurated.)

Somewhat ironically, the psalm that Paul echoes in 1:17 makes this point nicely. While in v. 2 Psalm 98 speaks of the saving deliverance that is being effected by God in plain view of the pagan nations, in v. 3 it goes on to articulate in a syntactical development that this action is an act of fidelity to the house of Israel. And just the same considerations seem to apply to the phrase δικαιοσύνη θεοῦ when Paul deploys it later in Romans with specific reference to Christ. Christians suggest of course that the resurrection of Christ is ultimately also an act of fidelity toward Israel and so is the supreme expression of covenant loyalty and fulfillment by God. But these claims are not implicit in the semantic content of the phrase itself; they are further related theological claims that must therefore be argued for (and of course in certain respects they are by no means obvious). So Paul himself goes on to attempt to make, in Romans 9–11, an extensive case that his christological claims *should* be so understood (cf. also 15:8)! And as his argumentative maneuvers unfold there, it becomes increasingly obvious that these implications are far

---

56. For further elaborations of these hints, see my *Deliverance of God*, esp. chs. 15-17.

57. Käsemann, "The Righteousness of God in Paul," in *New Testament Questions of To-day* (London: SCM, 1969 [1961]), pp. 168-82. I hope that this essay can be viewed as an attempt to build on Käsemann's central insights, and not to overthrow or deny them.

from uncontested. Hence, to claim that he is merely semantically unpacking δικαιοσύνη θεοῦ in so doing is to overstrain his language (as well as to ignore what he does syntactically and argumentatively).

It needs to be emphasized in closing, then, that this reading does not exclude Israel from the Christ event for Paul — far from it. We have merely reached a semantic judgment that when Paul deploys the phrase δικαιοσύνη θεοῦ, and especially in the early argumentative stages of Romans, he is not speaking of something overtly and fundamentally covenantal and hence rooted in the past and in a certain conception of history. He is discussing a liberative and eschatological act of God in Christ — a fundamentally present and future event rooted in the resurrecting God (which therefore arguably introduces a reconceptualization of history). And this vital semantic and theological insight should ultimately be laid at the feet of Richard Hays. It seems that he was right, and profoundly so, in suspecting that an echo of Psalm 98 lies behind Paul's use of δικαιοσύνη θεοῦ in Romans 1:17. And I hope that he approves of the further suggestion made here: that, properly interpreted, this echo leads on to a broader resonance for the phrase via the ancient discourse of divine and human kingship that Paul is engaging in much of Romans. Located in that discourse, δικαιοσύνη θεοῦ seems to denote for Paul the deliverance of Christ by God through his resurrection — the right action that gives all other right actions their compass and true meaning.

From Toxic Speech to the Redemption
of Doxology in Paul's Letter to the Romans

Beverly Roberts Gaventa

First readers of Romans, especially first readers who have been taken in hand by the well-intentioned headings of English translations, may be forgiven for imagining that the letter consists of clearly identified "blocks" of argumentation. Romans 4 is "about" Abraham, for example. At 9:1, Paul takes up the vocation of Israel. Ethical admonition begins at 12:1. An eager novice once reduced the entirety of Romans to three words: "sin, salvation, and sanctification." More seasoned readers know, however, that the threads of Paul's argumentation are more delicate and are woven far more intricately than such labels might suggest. Applying a musical analogy, N. T. Wright characterizes Romans as a "symphonic composition," in which "themes are stated and developed (often in counterpoint with each other), recapitulated in different keys, anticipated in previous movements and echoed in subsequent ones."[1] Some of these subtle movements in Paul's argumentation are well known. The initial announcement about God's rectification at 1:16-17 reemerges not just at 3:21 but already at 3:5.[2] The question about the prerogatives of circumcision at 3:1 is not dropped but returns in robust fashion at the outset of chapter 9. The apparently abrupt reference to hope at 5:2 reemerges in the second half of chapter 8.

Another of these subtle argumentative threads is rarely noticed, and that

---

1. N. T. Wright, *Romans*, *NIB* 10 (Nashville: Abingdon, 2002), p. 396.

2. This point was made by Richard Hays in his first scholarly publication, "Psalm 143 and the Logic of Romans 3," *JBL* 99 (1980): 107-15. It is with genuine affection and respect that I offer this essay to honor a friend and colleague whose own life and work are characterized by care for words in general and doxological speech in particular.

concerns human speech. Crucial to what Richard Hays has astutely termed the "jackhammer indictment" of Romans 3:10-18 is its condemnation of human speech.[3] One of the reasons the word "jackhammer" fits the collection of Scripture passages so well is that it does not end as the audience is led to expect. Instead of turning at the end to praise for God's deliverance of the innocent or to thanksgiving for God's gift of wisdom, the collection continues to pound away, with a final declaration that *every mouth is stopped*. That condemnation can be traced back to the initial indictment of humanity for its refusal to glorify God (1:21), and the redemption of human speech stretches forward to the concluding eschatological vision of 15:8-13, with its anticipation of Jew and Gentile together praising God. In Romans, the corruption and redemption of human speech take us deep into Paul's diagnosis of the human problem as well as into his vision of God's new creation.

Romans 3:10-18

Our starting point is the collection of scriptural quotations at 3:10-18. This "anthology of condemnation"[4] stands at the end of the indictment that begins in 1:18 with Paul's declaration about the apocalyptic revelation[5] of God's wrath. At 3:9, the indictment comes to its most direct expression, when Paul asserts that all, Jew and Gentile alike, are under the power of Sin.[6] The catena and the interpretation provided in vv. 19-20 then offer the final step in the indictment. At 3:21, Paul will turn back to the discussion of God's rectification that began in 1:16-17.

Several distinctive features mark the catena, features that are seldom

3. Richard B. Hays, *Echoes of Scripture in the Letters of Paul* (New Haven: Yale University Press, 1989), p. 50.

4. Hays, *Echoes*, p. 50.

5. Admittedly, the redundancy of "apocalyptic revelation" grates on the ear. I find the redundancy necessary, however, since "revelation" by itself does not do justice to the invasive character of Paul's statements in 1:16-18. The "revelation" to which Paul refers is not simply an announcement of something that has been hidden; it is instead an event that *now* brings about a new situation (e.g., Rom. 3:21; 6:22; 8:1), what Paul elsewhere terms a "new creation" (2 Cor. 5:17; Gal. 6:15).

6. Although the word "power" does not appear in the text, Paul often employs the construction ὑπό τινα εἶναι to refer to being under the control or power of someone or something. See J. Louis Martyn, *Galatians,* AB 33A (New York: Doubleday, 1997), pp. 370-71. On Sin in Romans, see Gaventa, *Our Mother Saint Paul* (Louisville: Westminster John Knox, 2007), pp. 125-36.

noted in the scholarly literature. To begin with, the catena is the longest quotation from Scripture in any Pauline letter.[7] Even if Romans 9:25-29, with its interspersed introductions, is treated as a single quotation, 3:10-18 is still slightly longer. And unlike most other passages in which Paul quotes from a series of texts, here he identifies what follows as Scripture with just a single comment at the beginning;[8] "as it is written" introduces not one quotation but a collection of at least six quotations.[9] This introduction contrasts sharply with Romans 15:9-13, where Paul scrupulously informs his audience when he is switching from text to text:

- As it is written . . .
- And again it says . . .
- And again . . .
- And again Isaiah says . . .

The repeated announcements in Romans 15 are rhetorically effective, with their relentless reminder to Paul's audience that the voice being heard is that of Scripture and that various texts are being cited (as also in 9:25-29; 10:18-21). Yet the singular introduction in Romans 3:10-18 is also effective, because it invites the audience to hear this collection of passages as a unified text. Indeed, I shall argue below that it is crucial to Paul's argument that his audience hear this as a unified text since the catena lures the audience into imagining themselves exempt from its depiction, a response on which Paul springs the trap in 3:19.[10]

7. This point is noted also by Douglas Moo, *The Epistle to the Romans,* NICNT (Grand Rapids: Eerdmans, 1996), p. 202.

8. A singular introduction to a compilation of texts appears also in 2 Cor. 6:16b-18, but the authenticity of that passage is questioned by a number of scholars. See the discussion of the problem in Victor Paul Furnish, *2 Corinthians,* AB 32A (New York: Doubleday, 1984), pp. 371-83.

9. The qualifier "at least" reflects a scholarly dispute over the sources of some lines of the catena. James D. G. Dunn, *Romans 1–8,* WBC 38A (Dallas: Word, 1988), pp. 149-50, and Joseph A. Fitzmyer *Romans,* AB 33 (New York: Doubleday, 1993), pp. 334-35, for example, contend that the first line comes from Eccl. 7:20. Richard Bell, *No One Seeks for God: An Exegetical and Theological Study of Romans 1.18–3.20,* WUNT 106 (Tübingen: Mohr Siebeck, 1998), p. 217, argues that Paul has adapted Psalm 14 (13 LXX) to fit his theological purpose. Likewise, Francis Watson, *Paul and the Hermeneutics of Faith* (London: T. & T. Clark, 2004), pp. 58-59, identifies vv. 10-12 as Paul's "free handling" of Ps. 13:1-3 LXX.

10. However we resolve the contested question of the knowledge of Scripture in the various churches Paul addresses in his letters, it seems unlikely that they would recognize the variety of source texts Paul quotes here, especially on the first encounter with the letter.

These formal features of length and introduction mark the catena as distinctive, but its content is also unusual. None of Paul's other extended citations of Scripture deal so exclusively with the dispositions and actions of humankind. More typically, Paul's citations concern *God's* actions or *God's* promises. For example, the extended series of quotations in Romans 9:25-29 focuses on God's creation and election of Israel. Similarly, the quotations in 10:18-21, 11:8-10, and 11:26-27 directly address God's dealings with Israel and the Gentiles. Even 15:9-12 is not an exception, despite its announcement about the shared praise of Israel and the Gentiles, since it also celebrates the arrival of the "root of Jesse" in whom the Gentiles hope (15:12).[11] In Romans 3, however, God is not the agent; God is referred to largely in the negative sense that human beings have *not* sought God, have *no* fear of God. To put it starkly, it is hard to imagine a choral setting of Romans 3:10-18.

These features of the catena might have stimulated significant scholarly activity; in fact, however, relatively little attention has been given to this passage. Commentary after commentary passes over the catena with only the briefest of remarks.[12] The tacit assumption seems to be that this text serves little more than a decorative purpose; not unlike the obligatory poem tacked on to the end of the stereotypical three-point homily, the catena simply buttresses an argument that culminates at 3:9 and is repeated in 3:19-20.

Such scholarly discussion as has treated the catena has focused largely

---

11. If the speaker of the psalm here is Christ, as Richard Hays has argued, then the contrast with the catena in 3:10-18 is even sharper, as the point of the catena could be restated as humanity's refusal to pray. See Hays, "Christ Prays the Psalms: Paul's Use of an Early Christian Exegetical Convention," in *The Future of Christology: Essays in Honor of Leander E. Keck,* ed. Abraham J. Malherbe and Wayne A. Meeks (Minneapolis: Fortress, 1993), pp. 122-36.

12. See, e.g., Sanday and Headlam, *A Critical and Exegetical Commentary on the Epistle to the Romans,* ICC (Edinburgh: T. & T. Clark, 1902), pp. 77-79; Hans Lietzmann, *An die Römer,* HNT 8 (Tübingen: Mohr, 1933), pp. 47-48; Anders Nygren, *Commentary on Romans,* trans. C. Rasmussen (Philadelphia: Muhlenberg, 1949), pp. 141-42; C. K. Barrett, *The Epistle to the Romans,* HNTC (New York: Harper and Row, 1957), p. 66; Otto Kuss, *Der Römerbrief* (Regensburg: Pustet, 1963), pp. 106-8; C. E. B. Cranfield, *A Critical and Exegetical Commentary on the Epistle to the Romans,* 2 vols., ICC (Edinburgh: T. & T. Clark, 1975-79), 1:191-97; Heinrich Schlier, *Der Römerbrief,* HTKNT (Freiberg: Herder, 1977), p. 99; Ulrich Wilckens, *Der Brief an die Römer,* EKKNT (Neukirchen-Vluyn: Neukirchener Verlag, 1978), p. 173; Ernst Käsemann, *Commentary on Romans,* trans. and ed. G. W. Bromiley (Grand Rapids: Eerdmans, 1980), pp. 86-87; Brendan Byrne, *Romans,* SP 6 (Collegeville, Minn.: Liturgical Press, 1996), pp. 116-17.

on the question of its authorship and origin. As early as 1895, Hans Vollmer suggested that the catena was not constructed by Paul.[13] In an influential article, Leander Keck took the suggestion further, arguing that the structure of the catena seems independent of the structure of the surrounding argument and that the catena does not "match closely either the foregoing argument as a whole nor fit precisely its immediate context."[14] Adducing several texts as parallels to the catena's indictment of human sinfulness (e.g., *4 Ezra* 7:22-24; *T. Mos.* 5; CD-A 5:11-14), Keck concluded that the catena originated in Jewish apocalyptic circles and that the parallel in Justin Martyr (*Dial.* 27:3) offers evidence that Romans 3:10-18 once circulated independently. Finally, finding thematic connections between the catena and the surrounding text (1:18–3:9, 19), Keck concluded that Paul worked backward from the catena to compose the whole section of the letter as "a forensic indictment, a statement of God's 'case' against the world."[15]

Keck's arguments for non-Pauline authorship of the catena have been adopted by a number of scholars,[16] but the difficulties with this hypothesis are several. To begin with, the Jewish texts adduced by Keck as evidence of indictments parallel to the catena differ from Romans 3:10-18 in that they all specifically address law observance and temple practice, while the catena does not. In addition, Keck's arguments about the relationship between the catena and *Dialogue* 27.3 are reversible, as Richard Bell has demonstrated, which means that there is no clear evidence of an independent form of the catena.[17] Moreover, it is difficult to understand how Keck could argue *both* that the catena does *not* "match closely either the foregoing argument as a whole nor fit precisely its immediate context" *and* that Paul worked from the catena backward to compose his indictment of humanity. If the latter is the case, would one not expect a close fit between text and context? Problems

13. Hans A. Vollmer, *Die alttestamentlichen Citate bei Paulus: text-kritisch und biblisch-theologisch gewürdigt: nebst einem Anhang über das Verhältnis des Apostels zu Philo* (Freiburg i.B.: n.p., 1895), pp. 40-41. See also Martin Dibelius, "Zur Formgeschichte des neuen Testaments," *TRu* 3 (1931): 228; Otto Michel, *Der Brief an die Römer*, 4th ed., KEK (Göttingen: Vandenhoeck & Ruprecht, 1966), pp. 99-100.

14. Leander E. Keck, "The Function of Rom 3:10-18: Observations and Suggestions," in *God's Christ and His People: Studies in Honour of Nils Alstrup Dahl*, ed. Jacob Jervell and Wayne A. Meeks (Oslo: Universitetsforlaget, 1977), pp. 141-57, quotation p. 142. See also Keck, *Romans*, ANTC (Nashville: Abingdon, 2005), pp. 95-97.

15. Keck, "Function of Rom 3:10-18," p. 152.

16. Including Hays, "Psalm 143 and the Logic of Romans 3," p. 112 n. 21; although note that Hays is more cautious in *Echoes*, p. 204 n. 38.

17. Bell, *No One Seeks for God*, pp. 218-20.

with the thesis of non-Pauline authorship have prompted other scholars to conclude that Paul himself composed the catena with a view to the writing of the letter, and that seems the most reasonable explanation.[18]

Given this attention to questions of origin and authorship, it is regrettable but understandable that less attention has focused on the actual content of the catena. What stands out at first glance is the repetition of the phrase "there is not." Five of the six lines of vv. 10b-12 begin with the same two words, οὐκ ἔστιν.[19]

> There is not a righteous one, not even one,
> there is not one who understands,
> there is not one who seeks out God.
> All have turned away, together they have become worthless.
> There is not one who does the good,
> There is not even one.

These lines come, in slightly modified form, from Psalm 14:1-3 (13:1-3 LXX).[20] The final lines of the catena return to the phrase (v. 18) with a citation from Psalm 36:1 (35:2 LXX): "There is not fear of God before their eyes."

Between these opening and concluding assertions that "there is not," the catena repeatedly refers to organs of speech — throat, tongue, lips, mouth. Commentaries sometimes observe that after the first six lines, the catena turns in v. 13 to an itemization of body parts,[21] but that is a bit imprecise.

---

18. Dietrich-Alex Koch, *Die Schrift als Zeuge des Evangeliums: Untersuchungen zur Verwendung und zum Verständnis der Schrift bei Paulus*, BHT 69 (Tübingen: Mohr, 1986), p. 184; Christopher Stanley, *Paul and the Language of Scripture: Citation Technique in the Pauline Epistles and Contemporary Literature*, SNTSMS 74 (Cambridge: Cambridge University Press, 1992), pp. 88-89; Francis Watson, *Paul and the Hermeneutics of Faith* (London: T. & T. Clark, 2004), p. 63 n. 71. A. T. Hanson had earlier suggested that Paul himself composed the catena, but that he did so prior to writing Romans and not specifically for use in this letter; see Hanson, *Studies in Paul's Technique and Theology* (Grand Rapids: Eerdmans, 1974), p. 192.

19. A few witnesses (B 1739 syr^P Origen) omit the οὐκ ἔστιν at 3:12c, the final instance of the phrase in this list, so that the translation of the resultant text would be: "There is not one who does the good, not even one." The longer version more closely follows Ps. 13:3 LXX, which suggests that the shorter version may have been harmonized with the LXX; however, the final οὐκ ἔστιν may also have been omitted as a result of haplography. The argument I am making does not depend on the presence or absence of the phrase.

20. See above, n. 9.

21. Martin C. Albl, *"And Scripture Cannot Be Broken": The Form and Function of the Early Christian Testimonia Collections*, NovTSup 96 (Leiden: Brill, 1999), p. 173, contends

Verse 15 does refer to feet shedding blood, but neither v. 16 nor v. 17 refers to a body part. The body parts are concentrated in vv. 13-14, and all of them have to do with speech:

> An open grave is their throat,
> with their tongues they deceive,
> the venom of asps is under their lips;
> their mouth is filled with cursing and bitterness.

Three different psalm texts come together here to make for a powerful and vivid indictment of human speech (Pss. 5:9b; 140:3b; 10:7). The Psalter offers many lines that indict the speech of the wicked — for slander, for boasting, for lying, for denying God, and so forth. Indeed, Psalm 5, from which Paul takes the first two lines of v. 13, contains a number of other lines that implicate human speech (vv. 5, 6, 9a), but Paul has selected only the most graphic lines for inclusion.

In addition to their attention to organs of speech, these lines invoke death. The throat is itself an "open grave." Calvin contemplates this metaphor with typical frankness, imagining the throat as "a gulf to swallow men up. This is more than if he had said that they were man-eaters . . . since it is the height of enormity that a man's throat should be big enough to swallow and devour men entirely."[22] The notion of poison being under the lips is equally vivid, prompting Robert Jewett to observe that poison under the lips would not only kill by virtue of the poisonous words that come out but would also kill the speaker.[23]

The last line of the quatrain refers to cursing and bitterness. This statement may initially seem less evocative, especially in our present cultural setting, where cursing scarcely occasions a raised eyebrow, even when it spews from the mouths of children or in the most public settings. And "bitterness" seems merely whining; but even here there is a hint about death, since Scripture associates bitterness with death, as in the question of Abner to Joab

---

that the catena's reference to body parts is evidence of non-Pauline authorship, since the earlier indictment in 1:18-32 does not reference bodily organs, but this argument reflects a too literalistic assumption about what it would mean for the catena to suit its context. In addition, as argued below, the effectiveness of the move Paul makes at the end of the catena derives in part from the specificity of these lines.

22. John Calvin, *The Epistles of Paul the Apostle to the Romans and to the Thessalonians,* CNTC 8 (Grand Rapids: Eerdmans, 1995), p. 67.

23. Robert Jewett, *Romans: A Commentary,* Hermeneia (Minneapolis: Fortress, 2007), p. 262.

(2 Sam. 2:26): "Is the sword to keep devouring forever? Do you not know that the end will be bitter?" (NRSV). Even more evocative is Psalm 64:2-3, with its depiction of "evildoers, who whet their tongues like swords, who aim bitter words like arrows" (NRSV; see also Deut. 29:18; 32:24, 32; Eccl. 7:26).

The catena does not specify what sort of speech is to be regarded as toxic. Given the references to the shedding of blood, destruction, and wretchedness that follow immediately, it initially appears that the speech under consideration is largely "horizontal," speech to and about other human beings. Yet the larger framework of the catena locates this toxic speech in the context of humanity's relationship to God: *No one seeks God; no one fears God.* Here that relentless "there is not" of vv. 10-12 and v. 18 features prominently. Both human speech and human violence are integrally connected to humanity's refusal to seek God or to respect God.

The Catena and the Audience

To this point, I have established that the catena — and Paul, who composes it — is concerned about human speech, both speech as it afflicts other human beings and speech as it reflects lack of fear of God. Such a conclusion is scarcely startling or provocative; in fact, there is nothing new in what Paul says here. Much in biblical tradition reflects similar concerns about human speech, most obviously in the Wisdom tradition. A few examples will suffice to recall this important feature of Wisdom literature:[24]

> Lying lips conceal hatred,
> > and whoever utters slander is a fool. (Prov. 10:18)

> An evildoer listens to wicked lips;
> > and a liar gives heed to a mischievous tongue. (Prov. 17:4)

> A slip on the pavement is better than a slip of the tongue;
> > the downfall of the wicked will occur just as speedily.
> The wise person advances himself by his words,
> > and the one who is sensible pleases the great. (Sir. 20:18, 27)

---

24. See also, e.g., Prov. 2:12; 4:24; 10:6, 18-21; 11:9; Wis. 1:8-11; Sir. 14:1; 19:7-17; 20 passim; 23:7-15. Quotations from Psalms, Proverbs, and Sirach in what follows are from the NRSV.

In the New Testament, of course, concerns about speech come to expression most explicitly in the attack on the human tongue in the book of James:[25]

> The tongue is a small member, yet it boasts of great exploits. . . . It stains the whole body. . . . The tongue [is] a restless evil, full of deadly poison. With it we bless the Lord and Father, and with it we curse those who are made in the likeness of God. From the same mouth come blessing and cursing. (Jas. 3:5, 6, 8-10a NRSV)

Not surprisingly, concerns about human speech extend well beyond Jewish and Christian traditions. For example, Paul's near contemporary Epictetus advises silence when possible, and otherwise only the most necessary remarks. He advises against talking about athletics or food (a sobering thought in the contemporary scene), and then he goes on: "Above all, do not talk about people, either blaming, or praising, or comparing them."[26] Diogenes Laertius reports that Anacharsis taught his followers that the tongue is "both good and bad."[27] Similarly, Plutarch reports that the tongue is both the best and the worst organ, since "speech contains both injuries and benefits in the largest measure."[28] Plutarch also composes an entire treatise about the offensiveness of garrulous people, lamenting from the beginning that "the garrulous listen to nobody, for they are always talking." The garrulous "blame Nature because they have only one tongue, but two ears."[29]

At first glance, then, Paul's comments appear to be nothing more than conventional wisdom. Yet something else is at work in Romans 3. In the Wisdom tradition, whether inside or outside Scripture, alongside concerns about human speech stands the assumption that *human beings are capable of changing their own speech.* Control of the tongue is a sign of virtue, something that can be cultivated. Plutarch writes:

> Control over the tongue, which is no small part of virtue, is something which it is impossible to keep always in subjection and obedience to the

25. See Luke Timothy Johnson, "Taciturnity and True Religion: James 1:26-27," in *Brother of Jesus, Friend of God: Studies in the Letter of James* (Grand Rapids: Eerdmans, 2004), pp. 155-67.

26. Epictetus, *Ench.* 33.1-3 (trans. Oldfather, LCL).

27. Diogenes Laertius 1.105 (trans. Hicks, LCL).

28. Plutarch, *Mor.* 38B (trans. Babbitt, LCL).

29. *Mor.* 502B-C (trans. Helmbold, LCL).

reasoning faculties, unless a man by training, practice, and industry has mastered the worst of his emotions, such as anger, for example.[30]

Other Greco-Roman moralists similarly counsel control of the tongue.[31] Proverbs assumes that human beings can discipline their speech:

> To watch over mouth and tongue
> is to keep out of trouble. (Prov. 21:23; see also Job 27:4)

Proverbs also contrasts the speech of the wise with that of the foolish (and see Sir. 20:27, quoted above):

> Rash words are like sword thrusts,
> but the tongue of the wise brings healing. (Prov. 12:18; see all of
> 12:16-23)

> The tongue of the wise dispenses knowledge,
> but the mouths of fools pour out folly. (Prov. 15:2)

> A gentle tongue is a tree of life,
> but perverseness in it breaks the spirit. (Prov. 15:4)

The assumption at work here is that people can do better: some do, and others do not. Some people are wise, while others are foolish. Against this background, the statements in Romans 3:10-18 stand out sharply as Paul hammers away insistently, "There is not." There is not a place in this catena for humans who are capable of wise speech, for those who may train themselves to control the tongue, for those who may achieve virtuous expression.

In addition, if we return to the psalms that are quoted in the catena, we find that they routinely move from castigating the speech of the wicked to expressing confidence in God's judgment of the wicked and God's deliverance of the innocent. Psalm 5, which is quoted in v. 13a, moves from this critique of the speech of the wicked to urge:

> Make them bear their guilt, O God;
> let them fall by their own counsels;
> because of their many transgressions cast them out,
> for they have rebelled against you.

---

30. *Mor.* 90B-C (trans. Babbitt, LCL). See also *Mor.* 9B; 10E-11C.
31. E.g., Diogenes Laertius 1.70; 1.104; 8.23; Seneca, *Ep.* 40.3-4.

> But let all who take refuge in you rejoice;
>   let them ever sing for joy.
> Spread your protection over them,
>   so that those who love your name may exult in you. (Ps. 5:10-11)

The pattern is utterly familiar. Again and again the Psalms presuppose both (1) that there are innocent people whose speech is not vile and (2) that God will act against the wicked on behalf of the innocent.

This predictable pattern means that an audience even vaguely familiar with conventional wisdom about human speech will expect Paul to say something about the speech of the wise person. And an audience even vaguely familiar with the Psalms will expect this "psalm" to move to its final stage, in which God vindicates the godly and punishes the wicked. Indeed, Paul's comments in chapter 2 would appear to reinforce this expectation, since Paul has earlier posited the existence of people who do good (2:7-10, 13-15).

But, as we have seen, in Romans 3 there is no turn to the wise person, no reassurance for the innocent, no promise that God will punish the wicked. What follows instead is 3:19: "Whatever the law *says* to those who are in the law *it speaks so that every mouth might be stopped* and the whole cosmos might be under God's judgment."[32] Discussion of this verse in the scholarly literature is almost totally preoccupied with what Paul is saying about the law — and understandably so — but we ought not thereby neglect what is being said about speech. The vile mouth of v. 14 is now stopped in v. 19. The language about speech does persist here in v. 19: the law speaks (i.e., the catena supports the Torah),[33] and the law speaks to close every human mouth.[34]

---

32. Here I am drawing on the translation of 3:19 in Neil Elliott, *The Rhetoric of Romans: Argumentative Constraint and Strategy and Paul's Dialogue with Judaism* (Minneapolis: Fortress, 2007 [1990]), pp. 144-45. Elliot rightly observes that reading the indicative verbs λέγει and λαλεῖ as structuring the statement means that τοῖς ἐν τῷ νόμῳ "more naturally" modifies λέγει (p. 145). In addition, the customary translation ("whatever the law says, it speaks to those who are under the law," NRSV) is problematic, because it suggests that only those who are in the law have been indicted, but the point of 3:9 and certainly 3:10-18 is that all are under indictment. The point of 3:19 is that what the law says to some (to the Jews who have God's oracles, 3:2) it says in order to condemn all, Jew and Gentile alike (so also Elliott, *Rhetoric*, p. 145).

33. See Watson, *Paul and the Hermeneutics of Faith*, p. 58: "Paul hears scripture's negative verdict on human endeavour beyond the Law of Moses as well as within it, and, insofar as the later writers are all saying the same thing as Moses, they too articulate the voice of the law."

34. The connection between speech organs in vv. 13-14 and the shutting of the mouth in v. 19 is rarely noticed. Keck, "Function of Rom 3:10-18," p. 151, does notice the connection, but

What 3:19 produces, then, is a rhetorical feint.[35] If we were analyzing a piece of music instead of a written text, we might refer to deceptive cadence, the movement from a chord, not to the chord the ear naturally anticipates, but to a different chord, surprising the hearer. Paul has created a text that invites the hearers to wait for the stipulation that some speak wisely, that some are faithful. Paul has led us to expect a certain conclusion and offered another instead.

Paul has used similar strategies earlier in the letter. In 1:18-32, he sets up his audience to urge him on as he attacks the Gentiles for their idolatry and immorality, only to turn at 2:1 and accuse his addressee of doing "the very same things." In chapter 2, he destabilizes the categories of Jew and Gentile,[36] so that when he finally asks at 3:1, "What is the advantage of the Jew? What is the benefit of circumcision?" the only logical answer is, "There is none" — but he asserts instead, "Much in every way!"

In 3:10-18, the audience, having heard 2:12-16 and 25-29, and attuned to the conventional movement of the Psalms and the conventional content of Wisdom literature, is again led to expect a conclusion that does not follow.[37] Rather than the anticipated assurance that God will punish the wicked and rescue the innocent, Paul asserts that there are no innocent, that every mouth is stopped. Paul's audience need not know any of these lines or any of these particular psalms. It suffices that they are generally acquainted with the movement of psalm texts. This reading of the rhetorical feint within the passage also does not rely on unsubstantiated claims that these texts would usually have been read in synagogues as "bolstering the assumption that the (Jewish) righteous could plead against the (gentile) wicked."[38] Having heard

---

he does not develop it. It is one of the many strengths of Robert Jewett's commentary that he does discuss the relationship, even briefly referring to 15:6, 16; see Jewett, *Romans*, p. 264.

35. I am grateful to my colleague Leong Seow for his help in clarifying this important point in my argument.

36. This understanding of Romans 2 is influenced by John M. G. Barclay, "Paul and Philo on Circumcision: Romans 2:25-9 in Social and Cultural Context," *NTS* 44 (1998): 536-56.

37. Richard Bell does not make the argument I do about the movement of the text or the expectations created in 3:10-18, but he does conclude that 3:9 and 3:10-18 show that "any righteous Jews and Gentiles which may have been hinted at [in chapter 2] do not in fact exist"; see Bell, *No One Seeks for God*, p. 215.

38. Dunn, *Romans 1–8*, p. 157. Markus Barth, "Speaking of Sin," *SJT* 8 (1955): 288-96 makes a similar remark: "Paul is conscious that in the Psalms these sayings which he quotes might have concerned Gentiles exclusively; but he wants to have them understood as referring to God's own people, 'those under the law' (v. 19a)" (p. 294).

the singular introduction ("It is written") and recognized the language, they would expect the text to move in a certain way. Instead, there is only the silence of a world in which the human mouth has been stopped.

Stopping Every Mouth

Given the preceding argument, the question that presses is, Why? Especially in the larger context of Romans, why is it important to stop every mouth? If we read backward in the letter, the reasons for Paul's attention to speech as a symptom of Sin's power begin to emerge.

If we turn back to the beginning of chapter 3, we find that Paul contrasts the truthfulness of God with the lie of humanity: "Let God be true and every human a liar" (3:4). Humanity's faithlessness here consists in a particular speech act, the lie.[39] Chapter 2 may also be pertinent, since it refers to boastful speech (2:17, 23) and to hypocritical teaching (2:19-21). As we turn further back in the letter, we find that the practices Paul so relentlessly itemizes in the dirty-laundry list of 1:29-31 include corrupt acts of speech — including gossip, slander, and boasting.

These scattered references to speech may be construed as merely incidental, until we attend to the opening of this section of the letter. The indictment begins this way: "God's wrath is being apocalyptically revealed from heaven against every ungodliness and wrong of human beings who suppress the truth with that which is wrong" (1:18). While the truth could be suppressed in any number of ways, Paul explicates, after stipulating the ways in which God is revealed, precisely what he means: "For although they knew God, they did not glorify God or give thanks as if to God" (1:21). In Paul's analysis, at the very root of human entrapment in the power of Sin lies the refusal to glorify God, the refusal to give thanks to God. That is, speech that belongs to God in thanks and praise is foundational to the human condition. It should not surprise us, then, to find that Paul pulls this entire section together with the conclusion that the law itself "speaks" in order that "every mouth might be stopped." It is because of humanity's refusal to worship God that God hands humanity over to Sin (1:24, 26, 28).[40]

---

39. Richard Hays notes the interchangeability in 3:1-7 of the language of faithfulness and truthfulness (or faithlessness and falsehood); see "Psalm 143 and the Logic of Romans 3," pp. 110-11.

40. On the importance of the repeated declaration that God "handed them over," see Gaventa, *Our Mother Saint Paul*, pp. 113-23.

This thread reveals not merely something about speech in general but a very specific problem concerning speech, namely, doxology. The seemingly endless recent debate about particular lines in Romans 1:18-32 that have to do with sexual relations allows interpreters to focus on Paul's indictment of one portion of the human community and then to quarrel bitterly about that group. It also prevents seeing the much larger concerns at work in this text. Fundamentally, what is wrong with humanity is not simply a matter of the way in which certain people behave sexually; it is a matter of humanity's refusal to worship God, humanity's determination to be God, and that refusal comes to expression in corrupt speech, in distorted doxology.[41] Once we see that starting point in 1:18-32, it should not surprise us to find in 3:19-20 that all mouths are stopped as the law shows humanity's collective culpability.

Glorifying God with One Mouth

Paul goes on, of course, to speak of Sin in other ways — the powerful relationship between Sin and Death (ch. 5), the enslaving capacity of Sin (ch. 6), the ability of Sin to subvert even God's holy law (ch. 7). But he also speaks, and more powerfully, about God's rescue of humanity from Sin — God's love being poured into the human heart (ch. 5), rectification and life for all (ch. 6), the glory that awaits God's children (ch. 8).

Where, then, does Paul say anything that suggests that the human mouth is rescued? That it might be other than stopped? To be sure, he never makes this claim explicitly. He never says that the mouth that was shut up in 3:19 has been opened by Christ. (A neat, tidy conclusion of that sort would suit an advertising jingle but not Paul's "symphonic composition.") The letter does offer indications, however, of the redemption of human speech and

41. Paul Minear, "Gratitude and Mission in the Epistle to the Romans," in *Basileia: Tribute to Walter Freytag*, ed. Jan Hermelink and Hans Jochen Margull (Stuttgart: Evang. Missionsverlag GMBH, 1959), p. 46, puts this point well: "What is to the apostle the deepest, most stubborn root of sin, the root from which all sinning springs? What leaves men without excuse? How do we all become 'fools with darkened minds'? What is it which brings God's wrath against all the ungodliness of men? Why does God give them over to the lusts of their hearts? How do men suppress the truth? The answer to all these questions is the same. And until we understand that answer it appears to be both anticlimactic and inadequate: 'they did not honor him as God or give thanks to him' (1:21). It is quite usual for men to associate ingratitude with a breach of courtesy or simply a lack of good taste. By contrast Paul associates it with its worst fruits, and by implication views it as worse than all those fruits."

also indications of what that redemption accomplishes. The first comes in 8:15: "You did not receive a spirit of enslavement again to fear, but you received a spirit of adoption by which we cry out, 'Abba, Father.'" Whether κράζειν is understood here as referring to ecstatic speech or to a more reflective, more intentional sort of cry (as in prayer) is a contested detail,[42] but on either reading the children of God are characterized as being led by God's spirit (8:15), and the primary evidence Paul offers of their adoption is that they call upon God as Father. However feeble this cry may be, and however fragile it appears in a context of suffering and threat (8:18-39), it stands as an overturning of the "there is not" of 3:10-18. When the human mouth is finally delivered and enabled to speak, when the mouth is unstopped, it cries out to God.

And 8:23 perhaps also points toward the redemption of speech: "We groan together as we wait for adoption." Further on in the letter, in 10:8-9, as Paul comments on faith's rectification, he draws from Deuteronomy 30:14 to claim that the word of Christian proclamation is "in your mouth (στόμα) and in your heart" and then characterizes faith as confessing "with your mouth that Jesus is Lord." Later still, when addressing conflicts in the congregations about what food is to be eaten, Paul insists that those with different practices are nevertheless eating (or not eating) and giving thanks to God (14:6).

Most important, in 15:6, as Paul brings to an end his discussion of the disputes over food, he includes a prayer wish "that you might together with one mouth glorify the God and Father of our Lord Jesus Christ." That united glorification of God continues in 15:7-13, in what many regard as the culmination of the letter.[43] It is not just that two different groups, Jew and Gentile, are united, or that they are able to talk with one another. However important this reconciliation may be, what Paul celebrates is that together Jew and Gentile glorify God with one mouth:

> Rejoice, O Gentiles, with his people.
> Praise the Lord, all you Gentiles,
>   and let all the peoples praise him. (Rom. 15:10, 11)

The mouth that was closed by virtue of its unwillingness to acknowledge God is here redeemed by God's action in the gospel of Jesus Christ.

42. See the discussion in Moo, *Romans*, p. 502 n. 34, and the literature cited there.
43. See the literature cited by J. Ross Wagner in "The Christ, Servant of Jew and Gentile: A Fresh Approach to Romans 15:8-9," *JBL* 116 (1997): 473.

This eschatological redemption of human speech helps explain the presence in Romans of numerous doxologies, notably at 1:25; 9:5; 11:36; 15:33; and 16:25-27. One important characteristic of God's new creation is a humanity that is able, together with one mouth, to praise God. That this emphasis on eschatological doxology is not at all far-fetched is confirmed by reading the Philippians hymn, which concludes with the eschatological announcement that

> at the name of Jesus
> every knee will bow
> of things heavenly and things earthly and things under the earth
> and every tongue will confess that Jesus Christ is Lord
> to the glory of God the Father. (Phil. 2:10-11)

Conclusion

Far from being an afterthought or a meaningless flourish, the "anthology of condemnation" in Romans 3:10-18 moves Paul's argument about the universal extent of Sin to its conclusion. Drawing on familiar motifs about speech in the Wisdom tradition and on the movement of many psalms from condemnation of the wicked to praise of the righteous, Paul leads his audience to expect a turn that never comes. Instead of celebrating the righteous or anticipating God's vindication of the innocent, Paul declares that human speech is condemned, that every mouth is shut. Humanity's toxic speech is redeemed by God, whose adopted children, now led by the Spirit, can cry out to God as Father and can rightly give God praise.

Following this intricate thread through the twists and turns of Romans is an intellectual joy. Paul uses his rhetorical "jackhammer" in ways that turn out to be subtle, catching the audience at just the point where vindication is anticipated. And, as with other concerns in this letter, he returns to it again and again, so that the patient reader, particularly the scholar who joins company with a legion of other readers in previous generations, takes delight in seeing the fabric created by Paul's argument.

Yet there is far more here than a scholarly playground. In Romans Paul offers a deep analysis of the human condition, one prominent thread of which is the toxicity of human speech. To be sure, we do not need to read Paul's letter to the Romans to learn that there are problems with human speech. Anyone who overhears conversations in an airport waiting area or in a grocery store or at the local coffee kiosk surely knows of the corruption of our own speech, to say nothing of glancing at the day's headlines. Romans helps us grasp that these speech problems are not simply problems of human relations. What is at stake, as Paul understands it, is first of all theology rather than anthropology. What is wrong is that human speech is relentlessly self-referential and unwilling to give God thanks and praise. The withholding of praise renders human speech itself corrupt and results in the shutting of every human mouth, the judgment of all. Mouths that cannot praise God also cannot speak in a healthy, whole, constructive way with one another.

Perhaps equally important, in Romans Paul contends that the move from corrupt speech to doxology does not take place through human willing; this is not a task for speech therapy, as it were, but for God's intervention. Here the difference between Wisdom traditions about speech and Paul's treatment becomes crucial. Wisdom traditions imagine that there are people who do have control over their own speech: there are wise people who have learned to discipline their speech, and there are foolish people who have not. However much we look for it, that distinction is missing in Romans. Paul does not instruct the Romans about the proper use of speech, nor does he simply exhort the praise of God. First there must be deliverance, rescue, redemption, since only God can restore the human tongue. Only God's action, breaking into the world of human speech and its corruption, brings about doxology.[44]

44. I am grateful for the help of Carla Works and Brittany Wilson with research for this article. J. Louis Martyn, Paul W. Meyer, Kavin Rowe, J. Ross Wagner, and Patrick J. Willson all read drafts and offered important suggestions and criticisms. I gave an earlier version of this article as one of the 2007 Zenos lectures at McCormick Theological Seminary, and I appreciate the constructive conversations on that occasion.

Manna and the Circulation of Grace:
A Study of 2 Corinthians 8:1-15

John M. G. Barclay

For all their labors, few scholars manage to alter the default setting of a scholarly consensus, and it is one of Richard Hays's distinct achievements to have done just that with regard to the relationship between Paul and his Scriptures. Countering the presumption that Paul's use of the Jewish Scriptures was relatively perfunctory, Hays's *Echoes of Scripture in the Letters of Paul* has persuaded almost all Pauline scholars that Paul was deeply engaged theologically with the texts that he cited and echoed, together with the contexts from which they are drawn.[1] The greatest benefit of the Haysian project lies in its capacity to make audible the range of theological harmonics sounding within Paul's letters, and it is in pursuit of that same goal that I wish to revisit a text — 2 Corinthians 8:15 — whose rich tones have already been sensed by Hays, but which is well worth a further theological audition.

Second Corinthians 8–9 constitutes an extended appeal for Corinthian generosity toward Paul's Jerusalem collection, combining administrative instructions, acute rhetorical pressure, and an extended exposition of grace, indeed the highest concentration of χάρις-vocabulary outside Romans 5:12-21.[2]

1. Richard B. Hays, *Echoes of Scripture in the Letters of Paul* (New Haven: Yale University Press, 1989). Among Hays's subsequent works in this field, note *The Conversion of the Imagination: Paul as Interpreter of Israel's Scripture* (Grand Rapids: Eerdmans, 2005). The scholarly industry prompted by his paradigm-changing scholarship is, of course, immense. For a notable development of the project, see Francis Watson, *Paul and the Hermeneutics of Faith* (London: T. & T. Clark, 2004).

2. I leave to one side here the question of the literary integrity of 2 Corinthians 8–9. Against the hypothesis that each chapter was originally a distinct letter (so, e.g., H. D. Betz,

The passage begins with an account of the extraordinary generosity of the Macedonians (2 Cor. 8:1-5) as a foil to the Corinthians' reluctance to give, but it is characteristic of Paul that the agency in this matter is attributed in the first place not to the Macedonians but to God: "We make known to you, brothers, the χάρις of God which was given to the churches of Macedonia, that in a severe ordeal of affliction the surplus (περισσεία) of their joy and their profound poverty have overflowed (ἐπερίσσευσεν) in the wealth of their generosity (τῆς ἁπλότητος αὐτῶν)" (8:1-2). This already makes clear that Paul can detect the workings of divine grace wrapped up in human acts of generosity, whose surprising, indeed deeply paradoxical, expression bears witness to its divine enablement. If God's grace is abundant (9:8-10), it here abounds (overflows) through human agency, and in this matter will reach the "saints" (in Jerusalem), not directly, but through the medium of human givers. As Paul's appeal proceeds, it becomes clear that his understanding of divine grace finds its focus and its paradigm in the Christ event: "For you know the grace (χάρις) of our Lord Jesus Christ that, being rich, for your sake he became poor, so that by his poverty you might become rich" (8:9).[3] This christological confession is made sharply relevant to the present Corinthian case, both through its unique use of an economic metaphor and in its unusual expression in second-person form ("for your sake," "so that you might become rich") instead of the more usual generalized "for us." In other words, the Christ event should be "known" among the Corinthian believers not only in their intellectual apprehension but also in the formation of their behavior. Why else have they been made "rich" except so that, like Christ and in Christ, they might utilize that "richness" in self-giving for others? The Christ event is thus, for Paul, the key enactment and the focal expression of the *cascade* of divine grace, from God, in Christ, through believers, to others. Moreover, as the following verses (8:13-14) make clear, that flow of grace at the human level is not unidirectional but reciprocal: if the surplus (περίσσευμα) of one serves to meet the needs (ὑστέρημα) of another, that other's surplus will, in due time and context, serve to meet the needs of the first. It is this mutuality of need and gift-reciprocity that Paul dubs ἰσότης — a term used only here (twice in 8:13-14) in the undisputed letters (cf. Col. 4:1).

---

2 *Corinthians 8–9* [Philadelphia: Fortress, 1985]), see Stanley K. Stowers, "*Peri men gar* and the Integrity of 2 Cor. 8 and 9," *NovT* 32 (1990): 340-48; for full discussion, see Margaret E. Thrall, *A Critical and Exegetical Commentary on the Second Epistle to the Corinthians*, 2 vols., ICC (Edinburgh: T. & T. Clark, 1994-2000), 1:36-43. The place of these chapters within the sequence of the Corinthian correspondence is a matter too complex to discuss here.

3. For the nuances of the participial clause "being rich" (πλούσιος ὤν), normally translated "though he was rich," see below.

This pattern of the mutual sharing of grace-in-surplus is what Paul links to the scriptural sentence "He who [had] much did not have excess, and he who [had] little did not lack" (ὁ τὸ πολὺ οὐκ ἐπλεόνασεν, καὶ ὁ τὸ ὀλίγον οὐκ ἠλαττόνησεν, 2 Cor. 8:15). The sentence, clearly signaled as a citation (καθὼς γέγραπται), comes from Exodus 16:18, where it describes the gathering of the manna in the wilderness.[4] But, as is frequently observed, while the original context concerns an equalization of resources, it says nothing about generosity, mutuality, or reciprocal gifts. When God "rains" manna from heaven, the people are instructed to gather "as much . . . as each of you needs, an omer to a person according to the number of persons, all providing for those in their own tents" (Exod. 16:16).[5] They did so, "some gathering more, some less. But when they measured it with an omer, those who gathered much had nothing over, and those who gathered little had no shortage; they gathered as much as each of them needed" (16:17-18). It is clear here that the gathering happens first, the measuring after. What is less clear is how it comes about that, on measuring, it is found that each has gathered exactly what was instructed, an omer a head, "as much as each of them needed." One could interpret this as the result of proper restraint, accurate assessment, or proportionate effort on the part of the gatherers: they were neither greedy in gathering too much nor overmodest (or lazy) in gathering too little but ended up with exactly what they needed per head in their households, as instructed. So much might be implied by 16:17, after the receipt of Moses' instruction: "The Israelites did so, some gathering more, some less." Or one could find here evidence for a miraculous arrangement: just as the collection of manna on the day before the Sabbath mysteriously produced exactly double quantities (16:22-23, reported to Moses as if unexpected and unintended), so the normal daily gathering produced exactly an omer a head, by divine arrangement.[6] Both interpretations of the happy result of 16:18 might

---

4. For the minor variations from the LXX (e.g., change in word order and omission of the original "when they had measured"), see Christopher D. Stanley, *Paul and the Language of Scripture,* SNTSMS 74 (Cambridge: Cambridge University Press, 1992), pp. 231-33.

5. OT and Apocrypha quotations are from the NRSV.

6. The interpretation of Exod. 16:18 as a *miraculous* disposition by God is found in Rashi (M. Rosenbaum and A. M. Silberman, eds., *Pentateuch with Rashi's Commentary* [London: Shapiro, Valentine, 1946], ad loc.) and is assumed by many more recent commentators; e.g., H. Windisch, *Der zweite Korintherbrief,* KEK (Göttingen: Vandenhoeck & Ruprecht, 1924), p. 259; C. K. Barrett, *A Commentary on the Second Epistle to the Corinthians,* BNTC (London: A. & C. Black, 1973), p. 227; Murray J. Harris, *The Second Epistle to the Corinthians: A Commentary on the Greek Text,* NIGTC (Grand Rapids: Eerdmans, 2005), pp. 592-94.

be hinted at in the narrative context, though neither is spelled out. The text is simply silent on the means or mechanism for this fair collection of manna and, like any such narrative ellipsis, is open to many interpretations. But nothing in the context suggests a *sharing* of resources, by the redistribution of surplus; nothing indicates that those who had "much" did not have "excess" because they handed over their surplus to those who were underresourced. Yet this is apparently Paul's reading of this text, since he places it immediately after, and in illumination of (καθὼς γέγραπται), the ἰσότης created by the mutual redistribution of excess to meet the lack of others (2 Cor. 8:13-14).

As Hays notes in his illuminating discussion of this passage,[7] the (apparent) mismatch between the Exodus narrative and the Pauline citation has led most commentators to conclude that Paul wants this tag from Exodus 16:18 merely to illustrate a principle of equality: the words are useful for Paul, for his wholly different paraenetic purpose, but the original context is irrelevant.[8] But, as Hays rightly insists, this will hardly do. The manna story, the paradigm of God's gracious provision for his people, is well known to Paul and is alluded to within his extended typological configuration of the church as the people of God in the wilderness (1 Cor. 10:3). Its significance for Israel's self-understanding, as a nation dependent on God, is too important within the Scriptures and in subsequent Jewish interpretation (see below) to allow us to imagine that Paul was uninterested in its theological implications. If Paul sees here an economic parable, that is not, argues Hays, a misreading of the manna text. Just as the story condemns those who tried to keep the manna for the next day (Exod. 16:19-21),

> the narrative, without direct exhortation to the reader, posits and commends a value system in which radical dependence on God is good and stockpiling goods is bad. Consequently, Paul can use the manna story to good effect in depicting the Corinthians' material "abundance" (2 Cor. 8:14) as a superfluous store that could and should be made available to supply "the wants of the saints." . . . Thus, his application of the story taps and draws out hermeneutic potential that is already fairly oozing out of

7. Hays, *Echoes*, pp. 88-91.

8. Hans Lietzmann, *An die Korinther I, II*, expanded by W. G. Kümmel, HNT 9 (Tübingen: Mohr Siebeck, 1969), p. 135, is typically forthright: "Für die Anwendung ist wie gewöhnlich nur der Wortlaut, nicht der Zusammenhang des Spruches massgebend"; cf. Alfred Plummer, *A Critical and Exegetical Commentary on the Second Epistle of Paul to the Corinthians*, ICC (Edinburgh: T. & T. Clark, 1915), p. 245.

the Exodus narrative — or, more precisely, Paul taps Exodus 16 and then walks away, leaving the reader to draw out the sap.[9]

But there is a crucial Pauline move here that deserves further consideration. What Paul connects with the Exodus tale is not just radical dependence on God or a ban on stockpiling goods. It is also the assumption that those goods (the surplus caused by grace) should be passed on to others, with the implication that they are given "in abundance" precisely so as to be passed on to others, and are circulated within a system of need and reciprocity in which each is dependent not only on God but on one another — or, rather, is dependent on God's grace partly through dependence on one another. In other words, Paul appears to have combined with the manna narrative, or superimposed upon it, a model of gift exchange and mutuality in surplus distribution that is *not* already implicit in the text but is brought to it from elsewhere, apparently from his understanding of the Christ event and its social implications. It appears that there is more than one tree being tapped here, and it is precisely the *blend* of juices that makes this reading of Exodus so unusual and so theologically creative.

In order to explore this hypothesis we need to undertake a double investigation. First, we need to see how other early Jewish interpreters read the manna story, in order to assess where Paul's reading is or is not unusual: if there is a variety of interpretative trajectories, that will help sharpen the profile of each, including Paul's. Second, we need to explore more fully Paul's understanding of grace, especially in 2 Corinthians 8–9; only in this way can we assess whether his reading of the manna story through the prism of mutuality is an ad hoc phenomenon, adopted for a localized rhetorical purpose, or whether it represents something more fundamental in his conception of grace, and thus his understanding of God-in-Christ.

I. The Manna Story in Early Judaism

The placement of the manna story in Exodus 16, between the departure from Egypt and the Sinai revelation, already indicates its special significance for the formation of Israel's identity in her relationship to God. The narrative

9. Hays, *Echoes*, p. 90; I omit from the citation a parenthetical sentence comparing the warning in Deut. 8:11-20 about "the dangers of complacency that can accompany material prosperity." But we should note that there is no hint there of *reciprocity* among the beneficiaries of God's goodness.

begins with Israel's complaint against Moses and Aaron (16:1-3) but is quick to interpret this grumbling as a complaint against God (16:7-8): what follows concerns not the leaders' provision for Israel's needs but the character of the God who brought them out of Egypt (16:6, 32). Indeed, the provision of quail and manna is the context in which they will *"know"* this redemptive God (16:6), the site at which they will see "the glory of the LORD" (16:7). For the Exodus narrator, this very special provision of food is not simply the satisfaction of human hunger but part of the revelation of God. The people's reaction is astonishment in the face of this divinely created novelty ("what is it?" 16:15), and as a material sign of divine provision, a portion of the manna is kept forever "before the covenant" in memory of the exodus revelatory event (16:32-34).[10] This preservation of the manna indicates that the story has more than simply historical significance: it will be recalled "throughout your generations" (16:33) because of its continuing relevance. At first glance, however, it is not at all obvious in what respects it *is* relevant; the gift of manna was very explicitly a temporary phenomenon, lasting for forty years, but *only* for that long, and ceasing as soon as Israel came into habitable land and was able to grow crops for herself (16:35; cf. Josh. 5:12). So what continuing or contemporary lesson could be learned from such a divine provision, limited to a special time, a special place, and a peculiar set of circumstances? The pressure of that question may be felt in *all* the accounts of the manna that we will survey, but it is evident already in this foundational narrative. The gift of the manna, with its instruction for daily collection, is an opportunity to *test* Israel, "whether they will follow my instruction *(torah)* or not" (16:4). Accordingly, detailed instructions are given by Moses for the daily collection of the manna, some of which are observed (16:17) and some not (16:19-20). In particular, the daily supply of manna provides the opportunity for a very specific command concerning its *non*-collection on the Sabbath, a requirement already signaled to Moses in 16:5, which becomes the core of the narrative in 16:22-30. This is the first recorded instance of Israel observing the Sabbath, anticipating the Sinaitic law of Exodus 20:8-11. The gift of the manna is thus already placed within the framework of Torah.

The subsequent narrative in Numbers 11 gives prime attention to the quail rather than the manna (the opposite emphasis to Exodus 16), and the

10. For a discussion of the possible sources and their interweaving in this narrative, see Brevard S. Childs, *Exodus: A Commentary* (London: SCM, 1974), pp. 274-83; cf. the less plausible analysis of Bruce J. Malina, *The Palestinian Manna Tradition* (Leiden: Brill, 1968), pp. 1-20. The readings we shall trace in Second Temple Judaism all presuppose the final form of the text.

manna is mentioned initially as a matter of complaint, since it constitutes a monotonous diet (Num. 11:6). The narrator immediately counters this complaint with stress on its versatility and pleasant taste (11:7-9) but then focuses on the quail, which become an ironic form of *judgment* (11:10-34). The same emphasis on complaint and judgment features in the narrative of Psalm 78, where the gift of manna and quail is placed within the story of Israel's disobedience (78:17-31). Framed by statements relating God's wrath (78:21, 31), this portion of the psalm emphasizes the graciousness of God in giving his unfaithful people "the grain of heaven" and "the bread of angels" (78:24-25). Manna and quail stand out as tokens of divine gift, against the dark background of Israel's rebellion (cf. Neh. 9:9-31). Finally, within the Scriptures, Deuteronomy 8 offers a different lesson. Israel's long journey in the wilderness was a time of humbling and testing: both the hunger and the unprecedented feeding were providential, "in order to make you understand that one does not live by bread alone, but by every word that comes from the mouth of the LORD" (Deut. 8:3). The fact that the manna was *not* normal points Israel beyond material provision and human security. As she is poised to enter the land where she will "eat bread without scarcity" (8:9, 12), the manna symbolizes her ultimate dependence on the promises of God (8:1) and her total commitment to God's commands (8:2; both forms of "word from the mouth of the LORD").

Each of these biblical tellings indicates that the manna story, from as early as it can be traced, was always more than a historical account of a past, time-limited miracle. All the biblical accounts place it within a larger framework and draw from it broader lessons — about Israel's obedience or rebellion, God's grace or anger, Israel's commitment to Torah and Sabbath, or her dependence on God.[11] We should hardly be surprised if subsequent tellings repeat and expand such didactic traditions. Paul is on good biblical ground in drawing "lessons" from the manna story and in associating it with divine gift. But we have yet to see in what framework he places it.

The early translations of Exodus 16 are not especially remarkable. Both the LXX and the Targumim remain fairly close to the Hebrew original in sense, though the Targumim diverge at some points of little relevance to our inquiry.[12] There is evidence for wide familiarity with the manna story in

---

11. See Michael Fishbane, *Biblical Interpretation in Ancient Israel* (Oxford: Clarendon, 1985), pp. 326-29.

12. It is significant for Philo's reading that the LXX translates לפי אכלו ("as much as each of you needs") by εἰς τοὺς καθήκοντας (Exod. 16:16, 18; cf. 16:21: τὸ καθῆκον αὐτῷ). This

Second Temple Judaism, in sources as diverse as Artapanus (*apud* Eusebius, *Praep. evang.* 9.27.37), the *Sibylline Oracles* (frg. 3.49), *4 Ezra* 1:18-19 and *2 Baruch* (29:8: manna as eschatological food; cf. Rev. 2:17). For our purposes, however, the three most interesting accounts are to be found in Wisdom of Solomon, Josephus, and Philo, and it is worth noting each in turn.

Wisdom of Solomon 16:15-29. Manna features for the author of Wisdom in the fourth of his antitheses, displaying the ways in which God turns nature *against* his enemies and *in favor of* his children. On the one hand, against the ungodly, God sent rain, hail, and fire that was unquenchable even in the midst of water (the plague of Exod. 9:22-26); on the other, he "spoon-fed" his people with "the food of angels," which, though it was like frost, withstood the effects of fire (i.e., could be baked and boiled, Exod. 16:23; Wis. 16:22-23, 27; 19:21). Other miraculous features of this food are noted: it provided every pleasure and changed taste to suit everyone's liking (Wis. 16:20-21).[13] All of this teaches one great lesson: God provides his children with his all-nourishing gift (παντότροφος δωρεά, 16:25), demonstrating that "it is not the production of crops that feeds humankind but . . . your word sustains those who trust in you" (Wis. 16:26). The echo of Deuteronomy 8:3 is clear, though the "word" here seems to be God's command to nature to adapt itself to his children's needs, rather than his promises and commands to Israel (Deut. 8:1-2). A further practical lesson is also drawn: just as the manna had to be collected early in the morning, before it melted (Exod. 16:21), so "one must rise before the sun to give you thanks (εὐχαριστία), and must pray to you at the dawning of the light" (Wis. 16:28). That lesson is hardly on the surface of the text of Exodus 16, but the author of Wisdom, like Paul, is alert to details in the text whose rationale is not fully explained, and is ready to find a contemporary application (cf. Sir. 39:5).

Josephus, Antiquities 3.26-32. Josephus recounts the giving of the manna after the provision of quail (*Ant.* 3.22-25), drawing close parallels between the two. In each case, the food is "sent from heaven"; it is a resource provided by God in answer to the prayers of Moses. But each type of food is also, im-

---

shifts the focus from sheer hunger to what is (morally) "proper" or "fitting" and thus encourages application beyond the material to other sorts of "goods" supplied by God. This may be significant for Paul's reading as well, though the term τὰ καθήκοντα is rarely found in his letters (only in Rom. 1:28). For the Targumim, see Malina, *Manna Tradition*, pp. 42-93. Among later rabbinic readings, see *Exod. Rab.* ad loc. and *b. Yoma* 75a-76a.

13. For rabbinic comments on the variety of tastes experienced by those who ate the manna (based on Num. 11:7-8), see references in David Winston, *The Wisdom of Solomon*, AB 43 (New York: Doubleday, 1979), p. 299.

portantly, a *natural* phenomenon: the quail are a species of bird plentiful in the Arabian gulf and inclined to settle on the ground after their long flight (3.25), while the manna is a kind of "dew" (3.26) or "rain" (3.31), which remains a mainstay for those who live in that region "to this day" (3.31). In other words, Josephus combines the biblical language of "rain from heaven" (though not "the bread of angels") with naturalistic explanations of the quail and the manna. Although the manna was "divine and extraordinary" in its properties (θεῖον καὶ παράδοξον, 3.30), it was also a normal and continuing feature of the local environment. This is a typically Josephan move, anxious to keep within the biblical frame but without excessive dependence on the miraculous (cf. *Ant.* 1.106-8; 2.347-48). Also typical is the moral lesson he derives from the account, in this case concerning the distribution of the manna. Orders were issued to all "alike" (ἐξ ἴσου, 3.29) that each should gather only an "assaron" a day (Josephus's equivalent for an "omer"), and this was to ensure that "obtaining it might not be difficult for those who were feeble because of the prowess of those who were more capable in grasping while gathering it" (ἵνα μὴ τοῖς ἀδυνάτοις ἄπορον ᾖ τὸ λαμβάνειν δι᾽ ἀλκὴν τῶν δυνατωτέρων πλεονεκτούντων περὶ τὴν ἀναίρεσιν, 3.29).[14] He continues by saying that those who did collect more than the prescribed measure got no benefit from this effort, for they found "no more than an assaron" (ἀσσαρῶνος γὰρ οὐδὲν πλέον εὕρισκον, 3.30). These statements indicate that Josephus was interested in the very same text that we find quoted by Paul (Exod. 16:18). The principle of equality matters to him, as to Paul (with Josephus's ἐξ ἴσου compare Paul's ἰσότης), and he is acutely aware of the power dynamics in competitive acquisition of resources. But he suggests that the equalization takes place of itself (without human arrangement or redistribution); he does not find in the text the same moral vision as Paul, that "equality" results from the mutual sharing of surplus.

Philo. As we might expect, Philo comments on the manna story in various contexts and from several different angles. In his historical account of Moses' life, the tale is retold on the literal level: as Creator, God made the air bring forth food, a new and strange benefaction that also vindicated Moses. Philo is interested in the fact that the manna had to be collected each day, and could not be stored (God had decided to give his gifts ever anew — δωρεὰς ἀεὶ νέας . . . χαρίζεσθαι, *Mos.* 1.204), as he is interested also in the Sabbath provision (1.205) and other details. In a later context, where Moses'

---

14. Translation, slightly adapted, from Louis H. Feldman, *Flavius Josephus: Translation and Commentary*, vol. 3, *Judean Antiquities 1-4* (Leiden: Brill, 2000), ad loc.

prophetic role is in view (*Mos.* 2.258-69), Moses' prediction and identification of the Sabbath is also a central theme. In other treatises, Philo shifts to an allegorical mode; indeed, manna is readily susceptible to such a reading, as a heaven-sent gift already identified in Deuteronomy 8:3 with the "word" of God. The provision of manna depicts the feeding of the soul with heavenly wisdom (*Leg.* 3.162-76) — a day's portion at a time, since the soul cannot absorb it all at once, but remains daily dependent, in hope and trust, on the χάριτες θεοῦ (3.163-64). Many other details in the description of the manna draw out Philo's allegorical ingenuity (that it was like dew, like coriander seed, like hoarfrost, etc.), but the basic frame is secure: that the manna represents heavenly wisdom granted by God to those who yearn for it (cf. *Det.* 118; *Fug.* 137-39; *Congr.* 173-74). The very fact that it was not ordinary bread, the fruit of human labor, is critical in its definition as heavenly gift, which God alone creates (*Mut.* 258-60). The fact that the manna was distributed by equal measure, an omer a head, also interests Philo, as it interested Josephus. God gives what is sufficient (neither more nor less) and according to "just measures" (μέτρα δίκαια, *Leg.* 3.165-66). It is not surprising that this motif reappears as one of many illustrations of the virtue of ἰσότης in *Her.* 141-206 (at 191). The giving of the manna to all alike (ἐξ ἴσου; cf. Josephus above) means that God's gifts are distributed with forethought with a view to ἰσότης. This is witnessed by the statement in Exodus 16:18, cited by Philo as by Paul, indicating that God gives by a μέτρον ἀναλογίας. Ἀναλογία here means "proportion," and the composite phrase ἀναλογία ἰσότητος (*Her.* 192) indicates that Philo takes "equality" in this context to mean not numerical identity but differential quantity by proportion: more for the intelligent, less for the foolish (cf. *QG* 4.102). Thus, Philo can read the text to mean that some did have (quantitatively) "more" than others, but this was not "too much" or "excess" for them, because they were capable (or deserving) of a larger portion. Philo does not imagine here any system of mutuality, or any sharing of resources among the recipients of God's gifts; God pours out his blessings in just the right proportion, and it might be somewhat blasphemous to suggest that they should *need* any sort of redistribution at the human level.[15]

How, then, does Paul stand in comparison with these other Second Temple interpreters? Like others, he associates the manna with divine gift

---

15. For broader discussion of Philo's interpretation of manna, in relation to John 6, see Peder Borgen, *Bread from Heaven: An Exegetical Study of the Concept of Manna in the Gospel of John and the Writings of Philo,* NovTSup 10 (Leiden: Brill, 1965).

and grace; as we have seen, for Philo and the author of Wisdom it is a paradigm case of God's graciousness to his people. If Paul selects items from the narrative, so do his Jewish contemporaries: he makes no mention of Sabbath or Torah in this connection, despite Exodus 16, but neither do Wisdom and Josephus. Although the character of the manna is not clear in 2 Corinthians 8, its description in 1 Corinthians 10:3 as πνευματικὸν βρῶμα suggests that he would be no more likely to agree with Josephus's rationalization of the phenomenon than would the author of Wisdom, for whom (like Psalm 78) it is the "bread of angels," not a regular natural product. On the other hand, he is as distant from Philo's philosophical interest in the manna as is Josephus.[16] Like the author of Wisdom, Paul traces how "grace" (χάρις) issues in "thanksgiving" (εὐχαριστία, 2 Cor. 9:11-14), though the former's homiletic point about *early morning* prayer is absent from Paul. Unlike Wisdom, Paul, Josephus, and Philo are all fascinated by the distribution of manna, each of the latter three finding there some principle of "equality." But — and this is the point from which we began — amidst these multiple commonalities and crossovers, Paul alone connects the gathering of the manna with a human mechanism of (re)distribution. For Paul alone the receipt of grace figured by the manna is embedded in the work of human intermediaries, and for him alone these intermediaries are bound together by webs of mutual benefaction and the reciprocal sharing of surplus. It is not in itself remarkable that Paul sees something in the text that is "unique" to him; so, in his own way, does each of the Jewish interpreters we have surveyed. But it is potentially significant if this apparently unique element, which Paul *brings to* the text, and does not simply *read out of* it, is a token of a wider pattern in Pauline theology, if it represents, in other words, a characteristically Pauline interpretation of divine grace.

II. Grace and Mutuality in Paul

As has often been observed, 2 Corinthians 8–9 is notable for the *connections* it draws between the χάρις of God or Christ (four times: 8:1, 9; 9:8, 14) and the collection project as itself a χάρις (four times: 8:4, 6, 7, 19; cf. 1 Cor. 16:3). It

---

16. It is widely recognized that Georgi's attempt to draw close parallels between Philo's metaphysical notion of ἰσότης and Paul's use of this term is misguided; see Dieter Georgi, *Remembering the Poor: The History of Paul's Collection for Jerusalem* (Nashville: Abingdon, 1992), pp. 84-92.

does not strain Greek to use this term for both objects, but the combination can hardly be accidental. The Corinthians are being invited not just to imitate God's dynamic of grace toward the world but to embody it, to continue and extend it in their own giving to meet the needs of others. Indeed, so deeply entwined is their giving with the divine gift that the recipients will recognize within it "the surpassing grace of God on you" (9:14) and will thus direct their thanks (εὐχαριστία; not accidentally a cognate term) *not* to the Corinthian donors but to God (9:11-13).[17] Paul certainly wants the Corinthian believers to be active agents in this process; it matters greatly to him that they are not coerced into giving, but that their gift is voluntary (8:11-12; 9:7), even if not exactly spontaneous.[18] Yet this giving of theirs will be an extension of the grace of God within them, as they "pay forward" what they have received, and "give themselves to the Lord" (8:5) by giving generously to others.[19]

At the center of this momentum of χάρις is the Christ event celebrated in 8:9: "you know the grace of our Lord Jesus Christ that, being rich, for your sake he became poor, so that by his poverty you might become rich." It would be a mistake to read this as if "grace" were a transferable property, as though Christ, by dispossessing himself of something, enabled it to be transferred into the possession of others. Although the economic metaphor might encourage that reading, Paul in adopting it alters its normal economic terms. Paul clearly delights in the paradox that out of poverty can come riches (cf. 6:10 [himself] and 8:1-2 [the Macedonians]), and in the case of Christ, this is not because Christ's poverty was subsequently *overcome* by a later stage of wealth (i.e., his resurrection)[20] but because the apparently

17. It may be a symptom of this entanglement of agencies that, in the context of 9:8-10, it is difficult to determine who is understood by Paul to be the agent of the verbs in 9:9 (a citation of Ps. 111:9 LXX); see Margaret E. Thrall, *Second Corinthians,* vol. 2, ad loc. For a theological treatment of this phenomenon, see Kathryn Tanner, *Jesus, Humanity, and the Trinity: A Brief Systematic Theology* (Edinburgh: T. & T. Clark, 2001), pp. 70-75.

18. Paul exerts many kinds of rhetorical pressure (see Betz, *2 Corinthians 8–9,* passim; Kieran J. O'Mahony, *Pauline Persuasion: A Sounding in 2 Corinthians 8–9* (Sheffield: Sheffield Academic, 2000). Yet Paul directs it to win their will (8:11-12), even if the Macedonians outshine them by taking the initiative (8:4).

19. On the notion of "paying forward," see Miroslav Volf, *Free of Charge: Giving and Forgiving in a Culture Stripped of Grace* (Grand Rapids: Zondervan, 2003); for the entanglement of agencies, see his insistence that "God never works in us without us" (p. 51). For recent treatments of agency in Pauline theology, see John M. G. Barclay and Simon J. Gathercole, eds., *Divine and Human Agency in Paul and His Cultural Environment* (London: T. & T. Clark, 2006).

20. *Pace* Morna D. Hooker, *From Adam to Christ: Essays on Paul* (Cambridge: Cam-

"poor" self-sharing love of God is itself the greatest form of "richness," by re-ceiving which believers are themselves transformed ("become rich" in this same grace). Thus, the "grace of our Lord Jesus Christ" does not consist in the fact that he *was* rich but ceased to be so (for a while), transferring his wealth to others, but that *being* rich, indeed *because he was rich* (in the life and self-giving love of God), he "became poor" (i.e., "loved me and gave himself for me," Gal. 2:20), so that out of that self-giving (supremely on the cross) others might become "rich" (overflowing with grace, sufficient not just for themselves but for others, 2 Cor. 9:8, 11).[21] It is this inexhaustible sup-ply of divine "richness" (that gives without itself suffering depletion or loss) that is witnessed, embodied, and accessed in Christ.

In this light we can see that the Christ event is here not just an *exemplum* to be imitated by human observers (as if they independently had the resource or will to do the same) but the identification of a divine mo-mentum in which believers are caught up, and by which they are empowered to be, in turn, richly self-sharing with others.[22] God's giving does not in-volve, then, some transfer of "goods," completed at receipt, but a dynamic that flows on into our giving, branching out into myriad acts of generosity and grace. Paul can express this human response in terms of "obedience in confession of the gospel of Christ" (9:13) or transformation "from glory to glory" (2 Cor. 3:18), but in either case it is clear that believers are made "rich"

---

bridge University Press, 1990), p. 18; however, her emphasis on participation in the richness of Christ is entirely right.

21. My reading takes πλούσιος ὤν (8:9) not as a concessive clause ("although he was rich"), as is normal in translations, but in a temporal or even causal sense: "while being rich," or "because he was rich." For a similar reading of the equally paradoxical expression about Paul ("because I am free, I have made myself a slave of all," 1 Cor. 9:19), see Wolfgang Schrage, *Der erste Brief an die Korinther 2, 1 Kor 6,12-11,16*, EKKNT 7/2 (Zürich: Benziger, 1995), pp. 338-39. See also Kathryn Tanner, *Economy of Grace* (Minneapolis: Fortress, 2005), p. 79, glossing 2 Cor. 8:9 as follows: "by becoming one with us in Christ, the Word, while re-maining rich, acquires our poverty and neediness, for the purpose of giving to us what we as mere creatures do not have or own by nature — the very riches of God's own life, its holiness and incorruptibility." Later she writes: "Jesus entered into our poverty for the sake of the poor, but he did so as someone rich with the Father's own love" (p. 84).

22. If the self-giving of Christ is also, at the same time, the "inexpressible gift" of God (2 Cor. 9:15) — as much God's gift of his Son (Rom. 8:32) as Christ's giving of himself (Gal. 1:4; 2:20) — the Christ story reshapes our understanding of God and of God's relation to the world; see Francis Watson, "The Triune Divine Identity: Reflections on Pauline God-Language, in Disagreement with J. D. G. Dunn," *JSNT* 80 (2000): 99-124. Thus, the meaning of the manna story as the paradigm of God's gift to his people must be reconfigured by its new placement within the framework of the Christ event.

(8:9) not for their own sake but in order that they may make others rich also (9:11). In other words, believers are themselves, and more profoundly themselves, not in holding on to the grace they have received but in passing it on to others, and since God's grace in this way fans out in all directions, that "passing on" will involve the circulation of grace among its human recipients in a variety of forms. And since the "surplus" thus passed on does not arise out of any competitive grasping for advantage (but merely out of God's equal generosity to all), it is possible that it can circulate in ways that produce neither competition nor status inequality. At least, that seems to be Paul's expectation in 2 Corinthians 8:13-15.

Paul is anxious to assure the Corinthians in 8:13 that in asking for a gift from them he is not requiring that they enter some permanent status of inferiority, bringing relief to the recipients only by causing hardship to the donors. If gift giving were like this, it would merely shift a disequilibrium in favor of one to a disequilibrium in favor of the other, creating not only resentment but also a competitive power game in which each side continually tried to wrest advantage from the other. The ancient world was acutely aware of the power relations involved in the giving of benefits — the pressure exerted by the donor in giving a gift (which could not *demand* a return, but strongly implied it), the obligation on the recipient to "return" the gift in gratitude and in some countergift (in a suitable form, and at a suitable time), carefully calculated to oblige the donor to continue in his patronage, without forcing him to do so.[23] Paul's rhetoric and practice have much in common with this system of benefaction, but also key elements of difference.[24] The system for the circulation of grace envisaged in this passage entails, as a key component, *reciprocity* between one party and another, but the equality Paul has in mind is organized in a peculiar way. We might expect him to tell the Corinthians that having received blessings from Jerusalem, they are under obligation to give something back to them (cf. Rom. 15:27), or that if they give to Jerusalem, the "saints" there will be under obligation to make some return, first of all in gratitude, and later, no doubt, in some return gift. In fact, the language of debt and obligation is completely absent here, and in its place is a system for the *mutual sharing of surplus*: the Corinthians will, at the present time, give from their surplus to meet the needs of the "saints," so

23. Seneca's *De beneficiis* remains the most interesting, as well as the fullest, discussion of ancient systems of reciprocity, from a Stoic perspective.

24. For recent treatments of this topic, see Stephan Joubert, *Paul as Benefactor* (Tübingen: Mohr Siebeck, 2000); James R. Harrison, *Paul's Language of Grace in Its Graeco-Roman Context*, WUNT 2.172 (Tübingen: Mohr Siebeck, 2003).

that the "saints" from *their* surplus will meet the needs of the Corinthians (8:14). Although it is not clear what the "saints" will have in surplus to give (Paul's abstract noun could cover both material and nonmaterial benefits),[25] it is presupposed here that each party has some surplus, provided by the abundant outflow of divine grace (cf. 9:8), and it is also presupposed that *both* parties suffer, or will suffer, from needs, and will depend on the other for their satisfaction (*pace* 8:7). Rather than one side being permanently the patron, and the other the ever-grateful client, each is a patron to the other, or — perhaps better — each is equally the client of a surplus-providing patron (God), who gives, however, not in order to receive back but in order that grace be given on.[26] What Paul means by ἰσότης, then, is not Philo's proportionality (the bigger people getting more, the smaller less) but equality, in the sense of equal opportunity to give, equal need of the other, and processes of equalization by which giving in one direction is continually, though perhaps differentially, equalized by giving in the other. And this is how Paul reads Exodus 16:18: not as an equal apportionment of shares, but as a redistribution of surplus, which is not unidirectional (always the *same one* with too much, giving to make up the lack of the other) but bilateral. Each can expect, at some time and in some respects, to be in surplus (having too much), with enough to give to others, *and,* at some other time or in some other respects, to be in deficit (having little), requiring others to fill up that lack.

This dynamic of mutuality is, in fact, a fundamental constituent of Paul's vision of community.[27] As Hays has rightly insisted,[28] Paul's ethics aim toward the formation of community, and one of the most persistent motifs in this connection is reciprocity — doing things to or for "one another" (ἀλλήλοις or εἰς ἀλλήλους). This occurs so frequently (thirty-two times in the undisputed letters) that we are apt to overlook it, but I regard it as a highly significant principle, and the product of careful reflection. The call to freedom is a call to "love one another" (Gal. 5:13; Rom. 12:10; 13:8), and be-

---

25. See the full discussion in Windisch, *Zweite Korintherbrief,* pp. 259-60.

26. Since each has surplus only by divine supply, there is a sense in which neither party is the *owner* of the goods passed on to the other: each *has* goods (8:12), but only in transit, as it were, from God. This may also ease the problematic of power relations in gift exchange, though I do not find Paul taking this motif as far toward the dissolution of property claims as is proposed by Tanner in her *Economy of Grace.*

27. For its economic features, see Justin J. Meggitt, *Paul, Poverty, and Survival* (Edinburgh: T. & T. Clark, 1998), pp. 157-64; cf. Volf, *Free of Charge,* pp. 86-87.

28. E.g., in *The Moral Vision of the New Testament* (New York: HarperSanFrancisco, 1996), pp. 32-36.

lievers who greet "one another with a holy kiss" (Rom. 16:16; 1 Cor. 16:20, etc.) are expected to "encourage one another" (1 Thess. 4:18) and "warn one another" (Rom. 15:14) in systems of mutual support and correction. The notion of "bearing one another's burdens" (Gal. 6:2) implies that there is no strong man, self-sufficient, who helps the weak; all are bound together in need, as well as in support. There are clear signs that this emphasis on mutuality is a highly conscious social strategy on Paul's part, and not just a verbal tic in his articulation of ethics. At the beginning of Romans he starts to say how much he is looking forward to visiting Rome in order to strengthen them with some "spiritual gift" (χάρισμα), but then corrects himself to say how they will be "*mutually* encouraged by the faith that is in one another, both yours and mine" (Rom. 1:11-12). Since Paul's relationship with the Roman churches is delicate, this move clearly recognizes the power claim inherent in the promise to give something to someone: Paul backs off from making himself patron of the churches, anticipating instead a mutual patronage, where each will have something to contribute to the other. The same dynamic is evident later in Romans, when dealing with the fraught relations within the Roman churches (Romans 14–15). Where some ("the strong") are inclined to disparage others for their weak faith and dietary "superstitions," Paul advances the image of a community in which it is not a case of one side welcoming the other, merely tolerating them or enduring their foibles, but where they "welcome one another" ("as Christ has welcomed you," Rom. 15:7); the power of the host is distributed evenly and mutually (under the supreme host, Christ). And, of course, the fullest exposition of this principle of reciprocity, and of its political ramifications, is the Pauline metaphor of the body (1 Corinthians 12; Romans 12). Here, the members of the body are explicitly described as bound together in mutual contribution and mutual need: no part can say it is self-sufficient, and none can be dispensed with or disparaged as superfluous. In the Corinthian situation this is clearly directed against the development of internal hierarchy and division. That the parts of the body care for one another (ὑπὲρ ἀλλήλων), to the same degree and in the same way (τὸ αὐτό), is the practice that prevents the community from flying apart into mutual hostility or mutual indifference (1 Cor. 12:25).

This principle of reciprocity, then, has the capacity to complicate power relations, and to work against the emergence of one-sided systems of gift, patronage, or authority. When discussing honor, that highly precious commodity in the ancient world, Paul suggests not a neat hierarchy, in which the lesser honor the great, but a mutuality of honor-giving that could have highly paradoxical effects. He urges the Romans to "take the lead (προ-ηγούμενοι) in showing honor (τιμή) to one another" (Rom. 12:10) — using a verb that signals precedence and authority to encourage not the taking but the giving of benefit. Be first, he says, in being second — an instruction addressed not to one party but to all! This is not simply a normal honor hierarchy inverted; it is not that the honorable should be demeaned and the insignificant exalted, but something far more complex, and perhaps far more creative, in which community members continually invent ways to honor each other. The same phenomenon is present in Philippians 2, where believers are warned against vanity and contentiousness by the instruction that "in humility, you should consider one another above yourselves" (ὑπερέχοντας ἑαυτῶν, Phil. 2:3). Without that word "one another" (ἀλλήλους), this would look like a charter for the crushing of the weak, as they are conditioned to accept their "proper" place and consider others superior to themselves. But what does it mean if *everyone* does this, if the deference runs continually *both ways*?[29]

It is important to note that these reciprocal relationships are dynamic, that their goal is not order or unity in a static sense but the project, or process, of mutual enhancement or enrichment. David Horrell, in his recent book on Pauline ethics, *Solidarity and Difference,* has rightly drawn attention to the importance of differentiated unity in Paul's social vision, but I would suggest that for Paul unity is only a subordinate goal, not an end in itself, since it is part of a larger shared commitment to processes of mutual construction.[30] The building metaphor is a significant component of Pauline social ethics, including the instruction to "build up one another" (Rom. 14:19). What is in view here is a continuing project in which each party seeks to draw out the potential of the other, and both are committed to the construction of a community that is perpetually being remade and further developed. Neither party can flourish without the presence and contribution of the other; they are bound together by webs of need and of gift.

What may we conclude from this brief analysis of the manna in 2 Corinthians 8? We have seen that the reciprocity envisaged in 2 Corinthians 8:13-

29. Cf. the remarkable instruction δουλεύετε ἀλλήλοις (Gal. 5:13); on "making universalising egalitarianism pass through the reversibility of an inegalitarian rule," see Alain Badiou, *Saint Paul: The Foundation of Universalism* (Stanford: Stanford University Press, 2003), pp. 98-106 (at 104).

30. See David G. Horrell, *Solidarity and Difference: A Contemporary Reading of Paul's Ethics* (London: T. & T. Clark, 2005). For the stress on the dynamic process of mutual construction, see Rowan Williams, *On Christian Theology* (Oxford: Blackwell, 2000), p. 287.

JOHN M. G. BARCLAY

14 is not a random phenomenon in Pauline thought, concocted to reassure the selfish Corinthians, but a constituent element in Paul's social ethics. It is by this mechanism, and within the framework of Christology (8:9), that Paul finds "equality" in the distribution of the manna (8:15). The manna story is important to him, as to his contemporaries, as a paradigm of divine grace, and, as we have seen, he is not alone in finding in the distribution of manna a principle of "equality." But Paul's interpretative framework for reading this story is neither Torah observance nor the philosophical quest for wisdom. Grace for him has been redefined by the "inexpressible gift" of Christ. Thus, the "richness" received in this grace is expressed in self-giving for others; if there is a law at stake, it is "the law of Christ" (Gal. 6:2), the one who "loved me and gave himself for me" (Gal. 2:20); and if there is a wisdom imparted, it is the paradoxical wisdom of the cross. The manna must be not just enjoyed but shared, and its sharing enacted in a system of circulation fitting a community of mutual benefit constituted in Christ. In sum, the scriptural sap that Paul draws from Exodus 16 is blended with the richness of the christological economy; combined, they hint at an understanding of gift deeply significant for New Testament ethics.[31]

31. The contemporary discussion of gift among Christian theologians is extremely lively and offers many possibilities for dialogue with biblical scholars. See, besides the works by Tanner and Volf mentioned above, John Milbank, "Can a Gift Be Given?" *ModTh* 11 (1995): 119-61; Stephen H. Webb, *The Gifting God: A Trinitarian Ethics of Excess* (Oxford: Oxford University Press, 1996); Jean-Luc Marion, *Being Given: Toward a Phenomenology of Givenness,* trans. J. L. Kosky (Stanford: Stanford University Press, 2002).

Imitating Christ Imitating Us:
Paul's Educational Project in Philippians

Susan Eastman

I ask them to take a poem
and hold it up to the light
like a color slide

or press an ear against its hive.

I say drop a mouse into a poem
and watch him probe his way out,

or walk inside the poem's room
and feel the walls for a light switch.

I want them to waterski
across the surface of a poem
waving at the author's name on the shore.

But all they want to do
is tie the poem to a chair with rope
and torture a confession out of it.

They begin beating it with a hose
to find out what it really means.[1]

---

1. Billy Collins, "Introduction to Poetry," from *The Apple That Astonished Paris.* Copyright © 1988, 1986 by Billy Collins. Used by permission of the University of Arkansas Press, www.uapress.com. Collins reminds us of the difference between mastering a text and being

427

Billy Collins's description of reading and *mis*reading poetry should give any biblical exegete pause, and especially those of us engaged in teaching others to "read, mark, learn, and inwardly digest" the words of Scripture.[2] Perhaps no text in the Pauline corpus has been more susceptible to attempts to tie it down and "torture a confession out of it" than the densely allusive story of Christ in Philippians 2:6-11.[3] Scholars debate its genre, its background, its structure, the meaning of each theologically fraught word and phrase, and the function of the "hymn" within the letter as a whole. One approaches this text with fear and trembling, mindful of the sentiments expressed about it 130 years ago by A. B. Bruce:

> The diversity of opinion prevailing among interpreters in regard to the meaning . . . is enough to fill the student with despair, and to afflict him with intellectual paralysis.[4]

How ironic. For Paul's "students," surely hearing this "poem of Christ" was meant to have the opposite effect and issue in a hopeful and invigorating φρόνησις. And surely it is the foundation, indeed the heartbeat, of Paul's final summary imperative in the letter: "What you have *learned* and received and heard and seen in me, do these things, and the God of peace will be with you" (4:9).[5]

---

moved by it. Throughout his years of teaching the New Testament, the honoree of this *Festschrift* has modeled the latter, through his humility before the text and mutuality in the delight of exegetical discovery. How better to honor him, therefore, than by taking a fresh look at our mutual teacher, Professor Paul.

2. Proper 28, *The Book of Common Prayer* (New York: Oxford, 1978).

3. The text's dense allusions and rhythmic construction function powerfully in formative ways, as eloquently argued by Paul S. Minear, "Singing and Suffering in Philippi," in *The Conversation Continues: Studies in Paul and John*, ed. Robert Fortna and Beverly Roberts Gaventa (Nashville: Abingdon, 1990), pp. 202-19: "the song articulated in both verbal and musical terms a rich cargo of non-verbal affections and emotions. . . . [T]he hymn encouraged participation at a level beyond the reach of analysis, where the *phronēma* of Philippians saints was being shaped" (p. 205). Following Minear, I shall refer to the hymn as a "story," "poem," or "libretto."

4. A. B. Bruce, *The Humiliation of Christ* (Edinburgh: Hodder & Stoughton, 1876), p. 8. Morna Hooker quoted this in a 1975 article on the text, but it bears repeating in every generation. See Hooker, "Philippians 2:6-11," in *Jesus und Paulus: Festschrift für Werner Georg Kümmel zum 70. Geburtstag*, ed. E. E. Ellis and E. Grässer (Göttingen: Vandenhoeck & Ruprecht, 1975); reprinted in *From Adam to Christ* (Cambridge: Cambridge University Press, 1990), p. 88.

5. Gordon Fee, *Paul's Letter to the Philippians*, NICNT (Grand Rapids: Eerdmans, 1995), p. 419, claims that, in effect, "this sentence summarizes, as well as concludes, the letter."

That the apostle intends, through his own person, to educate them in the way of the God of peace is clear not only from this verse but also from 3:17-18. Nonetheless, the question arises: what *have* they learned, and equally important, *how* have they learned and received and heard and seen it "in Paul"? The short answer is that in this apostle, who says elsewhere, "Be imitators of me, as I am of Christ" (1 Cor. 11:1), the Philippians have learned and received and heard and seen Christ. But in what way? "Who is this Christ in whom the Philippians now live, and in whom they are exhorted?"[6] The answer pushes us back to Philippians 2:6-11. With some trepidation, then, I offer the following essay as a heuristic engagement with the story of Christ, suggesting a different slant on its role in Paul's mimetic "educational project" among the Philippians.

My thesis is bold (hence heuristic) and twofold. First, in the drama of Philippians 2:6-11, Christ assumes Adam's part on the stage of human history.[7] He does not play Adam at creation but rather Adam after the fall, Adam in exile from the garden, Adam as a stand-in for the human race in all its desperate bondage and contingency. Emptying himself, taking on the form of a slave, coming to be in the likeness of human beings, being found in appearance ὡς ἄνθρωπος, Christ "puts on" Adam and makes Adam's role his own. Having begun the part, he plays it to the end, humbling himself and becoming "obedient unto death, even death on a cross" (2:8).[8] This drama of salvation both displays and enacts the φρόνησις that Paul replicates in his own life (3:4-18) and confidently expects to see repeated in the Philippians' life as well.[9]

---

6. J. Louis Martyn, "De-apocalypticizing Paul: An Essay Focused on *Paul and the Stoics* by Troels Engberg-Pedersen," *JSNT* 86 (2002): 84.

7. This dramatic notion of imitation was pervasive in the Roman Empire in the first century, characterized as it was by a "dominant aesthetic of theatricality and spectacularity"; see Philip Hardie, "Coming to Terms with the Empire: Poetry of the Later Augustan and Tiberian Period," in *Literature in the Greek and Roman Worlds: A New Perspective,* ed. Oliver Taplin (Oxford: Oxford University Press, 2000), p. 429. As Florence Dupont notes in *L'acteur-roi, ou, Le théâtre dans la Rome antique* (Paris: Belles Lettres, 1985): "Imitation — not in the Greek sense of representation *(mimēsis)* — but in the sense of mimic buffoonery, the play of the comic double and of mirroring, was a fundamental component of Roman culture"; translated in Carlin A. Barton, *The Sorrows of the Ancient Romans: The Gladiator and the Monster* (Princeton: Princeton University Press, 1993), p. 137. See also L. L. Welborn, *Paul, the Fool of Christ,* JSNTSup 293 (London: T. & T. Clark, 2005), pp. 34-48.

8. See Hooker, "Philippians 2:6-11," pp. 98-99.

9. On Phil. 2:6-11 as the "drama" of salvation, see especially Ernst Käsemann, "A Critical Analysis of Philippians 2:5-11," trans. Alice F. Carse, in *God and Christ: Existence and Prov-*

Second, when Paul says to the Philippians, συμμιμηταί μου γίνεσθε (3:17), he "educates" them into Christ by bringing them onstage with himself, as a fellow "mime" of Christ.[10] He can do this because Christ, by taking Adam's part on the human stage, has reordered the mimetic structure of that stage and thereby rescripted the social interactions that take place in the πολίτευμα over which he rules.[11] We might approach those rearrangements from many angles; my concern here is limited to the educative impact of Christ's mimetic intervention in the human drama.

As we set about tracing the ways in which Paul's mimetic education is transformed by the drama of salvation, it will be helpful to begin with some brief observations about imitation and education in Hellenistic culture. We will then focus on the dramatic aspects of the Christ hymn in relation to Adam's story, finally bringing those aspects back into conversation with Paul's educational project.

Setting the Stage: *Mimēsis* and *Paideia* in the Ancient World

The topic of imitation and education in the ancient world is immense and complex. Imitation, or *mimēsis*, was the glue that held together the social or-

---

ince, ed. Robert W. Funk (New York/Tübingen: Harper & Row/Mohr Siebeck, 1968). In my view, Käsemann's interpretation of the "hymn" as telling the drama of salvation is correct, but I disagree that the soteriological function of the hymn excludes a formative, "ethical" function as well. Christ is not *"Urbild*, not *Vorbild"* but *Urbild and Vorbild* (p. 74).

10. Most commentators opt for some version of the NRSV: "join in imitating me." For the view that 3:17 should be translated "be my fellow imitators (of Christ)," see W. F. M'Michael, "Be Ye Followers Together of Me," *ExpTim* 5 (1894): 287; J. Ross Wagner, "Working Out Salvation in Philippians," in *Holiness and Ecclesiology in the New Testament*, ed. Kent E. Brower and Andy Johnson (Grand Rapids: Eerdmans, 2007), p. 267; Morna D. Hooker, "A Partner in the Gospel: Paul's Understanding of His Ministry," in *Theology and Ethics in Paul and His Interpreters: Essays in Honor of Victor Paul Furnish*, ed. Eugene H. Lovering Jr. and Jerry L. Sumney (Nashville: Abingdon, 1996), pp. 93-94. The term συμμιμηταί is rare, and it is worth noting that Plato used it to refer to people joining together in imitation of a third party (*Pol.* 274D). While commentators point to Paul's use of τύπος in 3:17b to argue that Paul means "imitate me," it is equally possible that he means "follow our example of imitating, or 'miming,' Christ." For discussion of Paul's use of theatrical imagery in reference to himself as a mimic fool in 1 Corinthians 1–4, see Welborn, *Paul, the Fool of Christ*.

11. Operative here is the notion that cosmological patterns of correspondence between macrocosm and microcosm go hand in hand with ethical formation in the Hellenistic world, including the world of the NT (*pace* Michaelis, who sharply distinguishes between "cosmological mimēsis" and ethical imitation; see "Μιμέομαι," *TDNT* 4:659-74).

der in a harmonious whole.[12] That harmony was underwritten by patterns of cosmological correspondence between God, ruler, and state:

> The king bears the same relation to the state as God to the world; and the state is in the same ratio to the world as the king is to God. For the state, made as it is by the harmonizing of many different elements, is an imitation of the order and harmony of the world, while the king who has an absolute rulership, and is himself animate law, has been transformed into a deity among men. (Stobaeus, *Ecl.* 4.7.61)[13]

Within that order, education — *paideia* — functioned as a means of enculturation into a "system of hierarchical difference" that differentiated the educated from the uneducated by training young men (mainly) to be partakers of the elite culture of the πεπαιδευμένοι.[14] To be educated was to distinguish oneself from those who were not and to secure one's identity on the "correct" side of the social polarities that structured Greco-Roman society. So, for example, Iamblichus observed:

> [I]t is thanks to upbringing that humans differ from beasts, Greeks from foreigners, free men from household slaves, and philosophers from ordinary people.[15]

The quotation reveals a certain ambiguity in the social role of education. On the one hand, Iamblichus did not describe differences between equals but rather presumed fundamental distinctions between classes, as between species. Within these different groups, education was a homoge-

---

12. For a still-useful synopsis, see Willis P. De Boer, *The Imitation of Paul* (Kampen: Kok, 1962), pp. 1-13, 24-28. For a thorough and nuanced discussion, see especially Tim Whitmarsh, *Greek Literature and the Roman Empire: The Politics of Imitation* (Oxford: Oxford University Press, 2001).

13. Translation from Elizabeth A. Castelli, *Imitating Paul: A Discourse of Power* (Louisville: Westminster John Knox, 1991), p. 79; see further pp. 78-81. Stobaeus is relatively late (fifth c.), but this quotation nicely summarizes a persistent and widespread worldview. For example, Plutarch warns aspiring politicians to exercise strict moral judgment in their personal as well as public lives, because through their performance on the stage of life, they will be models for those lower on the social scale: "But do you yourself, since you are henceforth to live as on an open stage (ἐν θεάτρῳ), educate your character and put it in order" (*Mor.* 800, trans. Fowler, LCL). In *The Letter of Aristeas,* the king is advised: "As God acts well towards all men, so you too in imitation of Him are the benefactor of all your subjects" (281, *APOT*).

14. Whitmarsh, *Greek Literature,* p. 90. On the education of women, see pp. 109-16.

15. Iamblichus, *Vit. Pyth.* 44 (trans. Whitmarsh, *Greek Literature,* p. 90).

nizing force.[16] On the other hand, "upbringing" promised to be the means of separating oneself from lesser mortals and climbing the social ladder: "The rewards for *paideia* could be considerable, ranging from patronage and awards of citizenship (at least in the late republican period) right through to political promotion."[17] Hence, education both reinforced hierarchical differences and instigated a potentially destabilizing social movement within that hierarchy.[18]

Paideia promised upward mobility through the imitation of excellent models that did double duty. As children learned grammar and then rhetoric through memorizing the stories of great heroes of the past, they were presented with literary examples to improve their linguistic skills and, simultaneously, ethical examples to improve their character. Through imitation, the pupils achieved increasing "assimilation," or likeness (ὁμοιότης), to the subject matter.[19] In this way, education was about the construction of identity through "editing the models that the student must emulate."[20] To be educated in rhetoric was to be educated in the skills and virtues most prized by Roman society and thereby to become a proper, constructive member of that society.[21]

16. Jane L. Lightfoot, "Romanized Greeks and Hellenized Romans: Later Greek Literature," in *Literature in the Greek and Roman Worlds,* ed. Taplin, p. 261. Seneca, it should be noted, provides a counterpoint to Iamblichus:

> For what is a Roman knight, or a freedman's son, or a slave? They are mere titles, born of ambition or of wrong. One may leap to heaven from the very slums. (*Ep.* 31.11, trans. Gummere, LCL)

Seneca here supports the larger point, however, articulating the hope of mobility as well as the reality of hierarchy. For the pervasive tension between differentiation and sameness, and between hierarchy and a yearning for equality, see Barton, *Sorrows of the Ancient Romans,* pp. 149-75.

17. Whitmarsh, *Greek Literature,* p. 96. Whitmarsh delineates examples of hierarchical socialization in the literature of Roman Greece but also notes uses of education to advance social status and empowerment (pp. 90-130).

18. For one example (among many) of such an attempt at upward mobility, see Herodas, *Mime* 3, "The Teacher," in which Kottalos, a poor son of a fisherman, attends primary school in order to better his chances in life.

19. Dionysius, *De imit.* frg. 6.1; see Whitmarsh, *Greek Literature,* pp. 73, 86.

20. Whitmarsh, *Greek Literature,* p. 93. Henri Marrou, while noting that "professors of eloquence loved to give their pupils their own productions to work on," also describes the "tyranny" of a fixed canon of great orators and poets from the past; see *A History of Education in Antiquity* (New York: Sheed & Ward, 1956), p. 274. See also pp. 234-35, on the use of poetry to teach morality.

21. This is a simplified statement about a complex subject. Plato blamed the poets for leading people astray from the truth through mimetic art that was at three removes from the

While the subject matter was drawn from the past, the skill and character of the present teacher also came into play as models for the student. From the viewpoint of the rhetorician, the teacher's job was to model skill in oratory; from that of the philosopher, to model the pursuit of excellence.[22] At the same time, as the pupil acquired the teacher's art, becoming more "like" the teacher, he also gained the tools potentially to "one-up" the teacher, to the degree that in some cases the student and the teacher could exchange places.[23]

Such "assimilation" required a high degree of presence and intimacy: no online extension courses here! Rather, as Seneca told Lucilius:

> [T]he living voice and the intimacy of a common life will help you more than the written word. You must go to the scene of action, first, because men put more faith in their eyes than in their ears, and second, because the way is long if one follows precepts, but short and helpful, if one follows patterns. Cleanthes could not have been the express image of Zeno, if he had merely heard his lectures; he shared in his life, saw into his hidden purposes, and watched him to see whether he lived according to his own rules. Plato, Aristotle, and the whole throng of sages who were destined to go each his different way, derived more benefit from the character than

---

reality of the eternal forms (*Resp.* 602D-603E; 605A-C). But even in Plato, one finds ambiguity regarding the value of *mimēsis,* as well as pictures of ethical formation through imitation that verges on participation (see, e.g., *Phaedr.* 253A-B). By the time of the first century, imitation as education in character formation was pervasive; see, e.g., Plutarch, *How a Young Man Should Listen to Poetry* and *On the Education of Children;* and Dionysius, *On Imitation.*

22. See, e.g., Dio Chrysostom, defending his view that Socrates was a follower of Homer:

> For whoever really follows any one surely knows what that person was like, and by imitating his acts and words he tries best he can to make himself like him. But that is precisely, it seems, what the pupil does — by imitating his teacher and paying heed to him he tries to acquire his art. (*Disc.* 55.4-5, trans. Crosby, LCL)

See also, e.g., Philo, *Sacr.* 64; Isocrates, *Soph.* 17; Xenophon, *Mem.* 1.2.3.

23. On the notion of the student achieving parity with the teacher and potentially "changing places," see Whitmarsh, *Greek Literature,* p. 93: "Teaching is both conservative, in that it replicates the social order, and subversive, in that it transforms statuses and redistributes social power. This duality is a widespread motif in ancient texts. In comedy, the pedagogical relationship is likened to a father-son relationship, whereby the son's maturity culminates in his taking on paternity and the role of instructor to another." See also Heliodorus, *Aeth.* 2.33.5, for a father-daughter example; and Petronius, *Satyr.* 87, where student and teacher exchange places as objects of desire.

from the words of Socrates. It was not the class-room of Epicurus, but living together under the same roof, that made great men of Metrodorus, Hermarchus, and Polyaenus.[24]

In other words, it was the relationship in which imitation occurred that both validated the subject matter and grounded the developing character of the student. For mimetic education to take hold, the student had to participate in the teacher's life. To be sure, the effect of that participation was not simply rote repetition that created a cookie-cutter copy of the teacher: the students "were destined to go each his different way," yet the character of each was shaped by his vital relationship with the teacher.[25]

Christ Imitating Us

Readers familiar with Paul will have recognized points of both convergence and divergence between his letters and the preceding brief overview of *mimēsis* and *paideia* in the ancient world. As we have seen, mimetic education tended toward the notion of an *upwardly* mobile assimilation by the imitator or student to the likeness of the virtuous model.At first glance, Paul's exhortation to the Philippians in 4:9 appears to support a positive comparison between his method of character formation and such a mimetic ascent to excellence in virtue: "Keep on doing the things that you have learned and received and heard and seen in me, and the God of peace will be with you." When we ask what these "things" are, we find in the immediately preceding verse a list of virtues that numerous commentators identify as "terms that were current coin in popular moral philosophy, especially in Stoicism."[26]

But as Stanley Hauerwas points out, the problem with reading Philip-

24. Seneca, *Ep.* 6.5-7 (trans. Gummere, LCL).

25. The limitations of space preclude discussion of the use of imitation as an act of resistance employed by minority groups within the empire. Imitation of models drawn from the history of such groups may aid in constructing a corporate identity as separate from and superior to the dominant Roman culture. Fourth Maccabees provides an excellent example of such imitation. For Philo as well, to imitate Moses is to belong to an alternative, all-encompassing and superior πόλις (*Mos.* 1.155-59). Similar moves may be noted in Greek literature; see Whitmarsh, *Greek Literature,* pp. 57-71.

26. Peter T. O'Brien, *The Epistle to the Philippians,* NIGTC (Grand Rapids: Eerdmans, 1991), p. 502. So also Fee, *Philippians,* p. 414; Markus Bockmuehl, *The Epistle to the Philippians,* BNTC (London: A. & C. Black, 1998), pp. 250-51; Karl Barth, *Epistle to the Philippians,* 40th anniversary ed. (Louisville: Westminster John Knox, 2002), p. 124.

pians 4:8 as a list of culturally accepted values is that Paul is writing from jail: "If the virtues Paul recommends are generally recognized as a 'good thing,' how in the hell did Paul get himself arrested?"[27] Similarly, Stephen Fowl rightly cautions against a straightforward equation between the language of 4:8 and Greco-Roman virtues:

> Christians and pagans will have irreconcilable differences on what counts as wisdom. . . . Rather than translating his exhortations into a "public" language of pagan virtue, Paul has throughout the epistle been providing the Philippians with the resources they need to deploy that language within the context of a Christ-focused, cruciform common life.[28]

If we expand the precedent for the "things" in 4:9 to include Paul's self-description in chapter 3, we bring into play the "resources" to which Fowl refers. In so doing, we are following Paul's own directions within the letter, when he tells the Philippians to "pay attention to (σκοπεῖτε) those who walk as you have an example (τύπον) in us" (3:17), in a clause that immediately follows and amplifies Paul's call to be his co-imitators (συμμιμηταί μου γίνεσθε). This example contains elements of both downward and upward movement. On the one hand, Paul has just set before his auditors the image of himself as a competitor in a race: "Forgetting what lies behind and straining forward to what lies ahead, I press on toward the goal for the prize of the *upward call* (εἰς τὸ βραβεῖον τῆς ἄνω κλήσεως) of God in Christ Jesus" (3:13b-14). The ascent language tempts one to see Paul's imitation language as also a call to an upward movement toward his own moral excellence. The commentary of J. H. Michael is typical of this temptation, when he says of Paul:

> How firm must have been his confidence in his own rectitude, how positive his certainty that he himself was copying Christ! His self-assertion is not enfeebled by any consciousness of moral poverty. . . .
> . . . The channel of education was chiefly the seen or remembered character of definite individuals, the advice and conduct of the best people.[29]

27. "True Gentleness," sermon preached at the Episcopal Church of the Holy Family, Chapel Hill, N.C., December 17, 2006.
28. Stephen E. Fowl, *Philippians* (Grand Rapids: Eerdmans, 2005), p. 187.
29. J. Hugh Michael, *The Epistle of Paul to the Philippians* (New York: Harper, 1929), p. 169.

But on the other hand, who would consider someone writing from jail to be one of "the best people"? The problem here is a failure to consider the shocking impact of Christ's *downward* mobility on any upward movement toward a virtuous life, including that of Paul. This relationship between Paul's story and that of Christ "is not that the two subjects have done the same thing or thought the same thoughts but that the dramatic structure of the two 'plots' is analogous, though not the same."[30] Indeed, in 3:6-8 Paul puts himself forward as Exhibit A of the impact of Christ's downward mobility on his own claims to public moral excellence, when he lists his blameless "righteousness under the law" among those things that he now counts as loss and refuse (σκύβαλα). Surely in turning away from his former status and excellence and seeking to be conformed (συμμορφιζόμενος) to Christ's death — death on a cross — Paul models a downward movement that is a kind of anti-*paideia*.[31]

That such is his intent is evident also from the verse immediately following his exhortation to imitation, in which he implicitly contrasts the τύπος of himself and his cohort with those who live as enemies of the cross of Christ. The significance of the contrast is too easily lost in our context. In

---

30. Wayne A. Meeks, "The Man from Heaven in Paul's Letter to the Philippians," in *The Future of Early Christianity: Essays in Honor of Helmut Koester,* ed. Birger A. Pearson (Minneapolis: Fortress, 1991), p. 333. See also Hooker, "Philippians 2:6-11," pp. 91-93; Minear, "Singing and Suffering," pp. 205-7; Fee, *Philippians,* p. 314; William S. Kurz, "Kenotic Imitation of Paul and of Christ in Philippians 2 and 3," in *Discipleship in the New Testament,* ed. Fernando F. Segovia (Philadelphia: Fortress, 1985), pp. 103-26. As N. T. Wright puts it, "the author of the letter had the material and language of 2.5-11 in his bloodstream"; see Wright, "Jesus Christ Is Lord: Philippians 2:5-11," in *The Climax of the Covenant* (Philadelphia: Fortress, 1993), p. 59; see also p. 88. For an opposing view, see Brian J. Dodd, "The Story of Christ and the Imitation of Paul in Philippians 2–3," in *Where Christology Began: Essays on Philippians 2,* ed. Ralph P. Martin and Brian J. Dodd (Louisville: Westminster John Knox, 1998), pp. 154-61.

31. Such a reversal was not inconceivable in the empire, as ascent up the social ladder became associated with groveling hypocrisy and loss of virility. Gladiators, for example, were of low status yet simultaneously praised for their bravery (see, e.g., Tertullian, *Spect.* 22; Cicero, *Tusc.* 2.17.41; Seneca, *Ep.* 37.1-2). Some aristocrats even volunteered to fight in the arena, despite laws to the contrary. For example, Dio describes numerous senators and knights who petitioned to fight in the games (43.23.4-5; 51.22.4; 56.25.7; 57.14.3; 59.10.2). For particularly helpful discussion, see Barton, *Sorrows of the Ancient Romans,* pp. 12-36; Anne Duncan, *Performance and Identity in the Classical World* (Cambridge: Cambridge University Press, 2006), pp. 211-14. As Barton puts it, "The arena, which seems to epitomize Roman 'decadence' when seen through modern eyes, also offered a stage on which might be reenacted a lost set of sorely lamented values" (*Sorrows of the Ancient Romans,* p. 33).

the Roman Empire, to be an enemy of one of its most feared and loathed modes of execution, one reserved for slaves and those guilty of rebellion against Caesar, was to be a friend of virtue. Of course, the converse held as well: one did not ascend the social ladder through close association with crucified criminals! In such a context, the "upward call of God in Christ Jesus" looks suspiciously like a call to ascend the cross.[32]

Indeed, one begins to suspect that the link between crucifixion and imitation turns mimetic education upside down. I suggest that this mimetic reversal is grounded in the drama of Philippians 2:6-11. That drama tells of Christ Jesus, who, being in the form of God, takes on the form of a slave.[33] In what follows, I shall set forth a heuristic image of this movement as Christ's mimetic impersonation of Adam: insofar as "Adam" is a stand-in for all humanity, Christ imitates us.[34]

To be sure, Paul does not call Christ Jesus either a mime or a μιμητής of Adam. He does, however, use the language of mimetic representation rather than full identification when he describes Christ as ἐν ὁμοιώματι ἀνθρώπων γενόμενος καὶ σχήματι εὑρεθεὶς ὡς ἄνθρωπος ("born in human likeness and found in appearance as a human being," 2:7). The possibility that Paul here is suggesting a nascent docetism has caused endless theological grief for his subsequent interpreters.[35] Most commentators emphatically reject that pos-

---

32. This reading links 3:14 with Paul's self description in 3:10-11, where Paul seeks to become conformed to Christ's death (συμμορφιζόμενος τῷ θανάτῳ αὐτοῦ), that if possible he might attain the resurrection. That is, the prize is resurrection, but the upward call passes through crucifixion. On crucifixion as ironic elevation, see Joel Marcus, "Crucifixion as Parodic Exaltation," *JBL* 125 (2006): 73-87. Commentators take ἡ ἄνω κλῆσις as a reference to "the heavenly dimension" of Paul's thought — so O'Brien, *Philippians,* pp. 430-33 — such that the upward call is identified with "the prize promised by God's heavenly call in Christ Jesus." See also the discussion in Bockmuehl, *Philippians,* pp. 222-23, who opts for a subjective genitive reading: the prize "pertains" to God's call. Neither connects that call with the cross.

33. That Paul should add the name Jesus to his appellation of Christ is somewhat unusual and may emphasize Christ's movement onto the stage of human history. Hooker, "Philippians 2:6-11," p. 91, rightly calls attention to Paul's insertion of "Jesus" but interprets it as referring to "the kind of life seen in Jesus Christ" as a pattern for Christians. Paul, however, does not typically refer to Jesus' earthly life as a pattern for Christian behavior.

34. Here I am employing the language of imitation in a theatrical context: μιμητής means, among other things, "one who impersonates characters, as an actor" (LSJ 1134 s.v. μιμητής II). See discussion in Welborn, *Paul, the Fool of Christ,* p. 90 et passim.

35. Hooker calls Paul's terminology here "shadowy" ("Philippians 2:6-11," pp. 98-99). Käsemann, "Critical Analysis," p. 70, helpfully notes that Paul was not fighting docetism and that importing later christological disputes into the text does not further our interpretation

sibility, agreeing with Bockmuehl's assessment: "The cumulative effect . . . is to stress that Jesus humbled himself to become human, and indeed lowly, *through and through.*"[36] At the same time, commentators rightly stress that in becoming human *"through and through,"* Christ also remained "in the form of God."[37]

But does the simple assertion of Christ's thorough identification with humanity fully do justice to Paul's puzzling language? If Paul wants to say that Christ became human "through and through," he certainly confuses his readers by inserting the language of "likeness" rather than equation. Ὁμοίωμα primarily has the sense of "copy" or "what is made similar." In distinction from εἰκών, it "emphasises the similarity, but with no need for an inner connection between the original and the copy."[38] In Plato, it is closely related to the idea of imitation, because people become "like" those they imitate through action.[39] To imitate is to become a copy, a ὁμοίωμα, and to move toward assimilation (ὁμοιότης) with the model, just as students become assimilated both to the subject matter that they study and to their teacher.

In Paul's use of this terminology elsewhere, he maintains a tension between likeness and difference. In Romans 8:3, he says that God sent the Son ἐν ὁμοιώματι σαρκὸς ἁμαρτίας to describe Christ's likeness to, yet not complete identification with, ἁμαρτία. In Romans 6:5 he uses the language of assimilation (τῷ ὁμοιώματι τοῦ θανάτου αὐτοῦ) to describe believers' growth into union with Christ's death. In Romans 5:14, all humanity suffers under the reign of death inaugurated by Adam's transgression — even those whose sins are not like (ἐπὶ τῷ ὁμοιώματι) that of Adam. Thus, the word occurs in contexts denoting a shared state and destiny rather than complete identification, whether of humanity with fallen Adam, Christ with fallen humanity, or baptized persons with Christ.

---

of it: "[T]hese sentences are not intent on giving a definition of the essence in the sense of the christology of the later church. They speak rather about the sequence of occurrences in an event unified in and of itself."

36. Bockmuehl, *Philippians*, p. 138. Hooker, "Philippians 2:6-11," pp. 98-99, suggests that Paul employs "the 'shadowy' language" in order to highlight the paradox of Christ as the true man, the true Adam, becoming as humanity really is — "a travesty of what man is meant to be."

37. Bockmuehl, *Philippians*, pp. 133-34; Fowl, *Philippians*, p. 117; Fee, *Philippians*, p. 213; O'Brien, *Philippians*, p. 225; Käsemann, "Critical Analysis," pp. 67-70.

38. J. Schneider, "Ὅμοιος," *TDNT* 5:191.

39. See, e.g., *Theaet.* 176E, 177A. See also the helpful discussion in De Boer, *Imitation of Paul*, p. 27.

Σχῆμα conveys even more emphatically the sense of outward appearance, as distinguished from the reality or essence of a thing. This focus on outward appearance is strengthened by association with the verb εὑρίσκω, so that the clause refers to "the quality of a person or thing *as it is discovered or recognized by others*."[40] Paul's terminology assumes the presence of an audience who will recognize Christ's particular human identity by virtue of his σχῆμα.

Liddell and Scott list a range of meanings for σχῆμα: *form, shape, figure; appearance (opp. the reality), show, pretence; bearing, air, mien; fashion, manner, dress, equipment; character, role; characteristic property of a thing; a figure (in dancing), gestures, postures.*[41] Seizing on its sense as the *characteristic property of a thing*, commentators have interpreted this term in Philippians 2:7 as referring to "the *way* in which Jesus' humanity appeared."[42] I agree, but argue further that the senses of the term as *bearing, mien, dress, role,* and *gestures* afford a far richer image of that mode of appearing, by situating it in the context of the theatrical and performative mindset that permeated Roman society.

Abundant evidence demonstrates that the Romans saw the world as a theater and human life as a drama on the world stage, with each person playing an appointed role. Marcus Aurelius, for example, speaks of "the greater stage" (*Med.* 11.6) and muses that death is simply dismissal from that stage by the show's director (*Med.* 12.36); Seneca speaks of "this drama of human life" (*hic humanae vitae mimus, Ep.* 80.7-10); and Epictetus advises, "Remember that you are an actor in a play" (*Ench.* 17).[43] According to Suetonius, Augustus approached his death asking how fitly he had "played the comedy of life" (*ecquid iis videretur mimum vitae commode transegisse*) — then answered himself:

---

40. Ralph P. Martin, *Carmen Christi: Philippians ii.5-11 in Recent Interpretation and in the Setting of Early Christian Worship* (Cambridge: Cambridge University Press, 1967), p. 208, emphasis mine. In a parallel movement, Paul regards his own advantages as garbage so that he may be "found" (εὑρεθῶ) in Christ (3:9).

41. LSJ 1745. See also the discussion in J. B. Lightfoot, *Epistle to the Philippians* (London: Macmillan, 1903), pp. 127-33.

42. O'Brien, *Philippians*, p. 226, emphasis original. See also Martin, *Carmen Christi*, p. 207.

43. I am indebted for these references to T. J. Lang, "'All the world's a stage': Theatrical Imagery in Clement of Alexandria's *Protrepticos*" (unpublished paper, Duke University, 2006). The theatricality of Roman life is widely noted and discussed; see, e.g., Duncan, *Performance and Identity*, pp. 188-217; cf. n. 7 above.

Since well I've played my part, all clap your hands
And from the stage dismiss me with applause.[44]

In the theatrical lexicon, σχῆμα denoted the various means by which actors displayed the identity of their characters. In Euripides' *Ion,* for instance, Creusa's royal stature is evident from her bearing (σχῆμα):

For in your appearance (μορφῇ) there is nobility,
and your bearing (σχῆμα) gives evidence of who you are, lady.[45]

Σχῆμα also applied to the dress that designated and revealed the identity of a character; an actor might change clothing to denote a change in identity or status or circumstance. Such usage of the word has a long lineage; in Aristophanes' *Equites,* Demos's transformation is made visible by his appearance in "grand old apparel" (ἀρχαίῳ σχήματι λαμπρός).[46] Theatrical movements and gestures, particularly those of pantomimic dance, were called σχήματα. In pantomime, a single actor would dance the roles of multiple characters to rhythmic music as a chorus sang the plot; moving silently, the actor would "refine his gestures to such a high degree and perform his movements so expressively that in him alone one could see embodied now a god and now a goddess, now a hero and now a heroine."[47]

These performative senses of σχῆμα as dance, gesture, apparel, and bearing extended beyond the theater proper into other aspects of public life as well. We find dance gestures described as σχήματα in accounts of games and triumphal processions.[48] We find σχῆμα in the sense of bearing or mien in the drama of the world stage, where one's self-presentation was an important as-

44. Suetonius, *Aug.* 99 (trans. Rolfe, LCL).
45. Euripides, *Ion* 236-38 (trans. Kovacs, LCL).
46. Aristophanes, *Eq.* 1331. See discussion in Lightfoot, *Philippians,* p. 127.
47. Margarete Bieber, *The History of the Greek and Roman Theater* (Princeton: Princeton University Press, 1961), p. 235. Pantomime and mime were immensely popular theatrical genres, attended by people of all classes and acted in a variety of venues. Pantomime was generally more "high-brow," enacting the classic dramas, and mime more "street theater." See Bieber, *History of the Greek and Roman Theater,* pp. 235-38; Mary T. Boatwright, "Theaters in the Roman Empire," *BA* 53 (1990): 184-92, esp. p. 188; Richard C. Beacham, *The Roman Theater and Its Audience* (Cambridge, Mass.: Harvard University Press, 1992), pp. 154, 188-89; Lightfoot, "Romanized Greeks," p. 260; Duncan, *Performance and Identity,* pp. 194-97; Barton, *Sorrows of the Ancient Romans,* pp. 107-75.
48. For example, one of the musicians dancing in a triumphal procession recorded by Appian "caused laughter by making various gesticulations (σχηματίζεται ποίκιλος ἐς γέλοτα)" (*Pun.* 9.66).

pect of one's role. For example, Josephus describes King Hezekiah taking off his robes of state, putting on sackcloth, and assuming a σχῆμα ταπεινόν at the news of Sennacherib's invasion (*Ant.* 10.11; see Isa. 37:1; 2 Kings 19:1). Like the costume of Demos and the bearing of Creusa, this is a public appearance that assumes the presence of an audience; it is Hezekiah playing his kingly role in the particular crisis facing Israel. Similarly, I would argue, Christ's assumption of the σχῆμα of a human being is a public act that assumes an audience.

Clement of Alexandria describes Christ as "putting on the mask of the human" in order to "act the drama of salvation" (*Protr.* 10.110.2). Following Clement's lead, and playing off Paul's use of σχήματι, the following comments gesture toward reading Philippians 2:6-11 as the drama — the libretto, if you will — accompanying Christ's enactment of Adam's story.[49]

The plot goes as follows: In act one, Christ is offstage, existing in the form of God and possessing equality with God (2:6). At this point, Christ is distinctly different from Adam, and Paul uses language that distances him from the Genesis account of the creation of the first human being.[50] In this regard, the scholars who oppose an Adam Christology in 2:6 are correct; as Fee puts it, here "there is not a single *linguistic* parallel to the Genesis narrative."[51] Indeed, although elsewhere Paul refers to Christ as the εἰκὼν τοῦ θεοῦ (2 Cor. 4:4) in language reminiscent of the creation of Adam in the image of God (Gen. 1:26-27), here he uses the rare term μορφή.[52] Had he

---

49. I will not review the immense literature on Christ and Adam in Phil. 2:6-11 but will refer to it in the notes. The classic summary and exhaustive discussion is in Martin, *Carmen Christi*, pp. 116-20, 128-33. For arguments in favor of an Adam motif, but with distinctive differences between them, see particularly Hooker, "Philippians 2:6-11"; Wright, "Jesus Christ Is Lord"; J. D. G. Dunn, "Christ, Adam, and Preexistence," in *Where Christology Began*, ed. Martin and Dodd, pp. 74-83. For arguments against the presence of such a motif, see Fowl, *Philippians,* pp. 114-17; O'Brien, *Philippians,* pp. 263-68; Bockmuehl, *Philippians,* pp. 131-33; Fee, *Philippians,* p. 209.

50. *Pace* Hooker, "Philippians 2:6-11"; Wright, "Jesus Christ Is Lord"; Martin, *Carmen Christi*, pp. 161-64; Dunn, "Christ, Adam, and Preexistence"; all of whom posit similarity between Adam and Christ in Phil. 2:6, reading it as an echo of Gen. 1:26.

51. Fee, *Philippians,* p. 209, emphasis original.

52. It is worth noting that, despite the voluminous amount of ink spilled in attempts to link μορφή with εἰκών in Gen. 1:26-27 as a reference to Adam, Paul never refers to Adam as either the image or the glory of God. The closest he comes to such a reference is Rom. 1:23, where "they exchanged the glory of the immortal God for a likeness of an image of a mortal human being (ἐν ὁμοιώματι εἰκόνος φθαρτοῦ ἀνθρώπου) and birds and animals and reptiles" — hardly an endorsement of Adam! Rather, Adam is "the first man, from the earth, a man of dust" (ὁ πρῶτος ἄνθρωπος ἐκ γῆς χοϊκός) whose image (εἰκών) we *now* bear, just as we *will* bear the image of the one from heaven (1 Cor. 15:47, 49).

441

wanted to echo the creation of Adam at this point, he could have used εἰκών here as well.[53] Instead, the only possible connection with the Genesis narrative here is the implicit thematic *contrast* with Adam implied by the negative οὐχ ἁρπαγμὸν ἡγήσατο; when ἁρπαγμὸς is translated as "something to be exploited," this implicit contrast also serves to distance Christ from Adam in his initial situation.[54]

Thus, the difficulty with arguments for an initial parity between Christ and Adam is that they stumble over the lack of linguistic parallels with Genesis in Philippians 2:6. Nonetheless, in my view there is indeed an enactment of Adam's part in the hymn, and we see it when we reverse the line of movement. Christ does not *begin* with likeness to Adam and then move in an opposite direction, becoming increasingly *dissimilar* as the plot progresses. Rather, in the dramatic image of Christ as actor, there is a reverse mimetic movement from difference toward similarity, and that movement is on the part of Christ himself.[55] In v. 6, Christ the divine actor has not yet put on Adam's mask, become his copy, and assumed his gestures — that is why there are not yet any positive links with the Genesis narrative.

Act two begins in v. 7, when, taking on the form of a slave, Christ is born in

---

53. See Bockmuehl, *Philippians*, p. 132; O'Brien, *Philippians*, p. 264.

54. Here I follow Roy W. Hoover's translation of ἁρπαγμός, in "The Harpagmos Enigma: A Philological Solution," *HTR* 64 (1971): 95-119. Hoover's analysis treats the clause as a unit and notes parallels with Rom. 15:3, as well as 2 Cor. 8:9. The meaning of ἁρπαγμός has generated its own stack of scholarly monographs. Does Paul mean that Christ did not snatch at equality with God, that he did not cling to it, or that he did not exploit it? The first option would place Christ in a position similar to that of Adam, grasping at an equality with God that he lacks. The second and third would support a reading that sees Christ as possessing equality with God at the outset. Most scholars now opt for the third; we may note, however, that the result is a distancing between Christ and Adam, unless one posits that Adam also possessed equality with God prior to the fall. For a chart laying out all the interpretive options and their variants, with a thorough discussion, see Wright, "Jesus Christ Is Lord," p. 81.

55. This dynamic movement on the part of the model ironically reverses Castelli's depiction of a mimetic relationship as involving "one element being fixed and the other transforming itself or being transformed into an approximation of the first. The favored movement is from difference toward similarity" (*Imitating Paul*, p. 21). In my reading of imitation in Philippians, there indeed is movement from difference toward similarity, but that movement is initiated and sustained by the *model's* movement to become like the imitator, initiating and sustaining the imitator's reciprocal *mimēsis*. In this drama, all the characters are in motion. For further discussion of mimetic reversal in Paul's letters, see my *Recovering Paul's Mother Tongue: Language and Theology in Galatians* (Grand Rapids: Eerdmans, 2007), pp. 25-61.

human likeness and through his actions reveals his human identity. It is here, rather than in the previous verse, that the verbal echoes of Genesis 1:26-27 come into play. There are two: ὁμοιώματι ἀνθρώπων and ἄνθρωπος, echoing the creation of humankind (ἄνθρωπος) in the divine likeness (ὁμοίωσις).[56] Now Christ becomes (γενόμενος) someone he was not previously; he assimilates to Adam, in a mirror reversal of Adam's creation in the likeness of God.[57]

That Christ takes on Adam's role is further suggested by the use of the singular ἄνθρωπος at the end of v. 7. In Paul's other letters, ἄνθρωπος is his name for Adam: Adam is "the first person" (ὁ πρῶτος ἄνθρωπος, 1 Cor. 15:47), the ἄνθρωπος through whom death came to all (1 Cor. 15:21). In Adam all die; in Christ all will be made alive. Similarly, in Romans 5:12-21, Adam is the "one person" (ἑνὸς ἀνθρώπου, 5:12, 19) through whose disobedience death comes to all people (εἰς πάντας ἀνθρώπους). In referring thus to Adam, Paul follows LXX Genesis, where Adam is ὁ ἄνθρωπος (1:27; 2:7, 8, 15, 18). In the words of Joel Marcus, "Adam is 'the man' par excellence, the first man, the person who

56. Genesis 1:26 uses ὁμοίωσις, a rare word that is not in Paul's vocabulary, and indeed occurs only once in the NT, in the citation of Gen. 1:26 in Jas. 3:9. Paul employs the cognate noun, ὁμοίωμα, his preferred word (Phil. 2:7; Rom. 1:23; 5:14; 6:5; 8:3). The words are extremely close in form and meaning: ὁμοίωσις is an action that makes like or similar; ὁμοίωμα is the result of such an action. In Rom. 1:23 and 5:14, Paul uses ὁμοίωμα in reference to Adam's original trespass. In Rom. 8:3, Christ was sent "in the likeness of the flesh of sin" — if not a direct reference to Adam, at the least a reference to the effect of Adam's trespass (Rom. 5:12-21).

57. The verb γενόμενος deals a fatal blow to Dunn's argument that Phil. 2:6-11 refers only to Jesus' earthly life as a second Adam ("Christ, Adam, and Preexistence Revisited," pp. 78-79). As O'Brien, *Philippians,* p. 267, points out: "The *contrast* clearly expressed between 'being in the form of God' and 'becoming in the form of human beings' is very odd if it is only between two stages in the career of a human being" (emphasis original). The phrase also creates difficulties for linking Adam at creation with Christ as a preexistent divine being. Hooker, "Philippians 2:6-11," pp. 98-99, deals with γενόμενος by interpreting v. 7 as meaning that Christ, already in his preexistent state being what Adam was meant to be — "true man" — becomes what humanity now is, in the condition of enslavement to sin and death; see also Wright, "Jesus Christ Is Lord," p. 59. That argument is weakened by O'Brien's observation that the aorist participle γενόμενος "stands in sharp contrast to the present participle ὑπάρχων of v. 6" and that the hymn moves from using two static verbs (ὑπάρχων and εἶναι) in v. 6 to using active verbs (ἐκένωσεν, λαβών, γενόμενος, ἐταπείνωσεν) in vv. 7-8 (*Philippians,* p. 224). It is doubtful whether a change from one "Adam" to another "Adam" captures the contrast implied by the text. Rather, the repetition of the verb brings to mind the double γενόμενος of Gal. 4:4: "born of a woman, born under law." This is Paul's verb for depicting the conditions attending the advent of Christ, and it is not descriptive of a preexistent state but of a "becoming." Galatians and Philippians depict movements from Christ's prior existence into the realm of human affairs, and that prior existence bears no similarity to the abject state of Adam and his heirs. See also Lightfoot, *Philippians,* p. 112.

determines all subsequent human destinies both by his very existence and by his act of disobedience."[58] This is the person whose exiled and condemned status Christ impersonates through stepping onto the stage of human history. He does this, not by miming Adam's disobedience — οὐχ ἁρπαγμόν makes that clear — but by taking on the destiny of a condemned rebel.

But because Adam is a stand-in for the human race, Christ is also born ἐν ὁμοιώματι ἀνθρώπων — in the likeness of all human beings.[59] As an echo of humankind's creation in the divine likeness, this "birth" or "becoming" reminds the audience that even in slavery, even bound by sin and death and cast out from the garden, Adam retains God's imprint. So Christ also retains his being in the form of God, and indeed expresses that being through performing Adam's role. Returning to our heuristic image of Christ as miming Adam, we can picture him as the actor who never loses his offstage identity yet at the same time plays the onstage role with complete and utter realism. He remains fully God; he becomes fully human *through* the gestures with which he plays Adam's part.[60]

So we come to the third act: impersonating Adam, Christ humbles himself, becoming obedient to the point of death — death on a cross. The object of Christ's obedience is not named, but within the plot of the drama, he is obedient to the role that is given him to perform, submitting fully to the conditions that govern the plot onstage. Those conditions have been established by humanity's initial exchange of God's glory given at creation for "a likeness of an image of a mortal human being and birds and animals and reptiles" (ἐν ὁμοιώματι εἰκόνος φθαρτοῦ ἀνθρώπου καὶ πετεινῶν καὶ τετραπόδων καὶ ἑρπετῶν, Rom. 1:23), and God's subsequent judgment. On the world stage, humanity's script has become a tragedy, "handed over" by God to destructive powers and ending in death (Rom. 1:24-32). Sent "in the likeness of sinful flesh" (Rom 8:3), the divine actor "who knew no sin" (2 Cor. 5:21) plays humanity's role in this script, accepting the condemnation that is its necessary ending (Rom. 8:3). Yet insofar as God is ultimately the author and editor of this drama, Christ's obedience to his role is ultimately obedience to God. When God reverses the ending of the story and exalts Jesus, the tragedy becomes a comedy.

58. Joel Marcus, "Son of Man as Son of Adam," *RB* 110 (2003): 45. Marcus also notes that rabbinic traditions refer to Adam as "the first man" (p. 45 n. 30).

59. So Lightfoot, *Philippians*, p. 112: "The plural ἀνθρώπων is used; for Christ, as the second Adam, represents not the individual man, but the human race."

60. Σχήματι here is read as an instrumental dative, with Martin (*Carmen Christi*, p. 208) and O'Brien (*Philippians*, p. 227).

In other words, for Christ to become ἐν ὁμοιώματι ἀνθρώπων is for him to share fully in the desperate contingency, suffering, and death of Adam's heirs, whom I take to be the entire human race.[61] Paul is describing Christ's mimetic movement, his assimilation, into the likeness of humanity enslaved to the sin that came into the world through Adam (Rom. 5:12). In *this* way he repeats, replicates, and reverses Adam's story. By ultimately taking on the likeness of Adam's sin and death, Christ opens the way for humanity to be joined to the likeness of his own death (σύμφυτοι γεγόναμεν τῷ ὁμοιώματι τοῦ θανάτου αὐτοῦ), through baptism (Rom. 6:5).

Whereas an actor may take off the mask at the end of the play and go back to another existence, Christ makes Adam's destiny his own. His obedience even to the point of death may seem to us to go beyond the heuristic image of him as Adam's mime. But such a melding of the actor's and the character's identity and destiny was not unheard of in the ancient world. K. M. Coleman, in her remarkable study "Fatal Charades: Roman Executions Staged as Mythological Enactments," discusses "the increasing taste for realism on the stage" by the time of the early empire.[62] Thus, when a mime artist in the role of Ajax "rampaged hysterically,"

> [t]he situation caused some to marvel, some to laugh, and some to suspect that perhaps in consequence of his excessive mimicry he had caught the real disease.[63]

As Bieber notes, the bloodlust of the Roman public created a thirst for increasing violence in the theater as well as the stadium, leading to an admixture of theater and spectacle in both venues.[64] For example, a popular mime

---

61. *Pace* N. T. Wright, "Jesus Christ Is Lord," p. 59, who argues that Phil. 2:5-11 puts forth an Adam Christology in which "Christ as last Adam takes on the role of Israel in the purposes of God . . . to be the means of solving the problem posed by Adam's sin."

62. K. M. Coleman, "Fatal Charades: Roman Executions Staged as Mythological Enactments," *JRS* 80 (1990): 68. This taste for realism included increasing audience participation, voluntary and involuntary, in both theater and spectacles. Caligula, for example, augmented the number of criminals condemned to be thrown to wild animals by conscripting spectators from the stands (Dio 59.10.3); see further Barton, *Sorrows of the Ancient Romans*, p. 63; Josephus *Ant.* 19.24.27.

63. Lucian, *Salt.* 83 (trans. Coleman, "Fatal Charades," p. 68).

64. Bieber, *History of the Greek and Roman Theater*, p. 238. Duncan, *Performance and Identity*, pp. 200-203, chronicles the "spectacular executions" of costumed criminals, concluding: "All of these spectacles drew their power and their interest from the complete collapse of theater and reality into each other" (p. 203).

included a mock crucifixion of a bandit named Laureolus, in which the stage ran with artificial blood.[65] But Martial tells of a criminal who was forced to take the part of Laureolus and suffer actual crucifixion: "in him, what had been a play became an execution."[66]

Most instructive is the way in which condemned criminals were dressed in finery and made to play the role of gods in a public spectacle before being executed. Tertullian referred to this practice when he said to his pagan auditors: "[C]riminals often adopt *(induunt)* the roles of your deities. We have seen at one time or another Attis, that god from Pessinus, being castrated, and a man who was being burnt alive had taken on the role of Hercules."[67] Here the criminal-actor is forced to assume the identity of the god and suffer the god's mythological fate. Plutarch remarks that the role-plays of criminals in the arena could be so realistic as to fool naïve spectators:

> Yet some there are no wiser than little children, who see criminals in the amphitheatre, clad often in tunics of cloth of gold and purple mantles, wearing chaplets and dancing Pyrrhic measures, and struck with awe and wonderment suppose them supremely happy, till the moment when before their eyes the criminals are stabbed and scourged and that gay and sumptuous apparel bursts into flame.[68]

If some punishments involved enforced role-plays, others were designed to mimic the form of the crime.[69] Crucifixion was one such punishment. As Marcus explains:

---

65. Suetonius, *Cal.* 57, cited in Bieber, *History of the Greek and Roman Theater,* p. 238; see also Josephus, *Ant.* 19.13; Juvenal 8.187-188.

66. Martial, *Spect.* 7 (trans. Shackleton Bailey, LCL). According to Martial, the time necessary for "Laureolus" to die was shortened by hanging him just in reach of a wild boar that tore him to pieces in front of the audience. See Coleman, "Fatal Charades," pp. 64-65; Allardyce Nicoll, *Masks, Mimes, and Miracles: Studies in the Popular Theatre* (London: Harrap, 1931), pp. 110-11.

67. Tertullian, *Apol.* 15.4-5 (trans. Coleman, "Fatal Charades," p. 60). Coleman notes that Tertullian's terminology implies "the assumption of a role: *induo* properly describes the act of putting on clothing, ornaments, chains, etc., and, by transference, the assumption of a role or appearance" (p. 60). On this, Marcus, "Crucifixion as Parodic Exaltation," p. 82, comments that "the verb . . . may imply that the line between performer and role sometimes became blurred for both criminal and audience."

68. Plutarch, *Mor.* 554B (trans. De Lacy and Einarson, LCL).

69. See Duncan, *Performance and Identity,* pp. 202-3; Coleman, "Fatal Charades," pp. 46-47.

[T]his strangely "exalting" mode of execution was designed to mimic, parody, and puncture the pretensions of insubordinate transgressors by displaying a deliberately horrible mirror of their self-elevation. For it is revealing that the criminals so punished were often precisely people who had, in the view of their judges, gotten "above" themselves — rebellious slaves, for example, or slaves who had insulted their masters, or people of any class who had not shown proper deference to the emperor, not to mention those who had revolted against him or who had, through brigandage or piracy, demonstrated disdain for imperial rule.[70]

When we return our attention to Christ, who, "being in the form of God . . . took on the form of a slave" and "became obedient unto death, even death on a cross," we see him in the guise of Adam, who "got above himself" in his self-exaltation and therefore was liable for crucifixion.[71] Christ suffers the punishment that corresponds to Adam's "uppity-ness" in rebelling against the divine authority. But paradoxically, as a victim of Roman crucifixion, he also enacts the role of Adam who is destined to rule the cosmos (Gen. 1:28; Phil. 2:11; 3:21) and who therefore cannot help but come into conflict with the claims of Caesar. Both the condemnation of Adam as the first sinner and the hope of Adam's exaltation were current in first-century Jewish traditions; in the libretto of 2:6-11, Christ assumes and transforms these dual roles of humiliation and exaltation.[72]

The resulting picture of Christ's earthly existence is of one that is radically contingent on divine miracle. "Emptying himself," he has made himself "null and void, powerless."[73] Therefore, it is not his own power but God's ac-

70. Marcus, "Crucifixion as Parodic Exaltation," p. 78.

71. Hooker, "Philippians 2:6-11," p. 99: "Moreover, having put himself into this position of helpless enslavement, Christ is content to continue the path to the end. The inevitable end is death — the punishment which came upon Adam because of his grasping."

72. For a thorough discussion of Jewish traditions about Adam, see Marcus, "Son of Man as Son of Adam," which traces three traditions about the phrase "son of man" in parallel with three traditions about Adam: as an exalted eschatological figure, as the one designated to rule over creation, and as the first sinner, who brought death to the world (pp. 57-61). Philippians 2:7-8 plays out the last tradition about Adam, but vv. 9-11 may play on the first two traditions as well. With regard to the political implications of Christ's crucifixion and exaltation, it is interesting to note that theater frequently functioned as a venue for political commentary and satire, particularly when the actor could hide behind the mask while mocking Caesar (see Bieber, *History of the Greek and Roman Theater,* p. 247). Sometimes mimes ended in libel trials, or worse. See Matthew Leigh, "Primitivism and Power: The Beginnings of Latin Literature," in *Literature in the Greek and Roman Worlds,* ed. Taplin, p. 308.

73. Hooker's translation ("Philippians 2:6-11," p. 98).

tion that exalts him in v. 9, because his obedience as a slave consists in his dependence on the God who raises from the dead. After the stunning crisis that concludes the first strophe of the hymn — "even death on a cross" — God takes over as the subject of the action, and Christ becomes the object, the recipient of God's powerful act of exaltation and God's gift of the name above every name.

Paul and *Paideia:* The Play's the Thing

> For Christ plays in ten thousand places,
> Lovely in limbs, and lovely in eyes not his
> To the Father through the features of men's faces.[74]

In the first section of this essay, we briefly sketched some characteristics of Hellenistic *paideia* and the function of *mimēsis* within that *paideia*. In the second, we posited a different context, that of the theater and the public arena, for interpreting Philippians 2:6-11 in relationship to Paul's imitative educational project. Unlike the mimes and spectacles of the empire in which actors and criminals mimicked the gods, the "libretto" of Philippians 2:6-11 tells of a reversal in which the divine, preexistent Christ mimics humanity.

Insofar as this reversal displays the φρόνησις that is "in Christ Jesus" and that Paul urges on his Philippian friends, it presents a *Vorbild* that is countercultural in the extreme. We have noted that ancient education used imitation as a way to shape the subjectivity of students by impressing them with virtuous models. The anticipated "product" of such imitation was a student who achieved self-mastery and gained social esteem and influence. But imitation of a Savior who plays the role of humanity in its most derelict and helpless state, of Adam condemned to death, surely leads in an opposite direction. In Paul's self-description to the Corinthians, it leads to his own public persona as a condemned criminal acting in a public spectacle (1 Cor. 4:9-10).[75] When he writes to the Philippians, "be my fellow imitators, and pay at-

74. Gerard Manley Hopkins (1844-89), "As kingfishers catch fire, dragonflies draw flame," in *The Poems of Gerard Manley Hopkins,* ed. W. H. Gardner and N. H. MacKenzie, 4th ed. (New York: Oxford University Press, 1967), p. 90.

75. The majority of commentators read θέατρον as "spectacle," such that Paul is referring to the fate of people in the arena or amphitheater. For the argument that Paul is depicting himself as a mimic fool, see Welborn, *Paul, the Fool of Christ.* The difference between these interpretations is immaterial to my argument: since public executions in the arena

tention to those who walk as you have an example in us" (3:17), we hear his call to join him in sharing that persona, by assuming Christ's role and sharing his destiny of humiliation and exaltation.

Christ himself relied not on his own divine rectitude or power but, through his obedience even to the point of death, relied only on God. Insofar as Paul imitates Christ on the stage of human history, he also becomes a τύπος, not of moral mastery and superiority, but of humble trust and solidarity. In Barth's words:

> What is to be seen in *him,* Paul, as a Christian, is in point of fact not anything positive on which *he* could pride himself, but *Christ* — that is, however, the traces of the *dynamis tēs anastaseōs autou* (the power of his resurrection), the fellowship of his sufferings, a *gap* so to speak, a lack, a defect: he is *not* holy, *not* righteous, *not* perfect, all for the sake of Christ. This *typos* (example) he can really without presumptuousness commend to them for imitation.[76]

In the context of ancient *paideia,* such an example can only be considered a kind of anti-education. In this regard, it is instructive to note that the term παιδεία does not appear in Paul's letters, and he uses its cognates sparingly.[77] He reserves the verb παιδεύω for the chastening action of God (1 Cor. 11:32; 2 Cor. 6:9) and arrogates to the law the menial work of a παιδαγωγός (Gal. 3:24-25).[78] It is true that there are "countless" unnamed others who are the Corinthians' παιδαγωγοί, but they are not to be compared or imitated, in contrast with Paul in his role as "father" (1 Cor. 4:15). Furthermore, despite its wide use in scholarship on Paul, παραινέω and its cognates never occur in his letters, an observation that ought to make us pause, at the least, in the pursuit of understanding paraenesis in Paul.[79]

The fact that Paul never refers to his communication as παιδεία, nor

---

were also turned into theatrical entertainment, sometimes including mime, the element of role playing is common to both.

76. Barth, *Philippians,* p. 112, emphasis original.

77. The one exception to this observation is in deutero-Pauline 2 Tim. 3:16, where all Scripture is profitable πρὸς παιδείαν τὴν ἐν δικαιοσύνῃ, as well as for teaching (πρὸς διδασκαλίαν), reproof, and correction. The verse appears to echo Rom. 15:4, where Scripture is for our instruction (εἰς τὴν ἡμετέραν διδασκαλίαν).

78. Throughout the NT, God is the subject of παιδεύω, and the verb is used with the sense of discipline or correction; see, e.g., Heb. 12:6-7, 10-11.

79. Noted by Troels Engberg-Pedersen, *Paul and the Stoics* (Louisville: Westminster John Knox, 2000), p. 321.

himself as a παιδευτής, nor indeed his readers as πεπαιδευμένοι, distances his letters and his communities from the elitist discourse of *paideia* in the ancient world — a *paideia* that, as we have seen, enculturates its pupils into a hierarchical system of difference. Paul neither endorses nor mimics such education in his goal of encouraging communities in Christ, in whom there is "neither Jew nor Greek, neither slave nor free, not male and female" (Gal. 3:28). Indeed, the heuristic experiment of reading Philippians 2:6-11 as Christ's impersonation of Adam provides a different image of Paul's converts: addressing them as the socially mixed audience of a Roman theater,[80] he invites them to become a troupe of mimes. Later Christians got the point; perhaps the most compelling portrait of "imitating Christ" comes from the story of an actor named Ardalion, who performed in a mime of Christ's crucifixion before the emperor Maximian. In the midst of his performance, he shouted out his confession of faith — "I am a Christian!" (ἐγὼ γὰρ Χριστιανός εἰμι) — and was burned for his boldness.[81]

Ardalion is miming Christ suffering the execution common to countless victims of Rome's bloodlust. Like his predecessor Paul, he becomes a kind of τύπος, displaying the way in which he himself has been "imprinted" by Christ. Indeed, Ardalion exemplifies Paul's countercultural project in character formation, a project that may be construed as a kind of reciprocal "impersonation" in a double sense. As Whitmarsh puts it, education "both creates the conditions wherein the student can impersonate the teacher and 'im-personates' (i.e. places the 'person' within) the student."[82] For Paul, the teacher ultimately is the crucified and resurrected Christ, who first "impersonates" Adam and thereby puts his "person" into Adam's heirs, so that they in turn may impersonate Christ.

Pondering this reciprocal "impersonation," and recalling the student's imitation of both subject matter and teacher in ancient education, we may

80. The seating in the Roman theater was arranged according to social status, but those arrangements were not always observed. Caligula, for example, had vouchers given to the lowest classes so that they would take the knights' seats (Suetonius, *Cal.* 26.4). See Beacham, *Roman Theater*, p. 192; Barton, *Sorrows of the Ancient Romans*, p. 155.

81. The story of Ardalion comes from the Menologium Basilianum 3.59 (PG 117:408) and is noted in Coleman, "Fatal Charades," p. 65 n. 182, and Nicoll, *Masks*, pp. 90, 94. For full citation and discussion, see Hermann Reich, *Der Mimus: Ein Litterar-entwickelungs-geschichtlicher Versuch*, 2 vols. (Berlin: Weidmannsche, 1903), pp. 83-84. Comic mimicry of crucifixion and Christian baptism was popular, and there were other such accounts of mimic actors among the Christian martyrs of the first few centuries. See extensive discussion in Reich, *Der Mimus*, pp. 80-109.

82. Whitmarsh, *Greek Literature*, p. 94.

consider further the way in which Christ's action restructures that mimetic process. It is striking, for instance, how often Paul is *not* precisely or solely the subject of the action when it comes to teaching. Even in Philippians 4:9, where Paul invokes himself as a model, he refers obliquely to "what you have learned (ἐμάθετε) . . . in me," shortly thereafter telling the Philippians that he himself has learned (ἔμαθον) to be content (4:11).[83] In other words, like spectator-participants at a Roman theater or arena, the Philippians are to learn from watching the ways in which Paul himself has learned, thus receiving and hearing and seeing what has happened "in" him and is thereby displayed to them.

Finally, therefore, there is a sense in which Paul as teacher is displaced by the Subject that he teaches, a Subject that is more a "who" than a "what." This Subject is not a literary or mythic hero from the past, as in Greco-Roman education, who may become the object of endless literary improvisations by ambitious students. This Subject strides onstage, takes hold of teacher and students alike (Phil. 3:12), and throws them into the ring with the rest of the human race. To be taught in this way, to imitate Christ imitating us, is to discover that Christian education takes place in the messiness of human relating and the mystery of human suffering. It is to discover that

> [u]ltimately, the subject-matter to be known is God; it is the Word, Jesus Christ, a Reality that must give itself to be known if it is to be known at all. . . . The object of which Paul speaks is not one we can lay hands on; it is a living Subject who must lay hold of us in the knowing process.[84]

In light of what we have found in Philippians, we might paraphrase this statement to say that in the imitation of which Paul speaks, Christ is the living Subject who lays hold of us in the mimetic process. This, in a nutshell, is Paul's educational project.

---

83. Professor Paul rarely assumes the title of "teacher," although he is given that title in 1 Tim. 2:7 and 2 Tim. 1:11. In 1 Cor. 4:17 he refers to teaching his "ways in Christ" among all the churches; in 1 Cor. 12:28-29 and Rom. 12:7, "teacher" is one of the gifts for ministry distributed by God. Elsewhere in Paul's letters, the Spirit (1 Cor. 2:13), God (1 Thess. 4:9), and Scripture (Rom. 15:4) teach.

84. Bruce L. McCormack, introduction to Barth, *Philippians*, p. xviii.

Resurrection and the Limits of Paulinism

Francis Watson

By the end of the second century, two collections of authoritative writings had been added to the ancient Scriptures the church shared with the Jewish community. On the one hand, there were the four Gospels (to which the book of Acts was attached); on the other hand, the writings of the Apostle Paul. Ambiguities remained: other gospels continued to circulate, the exact limits of the Pauline collection remained to be defined, and there was as yet no collection of "Catholic Epistles."[1] Yet the basic generic distinction between "Gospels" and "Epistles" was already clear, and remains so in the fully developed "New Testament" of the fourth century, with its twenty-seven books. In the Epistles section, the formation of a "Catholic" collection did little to check Pauline dominance. Historically, the four Gospels and the Pauline letters have retained their second-century primacy.

The coexistence of the two canonical genres has created a tension that is evident throughout the history of Pauline interpretation. Where Paul's texts serve as the primary source for theological construction, the tendency is to focus on what might be called (in Bultmannian terminology) "believing existence."[2] While the Pauline letters might in principle point their readers in a

---

1. On this point, see David R. Nienhuis, *Not by Paul Alone: The Formation of the Catholic Epistle Collection and the Christian Canon* (Waco: Baylor University Press, 2007). Nienhuis demonstrates that the Catholic Epistles collection was intended as a canonical counterweight to Paul, associated primarily with the three "pillar" apostles — James, Peter, and John.

2. Bultmann's theology is the most important and influential modern example of the "Paulinism" I here seek to criticize. While "Paulinists" can also appeal to non-Pauline theo-

number of different theological directions, their fundamental concern is to relate the crucified and risen Lord to the ongoing life of the Christian community and its members. In that sense, their dogmatic orientation is toward theological anthropology, as the Reformers rightly understood. Where theology has primary recourse to the canonical Gospels, however, the focus will normally be on Christology — as in the patristic attempts to articulate the divine-human identity of the subject of the fourfold Gospel narrative, and thus the triune divine identity itself. Different sections of the scriptural canon lend themselves to different theological appropriations, and in principle there is no reason why this should not be so. Yet the disjunction between Gospels and (Pauline) Epistles runs deep. The two sets of writings share a common focus on Jesus' death and resurrection yet locate those events within quite different frames of reference: biographical narrative on the one hand, communal experience on the other. The christological orientation of one set of texts is matched by the anthropological orientation of the other; and the primary orientation of the one is secondary and subordinate in the other.

It is this Pauline, anthropological orientation that comes to expression in Martin Luther's assertion that "[t]o know [Christ's] works and the things that happened to him is not yet to know the true gospel, for you do not yet thereby know that he has overcome sin, death, and the devil."[3] For Luther, the gospel is only imperfectly articulated in the Gospels — for it is here that we read of Christ's "works and the things that happened to him" and yet risk failing to find "the true gospel." (Luther makes an exception of the Gospel of John, on the grounds that it has little to say of Christ's actions but much of his life-giving words.) While Christ's actions belong to the past and are of limited relevance, his words continue to sound forth in the present, addressing the individual here and now with the promise of salvation. Judged by this criterion of present, saving relevance, "the epistles of St. Paul and St. Peter far surpass the other three gospels, Matthew, Mark, and Luke."[4] To confuse the gospel with the Gospels is no less an error than confusing Christ with Moses. As a corrective, we should turn especially to the letter to the

---

logical resources — e.g., John in the case of Bultmann, the historical Jesus in the case of Käsemann — these resources are identified as such only on the basis of Pauline criteria. There is little in Bultmann's interpretation of John, or Käsemann's of the historical Jesus, that is not already to be found within their respective readings of Paul.

3. Martin Luther, *Prefaces to the New Testament* (1522), in *Luther's Works*, vol. 35, *Word and Sacrament I*, ed. E. Theodore Bachmann (Philadelphia: Fortress, 1960), p. 361; hereafter cited as LW 35.

4. Luther, *Prefaces*, LW 35:362.

Romans, which "is really the chief part of the New Testament, and is truly the purest gospel."[5] What comes to light in Luther's remarkably forthright statements is the existence of a tension at the heart of the New Testament canon, which issues in a potentially fatal duality precisely as one seeks from the New Testament "the true gospel," the life-giving word that addresses us here and now. Seeking this transformative word, we encounter in the Synoptic Gospels a merely external history or biography, needlessly retold three times.

Following the Pauline model and rejecting the Synoptic one, Luther relocates the crucified and risen Christ within an account of believing existence, or "righteousness by faith." In that sense, we may say that he subordinates Christology to anthropology: for Christ is truly encountered only within the horizon of the believer's experience. It is by no means clear that Paul's texts are fundamentally misread here. Luther *rereads* Paul, radically reshaping the Pauline kerygma in a context quite different from its original one. At certain points, and from certain hermeneutical perspectives, one might wish to speak of a misreading. Yet this highly distinctive contextualizing of the risen Christ is no misreading but a realization of the semantic potential of Paul's own texts.[6]

Luther's theology of justification is the best known and most influential actualization of the canonical possibility of privileging Paul over the Gospels. Yet if it is correct to see this theology as realizing the texts' own semantic potential, this can hardly be the only such realization. Others before and after Luther have developed an anthropologically oriented theology in dialogue with Paul. In what follows, I shall consider an early and highly significant example of this interpretative move, occurring in *The Treatise on the Resurrection* (or *Epistle to Rheginus*), from the Jung Codex (Nag Hammadi Codex I).[7] Reflection on this ultra-Pauline text will prepare the ground for a critique of "Pauline" accounts of human existence in the light of the gospel.[8]

5. Luther, *Prefaces*, LW 35:365.
6. For further discussion of Luther, reading, and misreading, see my *Paul, Judaism, and the Gentiles: Beyond the New Perspective* (Grand Rapids: Eerdmans, 2007), especially the appendix.
7. Coptic text, with introduction, translation, and commentary by Malcolm L. Peel, in *The Coptic Gnostic Library: A Complete Edition of the Nag Hammadi Codices, I* (Leiden: Brill, 2000), 1:123-57, 2:137-215; hereafter *CGL I*. Translations of the treatise (hereafter cited as *TR*) are my own.
8. Richard Hays too is concerned with the disjunction between "subjectivizing" readings of Paul and the christological narrative, but he locates this disjunction in a different

The Spiritual Resurrection

The Treatise on the Resurrection displays a number of features that are typically labeled as "Gnostic." (Indeed, this text is widely held to be a product of "Valentinian Gnosticism.")[9] As a result of some original cosmic catastrophe, which here remains unspecified, the spirits of the elect have fallen from the divine realm of the Pleroma and have become entrapped in the alien realm of matter and the body, subject to hostile spiritual powers. The Savior therefore descends from the divine realm in order to communicate a saving revelation of the truth and to open up the way back to the Pleroma through his resurrection and ascension. In receiving this revelation, the elect become aware of their own origin and destiny as transcending their present embodied existence. This dualistic soteriology provides the framework for the author's exposition of the resurrection as "restoration (ΑΠΟΚΑΤΑϹΤΑϹΙϹ) to the Pleroma" (*TR* 44.31-32).[10] All this is characteristically, indeed classically, Gnostic — at least as this term has conventionally been understood.

Yet the term "Gnostic" is problematic if it is taken to imply that Christian language and motifs are here transplanted into a fundamentally alien context.[11] The author represents himself as one of "the philosophers of this

---

place. According to Hays, a christological narrative closely related to that of the Gospels belongs to the substratum of Paul's own theology; see especially Hays, *The Faith of Jesus Christ: The Narrative Substructure of Galatians 3:1–4:11,* 2nd ed. (Grand Rapids: Eerdmans, 2002). Thus, subjectivizing, anthropocentric readings of Paul fundamentally distort what the apostle intended to say. Although I read Paul differently from Hays (see his "Is Paul's Gospel Narratable?" *JSNT* 27 [2004]: 217-39, esp. pp. 236-39, and the exchange in *Pro Ecclesia* 16 [2007]: 126-40), there is theological common ground in the commitment to a narratively shaped Christology — though reached by different routes.

9. See Peel, *CGL I*, 1:133-35, 144-46. For a survey of Valentinianism, see Ismo Dunderberg, "The School of Valentinus," in *A Companion to Second-Century Christian "Heretics,"* ed. A. Marjanen and P. Luomanen (Leiden: Brill, 2005), pp. 64-99.

10. Greek loanwords such as ΑΠΟΚΑΤΑϹΤΑϹΙϹ constitute about a third of the vocabulary of this Coptic text, according to Peel (*CGL I*, 1:127).

11. The assumption that there is a distinct religious system know as "Gnosticism," independent of both Christianity and Judaism, is a legacy of the history-of-religion school — summed up in the title of Hans Jonas's classic work *The Gnostic Religion,* 2nd ed. (London: Routledge, 1992). On this premise, the appearance of recognizably Christian motifs within Gnostic texts will always represent a secondary "christianizing." Thus, with specific reference to *The Treatise on the Resurrection,* Hans-Georg Gaffron claims that the origins of Gnosis are to be found "in einer spezifischen, nicht ableitbaren Erfahrung des Daseins" and proceeds to ask: "Wie mögen Gnostiker . . . die christliche Botschaft von der Auferweckung Jesu Christi und der Auferweckung der Toten am Ende der Tage gehört haben?" Gaffron, "Eine

world" who nevertheless "believes" (46.8-9), yet, like other philosophically trained Christians of the second century, he aspires to write simply as a Christian.[12] Thus, in opposition to the suggestion that the resurrection is an illusion or fantasy (ϕαΝΤΑCΙΑ), he argues that "it is more fitting to call the world an illusion than the resurrection brought about by our Lord, the Savior Jesus Christ" (48.13-19). No non- or partially Christian author could have made such a claim. We may compare the equally arresting statement that opens Tertullian's treatise *On the Resurrection of the Flesh:* "The resurrection of the dead is the Christians' confidence: believing it makes us who we are."[13] The two authors (perhaps contemporaries) are at one in asserting the resurrection as the goal and meaning of the entire world process, in defiance of standard philosophical opinions. It is true that they disagree about what resurrection entails. The author to Rheginus develops the Pauline concept of a "spiritual resurrection" and rejects the (Platonic?) "psychical" resurrection and the (catholic) "fleshly" one (*TR* 45.39-46.2). The heavenly "flesh" of pleromatic existence will be quite different from the flesh of the present body (47.6-16). In contrast, Tertullian uncompromisingly affirms the resurrection of the present flesh, laboring long and hard to show that the apostolic claim that "flesh and blood cannot inherit the kingdom of God" (1 Cor. 15:50) is compatible with such a view (*Res.* 48-50).[14] For Tertullian, it is essential to assert the continuity of the present and future body — even though, as he acknowledges, many of our bodily organs will be redundant in the world to come. For the author to Rheginus, resurrection entails a sharp discontinuity between the present and the future body. The difference is

---

gnostische Apologie des Auferstehungsglaubens: Bemerkungen zur 'Epistula ad Rheginum,'" in *Die Zeit Jesu: Festschrift für Heinrich Schlier,* ed. G. Bornkamm and K. Rahner (Freiburg: Herder, 1970), pp. 218-27, quoting pp. 218, 219. It is assumed here that *The Treatise on the Resurrection* provides an answer to this question as to how the resurrection of Jesus will be understood, given a prior and continuing commitment to a *non-Christian* worldview.

12. I assume that in speaking of "one who believes among the philosophers who are in this world," the author is referring not just to "a particular believing philosopher" (Peel, *CGL I,* 2:169) but to himself.

13. Fiducia Christianorum resurrectio mortuorum: illam credentes hoc sumus (Tertullian, *Res.* 1.1); literally, ". . . believing the latter [i.e., the resurrection of the dead], we are the former [i.e., Christians]." For Latin text with translation, introduction, and commentary, see Ernest Evans, *Tertullian's Treatise on the Resurrection* (London: SPCK, 1960). Translations here are my own.

14. According to Tertullian, the analogy between Christ's resurrection and our own in 1 Corinthians 15 indicates that our own resurrection must be fleshly, as Christ's was. In v. 50, "flesh and blood" therefore has to do with moral conduct rather than physical constitution.

fundamental. Yet this difference has not come about because one of the two authors is an adherent of an alien religious system, that of Gnostic Christianity or Christian Gnosticism. From their own standpoints, both writers are Christians, and both agree that the resurrection of the dead is fundamental to the Christian confession.[15]

To a considerable extent, their difference is occasioned by divergent exegesis of the Pauline texts. Here, it is the so-called "gnostic" author who is at home with the Pauline concept of a "spiritual resurrection," at least as he himself understands it, whereas his "catholic" opponent is deeply embarrassed by it.[16] Introducing Paul's teaching on the resurrection, Tertullian initially claims that the apostle shares his own concern to maintain the identity of the present and future body:

> Since the proclamation of the previously unheard-of resurrection disturbed the Gentiles by its sheer novelty, and an understandable incredulity about such a thing began to torment faith with questions, the apostle took pains in virtually all his writings to strengthen faith in this hope, showing that this hope existed, that it was as yet unrealized, that it was corporeal (a point especially debated), and furthermore (most controversial of all) that this corporeality was none other than our own *(non aliter corporalem)*. *(Res.* 39.8)

Yet, in the very next sentence, Tertullian concedes that the apostle is not an entirely reliable ally:

> It is in no way surprising if counterarguments are drawn from these very writings [i.e., the Pauline texts], since we are told that "there must be heresies" — which could not be the case if the scriptures were not open to misunderstanding *(si non et perperam scripturae intellegi possent).* (40.1)[17]

---

15. Recent debate about the term "gnostic" suggests that it should be applied primarily to those who used it of themselves — as in the case of the "Gnostics" whom Irenaeus apparently distinguishes both from "Simonians" and from "the school of Valentinus" (*Haer.* 1.29.1, 31.3). On this see Alastair H. B. Logan, *The Gnostics: Identifying an Early Christian Cult* (London: T. & T. Clark, 2006), pp. 8-56. Logan further argues that Nag Hammadi Codex I (which contains *TR*) belongs to a group of codices (I, VII, and XI) comprising texts of a diverse character that stand apart from the "gnostic" mainstream of the library as a whole, which is centered on Sethian texts such as *The Apocryphon of John* and *The Gospel of the Egyptians* (pp. 22-23).

16. Compare N. T. Wright, *The Resurrection of the Son of God* (Minneapolis: Fortress, 2003), pp. 348-56.

17. The reference is to 1 Cor. 11:19 (δεῖ γὰρ καὶ αἱρέσεις εἶναι). The omission of ἐν ὑμῖν (also in D* F G lat Cyp Ambst) serves to generalize Paul's statement.

The heretics find support for their dualistic anthropology in Paul's distinctions between the "outer" and "inner" persons, respectively subject to decay and to renewal (2 Cor. 4:16); between the transitory body that is our earthly residence and the eternal body that awaits us in heaven (5:1-4); and between being "at home in the body" and "at home with the Lord" (5:6-8). Yet, Tertullian assures his readers, their arguments are specious. There is nothing in the disputed texts from 2 Corinthians (*Res.* 40-45), Romans (46-47), or 1 Corinthians (48-54) that compromises the authentic doctrine of the resurrection, which is that we shall be raised in our present bodies. In the last resort, however, it is only the Paraclete newly poured out on Christ's church who can dispel the ambiguities and obscurities of the scriptural texts and bring their true meaning to light (63.7). In the absence of the Paraclete, it can be conceded that Scripture has provided the heretics with "various materials" *(quasdam materias)* for their erroneous doctrines (63.8).

Heretical exegesis seeks to undermine the church's doctrine of the resurrection of the flesh by understanding the terms "death" and "resurrection" nonliterally. If the "death" in question is that of ignorance of God,

> then "resurrection" occurs when, in attaining the truth, one is reanimated and renewed by God, dispersing the death of ignorance and breaking forth from the tomb of the old humanity *(de sepulchro veteris hominis).* . . . It follows from this that people experience the resurrection by faith *(fide),* and are with the Lord when they put him on in baptism *(cum domino esse quem in baptismate induerint).* (19.4-5)

This summary of heretical teaching is replete with Pauline echoes. It is Paul himself who teaches that "we were buried with him through baptism into his death, so that . . . we might walk in newness of life" (Rom. 6:4; cf. Col. 2:12-13); that "our old humanity" died with Christ (Rom. 6:6); and that in baptism we "put on Christ" (Gal. 3:27; cf. Eph. 4:20-24; Col. 3:9-10). The objectionable nonliteral interpretation of death and resurrection stems from the apostle's own language. While Tertullian does not explicitly acknowledge this here, neither does he attempt to conceal it. Paul, it seems, is the root of the problem. Also to be noted is a further interpretative move, in which the heretics understand "resurrection" in connection with (physical) death, which is the soul's departure from the world, the realm of the dead (that is, of those who are ignorant of God), or from the body, the tomb of the soul (*Res.* 19.7). The resurrection is already anticipated in baptism, but it is fully realized only at physical death. Tertullian's opponents seem thoroughly familiar with the Pauline dialectic of "already" and "not yet."

This Pauline dialectic is fundamental to the understanding of resurrection proposed by the author to Rheginus. As in Paul, the dialectic is occasioned by Christology. The Savior, we are told, "swallowed up death," he "put aside the world which is perishing," he "raised himself up," thereby bestowing on us "the way of our immortality" (*TR* 45.14-23). The way of immortality is the way that leads out of this mortal world back to the eternal heavenly one, and it is the way of suffering and resurrection that Christ himself has undergone. Our way is also his, and his is ours: "Then indeed, as the apostle said, 'we suffered with him and rose with him and went to heaven with him'" (45.23-28). Underlying the Coptic verbs in this free citation are the characteristic Pauline συν- compounds. According to Romans 8:17, we co-suffer (συμπάσχομεν) with Christ; according to Ephesians 2:6, God co-raised us and co-seated us (συνήγειρεν καὶ συνεκάθισεν) in the heavenly places. What happened to Christ in his suffering, resurrection, and exaltation also happened to us, for the Savior is one with the saved. Yet, as the author proceeds to point out, the apostle's words have for us a primarily future application, referring us to the *post mortem* heavenward journey that is guaranteed by our present union with Christ:

> But if indeed we are revealed in this world as bearing him, we are his rays and are held fast by him until our setting — that is, our death in this life (ʙιοϲ) — and are drawn by him to heaven, as rays are by the sun. . . . This is the spiritual resurrection (ⲧ-ⲁⲛⲁⲥⲧⲁⲥⲓⲥ ⲛ̄-ⲡⲛⲉⲩⲙⲁⲧⲓⲕⲏ) which swallows up the psychical [resurrection] (ⲛ̄-ⲧ-ⲯⲩⲭⲓⲕⲏ) just as it does the fleshly one (ⲧ-ⲕⲉ-ⲥⲁⲣⲕⲓⲕⲏ). (45.28-46.2)

Christ is the sun whose rays make him manifest even in this dark world; we are the rays whom Christ will retract into himself at the moment of *our* setting (and not his). This slightly confused image makes its point about the identity of the Savior with the saved precisely in the confusion between the rays and the sun itself. Whereas for Tertullian the sun and its rays image the unity-in-distinction of the Father and the Son, the author to Rheginus traces here the consubstantiality of Christ and his elect.[18] Paul too can speak of the elect as participating in "the glory of the Lord" and as "transformed from glory to glory" (2 Cor. 3:18); and he too can find a parallel between the glory

18. For Tertullian's application of sun and ray to inner-trinitarian relations, see his *Prax.* 8.5-7.

of the sun and that of the resurrection (cf. 1 Cor. 15:41-43). That the author to Rheginus still has Paul in mind is evident from his reference to a spiritual as opposed to a psychical or fleshly resurrection, echoing Paul's insistence that the resurrection body is spiritual rather than psychical (1 Cor. 15:44-46, where the distinction occurs four times in three verses). "This is the spiritual resurrection" indicates that the image of the sun and its rays represent the author's exegesis of a well-known Pauline theme.

This spiritual resurrection "swallows up" the psychical and fleshly resurrections. The verb, which the author uses on four occasions,[19] is Pauline in origin (1 Cor. 15:54; 2 Cor. 5:4) and may suggest that the spiritual resurrection somehow transcends alternative accounts of resurrection as confined to the ϕγχн or to the flesh. Thus, the author does not simply reject fleshliness or bodiliness, any more than Paul does. He has learned from Paul that "not all flesh is the same flesh," and that "there are heavenly bodies and there are earthly bodies" (1 Cor. 15:39-40). There is an earthly flesh that was bestowed on us at our entry into this world, and there is also a heavenly flesh that will be bestowed on us at our return to the Pleroma:

> For if you existed without flesh and received flesh when you came into this world, why should you not receive flesh if you ascend into the Aeon? (*TR* 47.4-8)[20]

Like Paul, this author seeks "not to be unclothed but to be further clothed, so that what is mortal may be swallowed up by life" (2 Cor. 5:4). This bestowal of an ethereal flesh appropriate to the heavenly realm corresponds to the formation within us of a spiritual body analogous to the physical one: for "the visible members are dead and will not be saved, since it is the living mem[ber]s which are within them that will rise" (*TR* 47.38-48.3). As Paul put it, "if our outward humanity is being destroyed, our inner humanity is being renewed day by day" (2 Cor. 4:16). This spiritual resurrection, prepared even now, is illustrated by the teaching of the Gospel that on the Mount of Transfiguration

19. *TR* 45.14, 19-20; 46.1; 49.3-4.

20. In contrast, Bentley Layton ascribes the affirmation of fleshly resurrection in this passage to a hypothetical objector and translates it as follows: "Now (you might wrongly suppose), granted you did not preexist in flesh — indeed, you took on flesh when you entered this world — why will you not take your flesh with you when you return to the realm of eternity?" *The Gnostic Scriptures* (New York: Doubleday, 1987), p. 322; see also his *Gnostic Treatise on Resurrection from Nag Hammadi*, HDR 12 (Missoula, Mont.: Scholars Press, 1979), pp. 77-85. But there seems no reason to insert a hypothetical objector at this point.

"Elijah appeared and Moses with him" (*TR* 48.6-10).[21] The thought is presumably that Elijah and Moses were identifiable from their appearance, even though they were spiritual rather than earthly beings. They must therefore have had a flesh and a body corresponding to their spirituality.[22]

The spiritual resurrection is not yet, since it is a *post mortem* occurrence. As we have seen, however, the apostle taught that we have *already* risen with Christ and gone to heaven with him (45.25-28). What did he mean by this? In Romans 6, Paul states that "if we died with Christ, we believe (πιστεύομεν) that we shall also live with him, knowing that Christ being raised will no longer die . . ." (Rom. 6:8-9). Similarly, the author to Rheginus confesses: "We have known the Son of man, and we have believed (ⲁ-ⲣ̄-ⲡⲓⲥⲧⲉⲩⲉ) that he rose from the dead" (*TR* 46.14-17). For Paul, this interim period between Christ's resurrection and our own makes it possible and necessary for us to "consider ourselves dead to sin and alive to God in Christ Jesus" (Rom. 6:11). Once again, Paul's language and conceptuality are faithfully echoed by the author to Rheginus. The addressee is not to "live according to this flesh" (ⲡⲟⲗⲓⲧⲉⲩⲉⲥⲑⲁⲓⲕⲁⲧⲁ ⲧⲉⲉⲓ-ⲥⲁⲣⲝ), and must flee from the chains and fetters that bind him to this world: and so, "already (ⲏⲁⲏ) you have the resurrection" (*TR* 49.11-16). This recalls the (presumably fictitious) reference to Hymenaeus and Philetus, who falsely assert that "the resurrection has already (ἤδη) occurred" (2 Tim. 2:17-18). The parallel has led to the conclusion that the author to Rheginus is guilty of promoting an "over-realized eschatology."[23] Yet in speaking of the resurrection as "already" as well as "not yet," the author remains dependent on Paul. In his gloss on "already you have the resurrection," the Pauline exhortation to "consider yourselves . . . alive to God in Christ Jesus" is fused with the Hellenistic commonplace about living in the certainty of death:

> For if the person who is going to die knows of himself that he will die (for even if he passes many years in this life [ⲃⲓⲟⲥ], he will be brought to this), why do you not consider yourself as risen, and you will be brought to this? (*TR* 49.16-24)

---

21. The priority here given to Elijah over Moses recalls Mark 9:4 (contrast Matt. 17:3; Luke 9:30).

22. It is perhaps in response to some such appeal to the transfiguration story that Tertullian asserts that Moses and Elijah appeared in bodily form (*Res.* 55.10).

23. Thus Peel, *CGL I*, 1:144, argues that in this text "[t]he Pauline 'eschatological reservation' . . . has dissolved, with resurrection of all the faithful at the end-time being replaced with individually-experienced resurrection in the now."

This appropriation of Paul's teaching represents an "over-realized eschatology" only from the standpoint of Tertullian's hostility to nonliteral resurrection language. Here and throughout his letter, the author to Rheginus shows himself to be the apostle's faithful disciple.

As in Paul, the author's primary anthropological focus entails a Christology that corresponds precisely to the requirements of the human condition. There is the closest possible match between plight and solution, between what is needed and what is provided. Christ is who he needs to be if he is to help us, and nothing more or other than that. Paul emphasizes that Christ enters fully into our fallen situation, emptying himself and taking the form of a slave, being born under the law and in the likeness of sinful flesh (cf. Phil. 2:7; Gal. 4:4; Rom. 8:3). Similarly, the author to Rheginus acknowledges that the Lord lived "in flesh" (ϨⲚ ⲤⲀⲢⲌ) and "in this place where you remain" (*TR* 44.14-19). His being "under the law" comes to expression in his "speaking of the law of nature (Ⲡ-ⲚⲞⲘⲞⲤ Ⲛ-Ⲧ-ⲪⲨⲤⲒⲤ), which I regard as death" (44.19-21). Here, the Pauline association between the Mosaic law and death has been extended to the law of nature; Christ's "speaking of" this death-dealing law may reflect Synoptic traditions implying opposition between Christ and law, but it is also an expression of the κένωσις. There is no trace here of docetism. As Son of God and Son of man, the Savior possesses both humanity and divinity: it is by virtue of his divinity that he has the power to overcome death, whereas it is by virtue of his humanity that he brings about the restoration to the Pleroma (44.21-33). The author draws here on a tradition going back to Ignatius of Antioch, according to which the "Son of man" title emphasizes Christ's solidarity with ourselves, whereas "Son of God" emphasizes his uniqueness.[24] Yet "Son of man" is also associated here with an existence that predates the cosmos. As Son of man, Christ is able to restore us to the Pleroma "because he was at the first from heaven, a seed (ⲤⲠⲈⲢⲘⲀ) of truth before this structure (ⲤⲨⲤⲦⲀⲤⲒⲤ) came into being" (44.33-36). The author here paraphrases the Pauline assertion that "he is before all things" (Col. 1:17a).[25]

What is the connection between Christ's preexistence and his role as Savior? Does the apostle assert any such link? According to the author to Rheginus, Paul's concept of preexistence is to be connected to his under-

24. The Son of God/Son of man parallel occurs in Ignatius, *Eph.* 20.2; Justin, *Dial. Try.* 100.3-4; and frequently in Irenaeus (e.g., *Haer.* 3.10.2; 16.3, 7; 17.1; 18.3-4; 19.1-2).

25. That Colossians and Ephesians are probably "deutero-Pauline" is of no significance for the early history of interpretation, for which these are Pauline texts.

standing of the predestination of the elect. Our eternal well-being is assured on the grounds that

> we are chosen for salvation and redemption, predestined from the beginning not to fall into the folly of those without knowledge. (*TR* 46.25-29)

Once again, echoes of Pauline texts are clearly perceptible. The Thessalonians are told that "God did not appoint you to wrath but to attain salvation through our Lord Jesus Christ," and that "God chose you as first fruits for salvation" (1 Thess. 5:9; 2 Thess. 2:13). If the association of election and salvation echoes the Thessalonian correspondence, the association of election and predestination derives from Ephesians, which tells how God "chose us in [Christ] before the foundation of the world . . . , predestining us to sonship through Jesus Christ" (Eph. 1:4-5). If we are chosen and predestined "from the beginning," then we must presumably resemble Christ in *existing* "from the beginning," prior to the coming into being of the cosmos. In that case, Christ's own preexistence is fundamental to the solidarity with us whereby he becomes our Savior. The preexistence of the Savior corresponds to the preexistence of the elect, and it is a Pauline rather than a Platonic logic that underlies this correspondence.

Whether or not such a view was held by Paul himself (or by the author of Ephesians), the Pauline texts are clearly open to such a reading. In advocating a predestination without preexistence, Augustine and Calvin are not necessarily better readers of Paul than is the author to Rheginus. Arguably, this author has penetrated more deeply into the substance of Paul's thought than the later theologians, in taking the Pauline concept of participation in Christ to its logical conclusions and in giving full weight to the affinity between Christ and the elect. Again in contrast to later theologians, the author to Rheginus has noted that resurrection lies at the heart of Pauline theology, and he remains faithful to this insight as he develops his own theological position. Far from articulating an alien "Gnostic" conceptuality, this text is an impressive and creative reenactment of fundamental Pauline concerns — expressed, of course, in an idiom and a conceptuality that do not exactly reproduce Paul's own. It is a remarkably pure exercise in "Paulinism," that is, a theology that gives priority to the Pauline texts over the rest of canonical Scripture.[26] In proceeding from this methodological decision, *The Treatise*

---

26. Contra the claim of Layton, *Gnostic Treatise on Resurrection*, p. 5, that the "biblical parallels" in *The Treatise on the Resurrection* "are parallels of language, rarely touching upon fundamental structures of the author's thought."

on the Resurrection exemplifies a theological tendency that can be traced all the way from Marcion to Bultmann.

The question is whether this theological tendency is to be welcomed and approved. Tertullian thought not. Paul, he argues in opposition to Marcion, possesses no independent authority. While Paul himself claims that his apostleship is from no human source but directly from Jesus Christ (cf. Gal. 1:1), we can hardly take this at face value:

> Obviously anyone can make a claim about himself, but his claim can only be validated by the authority of another. One person signs, another countersigns; one person seals, another records. No one is both his own proposer and witness. (*Marc.* 5.1.3)[27]

According to Tertullian, it is essential to recognize that Paul became a disciple after the others. In his encounter with the risen Christ on the Damascus road, he became a disciple of necessity and not of his own free choice — and that at a time when the Twelve were already exercising their various missions. Paul, therefore, has no authority of his own, independent of the earlier apostles and the faith they preached:

> Even if Marcion had produced his gospel under the name of Paul himself, this single document would not be adequate for faith without the support of earlier authorities *(destituta patrocinio antecessorum)*. There would still be lacking that gospel which Paul himself found already in existence, to which he gave credence, and to which he so much wished his own to conform that he went up to Jerusalem to meet and consult the apostles, lest he should have run in vain — that is, lest he had believed otherwise than they did *(non secundum illos)* and had preached otherwise than they did. (*Marc.* 4.2.4-5)

It is in the canonical Gospels that the authentic apostolic gospel is to be found — and, in the context of this argument, especially in the Gospels of Matthew, Mark, and John, rejected by Marcion. It would be quite wrong to exalt the authority of Paul's texts over the canonical Gospels, for it is Paul himself who needs external validation (cf. Gal. 2:1-2).

Paul's subjection to the earlier apostles is, however, a less striking theme in Galatians 2 than his resistance to them in Antioch, where Cephas (di-

---

27. Latin text and translation, Ernest Evans, *Tertullian Adversus Marcionem* (Oxford: Clarendon, 1972). Translations here are my own.

rectly) and James (indirectly) are accused of failing to maintain the truth of the gospel (v. 14). Marcion finds in this incident a proof and illustration of Pauline priority over the apostolic Gospels:

> Marcion has obtained Paul's letter to the Galatians — where he rebukes the apostles themselves for failing to walk in line with the truth of the gospel, while accusing certain pseudo-apostles of perverting the gospel of Christ — and strives to undermine the status of those gospels which are given out as genuine and under the names of apostles or apostolic persons *(apostolicorum)*, claiming for his own gospel the trustworthiness that he denies to the others. (*Marc.* 4.3.2)

According to Marcion, the Gospels attributed to the first apostles (Matthew and John) or to their followers (Mark) are inherently untrustworthy — for the apostles are accused of failing to maintain the truth of the gospel — and are subject to further corruption by false apostles. The argument assumes that Pauline statements about errors in relation to the gospel (Gal. 1:7; 2:14) can be applied to the gospel in its written form. Thus, Galatians 2 becomes a charter for Pauline priority over the apostolic Gospels. Tertullian counters this reading by insisting that Paul's rebuke relates to conduct, not doctrine, and that he himself later practiced a similar sensitivity to Jewish scruples, becoming "a Jew to the Jews" (1 Cor. 9:20) just as Peter did at Antioch.[28]

The Treatise on the Resurrection is not a Marcionite text. Yet Tertullian would no doubt have seen in it a similar methodological error to the one he finds in Marcion: the error of isolating Paul from the other apostolic witnesses, and then pressing his ambiguous language toward radical and heterodox conclusions.

An Eclipse of Gospel Narrative

If we assume with Tertullian and other patristic theologians that the fourfold canonical Gospel is foundational to the New Testament witness, then theologies based on the assumption of Pauline precedence will seem inherently problematic. The Paulinism of the author to Rheginus can serve to illustrate the problems in question.

The author's Paulinism extends to the literary form of his text, which

---

28. *Marc.* 1.20.2-3; 4.3.3-4; 5.3.7.

uses epistolary format to communicate matters of fundamental concern (note the insistence that the subject matter is "an essential," ΟΥ-ΑΝΑΓΚΑΙΟΝ, *TR* 44.7).[29] While the standard epistolary opening is absent, a specific addressee is named at the outset and at three further points distributed evenly throughout the text:

- There are some, my son Rheginus, who are eager to learn many things . . . (43.25)
- Now the Son of God, Rheginus, was the Son of Man . . . (44.22)
- So then (ϨѠϹⲦⲈ), have no doubt about the resurrection, my son Rheginus . . . (47.3)
- So then (ϨѠϹⲦⲈ), do not think in part, O Rheginus . . . (49.10)

In the first passage, Rheginus is contrasted with those non-Christian inquirers into philosophical truth who know nothing of the resurrection. The author is writing in response to Rheginus's own request, and his relationship to his addressee constitutes the framework for his treatise on the resurrection. Thus, in the second passage, the addressee is named again as the author establishes the christological basis for his position. In the third and fourth passages, the author's dogmatic arguments are shown to be directly relevant to the addressee — an indication that the epistolary form is no mere convention but belongs to the substance of what this text seeks to communicate. Addressed to Rheginus, it has to do with how he is to think and live in the light of the resurrection — along with the other "sons" whom, at the close of the letter, the author includes within the scope of his address (50.1-16).

For this author, then, epistolary form is the appropriate vehicle for discourse on a topic of fundamental importance. Resurrection stands at the heart of Christian faith, for Christianity is nothing other than faith in the resurrection; and this faith is most appropriately articulated in the context of the present shared reality of author and addressee. This conjunction of literary form and theological content has profound implications for the manner in which the content is understood. While resurrection is rooted in the past, the time when the Lord lived in flesh and revealed himself as Son of God (44.13-17), and while it directs us to the future, when the return to the Pleroma is completed (47.6-8), it is the shared present of author and addressee that constitutes the horizon within which resurrection is to be understood. The past and future of resurrection are defined by their relation to

29. For a survey of views on the genre of this text, see Peel, *CGL I*, 1:128-30.

this present. While this bias toward the believer's existence in the present is a consequence of the text's epistolary form, we cannot conclude from this that the author's articulation of resurrection is *limited by* the epistolary form, as though he might have spoken quite differently had he chosen to present this theme within some other genre. Form and content cannot be so easily prized apart: it is not that the content is accommodated to the form but rather that the form is determined by the content. The horizon of the resurrection is the shared present of author and addressee, and this is so not because the author writes on this topic in the form of a letter but because the letter is the appropriate vehicle for an understanding of resurrection from the perspective of a shared present.

It is the Pauline letter collection that makes it possible for the later author to write his treatise on the resurrection in the form of a letter, and so to understand resurrection in the context of believing existence in the present. "Paulinism" — the hermeneutical privileging of the Pauline texts — is always characterized by this anthropocentric bias toward the present, so that every statement about Jesus the Son of God must demonstrate its value *pro me*. In the canonical Gospels, however, it is never the case that Jesus becomes a predicate of "my" present. Here, Jesus' identity is shaped by *his* present, which — like every present — is shared with others and yet limited by specific spatiotemporal coordinates. Jesus' life unfolds within a particular time and place that is *not* ours. If, through his resurrection, he is no longer *limited* by these coordinates and is free to be with us always, to the close of the age, that does not mean that the coordinates are simply obliterated. The Jesus who is with us always (Matt. 28:20) is none other than the Jesus whose life story Matthew and the other evangelists narrate.[30] Jesus does not leave that life story behind like a discarded husk, for it remains constitutive of who he is precisely as the one who has been raised. Or so the canonical Gospels would lead us to believe, in speaking of the one who lives by way of a narrative of what took place long ago in Galilee and Judea.

In contrast, a Pauline hermeneutic might — outside the canonical context — lead to a different understanding of resurrection, more closely aligned with that of the author to Rheginus. Here, the resurrection of Jesus will be assimilated to the experience of resurrection realized or anticipated in the lives of believers. In the absence of the canonical Gospel narrative, it is the experience of salvation that provides the hermeneutical key to Jesus'

---

30. On this, see Ronald F. Thiemann, *Revelation and Theology: The Gospel as Narrated Promise* (Notre Dame: University of Notre Dame Press, 1985), p. 143.

identity as the one who lives. Conversely, it is the pattern of Jesus' death and resurrection that shapes and determines the believers' experience of salvation. Christology and anthropology are indistinguishable as the distinct identities of Jesus and his followers are merged and become one: "As the apostle said, 'We suffered with him and rose with him and went to heaven with him'" (*TR* 45.24-28). The identities of Redeemer and redeemed are assimilated to one another: what is true of him is also true of us, and what is true of us is also true of him. The author to Rheginus faithfully reproduces the logic of the Pauline understanding of salvation.

This is an *assimilation* of identities, and not a one-sided projection of an experience of salvation into Christology. It would be quite wrong to conclude from the author to Rheginus that Christ has become a mere cipher for the experience of salvation, lacking a substantial being of his own. This author is no less convinced of the prior and foundational reality of Christ than Paul himself is.[31] As in the Philippians hymn, the author can on occasion speak of this reality independently of our participation in it:

> The Son of God . . . was Son of Man, and embraced both identities, possessing humanity along with divinity, so that he might overcome death in his capacity as Son of God, and as Son of Man achieve restoration to the Pleroma. (44.21-33)

When the author proceeds to cite the Pauline teaching that "we suffered with him and rose with him and went to heaven with him," it is ostensibly our identity that is conformed to Christ's, and not the reverse. Yet if this conformation or assimilation is to take place, Christ's identity must itself be construed in such a way as to make it possible for the elect to participate in it, and to derive from it their own transcendent identity. The assimilation of identities requires the removal of all particularities that might distinguish the Redeemer from the redeemed. Thus, his earthly life loses its distinctive features and is characterized in abstractly inclusive terms as an existence "in flesh" (44.15) that transpired "in this place (ΤΟΠΟΣ) where you remain" (44.18-19): Christ and his own share in an alienated physical constitution

---

31. Contrast the view of Gaffron, "Gnostische Apologie," according to whom this text "kennt keine qualitative Differenz . . . zwischen Erlöser und Erlösten," to such an extent that "[d]er nach seiner Identität suchende Mensch bleibt auf sich selbst gewiesen" (p. 227). Even where the author explicitly appeals to Paul, "[d]ie zeitliche und christologische Distanz, die das paulinische 'Mit-Christus' kennzeichnete, ist hier zugunsten einer Identifikation aufgegeben" (pp. 222-23).

within an equally alienated environment, and this emphasis on what is shared entails the suppression of what is distinctive and particular to each. The suppression is structurally necessary if the assimilation of identities is to occur. If Paul's christological statements show little awareness of the distinctive characteristics of the historical Jesus, the reason is not that these things were already well known to his congregations and did not need to be repeated.[32] The explanation is rather that Paul has only limited use for statements about Jesus that cannot be extended to incorporate ourselves. Admittedly, such statements do occur. Jesus was raised "on the third day" and "appeared to Cephas, then to the twelve" (1 Cor. 15:4-5). At such points, there is no analogy between Jesus and ourselves. Yet Jesus' resurrection derives its significance entirely from the analogy: for in his resurrection he becomes "life-giving spirit," so that "*as* is the man from heaven, *so* are those who are of heaven" (15:45, 48). *The Treatise on the Resurrection* is the product of prolonged meditation on this Pauline teaching.

In the canonical Gospels as in Paul, Jesus' identity is constituted above all by his resurrection. He is the one who lives, and we are not to seek the living one among the dead (Luke 24:5) — as though he were a mere figure of the past alongside others. Yet the Gospels make it clearer than Paul does that the resurrection in question is indeed the resurrection *of Jesus* — that is, of the bearer of that name who is also the subject of their narrative. The one whom God raised on Easter Day was "Jesus of Nazareth" (cf. Acts 4:10). The Gospels imply that the particularity of this event is *integral* to its universal significance and not a potential threat to it.[33] In Paul, however, the process of abstracting the event from its particularity is already far advanced, for only so can the identities of Christ and his own be assimilated to one another. It is true that Paul retains the name "Jesus," representing the individual identity. Similarly, the author to Rheginus can speak of "our Lord the

32. This well-known, commonsensical view is ably restated by J. D. G. Dunn, in his *Theology of Paul the Apostle* (Grand Rapids: Eerdmans, 1998), pp. 182-95. Dunn concludes that "knowledge of and interest in the life and ministry of Jesus was an integral part of his theology, albeit referred to only *sotto voce* in his written theology" (p. 195). Paul's "written theology" is, of course, the only Pauline theology still extant.

33. As Karl Barth argues, in *Church Dogmatics* III/2 (ET Edinburgh: T. & T. Clark, 1960): "It is as a man of His time, and not otherwise, that [Jesus] is the Lord of time. We should lose Jesus as the Lord of all time if we ignored Him as a man in His own time. It is in this history — the history which is inseparable from his temporality — that the man Jesus lives and is the eternal salvation of all men in their different times" (pp. 440-41). For Barth, it is his resurrection that discloses that "even as a man in His time Jesus is the Lord of all time" (p. 441).

Savior, Jesus Christ" (*TR* 48.18-19), "my Lord Jesus Christ" (49.38-50.1). Both writers can conceive of Christ as an individual who stands over against them, and not only as the bearer of a representative identity in which they have come to participate. Yet in both cases the process of abstraction is far advanced, to the extent that the particular identities not only of Jesus but also of his followers are subsumed within an abstract comprehensiveness. Jesus and Rheginus alike are deprived of their historicity, for historicity is precisely the condition from which they need to be liberated.

The author to Rheginus is an early exponent of "Paulinism," a term that can be applied to any theology that assigns foundational status to the Pauline texts at the expense of the Gospels and indeed the rest of Scripture. In certain respects, Paulinism may represent a misunderstanding of Paul — above all, in its persistent tendency to marginalize the role of scriptural interpretation in Pauline discourse.[34] Yet one should not be too quick to accuse the author to Rheginus or Marcion or later Paulinists of a mere "misunderstanding" of the apostle. What they have understood of Paul they have understood profoundly, even as they adapt it to social and intellectual contexts quite different from Paul's own.

As Tertullian rightly saw, the hermeneutical issue is most starkly illustrated by the autobiographical narrative of Galatians 2. Here Paul claims that even apostles, the revered disciples of the earthly Jesus, can misrepresent the truth of the gospel. Does this claim warrant the application of a "hermeneutic of suspicion" to the whole of non-Pauline Scripture, an insistence that this Scripture must conform to Pauline norms if its authoritative status is to be validated? Or are we to minimize the significance of the Galatians narrative, appealing instead to Paul's acknowledgement elsewhere that "whether it was I or they," the same gospel was preached (1 Cor. 15:11)? If, with Tertullian, we prefer the latter course, we are still compelled to admit that the Pauline texts themselves lend some credence to the alternative point of view. In a certain sense, Paulinism is indeed truly and radically Pauline.

Yet a canonical resolution of this difficulty is not far to seek. As the four-fold canonical Gospel already indicates, the gospel itself cannot be exclusively identified with any one of its literary embodiments. "The gospel" is never simply "the gospel of Jesus Christ" (in spite of Mark 1:1); it is always

---

34. For this crucially important point, see Richard B. Hays's groundbreaking *Echoes of Scripture in the Letters of Paul* (New Haven/London: Yale University Press, 1989); also, my own *Paul and the Hermeneutics of Faith* (London/New York: T. & T. Clark, 2004).

"the gospel according to . . ." The point applies to Paul no less than to Matthew, Mark, Luke, and John. Here too the relation between gospel and text is an indirect one, since the gospel of the risen Jesus can never be articulated on the basis of exegesis alone. Pauline exegesis may or may not lead to Paulinism, but Paulinism is not the gospel.

Faith, Virtue, Justification, and the Journey to Freedom

N. T. Wright

Introduction

The first time I met Richard Hays was at the Annual Meeting of the Society of Biblical Literature in Dallas, Texas, in December 1983. Dallas was having an ice storm at the time, but we were warm and safe in a huge hotel, along with thousands of other scholars, reading papers to one another and, equally important, making friends in the margins of the meetings. Richard read his (now well-known) paper on Romans 4:1, which I instantly recognized as solving the notorious translation problem in that verse and raising important questions about the reading of the whole chapter, questions that he and I have continued to explore in dialogue.[1] I introduced myself, and within minutes we were sitting in a cafe with a couple of expensive gin and tonics and, again equally important, open Greek Testaments. We were talking, particularly, about faith. Thus it began; thus it has continued. And thus, nearly a quarter of a century later, I come to be writing about faith as a small tribute, expressive of heartfelt thanks, to a great friend and a great scholar.[2]

We did not, however, talk in those days about faith as a virtue. "Virtue" was not a topic that Pauline scholars even considered back then, except per-

---

1. See Richard B. Hays, "Have We Found Abraham to Be Our Forefather According to the Flesh? A Reconsideration of Rom 4:1," *NovT* 27 (1985): 76-98; N. T. Wright, *Romans, NIB* 10 (Nashville: Abingdon, 2002), p. 489.

2. An earlier version of this paper was given as a lecture at the Priory of the Assumption, Bethnal Green, London, on February 8, 2007. I am grateful to my hosts on that occasion for warm hospitality and fascinating discussion.

haps in a sidelong allusion to "virtue lists" at certain points in the letters.[3] It is fair to say that the very idea of "virtue" would have at once aroused suspicions. This might be, after all, a way of smuggling in "works" by the back door, into Paul's soteriology (something we Paulinists are trained to watch out for, like sniffer dogs at an airport ready to detect the slightest whiff of hard drugs). And since one of the many things that Richard Hays and I had had in common from our early theological formation was an anxiety about some readings of Paul in which, it seemed to us both independently, "faith" might actually become a "work" in the sense of something a person does to earn God's favor, the idea of faith itself as a "virtue" would have seemed highly suspicious to us both.[4] (There is an irony in this. We were both conscious of thereby taking a more "Reformed" line, over against a prevailing "Lutheran" reading of faith, and insisting on the importance of grace. Yet it is from the "Reformed" camp that a good deal of criticism has come against the lines of thought that we have both subsequently pursued.)

Since then a good deal has changed, not so much at this point within the world of Pauline scholarship but rather in the world of current ethical discourse. Virtue has been making a comeback, not least among Richard Hays's colleagues at Duke Divinity School. Within an overall understanding of Christian life as generated and sustained by God's grace (in other words, ruling out from the start any suggestion that the "virtue" we are going to talk about is something that "we do" through self-effort, still less self-justification), thinkers like Stanley Hauerwas, Gregory Jones, and Samuel Wells have explored Christian behavior in ways that, though ancient enough in themselves, have until recently been dormant.[5] Christian behavior, they have insisted, is more than merely the "automatic" way in which Spirit-filled people find themselves acting, more than merely a Spirit-driven obedience to *this* moral precept in *this* situation, but instead more like what Paul him-

3. E.g., Col. 3:12-15.

4. See especially, of course, Richard B. Hays, *The Faith of Jesus Christ: The Narrative Substructure of Galatians 3:1–4:11,* 2nd ed. (Grand Rapids: Eerdmans, 2002 [1983]).

5. See, e.g., among many others, Stanley Hauerwas and Charles Pinches, *Christians among the Virtues: Theological Conversations with Ancient and Modern Ethics* (Notre Dame: University of Notre Dame Press, 1997); Samuel Wells, *Improvisation: The Drama of Christian Ethics* (Grand Rapids: Brazos, 2004); L. Gregory Jones, *Embodying Forgiveness: A Theological Analysis* (Grand Rapids: Eerdmans, 1995). A useful summary of recent work on virtue in the context of its classical background is Jean Porter, "Virtue Ethics," in *The Cambridge Companion to Christian Ethics,* ed. R. Gill (Cambridge: Cambridge University Press, 2001), pp. 96-111. A good deal of this work looks back with appreciation to Alasdair MacIntyre, *After Virtue: A Study in Moral Theory,* 2nd ed. (London: Duckworth, 1985 [1981]).

self calls δοκιμή, "character" in the sense of "a well-formed character, a tried and tested personality": a life formed by a long succession of choices that have become habit-forming, choices that are often difficult to make, and often involve pain and suffering, but choices that have enabled people eventually to exhibit a deep Christlikeness, structural and not merely on the surface.[6] This, broadly, is the discourse of "virtue," and in my judgment, as an interested onlooker of contemporary ethical discussions, it is potentially enormously fruitful.

But why *faith* as a "virtue"? To return to the anxious Paulinist: is this not just what we suspected? Might this not imply after all that faith itself, the faith by which we are justified, is something that we have to "work at," to generate from within? But at this point the theological tradition insists: in addition to the "cardinal virtues" of temperance, courage, justice, and prudence, some of the greatest ever Christian thinkers have added the "theological virtues" listed by Paul himself, not only in 1 Corinthians 13, but in other passages as well, indicating that he already thought of them as, in some sense, a set.[7] And my intention in this paper is to offer some creative reflections on how a Pauline scholar might reinhabit this tradition of "virtue" discourse, and perhaps even refresh it from its putative scriptural origins.[8] In doing so I am hoping, as it were, to throw a bridge across into the area of ethics and moral theology that Richard Hays has made his own but in which I have published almost nothing. One of the (to me) interesting and unresolved questions within our long friendship has been why Richard has moved on from Paul to ethics while I have moved on (back?) from Paul to Jesus. Perhaps this venture of mine into his field will tempt Richard to try his hand, in return, in the study of Jesus . . .

I. Virtue and Eschatology

Many discussions of virtue, and many discussions of faith, begin from where we presently are, as muddled, sinful, half-believing human beings, and explore the ways in which virtue (including "faith" in some sense) can help us move forward to become the people God wants and intends us to

6. On δοκιμή in Paul, cf., e.g., Rom. 5:4; 14:18; 2 Cor. 2:9; 10:18; Phil. 2:22.

7. 1 Cor. 13:13; Col. 1:4-5; 1 Thess. 1:3; 5:8.

8. I find, in rereading the paper at editorial stage, that I have subconsciously echoed various themes from Hays's seminal paper on 1 Corinthians, "The Conversion of the Imagination," now published in the book of that title (Grand Rapids: Eerdmans, 2005), pp. 1-24.

become. In this, as in many areas of theological exploration, I find it helpful to start instead from the far end, from the ultimate goal. I propose that we begin with the picture of what God intends us to be, and has promised that we shall be, and to work back from there to where we are. This is, I suppose, rather like the procedure adopted by some management consultants: to ask where the company ought to be twenty years from now, to imagine that we are already at that moment of presumed or anticipated success, and then to ask the question, How did we get here? What steps did we take on the way?

If that is the shape of my account, much of the raw material for reflection will be drawn from the Scriptures. Obviously, in the discussion of virtue both in general and in particular there is an enormous tradition stretching from Augustine through Aquinas to many interesting discussions in the modern period. But, though I am aware of the broad outline of this tradition, it has not been my specialty, and I hope that what I have to offer as scripturally based reflection will bring a fresh contribution to that tradition rather than a reevaluation of some part of it from within. And, as is perhaps predictable given the subject, my own specializations, and my desire to engage Richard Hays yet one more time, I will draw particularly on St. Paul.

To work back from the future that God intends for us is actually suggested already by the classic accounts of virtue. Aristotle spoke of the goal or end, the *telos*, of human moral behavior. We are on a journey toward that point, which he called εὐδαιμονία. That has normally been translated as "happiness"; but the meaning Aristotle had in mind was not the one that word often suggests in today's Western world (the feeling of contentment or pleasurable excitement) but the more organic one of becoming our full and true selves, discovering in practice the best and highest activity of which humans are capable. The virtues are the particular "strengths" (that is the meaning of the Latin word *virtus*) that enable us to grow into that full being, to advance toward that eventual goal. Taking the word "goal" in its obvious current sporting usage, the virtues are like the different skills that different soccer players possess (passing, tackling, dribbling, shooting, and so on), which are all aimed, eventually, at getting the ball into the net.

But Aristotle's description of that goal, not least in terms of "reason" as the highest human faculty (so that the highest goal is the clearest and best use of reason), is of course challenged by the early Christian writings. There, again and again, we find the New Testament writers emphasizing instead love, ἀγάπη, as the highest activity, the one that binds everything else together.[9] They speak of this "love" as the fruit, not of unaided human effort, but of two things: the work of grace of the creator God, and the individual human response to that grace, which consists of faith. And one of the key questions we thus have to consider in thinking of Christian faith as in some sense a "virtue" is the extent to which, once you add the "theological" Christian virtues of faith, hope, and love to the "cardinal" virtues of temperance, courage, justice, and prudence, the notion of "virtue" itself has subtly but deeply changed. But since within the ancient Hebraic worldview, and particularly within its Christian offshoot, the notion of a journey toward a goal remains central and vital, giving us a picture of an unfinished story whose intended conclusion can nevertheless be glimpsed, we can take Aristotle's idea of *telos*, and of the virtues as the steps by which we advance toward that goal, and reflect on the Christian version of this, starting from the *telos* itself and working back toward where we are, faced with the question of faith in our contemporary world.

But are Aristotle's goal and the Christian goal the same thing? Yes and no. Yes: it is the goal of discovering that for which humans were made, that in which they will find their deepest fulfillment. No: the Hebraic and early Christian sense of the ultimate goal is quite different from that of Greek philosophy. The New Testament is clear about the goal toward which we are journeying. It is not, as in Platonism, an ultimate disembodied immortality in a non-spatiotemporal world. It is, rather, the new heavens and the new earth promised by Isaiah, Revelation, and other biblical books; the redeemed, renewed cosmos spoken of by Paul in Romans 8; the "summing up of all things in heaven and on earth in Christ" spoken of in Ephesians 1:10. Despite the widespread and misleading impression today that being a Christian has as its ultimate goal simply "going to heaven," the early Christians, like many of their Jewish contemporaries, looked back to Isaiah and similar prophecies and spoke, with them, not of God's abandonment of the good creation, but of God's rescue of that good creation from corruption and decay, both physical and moral, and of God's creation of a new world out of the old one, a world in which the wolf would dwell with the lamb, in which peace and justice would flourish, and in which, above all, human beings would find their true fulfillment. This big picture is the soil in which the ancient Jewish belief in the resurrection of the dead flourished and grew, until the time when, to everyone's surprise, resurrection actually happened in the

---

9. Col. 3:14: love is "the bond of completeness," σύνδεσμος τῆς τελειότητος. This already includes the eschatological note, the sense of an envisaged ending or goal, a *telos*.

case of Jesus of Nazareth, causing his followers to declare that in him God's new creation had already begun, confirming the ancient Jewish expectation and indicating that it had already started to come true.[10]

This already gives to the Christian understanding of the journey a sense, as Eliot said, that "the end is where we start from."[11] The end, the *telos*, the goal, has already happened in Jesus. We are not merely journeying toward a distant, and largely unknown, destination; we have glimpsed it already in microcosm. A small but highly significant part of the future has come forward to meet us, and is now firmly embedded in what is the fixed and unalterable past of this world. Having already been grasped by that *telos,* we now advance toward it in quite a different mood, quite a different mode, from those who travel without having already arrived.

This eschatological reshaping is closely cognate with the Christian redefinition of classical virtue in terms of a life lived through the calling of God's grace and in the power of his Spirit. We do not simply make ourselves good by learning about virtues and then trying hard to practice them, ending up producing a self-made human being that could, in the end, be presented before God for inspection and approval. Rather, we find ourselves caught up by the story of Jesus, by the events of his life, his kingdom announcement, his death, and his resurrection, and we find both that he is himself the goal, the fullness of humanity as well as the fullness of divinity, and that he himself is the way, the journey by which we may ourselves come to that goal.

II. Virtues, Pagan and Christian

All of this does not mean, as Augustine seems to have thought, that virtue seen from a Christian point of view is completely discontinuous with virtue seen from a pagan point of view (whether Aristotelian, Stoic, or any other). On the contrary. The early Christian view, built foursquare upon the ancient Jewish theology, was that the one God known to the Jews as the God of Abraham, Isaac, and Jacob, the God of the exodus, of Moses, of David and the prophets, was the Creator of the whole world, heaven and earth alike, and had made all humans in his own image. The ancient Jews thus assumed

---

10. On all of this, see my *Resurrection of the Son of God* (London/Minneapolis: SPCK/ Fortress, 2003), and now also *Surprised by Hope* (London: SPCK, 2008).

11. T. S. Eliot, "Little Gidding," in *Four Quartets* (London: Faber, 1959 [1944]), p. 47.

(and the early Christians carried on this assumption) that in all kinds of ways the vision of genuine humanity that they glimpsed in God, in Torah, and in Wisdom constituted the overarching goal that included within itself, even though it also transcended, the goal glimpsed by pagan philosophers.

Some Jewish writers, such as Philo or the author of 4 Maccabees, explored this explicitly. Often it is assumed, taken in en route. The result is that temperance, courage, justice, and prudence are seen, not as irrelevant or dispensable for the Christian, but rather as intermediate goals, steps on the road to the higher and in some ways quite different goal marked out by faith, hope, and love. What is more, they are seen as intermediate goals that are themselves to be reached, not by sheer unaided moral effort, but by the grace of the creator God, and the renewal, by that grace and through faith, of the image-bearing capacity of all human beings. More in line with Aquinas than with Augustine, this means that the classical virtues, like every other aspect of God's created world, can themselves, as it were, be redeemed — but only if they submit, as all creation must submit, to the process of baptism, being put to death with Christ and being raised again. This, I think, is more or less what Paul means when he speaks of "taking every thought captive to obey Christ" (2 Cor. 10:5).

But whenever that putting-to-death and raising-to-life takes place, there are some things that are left firmly behind, and other things that emerge in quite a new light. One of the obvious results of putting to death in Christ the classical notions of virtue, and of the individual virtues themselves, is immediately apparent: pride is stood on its head. Pride was a virtue in the classical world. It was the sense of self-worth that came from knowing one's own value and position, particularly from contemplating one's own social, cultural, military, personal, moral, or other achievements. And pride is the great casualty of the Christian journey; that is one of the main thrusts of Paul's two letters to Corinth. If the goal has already been given in Jesus Christ, our journey is not one of achievement but of implementation, not of unaided goodness but of unmerited grace. And this leads us back to faith, hope, and love, the theological virtues, which Paul lists in that way precisely in the first letter to the Corinthians at the point where he confronts the pride of the community and shows them "a more excellent way" (1 Cor. 12:31). Indeed, Aquinas takes the daring step, as well as dethroning pride, of reinhabiting passion: over against the Stoics, with their desire for ἀπάθεια, he declares that the ultimate goal is the passionate love of God. Nothing that is put to death cannot be raised, but nothing that is not put to death can or will be.

This is the point where we glimpse one of Paul's many visions of the ultimate end, the *telos*. Now, he says, these three things abide: faith, hope, and love; but the greatest of these is love (1 Cor. 13:13). The point he is making, in that fascinating and powerful poem on ἀγάπη, is precisely not that love is a virtue to which you should aspire in the old sense of a hard, unaided moral struggle. Half of the chapter consists in his attempt to explain to the Corinthians, who were used to thinking in that static pagan way, that for a fully Christian virtue you need a fully Christian eschatology. He contrasts the "now" with the "not yet": now we see through a glass darkly, but then face to face; now I know in part, but then I shall know as I am known. Paul is drawing on the picture of the ultimate future, the resurrection life, which he will expound in detail two chapters later, in order to insist to the Corinthians both that the highest form of virtue is love and that the way to this virtue is to recognize it *as an eschatological reality,* that is, something whose *telos* lies in the ultimate future but something that is already given in Jesus Christ and given to others in Christ and by the Spirit. Thus, the eschatological nature of Christian virtue provides the key to understanding both the convergence and the divergence between pagan and Christian.

That sense of a reality given in Christ and through the Spirit is, by the way, the biblical reality that lies behind the rather fuzzy talk in some Christian circles about Christian behavior being a matter of allowing the Spirit to work in one's life. This can sometimes degenerate into the romantic or existentialist idea, a kind of parody of the theology of grace, that sees the only good deeds as those that "come naturally," those in which one is being "true to oneself," living "authentically" in the sense of there being a close fit between deep intention and practical action. The trouble with that, of course, is that it would be all right if we were already at the goal in the sense of already being completely filled with the Spirit, already raised from the dead; but at the moment we are still on the way, *in via*. The resurrection has not already occurred, except in the case of Jesus, and for that reason moral effort (always with the Pauline proviso, "not I, but God's grace"; cf. 1 Cor. 15:10) is still essential.

This, I think, is the reason why there has been in our day a renewed emphasis on the virtues, as we noted at the start. It stems from a recognition that Christian romanticism is not enough. You can have as strongly inaugurated an eschatology as you want *as long as you realize that it is not yet complete,* as Paul himself insists throughout 2 Corinthians and in Philippians.[12] Every time you say "already," you must always insist "not yet" (and vice

12. Cf., e.g., Phil. 3:12-16.

versa, but that is not my present point). Not that Christian experience is simply an undifferentiated muddle, though it may sometimes feel like that; but that we can understand clearly what it means to live between the resurrection of Jesus Christ (and the power of the Spirit that flows from that) and the final renewal and resurrection that has clearly not yet taken place. And those who live in that intermediate time need a framework of thought-out and understood moral shaping: not just individual commands for individual situations, to be obeyed (or perhaps disobeyed) in a kind of ad hoc fashion, but a sense that, in order to obey those commands, we are not simply miscellaneous Christians who happen to obey or disobey, but that we can actually *become the kind of people* who are more likely to obey than not, and that this will come as we cultivate the habits of mind, heart, body, and life — in short, the virtues — that will dispose us to obey. We can become, in other words, people for whom the romantic or existentialist dream might eventually begin to come at least partially true. But this is not, or not for the most part, something straightforwardly and completely given in baptism and in initial Christian faith.

The Christian teaching and practice of virtue, then, can be understood in terms of the life that is lived within the story whose goal, whose *telos,* is that complete, redeemed, renewed, and perfected human life, within God's new and redeemed heaven and earth and among God's ultimately restored people. For the Christian, virtue is the practiced art of being the sort of person who is already anticipating, in the present, the life of the coming age. The point of 1 Corinthians 13 is that love is not our duty; it is our *destiny.* It is the song they sing in God's new world, and we are to become the sort of people who practice it in the present (even against the other jangling tunes the world is singing) so that we are all the more ready to sing it in the future, and so that we can be a sign of that future coming already into the present.

When we grasp this shaping of the Christian moral life, we may perhaps suggest that the relationship between the cardinal virtues and the theological virtues (and, behind them both, the pagan and Christian ideals of moral habit-forming) is not simply that the latter, by supplementing the former, give them a new context, changing the abstract idea of virtue itself. It may also be that some of the thrust of the former is transformed, by that putting-to-death and bringing-to-life we noted earlier, into the thrust of the latter. Thus, most obviously, the cardinal virtue of justice, giving to each person what is his or her due, is transformed into ἀγάπη, giving to each not simply what is due but more besides, including "justice" itself (since ἀγάπη will never wrong anyone, as Paul says elsewhere[13]), but going beyond it into generosity, giving to each in the way God gives to each, that is, lavishly and without thought for cost. That transference, that taking up of the lesser (justice) into the greater (love), works more or less in that particular case. It is not so obviously the case, or not to me at any rate, when we consider the relationship between faith and hope, the other two "theological" virtues, on the one hand, and temperance, courage, and prudence, the other three "cardinal" virtues, on the other. Maybe this is a sign that we should not be overly restricted by the fourfold and threefold pattern of classical pagan and Christian virtue discourse. Indeed, if we ask where "prudence" comes within early Christian ethical thinking, the straightforward answer is "wisdom," which itself, as has been argued, is a matter of recalibrating pagan prudence in the light of the command to love: that is, that knowing the love command to be the highest there is, we drastically reorder our sense of priorities.[14] And one could easily argue that what Aristotle meant by "courage" is included en route within Paul's exhortations to live by faith, patience, and hope; also, that "temperance" corresponds quite closely to what Paul meant by "self-control," which is a fruit of the Spirit (Gal. 5:23).[15] But to pursue any of this would take us too far afield.

III. Faith Among the Virtues

With this framework of eschatological virtue, and of the convergence and divergence between pagan and Christian virtues both in themselves and in the way they "work," I return more specifically to the question of faith as a virtue. It is fascinating to see in 1 Corinthians 13:13 that faith and hope, like love, are among the things that "abide," that last into the future, that are (in other words) among the things that form bridges from the present age into the age to come. Putting this the other way round, it seems that for Paul, faith is a quality that we shall possess in God's new age, and that we anticipate in the present. Paul, indeed, gives both faith and hope as qualities of love: love bears all things, *believes all things, hopes all things,* endures all things (13:7).[16]

13. Rom. 13:10.

14. See Charles Pinches in *Oxford Companion to Christian Thought,* ed. A. Hastings (Oxford: Oxford University Press, 2000), p. 742.

15. So, of course, for that matter, are "love" itself, and also "patience" (μακροθυμία); Gal. 5:22.

16. Again, note the presence of patience in this catalogue of what "love" will do.

Most people do not, I think, see "faith" in this Pauline way. A well-known hymn specifically differentiates between faith and hope on the one hand and love on the other:

Faith will vanish into sight,
Hope be emptied in delight;
Love in heaven will shine more bright,
Therefore give us love.[17]

There is some justification within Paul himself for saying something like this in relation to hope: "Who hopes," he asks, "for what he sees?" (Rom. 8:24). But if we explore what that means, we discover that hope is not so much emptied as fulfilled. If "hope" is the longing to possess what God promises in the future, when we possess it *we do not abandon our hope; we fulfill it.* "I've got what I hoped for," we say, and hope is thereby affirmed. (There is a potential semantic catch here: when we speak of "gaining our hope," what we really mean is "gaining the thing we had hoped for," leaving it open in what sense the activity of hoping still continues.) It is of course possible, too, perhaps even likely, that in God's new creation there will be new projects and aspirations, tasks to work on, plans to fulfill.[18] In that case, "hope," which at present is always darkened by the shadow of uncertainty, will be a glad looking-forward from which that shadow has been removed, since we shall then want and intend what God wants and intends. Perhaps there is, in that sense as well, a future for hope, a future in which hope itself will be transformed, not abandoned.

What then about faith? Is faith part of our present journey, which will be unnecessary when we arrive, in the way that a boat becomes unnecessary when we reach the opposite shore? Or is it like love, something we know in part at the moment, which will be given more fully and richly in the future, in the way that the giant cluster of grapes offered the weary Israelites a foretaste of the promised land? I think it is both. For this we need some kind of typology of the New Testament idea of "faith," which is more polymorphous than many readers, I think, give it credit for. We need to set this out before we can understand what exactly faith is from the Christian point of view, in

17. "Gracious Spirit, Holy Ghost" (1862), by Christopher Wordsworth (1807-85), bishop of Lincoln (and a nephew of Wordsworth the poet).

18. That seems to me at least to be implied by passages like Revelation 21 and 22. In 22:2 the leaves of the tree of life, growing by the water of life that flows from the New Jerusalem, are to be "for the healing of the nations." Who will administer that healing?

what sense it may be classified as a virtue, and (presuming a positive answer to the latter question) what the effects of practicing this virtue may be in personal and public life.[19]

The word πίστις and its cognates cover, in fact, quite a wide semantic range, with four main and broad areas that merge into one another, and that thereby provide a large open field across which one can move in various directions, while each retains something of its individual flavor. All four senses are important if we are to understand the full early Christian picture of faith; not that we can parcel each occurrence of the relevant words confidently into one or another of the categories, but that all these meanings are readily available as part of the immediate field.

First, there is faith as *trust:* relying on someone or something, a person or a promise. Here "faith" denotes both a single action, an act of trust, and also a wider attitude, a trusting approach to God, to a particular person (not least, in the Gospels, to Jesus himself), and hence more or less an attribute of the person doing the trusting. In this sense, "faith" becomes as it were a *property* of the person concerned. Such a person becomes a "trusting" person, a "faithful" person in that sense.[20]

Second, there is *belief*, in the sense of believing a particular statement to be true (which will often, but not always, involve believing, or trusting, the person making the statement). This is, if you like, a more focused aspect of the more general "trust": believing *that* as opposed to simply believing *in*.[21] (In case anyone should try to play these two senses off against one another, we should note that both belong together in central New Testament formulations: in Rom. 4:24-25 Paul speaks of "believing *in* the God who raised Jesus from the dead," and in Rom. 10:9 he speaks of "believing in your heart *that* God raised him from the dead.") The famous *fides qua creditur*, the faith "by which" one believes, is in the New Testament a combination of these first two senses.

Third, there is *fides quae creditur*, the faith itself *that is believed*. Here "the faith" has become the proposition, or the set of propositions, or indeed the entire potential and later actual multivolume corpus of systematic theol-

19. There are of course many typologies of "faith" on offer, not least Bultmann's classic (though in my view flawed) account in *TDNT* 6:174-228. This is not the place for detailed engagement with different ways of organizing the material.

20. Several of the occurrences in Romans 4 clearly belong here, while shading also into the second sense by the end of the chapter at least. Cf. too, e.g., 1 Cor. 2:5; 2 Cor. 5:7; Col. 1:4. For a "faithful" person, cf., e.g., Gal. 3:9 ("those of faith").

21. Cf., e.g., Rom. 4:3, 18; 6:8; 10:9; also in a related sense 14:2; 1 Cor. 15:11; 1 Thess. 4:14.

ogy, that is thought to form the substance of that which Christians believe. Paul uses this, too: "the one who formerly persecuted us," say the Jerusalem Christians according to Galatians 1:23, "is now *preaching the faith he once tried to destroy.*"[22] Here "the faith" is more or less "the Christian message" or "the gospel." At this point, obviously, "faith" in this sense cannot be a "virtue," since it has shifted from describing the act or attitude of the believer to describing its correlate, the thing believed. It might be possible to argue that "the faith" in this sense includes or presupposes the virtue of "faith" in the other senses, but "the faith" itself in this sense cannot be a virtue.

This is emphatically not so in the fourth sense. Here "faith" and its cognates mean, more or less, faithfulness, loyalty, reliability, trustworthiness, and even, in consequence, something like our word "integrity": the quality of being so fully in tune, all through one's thinking and acting, that others know they are with someone on whom they can lean all their weight. (This is perhaps part of what Revelation means in calling Jesus the "faithful" witness.)[23] More particularly, to put it anthropomorphically, someone of utter faithfulness is someone on whom *God* knows that he can lean all his weight.[24] In this sense, of course, none of us (except Jesus himself) is fully trustworthy in the present life. But part of the point of the eschatological perspective is that when we shall know as we are known, we shall have become people of utter faithfulness, utter reliability. Just as there is a striking contrast between Peter on the night Jesus was betrayed and the same Peter standing boldly before the crowds and the high priests in Acts, so there will be a contrast between our present fickleness and our utter integrity and reliability in God's new creation.

And, once more, Paul uses the πίστις root in this sense, both of God and of Israel. In Galatians 2, he speaks of having been "entrusted" with the gospel to the Gentiles. In Romans 3:2-4, he speaks of Israel being "entrusted" with God's oracles, and of some proving unfaithful to that trust — not, in other words, of them simply not believing in God's oracles themselves, but in being unreliable, untrustworthy, "unfaithful" in the sense of "unfaithful to their commission": they should have passed on "the oracles" to the world, but they did not. This "infidelity" in the sense of unreliability does not, Paul declares, call into question the "faithfulness" of God himself, because God

22. Cf. too, e.g., Acts 6:7; Rom. 10:8?; 1 Tim. 5:8. And 1 Cor. 15:14, 17 appear to belong here, though with strong overtones of 1 and 2; also 2 Cor. 13:5; Gal. 6:10 (though again, in the context of the whole letter, we must assume that echoes of 1 and 2 are also present); Eph. 4:5, 13; Phil. 1:27.

23. Rev. 1:5; 3:14; 19:11.

24. For "faithful" in this sense, cf., e.g., 1 Cor. 4:2, 17; 7:25; Eph. 6:21; Col. 1:7.

will be true even if all humans are false. (At this point, we note, the concepts of faith and faithfulness need to be calibrated against the concepts of truth and truthfulness, but that too would take us too far afield, except to note the use of the older word "troth," where "I give you my troth" means, more or less, "I put my truthfulness on the line by making a promise to which I will be faithful.") A further example may be in 2 Corinthians 4:13, where Paul quotes Psalm 116:10, which may be best translated here, not "I believed, and so I spoke," but "*I kept faith, and so I spoke.*" The point of the passage, and of the psalm being quoted, is not so much a statement of "faith" in the second sense, as is often assumed, but in the fourth: "I remained loyal," even under all the pressures and suffering that might have blown me off course.

How then does "faith," in any of these senses, constitute a proper anticipation of an aspect of the ultimate future life, the resurrection life in God's new heavens and new earth? How, in other words, can "faith" be seen to be the practice of something that will last, something that is a necessary part of that growing of a human being toward the full *telos* for which God has made us? Is faith, after all, also among the virtues?

We must face, to begin with, the problem that Paul and others sometimes speak of "faith," in parallel with "hope" in Romans 8:25, as something that will not be needed in the age to come: "We walk by faith, not by sight" (2 Cor. 5:7). But the apparent conflict between this passage and 1 Corinthians 13:13 is only superficial. If "faith" means trust (more specifically, for the Christian, trust in the God who raised Jesus), this trust will obviously continue and be perfected in the age to come. If it means "belief that Jesus is Lord and that God raised him from the dead," that too will not be abandoned but rather celebrated in the age to come. If it means "loyalty to this God," and utter trustworthiness of character as a result, then this too will be consummated and perfected in the coming age. (And the one remaining sense, "the faith," *fides quae,* will of course remain just as true in the coming age as in the present one.) In every sense, then, "faith" is something that will last into God's new world, and indeed be enhanced there.

Of course, part of the thrust of "faith" at the present time, as in 2 Corinthians 5:7, is precisely that it is trust, belief, and trustworthiness precisely under conditions that threaten to destroy trust, to deny belief, and to undermine trustworthiness. And perhaps, to jump to our conclusion, this is what gives "faith" its peculiar character precisely as a virtue, but a virtue precisely leading toward a *telos* in which, when perfected, the activity to which the virtue leads will "come naturally," while in the present it does not. At the moment, to put it bluntly, "faith" in any specifically Christian sense appears difficult or impossible. The observed fact of universal death — observed and commented on, of course, not just since the Enlightenment, but as early as Homer and Aeschylus! — makes it difficult if not impossible to believe in the resurrection, either of Jesus or of his people. At the moment the fact of evil in the world makes it difficult for many, and impossible for some, to believe in a good Creator. At the moment the changes and chances, the problems and pressures of life make it difficult for any of us to be utterly trustworthy, utterly loyal, utterly faithful in any sense or context. It is true that being trustworthy in general terms might be thought an aspect of the cardinal virtue of justice, part of giving to each his due (we owe to each a duty of being true to what we have said, to what she may properly expect from the sort of person we have presented ourselves to her as being), and for that matter part of the virtue of temperance (controlling one's desire to behave in an untrustworthy manner) and indeed prudence (reckoning that trustworthy behavior is more likely to have desirable consequences). It could thus be argued that there might be some aspects of "faith" that could be seen as virtuous even outside a Christian context. But the demands of the Christian meanings of "faith," in the senses explored above — faith as trust, belief, and loyalty to the God revealed in Jesus — are such as to transcend this completely. The gospel, as Paul knew, is folly to pagans. Trusting it would appear, not as a virtue, but as a vice. "Faith" of this Pauline sort can therefore come about only *in response to the grace and revelation of the God of Abraham, the God who raised Jesus from the dead.*

This mention of Abraham and resurrection leads us to one of the most central Pauline statements of faith. In Romans 1 Paul declares that all humans have an innate knowledge of God but that they suppress this knowledge: they refuse to acknowledge God or give glory or thanks to him, even though they can see his eternal power and deity in the created order. As a result, he says, their humanness deconstructs and they become futile (Rom. 1:18-23), worshiping lifeless idols and so courting death. By contrast — and recent studies have made it clear that Paul fully intends this contrast at the end of the epistolary section of which Romans 1:18 is the opening — Abraham believed God's promise, since despite the counterevidence he trusted God as Creator, gave glory to him, and was "fully convinced that God could do what he had promised" (Rom. 4:16-22).[25] That was why he became fruitful despite his and Sarah's old age.

---

25. On the links between Romans 1 and 4, cf. my *Romans*, pp. 500-501, and, e.g., Edward Adams, "Abraham's Faith and Gentile Disobedience: Textual Links between Romans 1 and 4," *JSNT* 65 (1997): 47-66.

Paul designed this rather careful analysis of Abraham's faith, of course, in order to demonstrate that Christians share essentially the same faith, because they are trusting the same God to be the Creator and life-giver (4:23-25). This is the point at which one of the most important features of Christian faith comes into view: *Christian faith means responding in trust to the trustworthy God,* who is trustworthy precisely as Creator and Redeemer, as maker and judge, as the one who calls all things into being and promises to set all things right at the end. Here the first, second, and fourth senses of "faith" all come together. Christian faith is not a thing in itself, an independent decision to pin one's flag on God's map, but is always and necessarily the answer to an invitation, the gratitude for grace, the response to a call. This is part of the very grammar of "faith" in the Christian sense. And the third sense of "faith," *fides quae,* is not left out of this picture, since Paul's formulation insists upon it: Christian faith is not a general trust in a divine presence or possibility but belief in *this* God, the God who raised Jesus, that is, belief in "the faith" that Jesus is Lord, that God raised him from the dead, and that God's new age, his new creation in which all is judged and all is set right, has already begun in him.

From this perspective, we should not be surprised to see Paul describing faith itself as a gift, as one of the results of the sovereign "word of God" preached in the gospel, one of the consequences of the Spirit's working. "By grace you are saved, through faith; and this is not of yourselves, it is God's gift" (Eph. 2:8). This raises, of course, but does not answer, the puzzling question of predestination: "the word of God, which is at work in you believers" (1 Thess. 2:13; cf. 1:4-5); "no one can say 'Jesus is Lord' except by the Holy Spirit" (1 Cor. 12:3). This has been a bone of contention in much Protestant dogmatic theology. Reformed thought has strongly emphasized faith as the gift of God, ruling out any sense that "faith" is something that "I do" to become pleasing to God — in other words, preventing "faith" from becoming "a work." Lutheran and Arminian thought has sometimes apparently insisted on faith as free, uncaused human belief — not least in supposed reaction to a perceived medieval Roman view of faith as an infused virtue.[26]

But if faith is in any sense a gift, we are back with Augustine's paradoxical and (to some people) disturbing formulation: give what you command,

---

26. The idea of "infused virtue" in medieval thought seems to be the result of Aquinas's drastic modification of Aristotle by the inclusion of Rom. 5:5 read in an Augustinian sense (i.e., taking "the love of God has been poured into our hearts through the Spirit" to mean that the gift of the Spirit has enabled *us* to love *God*).

and command what you will! While some might hear this as a shoulder-shrugging excusing of moral incapacity ("God simply hasn't given me the grace to keep this particular commandment, so clearly he can't want me to do so"), Augustine's saying can, and in this case certainly should, be read in the much more bracing sense: the sign that God is indeed commanding this virtue, and also giving it, is that we now clearly perceive our inalienable obligation to be working at it in the power of the Spirit. Simply to pray for a particular virtue (or for the disappearance of a particular vice) and then to expect it all to be done for us without our having to think about it, or to undertake particular and no doubt very difficult acts of will and moral self-discipline, is to capitulate once more to a romantic dream of what the moral life ought to be like. Such a dream would be the moral or even emotional equivalent of a poor person suddenly winning the lottery: without effort, suddenly all your problems are over! Just pray about it and there won't be any more moral battles!

But virtue is not like that, and Christian moral living is not like that either. The romantic dream of an inner transformation that will make moral effort unnecessary is untrue both to the New Testament and to worldwide and millennia-long Christian experience. Romantics may suppose that they have been installed in a hotel where everything they want is brought by room service at the touch of a button, but in fact they inhabit a house with a well-stocked larder from which they must choose ingredients and do their own cooking. The point of virtue, in other words, is the recognition that there is such a thing as building up a habit of taking regular small decisions to be a certain type of person, so that gradually one becomes that type of person indeed. And the point of virtue within a Christian frame of reference is that recognizing the utter gift character both of the new age itself (the new age that has broken in with Jesus' resurrection) and of our own participation in that new age (the gift of faith and baptism, of membership in the eschatological people of God) does not take away but rather sets in its proper context the life of moral effort, of virtue that really does flow from the new life of Jesus' resurrection and that really does anticipate the *telos* to which it tends, the fully redeemed life of our own resurrection within God's new world. And, once again, this contextualizing of Christian virtue within the redemptive eschatological framework underscores the great revolution in virtue ethics that took place from Paul onward, or as Paul would say, from the cross of Jesus Christ onward: the dethroning of pride and the enthroning of humility and gratitude. Not for nothing are Paul's two chapters on fundraising, on giving money as a sign of gratitude to God, framed within the letter where above all Paul stands ancient pagan virtue culture on its head: when I am weak, then I am strong![27]

Faith, then, is indeed a virtue. It demands hard work, not because it isn't a gift, but because it is; not because it isn't authentically flowing from within us, but because it is. The gift is the gift of the path to a richer, more responsible humanness; authenticity includes the choice to make an act of will despite desire, not simply bringing desire and will into line. To choose to believe, to choose to continue to believe, to choose to be faithful, loyal, and trustworthy, despite all the pressures to unbelief and disloyalty, is typical of the choices that constitute, or contribute toward, the life of Christian virtue.

IV. Faith, Virtue, and Justification

It is in this light that we can, I believe, make some fresh sense of "justification by faith" itself. At first sight, as we said earlier, the traditional reading of, and language about, justification by faith would seem to exclude all talk of "virtue" as being dangerously prone to human pride and self-glorification. That, it seems, is why Augustine wanted to deny that there could be such things as "natural virtues" apart from faith, hope, and love; and why Karl Barth, the greatest Augustinian of modern times, avoided the language of virtue altogether (though the substance of virtue discourse is still to be found in his work). Let it be said again, as clearly as possible, that in attempting to put justification by faith and our discussion of faith-as-virtue into some kind of mutual correlation, I have no intention of "smuggling in 'works' by the back door."[28] But justification by faith, as Paul makes extremely clear in a way that has sadly remained opaque to many of his ardent followers, must itself be understood quite strictly within its eschatological context. How does this work, and what will it say to our pursuit of faith as a virtue, a virtue that moreover will help us take large steps toward that freedom that God desires for his children?

---

27. 2 Corinthians 8, 9; cf. 12:10.

28. I have discussed this and cognate topics frequently, not least in the *Romans* commentary and in *Paul: Fresh Perspectives* (U.S. title: *Paul in Fresh Perspective*; London/Minneapolis: SPCK/Fortress, 2005), ch. 6. See in addition, e.g., "Redemption from the New Perspective?" in *The Redemption*, ed. S. T. Davis, D. Kendall, G. O'Collins (Oxford: Oxford University Press, 2004), pp. 69-100; "New Perspectives on Paul," in *Justification in Perspective: Historical Developments and Contemporary Challenges*, ed. Bruce L. McCormack (Grand Rapids: Baker Academic, 2006), pp. 243-64.

Paul's fullest statement of justification is of course in Romans, and despite what many think, the first statement of justification is actually about justification by works. In Romans 2:1-16, he sets out a classic Jewish framework of the final judgment, revised at every point around the gospel of Jesus Christ. There will come a day when God will judge the secrets of all through Jesus Christ, and in this judgment Jew and Gentile will stand on level ground. On that day, Paul declares — to the horror of those who would much rather he hadn't uttered such unreformed nonsense — that those who *do* what is right will be justified, will (that is) be declared by God to be in the right (2:13). (We later discover, in chapter 8, that the *form* of this future justification is precisely resurrection to immortal and eternal bodily life, the event through which God will declare who are his true children, just as, in 1:4, the resurrection of Jesus declared that he had all along been God's unique Son.) Paul does not, in Romans 2, explain how it is that, with all humans being roundly declared to be sinful (3:9-20), any at all can in fact be discovered "to have persevered in well-doing" (2:7). This causes problems for those who suppose, ahead of the evidence, that the sequence of thought in Romans corresponds to the sequence of ideas in a classic Protestant *ordo salutis*. Such readers normally suggest that Paul is here merely offering a hypothetical position, which he will then undermine in chapter 3. The mirror image of this is the suggestion that Paul is in fact cheerfully acknowledging that there are indeed some good pagans who, without the grace of the gospel, do what is right and will thereby be justified on their own merits on the last day.[29]

But Paul is far more subtle, and his writing is far more symphonic, than that. He has drawn attention, as a good theologian of inaugurated eschatology might well do, to the eventual picture, the future day when God will set all things right. Only in the light of that future day, now disclosed by its anticipation and inauguration in Jesus Christ, can we understand what God is up to in the present time. And it is precisely *in the present time* that the doctrine of "justification by faith," set out in 3:21-31, means what it means. The point is this: though all have indeed sinned and fallen short of the glory of God (3:23), God's gift of grace in the redemptive death of Jesus Christ (3:24-26) means that all who believe the gospel are declared to be in the right *in the present time*, in other words, as an anticipation of the future day when the secrets of all hearts are disclosed. Paul's double emphasis that this is the *present*

---

29. Perhaps the best-known example of the latter is C. H. Dodd, *The Epistle of Paul to the Romans* (London: Fontana, 1959 [1932]), p. 62.

reality[30] is meant to answer to the *future* reality set out in 2:1-16. Justification by faith is God's declaration, in advance of the final judgment, that all who believe in the gospel of Jesus Christ are already marked out as his people, being assured of forgiveness of sins. And part of the point of this declaration, in advance of the final judgment, is that by giving the believing Christian full assurance of this forgiveness, and of sharing in the sonship of Jesus Christ (8:29), the context is set for that life of moral effort that is spoken of so vividly in chapters 6 and 8: not, in other words, that being a Christian commits you after all to the unrelenting and anxiety-driven pagan search for perfection, which would only result in pride, nor that being a Christian means that you will now "automatically" behave in a manner that conforms to the gospel, but that being a Christian, believing in Jesus Christ and coming to understand justification by faith, creates a context of grace and gratitude in which the holiness of life commanded in Romans 6–8 is set, in which (in other words) virtues can be pursued without any shred of danger of lapsing back into Pelagianism or anything like it. And, in case there were any doubt about how all of this happens, Romans 12:1-2 makes it very clear: transformation through renewal of the *mind*. You will need to think differently in order that, through sustained moral effort, you may live differently. God, after all, wants redeemed humans, not puppets. Christian living demands that we become more fully human not only in what we do but in why we do it.

Equally, part of the point of justification by faith, here in Romans 3 as elsewhere, is the point I have labored in other places:[31] that because faith, rather than possession of Torah or the attempt to keep it, is the badge of membership in the eschatological people of God, this means that Gentiles as well as Jews are full and equal members within that people. This, indeed, sets the ecclesial context for Christian faith, which is important for Paul in a multiplicity of ways for which there is no space here. I want, rather, to probe further into the question, vital for our central topic of faith as a virtue, Why should *faith* be the badge that marks out Christians in the present as those who belong to God's eschatological people, those who are already assured of final vindication?

Two obvious initial answers, one negative and one positive, come to mind.

Negatively: the badge cannot be Torah or other signs of Jewish covenant membership, because if it were, as Paul says, only Jews could be members

---

30. Rom. 3:21: νυνὶ δέ; 3:26: ἐν τῷ νῦν καιρῷ.

31. Notably, *Paul: Fresh Perspectives*, ch. 6.

(3:27-30). Even then, this would remain a theoretical possibility only, since they too are in fact sinful (3:19-20). The universal badge must therefore be faith, because faith is open to all. This gets us so far but no further, since several other things are also open to all, such as (obviously) hope and love. Why not justification by hope, or by love?

Positively: faith in the God who raised Jesus has an obvious character, of responding to *this* gospel, the message about *this* God, and thus marks out Christians as persons who are placing their trust *here* rather than anywhere else, leaning all their weight on the events through which God actually accomplished the defeat of sin and death and the launching of his new creation. This too is important but insufficient.

I suggest that both answers point beyond themselves. Where they point, I suggest, is to the important and Pauline idea that actually defines faith itself — and launches it on its new career of being a (Christian) virtue! — namely, that Christian faith is the answering, faithful response to the faithful acts and word (both acts-as-word and word-as-acts) of the utterly trustworthy God. *Christian faith is thus the first sign that a particular human being is reflecting God's image,* so that when God speaks the faithful word of the gospel, the word that tells of his personal faithfulness to creation and covenant, in Jesus Christ and his death and resurrection, the human being who believes is answering God's faithfulness with faithfulness. (Some have read Paul's "from faith to faith" in Rom. 1:17 as expressing exactly this point.)[32]

What is more, the believing person is thereby reembodying *the faithfulness to death of Jesus Christ himself.* A long contemporary debate, in which Richard Hays has played the major role, has wrangled over whether by πίστις Ἰησοῦ Χριστοῦ and similar phrases Paul might actually mean "the faithfulness of Jesus Christ" rather than "faith in Jesus Christ."[33] Though there is no doubt more to be said, I regard this debate as in principle settled in favor of the former interpretation, which appears fresh to us only because of the heavy weight of the long Protestant tradition that has stressed the latter. Jesus, says Paul in Philippians 2:8, was *obedient* unto death, the death of the cross. The notions of *faithfulness* to God's plan and *obedience* to God's purpose are here very close. When, in Romans 5:12-21, Paul refers in summary form to what he has said in 3:24-26 and 4:24-25, "obedience" is the category he chooses, because of the desired contrast with Adam. But the point of

---

32. E.g., James D. G. Dunn, *Romans 1–8,* WBC 38A (Dallas: Word, 1988), pp. 43-44; and my *Romans,* p. 425.

33. See Hays, *The Faith of Jesus Christ,* especially the appendices in the second edition.

Romans 3:1-5 was that God always required a faithful Israelite to carry forward his purposes; and this is what he has now put forward in the person of his Son, the Messiah who represents Israel in himself.[34] *Christian faith is thus also the first sign of the Christ-life appearing within a person,* that faithfulness to God, his purpose, and his promise that is not just a miscellaneous religious awakening or awareness but a very specifically Christ-shaped refashioning of the person from the heart and mind outward.

This account of justification by faith will not, of course, satisfy those who are always on the lookout for semi-Pelagianism, ready to warn against the idea that God accepts us because of "something in us." But this reaction is a mistake. There is an irony here, not unlike the irony of traditional polemic over the eucharistic sacrifice: Protestants have always suspected Catholics of supposing that they were resacrificing Christ, because Catholics always insisted that the Mass was not something other than Christ's own sacrifice, while Catholics have suspected Protestants of adding merit of their own to the Lord's Supper, because they said that what they were doing was indeed something different from Christ's death. In the same way, many Protestants have suspected Catholics of semi-Pelagianism, because they say (as I have done) that the faith because of which God declares us to be in the right is itself a gift of God that we now have within us. Catholics, in turn, have suspected Protestants of adding to or even anticipating the gift of God, by insisting that faith is something in some way outside ourselves. I strongly believe that a properly eschatologically oriented account will bypass this difficulty (and for that matter, the problem about eucharistic sacrifice, though that again is a topic for another time).

Part of the problem has been, I think, that for many in the Protestant tradition there has been a large-scale muddling up of several things, including conversion, justification, receiving the Holy Spirit, coming into a "personal relationship with God," sensing and practicing the presence of God, and even "salvation" itself. Within this general muddle, "justification by faith" has often come to mean simply believing and trusting in God and coming to know him through Jesus Christ, and discovering that this personal relationship, not the attempt to perform moral good deeds or religious or liturgical actions, is the center of everything, and the guarantee and foretaste of final salvation itself. Theologians have often talked of "saving faith," or even of "salvation by faith," though Paul only once appears to use the latter formulation (Eph. 2:8). But Paul does not mean that one is "justified," that is, "declared to be in the right,"

---

34. See *Paul: Fresh Perspectives,* ch. 3.

by "coming to know God personally." Of course, "coming to know God in a personal way" is part of the complex event that includes "conversion," "regeneration," "being saved," and so on. But the slipperiness of popular language about this complex event should not allow us to blur the very precise and specific thing Paul is referring to when he speaks of justification. To be justified means to be declared "in the right" by God (i.e., [a] that one's sins are forgiven through the death of Jesus Christ and [b] that one is a fully accredited member of God's single, worldwide covenant family). This declaration takes place in the present time (Rom. 3:21-31) in anticipation of the declaration that will take place on the last day (Rom. 2:1-16). And this "justification," which is of course possible only because of the sheer grace and mercy of God acted out in the death and resurrection of his Son, is made not on the basis of a new "personal relationship with God" or some other religious experience but rather on the basis of the belief that Jesus is Lord and that God raised him from the dead. Such belief acknowledges that because of God's grace, the believer *finds him- or herself within the eschatological purposes, the eschatological people and the eschatological narrative of the one true God, known in and through Jesus Christ.* And when God makes exactly that declaration about believers — in the future, by raising them from the dead, and in the present, by declaring them in advance to be thus "in the right" — that declaration is what is called "justification."

V. Faith, Virtue, and Freedom

This at last opens the way for two important final points. First, the faith I have described, which includes trust, belief, and faithfulness, does indeed become a virtue in the Christian sense. Second, this faith leads to a freedom, both personal and social, that is vital to be grasped if Christian life is to be renewed and Christian freedom to be celebrated in the public square today.

First, this faith does indeed become a virtue, in the Christian sense. The initial reaching out in grateful response, itself precipitated by the work of the Spirit and the preaching of the Word, is the start of a lifelong reaching out, a faithfulness that, like the initial faith, is the answer to God's faithfulness in Jesus Christ and in the word of the gospel. But this lifelong faithfulness, sharing as it does the nature and character of the initial faith by which one is justified, is not (again, as in some romantic or existentialist dreamings) a matter of giving expression to how one happens to be feeling at the time. (One of the evils of our age is first to say "I feel" when we mean "I think";

then to pass, subtly, to the point where *actual* feelings have taken the place of *actual* thought; then to pass beyond that again, to the point where "feeling" *automatically trumps* "thinking"; then to reach the point where thought has disappeared altogether, leaving us merely with Eliot's "undisciplined squads of emotion."[35] At that point, one of the nadirs of postmodernity, we have left behind both the classical and the Christian traditions, though tragically you can see exactly this sequence worked out in various would-be Christian contexts, not least Synods.)

This lifelong faithfulness is a matter of practice. It means acquiring a *habit:* making a thousand small decisions to trust God *now,* in *this* matter, to believe in Jesus and his death and resurrection *today,* to be faithful and trustworthy to him *here and now,* in *this* situation . . . and so coming, by slow steps and small degrees, to the point where faith, trust, belief, and faithfulness become, as we properly say in relation to virtue, "second nature." Not "first nature," doing what comes naturally. No: *second* nature, doing from the heart that which the heart has learned by practice and hard work. Christian faith thus reaches out, by Spirit-inspired and eschatologically framed moral effort, toward the *telos* for which we were made, that we should be image-bearers of the faithful God. This means, in the terms I have posed in this paper, that faith is indeed one of the things we learn to do in the present time that truly anticipates the full life of the coming age. This is the sense, I think, in which lifelong Christian faith, though not different in kind or content from the faith by which one is justified (but only in temporal location, i.e., ongoing rather than initial), is indeed to be reckoned among the virtues.

Second, and perhaps still more urgently, Christian faith — belief and trust in the creator God who raised Jesus from the dead, and trustworthy loyalty to this God — sets us free in our personal lives from the need to worship or trust idols, and in our public lives from the pressure to serve the needs of an idolatrous state. In our personal lives, as Paul sees in Romans 1, what matters above all is worship, the worship that acknowledges that God is God, the Creator and life-giver, the all-powerful one. All sin proceeds from a diminution in this trusting faithfulness, and the replacement of some or all of it by the worship of idols of one sort or another. And idols, when worshiped, first enslave, then dehumanize, and then kill. I am not by training a spiritual director, but I know enough from pastoral work — not to mention the evidence of my own heart and life! — to know how idols work and how faith in the God who raised Jesus displaces and dethrones

35. From "East Coker," in *Four Quartets,* p. 26.

them, and thereby sets the Christian free to be, at last, the person God is calling him or her to be.

Likewise, in our public lives, as in the first century, to believe that Jesus is the Lord and that God has raised him from the dead is to believe that Caesar, in whatever form, is not Lord, and that Caesar's proper sphere of work is not to usher in the new world in which justice and joy dwell forever (as Caesar-figures often claim).[36] Only the one true God will do that, in a fresh and further act of grace, the final outworking of the achievement of Jesus Christ. Rather, Caesar's proper and limited task is to bring a measure of order to present society, to anticipate in specific acts of judgment (putting-to-rights) such elements of God's final putting-to-rights as can be done within the present age.[37] Part of our difficulty in today's world is that we are completely unclear about what it is that governments can do, and should try to do, and how they should go about finding a moral basis for doing it. We live in a confused time, with democracy in apparent decline and with the church and Christian consciences increasingly at risk from governments, in various parts of the globe, that, having made a mess of almost everything else, decide to distract attention by stirring up anti-Christian sentiment and passing laws designed to make life difficult for those who want to be faithful followers of Jesus Christ. This is where faithfulness, loyalty, and trustworthiness will stand out, where that fourth meaning of πίστις is needed over against the shrinkage of "faith" to merely "my personal belief." The rhetoric of the Enlightenment has been extremely keen to squash "faith" into "private, personal belief," so that it can then insist that such "faith" should stay as a private matter and not leak out to infect the wider world. But since the Christian's personal belief is in the creator God who raised Jesus from the dead, this personal belief can never remain *only* a personal belief but, rooted in the trust that is the first meaning of πίστις, must grow at once into the loyalty, the public trustworthiness, that is the fourth meaning. This too is part of the virtue of "faith": to take the thousand small decisions to be loyal, even in public, even when it is dangerous or difficult, and so to acquire the *habit* of confessing this faith (sense 3) both when it is safe and when it is dangerous. Just as Mother Teresa spoke of recognizing Jesus in the Eucharist and then going out to recognize him in the poor and needy, so we need to learn the virtue of affirming our faith in our liturgical and prayer life so that we

36. See *Paul: Fresh Perspectives,* ch. 4.

37. On this point, and the whole paragraph, see especially Oliver O'Donovan, *The Ways of Judgment* (Grand Rapids: Eerdmans, 2005).

can then go out and affirm it on the street, in public debate, in pursuit of that freedom for which the second-century apologists argued.

Christian faith, then, does indeed belong among the virtues. But we can only understand that in the light of the full biblical and eschatological narrative, in which God's eventual new creation, launched in Jesus' resurrection, will make all things new. Christian faith looks back to Jesus, and on to that eventual new day. It tastes in advance, in personal and public life, the freedom that we already have through Jesus and that one day we shall have in all its fullness. The *practice* of this "faith" is, on the one hand, the steady, grace-given entering into the habit by which our character is formed, a habit correlated with those resulting from the similar practice of hope and love. On the other hand, the practice of this faith is the genuine anticipation in the present of that trust, belief, and faithfulness that are part of the *telos,* the goal. That goal, already given in Jesus Christ, is the destination toward which we are now journeying in the power of the Spirit. Virtue is one of the things that happen in between, and because of, that gift and that goal.

The Conversion of Desire in
St. Paul's Hermeneutics

Markus Bockmuehl

> *O Almighty God, who alone canst order the unruly wills and affections of sinful men; Grant unto thy people, that they may love the thing which thou commandest, and desire that which thou dost promise; that so, among the sundry and manifold changes of the world, our hearts may surely there be fixed, where true joys are to be found; through Jesus Christ our Lord. Amen.*
>
> — *The Book of Common Prayer* (1662)
> Collect for the Fourth Sunday after Easter

Over three decades of teaching and research, and like scarcely another *Neutestamentler* of his generation, Richard Hays has combined a remarkable range of academically rigorous and often field-defining scholarship with a palpable sense of standing intentionally in the service of the community of Christian faith.[1] His major contributions to the field have deployed masterfully subtle and sophisticated literary and narrative skills in the work of exegesis, theology, and Christology, and perhaps above all in the study of the New Testament authors' understanding of faith, of ethics, and of the Hebrew Scriptures. His sense of churchly accountability speaks eloquently through-

---

1. I am grateful for comments and suggestions received from a variety of friends and colleagues, including David Lincicum, Kavin Rowe, Graham Stanton, Marianne Meye Thompson, Ross Wagner, and John Webster; and for Carol Shoun's patient and ever-vigilant editorial assistance.

out these writings, and finds a highly emblematic focus in his "ecclesio-centric" or "ecclesiotelic" understanding of St. Paul's biblical hermeneutic, developed over a number of years.[2]

The Conversion of the Imagination

In the course of preparing his respected commentary on 1 Corinthians for the Interpretation series,[3] he returned to the issue of Pauline hermeneutics in relation to the much-debated question of quite how Scripture "works" in the apostle's correspondence with the church at Corinth. The result was an article, first published in 1999, that went on to lend its programmatic and captivating title to a book published in 2005: *The Conversion of the Imagination.*[4]

The question of hermeneutics in 1 Corinthians arises especially in the face of the challenge, diversely posed but nonetheless pressing for both Paul and the Corinthian Christians, of an apocalyptic eschatology. Richard Hays's work on that question is drawn particularly to the eschatological and indeed "ecclesiotelic" implications of two key passages. The first of these concerns Paul's eschatological and Spirit-centered attack on the supposed self-sufficiency of philosophical and rhetorical "wisdom" (1 Cor. 1:18-31), while the second develops the apostle's warning that the Passover typology of Jesus' death entails the readers' identification with Israel and thus requires them to "cleanse out the old leaven" of sin and celebrate the feast of that new eschatological identity (5:1-13). In his powerful evocation of Israel-centered metaphors, here and elsewhere, Paul stresses that the Corinthian believers in Jesus are now to recognize Israel's story as one into which they themselves have been taken up. To be sure, "Israel" here functions for Hays not in terms of a seamless *Heilsgeschichte* but rather as "hermeneutically reconfigured by the cross and resurrection" (p. 5); nevertheless, "Israel's story is not some-

---

2. Richard B. Hays, *Echoes of Scripture in the Letters of Paul* (New Haven: Yale University Press, 1989), p. 86 et passim, refined in Hays, "On the Rebound: A Response to Critiques of *Echoes of Scripture in the Letters of Paul*," in *Paul and the Scriptures of Israel,* ed. J. A. Sanders and C. A. Evans (Sheffield: Sheffield Academic, 1993), pp. 77-78; cf. Hays, *The Conversion of the Imagination: Paul as Interpreter of Israel's Scripture* (Grand Rapids: Eerdmans, 2005), p. 11.

3. Richard B. Hays, *First Corinthians,* IBC (Louisville: John Knox, 1997).

4. Cf. Richard B. Hays, "The Conversion of the Imagination: Scripture and Eschatology in 1 Corinthians," *NTS* 45 (1999): 391-412. In the following discussion, page references to the book will be placed in parentheses within the text.

body else's history; rather, Paul addresses the Gentile Corinthians as though[5] they have become part of Israel" (p. 9). Indeed, according to passages like 1 Corinthians 10:1 and 12:2 (cf. Rom. 11:17-24), Paul, like other key New Testament authors from Matthew and Luke, via Hebrews, to 1 Peter, invites his readers

> to understand themselves now as descendants of the characters who appear in the pages of Scripture. . . . He considers them ἔθνη no longer. Within Paul's symbolic world, they are no longer among the *goyim*, because they have been taken up into the story of Israel. (p. 9)

Paul's hermeneutic in 1 Corinthians "makes sense if and only if the readers of the letter embrace the typological identification between themselves and Israel" (p. 24).

Hays's subtext throughout is his recognition of the self-involving nature of the New Testament authors' Christian biblical interpretation in its demands on the interpreters' moral, intellectual, and spiritual worlds. It is in this connection that Hays coins the powerfully evocative notion of a "conversion of the imagination." His own summary statement of this idea is worth quoting *in extenso* (pp. 5-6):

> Paul's missionary strategy in his confrontation with pagan culture repeatedly draws upon eschatologically interpreted Scripture texts to clarify the identity of the church and to remake the minds of his congregations. . . . In 1 Corinthians we find Paul calling his readers and hearers to a *conversion of the imagination*. He was calling Gentiles to understand their identity anew in light of the gospel of Jesus Christ — a gospel message comprehensible only in relation to the larger narrative of God's dealing with Israel. . . . The result was that Jew and Gentile alike found themselves summoned by the gospel story to a sweeping reevaluation of their identities, an imaginative paradigm shift so comprehensive that it can only be described as a "conversion of the imagination."

---

5. The phrase "as though" is potentially infelicitous here: however counterfactual it may have seemed to contemporary detractors, 1 Cor. 12:2 implies that from Paul's perspective (as from that of Hebrews, 1 Peter, etc.) there is nothing "virtual" about his construct. Hays himself rightly points in that direction (see the quotation below from p. 9 of Hays's book): Gentile believers in Christ are now part of the story of Israel. For the NT authors, God's raising of Israel's Messiah from death to life has the universalizing effect of vindicating the graft of "wild" branches of YHWH-believing Gentiles fully into the storied tree that is the Israel of God.

As the unfolding argument of 1 Corinthians shows, this "clarification" of the congregation's Israel-focused identity in Christ in fact necessarily entails "a critical confrontation" of the community's beliefs and practices with the gospel (p. 6), a confrontation that can be rightly understood only in eschatological terms, because it subjects the church's present experience to God's coming judgment (pp. 11-12). Thus, as for example, 1 Corinthians 1 shows in relation to secular culture, "the conversion of the imagination that Paul demands is fostered by placing σοφία in a *scriptural* framework of God's judgement; in light of Scripture, Paul is calling on the Corinthians to reevaluate their prizing of rhetoric" (p. 15, emphasis original).

The resulting thesis makes for an essay, and indeed a book, that justly bears one of the most evocative titles of any recent work of New Testament scholarship.[6] Richard Hays here puts his finger on a crucial feature of the Pauline hermeneutic, and indeed of the textual intention *(intentio operis)* of the New Testament writings more generally. There are no doubt other implications of this hermeneutical engagement, including some along the lines of what others have described in terms of "resocialization," or, for that matter, of the implied reader's intellectual and moral "conversion."[7] Within Paul's own framework, Hays appropriately cites recent discussion of 1 Corinthians 4:6 with its insistence "not to go beyond what is written," a warning against arrogance that expresses the apostle's wish "to remake the minds of his readers" in the light of Scripture.[8]

At the same time, we may suggest that this newer statement perhaps also serves as a restatement and refinement of Hays's own earlier thinking — for example, in *Echoes* — about the idea of Paul's writing as "hermeneutical model" for us as we "learn how to read Scripture."[9] That perspective is still

---

6. But see below, n. 16.

7. So also, rightly, Hays, *Conversion of the Imagination,* p. 6 n. 13, citing Wayne A. Meeks, *The Moral World of the First Christians,* LEC 6 (Philadelphia: Westminster, 1986), pp. 13-14, 126, 129. In more groping and inarticulate fashion, I myself have elsewhere attempted to draw attention to the authors' address to an "implied" readership assumed to have been converted to the moral and spiritual reality of which the text speaks (e.g., Bockmuehl, *Seeing the Word: Refocusing New Testament Study,* STI [Grand Rapids: Baker Academic, 2006], pp. 92, 232).

8. Hays, *Conversion of the Imagination,* pp. 17-18, citing J. Ross Wagner, "'Not Beyond the Things Which Are Written': A Call to Boast Only in the Lord (1 Cor 4.6)," *NTS* 44 (1998): 279-87, as well as Morna D. Hooker, "'Beyond the Things Which Are Written': An Examination of 1 Cor IV.6," *NTS* 10 (1963): 127-32 (cf. Hooker, "Beyond the Things That Are Written? St Paul's Use of Scripture," *NTS* 27 [1981]: 295-309), among others.

9. Hays, *Echoes,* pp. 178-92.

affirmed here (see, e.g., pp. viii et passim); but arguably there is also a subtle and unstated attenuation of the earlier assumption that this means reading all of Scripture in the same "metaphorical mode" and with the same "imaginative freedom" that Paul apparently deploys vis-à-vis the Old Testament.[10] In the earlier book, Hays writes: "we acknowledge that Scripture forms our identity, even while we read it with imaginative freedom."[11] Now, however, the proper working of such imagination is said, more explicitly than before, to be contingent upon its moral and spiritual *conversion* (pp. viii-ix).[12] In other words, we may venture to suggest that there has perhaps been a shift in emphasis in Hays's later work on this topic — from imagination's freedom seen as innate (however much also inspired) to the discovery of that freedom precisely in the discipline of its Spirit-led, ecclesiotelic *conversion*.[13]

"Conversion" and "Imagination": Charting the Problem

In pondering Hays's exposition of these matters, it is hard not to find oneself profoundly instructed about Paul's hermeneutical stance in 1 Corinthians and well beyond. Though at times less explicitly "ecclesiotelic," the same Pauline outlook finds comparable expression in the call to discern the will of God through a transformation of the mind (μεταμορφοῦσθε τῇ ἀνακαινώσει τοῦ νοός, Rom. 12:2; cf. the parallel to 12:3 in 1 Cor. 4:6), or in the later conviction that coming to faith involves a conversion from the deceitful desires of Gentile "futility of the mind" (ἐν ματαιότητι τοῦ νοός) to a renewed spirit of the mind (ἀνανεοῦσθαι δὲ τῷ πνεύματι τοῦ νοὸς ὑμῶν) that has "learned Christ" in the likeness of God (Eph. 4:17-24). At the same time, further reflection on the meaning of the terms "conversion" and "imagination" has led me to wonder whether the substance of what this account so powerfully captures may in fact be more adequately described, historically and perhaps theologically, in terminology *other* than that of "the imagination." It is that question to which the present essay intends to offer a modest contribution.

10. Hays, *Echoes*, pp. 186-89.

11. Hays, *Echoes*, p. 189; cf. *Conversion of the Imagination*, p. ix.

12. Cf. Hays, *Echoes*, pp. 146-49, where the element of "transformation" and "illumination" is set, more tentatively, within the context of a "hermeneutical freedom" that turns Scripture for Paul into "a metaphor, a vast [ecclesiological] trope."

13. So also Hays, "Reading the Bible with Eyes of Faith: The Practice of Theological Exegesis," *JTI* 1 (2007): 15: "the Spirit-led imagination, an imagination *converted by the word*, is an essential faculty for the work of theological exegesis" (emphasis mine).

Neither "conversion" nor "imagination" comes in for close scrutiny or definition in Hays's work. Even so, it is worth affirming from the outset that despite being somewhat "undertheorized," both terms are unquestionably effective in advancing the overall exegetical case. What I wish to examine here, then, is not so much the *de facto* exegetical and theological fruitfulness of appeals to "the imagination" in the work of Hays and others,[14] but rather the question whether this choice of terminology is serviceable to the historical (and theological) task.

Difficulties with the notion of a "conversion" of "the imagination" arise from historical and theological perspectives. Historically, both nouns depend for their contemporary meanings on relatively recent social constructs that remain to a significant extent debated. Nevertheless, the former is arguably somewhat less problematic in its range of reference. In relation to early Christianity and ancient Judaism, for example, phenomena of "conversion," "accommodation," and "apostasy" have in recent scholarship been much discussed from both social-scientific and theological angles; modern social-scientific categories like alienation, inculturation, resocialization, etc., have been widely applied, if perhaps also periodically questioned as to their methodological or conceptual adequacy.[15]

For all the requisite methodological caution, however, "conversion" in its biblical as well as ancient Jewish and Christian contexts is in the end a phenomenon known in outline to ancients and moderns alike, and relatively straightforward to identify in well-attested texts and terminology. A number of open questions would no doubt benefit from further debate about these issues; but the notion of a "conversion" or "transformation" of the Pauline

---

14. Luke Timothy Johnson, "Imagining the World Scripture Imagines," *ModTh* 14 (1998): 165-80, especially merits attention in this regard.

15. Following early landmark studies like A. D. Nock, *Conversion: The Old and the New in Religion from Alexander the Great to Augustine of Hippo* (Oxford: Clarendon, 1933), note influential works like Alan F. Segal, *Paul the Convert: The Apostolate and Apostasy of Saul the Pharisee* (New Haven: Yale University Press, 1990); and John M. G. Barclay, *Jews in the Mediterranean Diaspora: From Alexander to Trajan, 323 BCE–117 CE* (Edinburgh: T. & T. Clark, 1996); also more recently Kenneth Mills and Anthony Grafton, eds., *Conversion in Late Antiquity and the Early Middle Ages: Seeing and Believing*, StCH (Rochester: University of Rochester Press, 2003); Zeba A. Crook, *Reconceptualising Conversion: Patronage, Loyalty, and Conversion in the Religions of the Ancient Mediterranean* (Berlin/New York: de Gruyter, 2004); and, for conversion to Judaism, Louis H. Feldman, "Conversion to Judaism in Classical Antiquity," *HUCA* 74 (2003): 115-56. Patristic evidence is usefully surveyed in, e.g., Elisabeth Fink-Dendorfer, *Conversio: Motive und Motivierung zur Bekehrung in der Alten Kirche*, RST 33 (Frankfurt/New York: Lang, 1986).

reader's epistemological position and hermeneutical posture seems clear enough, and an important insight into the early Christian mind-set.

Here, therefore, we shall concentrate in particular on the question of the second notion — of what might fruitfully be meant by a converted *imagination*.

Imaginative Anachronism?

"Imagination" is a term whose contemporary usage and popularity seem to be deeply rooted in eighteenth- and nineteenth-century developments — one thinks here especially of the influence of Samuel Taylor Coleridge (1772-1834), William James (1842-1910), and others. It seems, at any rate, difficult to attest contemporary notions of the imagination before the Enlightenment, and striking to observe the transformation of notions of the imagination from the time of Blaise Pascal (1623-62), via Baruch Spinoza (1632-77), and leading eighteenth-century thinkers like David Hume (1711-76), Jean-Jacques Rousseau (1712-78), and Immanuel Kant (1724-1804).[16]

Part of the difficulty with identifying "imagination" as a heuristic organ of Pauline hermeneutics lies in the unstable nature of even modern definitions, which may owe much to romantic art or literature, to psychology or to philosophy. According to the *Oxford Dictionary of Philosophy,* imagination is fundamentally "the faculty of reviving or especially creating images in the mind's eye." In a wider sense, as Coleridge also thought, it is properly exercised in a disciplined, creative use of this faculty, as opposed to the mere indulgence of fancy. What is more, in the most general application, one may even find "imagination" involved rationally "in any flexible rehearsal of different approaches to a problem."[17]

---

16. In a study of strikingly similar title, Matthew William Maguire, *The Conversion of Imagination: From Pascal through Rousseau to Tocqueville* (Cambridge: Harvard University Press, 2006), surveys the history of notions of imagination in French thought between the seventeenth and nineteenth centuries. The most serviceable account of imagination in the history of ideas remains J. M. Cocking, *Imagination: A Study in the History of Ideas,* ed. P. Murray (London/New York: Routledge, 1991); also worth consulting are James Patrick Mackey, ed., *Religious Imagination: Festschrift for John McIntyre* (Edinburgh: Edinburgh University Press, 1986); and Mary Warnock, *Imagination* (London: Faber & Faber, 1976). Cf. further John Sallis, *Force of Imagination: The Sense of the Elemental,* SCT (Bloomington: Indiana University Press, 2000).

17. Simon Blackburn, *The Oxford Dictionary of Philosophy* (Oxford/New York: Oxford University Press, 2005), s.v. "imagination."

It seems significant that in pre-Enlightenment thought the appropriation of "imagination" as a valued, *positive* endowment of human anthropology is almost unheard of. This is especially clear in formative Christian texts of the early modern period. Thus, all twenty occurrences in the 1611 King James Version of the Bible, and all four in the 1662 *Book of Common Prayer,* appear without exception in the *negative* sense, as an expression of errant, deceitful, or wicked human proclivities.[18] "Imagination" in that sense appears closely linked to what the same Prayer Book's General Confession famously calls "the devices and desires of our own hearts."

Around the same time, Blaise Pascal similarly thought imagination the dominant and deceitful "mistress of error and of falsity," though not an infallible rule even of error, since it marks true and false with "the same character," distorted by the power of pride. Imagination, he argued, makes fools happy rather than wise; only those who are already wise can handle it with discretion.[19]

Used negatively, that is, *in malam partem,* at least the idea of the imagination (though not the term, with its distinctive semantic trajectory in English[20]) does have a measure of medieval and ancient Christian precedent, even if the eighteenth and nineteenth centuries' morally positive appreciation of the mind's free creative genius or framing of beauty is difficult to attest. For a morally neutral or positive picturing of the unseen, ancient (and, more generally, premodern) Jews and Christians tended to prefer the language of *memory,* of *wisdom,* of visionary and auditory *revelation* (or inspiration), and indeed of *desire,* a point to which we will return below. It seems that the cultural and conceptual space occupied in late modernity by *generative* (Promethean or neo-Gnostic) accounts of "the imagination" has

---

18. For "imagination" in the KJV, see Gen. 6:5; 8:21; Deut. 29:19; 31:21; 1 Chron. 28:9; 29:18; Prov. 6:18; Jer. 3:17; 7:24; 9:14; 11:8; 13:10; 16:12; 18:12; 23:17; Lam. 3:60, 61; Luke 1:51; Rom. 1:21; 2 Cor. 10:5; cf. "imagine" (16x) in Gen. 11:6; Job 6:26; 21:27; Pss. 2:1; 10:2; 21:11; 38:12; 62:3; 140:2; Prov. 12:20; Hos. 7:15; Nah. 1:9, 11; Zech. 7:10; 8:17; Acts 4:25. For "imagination" in the 1662 *Book of Common Prayer,* see Morning Prayer, the Magnificat; the Psalter, Pss. 5:11; 81:13; 140:8; cf. "imagine" in Pss. 2:1; 10:2; 21:11; 28:3; 35:4, 20; 36:4; 38:12; 41:7; 52:3; 56:5; 58:2; 62:3; 64:6; 83:3; 94:20; 119:69, 113, 118; 140:2.

19. See the discussion in Maguire, *Conversion of Imagination,* pp. 17-18.

20. German has no direct equivalent but relies on *Vorstellung, Phantasie,* and related compounds; French does use *imagination* but supplements the semantic range of the English with *fiction* and *fantaisie.* In Latin, *imaginatio* is rare (absent from the Vulgate) and denotes irrational designs or dreamlike fancies (e.g., *libidinum imaginationes in somno,* Pliny, *Nat.* 20.7.26 §68; *provincias secretis imaginationibus agitans,* Tacitus, *Ann.* 15, 36); alternate terms include *cogitatio* and *opinatio.* For Christian use, see below.

largely displaced the classic Christian experiential world once inhabited by Eastern icon painters and Western mystics alike, who *saw* and *heard* the realm of God with the eyes of the heart and mind illumined by charity.[21]

The term *imaginatio* was for the early church a powerfully fertile human expression of idolatrous hubris. The Vulgate never uses the term at all. Tertullian describes fascination with *imaginatio* pointedly as a mark of the Valentinian error.[22] *Imaginatio* is consistently evil or futile in Arnobius,[23] while Isidore of Seville considers it of uncertain and possibly Satanic origin, at work especially in dreams.[24]

Augustine's view of what modern writers might call "the imagination" is certainly complex and in part controversial, but it does not depart substantially from this patristic suspicion of imaginary worlds vis-à-vis the real (including the heavenly) created world. The mental picture Augustine employs in his search for the origin of evil (*Conf.* 7.5) is specifically associated with his *imaginatio:* his marshalling of the created order before the mind's eye *(constituebam in conspectu spiritus mei)* is part of an intrinsically misguided quest, evil *(malum)* in conception and wretched *(misero)* in effect, because it departs from the catholic faith of Christ. This is not to say that he denies a notion of mental perception altogether, but he expresses significant reservations about his friend Nebridius's fondness for imaginary worlds. In his *Epis-*

---

21. In this respect, Stanley Hauerwas, *Matthew,* BTCB (Grand Rapids: Brazos, 2006), p. 24 n. 1, writing on the project of Matthew the evangelist, quotes to good effect David Bentley Hart, *The Doors of the Sea: Where Was God in the Tsunami?* (Grand Rapids: Eerdmans, 2005), pp. 60-61, on the stance of Christian theodicy: "To see the world as it should be seen, and so to see the true glory of God reflected in it, requires the cultivation of charity, of an eye rendered limpid by love. . . . The Christian should see two realities at once, one world (as it were) within another: one the world as we all know it, in all its beauty and terror, grandeur and dreariness, delight and anguish; and the other the world in its first and ultimate truth, not simply 'nature' but 'creation,' an endless sea of glory, radiant with the beauty of God in every part, innocent of all violence. To see in this way is to rejoice and mourn at once, to regard the world as a mirror of infinite beauty, but as glimpsed through the veil of death; it is to see creation in chains, but beautiful as in the beginning of days." The stress on faith's renewal of hermeneutical vision is made explicit in Hays's own recent work, even while the appeal to "the imagination" is retained. Hays, "Reading the Bible with Eyes of Faith," p. 13, writes with reference to Paul S. Minear, *Eyes of Faith: A Study in the Biblical Point of View* (Philadelphia: Westminster, 1946): "We need to learn to stand where these witnesses stand and look where they point. Insofar as we do this, we will learn to see *as* they see; as Minear's *Eyes of Faith* promises, we will find our vision trained anew."

22. Tertullian, *Adv. Val.* 17 (PL 2.572); cf. Irenaeus, *Haer.* 5.1.

23. Arnobius, *Adv. Gen.* 1.46 (PL 5.778); 2.60 (PL 5.907); 3.15 (PL 5.958).

24. Isidore of Seville, *Sententiarum Libri Tres* 3.8, 11 (PL 83.670).

tle 7 (389 CE), Augustine objects to the idea that memory *requires* images generated by the imagination. In allusion to Socrates, he suggests that all thought is in some sense memory; but what we hold in memory is what we have seen, not what we now see by means of imaginary figments (7.1.2, PL 33.68). Specifically with respect to our understanding of eschatology, Augustine stresses that even eternity "does not require any image fashioned by the imagination as the vehicle by which it may be introduced into the mind. . . ." After considering three classes of images present to the mind, he concludes that the valid exercise of imagination is in relation to images derived from sense perception:

> When we were boys, born and brought up in a landlocked region, we could already form some idea of the sea, after we had seen water even in a small cup; but the flavor of strawberries and of cherries could in no wise enter our conceptions before we tasted these fruits in Italy.[25] (7.3.6, PL 33.70)

He concludes by earnestly warning Nebridius "for the sake of faith in the divine law itself" (*pro ipsius divini juris fide sedulo monuerim*) to break off without delay whatever friendship or flattery may have been begun between him and "those shadows of the realm of darkness" (*cum istis infernis umbris;* 7.3.7, PL 33.71).

The Greek Fathers appear to have no direct equivalent, although a study of terms like φάντασμα and φαντασία would reveal comparable results, driven in part by the negative overtones of those terms in most early and middle Platonic philosophy,[26] as also in the New Testament.[27] Similarly, one

---

25. Ita nos pueri apud mediterraneos nati atque nutriti, vel in parvo calice aqua visa, jam imaginari maria poteramus; cum sapor fragorum et cornorum, antequam in Italia gustaremus, nullo modo veniret in mentem.

26. Even for Plotinus and Porphyry, the pagan neo-Platonics most sympathetic to the role of "imagination," "*phantasia* stands to intellect as opinion stands to knowledge, and its impact on the soul is even deprecated in one place as 'a stroke of the irrational from without.'" M. J. Edwards, "A Portrait of Plotinus," *CQ*, n.s., 43 (1993): 488, citing, also *pace* John M. Dillon, "Plotinus and the Transcendental Imagination," in *Religious Imagination*, ed. Mackey, pp. 58-64.

27. NT usage is unambiguous: φάντασμα as a ghost (Mark 6:49 // Matt. 14:26; cf. Wis. 17:14); φαντασία as pompous display (Acts 25:23). For the ancient Skeptics, φαντασίαι are part of the subjective human cognition — but representing impression rather than reality, not to be sorted into truth or untruth. See Martha C. Nussbaum, *The Therapy of Desire: Theory and Practice in Hellenistic Ethics* (Princeton: Princeton University Press, 1994), pp. 291-93.

might note Origen's informed comments on wisdom's refusal to perceive the substance of God by "mere visions" and "human imaginations."[28]

Contemporary "Imagination" and Theological Anthropology

Theologically, too, the notion of "the imagination" as a neutral or positive human faculty has attracted considerable controversy. While in recent years the imagination as a fundamental engine of faith and theology has found prominent support, the associated proposals have come in for significant analytical criticism from a range of scholarly opinion.

One flash point of debate has involved eschatology, where writers like Trevor Hart and Richard Bauckham have strongly promoted the notion that Christian hope is accessible through "the imagination."[29] In that context, imagination supplies what is not seen, indeed what does not, or not yet, exist: hope, including Christian hope, is therefore "fundamentally imaginative," and its essence is to imagine things "that may or may not actually come to pass."[30] For Trevor Hart, as for David Brown and others, theology more generally becomes "a highly imaginative venture."[31]

In terms of Christian hope, John Webster finds this appeal to "imagination" questionable on a number of theological grounds:

> "Imagination" suggests something too projective or poetic, too little oriented to what has been accomplished and what is now being made known

28. Οὐ γὰρ ἐν ψιλαῖς φαντασίαις τοῦ θεοῦ καὶ πατρὸς τῶν ὅλων τὴν ὑπόστασιν ἔχει ἡ σοφία αὐτοῦ κατὰ τὰ ἀνὰ λόγον τοῖς ἀνθρωπίνοις ἐννοήμασι φαντάσματα (*Comm. Jo.* 1.34.243). Cf., e.g., Hippolytus, *Ref.* 7.38; the same usage occurs frequently in Gregory of Nyssa, Gregory of Nazianzus, Eusebius, Epiphanius, Athanasius, Basil, Cyril of Jerusalem, and many others.

29. Richard Bauckham and Trevor A. Hart, *Hope against Hope: Christian Eschatology at the Turn of the Millennium* (Grand Rapids: Eerdmans, 1999), pp. 84-88, 95-108, et passim.

30. The phrases, while characteristic, are taken from an interview given by Trevor A. Hart, "Gown," *The StAndard: University of St Andrews Staff Magazine* 11 (2007): 26. Cf. also William C. Spohn, "Scripture," in *The Oxford Handbook of Theological Ethics*, ed. G. Meilaender and W. Werpehowski (Oxford/New York: Oxford University Press, 2005), p. 98: "Christians become conformed to the 'mind of Christ' (1 Cor. 2:15) by using their imaginations under the grace of the Spirit."

31. Hart, "Gown," p. 26; note the trilogy of David Brown, *Tradition and Imagination: Revelation and Change* (Oxford/New York: Oxford University Press, 1999); *Discipleship and Imagination: Christian Tradition and Truth* (Oxford/New York: Oxford University Press, 2000); *God and Enchantment of Place: Reclaiming Human Experience* (Oxford/New York: Oxford University Press, 2004).

in the Spirit's revealing work. . . . Imagination is oriented more to possibility than to actuality, and it can make hope's envisaging of the future into a task to be undertaken, rather than the hearing of an authoritative divine judgement which has already been announced.[32]

Why should this necessarily be problematic? To understand John Webster's point about eschatology more broadly, it helps to consider that imagination concerns, by etymology and probably by definition, the making of images — whether graven or virtual. This aesthetically and culturally uncomfortable association of "imagination" with "images" is nevertheless one that finds plenty of echoes in Scripture and tradition. Kathryn Tanner makes this one of the linchpins of her incisive critique of the project of David Brown's *Tradition and Imagination,* for whom (understandably?) the programmatic affirmation of imagination and images requires one to marginalize Scripture's reserve in that department. "The incarnation as an endorsement of human creativity is in this way played off against the Bible," observes Tanner, which as a result "has no status qualitatively different from the other texts or stories thrown up by Christian creativity."[33] The insistence of Brown and others on such "image making" as a fitting means of theological perception is itself theologically problematic. More specifically, the widely encountered notion that it is somehow rooted in the incarnation tends to be a romantic misappropriation of Eastern orthodox theologies; in Brown's case, Tanner regards this as "wildly lopsided and quite inadequate soteriologically."[34]

Notably, what is lost in an approach to Christian doctrine by way of "imagination" is for Tanner summarized in precisely the terms Richard Hays wishes to safeguard for Paul:

> Lost is the soteriological importance of conversion, transfiguration, new creation, rebirth, or deification — indeed, the way of the cross and resurrection — the sense that we are in dire straits and radically transformable by God's grace.[35]

Here, then, our question must be this: to what extent is "the imagination" in the contemporary understanding proper to Pauline theological epistemol-

32. John Webster, "Hope," in *The Oxford Handbook of Theological Ethics,* ed. Meilaender and Werpehowski, p. 302.

33. Kathryn Tanner, review of *Tradition and Imagination: Revelation and Change,* by David Brown, *IJST* 3 (2001): 119, 120.

34. Tanner, review of *Tradition and Imagination,* p. 121.

35. Tanner, review of *Tradition and Imagination,* p. 121.

ogy, especially once it has been "converted" in the sense Hays so eloquently describes?

Ancient Philosophy and the Transformation of Desire

In pondering the possibility that contemporary appeals to "the imagination" may be an anachronism in the interpretation of ancient texts, it is worth taking a brief detour through Martha Nussbaum's landmark study *The Therapy of Desire*, which, like few other recent works of classical scholarship, manages to combine description with *aggiornamento* in analyzing and commending the pedagogical purpose of Hellenistic philosophy as a way to address the deepest challenges of human life, in both cognitive and affective terms. Nussbaum's nuanced and perceptive analysis has been widely acclaimed, even if in some quarters it has been thought to perpetuate certain "rhapsodic" anachronisms of its own. Critics have noted the privileging of a psychotherapeutic mind-set, the easy fugue of ancient with contemporary notions like the "unconscious," and the neglect of the widespread ancient linkage of εὐδαιμωνία with the goal of assimilation to the divine (ὁμοίωσις θεῷ).[36] What matters for our purposes, however, is Nussbaum's recognition that "transformation" of human cognition and affection is central to Stoic and other ancient philosophies. Although by no means averse to using the term "imagination" somewhat loosely and *en passant*,[37] she rightly focuses on the fact that the ancients addressed the pupil's passions — anxieties and angers, loves and hates — as susceptible to a transformation (in Nussbaum's terms, a "therapy") of *desire*. Despite some justified criticism of her preference for *therapeutic* metaphors (and her complete disregard of *Christian* thought in late antiquity), there has been widespread praise for her renewed emphasis on the link between ethics and εὐδαιμωνία, which is indeed pervasive in ancient thought. And in the case of Stoicism, the self-critical and reforming moral impulse is of course particularly potent both intrinsically and in the subsequent encounter with Christian moral and pastoral praxis: *Seneca saepe noster,* in this respect.[38]

---

36. E.g., Diskin Clay, review of *The Therapy of Desire: Theory and Practice in Hellenistic Ethics,* by Martha C. Nussbaum, *PhLit* 20 (1996): 503-4. The review by A. W. Price in *Mind* 106 (1997): 190 detects signs of "New Age rhapsody."

37. The term is not in her index, but pertinent references include pp. 28, 35-36, 40, 67, 68, 75, 107, 176, 312, 339, 344, 364, 415, 459, 462, 471, 476, and 487. Only a minority of these occurrences ostensibly paraphrase an ancient author.

38. Cf. Tertullian, *De anima* 20.1 ("Seneca is often on our side").

Transformation (if not always "therapy") of passion and *desire*, therefore, is to some extent an idea common to ancient philosophical as well as Christian moral reflection. It is here that we may see the contextual location of what Richard Hays identifies in Paul as the converted "imagination": indeed, the notion of a conversion of pagan into Christlike passions, like lust into charity and anger into joy, is a recurrent theme in the Fathers. Although perhaps most famous in Augustine, it is in fact strongly developed in Basil of Caesarea (ca. 330-379), Gregory of Nyssa (335-394), Maximus the Confessor (ca. 580-662), and eventually Gregory Palamas (1296-1359).[39] It is in this Christian revolution of the classical tradition that the New Testament's theological anthropology of a hermeneutical conversion of heart, mind, and identity arguably finds its most sophisticated exposition — a definitive point of reference in its *Wirkungsgeschichte*.[40]

Concluding Observations

The preceding musings cannot buttress a confident conclusion. But they do, perhaps, suggest that the theme of a hermeneutical conversion so powerfully described in Richard Hays's recent work could gain valuable definition from further study in the context of its premodern setting. Hays himself has masterfully expounded the implications for Pauline interpretation in relation to

---

39. See, e.g., Paul M. Blowers, "Gentiles of the Soul: Maximus the Confessor on the Substructure and Transformation of the Human Passions," *JECS* 4 (1996): 57-85, esp. pp. 60-61, 70-73, with copious references.

40. Space does not permit here a fuller exploration of *Jewish* parallels. Suffice it to suggest that Jewish piety too calls for a transformation of desires in close engagement with the divine will. OT passages like Ps. 37:4 point in this direction ("Take delight in the LORD, and he will give you the desires of your heart," NRSV), as does the tradition of Jewish prayer (including of course the Lord's Prayer). *M. Abot* 2.4 famously attributes to Rabban Gamaliel II the dictum "do His will as your will, that He may do your will as His will" (עשה רצונו כרצונך, כדי שיעשה רצונך כרצונו). For the "ecclesiotelic," that is, Israel-focused, dimension of Jewish hermeneutic, see also the insightful remarks of Rudolf Pesch, "Paulus und die jüdische Identität: 'Jeder, der den Götzendienst zurückweist, wird ein Jude genannt' (Meg 13A)," in *"Il Verbo di Dio è vivo": studi sul Nuovo Testamento in onore del Cardinale Albert Vanhoye, S.I.,* ed. J. E. Aguilar Chiu et al. (Rome: Editrice Pontificio Istituto Biblico, 2007), pp. 387-99, comparing R. Yohanan's principle that "a Jew is anyone who rejects idolatry" (*b. Meg.* 13a שכל הכופר בעבודה זרה נקרא יהודי, referencing Mordecai, described in Esth. 2:5 as both a Benjamite and a "Judahite") with Paul's view of Christian conversion in 1 Thess. 1:9 (cf. also Rom. 2:29, not nearly so far removed from this Talmudic sentiment as commentators typically suppose).

the hermeneutical stance of 1 Corinthians. Numerous other New Testament texts envisage a hermeneutic conditioned by the remaking of believers' ecclesial identity and affective world — a topic that was richly developed in the patristic period.

One of the effects of Richard Hays's attention to the Pauline theme of the converted interpreter is to problematize the conventional *Neutestamentler's* conception of the biblical author primarily *as a critic,* as a kind of creative genius who works his way upon a text. Without of course wanting to exclude or minimize that dimension of the hermeneutical reality, there is arguably a more important dimension whose force operates precisely the other way. As a matter both of phenomenological fact and of the biblical authors' self-conscious intent, their engagement with the Old Testament is partly a function of that text's own *claim and impact on them:* there is a distinct sense that they speak as they do because they are compelled by the pressure that Scripture *as a hermeneutical Other* exerts on their own view of things. In *Echoes of Scripture,* Hays rightly noted

> the extent to which the subtext is finally allowed by the poet to retain its own voice, to answer back, to challenge the poet's own attempts at integration. . . . Paul's proclamation needs the blessing of Scripture, and Scripture's witness to God's election of Israel stands in judgment of all formulations of the gospel. On the other hand, Scripture's witness gains its eschatological coherence only in light of the gospel, and the gospel stands in judgment of Israel's unbelief. The voices contend in counterpoint.[41]

What this also means, however, is that what would appear to the modern critic as a "device" or a "strategy" of manipulation will have struck the authors primarily as an expression of faithfulness to Scripture's evocative naming of the fresh reality God had worked in their midst. That impression of the biblical text's own directional energy is on a straightforward level true to what the authors say about their own encounter with it (Heb. 4:12 and 1 Cor 10:11 are just two among many instances). More than that, however, the New Testament's testimony to the force of that encounter shows the inadequacy of the sorts of Promethean conceptions of authors and "interpreters" that have been dominant in scholarship since the eighteenth century.

---

41. Hays, *Echoes of Scripture,* pp. 176-77. In a personal communication about this passage, Richard Hays tells me he now questions the appropriateness of the verb "contend" and would focus instead on Scripture's witness not only to Israel's election but also to the identity of Jesus Christ (e-mail correspondence, October 1, 2007).

A fuller study of these matters would exceed the scope of this essay, but would be well worth pursuing beyond the confines of Hays's initial focus on 1 Corinthians. Later in the Corinthian correspondence, for example, Paul sees the mark of the new creation partly in an epistemological conversion from a fleshly to a renewed and reconciled knowledge of Christ (2 Cor. 5:16; cf. 4:3-6; and see above on Rom. 12:1-2 and Eph. 4:17-24). Elsewhere, the use of an inclusive Pauline "we" in the hermeneutical articulation of the new "ecclesiotelic" incorporation of Jews and Gentiles is another significant pointer. Even while the apostles continue to acknowledge a distinction between "us" (apostolic Jewish Christians) and "you" (Gentile converts) in terms of ethnic origin, covenantal background, and perhaps (more controversially) Torah observance, when it comes to the identity of the united people of God as the body of Christ, Paul's hermeneutical stance is driven by his affirmation of a single hope for them all: "For whatever was written in former days was written for our instruction, so that by steadfastness and by the encouragement of the scriptures we might have hope."[42]

We find a similar correlation in later parts of the Pauline corpus and beyond. For Ephesians, the church's newly unified identity finds expression in the believers' striving to consolidate the Spirit-empowered unity represented in the full maturity of Christ, and characterized by a dramatic transformation of mind, understanding, and desire (Ephesians 2 and 4 passim). In the Pastoral Epistles, too, it is specifically the transformed desire for godly life in Christ that enables the believer to find the Scriptures "able to make you wise for salvation" (2 Tim. 3:12-15). And the notion of a rebirth of hope and desire recurs similarly in the latest writings of the New Testament; in 2 Peter, for example, the true Spirit-born prophetic reading of Scripture stands opposed to the misguided desires of the unregenerate (2 Pet. 1:19–2:3).

Once again, this cannot be the place to multiply such illustrations. Our conclusion here must be to offer this essay as a small birthday greeting to one whom this author owes a very considerable debt of gratitude, not only for unmerited and unstinting friendship, but also, and perhaps above all, for his inspiring exemplification of that spiritual and intellectual conversion of desire — indeed, of imagination — that marks the true student of St. Paul.

---

42. Rom. 15:4 NRSV, closely paralleling 1 Cor. 10:11 (on which see Hays, *Conversion of the Imagination,* pp. 8-12).

Walking through the Word of God:
Gregory of Nazianzus as a Biblical Interpreter

Brian E. Daley, SJ

Biblical studies really came into their own in the second half of the fourth century. As we look back, from the vantage point of modern scholarship, at the early development of Christian theology and at the scriptural interpretation on which it rests, most of us would probably identify Origen of Alexandria, in the early third century, as the first great Christian exegete. It was not until the last quarter of the fourth century, however, after the brief final threat of Julian's reign, when Christians were finally able to take on roles of leadership in the political and cultural life of the Roman Empire, that Origen's influence and example as a biblical interpreter would begin to bear abundant fruit. Basil of Caesarea's influential homilies on the biblical account of the six days of creation; Gregory of Nyssa's homilies on Ecclesiastes and the Song of Songs; Didymus of Alexandria's richly Origenistic commentaries on the opening chapters of Genesis, the Psalms, Job, and Zechariah; the self-consciously practical, less allegorical commentaries and homilies of the Antiochene interpreters Diodore of Tarsus, Theodore of Mopsuestia, and John Chrysostom, with their implied reserve toward Origen's style of thought; the elaborate Latin homilies and biblical essays of Ambrose of Milan, inspired by Origen, and inspiring in turn the exegetical works of his admirer Augustine of Hippo; and finally, the immensely productive exegetical work of Jerome, at once both Origen's imitator and his most virulent critic — all of these forays into biblical interpretation offered fertile ground, in a more peaceful and prosperous world, for the growth of the seeds Origen had labored to sow in the 230s and 240s.

In the context of this cultural and theological flowering, the one major

Christian thinker of the late fourth century who does *not* immediately come to our minds as a biblical interpreter is Gregory of Nazianzus. Always a paradoxical figure, Gregory stood out in his own generation — as well as for the later Greek Christian tradition — as a humanist, a supremely accomplished master of Greek literary style, most of all as the classical formulator of the deep implications of the Christian understanding of the person of Jesus and the persons of the triune God. Within fifty years of his death, Gregory had been labeled by Eastern Christianity as "the Theologian," the one who taught Greek-speaking Christians how to think and speak of God. Gregory left us a substantial literary legacy: 44 highly polished orations of various kinds; 249 elegant letters to friends and colleagues; some 17,000 lines of poetry, on Christian subjects but in impeccable classical meter and language. But his corpus includes no commentaries (except for a number of dubiously authentic fragments on biblical books attributed to him in the Greek catenae), and no set of homilies on a biblical book. Even his one oration directly focused on a single scriptural passage — Oration 37, on Matthew 19:1-12 ("becoming eunuchs for the kingdom of heaven") — is really not an exegetical homily but a reflection on marriage and celibacy in the turbulent Christian culture of Constantinople in 380, and on the appropriateness for Christians of the Roman law of divorce. A number of Gregory's theological poems deal with scriptural subjects: a longish hexameter description of the contents of the newly stabilized Christian canon,[1] several epigrams on Old Testament figures,[2] a poem on the genealogies of Christ in the New Testament,[3] another epigram on the twelve apostles,[4] and brief poetic presentations of the miracles and parables of Jesus in each of the four Gospels.[5] He has also left, in poetic form, a brief prayer for someone about to proclaim (ἀναγνῶναι) the Scripture liturgically, recalling the central importance of the biblical narrative of the economy of salvation for the lives of those gathered to listen to its

---

1. Gregory of Nazianzus, *Carm.* 1.1.12 (PG 37:471-74). The earliest full list and discussion of the canonically accepted books of the Bible by a Greek Christian writer is usually taken to be Athanasius's *Ep. fest.* 39.4-5, written in 367. Cyril of Jerusalem, in *Catech.* 4.35-36, dating from around 348, also lists the biblical books recognized by the church but leaves out the book of Revelation — as does Gregory Nazianzen. See Bruce M. Metzger, *The Canon of the New Testament: Its Origin, Development, and Significance* (New York: Oxford University Press, 1987), pp. 209-12.

2. *Carm.* 1.1.13-17 (PG 37:475-79).
3. *Carm.* 1.1.18 (PG 37:480-87).
4. *Carm.* 1.1.19 (PG 37:488).
5. *Carm.* 1.1.20-28 (PG 37:488-507).

words.[6] All of these poems deal with scriptural themes, but less by way of interpretation than as simple, catechetical summaries of Scripture's main stories and figures. To know the narrative, Gregory assumes, is to let oneself be touched by its content and be drawn into its movement toward God.

Yet in spite of this apparent lack of interest in biblical exegesis, Gregory still stands out as a theologian whose work is always rooted in the language and concepts of Scripture rather than in any philosophical system or strategy, and as a pastor whose sense of his own ministry is formed by the figures of the prophets and Paul rather than by any political or organizational paradigm. The Bible supplies Gregory, in his written legacy, not so much with material for explanation as with an imaginative world, a framework for thought and action and Christian self-understanding that emerges both from deep familiarity with the biblical text and from constant meditation on its implications.

By training, Gregory had learned to be above all a discerning reader of the formative literary monuments of his culture, from Homer and the tragedies, Demosthenes and Lysias, to the more recent representatives of Platonism. By training, too, he had been formed to use these literary sensibilities in moving his hearers and his correspondents to action — he was a rhetorician as well as a grammarian. And by decided preference, Gregory and his fellow Cappadocians had absorbed the biblical legacy of Origen. He and his friend Basil of Caesarea spent months together studying the Scriptures in Basil's family retreat in Pontus, and are traditionally thought to have compiled the *Philokalia Origenis,* a still-extant anthology of passages from Origen's scriptural commentaries and hermeneutical writings; it was at least a resource that they used, and shared with friends.[7] In his own distinctive way, then, Gregory was also imbued with the spirit and the project of Origen the exegete. Let us examine this more closely: first by considering his sense of the priestly and episcopal vocation as being essentially a call to proclaim the scriptural message; then by looking at his approach to the implied principles of biblical interpretation; and finally by considering a few examples of his use and treatment of Scripture in his orations.

6. *Carm.* 1.1.35 (PG 37:517-18).

7. In *Ep.* 115, to Bishop Theodore of Tyana, probably from Easter 383, Gregory says he is sending Theodore a copy of such a collection, "that you may have a memento of us and similarly of the holy Basil"; this has often been taken to mean that Gregory and Basil compiled the collection themselves, but it may simply suggest that it is something they found useful in their study of Scripture. See the introductory remarks of Marguerite Harl in her edition of the *Philokalia,* SC 302 (Paris: Cerf, 1983), pp. 20-24.

I. The Priestly Art

In a letter from sometime in the 360s to Basil's brother, Gregory of Nyssa, Gregory chides the younger man for abandoning his office of lector in the church in order to work as a grammarian — perhaps in the aftermath of the Emperor Julian's decree banning practicing Christians from teaching and interpreting Greek literature. "What is wrong with you, my good sage," he writes; "what do you regret about your life, that you have thrown away those holy, thirst-quenching books, which you once proclaimed to the people," and "have turned your hand to salty, undrinkable literature, and wish to be called 'rhetor' rather than 'Christian'?"[8] To proclaim and interpret the Bible in the context of the church's liturgy, in the office of a lector — to be a kind of liturgical *grammatikos* — obviously ought to take precedence, in Gregory of Nazianzus's mind, over any secular occupation, however similar the teaching skills the two positions may require; and to distance oneself from church ministry in order to teach Greek literature, whatever one's motives may be, amounts in Gregory's mind to a public scandal.

In Gregory's own complex career, the proclamation of the scriptural word clearly formed the center of his understanding of ordained ministry. "The distribution of the word (διανομὴ τοῦ λόγου)," he writes in his oration explaining his initial reluctance to be ordained a presbyter by his father (*Or.* 2), is "the first of our duties" — a duty so exalted that, in contrast to the theological rashness of some of his contemporaries, Gregory is seriously daunted by the prospect. "To me, indeed, it seems a task that is not for the lazy or for those small in spirit, to give to each one, 'in due season, their measured share' of the Word."[9] This role of providing biblical nourishment involves, for Gregory, not simply reading the text aloud to a congregation, but interpreting it within the wider context of the apostolic faith, as handed down in the church's tradition. Echoing the prologue to Origen's *On First Principles*, he immediately suggests that preaching involves "managing, with judgment, the truth of what we teach: what we speculate about the world or worlds, about matter, about the soul, about mind and intellectual natures, both good and bad, about the providence that binds all things together and leads them to their end."[10] But beyond these things, Gregory insists, full biblical procla-

---

8. *Ep.* 11, trans. Brian E. Daley, *Gregory of Nazianzus*, ECF (Abingdon/New York: Routledge, 2006), pp. 173-74.

9. *Or.* 2.35 (ed. Bernardi, SC 247, pp. 132-34). Except where otherwise noted, translations are my own.

10. *Or.* 2.35 (ed. Bernardi, p. 134).

mation involves underlining the place of Christ within salvation history, "his incarnation, sufferings, and death; with all that surrounds the resurrection, our end, judgment, and retribution, both sad and glorious; and most important of all, with what we must understand about the sovereign and blessed Trinity."[11] Interpreting the Scriptures means talking about God (θεολογία) from within the framework of the biblical narrative that begins with creation and ends with the second coming of Christ, who reveals God to us in the fullness of his Mystery, and has brought God's work to final realization.

Because it is centered on the "distribution" of this scriptural word to spiritually needy, often resistant human hearers, ministry, in Gregory's Second Oration, is painted as "the art of arts and science of sciences."[12] Comparing the church teacher's role to that of a physician,[13] even to an animal tamer,[14] Gregory sees the central purpose of recounting and interpreting the long scriptural narrative as discerning God's way of training and healing his hearers:

> This is why "the heathen rage and the people imagine vain things," [he argues at the end of a long litany of allusions to Old Testament texts and their fulfillment in the New], why tree is set over against tree, hands against hand — the one stretched out in self-indulgence, the others in generosity; the one unrestrained, the others fixed by nails; the one expelling Adam, the other reconciling the ends of the earth. This is the reason of the lifting up to atone for the fall, and of the gall for tasting, and of the thorny crown to rule over evil, and of death for death . . . , and of resurrection for the sake of resurrection. All these details are a training (παιδαγωγία) from God for us, and a healing for our weakness, restoring the old Adam to the place from which he fell, and conducting us to the tree of life, from which the tree of knowledge estranged us.[15]

But if the story the preacher tells is so central to human history, Gregory presents his own reluctance to take up the priestly ministry, in this oration, as coming from a deep awareness of what conveying this message requires from the preacher:

---

11. *Or.* 2.36 (ed. Bernardi, pp. 134-36).
12. *Or.* 2.16 (ed. Bernardi, p. 110).
13. *Or.* 2.16-22, 26-33 (ed. Bernardi, pp. 110-20, 124-32).
14. *Or.* 2.44 (ed. Bernardi, pp. 146-48).
15. *Or.* 2.25 (ed. Bernardi, pp. 122-24, trans. Browne and Swallow, *NPNF*[2] 7:210 alt.).

A person must himself be cleansed, before cleansing others; must himself become wise, that he may make others wise; become light, and then give light; draw near to God, and so bring others near; be made holy, and then sanctify them, have hands to lead others by the hand, have wisdom to give advice.[16]

So his models for priesthood, here and elsewhere, are almost exclusively prophetic rather than cultic: Paul in the New Testament,[17] the prophets in the Old.[18] Significantly, the final example he offers is that of Jonah, the reluctant prophet who tried to escape his vocation by running away, as Gregory himself was occasionally to do.[19] In Jonah's final, if somewhat coerced, obedience to God's call, Gregory finds comfort and hope for his own future work as a preacher and interpreter of the Gospel, despite his radical sense of inadequacy and unpreparedness. God makes the prophet who trusts in him into "a perfect leader."

II. Principles of Interpretation

Gregory's approach to scriptural interpretation, as revealed in countless passages where he attempts to make sense of texts and plumb their theological implications, is to assume — as Irenaeus and Origen had done — that the writings accepted as canonical by the Christian community, diverse though their origin was, formed a single coherent whole, with a single narrative and a single message centered on the fullness of redemption in Christ. For instance, in the last of his "mystery poems" *(Poemata arcana)* — eight densely constructed didactic poems, written in the 380s in the meter and language of Homer or Hesiod, which develop Gregory's mature views of the central subjects of Christian faith, as first set out by Origen in his treatise *On First Principles* — Gregory discusses "the Testaments and the coming of Christ," beginning with the question why God made two covenants with the human race. It is not that God has changed his plan, Gregory insists — "that is blameworthy even for mortals!" — but rather that "this is a loving God's way

16. *Or.* 2.71 (ed. Bernardi, p. 184, *NPNF*² 7:219 alt.).

17. *Or.* 2.52-56 (ed. Bernardi, pp. 158-66).

18. *Or.* 2.57-68 (ed. Bernardi, pp. 166-82). Gregory may be influenced here by Origen's conception of priesthood in terms of "laying open" the mysteries contained within the text of Scripture; see, e.g., Origen, *Hom. Lev.* 1.1, 4 (ed. Borret, SC 286, pp. 66-70, 78-84).

19. *Or.* 2.106-9 (ed. Bernardi, pp. 224-30).

of helping *me*."[20] Gregory goes on to summarize the biblical narrative from the fall, pointing to what he sees as the increasing infidelity both of humanity as a whole and even of "the race of holy Hebrews."[21] Eventually, in order to rouse Israel to a healthy jealousy and draw them to the fullness of faith, God sends his Son to become human as we are and, as the new Adam, to offer a share in Israel's honor to all humanity.[22] Christ's life and death, Gregory repeatedly emphasizes in this poem, is all "for my sake,"[23] makes available to me a new life in baptism; so both the early history of Israel — the exodus, the rescue from captivity, the messages of the prophets — and the whole career of Christ after the incarnation are meant to accomplish the same saving purpose of God, now not simply for Israel but for the whole of humanity, for *me*. "For mine is the blood Christ my Lord poured out, a ransom for primal ills, a recompense for the world."[24]

Gregory sees in the whole Bible, then, a message of salvation personally tailored to each of us, whatever our ethnic or religious origins — a message whose final explanation (to the degree that any explanation is possible) lies in the church's understanding of the incarnation and of the continuing ecclesiastical presence of the Word. It is that incarnation itself, when taken seriously, that enables the faithful reader to avoid the confusion generated by scriptural texts that seem to give mixed signals about who and what Jesus is, and thus about the salvation he brings us. He exists as Son of God in our human world, bringing into one story two infinitely incommensurable realities. So at the start of his Fourth Theological Oration (*Or.* 30), Gregory summarizes his interpretive strategy in dealing with the person of Christ in Scripture, "attributing to the deity the higher expressions, more suitable to God, and the lower and more human ones to him who is a new Adam for us, God made capable of suffering to overcome sin."[25] It is this perception of the Mystery of Christ's person, in turn, that enables Gregory to work out with unprecedented precision and subtlety his vision of God, as one ineffable substance or reality existing in three inseparably related centers of non-spatial "movement," which we have come to call "persons." "Therefore a Monad," as he boldly puts it, "set in motion 'from the beginning' in the direc-

20. *Arc.* 8.7-8, trans. D. A. Sykes, *Poemata Arcana*, ed. C. Moreschini, OTM (Oxford: Oxford University Press, 1997), pp. 40-41 alt.
21. *Arc.* 8.19 (trans. Sykes, pp. 42-43).
22. *Arc.* 8.25-33 (ed. Moreschini, pp. 42-43).
23. See, e.g., *Arc.* 8.26, 43, 69, 78-81, 93-95.
24. *Arc.* 8.80-81 (trans. Sykes, pp. 46-47).
25. *Or.* 30.1 (ed. Gallay, SC 250, p. 226).

tion of a Dyad, has come to rest in a Triad; and this is, for us, the Father and the Son and the Holy Spirit."[26] In all of Gregory's work, particularly his orations, the intertwined themes of the person of Christ and the Trinity of God recur like a kind of refrain;[27] it is the mutual inherence of these two schemata for formulating biblical faith that defines, for him, both the integrity of the church's faith and the central message of the preacher.

Like Origen before him,[28] Gregory bases his actual interpretive approach to Scripture on the conviction that a doggedly literal reading is usually a form of "enslavement."[29] Preaching (in *Or.* 37) on Jesus' saying about those who have "made themselves eunuchs for the sake of the kingdom of heaven" (Matt. 19:12), Gregory suggests that

> this passage distances itself from bodies, and symbolizes through bodies higher things. For to bring the passage to a stop at the meaning of bodily eunuchs is perhaps a small-minded reading, very weak and unworthy of the Word; we must, then, imagine something here worthy of the Spirit.[30]

In robust Origenistic style, Gregory is often willing to read passages in Scripture in imaginatively figural ways: to suggest, for instance, that the trees of paradise may really have been "immortal plants — divine thoughts, perhaps, both of a simpler and a more perfect kind," capable of nourishing the original human pair in their spiritual nakedness and simplicity by knowledge alone.[31] Moses' ascent of Sinai, and glimpse of the "back parts of God," suggests to him our ability to find God's law and even his glory through the contemplation of creation.[32] Even the otherwise obscure saying of Ecclesiastes 11:2 LXX, "Give a portion to the seven, and indeed to the eight," Gregory takes as an exhortation to live justly in the present world, created in seven

---

26. *Or.* 29.2 (ed. Gallay, p. 180).

27. For passages emphasizing, in some detail, right faith in God as Trinity as the center of Christian life and ministry, see, e.g., *Or.* 20.6-11; *Or.* 25.16-19; *Or.* 29.2; *Or.* 31.9; *Or.* 39.12; *Or.* 42.15. For Gregory's emphasis — primarily through chains of telling paradoxes — on the composite being of Christ, see *Or.* 29.18-20; *Or.* 37.2-4; *Or.* 38.13-14; *Arc.* 8.41-52; and his three celebrated letters criticizing the Christology of the Apollinarians: *Eps.* 101 and 102, to Cledonius, and 202, to Nectarius.

28. See, e.g., *Princ.* 4.2.2.

29. So *Or.* 31.24, arguing for the divinity of the Holy Spirit on the basis of scriptural passages that do not affirm it directly.

30. *Or.* 37.20 (ed. Moreschini and Gallay, SC 318, pp. 310-12).

31. *Or.* 38.12 (trans. Daley, p. 122).

32. *Or.* 28.2 (ed. Gallay, p. 102).

days, but also to anticipate authentically the world to come, signified by the "eighth day" of the new creation.[33]

For Gregory, too, the contemplation of what Scripture tells us about God's active presence among us, and especially what it tells us about the events of the life of Christ, is not merely an intellectual enterprise; like all ancient philosophy, it is knowledge that invites, even requires, active personal participation.[34] So toward the end of his great Christmas sermon *On the Theophany* (*Or.* 38), Gregory rapidly summarizes all the events the Gospels relate of Jesus' life as "mysteries" in which the believer is meant to share, emotionally and imaginatively:

> Journey (ὄδευσον) uncomplainingly through all the ages and miracles of Christ, as Christ's disciple. Be purified, be circumcised, remove the veil with which you were born. . . . And in the end, be crucified with him, die with him, be buried eagerly with him, so that you may also rise with him and be glorified with him and reign with him.[35]

At the end of the Fourth Theological Oration (*Or.* 30), after cataloging, in Origenistic fashion,[36] all the titles applied to Christ in the Scriptures, Gregory uses this same metaphor of a journey to suggest a meditative approach to these titles that goes beyond simple understanding, to admiring contemplation:

> These are the titles of the Son. Walk (βάδιζε) through them — those that are lofty in a godlike manner; those that belong to the body in a manner suitable to them. Or rather, walk completely in a godlike manner, that you may become a god, ascending from below for his sake, who came down from on high for our sake.[37]

To understand Scripture as revealing the single, life-giving Mystery of the trinitarian God, through the life and actions of the incarnate Son and by the gift and presence of the Holy Spirit, is to undertake a journey of ascent that

---

33. *Or.* 14.22; *Or.* 44.5.

34. See now Pierre Hadot's description of classical philosophy as primarily aimed at helping people live more freely and more virtuously, through learning to practice various "spiritual exercises": *What Is Ancient Philosophy?* trans. M. Chase (Cambridge: Harvard University Press, 2002).

35. *Or.* 38.18 (trans. Daley, pp. 126-27 alt.).

36. See, e.g., Origen's *Comm. Jo.* 1.16-40.

37. *Or.* 30.21 (ed. Gallay, p. 274, *NPNF*² 7:317-18 alt.).

transforms us utterly: to become a participant in a pattern of life that draws us beyond the physical and historical realm, into the eternal reality of God. It is our doorway to divinization.

III. Examples of Gregory's Exegetical Practice

We have already considered in passing a number of texts in which Gregory puts his techniques of scriptural interpretation into practice. It might be useful, however, to look somewhat more closely at two particular examples: works that reveal, in somewhat different ways, how Gregory uses the scriptural text as both a source of argumentation on the content of faith and a literary or cultural medium that defines the boundaries of his discourse.

The "Theological Orations"

Orations 27 through 31, probably composed in the summer of 380 during his embattled tenure as pastor of the Nicene community in Constantinople, are Gregory's best-known works: a closely connected set of treatises aimed at dismantling the attacks on the Nicene vision of faith then being mounted by the "Eunomian" Arians — anti-Nicenes whose main strategy was aggressive philosophical definition and analysis rather than a sustained, sympathetic consideration of Scripture and the tradition of faith. In the first of these orations (*Or.* 27), Gregory reflects briefly but trenchantly on what he sees as the conditions for carrying on any adequate theological discourse: spiritual maturity, moral probity, freedom from self-promotion, and a sense of the seriousness of the theme itself for human salvation. The main subject of the oration is what is required if one is to "philosophize about God" adequately as a Christian.[38] His critique is aimed mainly at those who allow this centrally intellectual inquiry to become simply a show, done for effect, like professional wrestling,[39] rather than as an expression of reverent religious searching. But even in this largely methodological piece, Gregory frames his question constantly in biblical rather than Platonic images, and with the help of biblical quotations. So he begins the oration with a quotation from Jeremiah 50:31: "'Behold, I am against you, insolent one' — insolent in education, in hear-

---

38. *Or.* 27.3 (ed. Gallay, p. 76, *NPNF*[2] 7:285).
39. *Or.* 27.2 (ed. Gallay, p. 72).

ing, and in understanding."[40] As he continues, Paul is his example of economical discourse, Jeremiah of compassion toward opponents, Moses of remembering God continually, Israel's exiles in Egypt and Babylon of letting reason lead one into alien territory.[41] Unseemly theological debate, in the language of this oration, is essentially pseudobiblical theatrics rather than biblical contemplation, "fighting over the word beyond what is pleasing to the Word himself."[42]

In the oration that follows (*Or.* 28), Gregory turns directly to the problems that face us in trying to conceptualize and verbalize our sense of the Mystery of God. God is "impossible to speak about (φράσαι)," he declares early in the oration, "and still more impossible to know intellectually (νοῆσαι)," because of the darkness of the human mind's present embodied condition.[43] So we must first content ourselves, as would-be theologians, with affirming *that* God exists, and with trying to define what God is *not*: God is simple, free from composition, incorporeal, incorruptible, unchanging.[44] But Gregory goes on to suggest that the human mind, embedded in time and space, must still try to reach out through its experience of the present world to find the God who both sustains and transcends it, and "through the beauty and good order of what is seen, to come to know God."[45]

The danger of seeking God through creatures, of course, is that of idolatry: mistaking a part of the world, or some image derived from the world, for its creator. No human being, in this present life, can hope for more than inexact glimpses of God's reality, affording one at best a greater awareness of God than may be accorded to one's neighbors: "so that if anyone has come to know God, or is attested as having known him, he knows only so much as to appear closer to the light than someone who has not been so enlightened."[46] Here Gregory seems clearly to be thinking about the witness to such privileged knowledge given in the Scriptures; and he goes on immediately to cite the examples of various Old Testament patriarchs and prophets, as well as of John the Baptist and Paul, as people whose graced experience of the reality of God in this life has at least allowed them to "prophesy in part" (1 Cor. 13:9). Even the language of Scripture, based as it is on the experience of di-

---

40. *Or.* 27.1 (ed. Gallay, p. 70).
41. *Or.* 27.1 (Paul), 2 (Jeremiah), 5 (Moses, the exiles in Egypt, and Babylon).
42. *Or.* 27.6 (ed. Gallay, p. 86).
43. *Or.* 28.4 (ed. Gallay, p. 108).
44. *Or.* 28.7-13 (ed. Gallay, pp. 112-28).
45. *Or.* 28.13 (ed. Gallay, p. 128).
46. *Or.* 28.17 (ed. Gallay, p. 136).

vinely guided but temporally bounded human beings, gives our minds only limited access to God's transcendent being. Still, the mind trained by biblical revelation should, Gregory implies, be able to grow more and more aware of God's reality in and through the diaphanous wonders of creation: the human self, and all the myriad of creatures that surround us. So Gregory invokes Solomon, Paul, and David as his authorities when, in the final third of the oration, he leads the reader through a contemplation of the natural world as evidence of the creative ingenuity of God.[47]

In the Third Theological Oration (*Or.* 29), Gregory turns directly to the received tradition of the Christian Scriptures: specifically, to classical "Arian" objections to Nicea's doctrine that the Son, incarnate in Jesus of Nazareth, is "of the same substance" as the God of Israel, whom he calls "Father." After discussing the language of generation and natural relationship at some length, he turns, as we have seen, to the titles and metaphors used for Christ in the New Testament, and to the paradoxical yet definitively important portrait of Jesus there, as a man beset with all our natural human limitations, yet powerful to do the works of God. Gregory's rule for making sense of this bewildering mass of scriptural assertions about Jesus and his works is stated simply toward the end of the oration:

> To sum up in a word, apply the loftier things to the divinity, to what is naturally superior to bodily passivities; but apply the more lowly things to the composite person, the one who emptied himself and became flesh for your sake . . . , so that you might break through the fleshly, lowly aspect of your theories and learn to rise above them, and to ascend to the divinity with him, . . . and might know what is said of him in virtue of nature, and what in virtue of the "economy."[48]

If one bases one's interpretation of the New Testament's portrait of Jesus on the church's acknowledged faith in the incarnation of the Word, rather than trying to move simply — in the opposite direction — from text to dogma, one has a guide that enables one to see the affirmations of Scripture as forming a consistent, if astonishing, picture of "God with us." A few paragraphs later, at the very end of the oration, Gregory brings his point home by boldly insisting that it is this biblically grounded rule of faith, as a principle of hermeneutics, that alone enables both philosophical reasoning and scriptural affirmations about God to be seen in their full meaning:

47. *Or.* 28.21-31.
48. *Or.* 29.18 (ed. Gallay, p. 216).

For when we cast faith aside and give priority to what is possible for reason, and destroy the authority of the Spirit by our investigations, so that reason is overwhelmed by the sheer size of the subject . . . , then what happens? The weakness of our reason appears to belong to the Mystery itself. In this way, the elegance of our reasoning is shown as "the emptying of the cross," as Paul realized [1 Cor 1:17]. For faith is what brings our human reason to its full realization (ἡ γὰρ πίστις τοῦ καθ' ἡμᾶς λόγου πλήρωσις).[49]

Faith — understood as both attitude and formulation — enables both philosophical analysis and exegetical inquiry to discover in the scriptural text God's word of revelation.

In the Fourth Theological Oration (*Or.* 30), Gregory turns his attention to particular scriptural passages that had been used throughout the fourth century to bolster the "Arian" arguments against the Nicene formula: ten classical texts in the Christian Bible that seemed to suggest that the eternal Wisdom is a creature (like Prov. 8:22) or that the Son is limited in power by his subjection to the Father (like 1 Cor. 15:25) or is dependent on the Father for his role as judge and Savior, in the way that a created intermediary might be (John 5:19 and 26; 14:28; 20:17). To all of these difficult passages Gregory applies the hermeneutical rule he has articulated in the previous oration: what speaks of the limitation and subordination of Christ refers to his human state, to the condition of humility and subjection the divine Word has freely taken on in the course of history for our salvation.

The Fifth Theological Oration (*Or.* 31), dealing primarily with the status of the Holy Spirit, is in many ways the most boldly speculative of the five, simply because the robust picture of the Spirit as a divine hypostasis, equal to Father and Son and bound with them in a substantial identity broken up only by interpersonal relationships — the conception of the divine Mystery as Trinity, in other words — was indeed new territory in the late fourth century. Here Gregory lays the groundwork for what still remains the classical Christian understanding of God, as radically one and irreducibly three.

The main objection to Gregory's presentation of the Spirit, as he acknowledges from the beginning, is that such a Spirit is "strange God, not mentioned in Scripture" (ξένον θεὸν καὶ ἄγραφον):[50] a Spirit both hypostatically distinct and fully divine seems to reach beyond the textual witness

49. *Or.* 29.21 (ed. Gallay, p. 224).
50. *Or.* 31.1 (ed. Gallay, p. 276).

of either the Old Testament or the New. Gregory devotes the first part of his oration to developing a trinitarian model for God that does not, in his view, violate the most basic affirmations about God's being that the whole of Scripture offers. He then returns to the question of the Spirit's divinity as ἄγραφον, unscriptural, in chapter 21. Much in Scripture is metaphorical, Gregory argues, and some of our principal present concepts for the Christian doctrine of God — concepts we assume to be more than simply poetic images — are only implied.[51] The careful reader, then, who seeks divine truth in the Scriptures, must avoid being "enslaved by the letter" and look beyond terms (τὰ λεγόμενα) toward their meaning (τὰ νοούμενα).[52] To do this, Gregory suggests, one needs to start from a broad sense of the history of God's work in the world, which is offered by the Scriptures taken as a single whole. There have been two great changes (μεταθέσεις) in humanity's religious consciousness since the beginning, he argues: first from idolatry to the law, in what we call the Old Covenant, and then from the law to the gospel, in what we call the New. These two spiritual "earthquakes" point to a third, which is still to come: "the change from the present world to the world to come, to a state that will no longer be moved or shaken."[53]

> The Old Testament proclaimed the Father, and the Son indistinctly; the New revealed the Son, and hinted at the divinity of the Spirit. Now the Spirit is present among us, offering us a clearer revelation of himself. . . . You see lights shining on us one by one, and an order in language about God (τάξιν θεολογίας) which it is best for us to observe, neither revealing things suddenly nor concealing them up to the end. . . . For our Savior there were some things which, as he said, the disciples "could not bear" at the time, even though they were filled with many teachings . . . ; one of these, I believe, was the very divinity of the Spirit.[54]

Gregory's argument, in the end, about the scriptural basis for the divinity of the Holy Spirit, and with it of the whole trinitarian doctrine he is laboring to formulate, is that Scripture is the source, surely, but does not present the final linguistic form of the creedal articulation of biblical faith. The very history that Scripture reveals, when it is understood as a coherent narrative of God's way with the world, must open the faithful reader to developments in

51. *Or.* 31.22-23 (ed. Gallay, pp. 316-20).
52. *Or.* 31.24 (ed. Gallay, p. 320).
53. *Or.* 31.25 (ed. Gallay, p. 322).
54. *Or.* 31.26-27 (ed. Gallay, pp. 326-30).

his articulation of faith that are governed by Scripture's logic but sometimes surprisingly new in language, content, and implications. The "earthquake" led by the Spirit still goes on.

Oration 14, On Loving the Poor

Other orations of Gregory deal less directly with the principles of hermeneutics or the criteria for finding in Scripture the basis of church doctrine, but show us other sides of Gregory's understanding and use of the Bible — especially, his relationship to the biblical text as an intellectual and cultural environment, a world of images and allusions in which his own exquisitely trained mind carries out its verbal craft. A good example of this is Oration 14, On Loving the Poor, a plea for understanding and compassion toward the marginalized and destitute, especially homeless lepers, that is one of his most powerful writings. This piece is probably one of Gregory's early works, dating apparently from the years 369-71, and seems to have been intended — along with two shorter sermons by Gregory of Nyssa — to support the campaign of Basil to improve the lot of the sick and poor in Caesarea during an outbreak of leprosy.[55] Gregory begins this centrally moral discourse by briefly discussing the virtues: faith, hope, and love; hospitality, jealous zeal for God's honor, chastity, self-control, frugality. For each of them, Gregory immediately offers a biblical example; each, he says, is a "path to salvation," enabling us to keep to Christ's way.[56] Yet if it is true, as Christ our Lord teaches, that "love is the first and greatest of the commandments, the crowning point of the law and the prophets," Gregory continues, "I must conclude that love of the poor, and compassion and sympathy for our own flesh and blood, is its most excellent form. For God is not so served by any of the virtues as he is by mercy, since nothing else is more proper than this to God."[57] Gregory goes on to describe the present condition of lepers in the city in vividly dramatic terms, drawing on all his skills as a trained rhetorician; what distinguishes his depiction from what one might find in Libanius or Themistius, however, is his constant reference to the Christian understanding of creation and redemption, and his constant

55. For the dating and context of this sermon, see my article "Building a New City: The Cappadocian Fathers and the Rhetoric of Philanthropy," *JECS* 7 (1999): 431-61, esp. pp. 454-56.

56. *Or.* 14.2-5 (trans. Daley, p. 78).

57. *Or.* 14.5 (trans. Daley, p. 78).

weaving of biblical references into his text. By a rough count, Gregory cites Paul twenty-six times in the oration, the four Gospels twenty-one times, the Psalms seventeen times, the Prophetic books seventeen times, even the book of Job four times — usually without reference to the source he is quoting. Like Augustine citing the Psalms in the *Confessions,* Gregory here is constantly working scriptural allusions as extra yarn into his tapestry, giving a distinctively Christian and biblical coloring to what he wants his audience to hear.

Ancient rhetoric was, among other things, the art of making well-chosen allusions: hints at a world of classical narrative and expression that placed both speaker and hearer in a familiar cultural milieu, in which each of them found affirmation and encouragement, models to steer by, examples to inspire and guide. Gregory uses this technique with consummate skill, but the world he invokes is not so much that of Homer and the tragedies (though he does this too, on occasion, especially in his letters), not the narrative of classical myth, but the language and narrative of the Bible. So toward the end of this oration, after a lengthy general reflection on divine providence and the instability of all human welfare — themes one might find in any philosophically literate piece of late-antique rhetoric — Gregory reinforces his appeal for *philanthrōpia* by a final, still more intensified reflection on Scripture. The reason for active mercy, in the end, is not simply philosophy or natural compassion but the "great commandment" of loving one's neighbor as oneself. Gregory then sweeps across a tissue of artistically quoted verses from the Psalms, allusions to sayings from Proverbs, and eloquent appeals to Isaiah and the Gospels — all urging the priority of love, all without explicit identification of the source, all readily recognizable to anyone accustomed to Scripture in the liturgy — and works toward his conclusion in a *stretto* of almost unintelligible compression:

> I revere greatly Christ's ointment-box, which invites us to care for the poor [presumably an allusion to John 12:3-8, and its reminder, "The poor you have always with you"], and the agreement of Paul and Peter, who divided up the preaching of the Gospel but made the poor their common concern [an allusion to Gal. 2:8-10], and the way of perfection of the young man, which was defined by the law of giving what one has to the poor [Matt. 19:21]. Do you think that kindness to others is not a necessity for you, but a matter of choice? That it is not a law, but simply an exhortation? I used to wish this very much myself, and supposed it to be true. But that "left hand" has instilled fear in me, and the "goats," and the re-

bukes that will come from him who raises them to stand before him [Matt. 25:31-46].[58]

Gregory's answer to this prospect of judgment, still echoing Matthew 25, is simply to see Christ in the poor, and minister directly to him in their persons:

> Let us take care of Christ while there is still time; let us minister to Christ's needs, let us give Christ nourishment, let us clothe Christ, let us gather Christ in, let us show Christ honor — not just at our tables, as some do, nor just with ointment, like Mary, nor just with a tomb, like Joseph of Arimathea. . . . But since the Lord of all things "desires mercy and not sacrifice" [Hos. 6:6], and since "a compassionate heart is worth more than tens of thousands of fat rams" [Mic. 6:7], let us give this gift to him through the needy.[59]

Scriptural allusion and imagery has become both the medium and the substance of Gregory's appeal, shaping the world of discourse in which his hearers may be persuaded to action.

IV. Conclusion

Why Gregory never attempted a biblical commentary or delivered a series of sermons on one biblical book is one of those questions, however much worth asking, that remains unanswerable. Perhaps it was simply that while his scholarly model, Origen, and his own contemporaries, Didymus and Jerome, always remained grammarians at heart — philologists, workers with texts — Gregory was, by preference, more of a rhetor; his interest in the art of words lay more in persuasion than in analysis and quiet discovery. Nevertheless, as I have tried to show, Gregory was a quintessentially biblical thinker and writer — someone whose understanding of God and Christ was couched in relentlessly biblical terms, just as his strategy for interpreting and proclaiming the Bible was always centered on his understanding of the incarnation and the Trinity, both doctrines central and unique to biblical Christianity. As a highly educated Greek Christian of the late fourth century, too, his intellectual and literary agenda was largely set by the reaction he and

58. *Or.* 14.39 (trans. Daley, p. 97).
59. *Or.* 14.40 (trans. Daley, p. 97).

so many of his contemporaries felt called to offer to the Emperor Julian's rescript of June 362 banning Christians from teaching Hellenic literature in publicly supported schools and thus suggesting that only those who personally affirmed the classical religious myths and practices interwoven with that literature could authoritatively represent Greek culture. For Gregory and for the whole new generation of Christian poets, Latin and Greek, who began to flourish in the late-fourth-century empire, the task was to begin creating a new body of classical letters, as perfect in form and diction as all that had been inherited from Homer and Virgil, but embodying Christian moral values and based on the true "myth" of the biblical narrative.

Gregory begins his poem *On the Genuine Books of Scripture* with what might be called a policy statement on how to use the Bible:

> Always be circling, in speech and in your mind,
> around the words of God: for God gave this
> to be a prize for labors, a light for seeing
> something hidden; or else, to be a blessing,
> that by the holy God's great laws you might be pierced;
> or third, that by these cares you might withdraw
> your mind from earthly things.[60]

The reason Scripture is so important, in Gregory's view, is that it is about us, that its words are meant to touch and change our lives. The narrative of Scripture, like the history of the church that has received it as the norm of its thinking and preaching, is really the story about each of us; it is the story of "my Jesus,"[61] whose life and whose death are "for *me*," the story of the Spirit sent to make *me*, and all of us, holy. And just as Origen, in the first book of his *Commentary on John*, could remark that "every good deed done for our neighbor by us is noted down in the Gospel, which is written on the tablets of heaven,"[62] Gregory too seems to assume that the text of Scripture really defines and evokes the world we live in: the place where we worship, surely, but also the place where we think and speak about our God, where we learn to love our neighbor, and where we follow our Christ. Perhaps he has relatively little of a technical, formally exegetical character to say about Scripture precisely because he speaks, most of the time, of little else.

---

60. *Carm.* 1.1.12.1-7 (PG 37:471-74), trans. Peter Gilbert, *On God and Man: The Theological Poetry of St. Gregory of Nazianzus* (Crestwood: St. Vladimir's, 2001), p. 85 alt.

61. See, e.g., *Or.* 37.4; *Or.* 39.1.

62. *Com. John* 1.11.68 (ed. Blanc, SC 120, p. 94).

The Domestication of Prophecy
in the Early Reformation

David C. Steinmetz

Martin Luther was sometimes hailed as a prophet by his admirers in the six-teenth century.[1] By identifying Luther as a prophet, no one meant to suggest he was a visionary whose predictions of future events had proven uncannily accurate. If accurate predictions were the final test of a true prophet, Luther would have been something of a disappointment. The unanticipated twists and turns of his improbable life often took Luther by surprise and would have confounded any seer. Even his prediction that the world would soon end — since he could not imagine how the world could grow any worse or be more ripe for a last judgment — proved in the end to be false. Luther died in Eisleben in 1546 and the world continued on its merry way into an indeter-minate future.

When Luther's allies called him a prophet, they were not calling atten-tion to his ability to foretell the future. They knew perfectly well Luther claimed no private revelations from God. Their definition of prophecy was somewhat more mundane. A prophet for them was primarily a messenger from God, someone who like the ancient prophets of Israel carried an im-portant and authoritative Word. In Luther's case, he was regarded as a prophet whose message had inaugurated a new evangelical age in the history of Christianity. Even if one differed with Luther over details — and many of his admirers did — no one could deny that his message had made a crucial

1. This essay was given as the Roland Bainton Lecture for 2006 at Yale Divinity School. I am grateful to Dean Harold Attridge and the members of the Yale community for their warm reception and generous hospitality.

difference. Had Luther remained silent, European history might very well have taken a different turn.[2]

Prophecy as a Transforming Word

There were, of course, a number of would-be reformers in the early years of the Reformation who claimed direct inspiration from God. Three of the most famous of these charismatic figures were the so-called Zwickau Prophets: Nicholas Storch, a weaver and lay preacher; Thomas Drechsel, a blacksmith of good character; and Markus Thomae (known more commonly as Stuebner), a sometime student at Wittenberg, whose father owned a bathhouse. The leading figure of the three was clearly Storch the weaver, who claimed to be instructed by the Holy Spirit (or by an inner Word) to oppose a religion that relied too much on such externals as sacraments and images of the saints. True Christianity is inward, argued Storch, and the truly devout rely on the inner voice of God.[3]

Luther, who thought himself second to none in his admiration for the work of the Holy Spirit in human life, nevertheless asserted that the inner activity of the Spirit is mediated by external signs, symbols, sacraments, and words.[4] The Word which God speaks to the human heart is always a mediated Word. It is invariably external before it is internal. The external Word provides a check on the tendency of human beings to confuse their inmost feelings with the voice of God.

Luther said as much in his polemical treatise *Wider die himmlischen Propheten.*[5] He ridiculed the prophets of inwardness, who pitted a fresh but untrustworthy inner Word against the ancient but reliable external Word of Scripture. Nor was Luther convinced by Storch's constant appeal to the Holy Spirit. Indeed, in Luther's view the Zwickau Prophets had so frequently

2. Which is not to deny that a Reformation of some kind might have occurred without Luther or to reduce the Reformation to a footnote in his life. It is only to affirm with Luther's contemporaries that the Reformation that did occur bore, for better and for worse, the marks of his active agency.

3. Older but still useful is E. Gordon Rupp, "Word and Spirit in the First Years of the Reformation," *ARG* 49 (1958): 13-26.

4. It is sometimes easy to overlook how much Luther had to say about the Holy Spirit. See especially the classic study by Regin Prenter, *Spiritus Creator* (Philadelphia: Muhlenberg, 1953).

5. WA 18:83.

claimed to have heard the voice of the Holy Spirit that a disinterested observer might easily get the impression "they had swallowed the Holy Spirit, feathers and all."

More important than Storch, Drechsel, and Stuebner was their radical pastor at St. Katherine's Church in Zwickau, Father Thomas Muentzer.[6] Muentzer was no admirer of Luther and called him such unflattering names as Doktor Lügner and Doktor Leisetritt (Dr. Liar and Dr. Pussyfoot). Muentzer differed sharply with Luther over nearly every issue. He could see no reason to think that God had ceased to make his will clear to believers by dreams, visions, and prophetic ecstasy. There were too many examples in the Old and New Testaments for Muentzer to concede that direct revelation by the Holy Spirit was impossible. He was therefore willing to defend in principle the proposition that fresh revelations from God do occur, even in Zwickau, and to offer in support his own claim that he had heard on more than one occasion the inner voice of God.

In actual practice, however, Muentzer was a good deal more conservative than his rhetoric implied. His extant works are full of biblical exegesis and notably devoid of fresh oracles from God. To be sure, Muentzer's exegesis is anything but standard and his interpretation of some texts must have left his congregations breathless. But imaginative exegesis, however unconventional, is not the same thing as a direct vision from God. In the end, Muentzer in Zwickau was no Daniel in Babylon. He was an interpreter, who offered fresh insight, rather than a seer, who delivered fresh oracles.

Luther and Muentzer agreed about one thing, however. They agreed that Christianity was not a scribal religion. For Luther this meant that Christianity was ultimately about realities that stood outside the biblical text. These realities were inaccessible apart from the Bible, but the Bible was always a means to an end and never the end itself. In an unforgettable image, Luther called Scripture the "swaddling clothes" in which the Christ child was wrapped.[7] Luther saw no way to gain access to Christ apart from the biblical stories in which Christ was presented, but warned that no one should confuse the wrapping with the priceless gift it contained. To master the biblical text and to miss its chief point was what Luther regarded as a fool's bargain.

What both Muentzer and Luther were listening for was the voice of the

---

6. For introductions to Muentzer's life and thought, see E. Gordon Rupp, *Patterns of Reformation* (Philadelphia: Fortress, 1969); Eric W. Gritsch, *Reformer Without a Church: The Life and Thought of Thomas Muentzer, 1488?-1525* (Philadelphia: Fortress, 1967).

7. WATR 6:16.

living God. To the extent they were intent on hearing that voice, they considered themselves less as scribes, custodians of a Word once spoken in the past, than as prophets, servants of a Word freshly spoken to their own generation. The principal issue between them was whether the voice of God was mediated by something external to the self. For Muentzer God spoke (or, at the very least, could speak) in a still small voice within. For Luther the Word God spoke afresh to the human heart had first been spoken by ancient prophets and apostles.

Which meant, of course, that Luther could not escape the scribal work he tended to regard as secondary. Even though careful work with texts was never more than a means to a larger end for Luther, it was nevertheless an essential means to that end. Accordingly, Luther's days were devoted to writing lectures and commentaries on the Bible, preaching on biblical texts, and even translating the Bible from Greek and Hebrew into Latin (the language of the classroom) and German (the language of the streets).

Luther observed that the Bible distinguished two kinds of words: *Heisselwörter,* or words that simply name and classify already existing things, and *Thettelwörter,* or words that effect whatever they signify.[8] When Adam named the creatures found in the garden of Eden, he used *Heisselwörter,* language as a symbolic system that orders a reality it did not create. But when God created the world, he used *Thettelwörter,* language that is indistinguishable from reality-transforming deeds. "Let there be light," said God, according to the book of Genesis. "And there was light." As Psalm 33 put it in a gloss on Genesis, "God spoke and it was done."

What made the Bible such an extraordinary book from Luther's perspective was that it is about words that alter reality and do not merely describe it. The ancient prophets of Israel seemed to Luther to bear a reality-altering Word from God. Like God who "spoke and it was done," prophets spoke a *Thettelwort* from God that changed whoever heard it — sometimes for the better, other times for the worse, but never without some effect. As with the prophets, so too with the later apostles and evangelists. Luther recommended that whoever wanted to hear the authentic voice of God should abandon reliance on what Luther regarded as an ill-defined and untrustworthy inner Word and listen instead to the voices of the prophets and apostles recorded in Scripture.

When Luther described the transforming Word of God as a *Thettelwort,*

---

8. Franz Hildebrandt discussed this distinction in *Est: Das lutherische Prinzip* (Göttingen: Vandenhoeck & Ruprecht, 1931).

he was using language more commonly associated in medieval Christianity with the sacraments. Medieval Christians believed a sacrament is a sign that effects what it signifies. Baptism, for example, does not in their view merely signify a ritual cleansing from sin. It effects what it signifies by washing away the guilt and punishment of original sin, including for adults the guilt and punishment of any actual sins committed prior to baptism.

Preaching, however, was never accorded by medieval theologians the status of a sacrament. Sermons could — and should — instruct parishioners about the nature of the church's sacraments and even warn them about the dangers of neglecting their use. But sins were forgiven in medieval Christianity by attending to baptism and penance, not by listening to sermons, however eloquent or orthodox. Medieval preachers prepared their congregations to receive the grace offered through sacraments, but saving grace was offered through sacraments and not through preaching. The prophetic task of the preacher in medieval Christianity was subordinated to the sacramental role of the priest. Good preaching benefited the church, but sacraments were essential to its life.

Luther saw matters differently. The Word of God was a *Thettel*, not a *Heisselwort*. It was Word as deed and not Word as adjective. The Word first spoken directly by God, then indirectly through prophets and apostles, was a powerful sign that effected what it signified. The same God who said "let there be light" also declared "your sins are forgiven you." Luther concluded that this Deed-Word of God is the fundamental sacrament and that baptism, Eucharist, and preaching are the three forms in which this fundamental sacrament is expressed in the practices of the church.

Baptism, as Luther pointed out in the *Small Catechism,* is not merely water; it is water joined to the transforming Word of God. Similarly, the Eucharist is not merely bread and wine; it is bread and wine joined to the same transforming Word. Even preaching is not merely human language; it is human language joined to and taken into the service of the Word of God. So far from subordinating the prophetic work of the church to its priestly functions, Luther redefined the priestly functions of the church in the light of its prophetic task. Priests, like prophets, bear the lively and life-giving Word of God to new generations.

Which meant, from Luther's perspective, that Muentzer and the Zwickau Prophets had it all wrong. Storch thought sacraments were a distraction that made it more difficult to hear the voice of God. Like the other Zwickau Prophets, Storch advocated inwardness over external practice. God, in his view, spoke directly to the human heart without external signs and symbols. But it was precisely the external signs and symbols Storch denigrated that offered Luther what he regarded as the only possibility for men and women to hear again the voice of God.

Luther was therefore happy to be called a prophet as long as everyone understood that modern prophets were bearers of a Word that did not arise from their own inward spirituality or prophetic visions but was mediated to them through Scripture. Unlike the ancient prophets of Israel, modern prophets were not the recipients of fresh oracles — Thomas Muentzer and the Zwickau Prophets to the contrary notwithstanding. But the fact that their prophetic proclamation was derived from Scripture did not make it any less a lively and transforming Word from God.

As Luther's career makes plain, early Protestants were interested not only in a renewal of the study of the Bible in its original languages but also in a renewal of its oral proclamation to the church. Preaching became such a central focus of the early Protestant movement that it overshadowed the celebration of the Eucharist, which had been the central focus of medieval worship for more than a millennium. Even sacraments were redefined as visible words of God. Heinrich Bullinger summed up the consensus of the early Protestants on their prophetic task when he wrote in the Second Helvetic Confession, "*Praedicatio verbi dei est verbum dei* — the preaching of the Word of God is the Word of God." Luther could not have put it better.

Prophecy as a Craft

While Protestants supported the renewal of preaching, they arrived somewhat late on the scene. Already in the fifteenth century many of the so-called imperial free cities in the Holy Roman Empire had taken matters into their own hands. Weary of uninspired preaching, they had invited gifted preachers to serve as *Leutpriester* (or people's priests) in their major churches. Unlike other parish clergy, the new class of skilled preachers was paid out of public funds rather than from church treasuries. They were excused from many of the pastoral duties other clergy were required to discharge in order to devote themselves to preparing sermons for Sundays and feast days.

The most famous of these *Leutpriester* was undoubtedly John Geiler of Kaysersberg, an Alsatian who preached in Strasbourg on the eve of the Reformation. Books of his sermons were immensely popular and circulated widely throughout German-speaking Europe. Geiler normally preached two sermons back to back on Sundays, each an hour long. One sermon was on the assigned pericopal lesson for the day and the other on a theme of Geiler's own choosing. Geiler once preached a famous thematic series on Sebastian Brant's *Ship of Fools*. His style could be fairly crisp. Commenting on war and peace, he observed: "Peace makes wealth, wealth makes one cocky, cockiness brings war, war brings poverty, poverty makes one humble, and humility establishes peace again."[9]

Geiler wanted to stress the importance of the prophetic task of preaching over the priestly task of presiding at the Eucharist. He did so by underlining the close link between preaching and the sacrament of penance. Preaching frequently casts the cold light of God's judgment on the failings and foibles of erring humanity, motivating the wayward members of Christ's flock to confess their sins to a priest. Penance, when correctly administered, is a powerful remedy for sin. It absolves sinners from mortal sins, i.e., serious infractions of God's law. The Eucharist, on the other hand, can only cleanse sinners from minor faults known as venial sins.

The conclusion seemed clear to Geiler. As mortal sin is more important than venial sin, so penance, which dissolves mortal sin, is more important than the Eucharist, which cleanses from venial. Therefore, the preacher who calls men and women to penance is more important than the priest who presides at Mass. It was an ingenious argument, but on the basis of Catholic principles, a theological nonstarter. Everyone knew that Eucharist was more important than penance, because it was the one sacrament in which Christ himself was substantially present. There was no way to top that. In medieval Christendom the priest at the altar was always more important than the prophet in the pulpit.

Although early Protestants had to provide their own ideology of preaching, they could admire the skill exercised by the late medieval masters of the craft. Even the young Philip Melanchthon, who had never heard Geiler preach in person, nevertheless wrote a Latin elegy to mark the occasion of his death. After hearing a sermon by Huldrych Zwingli, who was at the time a *Leutpriester* in Einsiedeln (and not yet a Protestant), Caspar Hedio remarked that his preaching was "elegant, learned, weighty, rich, penetrating, and evangelical, clearly such as to return to the effect of the ancient theologians."[10] Without a doubt there was much to admire in the work of

9. Still important for understanding Geiler is the study *Justification in Late Medieval Preaching: A Study of John Geiler of Keisersberg,* by E. Jane Dempsey Douglass (Leiden: Brill, 1966).

10. Hedio provides one of the important accounts of the debate between Luther and Zwingli over Christ and the Eucharist at the Marburg Colloquy in 1529.

Leutpriester like Geiler and Zwingli, not least their learning and skill. Preaching, after all, is a craft and not merely a charism.

Preparation for preaching required a different, more demanding, education than preparation to preside over sacraments. Most medieval clergy, especially parish priests, were not university trained. Clergy who studied at universities were often siphoned off for important posts in dioceses, religious orders, and government service. Protestants, however, wanted a preaching clergy who could read the Bible in Greek and Hebrew as well as in Latin translation and had studied rhetoric, philology, and the early Christian Fathers. When Calvin preached — which he did as often as seven times a week — he took the Greek and Hebrew Bible with him into the pulpit and translated the text into French as he spoke. It was a model for what the leadership of the movement hoped would happen on the smaller parish level as well.

What the Protestants had in mind became particularly clear in Zurich, where Huldrych Zwingli, formerly of Einsiedeln, now a *Leutpriester* in the Grossmünster (and an increasingly influential Protestant reformer), established a regular seminar called *Prophezei*. Later Puritans called similar seminars in England, modeled on the Zurich archetype, "Prophesyings." The seminar combined in one event the continuing education of clergy, religious instruction for schoolboys, and theological education for the laity.

The clergy of the city and canton of Zurich, together with boys from the Latin school, gathered early in the morning in the choir of the Grossmünster. If the biblical passage under consideration were taken, say, from the book of Genesis, it would be read first in Hebrew, then in the Greek translation of the Septuagint, and finally in Latin. One minister had been assigned to give a thorough exposition of the text. A second had been delegated to respond briefly to the first exposition and to offer corrections and suggestions of his own. A third minister discussed how the text might best be preached to the laity — at which point the doors of the church were opened and a fourth minister shared with the local congregation the results of the morning's studies in an extempore homily.

Prophesying in Zurich required hard exegetical work on the part of the would-be prophet. While Storch was correct to think that prophets should be devout, he neglected to mention they should be learned as well. The medieval church had not required parish priests to master Greek and Hebrew and demanded only enough Latin to get by. But the early Protestants, who redefined pastoral ministry as a prophetic office, set the educational bar much higher. By inducting all Protestant ministers into what an earlier generation would have regarded as a preaching order, the early reformers increased the prestige of parish clergy, while excluding from their ranks worthy candidates who could not meet the new educational standards. It is a nice question whether St. Augustine, who could never get his mind around Greek, would have qualified for ordination in one of the new Protestant churches.

Christ as Prophet

The model prophet was, of course, Jesus Christ. The early church had already identified him as a greater prophet than Moses. In the view of early Christians, he had been anointed by the Holy Spirit to bear witness to the truth, even at the cost of his own life. According to the Gospel of Luke, his public ministry began with the reading of Isaiah 61 in the synagogue at Nazareth, a passage descriptive of a prophetic calling: "The Spirit of the Lord God is upon me, because the Lord has anointed me to bring good tidings to the afflicted; he has sent me to bind up the brokenhearted, to proclaim liberty to the captives, and the opening of the prison to those who are bound." The account of the baptism of Jesus by John in the Gospel of Matthew alludes to a similar anointing, when it mentions a descent of the Spirit "like a dove alighting on him." The book of Acts also identified Jesus as a prophet, when it summarized a sermon of Peter in the Second Temple. According to Peter, Jesus was the prophet whom God had promised to raise up in the latter days. Although the Christology of the New Testament could hardly be summarized in the words of the liberal Protestant hymn, "O young and fearless Prophet of ancient Galilee, thy life is still a summons to serve humanity,"[11] it is nevertheless clear that the role of Jesus as a prophet was essential to the church's understanding of his identity.

Parish clergy in the later Middle Ages had not identified their work so much with Christ's role as prophet as with his role as priest. According to the book of Hebrews, Christ, who admittedly did not belong to the priestly tribe of Levi, was nevertheless described as a priest forever after the order of Melchizedek. Whenever Catholic priests were ordained, they believed they were inducted into that same non-Levitical order. Indeed, Christ shared his priesthood with them. It was not a common priesthood shared with the laity. Only a validly ordained priest could consecrate bread and wine in the confi-

11. "O Young and Fearless Prophet," words by S. Ralph Harlow (1931).

dence that God would transform the consecrated elements into Christ's body and blood. Every time parish clergy presided at the Eucharist, heard confession of sins, baptized the newly born, or anointed the dying, they were performing services of which Christ was the priestly source and archetype.

Protestants, on the other hand, identified with Christ as prophet, both because they regarded his priestly office as unique and unrepeatable and because they had redefined the priestly functions of the parish clergy as largely prophetic. Just as preaching was the spoken Word of God, so too were the sacraments the Word of God in visible form. In order for preaching to be a transforming Word of God, it must, of course, be derived from Scripture and conform to its central teaching. Christ as prophet — namely, as a teacher of saving truth — provided the norms according to which Scripture could be properly understood and apart from which it would inevitably be misinterpreted.

The fact that Christ was the final and definitive teacher of saving truth put an end for early Protestants to all free prophecy, including the new oracles touted by the Zwickau Prophets. No one wanted to deny that fresh insight was always possible, even from Storch and Muentzer. What Luther and Zwingli rejected was the claim of all radical visionaries to fresh revelation. Christ's prophetic office had put an end to free prophecy. True prophets were now governed by the rule of faith, understood not as an addition to Scripture but as its distillate.

In his classic treatment of the threefold office of Christ as prophet, priest, and king, John Calvin observed that Christ was anointed by the Holy Spirit as a prophet, not only in his own person, but also as the head of his body, the church.[12] The anointing of Christ was the act that authorized the preaching and teaching of the gospel by Christians. Sometimes the prophetic office of the church was discharged informally, as lay people spoke God's Word of judgment and grace to each other in private conversation. Sometimes it was discharged formally by clergy, who proclaimed the gospel publicly through sermons and the administration of the sacraments. But however discharged, it was an extension of the work of Christ as prophet.

It is difficult to overstate the importance of Christ's prophetic office for the early Protestant movement. Just as medieval priests regarded themselves authorized to preside at the sacraments through their participation in the priesthood of Christ, so Protestant pastors regarded themselves authorized

---

12. On Christ as prophet, see John Calvin, *Institutes of the Christian Religion* (Latin edition 1559) 2.15.1-2.

to preach and teach the Word of God through their participation in the anointing of Christ as prophet. The sermon, which had played a subordinate role in the medieval church, became the central act of Protestant worship. Laity, who had come to church under the old order to pray and adore the consecrated host, were now told to be quiet and to listen to the sermons that had once been optional. No wonder Calvin characterized the rightly ordered church as a school and not merely as a nurturing mother.

Conclusion

Which brings us, finally, to the title of the essay. Early Protestants domesticated prophecy by rejecting the dreams and visions of radicals like Storch and Muentzer, on the one hand, and by institutionalizing prophecy as a mediated and derivative activity, on the other. But while the Protestant reformers domesticated prophecy, they did not tame it. They were aware that the Word of God, understood as Luther had understood it, was a *Thettelwort Gottes*. It was a transforming Word that was never wholly under the control of the interpreter. God used human language to achieve God's purposes, which might — or might not — be identical with the aspirations of the would-be prophets who proclaimed them.

Set in this context, the claim that Martin Luther was a prophet seems a good deal less radical than it first appeared. He was, in the end, only one prophet among many, understood as the recipient not of fresh revelations but of fresh insights into an ancient and settled revelation. Indeed, viewed from one angle, the Protestant Reformation could be described as a prophetic movement in the late medieval Catholic Church. It transformed what had been a sacramental fellowship in which preaching had been regarded as beneficial but not essential into a worshiping assembly in which the public preaching of the Word became the central defining act. If Catholic priests were authorized to preside at sacraments by an appeal to Christ as a priest forever after the order of Melchizedek, Protestants were authorized to preach and teach by an appeal to Christ as a prophet and teacher of saving truth. The shift from sacrament to sermon had fateful consequences for both Protestants and Catholics. But that is the subject of another paper.

The Bard and the Book:
Shakespeare's Interpretation of Scripture

A. Katherine Grieb

> *"Kiss the book," slurs Stefano, the shipwrecked butler, in Act 2, Scene 2 of* The Tempest. *Spectators see him sharing a swig of wine from his homemade bark bottle with the drunken savage, Caliban. The words that he travesties with the language of the tavern originate in the house of worship, where they refer to a loving connection between a reader and a text. "The book," in English, signifies only one book, the Bible.*[1]

So begins Steven Marx's provocative study of Shakespeare and the Bible.[2] Marx reminds us that William Tyndale, the Protestant who first translated the Bible into English, was burned at the stake while hundreds of copies of his newly printed book fed the flames. Tyndale was one of the Marian martyrs, so named for Henry VIII's oldest daughter, the Roman Catholic queen who ruled England from 1553 to 1558. Mary's half-sister and Protestant successor Elizabeth, who made not a few martyrs of her own, reinstated the practice of reading the Bible politically as well as devotionally, "'kissing the book' herself in the course of a public ceremony at which she accepted a

---

1. Steven Marx, *Shakespeare and the Bible* (New York: Oxford University Press, 2000), p. 1.

2. An earlier version of this paper was given as the Presidential Address for the Annual Meeting of the Mid-Atlantic Region of the Society of Biblical Literature in March 2007. It is a pleasure to dedicate this to Professor Richard B. Hays, who has taught us all so much about the art of reading Scripture.

copy of the Bible from the allegorical figure of Truth and promised to read in it every day."[3]

Precisely what is Shakespeare doing here? Is he, as some readers have thought, approaching blasphemy when he has the drunken Stefano hand another drunk the bottle, urging him to "kiss the book"? Is he mocking the high doctrine of the Word of God written, held by conforming Protestants, nonconforming Protestant Puritans, and nonconforming Roman Catholics alike? Is he referencing a liturgical practice that would have been honored by old-fashioned crypto-Catholics and by some *Book of Common Prayer* Protestants like Elizabeth I, but not by Puritans? Is it a pointed "in" joke that only a certain portion of his audience would have understood? Or is he just fooling around, causing his clown Stefano to confuse the sacred and the secular in high comedy, something we see him doing often enough on other topics? Surely it would be a mistake to identify the speech of one of Shakespeare's clowns with the opinion of the playwright himself — or would it? This small incident points to the complexity of the topic of Shakespeare's multiple uses of the Bible, let alone what we might be able to discern from these about the playwright's hermeneutics and his theology of Scripture.[4]

Here we are only somewhat concerned with historical methodology (the question of the historical situation behind Shakespeare's texts and what we can recover about the author's intentions) and much more with intertextuality (in this case, the use of the books of the biblical canon as primary or predecessor texts in the secondary texts that make up the canon of Shakespeare's plays). As Luke Johnson notes in another essay within this volume, when present-day readers forgo attempts at historical reconstruction in order to focus on questions of canonicity and intertextuality,

> we are like theologians who read a Gospel in the context of the Bible as a whole rather than in the imagined context of its original audience, or students of Shakespeare who consider one of his plays as a textual composition within the complete works rather than as a drama performed before an Elizabethan audience.[5]

3. Marx, *Shakespeare and the Bible,* p. 4, citing Gail Paster, "The Idea of London in Masque and Pageant," in *Pageantry in the Shakespearian Theatre,* ed. David Bergeron (Athens: University of Georgia Press, 1985), p. 66.

4. Scripture quotations not otherwise identified are from the NRSV. Quotations from Shakespeare not otherwise identified are from *The Complete Works of William Shakespeare: The Alexander Text* (Glasgow: HarperCollins, 2006 [1994]).

5. Luke Timothy Johnson, "John and *Thomas* in Context: An Exercise in Canonical Criticism," his note 18.

This student of Shakespeare is far from claiming expertise in matters of the Shakespearian canon; attempting to understand the biblical canon is already the work of a lifetime! Nor is it possible to do justice here to the complexity of Shakespeare's use of the Bible within his complete works or even in one play. My aims in this essay are considerably more modest. After brief surveys of the scholarship with respect to Shakespeare's religious commitments, if any, and Shakespeare's citations of the Bible, I will suggest that Shakespeare's use of Scripture is an area where literary and biblical criticism might profitably combine forces. From the area of New Testament studies, and Paul's intertextuality in particular, I will draw on the work of J. Louis Martyn and Richard B. Hays to suggest a way forward on the question of Shakespeare's interpretation of Scripture. I will comment briefly on a few of Shakespeare's biblical references in the only play that directly alludes to Scripture in its title, *Measure for Measure,* one of the mature Shakespeare's most notorious "problem plays," concluding with a few thoughts about the significance of Shakespeare's use of the Bible for ethical debate.

I. Was Shakespeare a Christian? — And If So, What Kind of Christian?

There are many approaches to the question of Shakespeare and religion or Shakespeare and Christianity. We might consider first an ethics-of-reading question framed by doubts about whether Shakespeare should be called "Christian," and whether a Christian ought to read Shakespeare, on the part of certain conservative evangelical readers. An example is Rowland Cotterill's essay "Shakespeare and Christianity,"[6] where Cotterill worries about the contents of the plays, and notes many non-evangelical features within them, but argues that Christians can read Shakespeare with discernment, accepting what they can and rejecting what they must. Other Christian readers, both evangelical and more catholic, defend Shakespeare from charges of secularism, blasphemy, and heresy as they can. Since we have no knowledge that the playwright ever stepped in front of the curtain to comment on his plays, as, for example, Oscar Wilde did, the plays and the characters in them

---

6. Rowland Cotterill, "Shakespeare and Christianity," in *The Discerning Reader: Christian Perspectives on Literature and Theory,* ed. D. Barratt, R. Pooley, and L. Ryken (Grand Rapids: Baker, 1995), pp. 155-75.

require considerable discernment on the part of the hearer/reader who would inquire after Shakespeare's Christianity. A great deal depends on whether the speech of a particular character is taken to represent the point of view of the author himself.

Distinct from but related to the question about whether and how Christians ought to read Shakespeare (whether his work is "Christian" enough) is the historical question of Shakespeare's own religious beliefs. It is assumed by most literary critics that Shakespeare was a Christian, in response to Wordsworth and other critics within the romantic movement who contrasted the "secular" plays of Shakespeare with the theologically freighted work of Spenser and Milton. And it is usually assumed — or at least has been, until fairly recently — that he was a Protestant, but his apparent Protestantism can be played out in several ways.

One school of thought holds that Shakespeare may have been a "conforming Protestant," that is, conforming to the Elizabethan Settlement of the Church of England. Technically, the term "Anglican" is premature to describe an author living during the Shakespearean period, a slight historical anachronism. It is, however, convenient to speak of incipient or proto-Anglicanism and to contrast it with Puritanism, which was pushing English Protestantism to move in a more Reformed direction. Conforming Protestants were distinguished from "recusants" who failed to attend Church of England services. There are no records of Shakespeare's church attendance, as there are for many actors of his day.[7] Shakespeare's father, to be sure, had been indicted for recusancy, but Shakespeare himself never was, so he may actually have attended Church of England services.[8] It is the plays that provide the primary evidence of such familiarity with Anglican liturgy and other traditions that suggest firsthand experience of them rather than hearsay.

If Shakespeare was a proto-Anglican, that might explain why there are so many references not only to Scripture but also to the *Book of Common Prayer* and the two books of the *Homilies,* the first from the time of Archbishop Cranmer under Henry VIII and the second from Queen Elizabeth's

---

7. Peter Milward, *Shakespeare's Religious Background* (Bloomington: Indiana University Press, 1973), p. 104.

8. The Church of the Holy Trinity at Stratford records his baptism and burial there. In that church all three of his children were baptized and his two daughters were married. But there are no recorded personal connections with any church in London, only a tax assessment document linking him with St. Helen's, Bishopsgate, for the three years between 1596 and 1599. See Milward, *Shakespeare's Religious Background,* p. 104.

Archbishop Parker.[9] Further evidence for Shakespeare's "conforming Protestant" leanings is found in the significant attention his plays give to the notion of the divine right of kings and the horror of regicide,[10] a position supported by the monarchy, naturally, but also by conforming Protestant theologians from Thomas Cranmer on, with the notable exception of Richard Hooker, who insisted on the consent of the governed as an important foundation for the monarchy, both in law and in theology.

Another group claims that even if Shakespeare was forced to attend Church of England services, he may also have been a "recusant Protestant," or Puritan. This argument, based on the alleged historical evidence that Shakespeare quotes more often from the Geneva Bible, the Bible of the Continental Reformers, than from any other text,[11] was popularized by Richmond Noble, who wrote *Shakespeare's Biblical Knowledge* back in 1935.[12] Noble's study gave the impression that Shakespeare read English Protestant versions of the Bible, especially favoring the Geneva Bible later in life. But his work was not systematic and this question is tricky: it is notoriously difficult to tie Shakespeare's biblical citations to any one text, because the texts themselves varied so much. Naseeb Shaheen, who himself leans toward the position that Shakespeare was a nonconforming Protestant, and who has done a great deal of research in this area, reports that he has consulted seventy different editions of the Geneva Bible.[13] Such a plethora of versions makes it difficult to show Shakespeare's primary allegiance to one translation. Another, more serious problem for this argument is the number of spe-

9. Milward devotes a chapter to Shakespeare's allusions to the Prayer Book and the *Homilies;* see *Shakespeare's Religious Background,* pp. 104-25.

10. *Richard II* (published in 1597 but probably written in 1595) is a more complicated case than most of the plays on this point. Although it contains brilliant rhetoric concerning the divine right of kings, as in 3.2.36-62, and about the chaos that follows when the spiritual foundations of the monarchy are destroyed, as in 4.1.136-47, the legitimate king has squandered the land's resources and subverted national order while the usurper acts in the name of justice and proves a reliable and strong leader.

11. English translations of the Bible available to Shakespeare included at least the following: Tyndale's New Testament (1535), Taverner Bible (1539), Matthew Bible (1549), Great Bible (Archbishop Cranmer, 1553), Coverdale Bible (1553), Geneva Bible (1582), Rheims New Testament (Roman, 1582), Bishops' Bible (Archbishop Parker, 1584), and Douay Old Testament (Roman, 1609-10).

12. Richmond Noble, *Shakespeare's Biblical Knowledge and Use of the Book of Common Prayer as Exemplified in the Plays of the First Folio* (New York: Octagon, 1970 [1935]).

13. Naseeb Shaheen, *Biblical References in Shakespeare's Comedies* (Newark: University of Delaware Press, 1993), p. 10.

cifically anti-Puritan references in the plays, together with the well-known fact that the Puritans were trying to close the theaters — not just religious theaters but all theaters — and eventually succeeded in doing so under Cromwell's reign. It is hard to imagine any seriously Puritan playwright during the historical period in which Shakespeare lived.

A third group argues that Shakespeare may have been a conforming Protestant for political reasons but that personally he was a crypto-Catholic. Peter Milward set this agenda back in the 1970s with his book *Shakespeare's Religious Background*,[14] and it has been carried forward by David Beauregard[15] and other scholars. Their work has been considerably strengthened by the revisionist account of the Reformation spearheaded by Christopher Haigh,[16] J. J. Scarisbrick,[17] and especially Eamon Duffy, whose *The Stripping of the Altars: Traditional Religion in England*[18] showed that although Henry VIII and his successors (again, the Puritans were the worst) imposed drastic religious reforms, tearing down rood screens in local parishes, destroying liturgical vestments and accessories, breaking stained-glass windows, knocking off the heads of religious statues, and leveling monastic buildings, the common people, especially in the countryside, clung to the traditional Roman Catholic faith. They simply went underground to escape persecution and harassment. Shakespeare's daughter Susanna was charged with being "popishly affected" in 1606 when she failed to take communion in the Church of England.[19] Probable connections with important Jesuit leaders can be demonstrated for several members of Shakespeare's family and perhaps for Shakespeare himself, though, again, a lot of the argument depends on circumstantial evidence.

A last school of thought calls our attention to the history of England immediately before Shakespeare's birth: Henry VIII's break with Rome; the radical Protestantism of Edward VI and his advisors; the staunch Roman Catholicism of Mary Tudor; the religious settlement of Elizabeth I, which seems to have pleased no one entirely; and the short-lived hope of Roman Catholic restoration in the form of Mary, Queen of Scots. With all the see-sawing back and forth, and with martyrs on all sides, maybe Shakespeare

---

14. See n. 7 above.

15. David Beauregard, "Shakespeare and the Bible," *RelArts* 5 (2001): 317-30.

16. Christopher Haigh, *The Plain Man's Pathways to Heaven: Kinds of Christianity in Post-Reformation England, 1570-1640* (Oxford: Oxford University Press, 2007).

17. J. J. Scarisbrick, *The Reformation and the English People* (Oxford: Blackwell, 1984).

18. Eamon Duffy, *The Stripping of the Altars: Traditional Religion in England, c.1400-c.1580* (New Haven: Yale University Press, 2005).

19. Beauregard, "Shakespeare and the Bible," p. 317.

was simply cynical about the whole religious project. Perhaps he intended his plays to be "secular," not in the sense that they opposed religion or any one form of it, but "secular" in the sense that they took no one point of view and served primarily to raise questions about religious issues, such as the Anglican insistence on the divine right of kings, the Puritan doctrine of predestination, or the Jesuit theology of equivocation. Maybe, at least in this sense, the romantic movement critics were right after all. At any rate, whatever Shakespeare thought personally about theology and religion, he took it to the grave with him. The times he lived in suggested caution.

II. Shakespeare and the Bible:
Two Major Approaches to the Question

With respect to Shakespeare's use of Scripture, which is not perceived to be as controversial an issue as his religious affiliations (if any), there is considerably less scholarship to summarize. Two primary patterns of research are easily identified: the first systematically catalogues the biblical references in Shakespeare's plays, listing them next to the pertinent lines with a minimum of interpretive comment, while the second attempts to discover broad parallels between the larger thematic structures of biblical books or narratives and Shakespeare's plays.

Naseeb Shaheen is the contemporary scholar who has done the most to catalogue possible references to Scripture in Shakespeare. He has published three separate volumes collecting the biblical references in Shakespeare's tragedies, histories, and comedies, which have now been combined in a single volume, *Biblical References in Shakespeare's Plays*.[20] Everyone interested in this topic inevitably consults Shaheen's work with gratitude for his extensive efforts.

But there are glaring difficulties with his methodology. In the first place, perhaps because of his Protestant bent, he works primarily from the Geneva Bible in all its versions. Shaheen is careful to state that "although the Geneva Bible may have been the version that Shakespeare knew best and which he seems to refer to most often, the influence of other versions is also clearly evident, and no one version can be called 'Shakespeare's Bible.'"[21] Roman

---

20. Naseeb Shaheen, *Biblical References in Shakespeare's Plays* (Newark: University of Delaware Press, 1999).

21. Shaheen, *Biblical References in Shakespeare's Plays*, p. 44.

Catholic scholars such as David Beauregard have claimed that the evidence for Shakespeare's use of the Geneva Bible is far from compelling, because several of the citations Shaheen attributes to the Geneva Bible appear also in the Catholic Rheims Bible. Although Shaheen dismisses the Rheims/Douay versions as irrelevant because he assumes that Shakespeare was either a conforming or nonconforming Protestant and so would have used a Protestant Bible, his critics argue that this point is precisely what is contested.

Related to the issue of possible Protestant bias are some striking citation omissions, such as the word "penance." Gregory Martin, already in the late sixteenth century, had shown that the Greek word *metanoia* was uniformly rendered by Protestant translators as "repentance" instead of the "penance" used by Roman Catholic translators. For example, Matthew 3:2 in the Protestant versions reads, "Repent: for the kingdom of heaven is at hand," while in the Rheims translations it reads, "Do penance: for the kingdom of heaven is at hand." Overlooking this, Richmond Noble in 1935 failed to catalogue the nineteen times the word "penance" occurs in Shakespeare's plays, because he was not expecting to find the word in Scripture. There are other examples, such as the difference between "vengeance" (Geneva) and "revenge" (Rheims), as well as the "hard hearts" language of *King Lear* that (while it is not tied to a particular translation) Noble for some reason overlooked.[22] We can still be grateful for the work of these early researchers, even as we notice that much of it lacks the precision characteristic of scholarship on literary, and especially biblical, intertextuality today.

Perhaps the most important weaknesses of Shaheen's work are that, on the one hand, he fails to develop an adequate system for classifying proposed biblical references, or even to define what counts as a biblical reference, and, on the other hand, he fails to move beyond the mechanical task of identifying and listing possible references. With respect to the first problem, Shaheen uncritically takes over Noble's simplistic criteria as to what constitutes a biblical quotation, allusion, or echo: each biblical reference is listed as "certain," "probable," or "possible."[23] With respect to the second problem,

22. Beauregard, "Shakespeare and the Bible," pp. 322-23.
23. Shaheen describes his methodology in *Biblical References in Shakespeare's Comedies,* p. 28. For certain or highly probable biblical references (e.g., to named figures from the Bible or to unnamed figures like the prodigal son), he simply quotes the biblical text next to Shakespeare's lines; references he considers probable or possible are preceded by the word "compare"; references that seem remotely possible are preceded by "compare" with a comment that the Bible may function as an analogy rather than a reference; and instances where a common idea or phrase occurs in both Shakespeare and the Bible are identified

Shaheen never takes the next step to ask what these biblical allusions have in common, what patterns they reveal, what recurring themes or assumptions are characteristic of Shakespeare throughout the canon, and he never attempts any "close reading" of these texts to demonstrate such typical approaches or hermeneutical strategies. He never moves from the collection of micro-citations to the larger picture, the macro-theological vision of Shakespeare as a reader of Scripture.

The other dominant research pattern concerning Shakespeare's use of Scripture is exactly the opposite. Steven Marx, in his *Shakespeare and the Bible* (2000), works at discovering correspondences or parallels between biblical books or narratives and Shakespeare's plays. Using the hermeneutical strategies of typology and midrash, Marx discovers parallels, grand patterns of convergence and divergence, between Genesis and *The Tempest* on creation, posterity, and prosperity, commenting, for example, that both narratives begin with a storm at sea. (Marx understands the wind or spirit of God that hovers over the waters as a violent force.) He also reads *The Tempest* with the Revelation to John, understanding the Apocalypse as a masque. Marx goes on to compare and contrast historical figures: Moses and David are paired with Henry V. He reads the book of Job and *King Lear* together; he places *The Merchant of Venice* next to Paul's letter to the Romans; he compares *Measure for Measure* to the overall logic of the Gospels. Marx's project pays little attention to the historical context and the controversies swirling around Shakespeare's theological commitments. Instead, he is a creative reader of great patterns who tends to see the large picture first and has to work hard to make some of his details fit into it. As a Jewish scholar, he brings fresh readings to the biblical books by comparing them to Shakespeare's plays.

Marx notices a great deal by means of this approach and is well worth reading. No one can do everything, however, and what Marx cannot do with this reading strategy is the same kind of close reading of the play itself that is missing from Shaheen's collections of biblical references. Other literary critics have given powerful readings of Shakespeare's plays, and they have, of course, attended to the biblical allusions as those have interested them.[24] But

---

with notations of the overlapping words. Shaheen concedes that these are not hard-and-fast categories.

24. To mention only a few: W. H. Auden, *Lectures on Shakespeare,* ed. Arthur Kirsch (New Jersey: Princeton University Press, 2000); Harold Bloom, *Shakespeare: The Invention of the Human* (New York: Riverhead, 1998); Marjorie Garber, *Shakespeare After All* (New York: Pantheon, 2004); Frank Kermode, *Shakespeare's Language* (New York: Farrar, Straus & Giroux, 2000).

it is evident that there is a major lacuna here: what students of Shakespeare who are interested in his use of the Bible really need is work — on both the micro and the macro levels — that explores Shakespeare's historical setting, his language, and his interpretive strategies, then attempts to retrieve his theological convictions about Scripture. That is to say, what we still lack is a sophisticated overall view of Shakespeare's hermeneutics that describes the great complexity of his various uses of Scripture and then works backward to reconstruct his theology of Scripture.

III. Pauline Studies and Shakespeare Studies: Can We Talk?

This is a point at which literary critics and biblical scholars, especially those who have studied the citation of and allusion to the Old Testament in the New, might work more closely together than we often have. Two recent interpretive strategies in Pauline theology might be particularly helpful by way of analogy.

J. Louis Martyn, in his commentary on Galatians,[25] has taught us how to take our seats in the Galatian congregation and to listen to Paul's letter "with Galatian ears" in order to reconstruct Paul's own theology. Martyn insists that exegesis must be well grounded in historical research but deplores the failure of nerve of those scholars who are too cautious to engage in the imaginative work of historical reconstruction. He concedes that some overconfident scholars, who think they can reconstruct the entire face from just the mustache, have caused other, more cautious thinkers to avoid the project of historical reconstruction entirely. Martyn insists, however, that with reasonable controls and careful attention to the precise language used by the apostle, we can reason backward in slow, careful steps from the letter text that we see before us to the theological mind of Paul.

Martyn starts with the letter text precisely as we have it and first tries to imagine what it must have sounded like to the Galatians. Since the reading of Paul's letter would have been an oral and aural event, probably performed by a trusted ambassador who had been carefully coached by Paul on how to deliver the letter in his absence, Martyn asks what impression the letter would have made on the Galatians when they first heard it. What would they have heard in the particular words Paul chose and the way he put them to-

25. J. Louis Martyn, *Galatians: A New Translation with Introduction and Commentary,* AB 33A (New York: Doubleday, 1997).

gether? In order to get at that problem, Martyn studies the contemporary meaning of a word and then notices how Paul has often modified it in a way that is distinctive and theologically startling. Martyn assumes that these rhetorical effects, these attention-getting fresh word usages — Paul liked to coin words almost as much as Shakespeare did — were intentional on his part, not accidental.

For example, when Paul uses the word εὐαγγέλιον ("gospel" or "good news") in Galatians 1:6 ("I am astonished that you are so quickly deserting the one who called you in the grace of Christ and are turning to a different *gospel*"), Martyn reasons that the Galatians would almost certainly have heard the word before and that it would have had important associations for them. From his studies of the way the Greek language was used during the time of the Roman Empire, Martyn can show that the Galatians would have associated the "good news" with the report of victory from the battlefield or of the birth of an heir to the emperor, among other things. But Paul's usage of the word would have gotten their attention: the Galatians would always have heard it used in the plural ("good news"), while Paul strikingly uses it in the singular. Martyn translates εὐαγγέλιον as the "good *new*" to show us how startling and perhaps unsettling it would have sounded to Galatian ears. From the very beginning of the letter, Paul has the Galatians wondering how the singular "good new" to which God has called them differs from the perverse characterization of that gospel that Paul attributes to those troubling them.

In example after example, Martyn invites us to work backward from what appears in the text to what must have been heard by the Galatians to what Paul seems to have engineered that they would hear. Can we figure out from what Paul achieved rhetorically (what probably happened when the letter was performed) what he had intended to communicate, to distinguish, to warn against? Then, pressing back even further, can we attempt to reconstruct from Paul's rhetorical strategy the theological assumptions that might have motivated that strategy? The question remains open, of course, until Paul himself can confirm or deny that we have read him read him correctly. But it is safe to say that many if not most readers of Martyn's commentary on Galatians are impressed by what his demonstrated procedure has uncovered about Paul's use of language and his theology.

I suggest that we need something like this for Shakespeare studies to accomplish for Shakespeare's plays what Martyn has been able to do for Galatians. Specifically, we need patient linguists who know the language of Renaissance English well enough to work backward from the text as it has been reconstructed to spot the words that Shakespeare himself has coined or altered or spun in a new direction. We need to take our seats in the Globe Theatre and learn to listen with Elizabethan ears. Then we can imagine what the effects might have been, and then, reasoning backward, we can reconstruct something of what Shakespeare's intentions were, and perhaps something of the worldview behind them. Having done that work for each of Shakespeare's plays separately, we then need to look at all of the plays together, working backward still further to discover, if we can, based on the probable dating of the plays (which is considerably more straightforward than that of Paul's letters), evidences of change and development in Shakespeare's theology of Scripture or whatever else it is that we hope to learn.

Martyn's overall project of deducing from the text of Galatians at least some of the theological convictions of its author by careful attention to the way language is being used provides a framework for thinking about the role of Scripture in Galatians and in Paul's other letters. In my mind, Martyn's framework is best complemented by the careful attention to the quotations, allusions, and echoes found in Paul's letters that has been given to us by Richard Hays.

In *Echoes of Scripture in the Letters of Paul,*[26] Richard Hays has worked out an elaborate set of criteria for testing the volume of biblical "echoes" in Paul's letters and elsewhere that shows all too clearly the inadequacies of Noble's and Shaheen's comparable attempts in Shakespearian biblical studies. Hays has taught us, borrowing from contemporary literary theory, several ways to think about the relationship of the author to the parent or predecessor text. He has also shown us, again borrowing from the world of literary criticism, how a well-placed biblical quotation, allusion, or echo can change what the text around it says, strengthening it, adding to it, but also modifying it, even subtly contradicting it or problematizing it. He has demonstrated how the importation of a biblical quotation, allusion, or echo carries with it the textual material that surrounded it in its original setting. Not only the specific words quoted, but also other words remembered by the reader/hearer because of their proximity on the page or their similar verbal content, work to transform the quotation in its new setting, subtly limiting or expanding its meaning or changing its tone.

As a result of this work, we have come to see Paul's letters not so much as instances where Paul is "using" the biblical texts for his rhetorical purposes

---

26. Richard B. Hays, *Echoes of Scripture in the Letters of Paul* (New Haven: Yale University Press, 1989).

(though he surely frames his quotations with his argument in mind) but rather as examples of Paul and the Scriptures engaging in an ongoing and mutually shaping dialogue. The Word of God is alive for Paul, as it is for the author of Hebrews. Living and active, in the power of the Spirit, Scripture speaks directly to us, just as it preached the gospel to Abraham, reassured David, and challenged Moses.

In the present context, it is worth noticing that playwrights already have a mechanism by which they can complexify an idea and reflect on its many aspects by having different characters voice different opinions about it. And, like Paul's Scripture, they often find the characters talking back to them, as if they had a mind of their own. Students of Shakespeare could use something like this understanding of Scripture to sense the depth of Shakespeare's theological vision. For Shakespeare, the parent text of Scripture was honored and trusted, and not to be violated, as we will see. But it also was real enough that it could be argued with and pushed against; it was strong enough that it could hold its own in the conversation; it was deep enough that his characters could speak it on several levels at once and still not exhaust its meaning. Clearly, the larger project in Shakespearian studies that can only be dreamed of here will involve extensive collaboration among historians of the religious controversies of the Elizabethan era, linguistic experts in the subtleties of Elizabethan poetry and prose, and literary critics who understand how plays are constructed and how characters come alive in the process of drafting dialogue and grow from scene to scene.

IV. A Thought Experiment: Shakespeare's Use of Scripture in *Measure for Measure*

So far I have argued that we need a more thorough study of Shakespeare's use of Scripture that attends systematically to its complexity and variety. This brief essay in no way approximates that gigantic project, but it is interesting in the context of this collection of essays to imagine how the contributions of Martyn and especially Hays in New Testament studies might be useful in overcoming the present apparent impasses in Shakespearean methodology. What follows in the rest of this paper is the beginning of a thought experiment, a brief first attempt to explore what *Echoes of Scripture* might look like when applied to some biblical references in one of Shakespeare's plays.

I have chosen *Measure for Measure* (usually dated 1604, late in the canon) because it is the only play whose title is an unmistakable biblical reference and because it is notoriously difficult to understand: although it seems to be structured at least generally as a comedy (mistaken identity is an issue and everyone gets married at the end), it is one of the so-called "problem plays" (along with *The Merchant of Venice* and *Twelfth Night*) that has received a good deal of attention from literary critics, especially literary critics interested in theology and ethics, precisely because it seems to "work" somewhat like a parable and because the biblical text is prominently featured in its title, although to what point is not immediately clear.

The Literary Precursors: Shakespeare's Probable Sources

A brief introduction to the literary precursors of *Measure for Measure* may be helpful. Three features of the play were common literary material: (1) the disguised ruler who goes about spying among his people to find out what they really think about him; (2) the unjust official who demands sexual favors from a female supplicant who then has to choose whether to surrender her chastity in order to save the life of someone she loves; and (3) the bed trick, the substitution of one sexual partner for another in the dark of night that is at least as old as Laban, Jacob, Leah, and Rachel in Genesis 29.

The idea of the disguised ruler who goes about investigating the government of his own land was a commonplace in sixteenth-century England and can be traced back to legends about the third-century Roman emperor Alexander Severus. Shakespeare seems to have known at least two versions of this story, George Whetstone's *A Mirror for Magistrates* (1584) and Barnabe Rich's *The Adventures of Brusanus, Prince of Hungary* (1592).[27]

The second feature of the play — the unjust official who demands sexual favors — was apparently based on a historical incident that occurred in Italy in 1547. A judge who extorted sex from the wife of a condemned murderer by promising mercy for her husband afterward executed the criminal anyway. When the unhappy widow complained to the authorities, the judge was forced to marry her and then was executed. The story circulated in several languages and versions, including Thomas Lupton's *Too Good to Be True* (1581), which is echoed in Shakespeare's play in the dialogues between Angelo and Isabella in act 2.[28]

---

27. The information in this paragraph is taken from *The Wordsworth Dictionary of Shakespeare*, ed. Charles Boyce (Ware, Hertfordshire: Wordsworth, 1990), p. 412.

28. *Wordsworth Dictionary of Shakespeare*, p. 412.

There are also literary precursors closer to home. George Whetstone's *Promos and Cassandra* (published in 1578) has a plot very close to Shakespeare's play about Angelo and Isabella. Whetstone's *Promos and Cassandra* was a disaster, written in rhyming couplets in lines of fourteen syllables and shorter lines that do not scan. It was also, in Shaheen's words, "a dreary play with a simplistic moral lesson: evil will be punished."[29] Apparently, it was never performed. But Whetstone, however much he had failed to write a play that could be produced, believed in his story line and published a prose version of it in 1582. Shakespeare seems to have read both of Whetstone's versions, and he must have seen enough dramatic potential in them to warrant his own extensive labors on the story. He kept Whetstone's comic subplot involving prostitutes and pimps that provide contrast to the story of threatened virtue. Moreover, he followed Whetstone in making the seduction of the young criminal an act of love in the context of betrothal. But his changes made the plot and the characters considerably more complex, and apparently it was Shakespeare who saw that the bed trick could be used to turn the play from a morality play or a tragedy into a comedy of sorts.

Whetstone's play and prose narrative were not Shakespeare's only sources. He also apparently knew Whetstone's Italian source, Cinthio's "Story of Epitia," a work of fiction inspired by the historical event of the unjust judge in Italy, first published in 1565 in a collection of short stories. Cinthio had already modified the story: the criminal's offense was not murder but the seduction of a virgin; his sister, not his wife, pleads with the judge for mercy. At the end of the story she also pleads for the life of the unjust judge who had violated her and is now her husband. When her plea is granted by a virtuous ruler, a "happy ending" replaces the cycle of revenge. Cinthio later transformed his tale into a drama, *Epitia,* which was published posthumously in 1583. Shakespeare seems to have known Cinthio's play, which he would have read either in the Italian version of 1583 or in the French translation of 1584. In the play version, the young criminal is spared by a merciful official, who substitutes a dead man's head, and a second woman, the sister of the judge, also pleads for his life. By now, many of the elements of Shakespeare's play are in place.[30]

The most obvious literary precursor of *Measure for Measure* is the Sermon on the Mount, especially Matthew 7:2: "For with the judgment you make you will be judged, and the measure you give will be the measure you

29. Shaheen, *Biblical References in Shakespeare's Comedies,* p. 185.
30. *Wordsworth Dictionary of Shakespeare,* p. 412.

get." Since the play's very title is taken from Scripture, we might expect it to yield some information about Shakespeare's attitude toward Scripture — and it does. At the same time, the expression "measure for measure" had already become proverbial in the sense of the *lex talionis:* an eye for an eye, a tooth for a tooth, a death for a death; and it is clear that Shakespeare uses it in this sense. We might wonder: did he also read or remember the antitheses, where Jesus says, "You have heard that it was said, 'An eye for an eye and a tooth for a tooth.' But I say to you, Do not resist an evildoer. But if anyone strikes you on the right cheek, turn the other also" (Matt. 5:38-39)?

How these two statements within the same "sermon" relate to one another is a perennial hermeneutical concern for contemporary interpreters of Matthew's Gospel. But our concern here is historical, more precisely the history of interpretation. Did Shakespeare ignore Matthew 5:38-39 in order to read Matthew 7:2 in a particular way? Did he quote the one text and somehow imply the other as well? Or was the saying only vaguely biblical for him; did he choose for his title a popular proverb to the effect that "what goes around comes around" without attention to the larger narrative of Jesus into which that "proverb" and the entire Sermon on the Mount have been inserted? Shakespeare and his contemporaries knew about the Ferris wheel-like wheel of fortune: at the bottom, down and out, you can trust that Fate or Fortune will lift you higher; but beware of the pride that goes before a fall, for the one at the top of Fortune's wheel has nowhere to go but down. Perhaps all of these (scriptural text, proverb, and the wheel of fortune idea) are implied in Shakespeare's title, given the plot of the play.

What makes the question particularly important and intriguing is that Shakespeare's title and his other biblical references are not present in Whetstone and Cinthio, his two major sources. Anyone who has reflected on the Synoptic Problem and the project of redaction criticism will immediately appreciate the significance of that remark: we have Shakespeare's probable sources in the same way that we have the Gospel of Mark as the probable source for the Gospels of Matthew and Luke. Just as it is common in redaction criticism to focus on "Special Matthew" or "Special Luke" in order to recover the evangelist's distinctive theology, so when we notice that it is Shakespeare who has titled the story biblically and used the biblical bed trick to modify its ending, it is worth asking whether we can see in those changes something of Shakespeare's biblical theology.

Shakespeare and Scripture: Allied Against Hypocrisy

There is space here to make only a few comments on Shakespeare's use of Scripture in general before turning more specifically to his use of Scripture in *Measure for Measure*. In this brief overview, we will begin the project of trying to reconstruct Shakespeare's theology of Scripture by attending to what he has his characters say about it.

Shakespeare seems to have had a point he wanted to make over and over again in the plays, a point against hypocrisy and the rationalization of sin or vice by quoting Scripture. One of the clearest examples of general hypocrisy, a character using Scripture as a cover for wickedness, is Richard III in the play of that name. He is probably Shakespeare's worst villain — the one we love to hate — who is also strangely seductive, as evil frequently is. From the very beginning of the play, Shakespeare uses the device of the "inside view" (Richard speaks more soliloquies than any other character in the Shakespearean canon, including Hamlet), and we are shown the villain's delight in pretending reverence for Scripture while he is cheerfully murdering everyone who stands between him and the throne of England. Listen to him speaking characteristically in an aside to us in 1.3.334-38:

> But then I sigh and, with a piece of Scripture,
> Tell them that God bids us do good for evil.
> And thus I clothe my naked villainy
> With odd old ends stol'n forth of holy writ,
> And seem a saint when most I play the devil.

The Vice was a conventional figure from the medieval morality play who strove to seduce the Soul or Everyman into evil ways by means of hypocrisy and lies. Shakespeare develops the Vice into a comic character who entertains with lewd jokes, outrageous puns, slapstick antics, and humorous asides to the audience. He retains, however, two of the morality play's conventions: the Vice incarnates the habitual blindness of an unrepentant sinner, and his dishonesty is obvious to everyone except his victim.[31]

An example of a character who engages in endless rationalization of vice, quoting Scripture in support of his actions, is Falstaff in Henry IV, part I, modeled after Sir John Oldcastle, whom Foxe *(Foxe's Book of Martyrs)* had recognized as a forerunner of the Protestant Reformation. Shakespeare's

---

31. *Wordsworth Dictionary of Shakespeare*, p. 691.

character is considerably less noble. He is "reverend Vice" (as in 2.4), prepared for any occasion with a host of pious expressions. Falstaff may also participate in Shakespeare's warning about the dangers of Puritan proof-texting. From the beginning of the play, Falstaff defends his practice of stealing purses with an appeal to Scripture: "Why, Hal, 'tis my vocation, Hal: 'tis no sin for a man to labour in his vocation" (1.2.101-2). Later, he uses a scriptural warrant for his sins of the flesh:[32]

> Dost thou hear, Hal? Thou knowest in the state of innocency Adam fell; and what should poor Jack Falstaff do in the days of villainy? Thou seest I have more flesh than another man, and therefore more frailty. (3.3.164-68)

Shakespeare was passionately against Puritan "precision" and Scripture-twisting. Bassanio in *The Merchant of Venice* associates religious hypocrisy with the abuse of biblical texts:

> In religion,
> What damned error but some sober brow
> Will bless it, and approve it with a text,
> Hiding the grossness with fair ornament? (3.2.77-80)

Earlier in the same play, Antonio advises Bassanio in the presence of Shylock, who has just given a biblical warrant for usury, that even the Devil can quote Scripture:[33]

> Mark you this, Bassanio,
> The devil can cite Scripture for his purpose.
> An evil soul producing holy witness
> Is like a villain with a smiling cheek,
> A goodly apple rotten at the heart.
> O, what a goodly outside falsehood hath! (1.3.93-97)

Shylock takes on many aspects of the stage "Puritan" with his antisocial behavior and especially his insistence on following the "letter" of the law in claiming a pound of Antonio's flesh. After praising Portia (in disguise) as "a Daniel come to judgment" because she awards him the pound of flesh men-

---

32. Milward, *Shakespeare's Religious Background,* p. 155.

33. Professor Hays begins his book on ethical hermeneutics with an allusion to this speech. See Richard B. Hays, *The Moral Vision of the New Testament* (San Francisco: HarperSanFrancisco, 1996), p. 1.

tioned in the bond, when she asks him whether he has a doctor standing by to save Antonio's life, Shylock challenges her, "Is it so nominated in the bond?" She replies, "It is not so express'd, but what of that? 'Twere good you do so much for charity." Shylock responds only, "I cannot find it; 'tis not in the bond" (4.1.218, 254-57).

Perhaps the purest example of the stage "Puritan" in Shakespeare is poor Malvolio of *Twelfth Night,* the overly zealous good steward who is accosted by the prodigal Sir Toby Belch with the words, "Dost thou think, because thou art virtuous, there shall be no more cakes and ale?" (2.3.108). As a result of the machinations of Sir Toby and Maria, Malvolio is tricked into believing his mistress has invited his attentions by means of a letter purporting to be from her hand. We watch, together with the hidden pranksters, as he "interprets" the "Scripture," construing what is self-evidently nonsense in fantastic ways in order to arrive at the plain sense of the text that he himself wants so much to believe (2.5.76-159). Hilarious on one level, it is deeply painful on another as the results lead to Malvolio's unjust imprisonment and his refusal, at the end of the play, to join in the joke: "I'll be reveng'd on the whole pack of you" (5.1.364). Like Shylock, Malvolio wins our sympathy in spite of himself, at the same time that Shakespeare is instructing us against the dangers of an overly wooden interpretation of Scripture.

Over against the Puritan claim to know the mind of God directly through the reading of Scripture, Shakespeare's contemporary Richard Hooker wrote:

> Dangerous it were for the feeble brain of man to wade far into the doings of the most high; whom although to know be life, and joy to make mention of his name; yet our soundest knowledge is to know that we know him not as indeed he is, neither can we know him: and our safest eloquence concerning him is our silence.[34]

Hooker's statement "The least thing in the world hath in it more than the wisest are able to reach unto" (*Laws* 3.2) is echoed in Hamlet's mild rebuke to his skeptical friend, "There are more things in heaven and earth, Horatio, / Than are dreamt of in your philosophy" (1.5.166-67). If Hamlet speaks for Shakespeare here, he seems to be more at home with the church's traditional theological reserve and reverent agnosticism about the deep things of God

---

34. Richard Hooker, *Laws of Ecclesiastical Polity* 2.2, quoted in Milward, *Shakespeare's Religious Background,* p. 135.

than with the Puritan confidence that the mind of God can be fathomed because it is expressed directly in Scripture.[35]

Measure for Measure: *Shakespeare's Engagement with Puritan Ethics*

In one of the sermons from the *Homilies* entitled "Of the Misery of All Mankind," it is claimed that the Holy Spirit intends through Scripture "to pull down man's vainglory and pride" and, conversely, "to teach us the most commendable virtue of humility, how to know ourselves, and to remember what we be of ourselves."[36] Of ourselves, continues the homily, we "bring forth but weeds, nettles, brambles, briars, cockle, and darnel." Milward comments that this is undoubtedly the deep significance of the humbled Lear's mad attire,

> Crown'd with rank fumiter and furrow weeds,
> With burdocks, hemlock, nettles, cuckoo-flowers,
> Darnel, and all the idle weeds that grow
> In our sustaining corn.[37]

To a New Testament reader, another allusion suggests itself: Matthew's parable of the weeds and the wheat (the darnel and the corn?) at 13:24-30 (see also 13:36-43). Leander Keck, following Gerd Theissen, thinks the historical background behind this parable involves Q-type "wandering charismatic teachers and preachers who advocated a rigorous, absolutist, uncompromising attitude on a range of matters," who left the simpler setting of a Palestinian village for a major urban center such as Antioch and were horrified by the laxity of the Christianity they found there. Keck comments: "These, I believe, are the people to whom Matthew alludes in his parable of the weeds in the grainfield; that is, they are the ones who volunteered to weed out the church." In Keck's judgment, "Matthew affirms their uncompromising stand, but surrounds it with other material which has the effect of moderating it." He incorporates the Q radicals into the community without allowing them to dominate it.[38]

---

35. In agreement with Milward, *Shakespeare's Religious Background,* p. 135.
36. Quoted in Milward, *Shakespeare's Religious Background,* p. 121.
37. *King Lear* 4.4.3-6, quoted in Milward, *Shakespeare's Religious Background,* p. 122.
38. Leander E. Keck, "Ethics in the Gospel According to Matthew," *IR* 41 (Winter 1984): 42-43.

Did Shakespeare read the Sermon on the Mount in the larger literary context of Matthew's Gospel? The parable of the weeds and the wheat, which appears only in Matthew, arguably describes the perennial situation of the church throughout history, but it also describes the city of Vienna[39] at the beginning of *Measure for Measure,* which appears to the Duke and others as a garden left unweeded for too long.

Milward shows how Shakespeare appears to have borrowed from another of the *Homilies,* "Against Whoredom," which complains that "the outrageous seas of adultery, whoredom, fornication, and uncleanness have not only brast in, but also overflowed almost the whole world," to provide the setting for Vienna. Shakespeare has Elbow speak of "fornication, adultery, and all uncleanliness" (*Measure for Measure* 2.1.77-78).[40] The same homily continues:

> this vice is grown into such an height, that in a manner among many it is counted no sin at all . . . not rebuked but winked at, not punished but laughed at.

Again, the words of the homily are echoed at the beginning of the play, this time by those of the Duke:

> In time the rod
> Becomes more mock'd than fear'd; so our decrees,
> Dead to infliction, to themselves are dead,
> And liberty plucks justice by the nose. (1.3.26-29)[41]

The Duke, recognizing that his own disposition does not lead him to be an enforcer of sexual morality and that his popularity would be diminished if he should suddenly become one after a long period of nonenforcement of the laws, conveniently takes an extended leave, after appointing Angelo, his conscientious Puritan-minded Q-radical, to govern temporarily in his place.

---

39. To the delight of Harold Bloom, who provides a thoroughly Freudian reading of the play. See the citation in n. 24 above.

40. According to *The English Hexapla,* the Geneva Bible (1557) translates Gal. 5:19, "Moreouer the dedes of the flesshe are manifeste, which are, aduoutry, fornication, vnclennes, wantonnes. . . ." The Rheims Bible (1582) reads, "And the vvorkes of the flesh be manifest, vvhich are, fornication, vncleannes, impudicitie, lecherie. . . ." See *The English Hexapla, Exhibiting the Six Important English Translations of the New Testament Scriptures* (London: Samuel Bagster & Sons, 1841), at Gal. 5:19.

41. Quoted in Milward, *Shakespeare's Religious Background,* p. 122.

The remainder of the play retells the parable of the weeds and wheat in the social and moral context of sexual immorality described by the homily. We are invited to explore what might have happened if the owner of the field had allowed the rigorists to weed out the darnel after all.

As we move in that direction, it will be useful to contrast our present approach with that of Naseeb Shaheen, whose list of possible biblical references in *Measure for Measure* begins with the observation that

> Since the play's very title is taken from Scripture, we might expect to find strong religious overtones in the play, along with many biblical references. But that is only partly true. Although there are many lines in the play that express religious ideas, the number of biblical references is not exceptionally large. Moreover, many of the items that appear in the following list are parallels or analogies to Scripture, rather than actual references.[42]

The following few examples of why his methodology is so problematic are typical of the rest. Most of the entries read something like this:[43]

> 1.1.61: That we may bring you something on the way.
>   Compare Gen. 18.16: "Abraham went with them to bring them on the way."
>   Compare 1 Cor. 16.6: "That ye may bring mee on my way."
>   . . . Shakespeare was probably using a common expression rather than making a conscious reference to Scripture.[44]

This entry is typical of the cataloging approach designed earlier. In the interest of thoroughness, we might expect a list of such nonstarters. But where there should be extensive discussion of examples that tell us something about Shakespeare's theology of Scripture by locating the quotation within the context of the play's argument, we get the same cataloging:

> 1.2.122-23: The words of heaven: on whom it will, it will;
>   On whom it will not, so; yet still 'tis just.
>   The "words of heaven" are based on Paul's words at Romans 9.
>   Rom. 9.15-16: "For he saith to Moses, I wil haue mercie on him, to whom I will shewe mercie: and wil haue compassion on him, on whom I

---

42. Shaheen, *Biblical References in Shakespeare's Comedies,* p. 186.
43. In quoting Shaheen, I leave his citation numbers and quotations intact.
44. Shaheen, *Biblical References in Shakespeare's Comedies,* p. 189.

will haue compassion. So then it is not in him that willeth, nor in him that runneth, but in God that sheweth mercie."

God's words to Moses are the words at Ex. 33.19: "I will shewe mercy to whome I will shew mercy, and will haue compassion on whom I will haue compassion."

Rom. 9.18: "He hath mercie on whome he will, and whom he will, he hardeneth."

For "yet still 'tis just," compare Rom. 9.14: "Is there vnrighteousnes with God? God forbid."[45]

Here Shaheen has rightly noted that Shakespeare's line almost certainly echoes Paul's argument in Romans 9. But if he had studied with Richard Hays, he would have known that recognizing the echo is only the first step. In the context of Shakespeare's play, the words are spoken by Claudio, who has just been arrested for fornication, to his guard. A few moments later Claudio explains to his friend Lucio that he and Julietta were formally betrothed ("she is fast my wife") but that for lack of the dowry had postponed their wedding, hiding their love from their friends until they could raise the needed funds. With the discovery of Julietta's pregnancy, however, Claudio has been arrested at the order of "Lord Angelo" and sentenced to death for fornication. The context of Claudio's words is important:

> Thus can the demigod Authority
> Make us pay down for our offence by weight[46]
> The words of heaven: on whom it will, it will;
> On whom it will not, so; yet still 'tis just.

The guard's description ("Lord Angelo"), Claudio's "demigod," and the capitalization of the word "Authority" all suggest that Angelo has usurped God's prerogative of showing or not showing mercy. At this point it becomes crucial to see that in the context of Romans 9, the stress of Paul's argument is precisely upon God's mercy when no mercy would be expected. The story Paul remembers in his quotation of Exodus 33:19 takes place immediately after the golden calf incident in Exodus 32, when God has every reason to hate Israel. Paul reads the Exodus quotation to stress God's sovereign free-

---

45. Shaheen, *Biblical References in Shakespeare's Comedies*, p. 190.

46. The Harrison edition of the play notes that this line means to "pay heavily for" our offense. *Shakespeare: The Complete Works*, ed. G. B. Harrison (New York: Harcourt, Brace & World, 1952), p. 1105.

dom to be merciful and gracious to whomever God wills, whether they deserve it or not.[47]

The biblical echo reminds us that God's costly righteousness in Christ is accomplished as a way of showing mercy to Israel, to the nations, and to all of humanity. The contrast between God's mercy and the hardened heart of Angelo subtly suggests that Angelo is Pharaoh to Claudio's Israel or perhaps the Angel of Death who moves relentlessly through the land of Egypt to execute the death sentence. By contrast, even when Israel is caught in the act of adultery at the foot of Mount Sinai, God finds a way to go on with Israel. Claudio's offense is not nearly so serious as Angelo's harsh judgment implies. The disconnect between God's mercy and Angelo's death penalty is highlighted by the use of the biblical allusion.

Space permits treatment of only two more examples from Shaheen's list of possible references. That the first of these is complicated is not immediately evident from Shaheen's simple treatment of it:

> 3.1.42-43: To sue to live, I find I seek to die,
>   And seeking death, find life.
>   Compare Matt. 16.25: "Whosoeuer wil saue his life, shall lose it: and whosoeuer shal lose his life for my sake, shall finde it."[48]

Shaheen's "compare" is his signal that he doubts whether the biblical reference is intended because the words don't quite match and it doesn't make sense. He may be forgiven for wondering whether this is in fact the biblical allusion it clearly seems to be: somehow the logic has become garbled and the whole statement seems confused in its context. Once more, attention both to the context of the parent text and to Shakespeare's use of it in his play is important. Again, we wonder: did Shakespeare intend to bring the title of his play and its invocation of the Sermon on the Mount into conversation with the rest of the Gospel in which it is located? Did he expect his hearers to make the connection? In Matthew's Gospel, these words are spoken by Jesus to the disciples as part of his invitation to deny themselves, take up the cross, and follow him. The invitation follows immediately after Peter's objection that the words spoken in this first passion prediction must not come true. This word on the cost of discipleship, spoken by Jesus to his first disciples, is spoken to all subsequent disciples as well. It is precisely the most appropriate

---

47. A. Katherine Grieb, *The Story of Romans: A Narrative Defense of God's Righteousness* (Louisville: Westminster John Knox, 2002), pp. 92-93.

48. Shaheen, *Biblical References in Shakespeare's Comedies*, p. 198.

quotation to be spoken by a Christian martyr facing death at the hands of the state.

But Claudio is not dying for his faith; he confides in the Duke (disguised as a friar) that he hopes for a pardon so that he will not have to die at all, though he says he is prepared for death if no pardon arrives. The Duke (as friar) gives a long sermon on life and death that is not even remotely Christian. Claudio's sentence is spoken as a response to that speech. Politely thanking the friar for what the audience knows is quasi-stoical platitude and drivel, he then puts the best spin on the situation he can with his own philosophical statement, which captures at least something of the biblical paradox but may actually be a parody of it. What is Shakespeare doing here? Perhaps the condemned man receives from the church, as he thinks, nothing useful and tries to say back to the friar what he thinks he is supposed to feel. If so, the shallowness of that conviction is immediately exposed a few verses later when he begs Isabella to sacrifice her chastity to save his life. This action shows that he is actually terrified of death. Whatever else our playwright is doing, he manages to raise the question of what the "ghostly counsel" of the church is worth at a time of crisis. We are invited to reflect upon what should have been said and what difference it could have made to a troubled soul.

The final example from Shaheen's list of possible biblical references is clearly an allusion to Matthew 23, though once more Shaheen himself is doubtful about the match because the words are slightly different:

> 3.1.88-92:   This outward-sainted deputy,
>
>   . . . .
>
>   . . . is yet a devil;
>
>   His filth within being cast. . . .
>
> Were the words "outward," "filth," and "within" inspired by Matt. 23.27?
>
> Matt. 23.27: "ye are like vnto whited tombs, which appeare beautifull outwarde, but are within ful of . . . all filthines."
>
> [3.1.88, 94-95, "outward-sainted . . . cunning livery of hell": 2 Cor. 11.14][49]

Shaheen's method, simply comparing the words of the two texts to see whether they agree closely enough to count as an echo, without paying attention to the function of the possible biblical allusion in its dual contexts, provides him no ground for confidence in a situation like this. But these

---

49. Shaheen, *Biblical References in Shakespeare's Comedies*, p. 199.

words are spoken by Isabella to her brother Claudio about Angelo after he has tried to seduce her. The words borrowed from Matthew 23's sevenfold condemnation of the scribes and Pharisees as hypocrites are surely enough to associate Angelo with the charge of hypocrisy even though the word does not appear precisely at that point in Shakespeare's text. On the level of Shakespeare's text, we pick up Isabella's meaning even if we do not recognize the biblical allusion; with the reference in place, Isabella speaks the words of Jesus condemning religious leaders in an analogous situation to the theocracy of Vienna.

The name "Angelo" helps us to recognize the second allusion. In 2 Corinthians 11:14-15, speaking of false apostles who disguise themselves as apostles, Paul says:

> And no wonder! Even Satan disguises himself as an angel of light. So it is not strange if his ministers also disguise themselves as ministers of righteousness. Their end will match their deeds.

The biblical predecessor text probably provided Angelo with his name in the first place. In the present context of Isabella's indictment, it serves to frame the issue of injustice theologically (Isabella is about to enter a convent, so we would expect nothing less from her), as well as to remind the audience that God judges judges. Each of us will have to render an account of our actions at the end. Isabella's anger at this point consists of righteous fury at Angelo's wrongdoing: untempered in her judgment, she is more like Angelo than she knows. Only at the end of the play will she be persuaded to plead for his life. By weaving together these two biblical allusions, Shakespeare has shown Isabella assuming the prophetic mantle of Jesus exposing the scribes and Pharisees and the apostolic mantle of Paul denouncing the ministers of Satan. At the moment, these seem to suit her well, but in just a few verses, she will turn on her brother Claudio with language more cruel than Angelo's death sentence. Her own moral blindness will compete with that of the judge she condemns. Shaheen's system of cataloging possible biblical references misses all of this intertextual play and the invitation to self-examination that it engenders in the attentive reader. The biblical texts are there for a reason: they do substantive work in carrying forward the argument of the play.

V. Measure for Measure? The True Injustice of a Merciful God

When Polonius, who also has some of the characteristics of the stage "Puritan," assures Prince Hamlet that he will use the players "according to their desert," Hamlet replies:

> God's bodykins, man, much better. Use every man after his desert, and who shall 'scape whipping? Use them after your own honour and dignity: the less they deserve, the more merit is in your bounty. (2.2)

The reference to "God's little body" alludes first to the incarnation, and, by implication, also to the crucifixion, where "God proves his love for us in that while we still were sinners Christ died for us" (Rom. 5:8). Martin Smith confesses to a certain uneasiness with the current exaltation of justice as if it were the church's primary goal. Of course, Christians must be advocates for those who are dispossessed of wealth and power and must strive to remedy the many inequalities that plague our cultures, but the ideal of justice is inadequate to express the liberating message of the gospel.

Smith reminds us of Saint Isaac the Syrian, a seventh-century contemplative theologian in what is now Iraq, whose *Mystical Treatises* provoke his readers to question whether in the light of the radical teaching of the gospel it makes sense to call God just. Reflecting on Matthew 20:1-10, the Syrian says: "And how can you call God just when you come to the passage about the laborer's wages? Where is God's 'justice'?" And further:

> Mercy and just judgment in one soul is like a man worshipping God and idols in the same house. Mercy is the opposite of just judgment. Just judgment is the equality of equal measures, for it gives to each as he deserves, without inclining to one side or another, or having respect of persons when it repays us. Mercy, however, is pity moved by grace and inclines to all in compassion; it does not requite him who deserves harsh treatment and it fills to overflowing him who deserves good. And if mercy is on the side of righteousness, then just judgment is on the side of evil. As grass and fire cannot stay together in the same house, so neither can just judgment and mercy remain in one soul.[50]

---

50. Quoted in Martin L. Smith, "The True Injustice of a Merciful God," *The Washington Window,* November 2005, www.edow.org.

VI. Conclusion: The Bard, the Book, and Doing Ethics

Shakespeare seems to have figured out fairly early in his career that the genre of a play is particularly effective for provoking moral reflection. Just as ancient classical biographers used their books to instruct readers about virtues, vices, and the character of great leaders, so Shakespeare's historical plays show the audience what happens when a particular moral agent encounters a given set of circumstances. As Shakespeare matured in his craft, his characters became rounder, multisided, and more complex; they began to speak more often of ambiguity and uncertainty, allowing us to enter their hearts and minds as well as the events of their lives. As we see them change and grow, we are summoned to reflect on our own maturity as moral agents.

By Shakespeare's choice of genre and his mastery of it, he demonstrates once more the advantages of doing ethics by means of telling a story. He makes his case with a narrative rather than employing a set of propositions. In the case of *Measure for Measure,* the narrative framework allows Shakespeare to show us the moral blindness of well-intentioned zealots like Antonio and Isabella who cannot see or acknowledge their own frailty or susceptibility to temptation. Shakespeare's narrative also raises questions about rulers and religious leaders who think they are God or authoritative deputies of God.

There is no need for us, as some very literal Christian interpreters of the play have done, to read *Measure for Measure* as an allegory of divine atonement, where Angelo is Everyman, Isabella is the Soul, the Duke represents God incarnate as Christ, Lucio is Satan disguised as an angel of light, and so on,[51] any more than we need to read New Testament parables so allegorically that we end up with a God who tortures his servants and commends dishonesty in them.

It seems obvious, especially in the plays that seem to involve caricatures of Puritans, such as *Twelfth Night, The Merchant of Venice,* and *Measure for Measure,* that Shakespeare is making a plea for reading Scripture in a way that results in mercy rather than strictly enforced justice.

The open question about Isabella at the end (whether she will take the Duke's hand offered in marriage and renounce her vows of chastity), and the discomfort of many of us with marriage as a remedy for sexual violation, or as the solution to every problem, may be intentional on Shakespeare's part. He seems to be well aware of the limits of the form of comedy, exploiting

---

51. *Wordsworth Dictionary of Shakespeare,* p. 410.

both the form and the limits for his own purposes. He may even be using the conventions as a way of suggesting a certain tolerance for ambiguity and recommending a lack of closure that we find problematic.

Whatever we make of Shakespeare's use of the Bible in his plays, and in *Measure for Measure* in particular, our studies will benefit from close attention to the placement of these references in the context of his argument as well as their original context(s) within the biblical canon. For wisdom about this endeavor, as in other things, we are grateful to Richard Hays.

Is Matthew Arnold Also Among the Prophets?
A Victorian Critic Interprets Paul

Leander E. Keck

Matthew Arnold's interpretation of Paul can be as beneficial as it is instructive because, despite being forgotten for a century by New Testament scholarship,[1] it is unexpectedly contemporary. While it engaged the wider religious, ecclesial, and cultural issues in Victorian England that now are of interest primarily to historians, it also struggled with perennial issues in the interpretation of Paul. By understanding Arnold's interpretation, we can learn something about our own. Arnold himself pointed out: "To know how others stand, that we may know how we ourselves stand; and to know how we ourselves stand, that we may correct our mistakes and achieve our deliverance — that is our problem."[2]

Arnold's fecund mind and facile pen produced a vast corpus,[3] of which four items are most germane for this essay: *Culture and Anarchy, St. Paul and Protestantism, Literature and Dogma,* and *God and the Bible.* While they constitute a discrete group written during a distinct period in Arnold's career, they draw on ideas expressed before and elsewhere, though such matters cannot be pursued in this essay. Nor is it possible here to identify the many influ-

---

1. It appears that Sanday and Headlam's commentary (1st ed. 1895) was the last to take account of Arnold's interpretation of Romans.

2. Arnold's inaugural address as Oxford's Professor of Poetry discussed the modern element in literature, from which quotation is taken by Peter Allan Dale, *The Victorian Critic and the Idea of History: Carlyle, Arnold, Pater* (Cambridge/London: Harvard University Press, 1977), p. 106.

3. R. H. Super's standard work, *The Complete Prose Works of Matthew Arnold* (Ann Arbor: University of Michigan Press, 1960-77), needs eleven volumes.

ences that flowed into his thought. Because it is Arnold's own thought that is the matrix of his interpretation of Paul, this essay first highlights some aspects of Arnold's work and thought, then discusses seriatim the writings about religion, and concludes with some observations about Arnold's work as a whole. Of secondary interest here is the vast secondary literature about Arnold, which, like that concerning Paul, shows no sign of diminishing.

I

Matthew Arnold (1822-88), son of the famed headmaster at Rugby, Thomas Arnold (1795-1842), was at the height of his powers when he published *St. Paul and Protestantism* in 1870. He had been Inspector of Schools since 1851, a position he held for over three decades but often found dreary.[4] During this time, he gained a reputation as a poet and was named Oxford's Professor of Poetry (for two terms, 1857-67); he was the first occupant of the chair to lecture in English instead of Latin. In 1865 "The Function of Criticism at the Present Time" opened his first *Essays in Criticism.* After the death of two sons in 1868, he turned increasingly toward cultural criticism, publishing in 1869 his best-known book, *Culture and Anarchy: An Essay in Political and Social Criticism,*[5] as well as his famous poem "Dover Beach" (begun much earlier). Many themes in *Culture and Anarchy* were developed the next year in *St. Paul.* In *Literature and Dogma* (1873), Arnold sought to preserve the preeminent role of the Bible — in an England seen as polarized, secularized, and vulgarized — by arguing that it should be read as literature, not as a quarry for doctrines. Two years later he responded to critics with *God and the Bible,* which also engages in detail F. C. Baur's views of the Fourth Gospel and discusses the origin of the New Testament canon. His *Last Essays on Church and Religion* appeared in 1877. In 1883-84 he lectured in America, and

4. "He spent many dreary hours during the 1850's in railway waiting-rooms and small-town hotels, and longer hours still in listening to children reciting their lessons and parents reciting their grievances"; see Stefan Collini, "Arnold," in *Victorian Thinkers,* ed. Keith Thomas (Oxford/New York: Oxford University Press, 1993), p. 223. Based on his on-site visits, he published *Schools and Universities on the Continent* in 1869.

5. The book, actually six articles published in 1867-68, went through several editions, for which Arnold provided introductions and changing chapter titles. Samuel Lipman's edition, *Culture and Anarchy by Matthew Arnold* (New Haven/London: Yale University Press, 1994), summarizes the complex publishing history. Page numbers used in this essay refer to Lipman's edition.

in 1886 as well. In 1888, while in Liverpool to welcome his daughter's return from a trip to the States, he died suddenly from a heart attack. That morning at church he had joined in singing "When I Survey the Wondrous Cross," which he declared the finest hymn in the English language.

Arnold's writings concerned with religion, like Paul's letters, were produced within a decade (roughly 1869-77), and both writers provoked controversies,[6] though Arnold paid scant attention to those that engaged Paul. Still, like Paul, Arnold "thrived on controversy," and "it stirred his creativity and aroused him to some of his most imaginative and sustained writing."[7] Few aspects of Victorian life escaped his caustic judgments. Looking back in 1902, an interpreter noted: "There was plenty of salt in his wit, but not much pepper."[8] In "Dover Beach" he lamented that "the Sea of Faith," once at full tide, now is heard roaring away, leaving a world that

Hath really neither joy, nor love, nor light,
Nor certitude, nor peace, nor help for pain;

so that now we are

Swept with confused alarms of struggle and flight,
Where ignorant armies clash by night.[9]

Arnold once said that poetry is "the dialogue of the mind with itself."[10] He could have said the same of his thought as a whole — as could the apostle.

Arnold's mother maintained that "Matt is a good Christian at bottom,"[11] but "bottom" was a good deal below the level of traditional Christian beliefs avowed by his father, for the receding "Sea of Faith" took with it the supernaturalism on which Christianity had relied. "At bottom" he was a moralist, a humanist with religious sensibilities who viewed religion as "morality

6. In fact, each of the writings discussed here was a response to criticism and in turn generated more criticisms. For a detailed treatment, see Sidney Coulling, *Matthew Arnold and His Critics: A Study of Arnold's Controversies* (Athens: Ohio University Press, 1974).

7. Collini, "Arnold," p. 276.

8. See Coulling, *Arnold and His Critics*, p. 13.

9. A contemporary (R. H. Hutton) said of Arnold's poetry that "no one has expressed more powerfully and poetically its [generation's] spiritual weaknesses, its craving for a passion it cannot feel, its admiration for a self-mastery it cannot achieve, its desire for a creed that it fails to accept, its sympathy with a faith it will not share, its aspiration for a peace it does not know." Quoted in Collini, "Arnold," p. 244.

10. Arnold, preface to *Poems* (1853).

11. Collini, "Arnold," p. 296.

touched by emotion" and demythologized God accordingly.[12] Without a supernaturally derived Scripture, Arnold's religion relied on empirical evidence provided by moral experience. His interest in religion was thoroughly practical and anti-theoretical: logicians "imagine truth something to be proved, I something to be seen; they something to be manufactured, I as something to be found."[13]

Victorian Britain was absorbed with religion and controversies over it. Despite the upsurge of religion in the 1840s, Christianity was experiencing the painful impact of multiple upheavals in English society, which generated the much-discussed "crisis of faith."[14] The church was embroiled in debates over historical criticism,[15] disestablishment, broad church versus high church, the Tractarians (the "Oxford Movement"),[16] and the demands of the Dissenters (Presbyterians, Congregationalists, Methodists, and Baptists) for more rights. Thousands were listening to Spurgeon's and Moody's preaching (which Arnold heard), but also many were staying away from church altogether, more from the established church than from nonconformist chapels. Increasingly, Anglican clergy, though bound by oath to affirm the Articles of

12. After Arnold's death, a commentator noted: "He has been treated as a flippant and illusory Christian, instead of as a specially devout and conservative agnostic." Quoted in William Robbins, *The Ethical Idealism of Matthew Arnold* (Toronto: University of Toronto Press, 1959), p. 75.

13. Arnold, preface to *Essays in Criticism* (London: Macmillan, 1865), p. viii. In *Literature and Dogma* he will write disdainfully of what is "invented"; see below.

14. See, e.g., Frank Turner, "The Victorian Crisis of Faith and the Faith That Was Lost," in *Victorian Faith in Crisis: Essays on Continuity and Change in Nineteenth-Century Religious Belief,* ed. R. J. Helmstadter and B. Lightman (Houndmills/London: Macmillan Academic & Professional, 1990), pp. 9-38; also Hugh McCloud, *Religion and Society in England, 1850-1914* (New York: St. Martin's, 1996), ch. 4.

15. For example, George Eliot's translation of Strauss's *Life of Jesus* was published in 1846, and of Feuerbach's *Essence of Christianity* in 1854; in 1860 the articles in *Essays and Reviews* created such a tumult because they accepted "higher criticism" that its authors were called *Septem Contra Christum;* in 1863 John Colenso, bishop of Natal, published a study of the first six books of the OT in which he not only distinguished literary strata but argued that details made the narratives historically incredible (e.g., what sort of food did Noah supply for the predatory carnivores in the ark?), prompting forty-one bishops to call for his resignation. Even Arnold got into the fray.

16. Basil Willey notes that in 1840 John Henry Newman wrote his sister that "Protestantism leads to infidelity"; see *More Nineteenth Century Studies* (London: Chattus & Windus, 1956), p. 28. Though Arnold admired Newman personally, and admired his preaching, he could not agree with the thinking that led Newman to Rome. The influence of John Henry Newman on Arnold is emphasized by David J. DeLaura, *Hebrew and Hellene in Victorian England: Newman, Arnold, and Pater* (Austin/London: University of Texas Press, 1969).

Religion, no longer believed them as factual statements, and so wrestled with their own integrity.[17] More interested in the impact of the quarrels than in their actual content, Arnold focused on the misunderstandings and misuse of the Bible they reflected. His own view of Scripture was deeply influenced by Spinoza's *Tractatus Theologico-Politicus,* according to which "faith does not demand that dogmas should be true [but that they] will stir up the heart to obey."[18] Writing from the top of the cultural pyramid, he was a centrist, abhorring partisanship in religion, because he saw the Church of England as a national institution for promoting the good of all.[19] In his own way a deeply religious man, he was convinced that his father's orthodox Christianity was no longer viable. He was an apologist for a Christianity that he believed could retain its moral influence only when freed from its traditional supernaturalism and unverifiable dogmas.

And that goal needed criticism. "The Function of Criticism" expressed his grand view of its task: "in all branches of knowledge, theology, philosophy, history, art, science, to see the object as in itself it really is"; to "try to know the best that is known and thought in the world, irrespectively of practice, politics, and everything of the kind; and to value knowledge and thought as they approach this best, without the intrusion of any other considerations whatever"; and, by "making this known, to create a current of true and fresh ideas" (pp. 1, 17, 19). Until now, criticism has not fulfilled its "best spiritual work; which is to keep man from a self-satisfaction which is retarding and vulgaris-

17. See James C. Livingston, *The Ethics of Belief: An Essay on the Victorian Religious Conscience,* AARSR 9 (Missoula, Mont.: Scholars Press, 1974), as well as Elisabeth Jay, *Faith and Doubt in Victorian Britain* (London: Macmillan Education, 1986); Jeffrey von Arx, "The Victorian Crisis of Faith as a Crisis of Vocation," in *Victorian Faith in Crisis,* ed. Helmstadter and Lightman, pp. 262-82.

18. See Arnold, "A Word More about Spinoza," *Macmillan's Magazine,* December 1863, pp. 136-42 (reprinted in *Essays in Criticism,* 1st ed. [1865] as "Spinoza," expanded in 2nd ed. [1869] as "Spinoza and the Bible"). For the Spinoza quotation, see Dale, *Victorian Critic,* p. 122. Dale asserts that "the extent of Arnold's reliance upon Spinoza for the reinterpretation of religious truth which everywhere informs and ultimately crowns his career . . . cannot be overestimated" (p. 117). But Arnold also noted that "Spinoza's ideal is the intellectual life; the Christian's ideal is the religious life. Between the two states there is all the difference which there is between the being in love, and the following, with delighted comprehension, a demonstration of Euclid." See Arnold, "A Word More about Spinoza," p. 141.

19. His view was like that of A. P. Stanley, then at Christ Church Oxford and later Dean at Westminster, who in 1850 wrote that "the Church of England, by the very condition of its being, was not High or Low, but Broad, and had always included and been meant to include, opposite and contradictory opinions." Quoted in Willey, *More Nineteenth Century Studies,* p. 172.

ing, to lead him towards perfection, by making his mind dwell upon what is excellent in itself, and the absolute beauty and fitness of things" (p. 21). Understandably, given Victorian self-congratulation,[20] "whoever sets himself to see things as they are will find himself one of a very small circle; but it is only by this small circle resolutely doing its own work that adequate ideas will ever get current at all" (p. 25).

II

In *Culture and Anarchy* (hereafter *CA*), Arnold explained how through culture "adequate ideas will get current." For Arnold, "culture" differed significantly from what an anthropologist studies — the overall configuration of a society's characteristic and determining habits. Arnold used "culture" in the sense of a "cultured" or "cultivated" person; similarly, Germans say that *Bildung* produces a *gebildeter Mensch*.[21] The essays in *Culture and Anarchy* were written "to recommend culture as the great help out of our present difficulties"; and culture requires criticism, "the pursuit of our total perfection by means of getting to know . . . the best which has been thought and said in the world" (*CA*, p. 5). Further, culture "leads us . . . to conceive of true human perfection as a *harmonious* perfection, developing all sides of our humanity; and as a *general* perfection, developing all parts of our society" (p. 8),[22] for it moves by "moral and social passion for doing good" (p. 31).

Since religion "comes to a conclusion identical with that [of] culture" — it too locates "human perfection in an *internal* condition, in the growth and predominance of our humanity proper" — religion is "the greatest and most important of the efforts by which the human race has manifested its impulse

20. G. K. Chesterton observed that Arnold found the mood of the English to be "one of smug Radical mediocrity" and the "window of the English soul opaque with its own purple"; see Chesterton, introduction to Arnold's *Essays Literary and Critical* (London: Dent, 1906).

21. The *Bildung* dimension of Arnold's whole work, including his emphasis on progress toward perfection, is seen clearly by Ruth apRoberts's *Arnold and God* (Berkeley/London: University of California Press, 1983). See also W. H. Bruford, *The German Tradition of Self-Cultivation: "Bildung" from Humboldt to Thomas Mann* (Cambridge: Cambridge University Press, 1975). Arnold admired Humboldt.

22. Italics within quotations are Arnold's except where otherwise noted. Arnold's view of culture develops what Coleridge had said about "cultivation" — "the harmonious development of those qualities and faculties that characterize our humanity." Quoted in Raymond Williams, *Culture and Society, 1780-1950* (New York: Harper & Row, 1958), p. 61. Williams traces the history of this use of "culture."

to perfect itself" (pp. 31-32).[23] From this lofty view Arnold looks critically at English society, in which "faith in machinery is . . . our besetting danger"; indeed, without the "purging effect wrought upon our minds by culture, the whole world, the future as well as the present, would inevitably belong to the Philistines" — those who "believe most that our greatness and welfare are proved by our being very rich" (pp. 34-35).[24] Culture is "not satisfied till we *all* come to a perfect man, . . . until the raw and unkindled masses of humanity are touched with sweetness and light" — and this requires "*real* thought and *real* beauty, . . . [not] an intellectual food prepared and adapted" for the masses by the well-meaning (p. 47).

He traces English resistance to this lofty goal to "our preference of doing to thinking," a contrast that he explores in terms of "Hebraism and Hellenism"[25] — cultural forces that contend for supremacy in history and alternate in achieving it, though their final aim is the same: "man's perfection or salvation," that is, "that we might be partakers of the divine nature" (pp. 86-87).[26]

23. In *Hebrew and Hellene,* pp. xi-xii, DeLaura speaks of the "progressive *religionizing* of the idea of culture," evident also in Newman and Pater.

24. Arnold speaks of three "classes": Barbarians (the aristocracy), Philistines (the middle class), and Populace, each having a severer and lighter side. The Barbarian's graver side likes honors; its lighter side enjoys field sports. There are two kinds of Philistines: in one, the graver side likes making money, while the lighter enjoys comfort and "tea-meetings"; in the other, the graver side likes trade unions, while the lighter goes for deputations and hearing lectures. The Populace's sterner side likes "bawling, hustling, and smashing; the lighter [side], beer." But in each class, some want something more (p. 72).

25. For a discussion of this motif, see DeLaura, *Hebrew and Hellene.* See also Frank M. Turner, *The Greek Heritage in Victorian Britain* (New Haven/London: Yale University Press, 1981). Turner notes that "Arnold's Hebrews were not Jews but rather contemporary English Protestant Nonconformists. His Greeks were not ancient Hellenes but a version of humanity largely conjured up in the late-eighteenth-century German literary and aesthetic imagination" (p. 21) — especially by the poet Heinrich Heine, whom Arnold admired. Earlier, Winckelmann's writings had offered an idyllic view of Greek sculpture, though he had never been to Greece to see it. Turner sees that the Victorians simply assumed that the (idealized) Greeks were like themselves — rational and democratic. Thus, the Hellenes could be the norm for judging the coarse aspects of Victorian society.

26. Although he quotes only this line from 2 Pet. 1:4, its full weight is apparent when the whole verse is read, and in context: God's power "has given us . . . his precious and very great promises, so that through them you may escape from the corruption that is in the world because of lust, and may become participants of the divine nature. For this very reason, you must make every effort to support your faith with goodness, and goodness with knowledge, and knowledge with self-control. . . . For if these things are yours and are increasing among you, they keep you from being ineffective" (1:4-8 NRSV). Thus, Arnold anticipates Hays's point: one must not isolate Paul's quotations from their context.

Hellenism's goal is identical with criticism's: "to see things as they really are; the uppermost idea with Hebraism is conduct and obedience. Nothing can do away with this ineffaceable difference; the Greek quarrel with the body and its desire is, that they hinder right thinking, the Hebrew quarrel with them is, that they hinder right acting. . . . The governing idea of Hellenism is *spontaneity of consciousness;* that of Hebraism, *strictness of conscience.*" In Christianity "this essential bent of Hebraism to set doing above knowing" is continued, and expressed as "self-conquest, . . . the following not our own individual will, but the will of God, *obedience*" (p. 88).[27] Christianity's "boundless devotion to that inspiring and affecting pattern of self-conquest offered by Christ" actually "establishes the law" (pp. 88-89, adopting Rom. 3:31). Ultimately, however, Hellenism and Hebraism are complementary, for both are contributors to the development of human perfection. But "now, and for us, it is a time to Hellenise, and to praise knowing; for we have Hebraised too much" (p. 26); there may be a time, however, when their importance should be reversed (so at the end of the introduction to *Culture and Anarchy*).

Because the error of Puritanism (which Arnold equated with Protestantism) lies in thinking that the one thing necessary is obedience, the Puritan is "a victim of Hebraism, of the tendency to cultivate strictness of conscience rather than spontaneity of consciousness," but there is no one thing necessary. "The real *unum necessarium* for us is to come to our best at all points" (p. 100). But Puritanism's one-sidedness not only takes Paul's writings to be absolute and final but also distorts his terms, such as grace, faith, election, and righteousness, into a "grotesque caricature" of his real meaning (pp. 101-2). Arnold, the Apostle of Culture, will recover it.

III

Arnold himself points out that what was begun in *Culture and Anarchy* is completed in *St. Paul and Protestantism.*[28] Determined to "rescue St. Paul

---

27. The struggle against one's natural inclinations and temptations was a theme in his father's sermons. See John O. Waller, "Matthew and Thomas Arnold: Soteriology," *AThR* 44 (1962): 60-62. For a discussion of popular "muscular Christianity" and Thomas Hughes's *The Manliness of Jesus* (1879), see Norman Vance, *The Sinews of the Spirit* (Cambridge: Cambridge University Press, 1985); Peter Gay, "The Manliness of Christ," in *Religion and Irreligion in Victorian Society,* ed. R. W. Davis and R. J. Helmstadter (London/New York: Routledge, 1992), pp. 102-16.

28. The book consists of two articles on Paul, together with a historical survey, "Puri-

and the Bible from the perversions of them by mistaken men,"[29] he declares that "the over-Hebraising of Puritanism, and its want of a wide culture" — which he saw while inspecting Dissenter schools — has so narrowed its vision that it does not understand Paul (*St. Paul,* pp. 6-7). So the primary need is "seeing things as they really are, and . . . the greater importance of ideas than of the machinery which exists for them" (i.e., forms of church polity in non-Anglican denominations).[30] Concretely, "what in St. Paul is secondary and subordinate, Puritanism has made primary and essential; what in St. Paul is figure and belongs to the sphere of feeling, Puritanism has transported into the sphere of intellect and made formula." The latter error misunderstands Paul's language and argument; the former distorts "what really characterises him and gives his teaching its originality and power" (pp. 8-9).

Paul's thought has been perverted by Puritanism's penchant for describing God "as if he were a man in the next street" whose mind and acts it pretends to explain and verify. But when one sees things "as they really are," science can acknowledge God as "that stream of tendency by which all things strive to fulfil the law of their being" — thus using Aristotelian teleology to "demythologize," similar to Bultmann's use of existentialism to avoid "objectifying" God-language. Arnold recognizes that when religion tries to "describe what it loves," it does speak of God as "a sort of magnified and non-natural man" (pp. 10-12). But the two languages are not identical and

---

tanism and the Church of England," and a lengthy preface in which Arnold responds to criticisms of the articles, claiming — somewhat disingenuously — that his interpretation was not his discovery but "belongs to the 'Zeit-Geist'" (p. xi). It is the Zeit-Geist that reveals that the church of the Philistines is not "the essence of Christianity" (p. xxviii). Arnold, however, is not optimistic about the unification of Hebraism and Hellenism, because for that to occur, "more preparation is needed than man has yet had" (p. xxxix). The book, nonetheless, is part of that preparation. Page numbers here refer to the third edition (New York: Macmillan, 1875).

29. In addition to Puritanism's interpretation, Arnold has in view Ernest Renan's *Saint Paul* (ET 1869), which concludes: "After having been for three hundred years the Christian doctor in an eminent degree, thanks to orthodox Protestantism, Paul seems in our days near the end of his reign." From now on, the heart of Christianity is not Romans but the Sermon on the Mount (London: Temple, n.d.), p. 165. Arnold begins *St. Paul and Protestantism* by contesting Renan, whom he met in 1859, and proceeds to connect Jesus and Paul.

30. As Arnold sees it, non-Anglicans have created their distinctive polities in order to validate their theological differences from the Church of England. Consequently, they "guide politics, govern statesmen, destroy institutions; — and they are based upon a blunder" (p. 114). In "Puritanism and the Church of England," his broad church sympathies are clear. Viewing the Church of England as "a great national society for the promotion of goodness," he sees no reason why other churches should remain apart from it.

must not be confused, as they are in Puritanism's distortion of Paul's letter to the Romans.

Instead of walking his readers through Romans, Arnold proceeds as a literary critic, reading Paul "with the sort of critical tact which the study of the human mind and its history, and the acquaintance with many great writers [replacing Puritanism's narrowness], naturally gives for following the movement of any one single great writer's thought; reading him, also, without preconceived theories" (p. 29).[31] This entails understanding that Paul's language is not scientific but Semitic (he "Orientalises") — that is, it is figurative. But he also "Judaises" when he quotes Scripture arbitrarily, sometimes interrupting the argument (a fault of style, as in Romans 3), sometimes arguing badly (a fault of reasoning, as in Galatians 3). Puritanism misunderstands him when he Orientalizes, but he himself is partly to blame when Puritanism Judaizes with him.

To get at "what Paul really thought and meant to say, it is necessary for us modern and western people to translate him" — but not as in Puritanism, which directly recasts his letter into "the formal propositions of a modern scientific treatise." Rather, "his letter itself must be recast before it can be properly conveyed." This means discerning and following "the *order* in which, in any series of ideas, the ideas come," their logical order and the connections between them (pp. 34-35, emphasis mine). In effect, the critic who follows "the movement" of any single author's thought must proceed not as a historian who traces the origin of ideas but as a reasoning theologian.

So the key question is, "What is it which sets Paul in motion? It is . . . the master-impulse of Hebraism, — the *desire for righteousness*" (p. 35).[32] "To the Hebrew, this moral order, or righteousness, was pre-eminently the universal order, the law of God; and God, the fountain of all goodness, was pre-eminently to him the giver of the moral law. The end and aim of all religion,

31. Implicitly, Arnold agrees with Benjamin Jowett's assertion (in *Essays and Reviews*, 1860) that the Bible should be read like any other book — a view that caused a firestorm, though Coleridge had said much the same decades before. On the Continent, such ideas had been expressed often since Herder, whom Arnold read. For Herder's influence on Arnold, see apRoberts, *Arnold and God*, pp. 40-46.

32. Here Arnold applies to Paul what he has earlier said in "A Word More about Spinoza": "A philosopher's real power over mankind resides not in his metaphysical formulas, but in the spirit and tendencies which have led him to adopt those formulas. Spinoza's critic, therefore, has rather to bring to light that spirit and those tendencies of his author, than to exhibit his metaphysical formulas; . . . that which is most important, that which sets all his work in motion" (p. 140).

access to God, — the sense of harmony with the universal order — the partaking of the divine nature [2 Pet. 1:4 again] — that our faith and hope might be in God [1 Pet. 1:21] — that we might have life and have it more abundantly [John 10:10], — meant for the Hebrew, access to the source of the *moral* order . . . and harmony with it" (pp. 35-36). It was Paul's desire to establish the law as the basis of righteousness that "gave him the insight . . . that there could be no radical difference, in respect of salvation and the way to it, between Jew and Gentile. 'Upon every soul of man that *worketh evil,* . . . tribulation and anguish; to every one that *worketh good,* glory, honour and peace'" (Rom. 2:9-10; pp. 36-37). For Arnold's Paul, God's fair retribution/reward is not an issue that is addressed by the gospel (in the "justification of the *un*godly," Rom. 5:9) but *is* the gospel.

Given Paul's "piercing practical religious sense," he writes "lists . . . of moral habits to be pursued or avoided" (e.g., Rom. 1:29-31; Gal. 5:19-23). Indeed, into Paul's spirit, "so possessed with the hunger and thirst for righteousness," the teaching of Jesus "sank down and worked there even before Paul ceased to persecute, and had no small part in getting him ready for the crisis of his conversion." Jesus' teachings — for example, love for one another, and that sometimes (!) the last should be first — "enlarged the domain of duty of which Pharisaism showed him only a portion" (pp. 37-41). No Antinomian, Paul was "so possessed with the horror of Antinomianism, that he goes to grace for the sole purpose of extirpating it, and . . . cannot rest without perpetually telling us why he is gone there." To Calvin and Luther, who "have shut up" Paul "into the two scholastic doctrines of election and justification," Paul would say, "Election is nothing, and justification is nothing, but the keeping of the commandments of God" (p. 42, appropriating 1 Cor. 7:19).

Important for Arnold is grasping the *order* of Paul's ideas (the "movement" of his thought). Whether Puritanism "finds its starting-point . . . in the desire to flee from eternal wrath" incurred by Adam's fall or "in the desire to obtain eternal bliss" because of what God has done through Christ's death, for it righteousness *follows* as evidence of salvation instead of *being* salvation. But Paul starts "with the *thought* [emphasis mine] of a conscience void of offence towards God and man, and builds upon that thought his whole system." As Paul's governing idea, "this difference constitutes from the very outset an immense scientific superiority" over Puritanism, because Paul "does not begin outside the sphere of science; he begins with an appeal to reality and experience" — namely, "the *conception* [(!) emphasis mine] of the law of *righteousness,* the very law and ground of human nature so far as this nature is moral. Things as they truly are, — facts, — are the object-matter of science; and the moral law in human nature . . . is in our actual experience among the greatest of facts" (pp. 43-46). Moreover, the truth of Paul's emphasis on "the law of righteousness, the law of reason and conscience, *God as moral law*," is confirmed by Stoics, who also knew that "on our following the clue of moral order, or losing it, depends our happiness or misery" (p. 47, emphasis mine). They knew too of the internal opposition to righteousness — that is, that the experience of the conflicted self in Romans 7 (important for Arnold) is likewise universal.[33]

At just this point, says Arnold, Paul "enters the sphere of religion, . . . that which binds and holds us to the practice of righteousness."[34] This is critical "for the scientific worth of his doctrine," because in contrast with Puritanism, Paul does not rely for salvation on "theurgy" — magic-like divine acts of "election, justification, substitution, and imputed righteousness" (p. 51). Universally real as the human plight of Romans 7 is, "sin is not a monster to be mused on [as in Puritanism], but an impotence to be got rid of. All thinking about it, beyond what is indispensable for the firm effort to get rid of it, is waste of energy and waste of time" (p. 56). What gets rid of it is human effort.

To show that Paul adheres to "the undoubted facts of experience" (p. 55), the second part of *St. Paul* turns to a psychological account of Paul's experience of God, and that requires Arnold to explain how the understanding of God becomes an experience. Claiming that God, as "the universal order by which all things fulfil the law of their being," is "independent of our sense of having kept it," *as well as* "the power . . . [that] envelops us on every side" (citing Acts 17:24-28), Arnold infers that "this . . . element is very present to Paul's thoughts, and makes a profound impression on them (pp. 57-58). By this element we are *receptive and influenced* [emphasis mine], not originative and influencing. . . . So we get the thought of an impulsion outside ourselves which is at once awful and beneficent" (citing here Ps. 22:29 and Jer. 10:23). This is a *natural* feeling.[35] While Paul is not "overwhelmed" by God's awe-

---

33. In the preface to *Last Essays on Church and Religion* (1877), Arnold emphasizes this, saying that "all experience as to conduct brings us at last to the fact of two selves, or instincts, or forces, — name them how we will, and however we may suppose them to have arisen." One is the impulse to gratify every inclination, the other "leading us to submit inclination to some rule" (1903 ed. [London: Smith & Elder], p. xiii).

34. Arnold alludes to the etymology of "religion" in the Latin *religio*, based on *ligo*, to tie up or to bind.

35. Ruth apRoberts, *Arnold and God*, p. 222, observes: "Of the Victorians, . . . Arnold most of all develops this subjectivism — striving to be objective about his own subjective experience. If Wordsworth is self-conscious, Arnold is conscious of being self-conscious."

someness as was Calvin, "it is always before his mind and strongly agitates his thoughts. The voluntary, rational, and human world, of righteousness, moral choice, effort, filled the first place in his spirit," but the second, necessary place was the "mystical, and divine world, of influence, sympathy, emotion." In short, "the presence in Paul of this twofold feeling acted irresistibly upon his doctrine. What he calls 'the power that worketh in us' [Eph. 3:20], and that produces results transcending all our expectations and calculations, he instinctively sought to combine with our personal agencies of reason and conscience" (pp. 59-60).[36] Religion being that which binds us to the other, Arnold finds an analogy in the way loving a person influences and empowers the lover: "a powerful attachment will give a man spirits and confidence which he could by no means call up or command of himself; . . . in this mood he can do wonders which would not be possible to him without it" (pp. 61-62). Thus, "Paul felt himself to be for the sake of righteousness *apprehended*" (p. 62) — adopting Philippians 3:12, which does not mention righteousness, though it does refer back to v. 9, which speaks of the righteousness of God through the faithfulness of Christ.

But how is this quality of Christ established experientially? Evidently having the whole passage in mind, Arnold now writes of Paul's contemplation of Christ, which produced the *impression* that Christ was sinless (insisting again on the order of thoughts: it was Christ's sinlessness that "establishes his divinity," not the reverse, as in "scholastic theology"). "For attaining the righteousness of God, for reaching an absolute conformity with the moral order and with God's will," Paul "saw no such impotence existing in Jesus Christ's case as in his own [in Romans 7]." For Jesus, "the uncertain conflict between the law in our members and the law of the spirit did not appear to exist. . . . Obstacles outside him there were plenty, but obstacles within him there were none. He was led by the spirit of God." If *we* who are led by the spirit of God are sons of God (Rom. 8:14), how much more is this true of Jesus, "who lives to God entirely and who renders an unalterable obedience, the unique and only Son of God" (pp. 63-65; note the sudden capitalization!). Since "this is undoubtedly the main line of movement which Paul's ideas respecting Jesus Christ follow" (p. 65), the center of Paul's message is *"the righteousness of God, the non-fulfilment of it by man,[37] the fulfilment of it*

---

36. Later he will say that "we are saved through our affections; it is as beings *acted upon* and *influenced* that we are saved" (p. 97).

37. "Paul did not go to the Book of Genesis to get the real testimony about sin. He went to experience for it. '*I see,*' he says, 'a law in my members fighting against the law of my mind,

by Christ" (p. 67). Thus, the experiential base of Paul's thought about Christ is maintained.

Christ's divinity being inferred from his sinlessness, Arnold says that Paul's application of Jewish Wisdom theology to Christ (Col. 1:15-17) is secondary, "not an original part of his system, much less the ground of it," as is the case in John. "Paul's starting-point, it cannot be too often repeated, is the idea of righteousness; and his concern with Jesus is as the clue to righteousness, not as the clue to transcendental ontology" (pp. 65-66; in itself the statement is true, even though its logic is faulty: it excludes a false alternative). And while Paul did apply to Jesus also the ideas of Jewish eschatology, he spiritualized them as he came to think more and more of "a gradual inward transformation of the world by a conformity like Christ's to the will of God, than of a Messianic advent. Yet even then they are always second with him, and not first; the essence of saving grace is always to make us righteous, to bring us into conformity with the divine law, to enable us to 'bear fruit to God'" (pp. 67-69).

But how does Christ's fulfillment of God's righteousness affect us? Arnold quotes Titus 2:14 ("Jesus gave himself for us that he might redeem us from iniquity") before itemizing how this redemption occurs: (1) Jesus rendered "an unbroken obedience to the law of the spirit" that "makes men one" — that is, integrates the self, for "it is only by the law in our members that we are many";[38] (2) he had a sense of the solidarity of men (it is not God's will that any should perish); (3) he persevered in his obedience "even to the death"; and (4) in him was "that ineffable force of attraction which doubled the virtue of everything said or done by him" (p. 69). The last point is essential, for it serves as the empirical, experiential basis of Jesus' impact on Paul. Because Paul "felt this power penetrate him," he found a point in which "the mighty world outside man, and the weak world inside him, seemed to combine for his salvation," and to this "new and potent influence Paul gave the name of *faith*," more precisely, "faith that worketh *through love*" (Gal. 5:6). Religion being that which binds us, faith is "holding fast to an unseen power of goodness" by identification with Christ (pp. 70-71).

But how does one identify with Christ? By *nekrōsis* (2 Cor. 4:10): Paul's

---

and bringing me into captivity.' This is the essential testimony respecting the rise of sin" (p. 95).

38. Arnold insists that "the forces and tendencies in us are . . . in themselves beneficent, . . . not evil," though "evil . . . flows from these diverse [unharmonized] workings" (p. 48). Accordingly, he interprets the numberless iniquities mentioned in Ps. 40:12 as the "hydra-brood" of the "law in our members" that is activated by the law (p. 56).

central doctrine is *"to die with Christ to the law of the flesh, to live with Christ to the law of the mind"* (p. 76), which for Arnold is the spirit (not the Spirit!) as the voice of "the universal order . . . expressing itself in us" (p. 49). This affective identification with Christ is salvifically effective: now one "can do, and does, what Christ did" (p. 77), because what was effective for Christ is effective for all humans as well. So Arnold can use Romans 12:1-3 to say that "Christ throughout his life and in his death presented his body a living sacrifice to God." Moreover, the one who thus dies with Christ to "every self-willed impulse blindly trying to assert itself without respect of the universal order" is "transformed by the renewing of [the] mind, and [rises] with him" (pp. 77-78). The truth of this is demonstrated by experience throughout history: "In the midst of errors the most prosaic, the most immoral, the most unscriptural, concerning God, Christ, and righteousness, the immense emotion of love . . . inspired by the person and character of Jesus has had to work almost by itself alone for righteousness; and it has worked wonders" (p. 79).

So the three key words in Paul's thought are not Puritanism's *"calling* [election], *justification, sanctification"* but *"dying with Christ, resurrection from the dead, growing into Christ"* (pp. 81-82, citing Col. 2:20; Phil. 3:11; Eph. 4:15). Arnold now expands the discussion of resurrection begun in *Culture and Anarchy,* where he said that in nine out of ten cases Paul thinks of resurrection as "a rising to a new life before the physical death of the body, and not after it" (*CA,* p. 102). While recognizing that in the Thessalonian and Corinthian letters Paul *does* emphasize "the physical and miraculous aspect of the resurrection, both Christ's and the believer's" (*St. Paul,* p. 83), Arnold must show that Paul nonetheless thinks experientially — that is, without recourse to any supernatural act of God. Solution: since Paul (like Arnold!) seeks "a moral side and significance for all the processes, however mystical, of the religious life" in order to strengthen "their hold upon us and their command of all our nature," he treated also resurrection in practical terms: "Resurrection, in its *essential* sense, is therefore for Paul, the rising, within the sphere of our visible earthly existence, from death [i.e., "living after the flesh, obedience to sin"] to life"; still, this occurs as "mortifying by the spirit the deeds of the flesh, obedience to righteousness" (p. 84, emphasis mine).[39]

39. The word "essential" is basic here. While Arnold insists that Paul "accepted the physical miracle of Christ's resurrection . . . as a part of the signs and wonders which accompanied Christianity," he also denies that this "gives to his teaching its essential character." We "cannot know with any certainty" how far Paul carried through the distinction between what he accepted and the essential; but that he was aware of it, and moved toward the latter, is indicated by 2 Cor. 5:16 and by Romans, where he "rejects the notion of dwelling on the

Since what applies to the believer applies also to Christ, Arnold can say that "from the moment . . . that Jesus Christ was content to do God's will, he died. . . . Christ 'died to sin,'" and, "consequently, through all his life here, he was risen and living to God" (p. 85). Therefore, "when, through identifying ourselves with Christ, we reach Christ's righteousness, then eternal life begins for us; — a continuous and ascending life, for the eternal order never dies, and the more we transform ourselves into servants of righteousness and organs of the eternal order, the more we are . . . this eternal order.[40] . . . But the transformation cannot be completed here; the physical death is regarded by Paul as a stage at which it [the transformation] ceases to be impeded" (pp. 87-88). So even if Paul accepted Jewish eschatological and early Christian views, "what makes him original and himself, is not what he shares with his contemporaries and with modern popular religion, but this which he develops of his own; and this . . . [makes] his religion a theology instead of a theurgy, and at bottom a scientific instead of a non-scientific structure" (p. 91).

Clearly, then, "in St. Paul's essential ideas this popular notion of a substitution, and appeasement, and imputation of alien merit, has no place. Paul knows nothing of a sacrificial atonement; what Paul knows of is a reconciling sacrifice." The true substitution, for Paul, "is not the substitution of Jesus Christ in men's stead as victim on the cross to God's offended justice; it is the substitution by which the believer, in his own person, *repeats* Jesus Christ's dying to sin" (p. 103, emphasis mine). Thus, Christ's sacrifice (in not pleasing himself, consummated on the cross) is structurally archetypal and salvifically paradigmatic, for "it contained the means, the only possible means, of our being brought into harmony with [God's eternal] order," righteousness (p. 111). And when we, by identifying with Christ, "rise with him . . . to life, the only true life, . . . of following the eternal law of the moral order which by ourselves we could not follow," *then* "God justifies us" (p. 112).

In Paul's language, "figures of ransom, redemption, propitiation, blood,

---

miraculous Christ, on the descent into hell [!] and on the ascent into heaven" (pp. 88-90). Unfortunately, he notes, the translators of the AV pulled Paul in exactly the opposite direction, for by adding "and revived" to Paul's "Christ died and rose again" in Rom. 14:9, they made Paul revert to the resurrection as resuscitation (p. 82).

40. Note how Arnold not only combines "servants of righteousness" (Rom. 6:18) with "members [Arnold's "organs"] . . . to righteousness" (Rom. 6:19) but also equates "righteousness" with "the eternal order" and so interprets "that we might be made the righteousness of God in him" (2 Cor. 5:21) as the process of becoming this "moral order" — that is, as growth toward perfection.

offering, all subordinate themselves to his central idea of *identification with Christ through dying with him,* and are strictly subservient to it" (pp. 113-14). There is no need to turn his language into doctrines. "But if it is to be turned into methodical language, then it is the language into which we have translated it that translates it truly" (p. 114). Indeed, Arnold concludes, if Paul could hear how Puritanism speaks of predestination and justification each Sunday, he would see that again "the veil is upon its heart" (as in 2 Cor. 3:15-16); but when he is understood rightly, Puritanism will also "feel as though scales were fallen from its eyes" (p. 115).

IV

Within the same perspective, *Literature and Dogma* (hereafter, *LD*) devotes a long chapter to Jesus but needs only a few pages to repeat what was said in *St. Paul and Protestantism.* Whereas *St. Paul* sought to "rescue" Paul from Puritan misunderstanding, *Literature and Dogma* seeks to "restore" the Bible to those who abandon it (and Christianity with it) because they cannot accept the doctrines that orthodoxy says are based on Scripture and its miracles.[41] The language of the Bible "is not scientific, but the language of common speech or of poetry and eloquence, approximate language thrown out at certain great objects of consciousness which it does not pretend to define fully," though it "deals with facts of positive experience" (p. 114).[42] Indeed, the word "God" itself is not used scientifically but is "a term of poetry . . . *thrown out,* so to speak, at a not fully grasped object, . . . a *literary* term" (pp. 10-11).[43] So then, "if there

41. Arnold explicitly says that the book is not written for those who still accept the Bible on the basis of either popular or metaphysical theology (p. 114), noting also: "To walk on the sea cannot really prove a man to proceed from the Eternal that loveth righteousness" (p. 142). Page numbers here refer to the 1899 (Macmillan) edition.

42. Ruth apRoberts, *Arnold and God,* p. 229, sees here a parallel to "the Logical Positivists' classification of ethical and aesthetic 'propositions' as forms of emotive as opposed to referential language." She follows Epifanio San Juan Jr., who writes: "To Arnold, the language of the Bible functions metaphorically with its pseudo-statements, a pseudo-statement being 'a form of words which is justified entirely by its effects in releasing or organizing our impulses and attitudes'"; see San Juan, "Matthew Arnold and the Poetics of Belief: Some Implications of *Literature and Dogma*," *HTR* 57 (1964): 103, citing I. A. Richards, "Science and Poetry," in *Criticism,* ed. M. Schorer et al. (New York: Harcourt Brace, 1948), p. 518.

43. In the preface to *God and the Bible* (New York: Macmillan, 1875), Arnold writes of popular theology as "materialised poetry, which they give as science; and there can be no worse science than materialised poetry" (p. xlvi). In *Last Essays on Church and Religion,* he

be anything with which metaphysics have nothing to do, . . . it is religion. For the object of religion is *conduct*," which is three-fourths of human life (p. 13). In short, "conduct is the word of common life, morality is the word of philosophical disquisition, righteousness is the word of religion" (p. 18).

Next, Arnold asserts that "the real germ of religious consciousness . . . was a consciousness of *the not ourselves which makes for righteousness*" (p. 46).[44] Because this reality's power is enduring, Arnold says that the Tetragrammaton in Exodus 3:14 really means the Eternal, and that what it affirms is "real and verifiable" (p. 56).[45] Thus, the factual (hence scientific) basis of this consciousness is the sense of what we must do in order to fulfill the law of our being (as noted above). This consciousness is no more self-generated than we are self-created; we simply become aware of it. Moreover, since for science "God is simply *the stream of the tendency by which all things fulfil the law of their being*" (p. 37), there is no antithesis between revealed religion and natural religion, for "that in us which is really natural is . . . *revealed*."[46] The real antithesis, to natural and revealed alike, is *invented, artificial*" — that is, "a system of theological notions about . . . essence, existence, consubstantiality" which has been "invented by theologians, — able men with uncommon talents for abstruse reasoning" (p. 45).

It is important for Arnold that the meaning of "God" is verifiable[47] —

---

writes: "It is a great error to think that whatever is thus perceived to be poetry ceases to be available in religion. The noblest races are those which know how to make the most serious use of poetry" (p. 27). In "The Study of Poetry" (introduction to *The English Poets*, by T. H. Ward [London: Macmillan, 1880]), he foresees that humanity will "turn to poetry to interpret life for us, to console us, to sustain us. Without poetry, our science will appear incomplete; and most of what now passes with us for religion and philosophy will be replaced by poetry" (p. xviii).

44. Ruth apRoberts notes Arnold's debt to Thomas Carlyle's *Heroes and Hero Worship* (1840); see *Arnold and God*, pp. 224-25. In the first lecture, Carlyle traces the origin of religion to humanity's most rudimentary experience of the world: "That it is a Force, and thousandfold Complexity of Forces; a Force which is *not we*. That is all; it is not we, it is altogether different from *us*" (emphasis original).

45. In *God and the Bible*, Arnold claims that his definition of God as "the eternal power, not ourselves, which makes for righteousness" can be verified, whereas definitions like "God is a person who thinks and loves" cannot (p. 107). Moreover, "*Power* is a better word [than Being, which is not understood anyway], because it pretends to assert of God nothing more than effect on us, operation" (p. 108).

46. For Arnold, what is revealed is what is found; see the quotation in section I above.

47. He would have agreed with his friendly opponent T. H. Huxley, who said: "The man of science has learned to believe in justification, not by faith, but by verification"; quoted in Coulling, *Arnold and His Critics*, p. 217.

the enduring correlation between right conduct and experienced well-being, expressed in Proverbs 11:19: "righteousness tendeth to life" (together with its unstated correlate in the rest of the verse, "so that he that persueth evil persueth it to his own death"). However, the Hebrews experienced both contradictions and delays. To the former, Ecclesiastes responded with skepticism; to the latter, the prophets with hope — especially Daniel, whose messianic ideas included resurrection. But Proverbs 11:19 "has a firm, experimental ground, which the Messianic ideas have not," for they are a "kind of fairy-tale" beyond proof or disproof. Quoting his admired Goethe, "*Aberglaube* is the poetry of life," not science (pp. 69-70). But what is *Aberglaube*? Arnold renders it *"extra-belief"* (*aber* can mean "beyond"), surely knowing that the usual meaning of *Aberglaube* is superstition, but also suggesting that *Aber+glaube* is analogous to super+natural, and hence neither necessary nor currently credible. Thus, Israel's eschatological ideas, being *Aberglaube,* have no scientific value in providing experience-based certitude, for they refer "to a state of things not yet actually experienced" (p. 94). Although Jesus tried to extricate his disciples from such "phantasmagory of outward grandeur and self-assertion,"[48] *Aberglaube* returned as futuristic eschatology, miracles, and specious reasoning in the use of the Old Testament (pp. 94-96).

Lest readers abandon the Bible because of its abundant *Aberglaube,* Arnold points out that "the New Testament exists to reveal Jesus Christ, not to establish the immunity of its writers from error. Jesus himself is not a New Testament writer." Actually, the more one sees that the reporters were "fallible and prone to delusion," the more Jesus becomes "independent of the mistakes they made, and unaffected by them." Indeed, "the greater he was, the more certain were his disciples to misunderstand him" — a motif in many efforts to construct "the real Jesus" from the Gospels. Thus, if the Old Testament speaks of the Eternal without adequately understanding him, even more does the New Testament speak of Jesus without "accurately comprehending him" (pp. 134-35). Nonetheless, the evangelists reported a key sentence that they, being "full of the turbid Jewish fancies" (p. 137), could never have invented — "The kingdom of God is *within* you" (p. 140), in accord with culture's inner impact (see above, section II). Since the task of distinguishing what Jesus said from what is attributed to him cannot be carried

---

48. In fact, Jesus was always translating Jewish *Aberglaube* "into . . . the only sense in which it had truth and grandeur" (p. 200); for example, in John 11:23-24 he corrected Martha's *Aberglaube,* the traditional Jewish view of resurrection (p. 222).

out with complete success, what is really needed is criticism, and this requires knowing the history of thought, the way people thought and used words, and perception of the "Zeit-geist." Only with this knowledge can one show "the line of growth" of Jesus' doctrine (p. 160).[49]

Arnold finds that Jesus came "to *restore the intuition*," his way of saving and giving eternal life (p. 172). And "he restored the intuition of God through transforming the idea of righteousness"; and "to do this, he brought a *method,* and he brought a *secret*" (p. 174). The method is epitomized by repentance, "a great unceasing inward movement of attention and verification" expressed in conduct, since Jesus called for "a change of the inner man" when he said (in Mark 7:20, 21) that it is what comes from within that defiles, not externals (pp. 175-78). The secret was self-denial, epitomized by John 12:25 ("He that loveth his life shall lose it, and he that hateth his life in this world shall keep it unto life eternal") and Luke 9:23 ("Whosoever will come after me, let him renounce himself, and take up his cross daily, and follow me"; pp. 181-82).

This is exactly what Paul called "the word of the cross," or νέκρωσις (putting to death). His "rule of action" was stated in 2 Corinthians 4:10 — "Always bearing about in the body the *dying* of Jesus, that the *life* also of Jesus may be made manifest in our body!" (p. 181).[50] Indeed, the "word of the cross" *is* "the word of the kingdom" (the phrase in Matt. 13:19). Moreover, the sense of having the Eternal on our side and approving us (the consequence of righteousness) is what Jesus conveys with "*Therefore* doth my Father love me, because I lay down my life, that I may take it again" (John 10:17). This is not "theurgy" but the result of Jesus "himself having followed his own secret" (pp. 184-85); nor is it theory, "because *theory* Jesus never touches, but bases himself invariably on experience" (pp. 189-90). A doctrine like "God is a Person" cannot be applied as a practical rule or have the force of an intuition. Jesus, however, always exhibited his doctrine as "an intuition and practical rule . . . which, if adopted, would have the force of an intuition for its adopter also" (p. 191). Accordingly, the disciples were "not told to believe in his method, or to believe in his secret, but to believe in *him*" (p. 195). In a

---

49. While refusing to follow named German critics (Baur, Strauss, Ewald), his verdicts on unnamed English critics were caustic: not only do they maintain "their criticism against all questioners," but "it was a kind of impertinence in such professors to attempt any such criticism at all. Happily, the faith that saves is attached to the saving doctrines in the Bible, which are very simple; not to its literary and scientific criticism, which is very hard" (p. 162).

50. Arnold takes "the life of Jesus" as a reference to the Jesus of history, not to his resurrection life.

word, instead of doctrines like atonement and the "whole structure of materialising mythology" at the heart of traditional Christianity, "the true centre of gravity of the Christian religion is in the *method* and the *secret* of Jesus" (p. 218).

"All this is in Paul" — as well as what is not essential: "there is, besides, the *Aberglaube* . . . of the bodily resurrection, of Christ's second advent during the lifetime of men then living; there is the Calvinistical God 'willing to show his wrath' . . . [Rom. 9:22]; there is the Rabbinical logic, and the unsound use of prophecy and of the Old Testament" (p. 237). Nevertheless, when Paul said he was "in travail . . . till Christ be fashioned in them" (Gal. 4:19), he was talking about "the entire Christ, with his method, secret, and sweet reasonableness;[51] but the great stress is laid on the 'secret,' on *dying,* because this *was* Christ's secret, because the heart of the matter is indeed here" (p. 236).

V

In the preface to *God and the Bible,* Arnold asserts that "two things about the Christian religion must surely be clear. . . . One is, that men cannot do without it; the other, that they cannot do with it as it is" (p. xiv). Although his critics on the left would have disputed the first assertion and his opponents on the right the second, Arnold's verdict applies also to his own views. In fact, if biblical scholarship is to profit from reading him today, the verdict's distinction is essential. Without it, current scholarship might readily compile Arnold's omissions and errors — easy enough to do — and so simply reassure itself. But it is the distinction that makes reading Arnold profitable: on the one hand, identifying what we "cannot do without" not only acknowledges his achievement but also locates what we must continue; on the other hand, by specifying what we "cannot do with as it is" we clarify our own conception of the task by critical self-reflection.

Nothing illustrates better the inevitability of this self-assessment than asking whether we are better off without Arnold's view of criticism and its role, or whether it is something we "cannot do without" — namely, criticism's aim of finding "the best that is known and thought in the world, and by . . . making this known, to create a current of true and fresh ideas" that

---

51. "Sweet reasonableness" is Arnold's rendering of *epieikeia* (clemency, gentleness, courtesy), used once of Christ (in 2 Cor. 10:1) but often by Arnold.

over time can mitigate modern society's confusions. In the same essay, "The Function of Criticism at the Present Time" (1865), he also insists that if criticism is to "see things as they are" (p. 25), it must be detached from immediate practical concerns (not disinterested in them!); otherwise, it will be unable to "express dissatisfaction" with well-meant efforts or praise the desirable in the otherwise objectionable (p. 33). Without this necessary independence, people will applaud indiscriminately: "We are all in the same movement, we are all liberals, we are all in pursuit of truth." As a result, he adds sarcastically, "the pursuit of truth becomes really a social, practical, pleasurable affair, almost requiring a chairman, a secretary, and advertisements; . . . in general, plenty of bustle and very little thought" (p. 27). Many will reject this view readily — detachment for the sake of unbiased judgment — as elitist (who decides what is "best"?), as blind to the realities of a plural, multicultural society, and as abetting the already descried indifference of biblical scholarship to the needs of the church. But those who agree that we "cannot do without" Arnold's view of criticism also want an alternative to the culture wars, the internecine church conflicts, and the claims that praxis determines thought. In short, reaction to Arnold — as to any significant writer — discloses as much about ourselves as it does about him. That said, the judgments that follow intend to focus attention on Arnold.

To begin with, we cannot do without Arnold's insight that the Bible's language is "poetry," which, as he elsewhere said, "gives the idea, and it gives it touched with beauty, heightened by emotion."[52] The Bible's figurative character must be respected lest it be turned into the denotative language of science (as it is in the arguments over "creation science").[53] Indeed, even apart from the many-sided investigations of language in the twentieth century, probing its use in religion is especially urgent today, not only for professional interpreters of the Bible but also for those living on Dover Beach (which is more crowded now), as well as for those who resist living there. We cannot do without understanding that the Bible's language expresses ideas and experience imaginatively; that its depictions of God are "approximate" — that is, figurative imagery "thrown out" regarding a Reality that is acknowledged but never fully grasped by the reasoning mind; that it has the capacious ability to evoke a sense of the "not ourselves" because it was itself

---

52. Quoted by Nathan A. Scott Jr., "Arnold's Version of Transcendence — the *Via Poetica*," *JR* 59 (1979): 273.

53. Unfortunately, Arnold did not reckon with the Bible's language in law or historical narrative, which is hard to call "poetry."

evoked; that its religious power stems from its appeal to the imagination, distilled into art and music as well as into the formulations of theology. Nor can we do without what Arnold undertook — to state in conceptual language what the Bible refers to in its figures, images, metaphors, and tropes.

At just this point, however, it becomes evident that we "cannot do with" the results of Arnold's work "as it is," for while he recognized that poetry "gives the idea," his overarching apologetic aim prompted him to devise a non-theistic "Hebraic" definition of God ("the power, not ourselves, which makes for righteousness") for which he found a "Hellenic" equivalent ("the universal law by which all things fulfil their being"), expecting that whoever acknowledges the latter would also accept the former. In effect, by using the "Hellenic" to redefine the "Hebraic," he avoided having to choose one or the other (though leaving the door ajar to do so), just as he avoided combining them into language that would describe God as a "magnified . . . man in the next street." Nonetheless, the result is something one cannot do with "as it is," because it does not do justice to the referent of the Bible's figurative language about God, nor does it achieve its apologetic aim of an alternative language that is religiously adequate today. This dual deficiency is largely the result of Arnold's antipathy toward "supernaturalism" and the metaphysics traditionally used to undergird it; it also reflects his consistently functional understanding of religion reduced to "morality touched with emotion," whose goal is conduct.

The problem with his redefined referent of the Bible's language ("the power, not ourselves," etc.) is not that is wrong but that it leaves him with a deity that *is* but never *does*, who "makes for righteousness" through consciousness of law but does not *make* any situation or any person righteous, for that would be "theurgy," inseparable from speaking of God as a Person. Arnold's redefined biblical God neither initiates action in history (e.g., the exodus) nor responds to human action (other than as inevitable consequence); prayer is effective not because God "answers" it but because, by expressing aspiration, it energizes *our* action (*LD,* pp. 38-39 n.).[54] But the referent of the Bible's "thrown out" language is a deity whose existence and character are disclosed by deeds.[55] The Bible's deity is YHWH, a living, act-

54. Understandably, Bernard M. G. Reardon characterized Arnold's religion as "ethical deism"; see *Religious Thought in the Victorian Age: A Survey from Coleridge to Gore,* rev. ed. (London/New York: Longman, 1975), p. 272.

55. Oddly, although Arnold valued Isaiah 40–60 so highly that he translated these chapters for use in schools, he ignored the prophet's contemptuous polemic against gods who neither speak nor act.

ing Reality whose identity cannot be paraphrased as "the universal *law* by which all things fulfil their being."

Second, in our data-dominated era, we cannot do without reflecting on the nature and role of experience in religious perception and its language. Eschewing reliance on external authority (whether in Scripture or creed), Arnold emphasized experience because he was writing for those who expected religion to be based on verifiable evidence. So by tracing the Bible's understanding of God (as he had redefined it) to Israel's experience, he sought to show that the truth of the Bible is verifiable today.

But we cannot accept his construal of experience "as it stands." Not only does it fail to do justice to the richness of Israel's experience, but it also is unconvincing exegetically. He claims that the Hebrews "dwelt upon the thought of conduct and right and wrong, till the *not ourselves* which is in us and all around us [like the Stoic logos], became to them . . . *a power which makes for righteousness;* which makes for it unchangeably and eternally, and is therefore called *The Eternal.*" Further, there being "not a particle of metaphysics in their use of this name," he concludes that Israel "inferred nothing, reasoned out nothing; he felt and experienced" (*LD,* pp. 28-29), implying that Israel experienced God immediately, like Adam in the garden. But Israel did infer and reason about God in light of its wide range of experiences. Looked at more closely, Arnold implies that what Israel actually experienced was its own thinking about conduct. In addition, Arnold's view of verifiable experience is too limited to commend Christianity today as a vital religion to those who "will never interest themselves at all in our [merely] amended religion" (p. 294), for as Scott noted, it is "an account of the Christian witness that skips with a vengeance."[56] Concretely, it skips over much in the experience of both the evangelical's salvation and the existentialist's Angst. The significance of the narrow range of experience that Arnold takes into account becomes evident when one recalls his definition of sin as an "impotence to be got rid of," for this implies that sin is experienced as an incapacity by those for whom religion facilitates self-mastery. They are healthy, vigorous, relatively secure strivers who assume that their primary need is empowering their resolve to achieve as much perfection as possible and thereby "fulfill the law of their being." Whether sin is experienced as a failure to achieve or as a wound self-inflicted by ignoring or violating this law, it is eclipsed as complicity in collective guilt, be it inherited from the past or bequeathed to the future. In short, sin is experienced as it is construed — a personal prob-

56. Scott, "Arnold's Version of Transcendence," p. 281.

lem to be solved, not a feature of the given human condition that needs transformation (as it is for Paul). Viewing sin as impotence is reinforced by attributing failure to the inhibiting impact of external factors.[57]

Moreover, Arnold's limited experiential base generally ignores the deeper experiences that lie beyond right conduct's need of empowering emotion and example. Missing, from these writings at least, is life experienced as ever-deepening and unfathomable mystery, as the awesome enigma of finitude that is consummated — not simply terminated — by death, as the capriciousness of undeserved suffering, exploitation, and debilitating mental agony, as the power of evil to deceive good intentions and destroy good deeds. Conversely, also missing is the elemental experience of terrifying awe,[58] or bafflement at the ways the wholly unexpected turn of events exposes "the cunning of history" and thus mocks the design of the calculated life. Nor is the experience of self-fulfillment by deliberate, costly self-giving given its due. Consequently, Arnold's religion lacks power because it is not sufficiently in touch with the raw experience of life, including the inexplicable, the irrational, and the demonic, which are at least as much the motor of religious experience as awareness of obligation. To be sure, he lived long before the horrors of the Great War, which energized poets like Siegfried Sassoon and Wilfred Owen, but today reflection on experience — particularly in religious thought — cannot ignore the experienced illusions and agonies of the twentieth century.

The third element in Arnold's thought that we cannot do without pertains particularly to Paul — the centrality of Jesus. Jesus was as significant in Arnold's version of Christianity as he was in Paul's kerygmatic gospel — but in a quite different way. Arnold saw more clearly than many later interpreters of the apostle that Jesus — the actual Jesus of history, not the historians' Jesus — was absolutely essential in Paul's thought because solidarity with Jesus is at the core of salvation. Moreover, the portrayals of Jesus produced

57. Convinced that "a thing that *can* prove itself . . . *will* prove itself, because it is so" (*LD*, p. 300), Arnold explains why the world is not righteous: "the thwarting cause is the same now" as in Jesus' day — "the dogmatic system current, the so-called orthodox theology." Today, the chief priests, scribes, and elders are "our bishops and dogmatists, with their pseudo-science of learned theology," the Pharisees are the Protestant Dissenters, the Sadducees "are our friends the philosophical Liberals," and Pilate is the aristocracy, with "its complete inaptitude for ideas, its profound helplessness in presence of all great spiritual movements" (pp. 334-35).

58. Scott too readily equates Arnold's "the Eternal not ourselves" with Rudolf Otto's *mysterium tremendum et fascinans;* see Scott, "Arnold's Version of Transcendence," p. 270.

since the 1870s, diverse though they are, would induce few to fault Arnold for emphasizing Jesus' method, secret, "sweet reasonableness," and unalloyed obedience to God (his righteousness) that was completed on the cross, nor would many dispute that these traits, taken together, qualify him to be the exemplar of humanity at its best. And today, not a few would approve of Arnold's virtual elimination of the apocalyptic aspect of Jesus' message.

Nonetheless, one cannot accept Arnold's interpretation of Jesus in the thought of Paul "as it is," for once again, it does not do justice to the way Paul thought about Jesus, nor does it provide an adequate view of salvation today. True, Paul also emphasizes Jesus' obedience, but it was neither the moral achievement of Jesus' self-mastery nor the message and demeanor of the Jesus of history that triggered Paul's conversion and made Jesus the pivot of his gospel; rather, it was the meaning of the crucified Jesus' resurrection, apart from which Paul viewed him "according to the flesh" — that is, as offense. While Arnold rightly sees that for Paul resurrection was not physical resuscitation, he moves so quickly to resurrection as a metaphor of true life before death that he can only concede, somewhat reluctantly, that for Paul resurrection was an actual event — a view that he allegedly did not maintain (fortunately for Arnold). Consequently, it is virtually inevitable that Arnold would attribute to Paul a devotion to the Jesus of history as the prototype of both the righteous life and the sole way of achieving it — in short, a Jesuology.

In Paul's thought, however, Jesus was the focal point of a Christology, a theological understanding that correlates Jesus' identity, mission, and resurrection with the character and action of God. The distinction is important. In a Jesuology, the focus is on *Jesus'* relation to God, because it is inherently — that is, structurally, substantially, and experientially — distinguishable from ours only in the superior degree of his achievement (required for being our prototype); in a Jesuology, Jesus facilitates, by word and example, *our* relation to God but leaves God's relation *to us* unchanged. Not so in a Christology. A Christology correlates who Jesus is and what he does with the identity and character of God by speaking of him as God's act toward us and for us while one of us. Arnold's antipathy toward "supernaturalism" and metaphysics prevented him from seeing that for Paul it is precisely God's actual self-involvement in the whole event of Jesus that makes that event the Christ event that inaugurates salvation for those who become as truly involved in it as God, and who *therefore* emulate Jesus as the consequence of that participation, not as the means of attaining it. Arnold did not probe the rationale implied in Paul's figurative language in Christology, because he regarded it as *Aberglaube* — an expendable addition to what really matters — achievable, Jesus-like self-mastery that is basic for a right relation to God.

For a Christian religion determinatively oriented toward right conduct, an Arnoldian Jesuology may be quite adequate. It is certainly simpler than Paul's Christology. But for a Christianity that, like Paul's, is deliberately oriented toward resolving the human condition as well, it is quite inadequate. From the apostle's angle, the deep, troublesome dimensions of existence — the human condition "under" sin and permeated by death as well as dominated by Death before dying — are resolvable only by dual participation: God's involvement in Christ as precedent and pledge of redemption, and our involvement in Christ as participation in the pledge. For Paul, only God can change a condition that prevents "the law by which all things fulfill themselves" from being actualized. Without God's self-involvement, even achieving a Jesus-like righteousness leaves the depths of human existence unresolved.

VI

So, then, was Matthew Arnold also among the prophets, and not only among the critics? His writings are often oracular enough, were that the criterion. He would also qualify if provoking rejection by the contemporary religious "establishment" were the prime requirement. If a prophet is one who clearly foresees the future, the verdict is mixed, for on the one hand, by redefining the referent of God-language as well as the role of Jesus in ways that would not offend the Zeitgeist, he did anticipate much that became common; on the other hand, precisely as a poet he failed to see that it is the strangeness of *Aberglaube* that, by questioning the Zeitgeist, offers an alternative to its perception of reality. But if a prophet is one who disturbs what is so much taken for granted that it inhibits enlivening interpretation — a real re-saying — then one may indeed consider him among the prophets. What, then, does Arnold disturb? The assumption that by locating the Bible's thought ever more precisely and accurately in the past one can interpret it without engaging "the best that is known and thought in the world" and being engaged by it. The last word here, then, is provided by whoever wrote Mark 13:14: "Let the reader understand." In his own way, Matthew Arnold did. And so does Richard Hays. That is why this essay is offered in honor of his work.

Neither Devils nor Angels:
Peace, Justice, and Defending the Innocent:
A Response to Richard Hays

Allen Verhey

"The Devil can cite Scripture to his purpose."

— Richard Hays's grandmother[1]

Any academic book that begins by citing the author's grandmother may be regarded as promising. The problem that Richard's grandmother identified is well known to scholars, of course, but the scholars characteristically prefer less interesting ways to state it. But whether one talks about the Devil citing Scripture or the "inexhaustible hermeneutical potential" (p. 1) of a text, the problem is on display again and again in conversation and controversy when the Bible is cited as somehow normative for what Christians should do or leave undone.

Although Richard Hays did not solve his grandmother's problem with *The Moral Vision of the New Testament* (the Devil can still cite Scripture to his purpose), he did "clarify how the church can read Scripture in a faithful and disciplined manner so that Scripture might come to shape the life of the church" (p. 3). That was the project of *The Moral Vision of the New Testament*. If the church is to be the church, it is hard to think of a more important project. And for many of us, it is hard to think of a more important contribution to that project than Richard's book.

---

1. Richard Hays, *The Moral Vision of the New Testament* (New York: HarperSanFrancisco, 1996), p. 1. Subsequent page references to this volume will be placed in parentheses within the text.

I am grateful for the opportunity to thank Richard both for his friendship and for his scholarship by a modest contribution to this *Festschrift*. I
propose to celebrate *The Moral Vision of the New Testament* by quarreling
with a part of it, with his rejection of "violence in defense of justice." I hope
my quibble does not simply display one more time the truth of Richard's
grandmother's observation — with me playing the role of the Devil.

Violence is Richard's first "test case" when he turns to what he calls "the
pragmatic task," the last major section of the book. The question is this: "[I]s
it ever God's will for Christians to employ violence in defense of justice?"
(p. 317).[2] And Richard's answer is "No! Never!" He repudiates the use of violence. Richard admits that many Christian theologians, at least since Augustine, have accepted violence for the sake of preserving order and defending
justice. He acknowledges that the just war tradition has served to limit as
well as to license violence. But he insists that the just war tradition is not derived from the New Testament and "must be rejected or corrected" (p. 341)
in the light of the New Testament's repudiation of violence.

I agree with Richard that our lives and our common life must be constantly tested and corrected and re-formed in the light of Scripture. But in
response to Richard's question, I cannot bring myself to Richard's answer; I
cannot quite bring myself to say "No, never." I think there are times when
Christians may (and must) employ violence in defense of justice. I want to
defend something like the just war tradition. I admit that the criteria are not
found in the New Testament. But I think Augustine had it largely right:
Christians properly disposed to peace, to patience, and to the love of enemies will sometimes in this sad world have reason to injure a neighbor. The
Christian community's effort to discern when and how fidelity to the gospel
might license and limit such violence would have required the invention of a
category like "justifiable violence" (and criteria for it) if they had not found
the notion of just war lying around among the moral and political commonplaces of their time.

Let me be clear at the outset that Richard is absolutely right about
"countless grim instances in which Christians have mindlessly embraced the
logic of violence" (p. 318). He is absolutely right that we must resist the
"knee-jerk impulse that has afflicted humanity since Cain — the impulse to
impose our will through violence" (p. 318). He is absolutely right to lament

---

2. The question is focused on Christian participation in military service and the use of
"lethal weapons" against enemies, but it evidently includes the participation of believers in
police forces and in other governmental roles that may involve the use of violence.

the Christian blessing upon the violence by Serbs against Bosnian Muslims and by the United States against Nagasaki and Hiroshima. He is absolutely right to demand attention to "the things that make for peace" (p. 319). About these things we do not disagree. The tradition that would license (and limit!) violence in defense of justice would insist that the "things that make for peace" include justice; it would insist that noncombatants be protected; and it would condemn "ethnic cleansing" and indiscriminate bombing no less forcefully than pacifism has. The blood of Abel still cries out from the ground, calling upon God for justice.

Let me also be clear that I much prefer Richard's rejection of violence to our culture's addiction to violence. If the choices were just Richard's pacifism or Bush's violent crusade against "terror," I would choose to stand with Richard. And I do stand with Richard — and within a tradition of just war reflection! — when I object to a Manichean dualism that masquerades as "realism," when I object to preemptive war, when I object to the dismissal of codes of international law as arcane, quaint, and obsolete, and when I object to a policy that seems to find its inspiration in Dirty Harry's readiness to defy the law in order to defeat the bad guys.[3] But I think there is another choice, Augustine's choice.[4]

---

3. See George A. Lopez, "The Ethical Legacy of Dirty Harry," *America*, September 11, 2006, pp. 16-18.

4. Augustine's political thought is contested territory. According to Reinhold Niebuhr, Augustine was a "political realist"; see Niebuhr, "Augustine's Political Realism," in *The Essential Reinhold Niebuhr: Selected Essays and Addresses*, ed. Robert M. Brown (New Haven: Yale University Press, 1986). A similar, if more scholarly, account may be found in Herbert A. Deane, *The Political and Social Ideas of St. Augustine* (New York: Columbia University Press, 1963). According to William E. Connolly, *The Augustinian Imperative: A Reflection on the Politics of Morality* (Newbury Park, Calif.: Sage, 1993), Augustine's political thought is simply authoritarian and the source of the morally totalitarian ideologies and institutions in Western culture. A quite different account is provided by Jean Bethke Elshtain, *Augustine and the Limits of Politics* (Notre Dame: University of Notre Dame Press, 1995), who emphasizes the limits of political power in Augustine, the freedom of people, and the equal obligation of citizens to obey "external" rules of public order and civic virtue. John Milbank, in the last chapter of his *Theology and Social Theory: Beyond Secular Reason* (Oxford: Blackwell, 1993), uses Augustine persuasively to display his claim that "in the beginning there was peace." I do not claim to be able to resolve the disputes about the interpretation of Augustine (and I do not want to defend all of Augustine's political judgments — surely not, for example, his defense of the imperial coercion of the Donatists). My account of Augustine's political thought is most indebted to the masterfully brief account of Oliver O'Donovan and Joan Lockwood O'Donovan, *From Irenaeus to Grotius: A Sourcebook in Christian Political Thought 100-1625* (Grand Rapids: Eerdmans, 1999), pp. 104-13.

We might consider the possibility that there is no real disagreement here. Perhaps we do not disagree! Perhaps this is just a semantic quibble, hanging on the meaning of "violence." To defend "violence in defense of justice," it is necessary to presume the plausibility of a distinction between "violence" and "unjust violence." Pacifists, of course, are at least suspicious of that distinction. For them, "unjust violence" or "immoral violence" are redundant expressions. And in ordinary speech, too, "violence" is frequently used and understood pejoratively, as *unjust* force or as the *unjust* use of power. In the history of the Christian church, however, there is hardly a consensus that violence is always and in every circumstance immoral; in the history of the church the distinction seems plausible.

If "violence" is defined pejoratively as *unjust* force, if a distinction between "violence" and "unjust violence" is not allowed, then neither I nor anyone else should or could defend violence.[5] We might proceed in one of two ways. We might agree to allow the distinction between "just violence" and "unjust violence"; or, stipulating that "violence" simply means "unjust force," and admitting, then, that we should never do "violence," we might ask whether we may ever justly use force and injure a neighbor in defense of justice.[6]

Because Richard evidently intends his question about the use of violence in defense of justice to be a meaningful question, let's allow the distinction between "just violence" and "unjust violence." And let's define "violence" as the use of force that injures another.[7] If we define "violence" in this

5. Indeed, if the distinction is not allowed, then the rejection of "violence in defense of justice" is simply an analytical judgment.

6. The effort of Walter Wink, *Engaging the Powers: Discernment and Resistance in a World of Domination* (Minneapolis: Fortress, 1992), to identify a "third way" between just war and pacifism seems to me to illustrate this ambiguity (and confusion) about "violence." On the one hand, he rejects "violence"; on the other, he calls for not only resistance to injustice but also the coercion of those who do injustice. Indeed, he calls for "highly aggressive nonviolence" (p. 227). He even wishes success to those who are driven by desperation to resort to counterviolence and hints that such violence might "usher in a better society" (p. 224). This hope, however, stands in obvious tension with his earlier claim, *"Violence can never stop violence because its very success leads others to imitate it"* (p. 192). According to Wink, we may use force to defend justice. Force may be "a truly legitimate, socially authorized, and morally defensible use of restraint to prevent harm being done to innocent people" (p. 224). But he is hesitant to use the term "violence" to describe such force; "violence" is understood as excessive force, as unjustifiable force. Wink even suggests that the criteria for just war be used as "violence-reduction criteria" (p. 227). This looks to me less like the development of a "third way" than the election of the second of the two ways to proceed identified above.

7. We can injure another in a variety of ways, of course; there are physical injuries but

way, of course, instances of "just violence" or "justifiable violence" seem easy enough to imagine. There is Augustine's famous example of the discipline exercised by his parents and teachers.[8] There is the act of tackling the toddler about to run into a busy street. There is the surgeon ready with scalpel. There is (or was) the public policy requiring the vaccine against smallpox. I am sure that Richard too has little difficulty imagining situations in which the use of force that risks injuring another is justifiable.[9] So perhaps we do not disagree, or disagree much at any rate. Perhaps a pacifist who does not claim to "know in advance what may and may not be violence"[10] will not disagree — or disagree much at any rate — with a nonpacifist who does not claim to know in advance what may count as "just violence." Perhaps the disagreement is largely semantic — but perhaps not. One way to tell would be by reading Scripture together. And if there is genuine disagreement, one way to respond to it would be by continuing to read Scripture together in the context of a readiness to be formed by the church and by the story the church loves to tell and longs to live.[11] That would be Richard's invitation, at any rate. And I mean to accept the invitation.

Richard's chapter "Violence in Defense of Justice" in <i>The Moral Vision of the New Testament</i> follows the pattern of the book as a whole. It begins with the descriptive task, continues with the synthetic and hermeneutical tasks, and concludes with the pragmatic task and the question about "living the text." The same pattern will order my comments in conversation with Richard.

---

also emotional injuries, and they can be inflicted by individual actions but also by systemic injustice, as in the "systemic violence" of racism, sexism, and classism.

8. Augustine, <i>Conf.</i> 1.9.14. We need not affirm physical punishment as a method of discipline in order to see that discipline involves some kind of injury and that it contributes to the task of raising our children.

9. We may concede — and should affirm — that the injury done is foreseen but not intended. If the toddler is remarkably unhurt as well as "unhit" after being tackled, no one has any business seeing to it that she be hurt.

10. Stanley Hauerwas, "Explaining Christian Nonviolence: Notes for a Conversation with John Milbank and John Howard Yoder," in <i>Performing the Faith</i> (Grand Rapids: Brazos, 2004), p. 174: "So Yoder is not a pacifist if by that you mean someone who assumes that pacifists know in advance what may and may not be violence."

11. One may note here that both John Howard Yoder and Augustine agree that Christians are properly formed by the church and its Scripture, not by "the world" or "the earthly city."

The Descriptive Task and the Key Text: Matthew 5:38-48

The chapter begins with a careful examination of what Richard quite appropriately identifies as the "key text": Matthew 5:38-48.

> You have heard that it was said, "An eye for an eye and a tooth for a tooth." But I say to you, Do not resist an evildoer. But if anyone strikes you on the right cheek, turn the other also; and if anyone wants to sue you and take your coat, give your cloak as well; and if anyone forces you to go one mile, go also the second mile. Give to everyone who begs from you, and do not refuse anyone who wants to borrow from you.
>
> You have heard that it was said, "You shall love your neighbor and hate your enemy." But I say to you, Love your enemies and pray for those who persecute you, so that you may be children of your Father in heaven; for he makes his sun rise on the evil and on the good, and sends rain on the righteous and on the unrighteous. . . . Be perfect, therefore, as your heavenly Father is perfect.[12]

Richard argues that this passage "teaches a norm of nonviolent love of enemies" (p. 329). On the way to that conclusion he surveys and rejects a number of interpretations "that mitigate the normative claim of this text" (p. 320). When he includes in that number interpretations that regard the passage as the statement of an "impossible ideal," an "interim ethic," or a "counsel of perfection," I have no quarrel. But he also includes in that number the interpretation of Augustine, which he summarizes in this fashion: "These words literally forbid self-defense, but they do not preclude fighting in defense of an innocent third party" (p. 320). That is indeed a part of Augustine's position on violence.[13] Violence in self-defense displays that one counts one's own life more valuable than another for whom Christ died, but violence in defense of an innocent third party can be free from such inordinate self-love. That summary, however, is not an adequate account of Augustine's *interpretation* of this "key text." According to Augustine, "[W]hat is here required [in Matthew 5:39] is not a bodily action, but an inward disposition."[14] Given that interpretation, acts that resist an evildoer, including acts that injure the evildoer, may be compatible with the text — if the actor has

12. Scripture quotations not otherwise identified are from the NRSV.
13. Augustine, *Lib.* 1.5. That there are occasions, however, in which violence in self-defense may also be justified will, I hope, become clear later in the paper.
14. Augustine, *Faust.* 22.76 (trans. Stothert, NPNF[1] 4:301).

the proper "inward disposition." Dispositions, of course, are not unrelated to our actions. And Augustine may have emphasized dispositions too much, too exclusively, when he said, "The real evils in war are love of violence, revengeful cruelty, fierce and implacable enmity, wild resistance, and the lust of power."[15] But he was right, I think, to resist reading Matthew 5:39 as an unexceptionable moral rule.

As Augustine pointed out, if it were a rule, Christ evidently broke it not only when he resisted evildoers (and sometimes quite forcibly, as in John 2:13-16) but also when he responded to being struck not by turning the other cheek but by challenging the one who struck him, "Why do you strike me?" (John 18:23).[16]

Moreover, Augustine's reading fits the pattern of the other antitheses. As there was a context within which Jesus called the scribes and Pharisees "fools" (Matt. 23:17; cf. 5:22), so there might be a context within which forcible resistance to an evildoer would be permitted and required. As Jesus could allow oaths, even as he attacked the pettifoggery surrounding them (23:16-22; cf. 5:33-37), so he might allow resistance to the evil that threatens an innocent neighbor with violence. Like "Do not swear at all" (5:34) and "If you say, 'You fool,' you will be liable to the hell of fire" (5:22), "Turn the other [cheek]" is given not as a legal requirement but as a suggestive illustration of the sort of character and community Jesus establishes.

Finally, let it be said in defense of Augustine that Richard himself notes that this key text is "not simply a rule prohibiting a certain action; rather, it is a symbolic pointer to the character of the peaceful city set on a hill" (p. 326). According to Richard, the text "functions as more than a bare rule; . . . it functions metonymically, illuminating the life of a covenant community that is called to live in radical faithfulness to the vision of the kingdom of God disclosed in Jesus' teaching and example" (p. 329). Among the interpretations to be rejected we should place, by Richard's own account, that interpretation that takes the passage to be a simple and unexceptionable rule. When the metonymy is recognized, the requirements of "radical faithfulness" seem not to be captured by an unexceptionable moral rule against injuring a neighbor. Violent acts might be compatible with this passage, as long as the actors were not *disposed* to violence, not eager for revenge, but instead motivated by the love of a neighbor, even if the neighbor were an enemy.

That last claim requires some attention, of course, to the other part of

---

15. *Faust.* 22.74 (trans. Stothert, NPNF[1] 4:301).
16. Augustine, *Ep.* 138.2.13.

this passage, to the command "Love your enemies" (5:44). Can one love one's enemies and injure them? Can one love one's enemies and kill them? Richard says matter-of-factly that the practice of loving enemies is "incompatible with killing them" (p. 329). Augustine, as Richard notes, was not so sure. Surely loving one's enemies is incompatible with hating them, but is "Love your enemies" incompatible with injuring them? Surely one should restrain an enemy no less forcibly than a friend who is unknowingly about to step into traffic. And one should not just not let one's friends drive drunk; one should restrain enemies no less forcibly than friends who are about to drive drunk. But what about lethal violence? What about killing? It is not implausible, I think, that Bonhoeffer loved Hitler even while he plotted to kill him. At least it is not more implausible that Bonhoeffer loved Hitler than that German Christians truly loved Hitler while allowing him to become a successful mass murderer.[17] A good measure of fear and trembling is appropriate here, of course. Loving the enemy will first and usually not entail a choice to resort to violence. Perhaps the claim that Bonhoeffer loved Hitler is plausible only because we are so confident that Bonhoeffer was not disposed to violence. But this one who understood "costly discipleship" so well evidently also came to see resort to violence (and lethal violence) as a necessary (if tragic) act in order to protect the lives and well-being of other neighbors. The disposition to love his neighbors, *all of them,* led this model of "radical faithfulness" to use just war considerations in order to discern what he ought to do in those awful circumstances.[18] In such a beginning and in such a conclusion, Bonhoeffer seems not far from Augustine.

The question of Jesus' pacifism does not rest on a single verse, of course. The "key text" is not simply a "proof text." Indeed, Richard insists that the "key text" be read and interpreted in the "wider Matthean context" (p. 322).

---

17. For an account of Bonhoeffer's participation in the resistance as "an act of repentance for the guilt of his church, his nation, and his class" see L. Gregory Jones, *Embodying Forgiveness: A Theological Analysis* (Grand Rapids: Eerdmans, 1995), pp. 23-33.

18. See Larry L. Rasmussen, *Dietrich Bonhoeffer: Reality and Resistance* (Nashville: Abingdon, 1972). See also Geffrey B. Kelly and F. Burton Nelson, *The Cost of Moral Leadership: The Spirituality of Dietrich Bonhoeffer* (Grand Rapids: Eerdmans, 2003). Mark Thiessen Nation argues against any account that would suggest that Bonhoeffer simply "outgrew" his pacifism for the "realism" of his participation in the resistance; see Nation, "Discipleship in a World Full of Nazis: Dietrich Bonhoeffer's Polyphonic Pacifism as Social Ethics," in *The Wisdom of the Cross: Essays in Honor of John Howard Yoder,* ed. Stanley Hauerwas et al. (Grand Rapids: Eerdmans, 1999), pp. 249-77. For Bonhoeffer, as noted by both Rasmussen and Nation, "[w]hat really matters for ethics happens in character formation" (Rasmussen, *Bonhoeffer,* p. 158), and the test for character formation is conformity to Christ.

He calls attention to Matthew's narratives of the temptation, the arrest, and the cross as consistent with a reading of the key text as teaching "a norm of nonviolent love of enemies" (p. 329). Augustine too called attention to the "wider Matthean context," but especially to the Matthean emphasis upon the continuing validity of the law.

Against the Manichean Faustus, and against his Manichean objections to the Old Testament law compared with Christ's teaching, Augustine emphasized that the Old Testament law had not been discarded or contradicted by Christ's teaching.[19] On the contrary, as Christ taught (Matt. 5:17-20), the law holds. It was not the law that was rejected but an interpretation of the law that was satisfied with merely external observance. Even the antitheses did not undermine or supplant the ancient law. In the "key text," the famous *lex talionis* was given first, followed by a word spoken with Jesus' own authority. The ancient law itself was not rejected, Augustine insisted. What was rejected was an interpretation of the law that was satisfied with a vengeful spirit as long as revenge stopped at the boundary of "an eye for an eye." The *lex talionis* set a limit, a "restraint," on revenge;[20] it did not sanctify it. The limit still stands, and as a minimal standard it remains effective against revenge where hearts remain hard, that is to say, this side of the eschaton. But Jesus' words, with the authority of God's own coming rule, reach into the heart and form a readiness not to return insult for insult or blow for blow, a readiness not to insist on one's rights over against the neighbor, even if the neighbor is an enemy.

The law holds, and its minimal restraints remain important, given that people remain "hard-hearted" (Matt. 19:8). However, to be satisfied with the "righteousness" of such minimal requirements while we remain as mean-spirited and vengeful as ever is not acceptable. So, are some concessions of the law no longer conceded? Consider Matthew's account of Jesus' saying concerning divorce (Matt. 19:1-9). Jesus' words first call attention to the story of creation that should form a readiness not to divorce even when the law (Deut. 24:1-4) would permit it. But the concession to divorce is still there in Matthew's account (echoing Rabbi Shammai's interpretation of the law). As Richard himself says, "Matthew's exception clause . . . is a clear concession to the 'not yet': until the kingdom arrives in its fullness, human unfaithfulness will necessitate realistic measures to cope with pastoral problems" (p. 366). Analogously, according to Augustine at least, "until the kingdom arrives in

19. Augustine, *Faust.* 19.18-19.
20. *Faust.* 19.25.

its fullness," concessions to violence are still sometimes appropriate. They remain *concessions,* to be sure; violence is no more the cause of God than divorce is. But sometimes in this sad world, not yet God's good future, violence may be necessary to protect a neighbor from violence and injustice, to restrain some great evil or to protect some little good. Violence, even war, is sometimes appropriate in the political order given a just cause.[21] And Christ, with his call to a "surpassing righteousness," can be followed even in violence, even in war, if malice is avoided and love preserved. A double measure of fear and trembling is required here, for it is easy to deceive ourselves about our "inward dispositions," and it is hard to resist the temptations to malice and enmity in the wake of war. (It must be admitted that the just war criteria are frequently invoked without a sufficient measure of fear and trembling.)

The law holds, with its statutes and its sanctions, sanctions that may be regarded as permitting and requiring the use of force or "violence" only for the sake of order and justice and peace. The law, with its minimal standards, and the "surpassing righteousness" of Christ are not identical, but neither are they inconsistent. The law points toward Christ and restrains evil until the end. And love "fulfills" the minimal standards — and sustains them until the end for the sake of restraining evil, protecting the neighbor still threatened by greed or violence, preserving a political peace, and serving a worldly justice.

Following Matthew 5:17-20, Augustine insisted, against Faustus, that the law holds, that it is not supplanted or undermined or abolished. Against Richard's interpretation of the "key text," Augustine might make the same point. Richard would defend his interpretation of the "key text" by citing Deuteronomy 19:15-21, where the *lex talionis* does have a prescriptive function rather than a limiting function. In that passage, as a deterrent to false witness, judges are commanded to "do to the false witness just as the false witness had meant to do to the other." And it concludes, "Show no pity: life for life, eye for eye, tooth for tooth. . . ." Richard's comment on this passage is this:

> But where Deuteronomy insists, "Show no pity," Jesus says, "Do not resist an evildoer." The Law's concern for maintaining stability and justice is supplanted by Jesus' concern to encourage nonviolent, long-suffering generosity on the part of those who are wronged. This extraordinary

21. *Faust.* 22.75.

change of emphasis constitutes a paradigm shift that effectually undermines the Torah's teaching about just punishment for offenders. (p. 325)

Augustine would reply, I think, that to "encourage nonviolent, long-
suffering generosity on the part of those who are wronged" does not "undermine" the law's charge to judges to protect those who have been wronged.[22]
Those who are wronged should not seek revenge, but those who are charged
with protecting the innocent should not, on the pretext of "pity," renege on
their obligations, under God, to hear the case of the widow (cf. Luke 18:1-8)
or to see that justice is done for the powerless. According to Augustine, Jesus'
word does *not* "supplant" or "undermine" the law's concern for maintaining
stability and justice in the land.

Jesus clearly addressed a situation that ignites our incendiary desire for
revenge, a situation in which we have been treated unjustly. But he does not
here address the situation in which we are to defend a neighbor against an
attack or against some other form of injustice. Or to make the point differently, he does not demand of a police officer that he never interpose himself
and his authority between an attacker and the one attacked. He does not require of a judge that he turn a deaf ear when a victim of assault brings a
charge before him. The question, for Augustine, is whether the police officer
or the judge or anyone else can both love the attacker and use force to restrain the attacker from injuring the neighbor; and the answer, for Augustine
and for me, is yes.

Synthesis: Violence in Canonical Context

It is not enough to set this key text in the wider Matthean context. It must finally be set in the context of the whole canon. Indeed, it must be read as a
part of *that* whole. Earlier in *The Moral Vision* Richard has located the unity,
the wholeness, of the New Testament in this: that these diverse texts all, "in
various ways, retell and comment upon a single fundamental story" (p. 193).
And he has summarized that story in terms of three "focal images": community, cross, and new creation (pp. 193-200). In the present chapter Richard
takes up again "the synthetic task," and his conclusion is that these diverse
texts are "impressively univocal" (p. 329) concerning nonviolence. There is,
he says, from Matthew to Revelation, "a consistent witness against violence

22. See *Faust.* 22.75.

and a calling to the community to follow the example of Jesus in *accepting* suffering rather than *inflicting* it" (p. 332, emphasis original).[23] The whole, and not just one passage, requires the rejection of violence — at least the whole of the New Testament.

One can hardly complain that Richard does not attend very much to the Old Testament here. This is, after all, a book on New Testament ethics. Nevertheless, it is regrettable, I think, that Richard's attention to the Old Testament is limited to some "holy war texts" (p. 336).[24] Richard readily admits that the Old Testament does not require the rejection of violence, but he insists that the New Testament "trumps the Old Testament" (p. 336).[25] The regrettable result is that the relation of Old to New Testament on this question seems to be described simply in terms of discontinuity and con-

---

23. Willard Swartley, *Covenant of Peace: The Missing Peace in New Testament Theology and Ethics* (Grand Rapids: Eerdmans, 2006), provides now a book-length defense of Richard's claim. Swartley's thesis, as he says, "complements Hays's claim by showing that the NT not only consistently and pervasively renounces the use of violence, even to achieve our calculated justice, it presents also a positive calling for believers" (pp. 419-20). That positive calling is to be peacemakers. I am persuaded that we are called to be peacemakers, but I am not persuaded that such a vocation is inconsistent with the use of force to protect a neighbor threatened by violence or injustice.

24. With respect to war, the OT should not be reduced to the texts of holy war. Some have even found, in Exod. 14:14 and in the tradition, God as a basis for pacifism in the OT. See Millard C. Lind, *Yahweh Is a Warrior* (Scottdale, Pa.: Herald, 1980); John Howard Yoder, *The Politics of Jesus* (Grand Rapids: Eerdmans, 1972), pp. 79-89. But whether one accepts that interpretation of Exod. 14:14 or not, it is surely the case that Israel was finally to trust in God, not in "chariots" and "horses" (Ps. 20:7; Isa. 31:3). There is the prophetic vision of universal peace (e.g., Isa. 2:2-4; 11:6-9; 65:25; Mic. 4:1-4). There is the prophetic condemnation of "war crimes" (Amos 1:3-2:3). See Matthew Schlimm, "Teaching the Hebrew Bible amid the Current Human Rights Crisis: The Opportunities Presented by Amos 1:3-2:3," *SBL Forum* 4, no.1 (2006), http://www.sbl-site.org/Article.aspx?ArticleId=478. Even the texts of holy war themselves, for all their horror, contain certain restrictions on war: an offer of peace must be extended before battle, and trees are to be protected (Deut. 20:10-11, 19). The violence that is ordained (and done) by God is also *limited* by God. It is not unbridled bellicosity.

25. To be fair, it should be observed that in the section on the "hermeneutical task" Richard has argued quite persuasively that "within the canon the New Testament has a privileged hermeneutical function" (p. 309), but in that same context he has also insisted on the hermeneutical point that "[t]he story that the New Testament tells makes sense only as the continuation and climax of the story of Israel" (p. 309). My complaint is not with either of these two points but rather simply that Richard does not *here* take his second point seriously enough. In other contexts he displays that he is a gifted interpreter of the ways NT readings of the OT can be both radically new and in continuity with the earlier texts. See, e.g., Hays, *Echoes of Scripture in the Letters of Paul* (New Haven: Yale University Press, 1989).

trast. Augustine's complaint against Faustus would urge attention to continuity as well.

Surely the Old Testament's vision of *shalom* provides a subtext for the New Testament. It is a rich and varied notion, not to be reduced to the absence of hostilities. Still, two generalizations seem both plausible and relevant to the synthetic task. The first is this: that *shalom* is intimately related to justice. Justice is also a rich and varied notion,[26] of course, not to be reduced to the minimal standards of law-abiding conduct. A fundamental test of justice is the treatment of the poor and the oppressed. So, for example, Isaiah 1:16b-17: "cease to do evil, learn to do good; seek justice, rescue the oppressed, defend the orphan, plead for the widow." The relation of *shalom* and justice may be found, for example, in the prayer for the king in Psalm 72: "Give the king your justice, O God. . . . In his days may righteousness flourish and peace abound" (vv. 1, 7). It may be found in the promise of God in response to the community's lament in Psalm 85: "Steadfast love and faithfulness will meet; righteousness (צדק, justice) and peace will kiss each other" (v. 10). And it is underscored in Isaiah's vision of a time when the "spirit from on high is poured out on us": "Then justice will dwell in the wilderness . . . [and] the effect of righteousness (צדקה, justice) will be peace" (Isa. 32:15, 16, 17).

The second generalization is this: that *shalom* is intimately related to the reign of God, which is in turn intimately related (but not reducible) to Israel's politics. That God reigns was a central affirmation of Israel's account of the relation of God to the world, including the political world.[27] It could hardly be otherwise. The story, familiar in ritual and in Torah, was a story of God's rule. God had chosen them as a people, liberated them from their slavery in Egypt, made a covenant with them at Sinai, and brought them to the land. That covenant was a "suzerainty treaty,"[28] familiar enough in the an-

---

26. Both צדק and משפט — and δικαιοσύνη in the NT — can often be translated as "justice."

27. I have called this tradition of political discernment "theocratic." "Theocracy," after all, is formed from θεός and κράτειν. The fundamental sense of the word, then, is simply that "God reigns," that "God is king." The problem, of course, is that "theocracy" conjures up images of ancient and contemporary tyrannies, made more tyrannical by their claim to be holy, authorized by God. The biblical tradition, however, stands opposed to tyranny. In *Remembering Jesus: Christian Community, Scripture, and the Moral Life* (Grand Rapids: Eerdmans, 2002), pp. 351-87, I have traced the Bible's "theocratic tradition" through the various political circumstances and institutions of Israel. The summary in the paragraphs that follow is drawn from that account.

28. See, e.g., George E. Mendenhall, *Law and Covenant in Israel and the Ancient Near East* (Pittsburgh: Biblical Colloquium, 1955).

611

cient Near East in the pledges exchanged between kings and their vassals, pledges of loyalty and peaceableness. In those pledges the gods were frequently called upon to witness the promises and to guarantee their fulfillment. At Sinai, however, God was not just a witness to the covenant; God was a party to it. God was the great suzerain, the great king who had rescued them from slavery, who provided them with law, and who promised them land. And they were the people of God, a people created by God, a people constituted by the covenantal pledge of allegiance to God as their king.

Because God was king, political authority among the people was derived from God — and answered to God! Political responsibility was a responsibility *to* God, to the God whose works and ways were remembered in the community of faith, to the God who heard the cries of the slave, who loved justice, and who intended the security and peace of the land God gave. Through a variety of political circumstances and institutions, the test for political discernment remained always this affirmation of covenant that "God is king" joined with the memory of God's works and ways.

In the settlement, the faith that "God is king" was marked by a suspicion of conventional politics, the politics that had enslaved and oppressed the people in Egypt, and by reliance upon "judges," those charismatic leaders whom God raised up in times of political crisis. But the judges could not withstand the threats of chaos. The transition to monarchy displayed both a suspicion of royal despotism and a theocratic hope that a humble king might perform God's reign and serve God's cause. The monarchy itself provided a context for both the political vision of the Yahwist (and the Royal Psalms) and the prophetic oracles of judgment against despotism and its oppression of the poor. The prophets reminded both the king and the people of the covenant, of the great suzerain, and of their accountability to God. They called for repentance and reform, and the lawmakers sometimes heeded their call by revisiting the received legal tradition and revising it to make it "fit" the old story (and new circumstances) a little better.

In exile, the theocratic tradition continued to honor the authorities, to pray for them, and to "seek the welfare" of the city where God had sent them. Even the Babylonian rulers had their authority from God. But also in exile, the theocratic tradition continued to join suspicion to honor, recognizing the inhumanity (the bestiality) of a politics of oppression and enslavement. The faithful did not let go — even in exile — of the conviction that the authority of kings and emperors is "under God" and finally accountable to God. Fidelity to God required separation from the injustice and violence and idolatry of the Babylonians (and of the empires that followed), but it also called for political participation (as Daniel and Nehemiah and others displayed) in service to the welfare of others and to the cause of God. The community learned not to despise "small things" politically but also learned not to confuse them with the final cause of God. Sometimes "small things" and certain legislative "minimal standards" can secure real (if small) goods and may even give some little token of God's good future. But that future, as apocalyptic reminded them, will not be a human political accomplishment. It will be the work of God. In the meanwhile, both honor and suspicion were appropriate to political authorities. Political discernment where "God is king" recognized the limits and ambiguity of political power and would not let go of accountability to God.

Augustine was right, against Faustus, to reject too sharp a disjunction between the Old Testament and the New. The synthetic task should include attention to Israel's wrestling with the meaning of faithful politics. Jesus — and the whole New Testament — was heir, after all, to that "theocratic tradition" of the Old Testament. But is there within the New Testament, as Richard asserts, no basis for violence in defense of justice?

In his synthesis of the New Testament materials, Richard attends briefly to a number of narratives involving soldiers (Luke 3:14; Matt. 8:5-13; Luke 7:1-10; Mark 15:39; Acts 10:1–11:18). In the first of these, for example, when John the Baptist was asked by some soldiers, "What should we do?" he did not tell them to forswear the use of force or to put off their weapons or to quit the military; he told them to forswear the unjust uses of their power: "Do not extort money from anyone by threats or false accusation, and be satisfied with your wages" (Luke 3:14). Richard acknowledges that in none of these narratives are the soldiers instructed to give up soldiering. Indeed, he acknowledges that these narratives "provide the one possible legitimate basis for arguing that Christian discipleship does not necessarily preclude the exercise of violence in defense of social order or justice" (pp. 335-36).

Another (parallel) argument would start with Romans 13:1-7. In his single comment on this passage in the chapter on violence, Richard says: "Though the governing authority bears the sword to execute God's wrath (13:4), that is not the role of believers" (p. 331). He follows John Howard Yoder here, who reached a similar conclusion in *The Politics of Jesus:*

> Christians are told (12:19) never to exercise vengeance but to leave it to God and to wrath. Then the authorities are recognized (13:4) as executing the particular function which the Christian was to leave to God. . . . This

makes it clear that the function exercised by government is not the function to be exercised by Christians.[29]

But believers could and evidently did hold political office. In Romans 16:23, for example, Erastus, who sends greetings to the church, is identified as "city treasurer." And in Luke's account of the conversion of Sergius Paulus, "the proconsul" (Acts 13:7-12), there is no hint that he resigned his post. There is nothing to suggest that political authorities, any more than soldiers, had to surrender their vocation.

Moreover, Romans 13:1-7 is instructive concerning the political vocation of both rulers and Christians. Paul reminds the Roman Christians of a tradition that was probably familiar enough to them.[30] Political rulers have their authority from God (vv. 1-2); they are the "servants" of God insofar as[31] they serve the common good, protecting the innocent and punishing the guilty (vv. 3-6);[32] and they are answerable to God! Therefore, people should honor them and pay taxes to them. Conventional enough — but as Richard quite properly insists, this passage must be read in its literary context.[33]

Romans 12–13 is a unit. It opens and closes with eschatological appeals (12:1-2 and 13:11-14). Along with reminders of the duty to love (12:9-10; 13:8-

29. Yoder, *Politics of Jesus*, p. 199. Richard cites this passage and commends Yoder's account of Rom. 13:1-7 in his discussion of Yoder's hermeneutical strategy (p. 246).

30. For elements of the received tradition, see, e.g., Prov. 8:15; Wis. 6:1-11; Philo's *Embassy to Gaius;* on this received tradition and on Rom. 13:1-7 more generally, see Victor Paul Furnish, *The Moral Teaching of Paul: Selected Issues,* 2nd ed. (Nashville: Abingdon, 1985), pp. 115-39.

31. Reading the participle προσκαρτεροῦντες (NRSV: "busy with," Rom. 13:6) as a conditional participle. It is possible to translate the participle causally ("because" rather than "insofar as"), but I do not believe Paul was naïve about the evil a tyrant could do. He knew from his own experience that the authorities did not always protect the innocent. Moreover, the theocratic tradition we briefly surveyed above joined suspicion to honor. Paul called the Roman Christians to submit to the authorities in terms of their vocation to do justice, not in terms of some naïve assumption that they always do justice.

32. Elizabeth Anscombe once complained that "pacifism has corrupted enormous numbers of people who will not act according to its tenets," people who so emphasize the moral difference between *accepting* suffering and *inflicting* it that the moral difference between violence against the innocent and violence against the guilty is neglected. See G. E. M. Anscombe, "War and Murder," in *Nuclear Weapons and Christian Conscience,* ed. Walter Stein (London: Merlin, 1961), p. 56.

33. The historical context, also worth noting, was probably early in the reign of Nero (54-68), when there was considerable hope that Nero would conduct his administration with humanity and justice.

10), these reminders of the eschatological situation frame Paul's advice in this unit. Paul set the traditional material in this literary context. He set political responsibility in the context of the duty to love the neighbor in a world that is not yet God's good future. We must love the neighbor — even the remote neighbor, even the neighbor we don't know or care to know — in a world where that neighbor is still threatened by violence, theft, deception, and oppression. That duty grounds and *requires* political responsibility; it does not *repudiate* it. Because of our duty to love the neighbor, we can and must support and respect and submit to — and may participate in — government as the servant of God insofar as justice is sought and done *for the neighbor.*

If Romans 12–13 is a unit, then we must attend also, of course, to the relation of Romans 13 to the rejection of vengeance in Romans 12:17-21. It was that passage that led Richard and John Howard Yoder to conclude that "the function exercised by government is not the function to be exercised by Christians."[34] "Do not repay anyone evil for evil," it says (12:17). "[N]ever avenge yourselves, but leave room for the wrath of God" (12:19). This rejection of vengeance may remind us of the "key text," of Jesus' word in the Sermon on the Mount concerning the *lex talionis* (Matt. 5:38-48). And our reading there seems even clearer here. Those who are wronged should not seek revenge, but those who are charged with protecting the innocent should not, on the pretext of either piety or pity, renege on their political obligations, under God, to do justice. Love for enemies is not inconsistent with a concern for — or participation in — maintaining stability and justice in the land. The violence involved in maintaining justice is indeed a mark of the "not yet" character of our world, but it is not exercised to "avenge yourselves" but to protect the innocent, and it is not a reason for either rulers or Christians — whether rulers or subjects — to renege on their political vocations.

Having completed his overview of the New Testament, Richard asks a question critically important to what he has called the "hermeneutical task." How does this material fit with "the single fundamental story" of the New Testament? And how is it "brought into focus" (p. 337) by what he has identified as the three "focal images" of that story: *community, cross,* and *new creation*?

Through the lens of *community,* Richard says, "we recognize that the church as a whole is called to live the way of discipleship and to exemplify the love of enemies" (p. 337). No quarrel there. Moreover, the focal lens of

34. Hays, *Moral Vision,* p. 246; Yoder, *Politics of Jesus,* p. 199.

community can correct the vision of those[35] who treat violence "as though it were a question of individual moral preference" (p. 337). No quarrel there. Indeed, Richard's emphasis on community should help us see that the church is a community of mutual encouragement and admonition, a community of moral discourse and discernment in memory of Jesus. But I puzzle over Richard's claim in this context that "the place of the soldier within the church can only be seen as anomalous" (p. 337).

If violence is absolutely prohibited, absolutely inconsistent with Christian identity and community, then I suppose soldiers — and police officers[36] — should be disciplined, perhaps even excommunicated, not just regarded as "anomalous." The community's discipline, I suppose, should start with an honest conversation. Suppose the soldier — or the police officer — replies that he just loves violence and hungers for the power this role gives to shove people around. Then the church should call the soldier — or the policeman — to repentance, and if he adamantly refuses repentance, the church should declare that he has cut himself off from the community. But suppose the soldier — or the police officer — replies that she shares the vocation to peacemaking and the hunger for justice that characterize the church. Suppose he says that he has a vocation to protect and serve his neighbors, and especially those who are vulnerable.[37] Suppose she says that she hates it when her role requires the use of force, when she risks injuring one neighbor for the sake of protecting another, but acknowledges that it sometimes does. Then the church, I suppose, should continue the conversation. And in that conversation, I suspect, there will be talk about things like legitimate authority and a presumption against violence, about just cause, right intention, and last re-

---

35. Richard identifies mainline Protestants as those whose vision here is in need of a corrective lens (p. 337).

36. The recent work on "just policing" is a promising approach to the problem of violence in defense of justice and to the reconciliation of the traditions of "just war" and pacifism. See especially Tobias Winright, "From Police Officers to Peace Officers," in *The Wisdom of the Cross,* ed. Hauerwas et al., pp. 84-114; Winright, "Just Cause and Preemptive Strikes in the War on Terrorism," *JSCE* 26 (2006): 157-81; Gerald Schlabach, "Just Policing: How War Could Cease to Be a Church-Dividing Issue," in *Just Policing: Mennonite-Catholic Theological Colloquium, 2002,* ed. Ivan J. Kaufman (Kitchener, Ont.: Pandora, 2004), pp. 19-75.

37. Long ago John Howard Yoder raised the question whether a Christian could be a police officer. In his reply he suggested that the proper way to answer the question was not in legalistic terms but in terms of vocation. He insisted that because using force "requires an exceptional justification," the police officer must provide evidence to the church of "such a special calling." Yoder, *The Christian Witness to the State,* IMSS 3 (Newton, Kans.: Faith and Life, 1964), pp. 56-57.

sort, about proportionality and discriminating between the guilty and the innocent, and about vigilance against the evil we sometimes do in resisting evil. There will be talk, that is, that echoes the conversation about criteria for a just war. (Indeed, it may well be that the criteria for just war echo such conversations in the early church with soldiers in the community.) If Richard means simply to call attention to the necessity of such a conversation by calling the presence of the soldier in Christian community "anomalous," we have no quarrel here either. But at the end of such a conversation, I think, the community might well decide that there is nothing "anomalous" about a place for such a soldier or police officer in its midst. It might well discern that within the "vocation of the community" there is a place for those with a vocation to public justice,[38] because "the things that make for peace" include justice, and because the law and its sanctions make a small but real contribution to both justice and peace.

The *cross* seems to be the central focal image for Richard's account of nonviolence. "Whenever the New Testament is read in a way that denies the normativity of the cross for the Christian community, we can be sure that the text is out of focus" (p. 338). It is a powerful image, and a powerfully corrective lens through which to see the world. But one may ask how we should understand the cross — and its normativity. It is an image of more than one thing. It was, for example, a symbol of Roman imperial power before it was a symbol of the Christian church. And for the Christian church it is an image of Christ's suffering and of his nonresistance to his own suffering, an image of God's self-giving love and of Christ's, an image surely of Christ's readiness to love and to forgive his enemies. But it is no less surely an image of his solidarity with those who suffer, his identification with those who are least, with the poor and oppressed, with other victims of injustice and violence and those who remain vulnerable in this sad world. With the resurrection, it images the reversal that his announcement of the kingdom promised (or threatened): the last shall be first, the humiliated will be exalted. Such a list, moreover, hardly exhausts the significance of the cross. No one image may be allowed a monopoly on our account of Christ's cross or its normativity, and although it is a focal image, it is intelligible only as a part of the whole story that Scripture tells.

---

38. I do not mean here to adopt the mistaken dualism that regards the church as "private" and the state as "public." There are, as Reinhard Hütter observes, a "multiplicity of different publics"; see Hütter, *Suffering Divine Things: Theology as Church Practice* (Grand Rapids: Eerdmans, 2000), p. 159.

Richard's account of the significance of the cross focuses almost exclusively on the cross as "an act of self-giving love" (p. 197; see also 27, in his treatment of Paul). But one may worry that accounts of the cross that allow self-giving love (or self-donation, self-sacrifice, or the nonresistance to violence) to monopolize our attention may ironically not serve the kingdom of God but the interests of the powerful. At least, that is a worry expressed by some feminists and by a host of voices from the margins. When the cross — or the love commandment — is used simply to call people to self-sacrifice, one may well worry that the strong and powerful will say "Amen, brother" while finding reasons to exempt themselves from such sacrifice and reasons to require it from the relatively weak and powerless. Barbara Hilkert Andolsen, for example, has said that "[m]en have espoused an ethic [self-sacrificing love] which they did not practice; women have practiced it to their detriment."[39] Richard is alert to this problem; indeed, he calls a reading of Scripture that warrants "a husband's domination or physical abuse of his wife" a "bizarre — indeed, blasphemous — misreading" (p. 197). But his response to it seems to be simply that "men and women alike . . . must . . . renounce violence and coercion" (p. 197). In a world like this one, as I judge, it is sometimes necessary to restrain the violent, and sometimes necessary to restrain them violently. To say to an abused woman that "men and women alike . . . must . . . renounce violence and coercion" seems to me also to be "bizarre." A sacrifice by the relatively more powerful and more privileged on behalf of the less powerful and less privileged is worthy of the story of Christ and of his cross; conscripting the sacrifice of the powerless is not. When the cross and the love it displays are used to conscript sacrifice from those who are the victims of injustice, then the first stay first and the last, well, last.

It would help, I think, if we remembered that the story of the cross is not just a story of self-sacrifice but also a story of solidarity with those who are least, who do not count for much as the world counts. It might also help if we remembered that the story of the cross, as John tells the story at least, is the story of a life sacrificed *for friends* (John 15:13: "No one has greater love than this, to lay down one's life for one's friends"). To be sure, it is a death for enemies, too, as Paul reminds us (Rom. 5:10), but even the death for enemies was that they may be friends. Friendship, rather than sacrifice, is the primor-

39. Barbara Hilkert Andolsen, "Agape in Feminist Ethics," in *Feminist Theological Ethics: A Reader*, ed. Lois K. Daly (Louisville: Westminster John Knox, 1994), p. 152. On the paradigm of the cross, see Sally B. Purvis, *The Power of the Cross: Foundations for a Christian Feminist Ethic of Community* (Nashville: Abingdon, 1993).

dial account of Christian love. Sacrifice is not its own justification. The mutuality and equality of friendship, the mutual attention to the needs and dignity of the other in friendship, is the primordial pattern. Friendship will sometimes require sacrifices, to be sure, but friends will make an effort both to minimize the situations calling for sacrifice and to share the burdens of the sacrifices required. Sacrifice is not itself the norm but a symptom of a disruption in a primordial mutuality and a means to make it right.[40]

Let it be admitted that Jesus' rejection of violence on the cross makes it clear that violence is not "a means to make it right," not finally right at any rate. Violence is not likely to restore friendship, to retrieve a primordial mutuality, or to achieve the promised community. Jesus consistently rejected violence as a messianic strategy, as a means to achieve the good future of God. After he had fed the crowds, they were ready to take him "by force" to make him king, but Jesus would have none of it and withdrew (John 6:14, 15). He saw that the problem in Israel was that it was "possessed" not just by Roman colonialists and oppressors but by its envy of them, by the wish to lord it over those who had lorded it over them. And he saw that that demon would not be "exorcised" by violence. Jesus would not be co-opted by a popular movement "possessed" by its hunger for power itself rather than for the justice that belongs to the kingdom of God, "possessed" by a spirit of resentment and revenge. Violence is a mark of the "not yet" character of Rome's politics and Israel's politics — and of our politics!

That raises Richard's third focal image, the *new creation*. It is the lens through which we see the power of God that raised Jesus from the dead already at work in the world, and the lens through which we acknowledge the "eschatological reservation" (p. 198), the sad and obvious fact that God's good future is not yet. This focal image can provide corrective vision when we are tempted to a "foolish utopianism" or to "despair" (pp. 338-39). Richard is right to insist on the importance of this eschatological perspective, but it is the perspective also of some who acknowledge the sad necessity of violence in defense of justice.

One cannot read the story of Jesus, or own it as one's own, and celebrate violence. In memory of Jesus and in hope, the church will be suspicious of violence. God's good future will not be wrought by violence, and the church should continue to reject violence as a messianic strategy, reject it as a means to achieve the good future of God, and reject it from its own ecclesiastical polity. But while hearts remain hard, while it is still not yet the good future

40. See Andolsen, pp. 156-57.

of God, violence may remain a political means, a means to restrain evil, a means to love and protect the neighbor still threatened in this sad world by greed and violence. This eschatological perspective provides the basis, I judge, for political "realism" in Augustine and in many others.[41] Against the background of this eschatological perspective, Christians may see and affirm the "secularity,"[42] the this-worldly limits and the this-worldly calling, of public politics. Christians may discern that "secular" authorities are necessary to organize and orchestrate a common life in the earthly *polis* and that sometimes those authorities may need to resort to force, to coercion, and even to violence in order to resist injustice and violence. Such at least was the conclusion of Augustine and many others in the Christian tradition of "just war," and such is my conclusion.

Hermeneutics: Responding to the New Testament's Witness Against Violence

Richard's descriptive and synthetic work on violence here has invoked many of the hermeneutical guidelines developed earlier in the book (pp. 219-312), so he does not need to revisit them in the section of this chapter devoted to the hermeneutical task.[43] He does revisit two of them, dealing

41. One might distinguish this "realism" from the political realism of Reinhold Niebuhr, which found its basis in the doctrine of original sin and seemed to exile the power of God to an arena "beyond history." The danger of the latter type is that it may neglect the possibilities of the present by regarding the present not only as "not yet" the good future of God but also as beyond the reach of the God who raised Jesus from the dead.

42. It is worth noting in this context the observation of Oliver O'Donovan, *Common Objects of Love: Moral Reflection and the Shaping of Community* (Grand Rapids: Eerdmans, 2002), p. 42:

> "Secularity" is irreducibly an eschatological notion; it requires an eschatological faith to sustain it . . . , for the virtue that undergirds all secular politics is an expectant patience. What follows from the rejection of belief is an intolerable tension between the need for meaning in society and the only partial capacity of society to satisfy the need. An unbelieving society has forgotten how to be secular.

The book reflects on Augustine's famous observation that "a people" is united by common objects of love, and O'Donovan's observation is recognizably Augustinian.

43. Moreover, Richard assumes here the extensive analysis he has earlier provided concerning the different "hermeneutical strategies" of Reinhold Niebuhr, Karl Barth, John Howard Yoder, Stanley Hauerwas, and Elizabeth Schüssler Fiorenza (pp. 215-90), which frequently engaged the issue of violence.

with "the mode of normative appropriation" and the relevance of "other authorities."

Richard's guideline concerning "the mode of normative appropriation" is that *"New Testament texts must be granted authority in the mode in which they speak,"* including when that mode is moral rules (p. 339; see also 294).[44] He attends to rules, principles, paradigms, and the depiction of a symbolic world as the "modes" in which the New Testament speaks about morality and about violence. And he concludes that "in all four modes, the evidence accumulates overwhelmingly against any justification for the use of violence" (p. 340). My conclusion has been that the evidence is at least less overwhelming.

I have argued (like Augustine) that Richard's "key text" is not an unexceptionable rule of conduct and should not be used to dismiss the institutions of public justice Israel found in its law and its sanctions. I have argued that in canonical context, peace is intimately related to justice and to the "theocratic tradition" of politics. Any "peace" that is not linked to "justice" is not, I think, the peace of God. Our notions of peace and justice, even if we render them "principles," must be constantly tested by the story Scripture tells. I have argued that the paradigmatic significance and normativity of the cross should not be reduced to self-sacrificial love. It is also paradigmatic as Jesus' solidarity with the poor and oppressed. And with respect to the "symbolic world" of the New Testament, I have argued that the great claim that there is a new creation established by the resurrection of Jesus — accompanied honestly always by the "eschatological reservation" — could as well found a political "realism" as pacifism. Such a "realism" would insist on the "secularity" of political authorities, their "this-worldly limits," but it could also insist on (and participate in) the calling of the "secular" political authorities.

Richard's guideline concerning the relevance of "other authorities" — tradition, reason, and experience — is that *"extrabiblical sources stand in a hermeneutical relation to the New Testament; they are not independent, counterbalancing sources of authority"* (p. 341; see also 295-98). I have no quarrel here; I applaud the desire to allow Scripture the last word in conversation

---

44. In other contexts I have argued that the rules of Scripture are normative for the church less as rules than as part of the whole story. See *Remembering Jesus,* pp. 71-74; "Scripture and Ethics: Practice, Performances, and Prescriptions," in *Christian Ethics: Problems and Prospects,* ed. James F. Childress and Lisa Sowle Cahill (Cleveland: Pilgrim, 1996), pp. 18-44. I will not take up that argument again. It is hardly relevant here anyway, for Richard's claim is not focused on rules themselves but on the consensus against violence in all four of the modes he considers.

with other sources of moral wisdom; but "tradition," "reason," and "experience" seem abstractions compared with the quite concrete contributions people who use them sometimes make to the moral discourse and deliberation in churches. Richard attributes the license to use violence in service to justice and the development of the criteria for the just use of violence to these other sources, and he insists in his guideline that these other sources may not be used "to overrule or dismiss the witness of Scripture" (p. 341). I have suggested, however, that the context for the development of such criteria was the mutual encouragement and admonition of Christian churches reading Scripture together and remembering the story. The context was the conversation of the church and that soldier or police officer or judge or public official who had a vocation to do justice, to protect and serve the neighbor. It was not an effort to put Scripture aside or to dismiss it; it was an effort to think together and talk together about how to live the story Christians love to hear and tell in this community.

Any judgment that violence is justified should be made (or reviewed) in Christian community gathered around Scripture, remembering Jesus. To that conversation people will bring different gifts and passions, a gift and passion for peace, a gift and passion for justice. In that conversation, deliberation and discernment have been served and will be served, as I judge, by attention to the questions important to the tradition of "just war": Is there a *justifying cause* for violence? Is the violence undertaken with *right intentions*? Is it undertaken under the auspices of a *legitimate authority*? Is violence a *last resort*? Has there been an *announcement* of the intention to begin hostilities? Is there *a reasonable hope of success*? And in the midst of violence, is due *proportion* preserved, does the good to be accomplished or preserved outweigh the harm being done in violence? Is *discrimination* between combatants and noncombatants preserved? The point of such questions is not to sanctify violence up to the limit permitted by some scribal account of "just war" doctrine. The point is rather to discern the path of faithful discipleship in the ambiguities of this sad world, remembering and following one who loved both peace and justice, one who loved both the enemy and the weak.

Living the Text: The Church As Community of Peace

I want finally to revisit the remark of Richard's grandmother, "The Devil can cite Scripture to his purpose." I worried earlier that I might find myself in the role of the Devil or the Devil's advocate.[45] And I acknowledge at the end that there have been — and are — far too frequently devilish uses of Scripture to license violence. One need only think of the European invaders of more than one continent who drew analogies between their invasions and the Jewish conquest of Canaan in order to license their violence. The very ease with which one can provide additional and contemporary examples of a devilish use of Scripture to license violence should make one sympathetic to Richard's account.

I grant that Richard is on the side of the angels in this dispute. But I worry a little also about an "angelic" reading. Paul worried some, after all, about the Corinthian Christians who thought that they were already angels.[46] I worry that an "angelic ethic," by failing to acknowledge the "not yet" character of our existence, may also fail to protect the innocent victims of this world's violence and injustice. It is true, as Richard says, that the church is called to live "in the present time as a sign of the new order that God has

---

45. In a conversation in a class we taught together, Richard, with characteristic generosity, did not attribute my defense of violence in defense of justice to the Devil but to my "Calvinist DNA."

46. The spiritual enthusiasts in Corinth evidently claimed to participate already fully in the future age, claimed to be already fully spiritual, claimed to be already "angels." And some of them made the ascetic inference that participation in the life of the body with its sexual pleasures was forbidden to genuinely spiritual Christians; they prohibited sexual intercourse and made celibacy a duty, or at least a mark of the spiritually elite. "It is well for a man not to touch a woman" (1 Cor. 7:1) was probably a slogan of these enthusiasts. (This at least is the opinion of many recent commentators — and some ancient ones, notably Origen.) Paul did not disagree with the slogan; celibacy is indeed a signal that the ages have turned, that the future age has already made its power felt, that the rule of Christ in whom there is "no longer male and female" is real. But he immediately qualified their enthusiasm — and their understanding of the word of the Lord that would be recorded in Mark 12:25 and Matt. 22:30 — by the recognition that the rule of Christ is "not yet" unchallenged. He said, "But because of the temptation to immorality, each man should have his own wife and each woman her own husband" (1 Cor. 7:2 RSV). Paul was capable of providing other — and better — grounds for marriage than that it is "a remedy for concupiscence." But here, against the eschatological assumptions of the Corinthian enthusiasts, he reminded the Corinthians of the "not yet" character of their existence. The powers of evil, including *porneia,* have not yet laid down their arms and admitted defeat. Until they have, celibacy remains a "gift," not a duty. And until they have, marriage too, even though it is an indication that we are not yet angels, may be a context for displaying something of God's good future by the mutuality, equality, and fidelity of the partners. According to Paul, the "not yet" character of the world of our sexuality not only justified marriage (or the permission to marry, 7:2, 36-38); it is also what made celibacy itself sometimes prudent (7:25-35). Nevertheless, marriage too could be shaped by the gift of Christ's reign already.

promised" (p. 338). But to live "in the present time" is to live this side of the eschaton. And the "new order that God has promised" is marked by both peace and justice. On this side of the eschaton, no peace is exactly "God's *shalom.*" On this side of the eschaton, no justice is exactly God's final vindication of the least. On this side of the eschaton, moreover, peace and justice do not always embrace. We should not simply say that we will never do violence for the sake of justice, nor should we simply say that we will never accept some measure of injustice for the sake of peace. The pursuit of a relative peace and a relative justice while we are not yet angels will require prudence and will best be served by a community of mutual admonition.

Earlier I suggested that perhaps Richard and I did not disagree, that perhaps the disagreement was simply semantic. I guess we do disagree, and I guess that the disagreement is not simply semantic. But in Christian community gathered around Scripture, perhaps the disagreement may be part of a continuing conversation that would shape and limit, bless and correct, the work of both peacemakers and those who hunger for justice. Both are gifted; together they provide a limited "sign of the new order [of peace *and* justice] that God has promised."

The disagreement is that I judge that the inference to be drawn both from Jesus' saying about revenge and from his story is not an absolute prohibition of force or coercion or violence in defense of justice. Jesus did not make pacifism a legal requirement of those who would follow him; pacifism is not the new *halakah.* I judge the church's practice of an ascetic discipline to require sometimes "postponing questions of peace to questions of justice."[47] I see the community's vocation as including a place for the vocation of some to "secular" politics this side of the eschaton in order to protect the neighbor still threatened by violence and greed, even where the protection of the neighbor may sometimes require violence in defense of justice.

Nevertheless, Richard is surely right to insist that those who would follow Jesus will not delight in violence; they will delight in peace. They will not seek violence, limited only by the restrictions of the latest scribal account of a "just war." While hearts remain hard, while we are not yet angels, Christians will discern how hard their own hearts often are, and they will recognize how infrequently violence softens hearts. Christians will look for political alternatives to violence, alternatives that protect both justice and the neighbor while keeping the peace. They will be peacemakers, hungering and

---

47. Oliver O'Donovan, *Peace and Certainty: A Theological Essay on Deterrence* (Grand Rapids: Eerdmans, 1989), pp. 116-17.

thirsting for justice; they will be justice-makers, hungering and thirsting for *shalom*. They will be and form an international community that reaches across the boundaries and across the enmity of violence, correcting misinformation (or dis-information), rejecting the demonization of the enemy, repenting from their own sins, loving the enemy.

The last word, of course, belongs neither to Richard nor to me. The last word belongs to God — and the last word will be *shalom*.

The Poetics of Generosity

Ellen F. Davis

Reading and Ruling

What resources does the Bible offer those who would advocate a generous political stance toward the religiously "other"? Are there texts — more to the point, is there a strong textual trajectory — that would press a socially or politically dominant majority to move beyond mere tolerance of a minority that is judged (from the standpoint of the majority's religious orthodoxy) to be religiously deficient?[1] Or, to put the question in the strongest terms, as it was recently posed to me (not incidentally) in Jerusalem: Is it possible to build a biblical argument that those who exercise political hegemony — broadly speaking, "rulers" — have a religious obligation to advance the well-being of "the sinful other"? Does that obligation stand even where there is reason to see this other as a threat to the social order, and further, where

---

1. See, for example, the Declaration of the Roman Curia *Dominus Iesus* (August 2000), in which then Joseph Cardinal Ratzinger challenged "that mentality of indifferentism" that is (citing John Paul II) "characterized by a religious relativism which leads to the belief that 'one religion is as good as another.'" If it is true that the followers of other religions can receive divine grace, it is also certain that *objectively speaking* they are in a gravely deficient situation in comparison with those who, in the Church, have the fullness of the means of salvation" (par. 22). In Ratzinger's view, this "objective" acknowledgment of deficiency does not negate the possibility of interreligious dialogue. The paragraph continues: "*Equality*, which is a presupposition of inter-religious dialogue, refers to the equal personal dignity of the parties in dialogue, not to doctrinal content, nor even less to the position of Jesus Christ . . ." (www.vatican.va/roman_curia/congregations/cfaith/documents/rc_con_cfaith_doc_20000806_dominus-iesus_en.html, emphasis original).

there exists sufficient political and military power to contain the minority, to maintain them in a weak position if not to suppress them entirely? In various places around the globe the question is not an abstract one, and those who look to the Bible for guidance (Jews and Christians) appear in both the majority and the minority position with respect to it. Currently, Israel and Palestine may be unique as the only contemporary nations where two peoples of biblical faith — religious Israelis and Palestinian Christians — look to the text from political and social positions that are (generally) opposed, though both are agonized. At the same time, American Jews and Christians might stand quite close to each other in considering the question of suppression or generosity with respect to American Muslims in our "post-9/11" culture. France is a largely secular country, yet French Christians who are ethnically European and therefore part of the dominant culture might still consider what religious witness they might offer in support of the religious rights of French Muslims. Conversely, Christians who live under the domination of the militantly Islamic Government of Sudan know what it is to suffer as the religiously other.

Although Richard Hays has not (to my knowledge) directly addressed this question of a generous exercise of hegemony, he came close in a discussion of the church's centuries-long and almost unabated history of anti-Judaism. That discussion concludes with the observation: "One of the church's most urgent pragmatic tasks in the 1990s is to form communities that seek reconciliation across *ethnic and racial* lines."[2] Now, about ten years later, in the midst of an American "War on Terrorism" that Hays has judged from the first to be deeply misguided — not least in its quasi-religious motivation and rhetoric — he would, I believe, agree to add "religious" to that list of dividing lines that challenge people of biblical faith to act for reconciliation.

The simplest argument a Christian can make for political action that furthers the welfare of "the sinful other" is *imitatio Dei:* Do as God does, and especially God in Christ. As the Apostle Paul wrote to the church in Rome, Jesus died for us "while we were [God's] enemies" (Rom. 5:10, cf. 5:8), and even now God in Christ is reconciling the world to himself — despite the fact that the world, including the church, remains in its basic disposition largely hostile to God. So if we confess that Jesus Christ is *Dominus dominorum,* King of kings and Lord of lords, then we would seem to be ac-

---

2. Richard B. Hays, *The Moral Vision of the New Testament* (New York: HarperSanFrancisco, 1996), p. 441, emphasis mine.

knowledging that the proper exercise of power — even political power — is characterized by an unreasonable degree of generosity toward those who are religiously deficient.

However, imitating God is not something one can resolve to do in the morning and accomplish by teatime.

"My thoughts are not your thoughts,
nor your ways my ways," says YHWH. (Isa. 55:8)

Bringing our ways into closer conformity with God's involves a long process of rethinking — and it is worth noting that the "you" addressed here is a grammatical plural, designating the whole people Israel. So God through Isaiah is calling for a corporate change of heart, which in the metaphorical physiology of the Bible is the locus of thinking as well as affect, and likewise the "control center" for our actions. In short, the heart is the organ of moral vision. Therefore, to follow Richard Hays's argument in his important work on that subject, effecting any change of heart within the community of faith is a lengthy process that begins with fresh readings of Scripture, undertaken in light of changing situations and urgent needs. At the same time, stirrings in our hearts may, when submitted to proper exegetical discipline, lead to fresh readings; Hays points to "a hermeneutical feedback loop that generates fresh readings of the New Testament as the community grows in maturity and as it confronts changing situations."[3]

Hays's work both highlights and evidences an important aspect of the discipline that should inform exegesis, although he sees it as equally a source of freedom. Certainly, one of the chief strengths and beauties of his work as scholar, teacher, and preacher is his careful attention to biblical poetics, the literary dynamics within particular texts but also between texts, that convey theological meaning. Considering how contemporary Christian interpretation might look if we were to imitate the Apostle Paul in his formational readings of Scripture, he suggests that "we would begin to cherish the poetics of interpretation, allowing rhetoric to lie down peacefully with grammar and logic. In our own proclamation of the word, we would grant a broad space for the play of echo and allusion, for figurative intertextual conjunctions . . . ," that is, for various forms of trope on the scriptural tradition.[4] Further, Hays argues that fostering the growth of moral discernment in the

---

3. Hays, *Moral Vision*, p. 304.
4. Richard B. Hays, *Echoes of Scripture in the Letters of Paul* (New Haven: Yale University Press, 1989), p. 186.

church involves following Paul (and other biblical writers) in the practice of an imaginative style of exegesis whereby scriptural symbols, stories, and instructions are read in ways that bear upon and gradually reconfigure the life of the present community of faith.[5]

In this essay I focus on two aspects of biblical poetics — first character, and then point of view — that seem especially important for understanding how a text may awaken and instruct the moral vision of its readers.[6] My aim is to show how narrative and prophetic texts in both Testaments may open fresh perspectives, even in our own situations, on the relationship between the dominant community and the religiously other. The claim to disclose fresh perspectives would seem, on the face of it, either absurd or arrogant, since the texts themselves are ancient, and none comes from an obscure corner of the Bible. Yet with respect to its poetics, perhaps the most important thing that can be said about the Bible altogether is that this is exceedingly complex literature. Because of its subtlety and ambiguity, it continues to unfold new meanings to its readers. But the flip side of that claim is that biblical literature is on the whole highly susceptible to misunderstanding, or understanding so partial as to be misleading. After twenty years of teaching the Old Testament in seminaries, I am still fascinated, but equally frustrated and puzzled, by this poetic strategy, in which most biblical writers seem to collude.[7] The literary difficulty of the Bible keeps people like Richard Hays and me in work — but at the same time, it creates a difficulty for the church. For the poetic difficulty of Scripture means that almost inevitably people of good faith, reading the Bible in all sincerity, will construe its words in ways that work harm — or fail to work sufficient good — in and for the faith community as it relates to the religiously other. In short, it is easy to read the Bible sincerely and yet fail to arrive at the truth, for, as moral philosopher Iris Murdoch observes, truth is an "other-centred concept," in contrast to "the self-centred concept of sincerity."[8]

5. Aspects of this argument appear throughout Hays's *Moral Vision*. See, e.g., "The Church as Embodied Metaphor," pp. 304-6.

6. Primary attention is given to these two aspects of biblical poetics by Adele Berlin, *Poetics and Interpretation of Biblical Narrative* (Sheffield: Almond, 1983); and Shimon Bar-Efrat, *Narrative Art in the Bible* (Sheffield: Almond, 1989).

7. In his valuable essay "On Difficulty," in *On Difficulty and Other Essays* (New York/Oxford: Oxford University Press, 1978), p. 34, George Steiner notes the existence of "an entire poetic of tactical difficulty."

8. Iris Murdoch, "Against Dryness," in *Existentialists and Mystics* (New York: Allen Lane/Penguin, 1998), p. 293.

As someone who confesses that the biblical writings are ultimately the work of the Holy Spirit for the benefit of Israel, the church, and the world, I must believe that this complex poetic strategy reflects divine wisdom, for all the human frustration and real risk it entails. The psalmist, poised it seems between frustration and praise, exclaims:

> How great are your works, YHWH;
> Exceedingly deep your thoughts!
> A stupid person cannot know,
> and the fool cannot understand this. . . . (Ps. 92:6-7)[9]

God's thoughts and works are characteristically vast, and maybe that is the best explanation for why the poetics of Scripture are habitually difficult: the biblical writers are inspired to mimic the Reality to which they witness. So instead of setting out straightforward moral lessons, they put their readers to work, confusing and unsettling us, raising questions where we might previously have imagined there was clarity. If we stick with these texts, submitting ourselves to the work the Holy Spirit is doing through them even now, in the midst of our own fresh difficulties, then in the end they may well complicate our thinking in useful ways — useful, at least, if the goal is to think more like God.

Self and Other

I begin with a text that cannot be avoided, for it bears directly on the question of furthering the well-being of the other — and seemingly renders it moot. If any text in the Bible appears to be unambiguous, it is the commandment for Israel to obliterate the Canaanites:

> When YHWH your God brings you into the land that you are coming (there) to possess, and clears away great nations before you: the Hittite and the Girgashite and the Amorite and the Canaanite and the Perizzite and the Hivite and the Jebusite — seven nations greater and stronger than you — and YHWH gives them over to you and you defeat them, you shall utterly consign them to the ban (החרם תחרים אתם); you shall not make covenant with them and you shall have no mercy on them. (Deut. 7:1-2)

9. Citations follow the Hebrew versification where it differs from the English.

Yet for contemporary students of the Bible, the apparently simple commandment to get rid of the Canaanites is (or should be) doubly complicated, read in historical context and also in the larger context of the Deuteronomistic narrative. For the purposes of this essay, the historical complication can be treated briefly. It is widely acknowledged that for the Deuteronomists writing in the seventh century, the extermination of the Canaanite nations was an ideological construct rather than a historical possibility, and an afterthought at that. Whatever the political status of these seven peoples might once have been (something not clearly known for most of them), they had long been assimilated into other populations, including Israel's (e.g., Uriah the Hittite). The real seventh-century threat was the neo-Assyrian Empire, with its efficacious policy of erasing national identity by transporting and intermingling the populations of its vassal states. Yet the idea of the seven other "-ites" could still be adduced to remind Israelites of the abiding danger of their own religious assimilation.

Even in the eyes of those lacking a historical-critical perspective on Pentateuchal composition, the commandment to exterminate without mercy has not always been taken at face value. According to one well-known rabbinic tradition, Joshua modifies the absolute ban against the Canaanites, applying instead the more lenient prescription of Deuteronomy 20:10-15, which allows for peace negotiations with pagan cities, but only those "distant from you."[10] This bending of the rules is more than the biblical account records, yet it is reasonable to speculate that the rabbis, careful readers that they were, took their inspiration from the book of Joshua itself. In contrast to Deuteronomy, the book that follows offers a much more complex view of Israelite and Canaanite and the relations between them. The fact that there is overall a genre difference between the two books is relevant here. While Deuteronomy is mainly a collection of simple, repetitive speeches framing a lengthy legal code, Joshua is a book of stories, complex narratives with developed characters. It is noteworthy, indeed, that among its many narrative representations, Joshua does not include a single developed picture of

---

10. "Rabbi Shmuel b. Nachman said: Yehoshua bin Nun fulfilled the laws of this section. What did Yehoshua do? Wherever he went to conquer, he would send the following proclamation: 'He who wishes to make peace, let him come forward and make peace; he who wishes to leave, let him leave and he who wishes to make war, let him make war.' The Girgashim left the Land of Israel. The Givonim made peace. Thirty-one kings who did not want to make peace came to wage war and were destroyed. If the kings had wanted to make peace, the Israelites would certainly have made peace with them" (*Devarim Rabbah* 5:14, *Tanchuma Shoftim* 18, *Yerushalmi Shevi'it* 6:1).

wicked Canaanites. Most of the Canaanites are simply the nameless, faceless, unstoried opponents of Israel, who fight the invaders and meet their fate as legally prescribed in Deuteronomy. Yet there are in Joshua some stories that seem designed to complicate the view that Deuteronomy purports to make normative, namely, that the one great threat to Israelite faithfulness is the external threat from the pagan Canaanites.

These complicating stories begin immediately. Already in the second chapter of Joshua it is evident that Israel owes its safe entry into the promised land, not to any good work done by the Israelite spies whom Joshua sends out "on the sly" (חרש, Josh. 2:1), but rather to the insight, loyalty, and even the Yahwistic faith of the Canaanite harlot Rahab. Indeed, it would seem to be due to the spies' dereliction of duty that Rahab enters the story at all. In response to Joshua's command, "Go, see the land, and especially Jericho," they "went and came to the house of a prostitute-woman (אשה זונה) . . . and they lay there" (Josh. 2:1) — taking their ease and pleasure under the very nose of the king of Jericho, who heard about them soon enough. To immediate appearances, Rahab represents in her person everything that is, from an orthodox Israelite perspective, dangerously attractive and reprehensible about Canaanites, namely, their supposedly rampant sexuality, associated with the cults of the ba'alim.[11] Not only her job description but even her name suggests it. As Hans Barstad notes, רחב is morphologically unique for a female personal name; it does not appear to be a real name at all but rather a common noun used as a nickname. In ordinary biblical usage, the root denotes width; in Ugaritic, medieval Arabic, and even perhaps biblical Hebrew poetry, the root is used with reference to the female genitalia.[12] Rahab is labeled a "broad" in the coarsest sense of that twentieth-century American slang term.

The narrator is pleased with the sexual joke and continues to amplify it.

---

11. Recently, scholars have cast serious doubt on the former consensus that sexual rituals, including sacred prostitution, dominated Canaanite fertility religion, including Baal worship within Israel. Alice Keefe, "The Female Body, the Body Politic, and the Land: A Sociopolitical Reading of Hosea 1–2," in *A Feminist Companion to the Latter Prophets*, ed. A. Brenner (Sheffield: Sheffield Academic Press, 1995), offers a good review of the (lack of) evidence and proposes that it is necessary to consider "how sexual imagery . . . functions within the symbolic order of ancient Israelite society and literature" (p. 89). See also Gale A. Yee, *Poor Banished Children of Eve* (Minneapolis: Fortress, 2003), pp. 81-109.

12. H. M. Barstad, "The Old Testament Feminine Personal Name Rahab: An Onomastic Note," *SEÅ* 54 (1989): 43-49. Barstad cites Isa. 57:8 as a likely occurrence of this usage in the Bible.

When the king's agents come looking for the Israelite spies at her house, they issue the command: הוציאי האנשים הבאים אליך אשר באו לביתך ("Bring out the men who entered you — that is, who entered your house!" Josh. 2:3; cf. 2:4).[13] Rahab parries deftly: "True, the men did come into me (באו אלי)" — a pun that works in biblical Hebrew just as it does in English[14] — "but I don't know where they are from . . . and the men went out. I don't know where the men went. Go after them quickly . . ." (2:4-5). Her ignorance, albeit feigned, is a mark of her professionalism; a prostitute or madam should not know anything of her clients beyond the moment of encounter.

Rahab is the first actual Canaanite with whom any Israelite has an encounter (here, apparently, in the strong sense) in the land. As the narrator initially represents her, and as she represents herself to the king's men, she is everything she ought to be to fulfill the Deuteronomic stereotype of the seductive Canaanite. Yet as her character develops (and Rahab may be the most developed character in this book), readers are drawn to admire and empathize with the prostitute-woman, far more than with the Israelite men in her story. She has the shrewdness, the boldness, and the survival instinct essential for a woman in her liminal social position, yet all those aspects of her situation and character manifest themselves in ways that expose the hollowness of the stereotype.

Although religious seduction is the ostensible Canaanite threat, when Rahab "propositions" the Israelite spies, she does so in the context of confessing her own orthodox Yahwistic faith, the first such confession made in the promised land. She proclaims it literally from the housetop (cf. Matt. 10:27; Luke 12:3):

> I know that YHWH has given the land to you and that dread of you has fallen upon us. . . . For we heard that YHWH had dried up the waters of the Reed Sea on account of you. . . . And we heard, and our heart melted, and the breath no longer rose in anyone on account of you, for YHWH your God, he is God in the heavens above and on the earth beneath. And now, swear to me by YHWH that if I act in good faith (חסד) with you, you yourselves in turn will act in good faith with my father's house . . . , and you will keep alive my father and my mother and my brothers and

13. See Frank Anthony Spina, *The Faith of the Outsider: Exclusion and Inclusion in the Biblical Story* (Grand Rapids: Eerdmans, 2005), p. 55.

14. Among the numerous occurrences of the sexual sense of the phrase בוא אל, in the Deuteronomistic History and beyond, are Judg. 15:1 and 16:1.

my sisters and all theirs — and you will deliver our lives from death (וְהִצַּלְתֶּם אֶת־נַפְשֹׁתֵינוּ מִמָּוֶת)! (Josh. 2:9-13)

The Deuteronomic demand for the extermination of the Canaanites bespeaks cultural fear, a deep sense of religious vulnerability. So it is noteworthy that this story, embedded within the Deuteronomistic History, places emphasis on Rahab's extremely vulnerable position: "Her house is *in the casement of the city wall;* right *on the wall* she sits" (Josh. 2:15). Maybe the repetition implies what is in fact the case: her location on the wall is ambiguous, for it both gives Rahab an opportunity to ally with the Israelites and places her on the front line of the impending battle when the Israelites "come" — this time, "come against" the land (בָּאִים ב, 2:18).[15] And for those who have ears to hear, there is a deep poignancy in Rahab's appeal to the Israelites, for she speaks Israel's own peculiar language of vulnerability. Her appeal echoes the voice of Israel at prayer, in its psalms of lament and thanksgiving: "For you [God] deliver my life from death" (הִצַּלְתָּ נַפְשִׁי מִמָּוֶת, Ps. 56:14; cf. 116:8). As so often happens in the Psalms, the articulation of faith in Israel's God comes by way of desperation. Indeed, Rahab, sitting on Jericho's wall, should be the very first to fall under the death sentence that Deuteronomic law imposes on Canaanites living in the territory God has granted to Israel: "You shall not keep a breathing thing alive" (Deut. 20:16).

The way Rahab escapes that fate is, one might say, peculiarly Deuteronomic; she uses persuasive rhetoric. She adopts the language of an insider to the Israelite covenant community:[16] the language of confession, of prayer, and of covenant loyalty (חֶסֶד). Far from seducing Israelites into apostasy, she insinuates herself into the household of Yahwistic faith by speaking as one who belongs. And her belonging becomes complete and permanent, in biblical tradition and thereafter. Jericho and everything in it are torched, "but Rahab the prostitute and her father's house and all of hers Joshua kept alive, and she has dwelt in the midst of Israel (בְּקֶרֶב יִשְׂרָאֵל) until this day . . ."

15. My interpretation of this emphasis on Rahab's location is in line with the argument developed in Nehama Aschkenasy's study of "biblical tales that interpret the woman's life through the medium of space" — *Woman at the Window: Biblical Tales of Oppression and Escape* (Detroit: Wayne State University Press, 1998). Although Aschkenasy does not treat Rahab, that story might be considered in light of her observation that "in many of these tales, . . . the woman is translated into a spatial element, an object with an opening, or *a territory to be invaded*" (p. 18, emphasis mine).

16. On Rahab's use of "insider language," Spina, *Faith of the Outsider,* p. 61, observes: "If all one had to go on was Rahab's use of vocabulary and phraseology in her confession, one would have to conclude that she is an Israelite of the first order."

(Josh. 6:25). The rabbis celebrate her absorption into the community by midrashically marrying her to Joshua;[17] Matthew (1:5) knows her as the mother of Boaz, placing her in the messianic lineage of the house of David.

Thus, the encounter with Rahab disturbs the neat Deuteronomic category of the reprehensible Canaanite, the other who must be kept at a distance or, at close quarters, either exterminated or enslaved.[18] Maybe this first disturbance of the prescriptions established by Torah is what underlies the enigmatic account — more a fragment than a story — of another encounter that occurs shortly thereafter:

> And it happened, when Joshua was at Jericho, that he looked up and saw — and here, a man standing opposite him, with his sword unsheathed in his hand. And Joshua walked up to him and said to him, "Are you for us or for our adversaries?" And he said, "Not at all!"[19] I am commander of YHWH's army; now I have come!" And Joshua fell on his face to the ground and prostrated himself. And he said to him, "What [word] would my lord speak to his servant?" And the commander of YHWH's army said to Joshua, "Remove your shoes from your feet, for the place where you are standing is holy!" And Joshua did so. (Josh. 5:13-15)

While the commander's final word recalls God's instruction to Moses at the burning bush, this encounter is nevertheless strangely inconsequential. There is no further message for Joshua or Israel, and the narrative moves right along as it had been moving before, to the attack on Jericho. Yet it hovers in the background, just at the edge of memory, this repudiation of Joshua's own attempt to assign the heavenly being to one of those neat categories: our side or our enemies'. Fleming Rutledge comments: "The startlingly irrelevant answer is neither one or the other, but simply '*No*.' God is not to be captured in any of our concepts."[20] Somehow that divine repudiation of the clear divide between self and other is connected with the recognition that the land now opening before Israel at Jericho is holy. Although the account of Jericho's fall (immediately following) takes no notice of this en-

17. Leila Leah Bronner, *From Eve to Esther: Rabbinic Reconstructions of Biblical Women* (Louisville: Westminster John Knox, 1994), p. 149.

18. On enslavement, see Josh. 9:3-27 (the case of the Gibeonites) and 1 Kings 9:20-22; in the Priestly tradition, see Lev. 25:44-46.

19. The particle of negation followed by כִּי is a strong adversative. See, e.g., Ronald J. Williams, *Hebrew Syntax: An Outline* (Toronto: University of Toronto Press, 1976), pp. 72-73.

20. Fleming Rutledge, "What the Angel Said," in *The Bible and The New York Times* (Grand Rapids: Eerdmans, 1998), p. 12, emphasis original.

counter, that account is framed on the far side by another story that may help spell out the connection. It is the story of "Achan ben Karmi ben Zavdi ben Zerach, belonging to the tribe of Judah" (Josh. 7:1, 18), who violates the ban (חרם) and takes some of the plunder from Jericho. As a result, Israel begins to fail in its conquest of the land.

Joshua's final instruction to the Israelites at Jericho, a moment before the trumpet blast and the shout that bring down the wall, provides the explicit link between the stories of Rahab and Achan: "The city will be חרם . . . ; just Rahab the prostitute will live. . . . And you, just watch out for the חרם, lest . . . you take anything . . . and turn the camp of Israel into חרם" (6:17-18). If Rahab is the Canaanite who comes to dwell "in the midst of Israel," to the benefit of both, then Achan, from the ruling tribe of Judah, is the native son who threatens the very existence of the community by effecting "חרם in [its] midst" (7:13). "Achan's story completely reverses the Rahab story," as Frank Spina has shown.[21] At the same time, it fulfills Moses' extended instruction about how Israel is to handle the various forms of evil that will arise "in [its] midst" (Deut. 13:2, 12, 15; cf. 6, 14). The people must "burn away" (ובערת, 13:6) the false prophet and the dreamer of dreams, "pelt with stones" (וסקלתו באבנים, 13:11) the brother or son or daughter or wife or best friend who incites to apostasy. As for the whole Israelite city that follows the most worthless of its citizens into false worship — it and all within it — they must treat as חרם and "burn with fire" (ושרפת באש, 13:17). Notably, the punishment for Achan and his family aligns his crime with these community-destroying actions. God decrees the ban, and "all Israel stoned him with stones (אבן . . . וירגמו אתו) and burned them with fire (וישרפו אתם באש) and pelted them with stones (ויסקלו אתם באבנים)" (Josh. 7:25). The multiple facets of the execution recapitulate the several punishments decreed for the apostate individual or the Israelite city that follows other gods.[22]

So the narrative shows the intra-Israelite threat quickly fulfilled, while the touted Canaanite threat to Israel is converted to mutual benefit and expansion of the covenant community. These two carefully crafted stories, which feature the most carefully developed characters in the book, shake our confidence that the two apparently fixed identities, the ban-bound Canaan-

---

21. Spina, *Faith of the Outsider,* pp. 52-71, quotation p. 70.

22. Spina, *Faith of the Outsider,* p. 69, suggests that Achan dies as "the quintessential Israelite-turned-Canaanite"; the double form of execution recapitulates the falling of Jericho's stone walls and the burning of the city. While this view might be seen as complementing my own, the closer verbal connections with Deuteronomy 13 suggest to me that Achan is rather the quintessential Israelite *apostate.*

ite and the covenant-bound Israelite, are in fact firm. Both the contrast and the blurring between these two — Rahab the whore of Jericho and Achan ben Karmi ben Zavdi ben Zerach from the ruling tribe of Judah — illumine the divine "No!" that the commander of YHWH's army returns to Joshua's dichotomizing question: "Are you for us or for our adversaries?" God's refusal to take a side points to the larger narrative picture that is emerging: there is no essential difference between Canaanite and Israelite as fixed religious or national identities; all depends on the decision for and practice of fidelity to God. Maybe that is the unarticulated message behind the commander's assertion that this is *holy* land into which Israel is now entering, a place that demands a radically new understanding of self and other.

In contrast to the relatively simple rhetoric of Deuteronomy — formulated almost entirely as direct address in which are embedded prescriptions and prohibitions, lapidary in style — Joshua contains the first real narratives in the Deuteronomistic tradition, and as I have argued, their effect is to complicate what may have previously (in terms of canonical order) seemed straightforward. Noting that difference in the poetics of these two books is, I believe, crucial for reading them well, and further, it bears on the question of how we exercise moral judgment in our communities. Philosopher Martha Nussbaum argues that artful literature can make a critical contribution to "public reasoning." She proposes that the best poets and novelists express a moral sensibility that goes beyond simple moralistic formulas and prescriptions. With carefully wrought words, images, characters, stories, they develop "a rich and concrete vision that does justice to human lives."[23] "Poetic justice" accords individuals or peoples the full dimensions of real human lives and thus views them in their distinctiveness rather than through the application of abstract principles. Serious literature is "an essential bridge to social justice," insofar as it cultivates in readers a "compassionate imagination,"[24] making us care about characters who could be real, and further, countering our prejudices by enabling us to see from perspectives we would never have inhabited on our own.

The practical consequence of reading such complex literature habitually is that we may bring "our evolving sense of principle and tradition to bear on a concrete context."[25] The particular context Nussbaum herself knows best is

23. Martha C. Nussbaum, *Poetic Justice: The Literary Imagination and Public Life* (Boston: Beacon, 1995), p. 81.
24. Nussbaum, *Poetic Justice*, p. xviii.
25. Nussbaum, *Poetic Justice*, p. 84.

the practice of law. As a professor of law and ethics at the University of Chicago, she sets forth the ideal of the "literary judge," in contrast to one who maintains a skeptical detachment, or adopts the scientific model of formal reasoning, or "cultivates a lofty distance from particulars for reasons of judicial neutrality." Rather, the literary judge pursues neutrality in a manner that requires "sympathetic knowledge of value-laden human facts"; from the common-law tradition she derives a preference for "an evaluative humanistic form of practical reasoning" over pseudomathematical or quasi-scientific models.[26]

The wider interest of Nussbaum's argument lies in her suggestion that all readers of serious literature are

> constituted . . . as judges of a certain sort. As judges we may dispute with one another about what is right and proper; but insofar as the characters matter to us, and we are active on their behalf, we do not feel that the dispute is about nothing at all[,] that we are merely playing around. . . . [F]or as concerned readers we search for a human good that we are trying to bring about in and for the human community. . . . What we are after is not just a view of moral education that makes sense of our own personal experience, but one that we can defend to others and support along with others with whom we wish to live in community.[27]

While Nussbaum may not herself endorse the usefulness of the Bible in promoting that kind of moral vision,[28] readers of the Bible may appreciate both the seriousness she ascribes to the reading enterprise and the goal she articulates. Nonetheless, people of faith would want to amplify or modify her notion of "a human good that we are trying to bring about." Stanley Hauerwas's comments on reading the Gospel according to Matthew suggest something of this difference:

> Our task is not to understand the story that Matthew tells in light of our understanding of the world. Rather, Matthew would have our understanding of the world fully transformed as the result of our reading of his

26. Nussbaum, *Poetic Justice*, p. 82.

27. Nussbaum, *Poetic Justice*, pp. 83-84.

28. I do not locate among her writings any studies of biblical texts. However, Nussbaum gives sensitive readings of at least two writers whose work draws its primary inspiration from the Bible, namely, Augustine and Dante; see Martha C. Nussbaum, *Upheavals of Thought: The Intelligence of Emotions* (New York/Cambridge: Cambridge University Press, 2001), pp. 527-90.

gospel. Matthew writes so that we might become followers, be disciples, of Jesus. To be a Christian does not mean that we are to change the world, but rather that we must live as witnesses to the world that God has changed. We should not be surprised, therefore, if the way we live makes the change visible.[29]

My argument is that the rich specificity and complex perspectives offered by the Bible's narrative and prophetic traditions may indeed inform our ethical thinking, here about the political question of advancing the well-being of the religiously other. The delineation of character in the linked stories of Rahab and Achan provides an outstanding (though not isolated) example of the exploratory capacity of biblical narrative. Here that genre is used to disclose the slipperiness of categories — builder vs. destroyer of covenant community, righteous self vs. sinful other — that often appear firm in other genres (legal prescriptions, proverbs, psalms of lament and imprecation). The book of Joshua attests to the existence of a different social and political reality, represented by the holy land of Canaan and those of its inhabitants who recognize what God is doing there. The job of faithful readers is to make that changed reality visible.

Looking from the Other Side

A second literary means by which biblical texts may challenge and change our thinking is manipulation of point of view, so that readers are invited to stand in an unaccustomed place as we listen for God's word. Here I highlight texts that enable us to "overhear" God's address to the powerful foreigner, to those who exercise hegemony over Israelites, the underdogs with whom readers of the Bible would normally identify. Because the Bible does not say much about how Israelites conducted themselves as sovereigns over foreign peoples, we must look for an oblique answer to the question of how those who claim to be the people of God should witness to their faith when exercising political hegemony. From the numerous biblical representations of rulers, the primary theopolitical truth that becomes visible is that no ruler, Israelite or otherwise, can be presumed beneficent. The presence of an Israelite on the throne is no guarantee of blessing even for the people Israel. In a psalm associated with Solomon, Israel prays:

29. Stanley Hauerwas, *Matthew* (Grand Rapids: Brazos, 2006), p. 25.

> Give to the king your capacity for judgment, O God,
> and your righteousness to a king's son. (Ps. 72:1)

Yet a careful reading of the Deuteronomistic account of Solomon's reign makes it clear that many of his own people, Israelites of the Northern Kingdom, did not receive justice from that king of conventionally blessed memory (1 Kings 5:27-30; 12:4). How much more would this be true of the foreign peoples whom the psalmist portrays as bowing or cringing before the king (Ps. 72:8-11) — if only we had their stories?

Nonetheless, the Bible does enable us to imagine ourselves into the perspective of the oppressed other, at least partially and indirectly, through what it reveals about the experience of Israel and the early church at the hands of foreign sovereigns. The texts to which I now turn, from exilic Isaiah and Acts, articulate God's demand for generous hegemony when "our side" is in the down position. However, I suggest that many first-world Christians will hear more truth if we identify ourselves with the powerful non-Israelites, with the Babylonian and Roman rulers whom God addresses through the prophet and the narrative character Paul, and further, that the poetic design of the texts themselves supports such a change of perspective.

Thus exilic Isaiah speaks for God to Babylon:

> I was angry with my people; I profaned my inheritance
> and gave them into your hand. You did not grant them mercy.
> Upon the elderly you made your yoke very heavy.
> And you said, "I will always be a great lady, forever."
> You did not take these to heart; you did not give thought to its
> aftermath. (Isa. 47:6-7)

What follows is an oracle of doom for Babylon. Since it is unlikely that any Babylonian ever heard those lines of Hebrew poetry, we must assume that they were recorded for the benefit of an Israelite audience, and secondarily for ourselves. The prophet puts the exiles in the position of overhearing God's condemnation of Babylon: "You did not grant them mercy." Mercy is the condition for retaining sovereign power. But what cogency does this overheard message have for Israelites — in historical context, an audience of vassals?

First, the message brings comfort to Israel, as one would expect with exilic Isaiah, above all others the prophet of consolation. There is the comfort of knowing that tyranny has a terminus; Babylon's greatness is not "forever." But there is also the further and deeper comfort of divine compassion, for surely that must underlie God's indictment of the Babylonians: they misread God's temporary anger as the eclipse of abiding compassion for Israel. From these lines, one might even infer that God expects *Babylon* to show the compassion that — for an instant — God has refused to show. If that is so, then this accusation occasions a remarkable rereading of the prophet's opening words: "'Comfort, comfort my people,' says your God" (40:1). Could the audience for that charge, unspecified but formulated in the plural, include even the Babylonians? If we can overhear God challenging the Babylonians to exercise compassion even toward those who on account of their sin seem to have been cast off by God, then is any people who worship Israel's God exonerated from the charge to comfort the weak? And if God's compassion is the determinant of who is to be shown mercy, then is any people ineligible for generous treatment?

In addition, this condemnation of the merciless Babylonians puts pressure on Israelites and upon the Christian readers who normally identify with them, because it can be grounded in Torah. Repeatedly in Exodus, Leviticus, and Deuteronomy, God insists that tenure in the land of promise depends on Israel's showing mercy to the vulnerable — widows and orphans, sojourners and the poor — "For you yourselves know the very being of the alien (נפש הגר)" (Exod. 23:9). And yet, Isaiah charges triumphant Babylon, "you did not give thought to its aftermath" (Isa. 47:7). Both Torah and the prophet are mindful of the vacillations of history: those who now have power to do good to others were once weak themselves; those who currently have power to do harm to others will someday be deprived of it. God "has brought down the mighty from their thrones and lifted up the lowly" (Luke 1:52). And it does not take long for that reversal to occur. Likely, when the prophet penned that divine accusation against Babylon, no Israelite was in a position to exploit anyone, and so overhearing the message as addressed to themselves seemed unnecessary. But no more than a dozen chapters and maybe a generation later, disappointed Israelites are directly chastised (through the same prophet?[30]) for their own failure to show mercy:

"Why do we fast, and you do not see? We afflict ourselves and you are not aware?"
Look, on your fast day you are doing business, and all your laborers you oppress. (Isa. 58:3)

---

30. Benjamin D. Sommer argues that the sections conventionally assigned to Second and Third "Isaiahs" in fact reflect the work of a single prophetic poet; see *A Prophet Reads Scripture: Allusion in Isaiah 40–66* (Stanford: Stanford University Press, 1998).

Even as vassals of the Persian Empire, some Israelites commanded enough power to be able to oppress others. So this pair of prophetic denunciations raises the question, Is there *any* situation in which people of faith do not need to be vigilant in the practice of mercy?

My final example of a text that instructs a Christian view of sovereignty is the story of Paul's teaching in the court of the Roman governor Felix in Caesarea. It stands as a lesser parallel to the account of Jesus' appearance before Pilate, that definitive encounter between hegemonic power and the one who speaks the truth of God. Initially summoned before Felix on the charge of being a public agitator, Paul offers his defense eagerly (εὐθυμῶς, Acts 24:10). Felix declines to decide the case and places Paul in custody on minimum-security conditions. According to Luke's representation, Felix is a relatively promising Roman; he has a spiritual bent, being "rather well informed about the Way" (24:22 NRSV), and he summons Paul for theological conversation. Their further exchange is briefly recounted:

> Some days later when Felix came with his wife Drusilla, who was Jewish, he sent for Paul and heard him speak concerning faith in Christ Jesus. And as he discussed justice, self-control, and the coming judgment, Felix became frightened and said, "Go away for the present; when I have an opportunity, I will send for you." At the same time he hoped that money would be given him by Paul, and for that reason he used to send for him very often and converse with him. (24:24-26 NRSV)

Luke's account offers a subtly ironic characterization of Felix. As Linda Hutcheon observes, irony comes into being "through the semantic playing off of the stated against the unstated," but "it is asymmetrical, unbalanced in favor of the silent and the unsaid."[31] Further, irony is a "relational strategy"[32] that operates within a community of shared reference. Luke's Judean audience might have smiled at the allusion to Felix's religious interest, being familiar with the story Josephus tells of the circumstances of his marriage:

> While Felix was procurator of Judea, he saw this Drusilla, and fell in love with her; for she did indeed exceed all other women in beauty; and he sent to her a person whose name was Simon, one of his friends; a Jew he was, and by birth a Cypriot, and one who pretended to be a magician; and en-

---

31. Linda Hutcheon, *Irony's Edge: The Theory and Politics of Irony* (New York: Routledge, 1995), p. 37.

32. Hutcheon, *Irony's Edge*, p. 58.

deavored to persuade her to forsake her present husband, and marry him; and promised, that if she would not refuse him, he would make her a happy woman. Accordingly she acted ill. . . .[33]

Tacitus gives a different but equally unflattering account of his marriage and personal character: "Antonius Felix exercised the prerogatives of a king with the spirit of a slave, rioting in cruelty and licentiousness. He married Drusilla, the granddaughter of Antony and Cleopatra, that he might be grandson-in-law of Mark Antony, who was the grandfather of [Emperor] Claudius."[34] Ambitious though he was, Felix was a failure as governor. His toleration of crime and even pitched battles among the inhabitants of the province, together with ill-timed penal measures and his own criminal conduct, brought the whole province to the brink of war, averted only by the intervention of the governor of Syria.[35] These contemporary histories of Roman Judea suggest that Luke's own understated history of the church's beginnings is "fraught with background." Likely, he expected his readers to know more than he says and therefore to share (what I take to be) his wry view of Felix's reaction when Paul discusses "justice, self-control, and the coming judgment."

Yet Luke's representation of Felix is not without generosity, however undeserved. He omits the unsavory personal details and implies that the governor, venal though he was, was neither impious nor inhumane; Paul's friends were allowed to minister to his needs in prison (Acts 24:23). By thus reducing the moral abhorrence his audience might otherwise feel, Luke makes it possible for us to stand more or less beside Felix and overhear when Paul formulates the basic construction of reality as the religious person experiences it: justice, self-control, and the coming judgment. But even those three nonsectarian essentials are too much for the Roman. So, as with Isaiah's denunciation of Babylon, that outline of Paul's instruction must be recorded for the benefit of those who overhear and may yet commit themselves — or commit themselves more fully, with greater understanding — to following the Way(s) of Israel's God. What Paul lays out for Felix is not the gospel message itself but the foundation for comprehending, living, and communicating the gospel. Justice, self-control, and the coming judgment — those mark for Christians the *starting point* in thinking about our public responsibilities.

---

33. Josephus, *Ant.* 20.7.2, trans. William Whiston, *Josephus, Complete Works* (Grand Rapids: Kregel, 1960), p. 420.

34. Tacitus, *Hist.* 5.9 (BCL 2:273).

35. Tacitus, *Ann.* 12.54 (trans. Dudley, NAL, p. 262).

So when we find ourselves in the position of exercising sovereignty — a situation that probably exceeded Paul's (and maybe Luke's) own vision for any substantial number of the Christian community — then these three must condition our own conduct toward the other, even the one whose religion, or lack of it, we judge to be sinful. (It is worth noting that from an orthodox Roman perspective, Paul himself was an atheist.)

The primary consideration Paul presents is "justice," the chief of the virtues in classical (Roman) tradition, in postbiblical Christian tradition, and also in the American political tradition.[36] Josef Pieper, drawing on Aquinas, offers a definition that pertains directly to our considerations here:

> To be just means to recognize the other *as other;* it means to give acknowledgment even where one cannot love. Justice says: That is another person, who is other than I, and who nevertheless has his own peculiar due. A just man is just, therefore, because he sanctions another person in his very separateness and helps him to receive his due.[37]

Such just acknowledgment of the other is the basis for exercising a generous hegemony — and, as Paul implies to Felix, the basis on which we will stand (or not) in "the coming judgment."

*　　*　　*

36. See Ted Sorenson's remarks in "A Time to Weep," his "lamentation for the loss of this country's goodness and therefore its greatness" (commencement address at the New School University, May 2004):

> Last week, a family friend of an accused American guard in Iraq recited the atrocities inflicted by our enemies on Americans, and asked: "Must we be held to a different standard?" My answer is YES. Not only because others expect it. WE must hold ourselves to a different standard. Not only because God demands it, but because it serves our security.
>
> Our greatest strength has long been not merely our military might but our moral authority. Our surest protection against assault from abroad has been not all our guards, gates and guns or even our two oceans, but our essential goodness as a people. Our richest asset has been not our material wealth but our values.

Sorenson goes on to cite President Kennedy's address at American University, just after the Cuban missile crisis: "This generation of Americans has had enough of war and hate. . . . [W]e *want to build a world of peace where the weak are secure and the strong are just.*" (Emphasis mine; for the full text, see www.commondreams.org/views04/0621-13.htm.)

37. Josef Pieper, *The Four Cardinal Virtues* (Notre Dame: University of Notre Dame Press, 1965), pp. 54-55, emphasis original.

To summarize my proposal: Because the narrative and prophetic texts of the Bible are both widely authoritative texts and very good literature, reading them well is a skill and practice with enormous public consequence. Complex and demanding literature requires that we perform certain feats of mental agility, such as tracing ironic narrative inversions (Rahab and Achan) and hearing ourselves addressed indirectly, through "characters" (including Babylon and Felix) with whom we might not choose to identify. Making those moves takes literary skill, yet the interest of the biblical writers is not literary in the narrow sense. Their aim is nothing less than to "enlighten the eyes of our heart" (cf. Eph. 1:18), to change our perceptions of ourselves in relation to God and others, and accordingly, to change our actions. In the case I have outlined here, the desired consequence of that change is that we might exercise political and military power, not in a spirit of slavery to prejudice and fear, but generously, faithfully, and justly.

A Resting Place

Sarah Hays Coomer

My father sang me to sleep every night for the first twelve years of my life, until I grew too old and too cool for such things. He took me to see Billy Joel, James Taylor, Paul Simon, Judy Collins, Pete Seeger, Tom Paxton, and many more. When I begged and pleaded, my father even took me to see the New Kids on the Block. I believe we saw them four times . . . a true show of fatherly love and devotion.

When I was thirteen, Dad and I rehearsed "Leavin's Not the Only Way to Go," a duet from *Big River,* and performed it at the Yale Divinity School coffeehouse/talent night. To this day, he gets out the guitar at family gatherings and asks me to sing it with him. Neither of us remembers the harmonies . . . or the words for that matter, but we sing it anyway.

On my eighteenth birthday, he bought me a Yamaha acoustic guitar and a chord book. The guitar sat mostly untouched for a few years until I moved to New York City during an extremely rough time in my life. Wandering through the streets of New York, in and out of coffeehouses and small acoustic clubs, I found a deeply soothing satisfaction in the sound of a simple acoustic guitar, played alone with nothing but a voice. I picked it up and slowly taught myself G . . . C . . . D . . . A minor . . .

Over the years since then, writing and playing music has become my solace, my passion, and my career. It has brought me from New York to Los Angeles and from Los Angeles to Nashville, closer to my family and, especially, closer to my father.

He instilled in me something greater than a mere love of music. It is a resting place in his world and in mine. Whether he is playing guitar, rooting through old LPs, silently focused on the sound streaming through his enormous headphones, decking the halls with Christmas carols, or making lovingly chosen mixes for my mom, there is always music in my dad's world.

For him, music also connects deeply with worship. Many years ago, he helped found a church in a very rough neighborhood of Chicago. When I was visiting colleges in 1993, we went back to see the church on a Sunday morning. We were welcomed with open arms and serenaded by the congregation singing songs my father had written for them before I was born. His music lived on in that community long after he had moved on to other cities, other ministries, and other students.

My father has always been kind, calm, judicious, loving, and present. He and my mom took my brother, Chris, and me to church every Sunday until we were old enough to rebel, and then they gave us the gift of choice. Of course, they made it clear that they wanted the family to go to church together, but they did not force us. Also, they did not baptize us as infants, giving us the choice to do so on our own, in our own time, as cognizant adults.

Ahead of myself as usual, I chose at the ripe old age of six to be baptized. Even then, they brought in our minister to sit me down, make sure I knew what it all meant, and help me think through the decision. That period and the year surrounding my fourteenth birthday were my primary forays into Christianity. As an adult, I found myself drawn to the writings of the Buddha, the Bhagavad-Gita, the Tao, Rumi, Alan Watts, and Ram Dass.

Fortunately, my father holds exploration and thought in high regard, always encouraging my search, even as it has led me to faiths and philosophies quite different from his own. In college, when I began exploring Eastern philosophy, Dad and I wrote a series of long letters back and forth to each other outlining, defining, and illuminating the differences and similarities in these very distinct faiths. His involvement in my exploration pushed me to go deeper, to understand more fully, and to articulate more concisely how and why those strange words from the Far East touched my heart.

As recently as two years ago, my parents flew out to Los Angeles to sit down with me and try to understand how I continued to find so much peace inside this foreign worldview. They challenged but they did not condemn. To this day, we differ in our faiths, but we share a profound sense of spirit in our daily lives.

My father taught me reverence for what lies beyond human understanding and the importance of living life with purpose, compassion, and a heart eternally open to . . . to use his word . . . guidance. He also taught me that sound, crafted in its endless forms, can reach beyond families, cultures, languages, tragedy, joy, and worship.

As a little girl with my father singing by my bedside, I buried my face in the pillow and wept quietly, trying to hide my tears every time Puff, the magic dragon, "ceased his fearless roar." As a grown woman on Christmas Eve with my father standing beside me at Duke Chapel, I find myself blinking back tears as "Silent Night" seeps through the giant organ over our heads. The tears come partly because the church and that song are buried so deep in our common history that I can't help but be touched by them, and partly because I regret that, in my heart, I know that the church will never be for me what it is for him.

In many ways, I wish that I could give him the gift of my own Christianity. I can't do that because it would be dishonest, but I can give him another gift. I can root myself securely on the earth, clumsily play my acoustic guitar, and raise my voice to the heavens in search of a meeting place where my father and I and the communities that surround us can know spirit, each in our own way. We are finding it a little easier with each passing holiday, each song, each witnessing. Every day his faith and my upbringing seep seamlessly into my lyrics, and I welcome their arrival.

> There's a burden in your slumber, buried in your bones,
> A burden in this heart attack you're living every morning.
> Ease your burden on the long way home.
>
> There's a tractor-trailer headlight heading for the center of your eyes.
> A holy angel waiting for the Lord above to give her a sign
> That it's time for the long way home.

— "The Long Way Home," © 2006 Sarah Hays

The Christian Practice of Growing Old:
The Witness of Scripture

Richard B. Hays and Judith C. Hays

EDITORS' NOTE: We are pleased to be able to reprint here the following essay, which represents in a small way the fruitful partnership that has characterized Richard and Judy's marriage of nearly forty years. Its challenging and hope-filled call to Christian discipleship through every stage of life provides a fitting conclusion to a volume that celebrates not the end of a journey but an important milestone along the way.

Introduction

In contrast to American culture's recent preoccupation with the problem of aging and care of older persons, the New Testament has surprisingly little to say on the topic. The relative silence of these texts may be explained, at least in part, by the very different social and cultural world in which the New Testament writers lived: fewer people lived to an advanced age,[1] and those who

1. On life expectancy in the ancient Mediterranean world, see Tim G. Parkin, *Roman Demography and Society* (Baltimore: Johns Hopkins University Press, 1992). Parkin estimates that life expectancy at birth was about 25 years, due largely to high infant mortality rates, and that "in Roman society those over the age of 60 years represented some 5 to 10 percent of the total population" (p. 134). Roger Bagnall and Bruce Frier (*The Demography of Roman Egypt* [Cambridge: Cambridge University Press, 1994]) calculate that for Roman

Originally published in *Growing Old in Christ*, ed. Stanley Hauerwas, Carol Bailey Stoneking, Keith G. Meador, and David Cloutier (Grand Rapids: Eerdmans, 2003), pp. 3-18.

did were honored and esteemed within the community. Aging, therefore, was not seen by the early Christians as a "problem" to which some sort of religious solution was required. Consequently, the New Testament documents provide few answers to questions that may seem of urgent concern to us: how to forestall the physical appearance of advancing age; how to cover the costs of long-term care for the aged; how to promote the preferences of dying patients. By comparison to the New Testament, the Old Testament tells more stories about characters of great age — from Methuselah to David — but here again the cultural context within which aging is understood differs so dramatically from ours that the fit between our concerns and the concerns of the writers is rough. Does this mean, then, that the Bible is of limited usefulness for our theological reflection on the Christian practice of growing old? On the contrary, because the scriptural texts provide a different evaluative framework for understanding aging, they may cause us to pause and reframe our own reflections.

This chapter will focus on the New Testament material, but we must always remember that the church's Scripture includes the twofold canon of Old Testament and New Testament together. The New Testament texts belong to the longer story of God's dealing with Israel, as disclosed in the Old Testament. The New Testament writers narrate the continuation of that story and offer particular sets of lenses through which to interpret it. Consequently, our discussion of aging, while focusing on the New Testament, will keep the wider biblical perspective in view.

Our discussion is divided into four parts. We begin with lexical observations about the terms employed for "old" and "aging" in the New Testament and with some observations about their significance. Then we will survey

---

Egypt, female life expectancy at birth was between 20 and 25 years, but that females who survived to age 10 enjoyed a life expectancy ranging from 34.5 to 37.5 years, meaning that they would, on average, die between the ages of 44 and 47 (p. 90). See also Evelyne Patlagean, *Pauvreté économique et pauvreté social á Byzance, 4e-7e siècles* (Paris: Mouton, 1977), pp. 95-101. According to her figures, half of the populace died before reaching the age of 44. By way of comparison, in the United States life expectancy was 76.7 years for those born in 1998 (National Center for Health Statistics, *Health, United States 2000 with Adolescent Health Chartbook* [Hyattsville, Md.: FIFARS, 2000], p. 4). In addition, by the year 2000, 13 percent of the population of the United States had attained the age of 65 or older (Federal Interagency Forum on Aging Related Statistics [FIFARS], *Older Americans 2000: Key Indicators of Well-Being* [Hyattsville, Md.: FIFARS, 2000], p. 2). Girls who were 10 years old in 1998 could expect to live an average of 60.2 more years, and the median age of survivorship for the total U.S. population was 80 years (Centers for Disease Control: National Vital Statistics Report 48:18, pp. 2, 4).

the New Testament's portrayal of aging characters and offer theological reflections on the themes highlighted in these stories. The third section of the chapter will take up the striking fact that Jesus, the New Testament's paradigm for a life lived faithfully before God, was executed as a young man and never experienced advanced age. What is the significance of this fact for theological reflection about aging? Finally, we will suggest that the matter of greatest concern to the biblical writers was not aging as such but the *telos* toward which the aging process leads: mortality. A biblical perspective on growing old will cause us to focus on death as the end toward which we move — and yet as the last enemy confronted by God's redemptive power.

Biblical Terminology for Aging

In the New Testament we encounter several different terms that refer to aging or to persons of advanced age, though none of the terms appears frequently. The word *presbytēs* ("old man") appears three times; in two of these cases the term is offered as a self-description, once by Zechariah (Luke 1:18) and once by Paul (Philem. 9). The third occurrence of the term refers to "old men" in the church in Crete, to whom Paul's emissary Titus is to provide instruction (Titus 2:2). The equivalent feminine noun, *presbytis* ("old woman"), appears in the same context (Titus 2:3), its only appearance in the New Testament. The closely related term *presbyteros* ("elder") is used with some frequency as a term for those who are recognized as community leaders in the synagogue (e.g., Matt. 21:23; Luke 7:3; Acts 25:15) or in the church (e.g., Acts 15:2; 1 Tim. 5:17; Titus 1:5; James 5:14). This usage presupposes that leadership is linked to seniority in the community. Sometimes, however, the term *presbyteros* — actually a comparative adjectival form, as the English translation of "elder" rightly suggests — refers to older people without reference to any office of leadership, as in Acts 2:17, 1 Timothy 5:1 (cf. also the feminine plural form *presbyteras* in 1 Tim. 5:2), and perhaps 1 Peter 5:5.

The noun *gerōn* ("old man," whence our English word "gerontology") turns up only once, in Nicodemus's question to Jesus (John 3:4). Related terms are *geras* ("old age": Luke 1:36) and the verb *geraskō* ("grow old": John 21:18; Heb. 8:13). This term appears to refer simply to chronological age without carrying any of the connotations of dignity that attach to *presbytēs/presbyteroi*.

Finally, the adjective *palaios* (from which words such as "paleontology" are derived) means "ancient, having been in existence for a long time," and it often carries the "connotation of being antiquated or outworn."[2] It can refer to an old, torn garment or old, brittle wineskins (Mark 2:21-22 and parallels), to the old leaven that is discarded in preparation for Passover (1 Cor. 5:7), to the "old covenant" read in the synagogue (2 Cor. 3:14; cf. Rom. 7:6), or, figuratively, to the old unregenerate self now put to death (Rom. 6:6) or removed like an outworn garment and replaced by a new identity in Christ (Eph. 4:22; Col. 3:9). Less frequently in New Testament usage, *palaios* refers to a teaching that is valuable and venerable because of its age (Matt. 13:52; 1 John 2:7). Significantly, the term *palaios* is never used in a literal sense to describe a person of advanced age. Unfortunately, because the single English word "old" is used to translate this term as well as the word "families" linked to *presbytēs* and *gerōn*, the pejorative connotations of *palaios* can bleed over and cause English readers to assign inappropriately negative associations to the other terms discussed above.

Older Characters in the New Testament

Older characters play a significant role in the opening chapters of Luke's Gospel. The first characters who appear on stage in Luke's story are the priest Zechariah and his wife Elizabeth, who were both "advanced in years" (Luke 1:7). Although they were both "righteous before God, living blamelessly according to all the commandments and regulations of the Lord," they remained, to their dismay, childless (1:6-7). When the angel Gabriel appears to Zechariah in the Temple and promises that Elizabeth will bear a son named John who is to play the role of Elijah in calling Israel to repentance (1:13-17), we hear echoes of the Old Testament stories of Abraham and Sarah (Gen. 18:1-15; 21:1-7) and of Hannah and her husband Elkanah (1 Sam. 1:1-20). In these stories, the surprising grace of God is made manifest through the promise and birth of a child to a previously barren couple. The parallel to the Abraham-Sarah story is especially strong because of the advanced age of the pair to whom the promise is made. The motif of surprising fruitfulness in old age highlights the power and freedom of God: "Is anything too hard for the Lord?" (Gen. 18:14; cf. Luke 1:37).

Nonetheless, like Sarah, who greeted the divine promise with skeptical laughter, Zechariah finds the promise incredible; consequently, Gabriel

---

2. F. W. Danker, *A Greek-English Lexicon of the New Testament and Other Early Christian Literature,* third ed. (Chicago: University of Chicago Press, 2000), p. 751.

strikes him temporarily speechless (Luke 1:18-23). Almost immediately, however, Luke also narrates the fulfillment of the promised good news: "After these days, his wife Elizabeth conceived" (1:24). As the plot unfolds, we find a continuing emphasis on the advanced age of the new parents. In Gabriel's annunciation speech to Mary, he discloses to her that "your relative Elizabeth in her old age has also conceived a son" (1:36).

Despite Zechariah's initial doubts, both he and Elizabeth become prophets who discern the new thing that God is doing. They are the first two figures in Luke's story who are said to be "filled with the Holy Spirit" (1:41, 67). Elizabeth pronounces Mary "blessed among women" and describes her prophetically as "the mother of my Lord," thereby becoming the first to ascribe the title *kyrios* to Jesus (1:42-43). Zechariah, in turn, finds his tongue loosed after the birth of John and utters a prophecy that summarizes the epic sweep of the biblical narrative and declares that God's promises to redeem Israel are now being brought to fulfillment (1:67-79). Thus, in Luke's carefully structured narrative, the older figures Elizabeth and Zechariah become both the instruments of God's purpose and — alongside Mary — the first interpreters of God's saving acts.

As Luke's story of the birth and infancy of Jesus continues, we encounter two more aged characters who serve as prophetic voices: Simeon and Anna become the prophetic chorus welcoming the child Jesus on the occasion of his purification in the Temple (Luke 2:22-38). The old man Simeon, who has long been hoping for "the consolation of Israel" (i.e., its deliverance from oppression), has been promised by the Holy Spirit that he will not die before he has seen the Lord's Messiah. Upon seeing the infant Jesus, he recognizes him as God's chosen one and movingly declares,

> Master, now you are dismissing your servant in peace,
>   according to your word;
> for my eyes have seen your salvation,
>   which you have prepared in the presence of all peoples,
> a light for revelation to the Gentiles
>   and for glory to your people Israel. (Luke 2:29-32)

Furthermore, speaking under the guidance of the Spirit, he intones to Mary a dark prophecy of the Passion, foretelling both her own suffering and the role of her child Jesus as a polarizing sign "for the falling and the rising of many in Israel" (Luke 2:34). Similarly, Anna — an eighty-four-year-old prophetess who frequents the Temple to worship and pray night and day —

recognizes Jesus, gives thanks to God, and declares the news about him "to all who were looking for the redemption of Jerusalem" (2:38).

Thus, Luke's narrative provides a matched pair of older male and female witnesses prefiguring Jesus' messianic vocation and the conflict that his mission will engender. The advanced age of Simeon and Anna signifies their time-tested wisdom, while at the same time symbolizing Israel's long-suffering expectation of deliverance. These two aged figures also suggest that radical openness to the redeeming power of God may be found among elders — perhaps particularly there.

In John's Gospel, we encounter an aged character who exemplifies a more ambiguous reception within Israel for Jesus. Nicodemus, a "ruler of the Jews," seeks out Jesus by night to question him (John 3:1-21). We are not told his age, but his response to Jesus' mysterious declaration about the necessity of being born again suggests that he may be well advanced in years: "How can a man be born *when he is old?* Can he enter a second time into his mother's womb and be born?" (John 3:4; emphasis added). Jesus' answer indicates that Nicodemus should not marvel at this call to be born again, even in late life, because the new birth is the work of the Spirit, which blows freely where it will.

In this story, in contrast to the account of Simeon and Anna, age confers no special wisdom or insight. Indeed, Nicodemus's role as an established "teacher of Israel" seems to stand in the way of his comprehension of the word of God embodied in Jesus, and his coming "by night" associates him symbolically with those who "loved darkness rather than light because their deeds were evil" (John 3:19). Nicodemus fades out of the scene in John 3, and we are not told how he responds to Jesus' elusive challenge. His last recorded words express a bewildered skepticism: "How can this be?" (3:9). Yet, if we read this story in a canonical context, we may note the similarity between Nicodemus's response and the response of Mary to Gabriel's promise that she will bear a child who will become the new Davidic king: "How can this be, since I have no husband?" (Luke 1:34). Perhaps, then, Nicodemus's question is no more his final response than is Mary's. Indeed, two other references later in the story suggest that Nicodemus continues to be at least a secret believer in Jesus: he speaks up — albeit noncommittally — in defense of Jesus before the chief priests and Pharisees (John 7:45-52), and he joins Joseph of Arimathea in anointing the body of Jesus for burial (19:38-42).

The last chapter of John's Gospel, in its depictions of Peter and the Beloved Disciple, offers evidence of some importance for a survey of aged characters in the New Testament. Here the risen Jesus prophesies Peter's eventual death as an old man: "Truly, truly, I say to you, when you were young, you girded yourself and walked where you would; but *when you are old,* you will stretch out your hands, and another will gird you and carry you where you do not wish to go" (John 21:18; emphasis added). This prophecy of martyrdom as an old man provokes Peter to ask about "the disciple whom Jesus loved." Jesus' evasive answer provides the occasion for the narrator to comment that, contrary to some rumors, Jesus had not predicted that the Beloved Disciple would not die (21:23). This authorial comment seems to presuppose a situation late in the first century when the Beloved Disciple, after a long life of bearing witness and serving as the source of community tradition (21:24), has in fact died. Thus, the story implies that both Peter and the Beloved Disciple, despite their different manners of death, continued into their old age as witnesses for the gospel and key leaders of the early Christian movement.

Turning to the Pauline Epistles, we find only a few passages dealing with aged characters. The most important of these is Paul's recounting in Romans 4 of the story of Abraham and Sarah. In the course of explicating the faith of Abraham, Paul highlights his advanced age: "He did not weaken in faith when he considered his own body, which was as good as dead because he was about a hundred years old, or when he considered the barrenness of Sarah's womb" (Rom. 4:19). Despite these seemingly hopeless circumstances, Abraham continued to trust "that God was able to do what he had promised," and his faith was reckoned to him as righteousness (4:21-22). Thus, Paul casts Abraham as an exemplar of faith, not merely for elders but for the whole world.

Paul makes one passing reference to himself as an "old man" who is now a "prisoner for Christ Jesus" (Philem. 9). This self-description may be intended to elicit sympathetic respect from the letter's addressees, whom he is seeking to persuade to deal mercifully with the slave Onesimus. Elsewhere, Paul's references to himself as the "father" of his converts serve a similar purpose of appealing for the respectful obedience due to an older parent (e.g., 1 Cor. 4:14-16; 2 Cor. 6:13; Gal. 4:19-20; 1 Thess. 2:11-12) — though the emphasis here is less on Paul's age than on his metaphorical "paternity" of his churches.

The respect due to older members of the community is emphasized in the Pastoral Epistles. See, for example, 1 Timothy 5:1: "Do not rebuke an older man, but exhort him as you would a father." Here we find also specific directives that the community should provide assistance to widows over the age of sixty, and that women recognized by the church as widows should devote their energies to prayer, hospitality, and service to the afflicted (1 Tim.

5:3-16). The letter to Titus adds that older women should be instructed "to be reverent in behavior, not to be slanderers or slaves to drink," and that they should train the younger women in their domestic duties, so that "the word of God may not be discredited" (Titus 2:3-5). The older men, on the other hand, are to be instructed, in a more general way, to be "temperate, serious, sensible, sound in faith, in love, and in steadfastness" (Titus 2:2). These unexceptional moral teachings for the elderly are part of a larger concern in the Pastorals that the church community be respectable in the eyes of the wider culture, but they offer little in the way of specifically Christian moral vision for growing old.

As we survey these scattered references to aging characters in the New Testament, can we make any general observations or discern any general themes?

First, the New Testament writers deem elders worthy of honor, respect, and special care. When elders are alone and in need, the church community is called to provide for their care, and those who fail to provide for their own older family members are harshly condemned: "they have denied the faith, and are worse than unbelievers" (1 Tim. 5:8). According to the Epistle of James, "religion that is pure and undefiled" devotes its attention to caring for widows and orphans (James 1:27). One of Jesus' sternest judgments against the scribes and Pharisees is directed against the casuistry they employed to abdicate responsibility for caring for parents (Mark 7:9-13). Even at the time of his crucifixion, Jesus showed concern for his mother Mary by commending her into the care of the Beloved Disciple, who then "took her into his own home" (John 19:26-27).

In turn, older persons bear a particular responsibility. They are to be paradigms of faith, role models exemplifying reverence and temperance (Titus 2:2-5). They are to exercise leadership in the community, especially in teaching and counseling. They may even find a special vocation to suffering, to face death, even martyrdom, without seeing the fulfillment of God's promises to his people. If so, their example of faith nonetheless continues beyond their deaths as a witness to later generations (Heb. 11).

This sort of exemplary faith is embodied by the older characters in Luke's infancy narrative and in Paul's account of Abraham and Sarah: they are well practiced in watchfulness for God. Precisely as people who have clung to God's promises over many years, they embody the virtues of long-suffering patience and trust in God's ultimate faithfulness. They also exemplify faith and hope, even when circumstances seem hopeless.

Finally, the older biblical characters signal the possibility of unanticipated fruitfulness in old age: Zechariah and Elizabeth, Abraham and Sarah, and perhaps even Nicodemus in John's story, demonstrate the possibility of change, new life, and the fruition of hopes at the end of the life span. Those who trust in God are not locked into the past — neither into traditional social roles nor into well-worn paths chosen earlier in life. Rather, they remain open to receive what God desires to give, open to the fresh, surprising working of God's Spirit. As in the prophecy of Joel, quoted by Peter in his Pentecost sermon, "Your young men shall see visions, and your old men shall dream dreams" (Acts 2:17, quoting Joel 2:28).[3] Unlike the old priest Eli (1 Sam. 3:1-9), the aged characters spotlighted in the New Testament remain open to hear the voice of God and to act on what they hear. They are the righteous people described in Psalm 92:

> The righteous flourish like the palm tree,
>   and grow like a cedar in Lebanon.
> They are planted in the house of the LORD;
>   they flourish in the courts of our God.
> In old age they still produce fruit;
>   they are always green and full of sap,
> showing that the LORD is upright;
>   he is my rock and there is no unrighteousness in him. (Ps. 92:12-15)

The Scriptures are filled with stories of God's breaking into the individual lives of older persons to confer a particular gift or vocation.

Equally important, perhaps, are the things *not* said about older characters in the New Testament. Nowhere in the biblical canon are they pitied, patronized, or treated with condescension. Nowhere is growing old itself described as a problem. Nowhere are elders described as pitiable, irrelevant, or behind the curve, as inactive or unproductive. Nowhere are they, as in so many Western dramas and narratives, lampooned as comic figures. On the contrary, they are seen as the bearers of wisdom by virtue of their age. Death is treated as an enemy to be conquered by Christ at the eschaton (e.g., 1 Cor. 15:24-26), but it never seems to occur to the New Testament authors to characterize the aging process itself as an evil to be overcome. Thus, the New Testament offers us an alternative vision in which the modern, popular view of aging as a "problem" might appear puzzling and unhealthy.

---

3. This verse is numbered as Joel 3:1 in the Hebrew text and in the Septuagint. Luke's citation of the passage in Acts 2:17 reverses the clauses, placing the climactic emphasis on the "old men" *(presbyteroi)*.

Reflections on a Messiah Who Died Young

Jesus did not grow old. The church has looked to Jesus of Nazareth as the definitive model for true humanity, the model for a life lived faithfully. Yet he did not live into what we would normally consider "late life." Luke tells us that "Jesus was about thirty years old when he began his work" (Luke 3:23), and within the span of three years he had aroused such controversy that he was put to death by the Roman authorities. To be more precise, Jesus was probably born between 6-4 B.C.E., under the reign of Herod the Great (who died in 4 B.C.E.), and was probably executed in 30 C.E. under the Roman governor Pontius Pilate. By this reckoning, he would have been no more than thirty-six years old at the time of his death.[4] Thus, Jesus died in the prime of his life, without experiencing old age. Does this mean that we are left with no christologically informed pattern for the Christian practice of growing old? If so, what is the theological significance of this state of affairs?

First of all, the manner of Jesus' death stands as a permanent reminder that fidelity is more important than longevity. Length of years is a blessing (Prov. 16:31; 20:29), but we should not presume that we have a right to a long life. God may call us to surrender our lives. The way of discipleship, as Jesus repeatedly taught his followers, leads to the cross (e.g, Mark 8:34-38; Luke 14:25-27). Jesus models for us a resolute trust in God that empowers us to act freely and to bear witness to the truth, even if such witness-bearing may lead to death. The book of Revelation extols the faithful martyrs who have conquered the great dragon Satan "by the blood of the Lamb and by the word of their testimony, for they did not cling to life even in the face of death" (Rev. 12:11). Thus, Christians are taught by the example of Jesus that we do not have to live in a cautious mode of self-protection, clinging to our lives desperately at all costs, making an idol of our own physical survival. We are free to let go of our lives when the time comes, because we believe that God will vindicate us in the end. (See also the final part of this chapter below, on death and resurrection.)

A corollary of this point is that, because we cannot necessarily count on a long life, we should live each moment of time in its fullness, whether we are

---

4. On the complicated issue of establishing the precise dates of Jesus' birth and death, see John P. Meier, *A Marginal Jew: Rethinking the Historical Jesus,* Anchor Bible Reference Library (New York: Doubleday, 1991-2001), vol. 1, pp. 372-433. In John 8:57 Jesus' skeptical interlocutors say, "You are not yet fifty years old, and have you seen Abraham?" This does not mean that Jesus was approaching fifty: it is merely an approximate yardstick to indicate how outrageous they consider the assertion that Abraham saw Jesus' "day" and was glad.

nineteen or ninety. Jesus' remarkable teaching that we should not be anxious about our lives or about tomorrow (Matt. 6:25-34) is to be understood not only in light of Jesus' radical trust in God's righteousness but also within the context of the story of the Passion. Precisely because we cannot control tomorrow and cannot choose the time of our own death, we are to receive each day as a gift, looking to God for our daily bread and making sure that we seek first the kingdom of God rather than squandering our time and energy on secondary concerns.

Second, even though Jesus died young, his suffering both represents and redeems all human experience, all human suffering. As the Son of Man, he bears all human destiny in himself. In the course of articulating their understanding of the incarnation, early Christian theologians insisted that Jesus was not only truly God but also truly human, for only by taking on human nature fully could he redeem it fully. As Gregory Nazianzen formulated this conviction, "What is not assumed is not made whole, and what is joined to God is saved."[5] This means that Jesus' life and death are to be understood as paradigmatic for all human experience. It does not matter that Jesus was not female, not a Gentile, not highly educated, not aged. It does not matter, for in his suffering, death, and resurrection we are all mysteriously included; his experience absorbs ours and becomes the key to understanding our own experience. This is true whether we are male or female, African or Chinese, illiterate or learned, young or old. Therefore, the Christian practice of growing old requires us to learn the imaginative skill of employing the cross and resurrection as the lens through which we view our own aging and dying. We learn to interpret the suffering that we experience — if in fact old age brings us suffering — as "always carrying in the body the dying *(nekrōsis)* of Jesus, so that the life of Jesus may also be made visible in our bodies" (2 Cor. 4:10). Our goal, as Paul puts it, is "to know Christ and the power of his resurrection and the sharing *(koinōnia)* of his sufferings, becoming like him in his death" (Phil. 3:10).

All of this runs contrary to the current widespread tendency to suppose that we can share deep solidarity only with those who participate precisely in our own particular experience of culture, race, class, gender, or adversity. The gospel teaches us another way: all of us are to understand our lives as grounded in the story of Jesus, and we find there a commonality that we could otherwise never have discerned. Thus, paradoxically, the elderly will find in the story of Jesus, who died in his mid thirties, a pattern

5. Gregory Nazianzen, Epistle 101 *(Ad Cledonium), Patrologia Graeca* 37:181C-184A.

that will continue to shape their own lives as they confront the challenges of growing old.

This pattern, as interpreted for us by the New Testament, is the pattern of self-giving for the sake of others. The Christian practice of growing old is shaped by the example of Jesus, who emptied himself and became obedient, even to the point of death, for our sake (see Phil. 2:1-13). Thus, Paul can write of himself:

> I have been crucified with Christ; and it is no longer I who live, but it is Christ who lives in me. And the life I now live in the flesh I live by the faithfulness of the Son of God, who loved me and gave himself for me. (Gal. 2:19b-20)[6]

Consequently, as we grow old, we should seek to discern how to give our lives for others. Old age is not a time simply to relax and play golf, nor is it a time only to reminiscence about the past. (Though relaxation and reminiscence surely have their rightful places in our lives.) Instead, in old age, as throughout our lives, we must continue to pursue the way of service, conforming our own lives to the self-giving pattern of Jesus. This christological pattern for the years of late life challenges and subverts many of the conventional models for aging that we see around us: old people as helpless, useless burdens on society, or old age as a time to sit back and reap the rewards we have earned through a lifetime of work. To understand late life in light of the pattern of a Messiah who died young is to embrace T. S. Eliot's counsel: "Old men ought to be explorers"[7] — with the proviso that the territory we are exploring is the way of discipleship that Jesus has charted for us.

The Defeat of Death, the Last Enemy

While the Bible shows little concern with *aging* as a problem, *death* is another matter. The biblical writers have a sober and realistic view of death as a grim shadow cast over the world. The psalmist laments the brevity of life and the inevitability of mortality:

---

6. On this translation, see Richard B. Hays, *Galatians,* New Interpreter's Bible, vol. 11 (Nashville: Abingdon, 2000), pp. 242-45.

7. T. S. Eliot, "East Coker," in *The Complete Poems and Plays* (New York: Harcourt, Brace and World, 1962), p. 129.

> For all our days pass away under your wrath;
>   our years come to an end like a sigh.
> The days of our life are seventy years,
>   or perhaps eighty, if we are strong;
> even then their span is only toil and trouble;
>   they are soon gone, and we fly away. (Ps. 90:9-10)

For the Old Testament writers, let it be said clearly, "flying away" does not mean the ascent of the soul to heaven. It is, rather, simply a description of the transient passing of human life, like a withered flower blown away by the wind (Ps. 103:15-16). If there is any thought of "life after death" in the Old Testament, it is primarily envisioned in terms of the image of going down to Sheol, the gloomy underworld realm of the departed. In the memorable imagery of Isaiah, death is "the shroud that is cast over all peoples, the sheet that is spread over all nations" (Isa. 25:7). Isaiah prophesies the day when God will destroy this shroud and "swallow up death forever" (Isa. 25:8), but that day remains, within the narrative world of the Old Testament, only a future hope.

The aversion to death is not found only in the Old Testament; if anything, it is even clearer in the New Testament that death is a great evil. In contrast to the serene detachment of Socrates facing his own death with imperturbable equanimity, Jesus prays in the Garden of Gethsemane in a state of agitation and grief as he contemplates his impending arrest and execution. He begs God to spare him from death (Mark 14:32-42). According to some manuscripts of Luke's Gospel, "In his anguish he prayed more earnestly, and his sweat became like great drops of blood falling down on the ground" (Luke 22:44). This point must be emphasized, because sentimental Christian piety sometimes lapses into careless talk about death as a smooth passage into a better world. But nothing could be further from the perspective of the New Testament writers. Jesus weeps at the tomb of Lazarus (John 11:32-37). Paul characterizes death as "the last enemy," which remains to be destroyed by Christ in the eschatological future when all things will at last be made subject to God (1 Cor. 15:26-28). Thus, in a world that still does not see all things in subjection to Jesus (Heb. 2:8), the process of aging carries with it the fearful prospect of death.

The New Testament's answer to the problem of death is firm and consistent: God will overcome the power of death by the resurrection of the body at the last day. The resurrection of Jesus is both the firstfruits of this final resurrection and the sign of the eschatological resurrection in which all Christ's people will share (1 Cor. 15:20-28). Thus, the hope of resurrection lies at the heart of the way in which Christians embody the practices of growing old. The resurrection shapes our understanding of aging in at least two decisive ways.

First, the doctrine of resurrection affirms God's unwavering fidelity to the creation, God's determination to redeem what he has made. For that reason, Gnostic indifference to the body is the farthest thing from Christian thought and practice. Christians, as Paul writes, groan in solidarity along with the created order awaiting redemption: "We know that the whole creation has been groaning in labor pains until now; and *not only the creation, but we ourselves,* who have the first fruits of the Spirit, groan inwardly while we wait for adoption, *the redemption of our bodies*" (Rom. 8:22-23; emphasis added). Note that those who have the Spirit long not for redemption *from* their bodies but rather for redemption *of* their bodies. This fundamental element of Christian doctrine gives rise to a wide range of practices that honor and care for the physical body, in life and in death.[8] We expect that the body will not be discarded but rather transformed in the resurrection. Therefore, life in the body continues to matter greatly as we grow old.

Second, because the resurrection of Jesus proclaims God's triumph over the power of death, we are set free from fear, no longer paralyzed or controlled by fear of aging and dying. This good news is movingly articulated by the Letter to the Hebrews:

> Since, therefore, the children share flesh and blood, [Jesus] himself likewise shared the same things, so that through death he might destroy the one who has the power of death, that is, the devil, *and free those who all their lives were held in slavery by the fear of death.* (Heb. 2:14-15; emphasis added)

As we grow old, we face death in and with Christ; therefore, while death remains a terrible enemy of human flourishing and of God's redemptive will for the world, we know that its "sting" has been taken away, as Paul declares in 1 Corinthians 15:55. We live no longer under slavery to fear. John Donne, the great seventeenth-century metaphysical poet, takes up Paul's taunt to Death, personified as a power that seeks to destroy us:

---

8. For an extended discussion of church sponsorship of establishments to shelter and feed the poor, and care for the sick, the aged, and the dying, from the fourth century to the present, see Guenter B. Risse, *Mending Bodies, Saving Souls: A History of Hospitals* (New York: Oxford University Press, 1999).

Death be not proud, though some have called thee
Mighty and dreadfull, for, thou art not soe,
For, those, whom thou think'st, thou dost overthrow,
Die not, poore death, nor yet canst thou kill mee.

. . . .

One short sleep past, wee wake eternally,
And death shall be no more; death, thou shalt die.[9]

In such confidence inspired by the New Testament's testimony, we are set free from the paralysis that the fear of death produces in our culture: we need not deceive ourselves with costly amusements that distract us from the truth of our mortality and foster the illusion that we are immortal. Likewise we are set free from the frantic urgency to forestall death at all costs: we need not grasp at life or harness every medical technology at our disposal. We can look death in the face without fear, because we trust in the promise of resurrection. This means that the practice of growing old can be characterized by a sober confidence, no matter what trials and complications we face. As Christians, we are people trained to die.[10] We have been trained for this from our childhood by focusing, week in and week out, on the story of the cross and resurrection. We need not avert our eyes from our own death, for our identity is grounded in the crucified Messiah who has gone before us through death and resurrection. That is why Paul can encourage the Thessalonians not to be afraid of death's power to separate them from their loved ones:

But we do not want you to be uninformed, brothers and sisters, about those who have died, so that you may not grieve as others do who have no hope. For since we believe that Jesus died and rose again, even so, through Jesus, God will bring with him those who have died. . . . Therefore encourage one another with these words. (1 Thess. 4:13-14, 18)

Conclusion

In light of this survey of biblical visions of old age, what can we say about how Scripture might inform our own understanding of aging? We conclude

9. John Donne, "Holy Sonnet X," in *The Complete Poetry and Selected Prose of John Donne*, ed. C. M. Coffin (New York: Modern Library, 1952), pp. 250-51.
10. Stanley Hauerwas, *A Community of Character: After Christendom*, 2nd ed. (Nashville: Abingdon, 1999), p. 43.

this chapter by offering a few reflections on the Christian practice of growing old, as it is shaped by the witness of Scripture.

The weight of the biblical witness is on the side of similarity rather than difference between aged and younger Christians. All followers of Jesus are to practice watchful waiting on God across the span of their years. At its heart, watchful waiting includes regular participation in corporate worship. The recitation of the historic creeds, the hearing of the Word, and the cycle of the liturgical year provide constant rehearsal of the life story to which all Christians find their lives conformed. Through rehearsal, we come to experience the mystery of which Paul testifies: "it is no longer I who live, but it is Christ who lives in me" (Gal. 2:20).

Should Christians reach old age, the accumulation of waiting bestows upon them a wisdom about the kingdom of God to which younger Christians should attend closely and defer. The special responsibility of older Christians is to lead, to teach, to counsel, as their gifts allow and as opportunities arise. Should older Christians become physically incapable of caring for themselves and have no family to attend to their needs, the church is responsible for their care. Even in debilitation and illness, however, their ministry of example may intensify: they embody the way of the cross and gratefully receive the service of others.[11]

In late life, Christians remain subject to the possibility that God will act decisively in history and in their lives in such a way as to turn their lives upside down. They may be called to a new ministry. They may receive new revelation. They may see the fulfillment of a long-awaited hope. In this they do not differ from younger Christians.

Finally, in old age as in youth, Christians are to take the Lord Jesus Christ as the model for their daily lives and interactions with others. When facing death, as they are more likely to do than are young Christians, elders with long practice of self-sacrifice and loving obedience to Jesus may repudiate fear and embrace hope more gracefully than those less practiced. Having long remembered and rehearsed the Passion of Jesus, they face death with the expectation that their story, like his, will continue in the life of the resurrection. But their confidence is not a natural fruit or reward of age itself; rather, it is a consequence of practice. Therefore, the Christian practice of growing old is a lifelong habit of believing God's witness in the Scriptures and acting on it, for as long as God gives life.

---

11. On these themes see Audrey West, "Whether by Life or by Death: Friendship in a Pauline Ethic of Death and Dying," chap. 3 (Ph.D. diss., Duke University, 2001).

Index of Modern Authors

Index of Scripture and Other Early Writings